Preface

The subject of this book is the *use* of computer-based services in support of scientific activities. The term "science" is intended in the broad sense—to include technological, governmental, and industrial activities not always thought of as "scientific," but which in fact have been permeated by the methods and techniques of the scientific process.

The reason for the book is that the field of computing systems and services is rapidly increasing in complexity—thereby offering a sometimes bewildering variety of computing services from which the user can choose to help him solve his problem. Similarly, there now exists a spectrum of facilities from which the computing installation planner or manager can choose to provide the needed service. There is a surprising dearth of literature on this subject, considering its importance. My personal contacts with others responsible for providing or using computing services convince me that there is a strong interest in the exchange of information on this subject. It is my hope that this book will encourage others to document and exchange their experiences.

Wherever possible, the book uses actual case studies to make various points and to demonstrate their feasibility. It is hoped that the collection of case studies will be useful in facilitating the transfer of usage experience between disciplines, from large to small organizations, and from industrialized to developing nations.

To understand this subject, we must consider the interaction among three elements or forces:

1. Existing computing equipment and software. We assume the availability of state-of-the-art general-purpose computing equipment.
2. A body of workers, professional and technical, who have a need for computing services.

3. An organization charged with the responsibility for operating and controlling this equipment to provide the desired services (and for analyzing and justifying the cost of doing so).

This book is intended both as a text and a reference. Sections I and II can serve directly as the text for a one-semester course on computer usage, or as a source book for a course on methods of science and technology. The material of Section III can be included in the computer usage course mentioned above, or covered in a course on systems management or systems modeling.

As a reference, the book is designed to be helpful both to the user of computer services and those responsible for the planning, management, or design of computer systems.

The introductory section of the book describes the general phases of scientific activity on one hand, and, on the other, the classes of computing services. An attempt is made in Section I to provide the background and terminology necessary to comprehend the remainder of the book.

Section II, "Current Usage," is presented from the user's point of view, structured in terms of the phases of scientific activity. It starts with the collection of data and goes through to the documentation and distribution of the resulting reports or products. For each phase of the scientific process, the use of various types of computing aids is introduced via case studies of existing applications. Lessons from this usage, both benefits and problems, are discussed and generalizations from these particular experiences are considered.

Section III, "Issues of Management," offers a methodology for planning and managing the use of computer services. It includes guidelines and models of the dynamics and economics of man-machine service systems. Again, real-world examples are introduced to demonstrate the feasibility of the approaches proposed. This material is intended for individuals in managing their personal use of computer services, as well as for those professionally responsible for computer system management.

This volume is based on 20 years of personal use of computer services in various engineering and research assignments, and 4 years as Director of Computing Systems and Services at IBM's T. J. Watson Research Center. I have drawn heavily on experience of the personnel of the Computing Systems Department and of the Research Staff Members who use the systems there. However, the judgments and opinions expressed herein are my own and I solely and personally am responsible for them.

DONALD N. STREETER

Yorktown Heights, New York
October 1973

Acknowledgment

I thank Arthur Anderson and Ralph Gomory, past and present directors of IBM Research, respectively, for the opportunity and freedom to undertake this study and write this book.

I acknowledge the valuable advice and assistance of Dan McCracken. Frank Smith, Harlow Freitag, Vin Vitagliano, and Dick Seymour kindly reviewed and criticized various sections of the manuscript. Special thanks go to Doris Crowell and Katherine Chandri for inputting and editing the manuscript. I also thank Ed Kopley and his staff at the Systems Research Institute for their support during my sabbatical year there.

Many others have contributed materials, ideas, and criticisms to this effort—too many to mention all by name—so I must express my indebtedness and gratitude collectively.

Contents

1. **Introduction**   1

    A. Methods of Science and Technology, 1
    B. Roles of Computer-Based Services, 7
    C. Relative Capabilities, Man versus Computer and Combined Capabilities, Man and Computer, 31

2. **Current Usage: Case Studies and Critiques**   34

    A. Data Collection, 35

        CASE STUDY 1. DATA ACQUISITION—IBM SAN JOSE LABORATORY, 35
        CASE STUDY 2. DATA CONDITIONING AND ENHANCEMENT—JET PROPULSION LABORATORY, 44
        CASE STUDY 3. DATA SHARING—NATIONAL OCEANOGRAPHIC DATA CENTER, 54
        CASE STUDY 4. DOCUMENT RETRIEVAL—IBM ITIRC SERVICE, 58

    B. Examination, 66

        CASE STUDY 5. PATIENT MONITORING—PACIFIC MEDICAL CENTER, 67
        CASE STUDY 6. PETROLEUM EXPLORATION—WESTERN GEOPHYSICAL COMPANY, 77

CASE STUDY 7. DATA ANALYSIS, MARKET RESEARCH—GENERAL FOODS, 86
CASE STUDY 8. MEDICAL DATA ANALYSIS—ALBERT EINSTEIN COLLEGE OF MEDICINE, 97

C. Problem Formulation, 105

CASE STUDY 9. LARGE MATHEMATICAL PROBLEMS, METEOROLOGY—IBM PALO ALTO, 106
CASE STUDY 10. DATA-DEPENDENT PROBLEM FORMULATION—IBM YORKTOWN LABORATORY, 113

D. Design, 122

CASE STUDY 11. AUTOMOTIVE DESIGN—GENERAL MOTORS, 123
CASE STUDY 12. COMPUTER-AIDED CIRCUIT DESIGN—FAIRCHILD SEMICONDUCTOR, 136
CASE STUDY 13. ARCHITECTURAL DESIGN—PERRY, DEAN & STEWART, 141

E. Analysis and Optimization, 154

CASE STUDY 14. ELECTION DISTRICT DELINEATION—WASHINGTON UNIVERSITY, 155
CASE STUDY 15. STRUCTURAL ANALYSIS—NASA, 169
CASE STUDY 16. CIRCUIT OPTIMIZATION AND SENSITIVITY ANALYSIS—IBM YORKTOWN LABORATORY, 184

F. Experimentation, 195

CASE STUDY 17. AUTOMOBILE TRAFFIC CONTROL—LINCOLN TUNNEL, 195
CASE STUDY 18. CONTROLLING MANUFACTURING PROCESSES—IBM BOULDER, 201
CASE STUDY 19. CONTROL OF THERMONUCLEAR FUSION EXPERIMENTS—PRINCETON UNIVERSITY, 210

G. Modeling Simulation, 220

CASE STUDY 20. SIMULATION OF AUTOMOBILE DYNAMICS—CORNELL AERONAUTICAL LABORATORY, 220

CASE STUDY 21. SIMULATED CHEMICAL REACTIONS—IBM SAN JOSE LABORATORY, 234
CASE STUDY 22. CALCULATION OF RADIATION TREATMENT DOSAGE—MEMORIAL HOSPITAL, 247

H. Documentation, 253

CASE STUDY 23. TOTAL SPECIFICATIONS INFORMATION SYSTEM—CHEVROLET MOTOR DIVISION, GM, 254
CASE STUDY 24. LEGISLATIVE INFORMATION SYSTEM— WASHINGTON STATE LEGISLATURE, 277

J. Continuing Responsibility, 288

CASE STUDY 25. QUALITY ASSURANCE SYSTEM—GENERAL DYNAMICS, 288

3. **Issues of Management**   **303**

   A. Definition of Objectives, Attributes, and Measures, 306

   B. Quantification of Value of Services, 308

   * Cost/Benefits of Computing Services, 310
   * Matching Task and Computing Device, 326

   C. Location/Allocation Problems, 336

   * Centralization or Dispersion of Computing Facilities, 338
   * Networks, 358
   * Internal Organization—Distribution of Function, 366

   D. Evaluation, 374

   * Reports and Queries, 374
   * Prediction via Simulation, 386
   * Of Usage Practices, 409

   E. Control, 418

   * Pricing, 419
   * Scheduling, 426

F. Quality of the Man-System Interface, 431

Application Languages, 431
Specialized Man-System Interface—a Case Study, 448
Expanding the User Community—Interactive TV and Computers, 456

Bibliography   461
Author Index   465
Subject Index   467

THE SCIENTIFIC PROCESS
AND THE COMPUTER

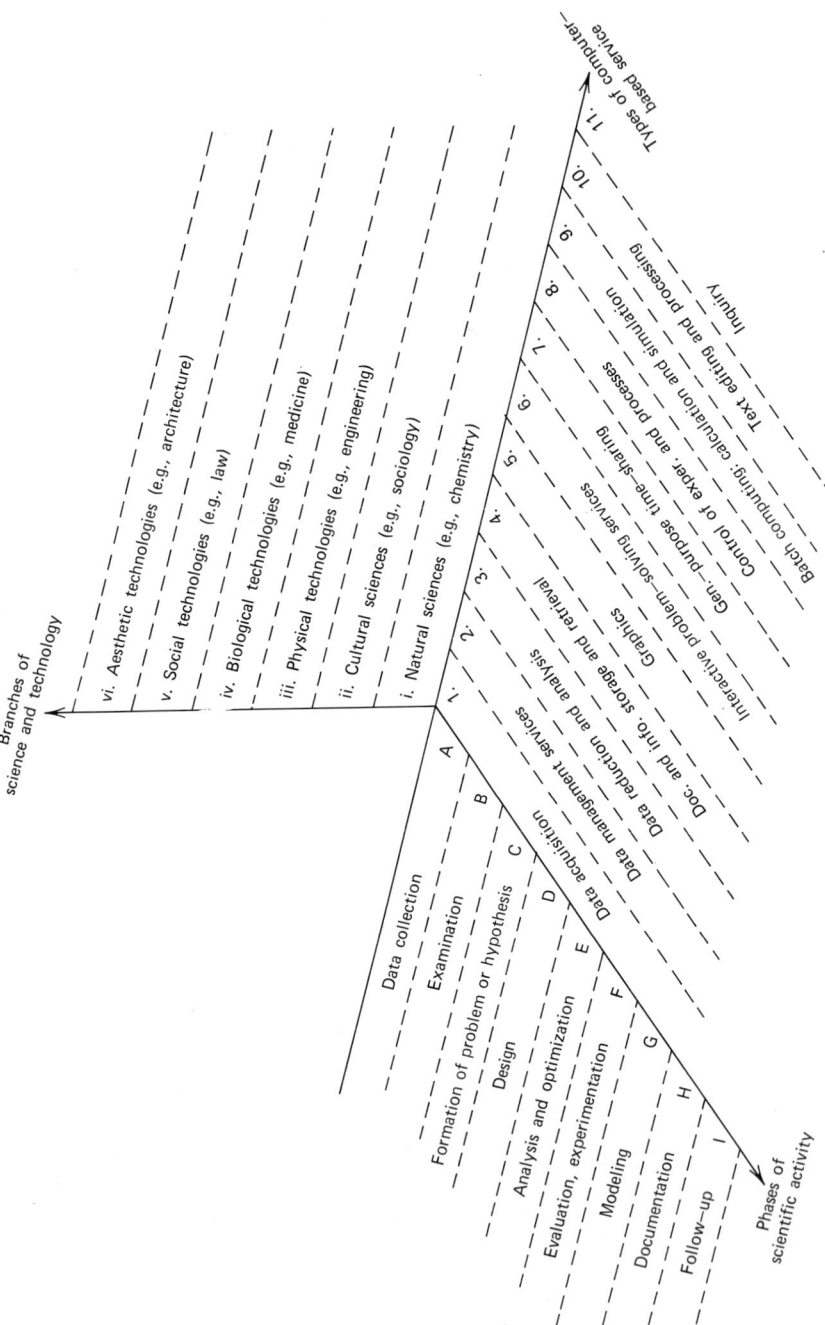

Figure I-1. Three dimensional structure.

SECTION ONE
Introduction

A. METHODS OF SCIENCE AND TECHNOLOGY

The scientific method has, over the past several centuries, provided a means of radically transforming the world and our comprehension of it. The products of the application of this method affect us all, directly and indirectly.

Scientific method is the strategy of scientific research; it bears on any whole research cycle and is independent of subject matter. The actual execution of each one of the strategic moves, however, depends on the subject matter and on the state of our knowledge regarding that subject matter.

In this section we develop an idealized description of the phases of scientific activity, which will provide a structure for the exposition of computer usage.

First, it is useful to define our terminology carefully.

Science, Research, Technology

The term science is generally construed to include both the process of applying the scientific method, and the body of knowledge thus obtained.

The process (or work) of applying the scientific method is called research. In general, the primary goal of scientific research is the advancement of knowledge. However, a useful distinction can be drawn

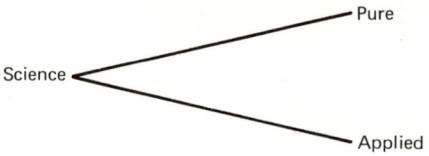

Figure IA-1. Science.

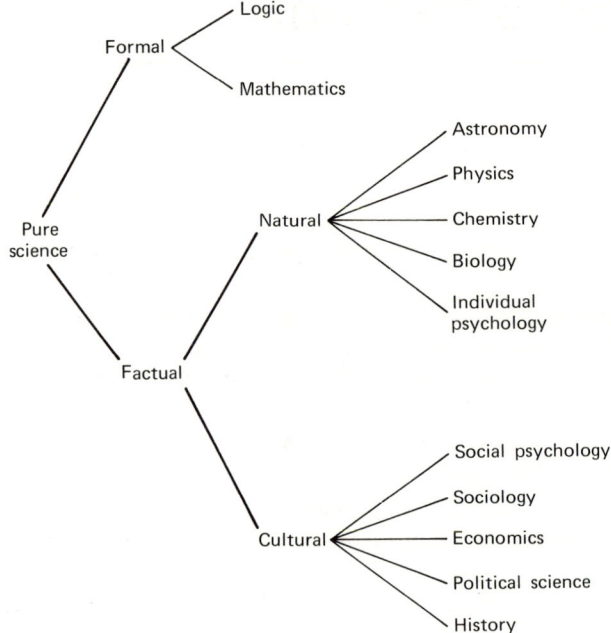

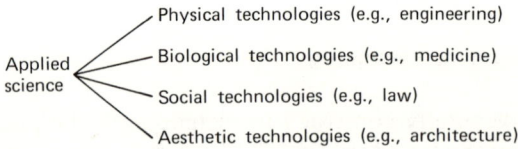

Figure IA-2. Branches of science.

between pure science, in which a purely cognitive aim is pursued, and applied science (or technology), which aims ultimately at practical goals such as increasing our welfare and power.

Figures IA-1 and IA-2, based on the classifications of Bunge (1), help clarify these definitions.

The Phases of Scientific Activity

The phases of pure research have traditionally been identified as (2):

1. The observational stage.
2. The experimental stage.
3. The theoretical and mathematical stage.

Ackoff (3) perceives the need of a finer breakdown to describe applied research, and uses:

1. Formulating the problem.
2. Constructing the model.
3. Testing the model.
4. Deriving a solution from the model.
5. Testing and controlling the solution.
6. Implementing the solution.

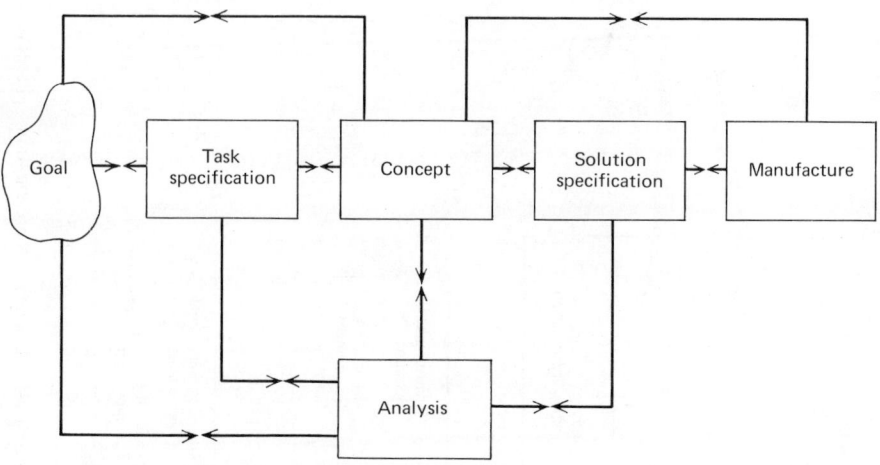

Figure IA-3. Engineering design process.

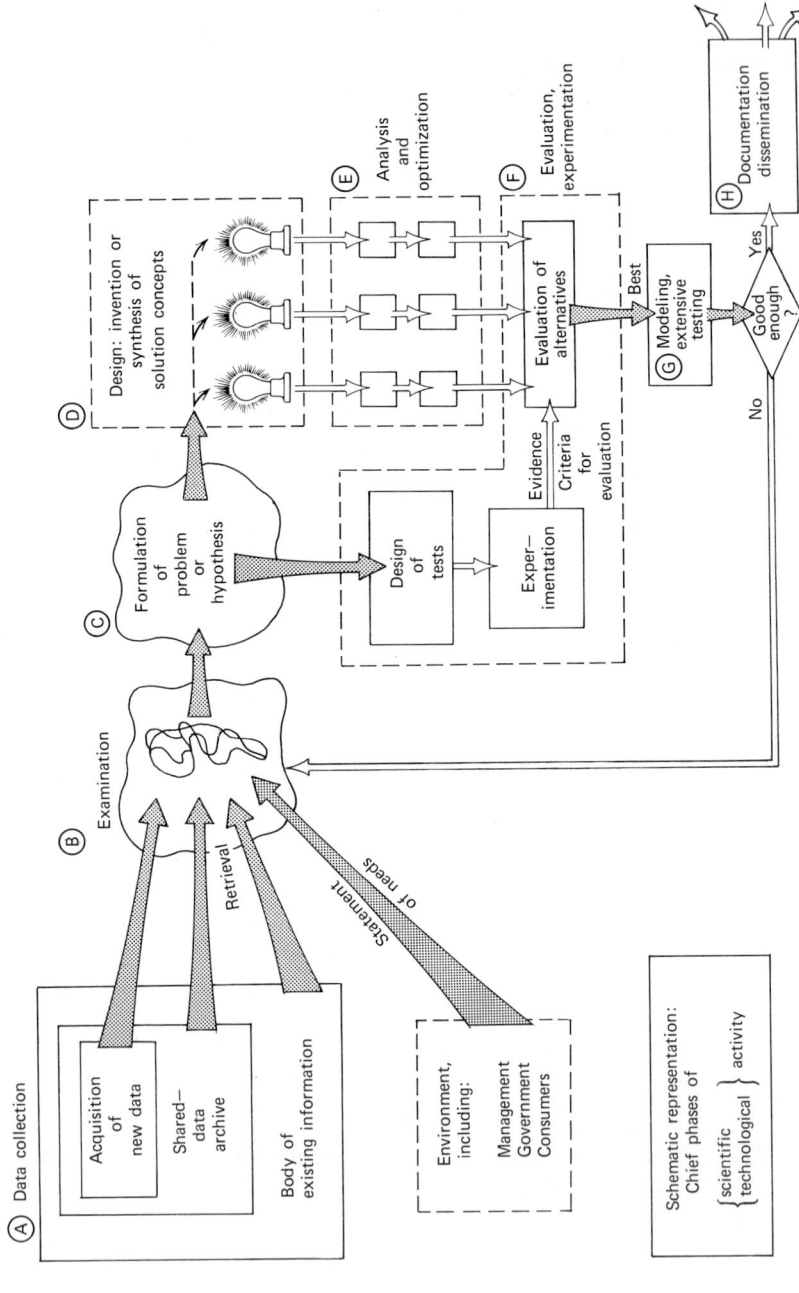

Figure IA-4. Schematic representation—phases of scientific activity.

A. METHODS OF SCIENCE AND TECHNOLOGY

Siders (4) characterizes the engineering design process as shown in Figure IA-3.

After reviewing such representations and examining the working habits of numerous scientists and technologists, we have been led to the schematic representation shown in Figure IA-4. This representation was chosen because:

1. It seems comprehensive enough and yet basic enough to describe the major activities of both pure and applied scientists, including design engineers, diagnosticians, and so on.
2. It is sufficiently detailed to serve the purpose of this book—examining the various roles of computer-based services in these processes.

The major phases of scientific activity, then, are as follows.

A. Data Collection. The data and information comprising the raw material for a scientific enterprise are collected from various sources. New data may be acquired from experiments being conducted in the laboratory or from measurements or surveys taken in the field. These new data are often contrasted with, or used in conjunction with, data that has been acquired sometime previously by the scientist or a colleague and stored in some kind of archive for future reference. Information—in the form of technical reports, articles in technical journals, or books—is retrieved from a file or library. Last, or perhaps first, information comes from a statement of need—for a new or improved product or idea—which stimulates or provokes the activity.

B. Examination. During and after collecting the various chunks of data and information, there is a period of examination, incubation, and speculation. This frequently involves a search of the data by the scientist for some pattern or regularity, or for some exceptional or surprising event. In many cases the examination primarily shows the need for additional data, which then leads to a new round of experimentation and data collection. Eventually, however, the examination process converges to the formulation of the problem.

C. Formulation of Problem or Hypothesis. At this point the problem must be stated narrowly enough to give direction and economy to the resulting activities, yet broadly enough to include the solutions of interest. Finding such a formulation often involves iterations of tentatively stating a hypothesis, testing the consequences, finding flaws, revising the hypothesis, and so on. This continues until one is confident enough to proceed on a more formal basis. The formulation of the problem leads to two separate activities: the design or invention of solutions to the problem on the one hand, and the development of criteria and means for evaluating the tentative solutions on the other.

D. Design. The design phase involves the invention or synthesis of tentative solutions to the problem that has been posed. Except in very routine problems, this is a creative rather than a logical process; that is, the generation of various solution concepts does not follow in any formal deductive fashion from the statement of the problem. It more often involves intuition or insight in which the scientist calls on his experience and imagination to associate a variety of possible solutions with the problem.

E. Analysis and Optimization. The several proposed solution concepts are individually subjected to a process of analysis, modification, and refinement, in an attempt to extract the most from each of the candidates. In the execution of this process, it usually becomes evident that some of the concepts are unsound, and they are eliminated from consideration. The surviving solutions are then evaluated by various tests and criteria.

F. Evaluation, Experimentation. The formulation of the problem also leads, in a somewhat more structured way, to the means of evaluating the proposed solutions. This phase involves the formulation of the criteria and specifications by which the designs or solutions will be evaluated. Then tests and experiments are designed to apply these specifications to the proposed designs.

G. Modeling, Extensive Testing. The evaluation process may reveal that none of the proposed solutions is good enough. In that case the scientist must either invent better solution concepts, or reformulate the problem. When the evaluation process finally yields a best, and apparently good enough, solution a phase of modeling and extensive testing is usually undertaken. The model may be a physical prototype, or an analog or symbolic representation. The objectives are to determine the range of suitability of the solution, to predict the consequences of the solution, and to determine the adequacy of the solution.

H. Documentation and Dissemination. When the modeling and testing conclude positively, the next step is the documentation of the results of the entire process, and the distribution of this documentation to those who will make use of it. The form of this documentation is primarily drawings and parts lists in the case of architects and engineers, and technical reports in the case of pure scientists. In addition to the transfer of this information to those for whom it is directly intended, its publication adds to the existing body of scientific knowledge.

Examination of this augmented body of knowledge leads another scientist to formulate a hypothesis, and so on.

1. Follow-up, Continuing Responsibility. The scientist's or engineer's responsibility does not completely terminate at any particular point in time or in the product cycle. This continuing responsibility has been spotlighted by the growing public sensitivity to the quality of technological products and the effect of these products on man and the environment.

References

1. Mario Bunge, *Scientific Research*, Vol. 1, Springer-Verlag, Berlin, 1967.
2. A. D'Ambro, *The Rise of the New Physics*, Dover, New York, 1951.
3. R. L. Ackoff, *Scientific Method*, Wiley, New York, 1962.
4. R. A. Siders, "Computer-Aided Design," *IEEE Spectrum*, November 1967, pp. 84–91.
5. T. T. Woodson, *Introduction to Engineering Design*, McGraw-Hill, New York, 1966.
6. M. Asimow, *Introduction to Design*, Prentice-Hall, Englewood Cliffs, N.J., 1961.

B. ROLES OF COMPUTER-BASED SERVICES

In the previous section we pointed out that a basic *methodology* is common to the various branches of pure and applied science. However, the *tactics* of execution, the techniques and tools employed in conducting the research and technological activities, vary widely among and within the branches. A stroll through a modern laboratory makes evident the seemingly infinite variety of tools of research and engineering.

The unique property of the general-purpose digital computer is that, for the first time, we possess a tool of such versatility that it can be used in all phases of the scientific process. This is *not* to say that computers *should be* used in any particular phase of a given scientific endeavor. Whether, and how, computer-based services should be used in any particular instance, is a complex technical/economic/social question on which, hopefully, this book will shed some light.

In this section we briefly describe, and give the motivation for, 11 types of computer-based services currently being provided in support of scientific activities. They are:

1. Data acquisition.
2. Data archive and data management services.

3. Data reduction, preprocessing, and analysis.
4. Document and information storage and retrieval.
5. Graphics.
6. Interactive problem-solving facilities.
7. General-purpose time-sharing.
8. Control of experiments and processes.
9. Batch computing: calculation and simulation.
10. Text editing and processing.
11. Inquiry.

It is interesting and instructive to introduce these various computer-based services in a historical fashion, giving some attention to the sources and timing of their development.

An interesting pictorial history of the pre-1950 period is presented in a recent book: *A Computer Perspective* (12). In it the digital computer is described as the offspring of the merging of three technological streams:

Statistical Machines. Machines used to find relationships within information by storing, sorting, and tabulating masses of data (e.g., punched-card equipment).

Logical Automata. Machines that use information about their past performance to determine their next action (e.g., gyroscopes, servomechanisms).

Calculating Machines. Machines used in performing mathematical operations (e.g., mechanical calculators, analog computers).

Some of the key developments of this early history are shown in Figure IB-a.

By the late 1930s the foundations were in place for the general-purpose computer. Actualization took place via a series of overlapping machine development projects, each of which took several important steps forward.

In Germany, Konrad Zuse built three relay calculators between 1936 and 1941. The Z-3, completed in 1941, was the first program-controlled computer. Program control, using 8-bit, one-address instructions, was punched on 35-mm cinefilm.

Between 1939 and 1944, Howard Aiken, of Harvard, and four IBM engineers designed and built the first large-scale automatic calculator—the Automatic Sequence Controlled Calculator known as the MARK I. Placed in operation at Harvard in 1944, the MARK I performed operations by following a sequence of instructions prepared by a programmer. Instructions were fed into it on punched paper tape, and the numbers on which the instructions were to operate were stored in registers. The MARK I was an

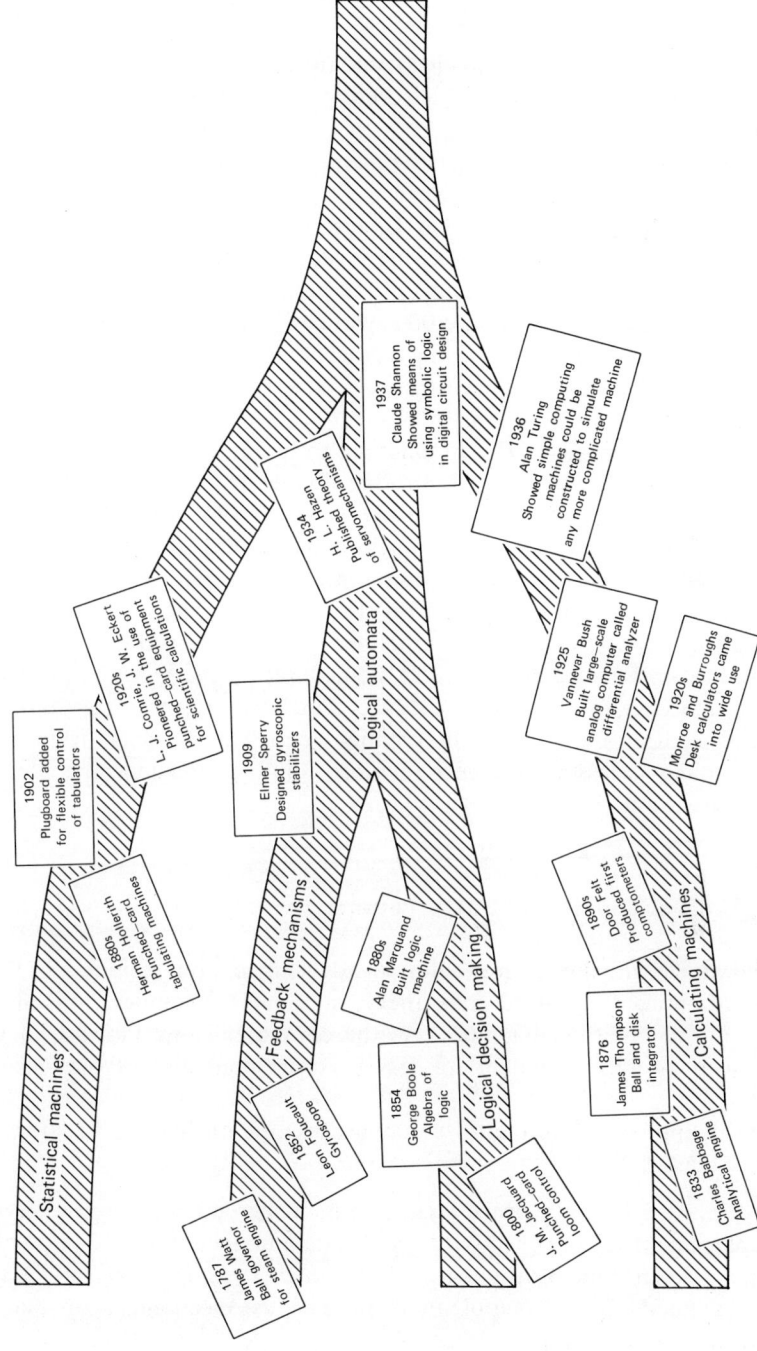

Figure IB-1. Prehistoric developments.

electromechanical rather than an electronic machine. Basic operations were performed by mechanical parts which were controlled electrically by about 3000 relays.

Between 1942 and 1946, J. Presper Eckert and John W. Mauchly, of the Moore School of Electrical Engineering at the University of Pennsylvania, developed the Electronic Numerical Integrator and Calculator known as ENIAC. Instead of relays, ENIAC used vacuum tubes and contained no moving parts except for the input-output gear. It had 500,000 soldered joints, 18,000 vacuum tubes, and 6,000 switches. It operated on the decimal system of numbers, the input was electromechanical, and the output was on punched cards. Counting was performing by electronic pulses.

In 1945, John von Neumann led a group which proposed a stored-program concept for the EDVAC machine to be built at the University of Pennsylvania. The EDSAC at Cambridge University was the first stored-program machine actually to become operative, in 1949. For the first time instructions were stored inside the machine and could be modified by the computer in the course of solving a problem.

Space does not permit more than this brief history. The references listed at the end of this section are recommended for further reading. It suffices for our purposes to note that by 1950 the general-purpose, stored-program digital computer had come into existence. Furthermore, its form than was essentially as it is today—the intervening years have largely been spent trying to make it less expensive and more reliable, and learning how to program and use it.

The Development of Usage Patterns

As noted above, the digital computer was developed from elements of three families of more specialized machinery: statistical machines, logical automata, and calculating machines. As the computer came into use, it was usually seen as a replacement for less versatile machines of one type or another.

Thus the application of digital machines became more or less segregated into three classes:

1. Administrative data processing, in which the computer was seen as a replacement for punched-card tabulating and accounting equipment.
2. Operational control applications, in which the computer served as a replacement for or supplement to various mechanical or manual means of controlling a process.

3. "Computing services" which grew out of the use of computers in replacing various sorts of calculating machines.

Figure IB-2 is an attempt to represent this symmetry between the sources of the computer and its domains of application.

The point that requires emphasis is that this segregation of computer usage is not absolute nor essential. In fact, the versatility of the computer offers a means of coordinating these different classes of activities. For example, administrative data processing and some operational control functions are being merged through the development of integrated information systems.

Until such integration is accomplished more generally, it is important that we take cognizance of the diverse roles the computer presently plays.

This book examines the class of computer usage referred to above as computing services. The characteristics of computing services are contrasted with those of data processing and operational control usage later, when issues of management are considered. Finally, we consider the potential benefits in the integration of personal computing services with information systems.

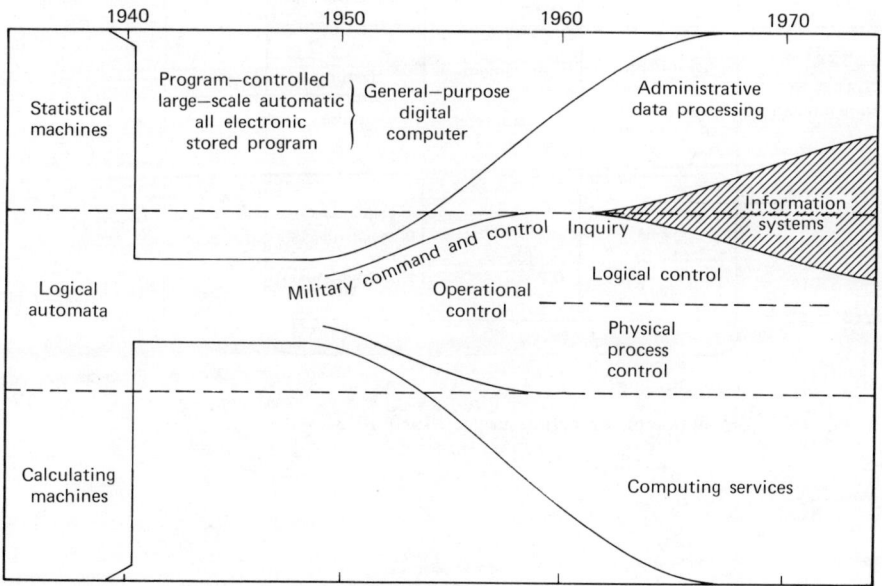

Figure IB-2. Domains of application.

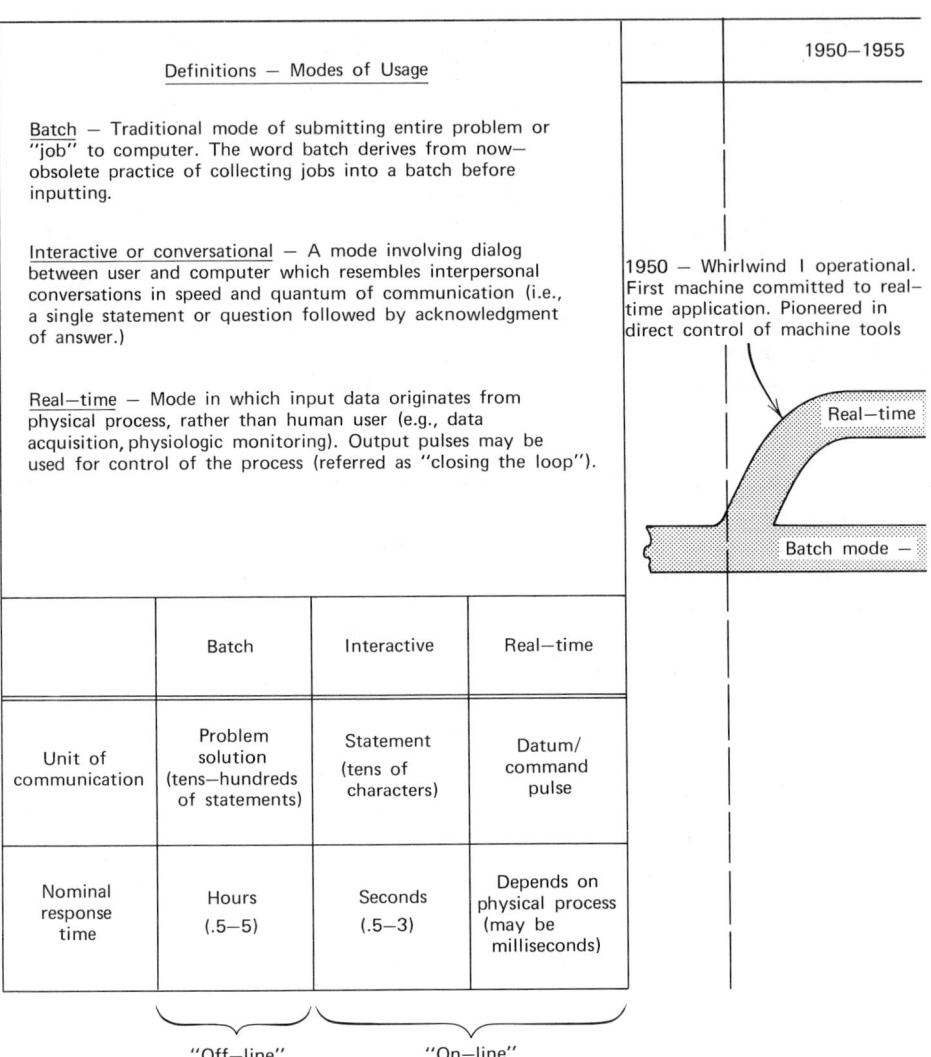

Definitions — Modes of Usage

Batch — Traditional mode of submitting entire problem or "job" to computer. The word batch derives from now-obsolete practice of collecting jobs into a batch before inputting.

Interactive or conversational — A mode involving dialog between user and computer which resembles interpersonal conversations in speed and quantum of communication (i.e., a single statement or question followed by acknowledgment of answer.)

Real—time — Mode in which input data originates from physical process, rather than human user (e.g., data acquisition, physiologic monitoring). Output pulses may be used for control of the process (referred as "closing the loop").

1950–1955

1950 — Whirlwind I operational. First machine committed to real-time application. Pioneered in direct control of machine tools

Real—time

Batch mode —

	Batch	Interactive	Real—time
Unit of communication	Problem solution (tens–hundreds of statements)	Statement (tens of characters)	Datum/command pulse
Nominal response time	Hours (.5–5)	Seconds (.5–3)	Depends on physical process (may be milliseconds)

"Off—line"   "On—line"

Figure IB-3.   Evolution of computing services. 1950–1973.

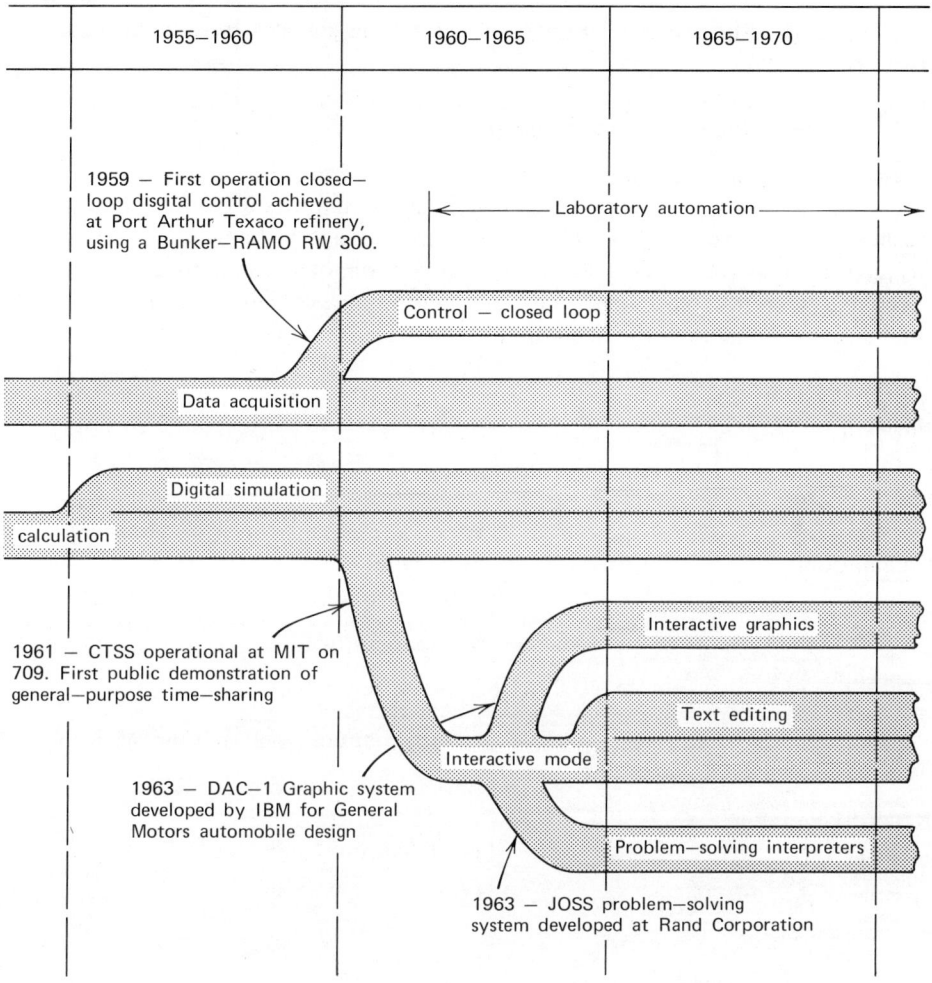

Figure IB-3 shows the flowering of computing services during the past two decades.

The State of Scientific Usage in 1950

Despite all the activity outlined in the previous discussion, at midcentury the computer was not being used by the great majority of scientists and technologists in their work. The revolution had not yet begun, so far as usage was concerned. The processes of calculation, experimentation, record keeping, reference searching, and documentation were almost completely manual, as indicated in the accompanying table.

Phase of Activity	Tools Used circa 1950
Calculation	Paper and pencil / Slide rule / Desk calculator
Experimentation	Manual control / Chart recorder with manual reduction and plotting
Record-keeping	Laboratory notebook / Filing cabinet
References	Library / Card index
Documentation	Manual / Technical assistance: Draftsman, Secretary

The following pages (Figures IB-4 through IB-8) outline the changes that have taken place in the intervening two decades and the roles that computers play in scientific activities today.

OVERVIEW: SUPPORTING ROLES OF COMPUTER SERVICE SYSTEMS

The following pages review the development of the various supporting roles played by the computer. A broad overview is herein presented of the functions available from current systems. References are made to the case studies that describe the particular function in use.

THE COMPUTER'S ROLE AS CALCULATOR AND SIMULATOR

The first use of computing machines in science was to perform involved, repetitive arithmetic calculations, such as the calculation of astronomical tables. Another early application, pioneered by Henry Wallace in Iowa in the mid-1920's, was the calculation of statistical correlations between various fertilizers and corn yields.

The high cost of computer equipment and difficulty in programming limited use of the early machines to long, repetitive jobs which otherwise would have been impossible.

The basic hardware and computational function available have changed surprisingly little since the late 1940s. The changes of paramount importance since that time have been reductions in the cost per calculation and in the difficulty of application programming.

Several recent studies* indicate a two-decade record of near annual doubling of scientific calculations per dollar. The reductions in application programming effort have resulted from the development of higher-level languages and program libraries. Figure IB-4 shows the general cost-performance trend, along with typical systems and application languages developed during the various time periods.

The early scientific use of the computer, as described above, was as a *calculator;* that is, a machine transformed numbers into numbers. Shortly, however, its use as a *simulator* began. Simulation is the process of conducting experiments on a "model" of a device or system, rather than conducting the experiments on the real object; the model is a mathematical or logical representation of the real thing. Solving a simulation problem involves not only calculation of the behavior of the model, but also establishment and checking of a faithful correspondence between the behavior of the model and that of the

---

* For example, Knight (5).

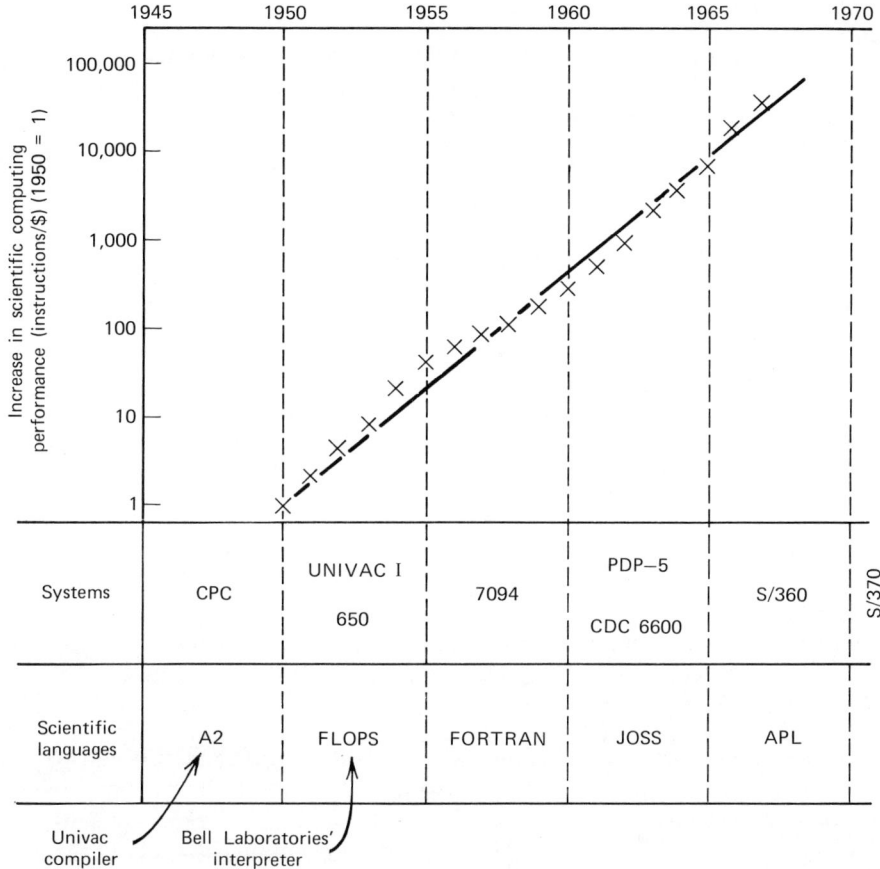

Figure IB-4. Historic trend in cost performance.

real thing. This is referred to as calibration and validation of the model. The following case studies illustrate the computer's use as a calculator and simulator.

Case Study 20. Simulation of Automobile Dynamics.
Case Study 21. Simulated Chemical Reactions.
Case Study 22. Calculation of Radiation Treatment Dosage.
Case Study 9. Formulation of a Large Mathematical Problem.

HISTORY OF THE COMPUTER IN THE LABORATORY

During the 1950s the digital computer was not being used in the laboratory. However, developments were underway which led to such application, namely:

1. Scientists were becoming familiar with programming and using computers—for their calculations.
2. The technology of real-time computer systems was being developed in other fields—including airline reservation systems, military command and control systems, and industrial process— and machine-tool control.

Gradually, then, more scientists were going through a process of manually recording experimental results and then converting them to machine-readable form via punched cards or punched tape for subsequent analysis. Naturally, the desire grew for automatic entry of the experimental data into the computer.

This was accomplished first in off-line fashion by connecting the experimental sensors, through an analog-to-digital converter, to a paper tape or card punch. The tape or cards, then, were carried to the computer and run in off-line, batch processing mode. The next step was to eliminate the cards or tapes by augmenting the computer with a "front end" which would accept the sensor data directly in a real-time mode.

The next major step in this evolution was to close the loop by feeding control signals from the computer back to control directly various parameters of the experiment. In this mode of operation control of the experiment is dependent on the data being acquired.

The final stage of laboratory automation is real-time or almost real-time data analysis and interpretation.

The Computers Roles in the Laboratory:

Data Acquisition—Case Study 1

Screening and Monitoring—Case Study 5

Controlling Experiments and Pilot Processes—Case Study 19

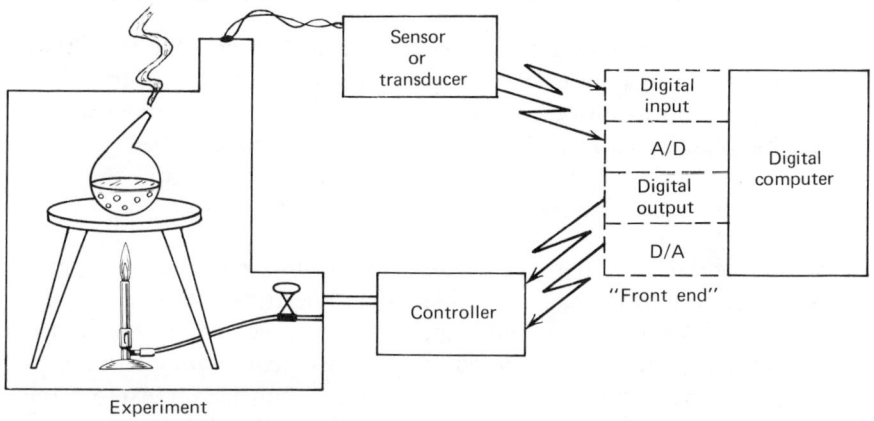

Figure IB-5. Schematic of digital data acquisition and control.

Figure IB-5 illustrates how the computer can be coupled to an experiment or pilot process. A sensor or transducer converts the physical variable(s) to be measured or controlled into a proportionate electrical voltage. An analog-to-digital (A/D) converter periodically samples the fluctuating voltage and converts it to a digital signal which can be read and stored by the computer as easily as if it came from a punched card.

In similar, but reversed, fashion, the computer, after operating on the input signal as programmed, can transmit output signals which adjust the experiment's control variable.

The addition of a conversational terminal to the digital control computer provides the scientist with an opportunity to monitor the progress of an experiment and, when desired, to modify the data collection, analysis, or control algorithms (see Case Study 10).

THE COMPUTER'S ROLE IN THE SCIENTIST'S OFFICE

The advent of remote access time-sharing makes possible the situation indicated in Figure IB-6-in which the full resources of the computer are continuously and conveniently available. Some of the possible functions afforded by this arrangement are described.

PROBLEM SOLVING (CASE STUDY 10).

An interactive terminal can be used like a desk calculator—to give quick answers to logical or mathematical questions. More generally, however, this interactivity can support a new mode of machine-aided problem solving. In such a mode the scientist can, without interruption, use the power of the computer to test hunches or explore the consequences of many ideas or designs. In such use, the computer serves to support human intuition—as earlier batch-type usage served to support human logical and analytical powers.

FILING. (CASE STUDY 8).

Using the on-line file storage facilities, information can be updated and retrieved on demand and shared with others. Many files heretofore manually committed to paper (e.g., data logs, project files, reference lists) can thus be more readily kept current and available.

REMOTE JOB ENTRY.

Even when one's problem requires only batch processing service, it is often expedient to write or revise and debug the program interactively, and to submit the program and data to the batch queue via the terminal. Upon completion the output, or at least a message, can be sent to the terminal.

Figure IB-6. The computer terminal in the right place.

TEXT EDITING AND PROCESSING (CASE STUDY 24).

The generation or revision of proposals, data logs, bills of material, reports, etc., can be accomplished on-line. This is indicated when frequent revisions are anticipated, or when speed of publication is critical.

COMMUNICATION.

The terminal can be used to communicate with colleagues and supporting workers, as well as with the computer. Thus it can serve as a high-speed interoffice mail service.

The new and exciting concept of computer conferencing offers the prospect of scientists actively collaborating in the solution of complex problems without physically assembling.

THE COMPUTER'S ROLE IN THE TECHNICAL LIBRARY

The computer's roles here are in storing, searching, retrieving, and summarizing technical information and data. Logically, these are library functions; in actuality these services usually have been provided by groups outside the traditional library organization.

SERVICES PROVIDED

Computer-Produced Abstracts and Indexes

Human readable: The production of secondary documents which, by their conciseness or organization, facilitate a personal search of the literature (e.g., *Engineering Index Monthly, Psychological Abstracts, and Information Science Abstracts*. Organizations engaged in providing these services generally are members of the National Federation of Science Abstracting and Indexing Services).

Machine readable: Magnetic tapes for bibliographic retrieval are now produced for practically all technical fields. Reference 14 describes 40 such magnetic tape technical document files which are available for lease or subscription services.

SDI (Selective Dissemination of Information)

A service that searches additions to the technical literature, and periodically provides each subscriber with a listing of citations to match his particular interest profile. (Case Study 4 describes the use of such a system.)

THE COMPUTER'S ROLE IN THE TECHNICAL LIBRARY

Retrospective Search

An in-depth search of the current and past literature on a specified subject. The query that directs the search can be specified in great detail by a subscriber in order to control the breadth, volume, and age of the information retrieved. An information retrieval specialist is often consulted in the formulation of such a query.

Data Archive

A repository for technical data collected from various sources. The data is stored, documented, and cataloged to facilitate secondary usage. The increasing cost of data and the need for data that may have been collected by another organization, for another purpose, has stimulated the creation of industry-wide, national, and international organizations dedicated to data achieving and exchange. Case study 3 illustrates the use of a data archive in the field of oceanography.

Technical Data Base or Bank

This type of service is built around a machine-readable collection of data on a particular subject. For example, the American Society for Testing Materials maintains four banks of materials data. The largest of these is the Infrared Spectral Index, which indexes the significant absorption bands of 102,000 organic and inorganic compounds.

THE COMPUTER'S ROLE IN THE TECHNICAL LIBRARY

PACE-SETTING SYSTEMS

Chemical Abstracts Service

A division of the American Chemical Society, has been providing chemical and chemical engineering information services since 1907. Computer technology plays a major role in the formation of abstracts and indexes, searching, and the generation of magnetic tapes, reports, manuals, and "hard" documents, as indicated schematically in the illustration.

MEDLARS (Medical Literature Analysis and Retrieval System)

A computer-based system at the National Library of Medicine. It became operational in 1964 with the publication of the first computer-produced issue of *Index Medicus*, a comprehensive subject-author index to articles from approximately 2300 of the world's biomedical journals.

MEDLARS provides references to the biomedical literature for researchers, clinicians, and other health professionals through:

a. Preparation of citations for publication in *Index Medicus* and current catalog.
b. Preparation of recurring bibliographies on specialized subjects of wide interest.
c. Preparation of retrospective one-time bibliographies (demand searches). This is achieved by rapid search through the file of citations to journal articles in response to specific requests submitted by health professionals.

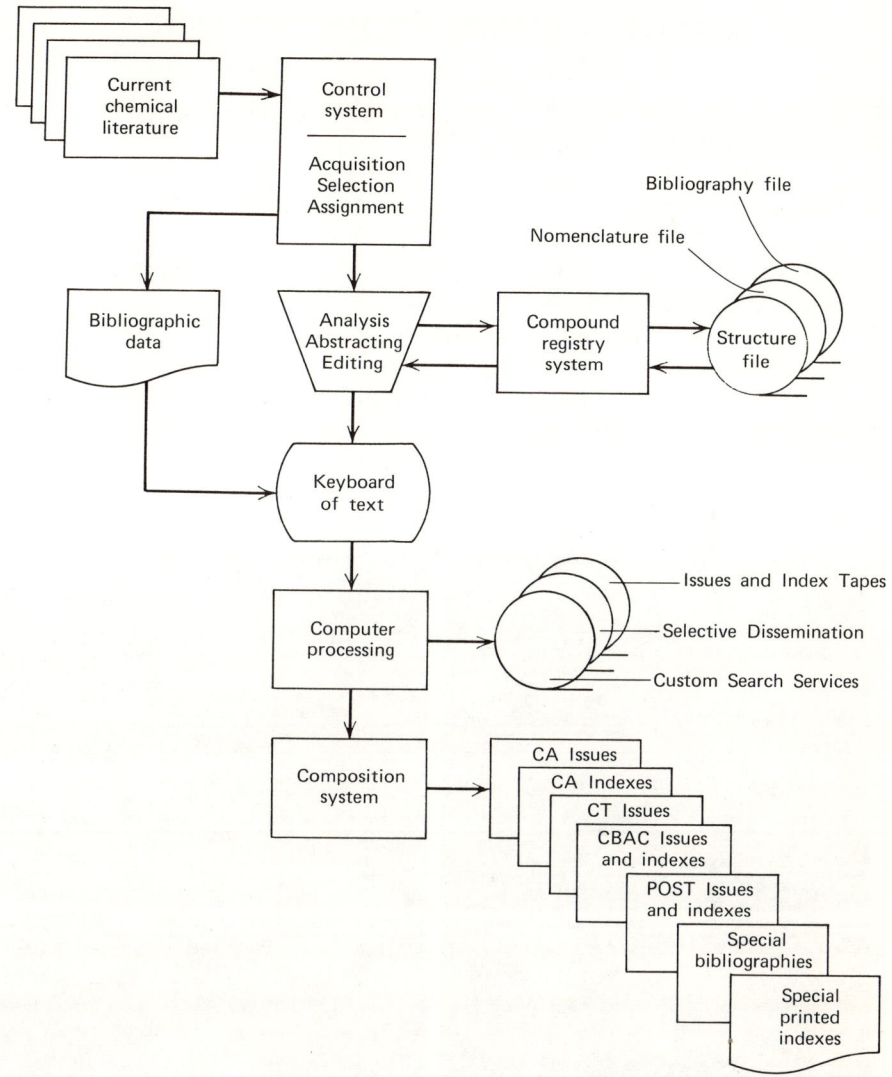

Figure 1B-7. CAS Unified Information System. The source documents are analyzed, and selected information is fed into the computer via a single keyboarding step. With little additional human work the computer can then organize the information into numerous forms for output. Thus digested and indexed information will be available more rapidly than in the past, coverage will be more complete, and details will be more accessible. Chemists, chemical engineers, and others needing the information will be able to obtain it in whatever form best suits their needs: a full printed record; an alerting publication, bibliography, or special printed index geared to their field of interest; or an individually constructed search of the computer files to answer specific questions.

COMPUTER-GENERATED GRAPHIC PRODUCTS

In many branches of science, the pictorial or grapical representation of data is either essential or desirable.

After the scientific use of computers became widespread, a scientist often found himself laboriously plotting the tabulated output of his problem by hand. The inconsistency of tedious manual plotting after high-speed automatic calculation demanded that the computer output be made available in the desired form.

There is no universally satisfactory graphic output device at the present time. Instead, a number of different devices must be employed to cover the range of requirements (speed, resolution, accuracy, cost, etc.).

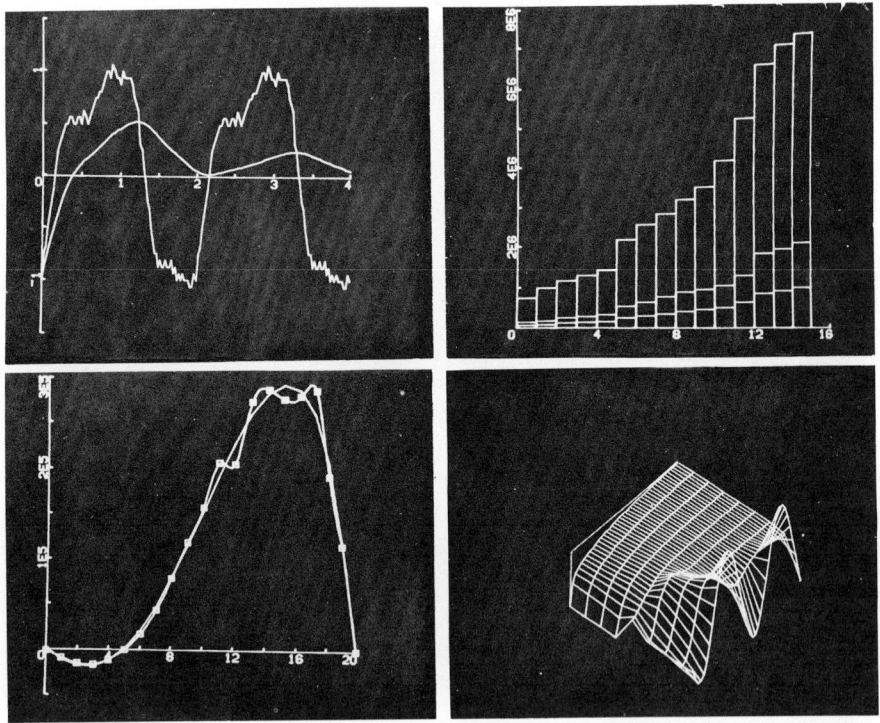

Figure IB-8*a*. Computer-generated graphic products.

Figure IB-8b. A computer-generated stereoscopic pair for crystal structure analysis.

Figure 1B-8c. Petroleum exploration—Case Study 6.

Figure IB-8*d*. Simulated chemical reaction. Case Study 21.   Figure IB-8*e*. Architectural drawing. Case Study 13.

THE COMPUTER'S ROLE AS COORDINATOR OF COMPLEX OPERATIONS

As technological operations become more complex, dynamic, and dispersed the need for overall coordination becomes a larger problem. Computer-based integrated information systems are used increasingly to coordinate these activities. The computer serves here primarily as a reservoir of up-to-date information. This widely accessible body of information makes it possible to make decisions continually on a decentralized basis without violating constraints and conditions imposed by the overall operation.

The following case studies illustrate the coordinating functions provided by some existing integrated information systems:

Case Study 18. Controlling Manufacturing Processes
Case Study 23. Total Specification Information System
Case Study 24. Legislative Information System
Case Study 25. Quality Assurance System

References

1. Anonymous, "The Evolution of the Computer from the Abacus to the ENIAC," an exhibit presented by the Johns Hopkins University Applied Physics Laboratory, Silver Spring, Md.
2. William J. Worlton, "Pre-Electronic Aids," in *Computers and the Physical Sciences,* Gordon and Breach, New York, 1970.
3. Herman H. Goldstine, *The Computer from Pascal to von Neumann,* Princeton University Press, Princeton, N.J., 1972.
4. Saul Rosen, "*Electronic Computers: A Historical Survey,*" *Computing Surveys,* **1,** 1 (March 1969).
5. Kenneth E. Knight, "Changes in Computer Performance," *Datamation,* September 1966.
6. Anonymous, "EDP Almanac," *Data Management,* January 1971.
7. R. R. Everett, "The Whirlwind I Computer," *Electrical Engineering,* **71** (August 1952), 681–686.
8. F. J. Corbato, M. Merwin-Daggett, and R. C. Daley, "An Experimental Time-Sharing System," Proceedings Spring Joint Computer Conference, 1962, pp. 335–344.
9. C. C. Hurd, "The IBM Card-Programmed Electronic Calculator," Seminar on Scientific Computation, IBM, November 1949, pp. 37–41.
10. J. W. Backus et al., "The Fortran Automatic Coding System," Proceedings Western Joint Computer Conference, 1957, pp. 188–198.
11. J. C. Shaw, "JOSS: a Designer's View of an Experimental On-line Computing System," AFIPS Conference Proceedings, Vol. 26, 1964, p. 455ff.
12. The Office of Charles and Ray Eames, *A Computer Perspective,* Harvard University Press, Cambridge, Mass., 1973.
13. Z. W. Pylyshyn, *Perspectives on the Computer Revolution*, Englewood Cliffs, N.J., Prentice-Hall, 1970.
14. C. G. Gechman, "Analysis of Technical Data Bases and Processing Services," *Proceedings of the ASIS*, Greenwood Publishing, Westport, Conn., 1970, pp. 97–99.

C. RELATIVE CAPABILITIES, MAN VERSUS COMPUTER AND COMBINED CAPABILITIES, MAN AND COMPUTER

Most scientific activities at the level of discussion in this book (e.g., data acquisition, problem formulation) are complex, being in fact composed of many tasks. At the present time many of these tasks can be performed "better" in some sense by a computer-based system than by a human (e.g., faster, cheaper, more accurately). However, many of the tasks still cannot, and perhaps never will be, executed as well by a machine as by a human.

The complexity of these scientific activities is such that most of interest to us include some tasks in each of these two categories. All other things being equal, an optimal strategy is to have the human and the computer each execute those tasks that it does "best."* All things are not equal, however, since there are two overhead costs to be considered:

1. The cost of preparation: The cost of programming the computer, or of training the humans, must be written off over the expected life of the task execution. This cost, when in the form of programming costs, may weigh against computerization in some short-lived applications.
2. Interaction overhead: Each time control is transferred from human to computer or back, some cost/time loss/inconvenience is incurred, which must be taken into consideration.

Before discussing these complications, however, let us review the relative strengths and limitations of humans and computer systems:

Basic Strengths and Limitations

Man performs operations in parallel, in milliseconds; his response time is > 100 msec.	Computers perform their operations serially, in nano- (10^{-9} sec) or microseconds (10^{-6} sec).
Man's languages are imprecise, redundant, and context-oriented.	Computer languages are unambiguous and have minimal context modification.
Men are flexible and adaptable, capable of "programming themselves contingently" on the basis of newly received information.	Computing machines are explicit, constrained by their preprogramming completely.
Man is quite good at inventing and organizing ideas, making associations between apparently unrelated notions, and recognizing patterns and stripping away irrelevant detail.	
Man is creative, unpredictable, sometimes capricious, and sensitive to human values.	The computer is capable of paying undivided attention to unlimited detail; it is immune to distraction, boredom, or fatigue.
The human memory for detail is quite limited, losing the majority of detailed information within a few minutes.	The computer's memory is, for all practical purposes, infallible.

In summary: Man is inventive and flexible. He perceives, abstracts, and associates quite well, drawing on broad experience to make decisions and check reasonableness. However, he is forgetful of detail, inaccurate, and subject to boredom and fatigue.

Computer systems, compared to humans, are fast, accurate, and consistent in recalling and processing information, but are inflexible, requiring detailed preprogramming for all situations to be dealt with.

Given the basic capabilities described above, we now can identify certain common scientific tasks that can generally be handled better by humans or by computer systems:

---

* This, of course, requires that we can determine the "best" for the tasks in question—a problem we address later.

Relative Abilities in Executing Scientific Tasks

Humans are generally "better" in their ability to:	Computer Systems are generally "better" in their ability to:
Set goals, define criteria, supply motivation.	Process quantitative information according to a specified program.
Improvise in cases of unanticipated types of events.	Monitor for prespecified events, especially when infrequent.
Make decisions using context and drawing upon varied experience.	Make rapid and consistent responses to input signals.
Reason inductively, generalizing from observations.	Carry out several programmed activities concurrently.
Make subjective estimates and evaluations.	Store coded information quickly and in great quantities. Retrieve coded information quickly and accurately when specifically requested.
Recognize gross errors or mistakes.	Count or measure physical quantities.
Identify the structure of a complex situation.	
Handle very low-probability situations.	Handle the application of simultaneous criteria and trace the interactions of any specified set or relationships without doubt or error when given a model of a complex system.

References

1. J. C. R. Licklider, "Man-Computer Symbiosis," *IRE Transactions on Human Factors in Electronics, HFE-1*, No. 1 (March 1960), p. 4–11.
2. John R. Pierce, "What Computers Should be Doing," in *Perspectives on the Computer Revolution*, Z. W. Pylyshyn, Ed., Prentice-Hall, Englewood Cliffs, N.J., 1970.
3. E. E. David, "Physiological and Psychological Considerations," in *On-Line Computing*, McGraw-Hill, New York, 1967, pp. 107–128.
4. E. J. McCormick, *Human Factors Engineering*, 3rd ed., McGraw-Hill, New York, 1970.
5. E. C. DeLand, R. W. Stacy, and B. D. Waxman, *Computers and the Delivery of Medical Care—Introduction to Computers in Biomedical Research*, Vol. III, Academic Press, New York, 1969.
6. S. A. Coons, "The Uses of Computers in Technology," in *Information*, A Scientific American Book, W. H. Freeman, San Francisco, 1966, pp. 131–142.

SECTION TWO

Current Usage: Case Studies and Critiques

As discussed in the previous section, the relative capabilities of humans and computers—in the execution of scientific tasks—are quite complementary. There is much to be gained, therefore, by accurately determining which tasks are best performed manually, which are susceptible to complete automation, and which are best performed by some man/machine collaboration.

The scientist's problem in making such determinations is complicated by the following factors:

1. There are many distinct phases of scientific activity.
2. There are now many types of computer-based services.
3. The field has developed so rapidly that there is little in the literature or, in personal or group experience, to provide practical guidance.

In view of this predicament, and in the absence of any broad constructive theory to guide the design of man-computer procedures, we attempt in this section to provide some such guidance by means of a retrospective review.

Our aim is to present a sampling of the results of the computer evolution that has taken place in science and technology over the past two decades. This is done via actual case studies, each one describing the result of a trial-and-error process undertaken by some scientist groping toward a practical exploitation of computer services in his particular environment.

These case studies are usually presented in the words of the designer or user of the system in question. Several case studies are included in each of the phases of scientific activity. Figure II-1 shows, for all case studies, the phase of activity involved, as well as the types of computer services utilized.

It should be noted that there is a definite bias implicit in this sort of presentation. That is, we are examining the survivors of a competitive process. The less successful have either not survived or have not chosen to publish. One must remember that computerization has *not* worked in many other cases, and that in few cases is it easy to introduce the computer intimately into the creative scientific process.

The reader should bear in mind that the case study approach, taken over many fields of application, leads to the introduction of some material describing the applications, which is not understandable in detail to the nonspecialist. It is important to avoid becoming hung up on this detail— read on. The case studies have been chosen to be understandable in a general way with respect to the use of computer-based services. It is hoped that, from this set of experiences, a commonly held intuition will develop which will be of some general practical value.

A. DATA COLLECTION

The data and information that provide the raw material for a scientific activity come from many sources. This section uses four case studies to cover several quite varied aspects of the collection process.

The first case study deals with the acquisition of measurement data from laboratory experiments. Case study 3 describes the means of obtaining existing data from a computerized data archive. Case study 4 describes a document searching and retrieval system which helps a scientist find the reports, books, and journals relevant to his current interest.

The second case study shows how computers can, by means of normalization and enhancement routines, serve to improve the quality of the data acquired.

CASE STUDY 1   Data Acquisition*

Introduction

The automation of chemical, biological, and physical instruments, and, in fact, whole laboratories has become widespread in recent years for a number of reasons. A wide diversity of concepts, approaches, and so-

---

* This case study is an excerpt from Swalen et al. (5).

Types of computer-based services	① Data acquisition	② Data management	③ Data reduction and analysis	④ Doc. and info. storage and retrieval	⑤ Graphics
Ⓐ Data collection	① San Jose Laboratory automation	③ NODC	② JPL Image proc.	④ ITIRC	
Ⓑ Examination	⑤ Patient monitoring		⑥ Seismic signal proc.		⑦ Market research
Ⓒ Problem formulation					⑩ Data-dep. problem form.
Ⓓ Design					⑪ GM / ⑬ Architec.
Ⓔ Design and optimization					
Ⓕ Testing and experimentation	⑱ Manuf. control				
Ⓖ Modeling					⑳ Auto dynamics / ㉒ Radiation
Ⓗ Documentation		㉓ TSIS / ㉔ WASH		㉓ TSIS / ㉔ WASH	
Ⓘ Follow-up		㉕ PAAC			

Figure II-1. Case study map.

⑥ Interactive terminal	⑦ Gen. purpose time—sharing	⑧ Control of exper. and processes	⑨ Batch computing and simulation	⑩ Text editing and processing	⑪ Inquiry
		⑧ Medical diagnosis			
⑨ Math. prob. form ⑩					
	⑪ GM — auto design		⑫ Fairchild CKT design		
			⑭ Election		
			⑮ NASTRAN		
			⑯ Circuit anal.		
		⑰ Traffic			
		⑱ Manuf.			
		⑲ Fusion			
			⑳ Auto dyn.		
			㉑ Clementi		
			㉒ Radiation		
				㉔ Wash. state	㉓ CHEVVY TSIS
					㉔ Wash. state
					㉕ PAAC

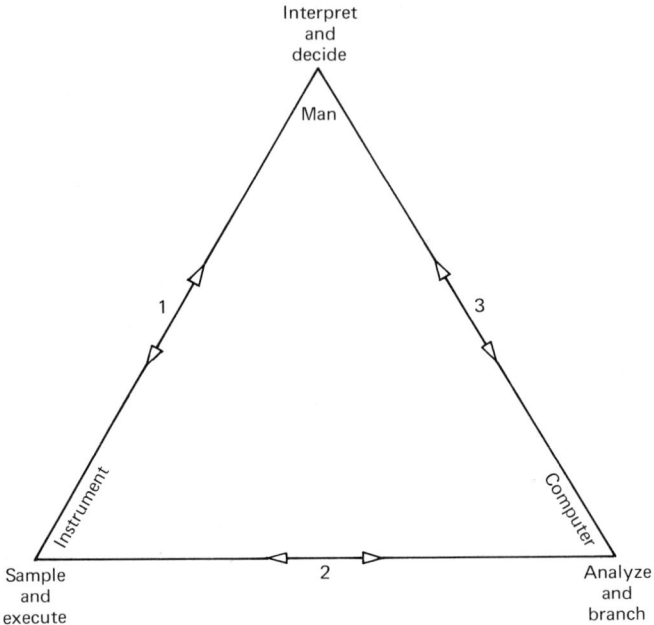

Figure IIA1-1. Laboratory Automation as a communications problem.

phistication are in evidence. To some, laboratory automation is connecting a single analog controller to some instrument variable, and to others it means the complete control and data processing of, for example, a nuclear accelerator. For the purposes of this discussion, we will primarily consider automation by digital computers of instruments in an analytical chemical laboratory and in a physics and chemistry research laboratory.

Many reasons can be given for automating a laboratory, whether it contains one instrument or several. First, one expects that more work can be done with the same amount of manpower. This might, perhaps, generate concern on the part of some, who fear that fewer jobs would be available because of the increased productivity. However, it is the tedium and monotony of laboratory work which is most dramatically reduced, not the generation of ideas nor the innovation of technique. On the contrary, since the professional experimenter can spend more time away from his laboratory, he is freed to design more experiments for his associates and himself to carry out—thereby increasing the number of jobs available.

Secondly, the work is better. It is more reliable, since the probability of error on the part of the computer is far less than that of the human. It is more accurate, since the computer can work at much greater arithmetic precision than its human counterpart. Further it is more reproducible under computer control than it would be otherwise, because the same sequence of precise instrument settings and readings can be guaranteed to occur repeatably.

Finally, new experiments can be performed that would not be feasible without automation. Some examples of these are the control of high speed and high data instruments, the improvement of signal-to-noise ratios allowing the observation of very weak signals and the ability to control and combine variables in a more complicated way to make difficult measurements. Although all contribute, the last factor more than the other two enhances the experimentalist's analytical and judgement powers.

The design of a laboratory automation system must take into account a number of communications requirements. Figure IIA1-1 portrays laboratory automation as a three-way communications problem. One concern is the communications between the instrument and the computer in terms of the actual recording of the experimental data and the physical control of the instrument. Another side of the triangle represents communications between man and the instrument which cannot be eliminated. There will probably always be some controls that will never pay to interface with the computer. The third side of the triangle, representing the man-computer interaction, is a matter of general concern throughout data processing. We will discuss briefly those man-computer communications specific to the problem of laboratory automation.

Data Acquisition

What are the general characteristics of the instruments we are attempting to automate? In nearly every case the investigator is interested in measuring the effect caused by the variation in some independent variable, such as wavelength, magnetic field, temperature, etc. on some physically observable phenomena, the dependent variable, for example, light absorption, or transmission, pressure variation, etc. However, because of the complexity of laboratory instruments today, this can become a tedious and time-consuming process. Often a number of other parameters must be constantly monitored during the course of an experiment to prevent instrument drift and subsequent loss of data. Moreover, on completion of the experiment a thorough understanding of the results may require the application of a number of data reduction algorithms and in some cases ultimately digitizing a significant fraction of the data for subsequent analysis on a digital computer. A common problem facing the physical scientist is

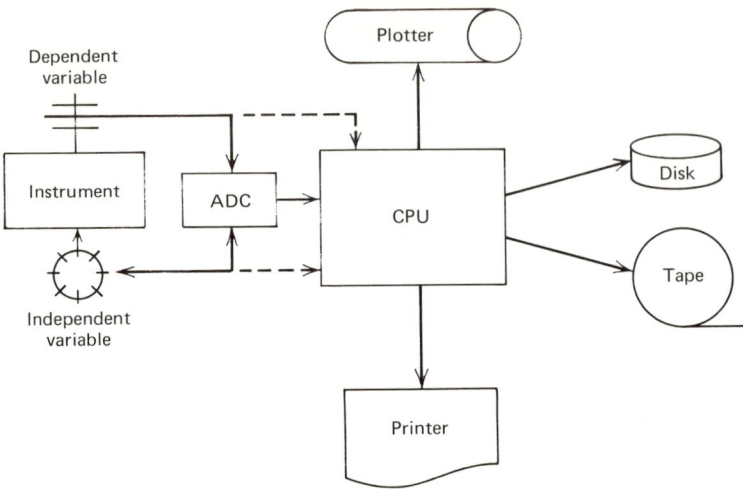

Figure IIA1-2. Schematic diagram of the instrument–computer interface.

the understanding of phenomena which manifest themselves as only small differences between a standard and the sample of interest. In these cases the major limitation is usually electrical or mechanical noise which limits the ultimate signal-to-noise ratio or sensitivity attainable in any instrument. One may reduce the effects due to noise, and, therefore, increase the resultant signal/noise ratio, by performing multiple scans over the region of interest and averaging the accumulated data. If the noise has a random distribution, the signal/noise ratio increases by the square root of the number of scans. This technique, commonly referred to as time or digital averaging, is one of the more frequent applications in lab automation. It is clear also that the experimenter can utilize a technology that handles the tedium of monitoring the experimental parameters and the multiple repetition of the experiment often necessary to render the data useful.

Let us consider the data acquisition step of automating an instrument using a digital computer. First, of course, we must provide the computer with digital values related to the parameters we wish to monitor. In practically all laboratory instruments the experimental data is recorded on a strip chart recorder, driven by analog signals proportional to measured variables. These analog voltages are usually suitable with little modification in terms of amplification or voltage division as input to an analog-to-digital converter (ADC) which may then interface to the digital logic of the computer (Figure IIA1-2). The ADC may be located at the instrument or may be an integral part of the computer as, for example in the IBM 1800.

There are now a number of techniques available for the recording of the experimental data. Conceptually the most obvious method is to dedicate the computer to the instrument, continuously monitoring and recording the necessary data during the entire length of the experiment. A second method is to have the computer sample the experimental parameters at fixed intervals, performing other processing tasks during the remaining available time. A third mode is to have the computer sample the data only in response to an interrupt from the instrument. In this manner, for example, data are recorded only when the interesting variable exceeds, in a positive or negative sense, some threshold value. Again, the remaining CPU time is available for other processing tasks.

The point of importance in this discussion is that the data sampling technique must be well matched to the instrument requirements, and in installations having more than one type of instrument, the lab automation system must be capable of providing the techniques that best support these instruments.

An Example of a Laboratory System

We will now give an example of how the criteria discussed above was established and implemented to meet the laboratory automation needs of the IBM San Jose Research Laboratory. This laboratory is relatively small (150–200 total personnel) providing research among others in the physical sciences. The experiments for which the lab automation system is designed are:

		Class
1.	Electron paramagnetic resonance spectrometer	I
2.	Vacuum ultraviolet spectrophotometer	I
3.	Visible-region monochromator	I
4.	Gas-liquid chromatograph	II
5.	Far-infrared interferometer	I
6.	Low-resolution mass spectrometer	III
7.	High-resolution Stark spectrometer	I
8.	Nuclear magnetic resonance spectrometer	I
9.	Gel-permeation chromatograph	II
10.	Photoconductive decay studies	III
11.	Differential scanning calorimeter	I

Each may be classified as belonging to one of three general categories:

I. Slow scanning and time independent,
II. Slow scanning and time dependent, and
III. Fast scanning.

The machine on which this system has been implemented is a 32K, 2 microsecond, IBM 1800 with 24 levels of priority interrupt. It is equipped with three 512K-1810-disks, a line printer, a card-read punch, an incremental plotter, a keyboard typewriter, three output typewriters, and three internal timers, one with a time base of .125 msec and two with 1 msec time bases. In addition, the 1800 is equipped with digital I/O, both high and low speed analog I/O, and external or process interrupt terminals. The laboratory automation system was written as a special purpose submonitor of the 1800-TSX (Time-Sharing Executive) system control program. The individuals responsible for the instruments above are for the most part scientists with limited computer and programming background.

A number of subroutines provide for disk file transmission and communication, examination of the data from a partly completed run, termination of tasks in the event of failures, time-averaging plotter subroutines, and debugging aids. In addition, a general purpose library of subprograms has been developed for interpolation, integer arithmetic, normal equation solution, Fourier-transform, numerical integration, smoothing, baseline correction, peak-picking, nonlinear least squares fitting, etc.

As an example of the mechanics involved in actual usage, we give below a listing of the FORTRAN subroutine, "DATIN", used for initiating data collection for the gas liquid chromatograph.

```
SUBROUTINE DATIN (IDT, NPTS)
INTEGER OP(12), DEV(2),LOAD(2)
DATA OP/1,1,8,10,2,5,2,14,1,5,10,0/
DATA LOAD/8,50/
DATA DEV/18,19/
OP (1) = NPTS
OP (2) = IDT
CALL INIO (OP,DEV,LOAD)
RETURN
END
```

The argument sequence for INIO consists of three vectors, OP, DEV and LOAD, which communicate the data acquisition parameters to the monitor. OP(1) and OP(2) are, respectively, the number of points and the time increment in milliseconds between points. Generally, 1200 points are collected at a rate of 1-2 points per second. OP(3), which has a value of 8, is the logical number of the typewriter used for output messages. OP(4-7) and OP(8-11) are grouped together and specify the operations to be performed.

Group 1 OP (4) = 10 OPERATION *10*, analog input sequential
         (5) = 2   READ *2* analog input points
         (6) = 5   Transmit the data to disk file *5*
         (7) = 2   Start the data transmission at record *2*
Group 2 OP (8) = 14 OPERATION *14*, record time interval (msec)
         (9) = 1   1 word needed for time data
        (10) = 5   Transmit the data to disk file *5*
        (11) = 10 Start the data transmission at record *10*

DEV is the device table. In this case DEV(1) and DEV(2) indicate that analog input multiplexer addresses 18 and 19. When data acquisition is completed, the interrupt core load EX10 releases the assigned resources and queues the user's program from the set of names EXIxx; the number and priority determined by the vector LOAD. Thus, EX108 is queued with a priority of 50.

This system, with the maximum of six simultaneous users and the limitations described above, has proven quite satisfactory in serving the needs of the San Jose Research Laboratory. The nature of the laboratory is such that most of the applications do not require continued use of the instrument over an extended period of time. The number of users has increased at a steady pace from one initially in late 1967 to the eleven present instruments online today.

References

1. S. P. Perone, "Computer Applications in the Chemistry Laboratory." *Analytical Chemistry*, August 1971, 1288–1299.
2. Don Secrest, *On-Line Use of Computers in Chemistry*, S. Fernbach and A. Taub, Eds., Gordon and Breach, New York, 1970, pp. 437–462.
3. H. Cole, "Computer Operated Laboratory Equipment." IBM Research Report, RC 2130, July 8, 1968.
4. H. A. Reich, *An Experimental System for Time-Shared, On-Line Data Acquisition, IBM Journal of Research and Development,* January 1969, 114–18.
5. J. D. Swalen, D. L. Raimondi, D. C. Clarke, P. M. Grant, R. J. Gritter, and T. R. Lusebrink, "Laboratory Automation, IBM Research Report, RJ 746, August 18, 1970.
6. K. L. Konnerth, *Use of a Terminal System for Data Acquisition, IBM Journal of Research and Development,* January 1969.
7. H. M. Gladney, "A Simple Time-Sharing Monitor System for Laboratory Automation," Journal of Computational Physics, February 1968.
8. A. Segmuller, and H. Cole, Procedures to Run on Automated Micro-Densitometer on a Shared Computer System, *Advances in X-Ray Analysis,* Vol. 14, Plenum Press, New York, 1971, pp. 338–351.
9. P. M. Grant, "Automation of a Wide-Range, General-Purpose Spectrophotometric System, "*IBM Journal of Research and Development,* January 1969.

CASE STUDY 2 Data Conditioning and Enhancement

Once data have been acquired from an instrument and stored in digital form, the computer can be used to improve the quality of the data by correcting or compensating for imperfections or limitations of the measuring instrument.

In some cases the imperfection of the instrument is inherent and unchanging, and can be compensated for by a fixed program. More frequently, the distortions are variable, as a result of changes in the instrument, environmental changes such as spurious "noise" signals, or because of the nature of the data and its relation to the instrument. In these cases, the amount and type of distortion must be deduced somehow, and the compensating transformation adjusted accordingly.

The case study presented here deals with the enhancement of pictorial data. The same principles and motivations apply to other data types, such as numbers or time signals. Pictorial data were chosen because it is easy to see the result of the enhancement, and because of the outstanding work done with this form of data as a result of the NASA space program.

Enhancement of Image Data*

INTRODUCTION. In recent years the ability to process images to emphasize details, to sharpen the picture, to modify the total range, to aid picture interpretation, to remove anomalies, and to detect differences between pictures has evoked interest in a number of different scientific fields. This paper is a discussion with illustrations of the kinds of processing which can be accomplished, a discussion of some of the parameter boundaries and limitations, and finally, a discussion of some of the system techniques which have proven helpful at JPL.

Initially, the concepts and understanding of the requirements of image processing were developed for the processing of pictures as returned from the NASA space vehicles to JPL. (The author is with the Image Processing Laboratory, Jet Propulsion Laboratory, California Institute of Technology, Pasadena, California.) In general, these same concepts and, to a very large extent, even these same specific programs, have been utilized to process pictures from the electron microscope, light microscope, medical and industrial x-ray photographs, various telescope pictures, and others.

APPROACH. It was decided that the required operations on the pictures could be best performed in a digital computer. Digital processing has the

---

* This case study is exerpted from Billingsley (2).

A. DATA COLLECTION   45

advantages of being extremely flexible and of being rather troublefree and easy to use once the programming system has been worked out, has the ability to handle problems which are nonlinear in both intensity and geometry, and can do these with an accuracy limited only by the user's knowledge of the incoming data. To gain the advantages of digital processing requires high-quality signals with low noise and associated accurate analog-to-digital conversion equipment for scanning film and digi-

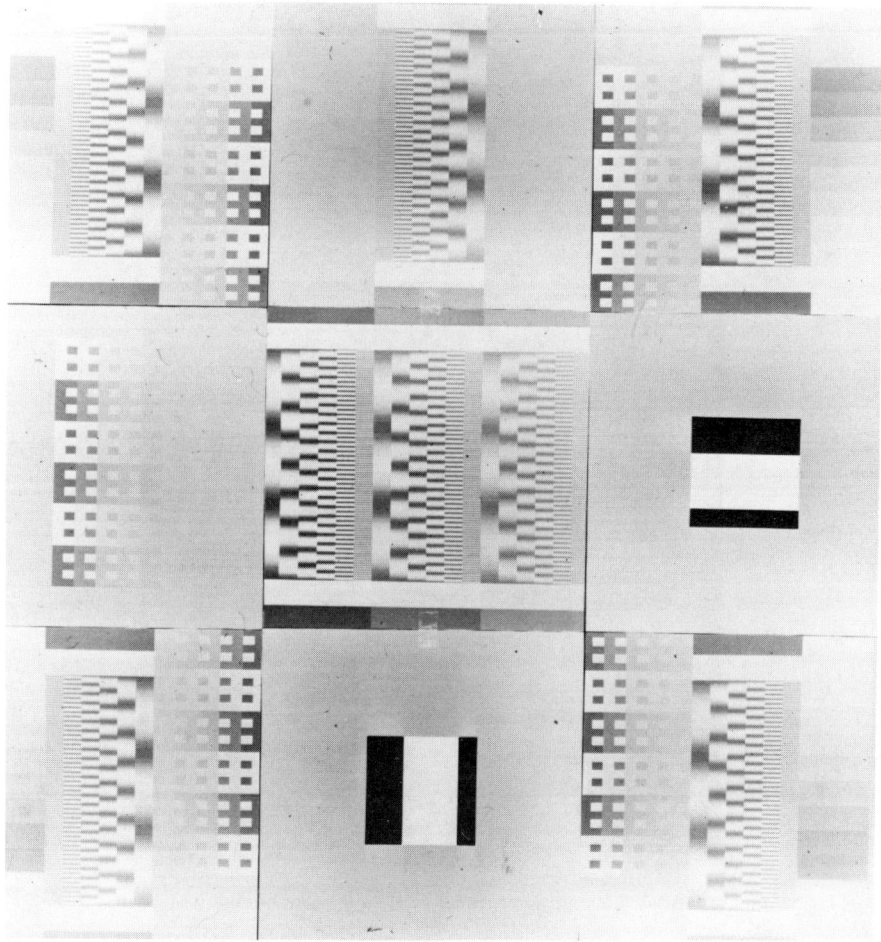

Figure IIA2-1. Computer-generated test target.

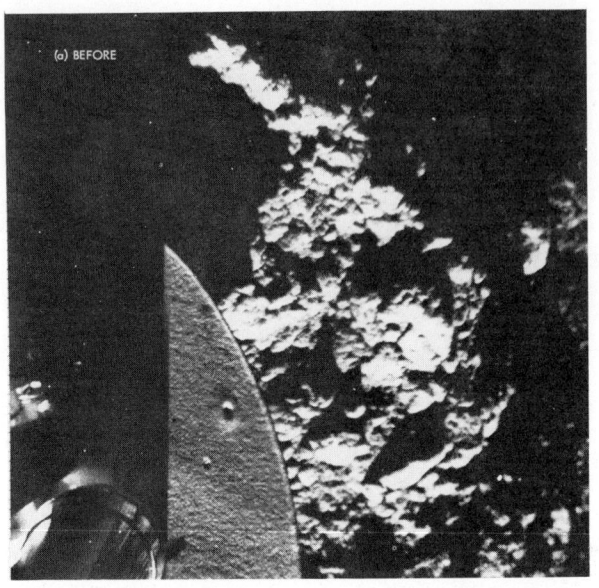

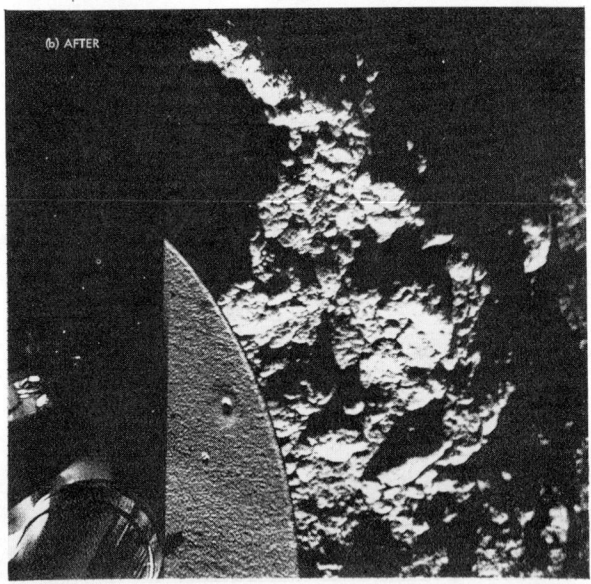

Figure IIA2-2. Picture sharpening by enhancement of high frequencies.

Figure IIA2-3. Removal of glare by partial removal of low frequencies.

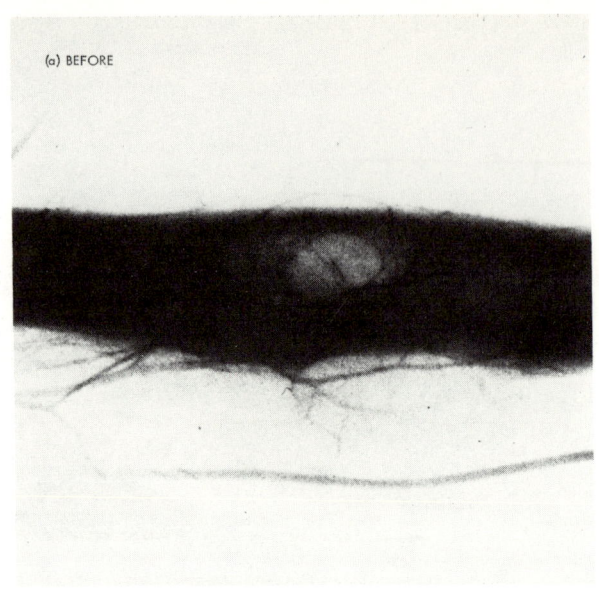

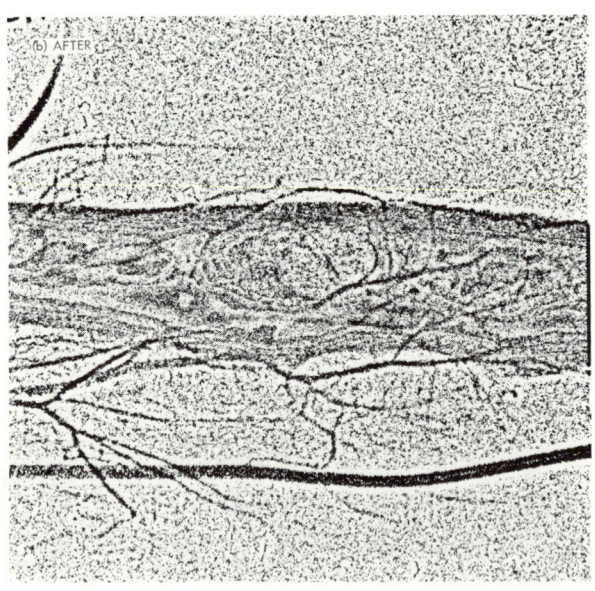

Figure IIA2-4. Edge enhancement by removal of all low frequencies (tumor).

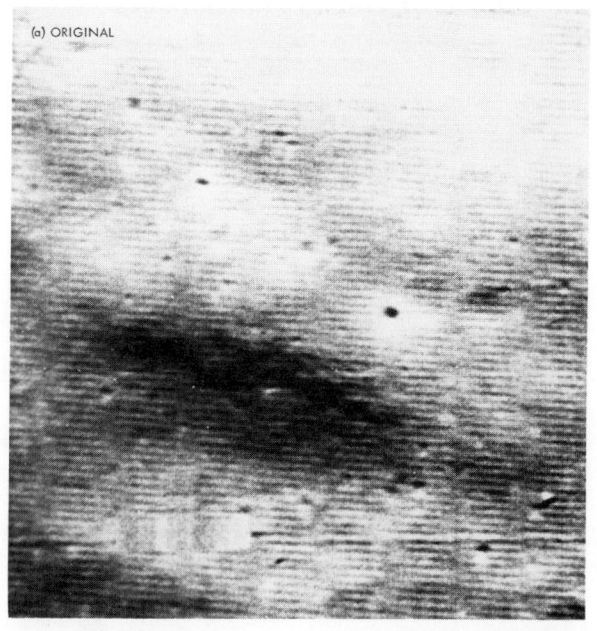

(a) ORIGINAL

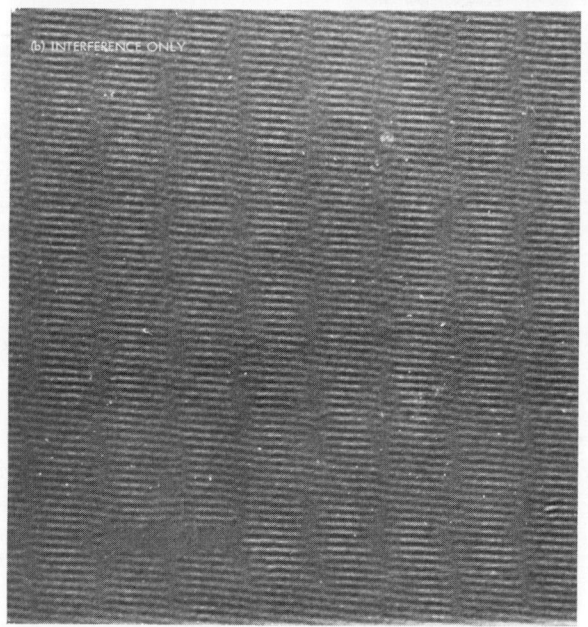

(b) INTERFERENCE ONLY

50 CURRENT USAGE: CASE STUDIES AND CRITIQUES

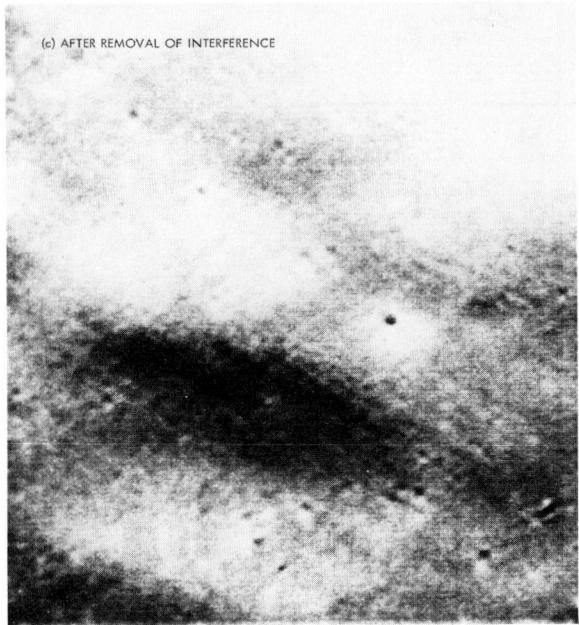

Figure IIA2-5. Location and removal of discrete two-dimensional sinusoids (Ranger).

tizing analog magnetic tape signals. Although the possible high cost of a digital computer system is a potential disadvantage, this cost can be traded for processing speed by using a smaller computer which will require longer to do the processing.

Spatial Frequency Operations

High spatial frequency response of a system is commonly limited within the passband defined by the Nyquist sample spacing, resulting in a loss of high-frequency detail. The amount of this loss may be measured in the x and y directions by photographing sinusoidal test charts such as shown in Figure IIA2-1. The two-dimensional inverse of this rolloff curve is produced and then Fourier-transformed. The high spatial frequency enhancement allowable, and hence the restoration and picture detail, is limited by the accompanying noise amplification at high spatial frequencies in a manner analogous to other equalization corrections. The filter is then applied by convolution to the picture, resulting in a restoration of the high-frequency details. The effects of such a process is shown in Figure IIA2-2.

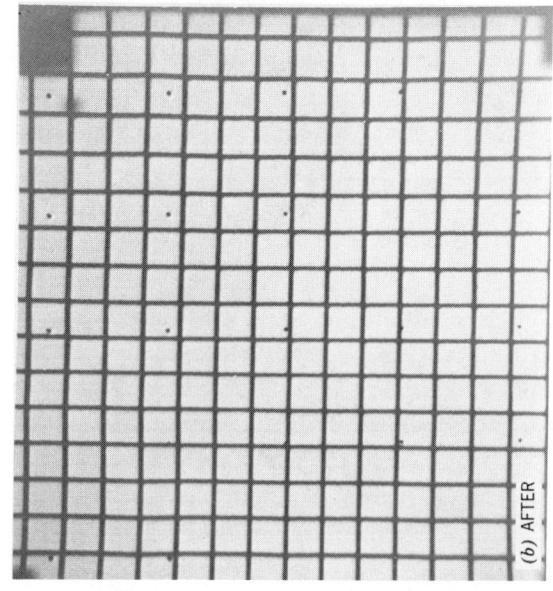

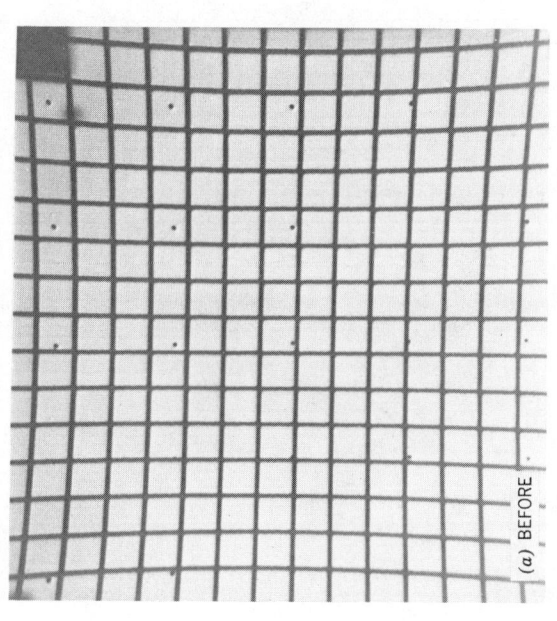

Figure IIA2-6. Correction of geometric camera distortion (Surveyor). (*a*) Before. (*b*) After.

Figure IIA2-7. Use of geometric correction for correction of perspective.

Other manipulations in the spatial-frequency domain may be accomplished. Figure IIA2-3 illustrates the removal of glare from a Surveyor III picture by a partial elimination of the low-frequency components. The low-frequency components may be completely eliminated as shown in Figure IIA2-4, resulting in the loss of all shading and the reproduction of only fine details and edges. Figure IIA2-4 shows the enhancement of this fine detail in the x-ray photograph of a tumor of the arm.

Shading operations need not be done linearly. Oppenheim and his co-workers at the Massachusetts Institute of Technology have used nonlinearly distributed digital steps of intensity. These when processed, result in a shading removal which has some advantages in the enhancement of the visual appearance.

The spatial frequencies to be removed may be isolated sinusoids. Figure IIA2-5 is a portion of a Ranger VII picture in which a sinusoidal interference is present in the transmitted picture. A convolution filter was used to isolate this noise (shown alone in Figure IIA2-5).

Geometric Manipulation

Typical camera systems will have some degree of geometric nonlinearity. This may be determined by measurement of the distortion in a photograph of a test target such as a known rectangular grid or a known array of stars. A known grid photographed by the Surveyor camera system before and after correction is shown in Figure IIA2-6.

The GOEM-type program may be used to reproject a photograph for rectification or other purposes. Figure IIA2-7 illustrates the application to an earth-based photograph of a building.

REFERENCES

1. Robert Nathan, "Digital Video Data Handling," J.P.L. Technical Report No. 32–877, January 5, 1966.
2. F. C. Billingsley, "Applications of Digital Image Processing," *Applied Optics,* **9**, 2 (February, 1970), 289–299.
3. C. Bristor, W. M., Callicott, and R. E. Bradford, "Operational Processing of Satellite Cloud Pictures by Computer," *Monthly Weather Review,* **94**, 8 (August 1966), 515–527.
4. J. A. Leese, A. L. Booth, and F. A. Godshall, "Archiving and Climatological Applications of Meteorological Satellite Data," ESSA Technical Report NESC 53, U.S. Dept. of Commerce.
5. B. S. Lipkin, and A. Rosenfeld, *Picture Processing and Psychopictorics,* Academic Press, New York, 1970.

CASE STUDY 3 Data Sharing*

The value and accuracy of a scientist's efforts are often limited by the amount of relevant data obtainable. In some fields, such as the social sciences, the gathering of data is frequently the most expensive component of the research project.

Therefore there is a great benefit to be realized from the exchange of scientific and technical data between individuals and organizations. It is surprising, however, to find how difficult it is to reconcile data that have come from several sources. The difficulty arises partly from the variety of styles and formats used in collecting and recording the data, and partly from the inadequacy of the documentation (if any) describing the data.

The personal use of computers by scientists has imposed some discipline on the management of their data to make it machine-processable, at all. On the other hand, the availability of computers has created a need for larger and larger quantities of data.

This need has, during the past several years, stimulated the establishment of organizations dedicated to the archiving and exchange of scientific data.

Within the government, the recent interest and concern over environmental issues called attention to problems of data coordination in this area. According to a Study of Environmental Quality Information Programs conducted during the spring of 1970, "there were 75 identified sources of environmental quality information located in agencies of the U.S. Government or in programs operating under the direct sponsorship of the government.

To help cope, with this problem, the Environmental Data Service was established as the first major line organization devoted to scientific data management in a government agency.†

Robert Freeman of EDS, in the referenced paper (1), delineates several problems which complicate the sharing of scientific data:

First, data are related to the time and place at which observations were made. Thus, while time series analyses and other statistical techniques may be applied for data reduction purposes, it is difficult to approach the well-known reproducible reference data found in the basic sciences.

Second, data generally are collected either for research or real-time forecasting, without much thought being given to possible future uses of no direct benefit to the collector. Consequently, variances in methods, instru-

---

* This case study was exerpted from References 1, 2 and 3, provided by Robert Ochinero of the National Oceanographic Data Center.

† EDS is one of six major elements in NOAA, the National Oceanic and Atmospheric Administration, in the U.S. Department of Commerce.

ments, and parameters measured make it difficult to piece together seemingly similar collections.

Third, a wide variety of storage media is made available to the data manager. The media include publications, punched cards, magnetic tapes, photographs, maps, charts, microfilm, handwritten forms, and autographic traces.

The fourth and final characteristic problem is access to the data. Feelings of proprietary interest and sheer lack of glamour in data archiving complicate the matter of making data available. Some data are relatively well hidden in thick publications. Consequently, obtaining access and keeping track of the location of the data may be as important as being able to produce the actual data values.

To illustrate the functioning of a Data Archive, we will examine the operation of the National Oceanographic Data Center (NODC), one of the Environmental Data Service's five major facilities, part of the world's largest usable collection of marine data. Established in 1960 to acquire and disseminate oceanographic data, the Center is a national service facility for the United States; it also administers World Data Center A, Oceanography.*

For researchers in government, private institutions, and industry, for marine scientists and engineers, and for all who take their talents to the sea, it is a central source of marine information and related products.

The National Oceanographic Data Center receives information for all oceans, seas, and estuaries from hundreds of sources, domestic and foreign, including the national data centers of other countries. Under the World Data Center system, World Data Center A receives material from international cooperative investigations, Declared National Programs (for example, the Eastern Gulf of Mexico Expedition), and other activities.

Data and publications are also obtained by exchange between the Center and individuals and organizations in 45 countries and such groups as the ICES, the International Council for the Exploration of the Sea, as gifts from scientists and organizations wishing to share their data,† and through the purchase of valuable marine data collections.

Incoming data are handled by the Operations Division, which accessions, processes, and performs quality control. A records control center provides inventories of all data entering the Center and notes their processing status and location. Data leave the Center through the Services Division, which

---

* Others are the National Climatic Center Asheville, N.C.: the National Geophysical Data Center and the Aeronomy and Space Data Center, Boulder, Colo.; and the Environmental Science Information Center, Rockville, Md.
† See the "Guide to Submission of Data," available from NODC.

provides copies, summaries, and analysis and information services on request. Archives include automated, miniaturized, and hard-copy forms. The Development Division carries forward the Center's work on innovative data processing, archiving, and retrieval systems. An IBM 360/40 operated by the Computer Systems Division provides high-speed processing, direct-access retrieval, and cathode-ray tube displays of the holdings.

The Center collects the National Marine Data Inventory (NAMDI), which contains information on quantities and types of data, area of operations, and responsible personnel. Input is received from major United States activities contributing to the national effort in the marine sciences. The inventory, initiated in 1967, is queried through a computer system.

Oceanographic Data Available from NODC

- Mechanical and expendable bathy-thermograph data in analog and digital form.
- Oceanographic station data, for surface and serial depths, giving values of temperature, salinity, oxygen, inorganic phosphate, total phosphorus, nitrite-nitrogen, nitrate-nitrogen, silicate-silicon, and pH.
- Continuously recorded salinity-temperature-depth data in digital form.
- Surface current information obtained by using drift bottles or calculated from ship set and drift.
- Biological data, giving values of plankton standing crop, chlorophyll concentrations, and rates of primary productivity; also papers on marine biology.
- Geological sampling inventory, primarily for the New England Continental Shelf.
- Bottom sample information.

NODC Services

- Data processing.
- Data reproduction, including computer printouts, punched cards, magnetic tapes, and other forms.
    - Analysis and preparations of statistical summaries based on archive holdings.
- Evaluation of various data records for specific analytical requirements.
- Library search for bibliographic references, abstracts, and documents.
- Referral to organizations holding requested information.
- Provision of general marine sciences information.
- Supply of publications, including data processing manuals, catalogs of holdings, data reports, and atlases.

A. DATA COLLECTION

Philosophy and Mode of Operation

Over the past years, the National Oceanographic Data Center (NODC) has sought to foster the exchange of oceanographic data by the design of standard NODC coding and reporting formats. This approach has been highly successful for certain physical and chemical, mainly serial depth and BT data, and has enabled NODC to build the world's most complete computer-linked data bases.

To be responsive to today's needs of the oceanographic community and to industry's expanding interest in the oceans, NODC is now striving to diversify its data bases and to cover a reasonably complete spectrum of data and information from the hydrosphere.

In line with its expanded acquisition effort, NODC is instituting a new and versatile processing system, referred to as the General Data System (GDS). The system is being designed to provide the processing capability to:

1. Accept data in a wide variety of locally established formats and to translate these into the standard formats maintained at the National Marine Data Bank.
2. Accept, store, and release, on a systematic basis, relevant supplementary and descriptive information.
3. Release data in formats adapted to local use and requirements.

It is NODC's belief that for the present the imposition of national standard formats is not practicable for many types of data. To facilitate the flow of data into the national repository and to make them available to the general user, NODC is now shifting its emphasis from standard formats to a flexible two fold approach:

1. The originator may send data in his own format, which subsequently will be standardized, and the data will be incorporated into the National Marine Data Base through NODC's General Data System.
2. NODC will accept a greater variety of oceanographic material that does not readily lend itself to computerization.

The preceding should not be misconstrued: NODC continues to support actively all efforts to standardize formats and observational or analytical procedures and will avail itself of any standards as they become accepted; the lack of national or international standard formats, however, need not and should not be a major deterrent to the exchange of data.

Data may be submitted in any local, regional, or national format, provided that the format is completely described. Include sufficient "housekeeping" sequencing or other simple numbering schemes to allow computer handling of the data by other installations.

Data submitted should be accompanied by sufficient descriptive information to ensure their proper use and understanding by future recipients of data or analytical products from the National Marine Data Base.

Ideally, data should be submitted after all reductions and adjustments have been performed, quality and plausibility have been reviewed, and the data have reached their most advanced state of processing or automation without significant loss of information content.

References

1. Robert R. Freeman, "Environmental Information: New Developments in NOAA," Proceedings ASIS, 1971, pp. 115–119.
2. Anonymous, "NODC: The National Oceanographic Data Center," NOAA/PA 71052, 1971.
3. Anonymous, "NODC—Guide to Submission of Data," Technical Bulletin Series, Publication B-1, 1969.
4. Ralph L. Bisco, *Data Bases, Computers, and the Social Sciences*, Wiley, New York, 1970.

CASE STUDY 4 Document Retrieval

One continuing responsibility of the scientist is keeping abreast of the literature in his field. The time and effort required to "keep up" increases each year with the exponential increase in scientific publication rate.

Despite these efforts, one often finds that he has missed articles of interest which have appeared in new journals, or in journals not usually read in his branch of science.

These difficulties provide the motivation for using computer-based searching and retrieval services in two ways:

1. Current awareness, which is a periodical search of new literature to select those items of possible interest to the individual scientist, in accordance with a "profile" of interest which he has written. This search, in effect, reduces an unmanageable volume of literature to a subset which can be perused by the scientist in a reasonable time to select those items to be obtained and read.
2. Retrospective search, which is a thorough search of present and past literature on a particular topic. This provides a means of determining the "state of the art" with some confidence, despite one's personal limitations in awareness of the literature.

IBM TECHNICAL INFORMATION RETRIEVAL CENTER
DATA SHEET
CURRENT INFORMATION SELECTION

1. PERSONAL DATA

Name _____ D.N. STREETER _____ Man No. _____

Position or Title ___ RESEARCH STAFF MEMBER _____

Department Name ___ STAFF—DIRECTOR OF RESEARCH _____ Dept. No. _____

Building No. or Street Address ___ T.J. WATSON RESEARCH CENTER _____

City and State ___ YORKTOWN HEIGHTS, N.Y. _____

Telephone No. _____ Division _____
      (Area Code) (Exchange) (Number)

                      (Tie-Line)

2. JOB DATA

Present job or project description and <u>associated information needs</u>:

3. SPECIAL SEARCH FEATURES

List any of the special technical terms, phrases, acronyms, authors, etc., related to your field of interest.

      I want information on the use and management of computer—based services for scientists and technologists. This would include descriptions of such use by physical and life scientists, engineers, architects and designers, clinical and laboratory technicians, operations researchers and urban planners. The services of interest include data acquisition and control, information and data retrieval, simulation, calculation, time sharing and text editing.

      I also want information reviewing experience gained in providing such services on topics in— cluding cost/benefits or cost/effectiveness; measurement and analysis; allocation, charging and control of computing resources; planning, justification; operations management; and ease of learning and use by non—programmers.

I authorize that _____ D.N. STREETER _____ , Man No. _____
                      (NAME)   (MAN NO.)

has my approval to become a CIS user in the IBM Technical Information Retrieval Center.

Signed _____ Position _____

Print Name _____ Date _____

NOTE: Many of the IBM documents processed by ITIRC are classified IBM CONFIDENTIAL. Please sign below if you certify that his need to know should enable him to receive abstracts of IBM CONFIDENTIAL reports. Also, if he requests them, complete copies of such documents will be made available to the individual through his local library or from ITIRC, in accordance with your location's security procedures.

      APPROVAL _____

If you do not certify a need to know, the profile will still be matched against all the non-confidential material in the system, about 90 percent of the total input.

RETURN TO: IBM Technical Information Retrieval Center
                  Old Orchard Road
                  Armonk, New York 10504

Figure IIA4-1. Technical information retrieval center data sheet.

CURRENT USAGE: CASE STUDIES AND CRITIQUES

The case study chosen to illustrate the document retrieval function is called ITIRC, *I*BM *T*echnical *I*nformation *R*etrieval *C*enter. Its capabilities are demonstrated by processing a profile written to cover the subject matter related to the writing of this book.

Itirc

ITIRC is a company-wide, computer-based retrieval and dissemination system established in 1964.

CURRENT INFORMATION SELECTION. More than 4000 IBM scientists, engineers, and managers who subscribe to ITIRC are alerted weekly to current information added to the ITIRC files. To become a subscriber, an employee completes a form (Figure IIA4-1) requiring his manager's signature. He describes his job and work-related interests using the language of his specialty or scientific discipline. He can request information on authors, companies, equipment nonenclature, and acronyms, as well as subjects in his profile of interest. Conversely, he can restrict output through a "negate" feature to eliminate words, phrases, journal titles, selected groups of publications, or even entire data bases. The search logic permits great flexibility. The ITIRC information specialist or ITIRC representative at a local library then prepares a "profile" (Figure IIA4-2). As new data are added to the stored information of the file, the user's "profile" is matched

```
    1   A  ON STREETER       05/69 8-862-1758      YKTN RES 400 801 06/72 06/72  01
  CON1    DATA WITH PROCESSING WITH MANAGEMENT OR SYSTEM$ OR SERVICE$            02
  CON2    COMPUTING WITH SYSTEM$ WITH RESEARCH OR SERVICE$                       03
  CON3    PROGRAMMING WITH MANAGEMENT                                            04
  CON4    REMOTE ADJ ENTRY OR PROCESSING                                         05
  CON5    SYSTEM$ WITH RELIABILITY OR AVAILABILITY OR SERVICEABILITY             06
  CON6    SYSTEM$ ADJ MEASUREMENT OR ANALYSIS OR OPERATING                      C07
          OR MODELLING                                                           08
  CON8    INFORMATION OR DATA ADJ MANAGEMENT OR STORAGE OR                      C09
          RETRIEVAL                                                              10
  CON9    COMPUTER$ WITH HARDWARE OR PROCESSOR$ OR                              C11
          PERIPHERAL                                                             12
  CON7    EXECUTIVE OR SUPERVISOR OR CONTROL ADJ PROGRAM$                        13
  CON11   DISPLAY ADJ TERMINAL$                                                  14
  CON12   CONVERSATIONAL ADJ LANGUAGE OR SYSTEM$                                 15
  CON13   INTERACTIVE ADJ SYSTEM$                                                16
  CON14   TIME ADJ SHARING ADJ SYSTEM$                                           17
  CON15   TSS OR APL OR CTS OR CPS                                               18
  A1      ECONOMICS                                                              19
  A2      COST ADJ EFFECTIVENESS                                                 20
  A3      A1 OR A2                                                               21
  A4      COMPUTER ADJ USAGE$ OR SERVICE$                                        22
  CON16   A3 AND A4                                                              23
  CON17   NOT CIRCUIT$$ OR WIRING OR ELECTRONIC$ OR                             C24
          SEMICONDUCTOR$ OR COMPONENT$ OR RC$$$$ OR RJ$$$ OR RZ$$$               25
  CON18   LABORATORY WITH AUTOMATION                                             26
  CON19   DATA ADJ ACQUISITION ADJ SYSTEM$                                       27
  END                                                                            ??
```

Figure IIA4-2. User "profile."

against this current input. When a match occurs, a notification card is printed. Samples of such notifications are shown in Figure IIA4-3.

SOURCES OF INPUT TO THE DATA FILE. Input to the ITIRC data file comes from many locations and organizations. Typical documents are:

Engineering reports
Patent applications
Programming manuals
Test reports
Application write-ups
Employee suggestions
Education materials

Materials obtained from outside sources include:

Selected technical journals
University reports
Government bulletins
Conference proceedings
Special reports

If all the details are wanted, the complete text is available on microfiche. When an information retrieval system alerts a subscriber about an important or timely report, he naturally wants a copy of the complete text. ITIRC has microfilmed as much of its input as possible to supplement the often limited supply of printed copies and to reduce costs.

Over 60,000 documents are now in the collection in microfiche form, and another 30,000 older times are on 16-mm film. More than 1000 new documents are added to the microfiche file each month.

This collection, nearly 3 million pages of information, is available in most IBM libraries for instant local reference. It is the equivalent of 130 five-drawer file cabinets filled with documents—but it is contained in two tab card files.

ITIRC supplies personal microfiche copies on request—via response cards, search listings, calls, and memos. Nearly 200,000 reports on microfiche have been sent to individual users since 1966.

A fundamental principle in the ITIRC system from the beginning has been the use of normal text-searching logic. The entire text of the input data is searched—in most cases an abstract of 200 to 300 words, plus title and all relevant bibliographic data. Searching is not limited to descriptors or key words. Thus, since the data base contains the language of the original document abstract (and author), the search questions or profiles can be phrased in the same kind of normal English or accepted technical language.

Cost/Effectiveness

The average profile now operates at a cost of only $130 a year. The average user received 550 abstract notifications during 1970—selected for him by a computer out of 38,000 new documents added to ITIRC that year—and he expressed a satisfaction level of better than 80 percent.

```
THE ATTACHED ABSTRACTS WERE SELECTED FOR YOUR REVIEW         687780
AFTER SEARCHING A TOTAL OF 3458 JOURNAL ARTICLES   04/13/73



              DN STREETER                   687780
              IBM CORPORATION
              787 UN PLAZA
              NEW YORK, NY   10017




IF THE MAILING ADDRESS SHOWN IS INCORRECT, PLEASE INDICATE THE CHANGES
ON THIS CARD AND RETURN IT TO ITIRC.


730000201                            JOURNALS   04/13/73    687780

     INFOS 01-73 P20-21.  CRYSTAL BALLING- TRENDS IN EDP MANAGEMENT.
JANUARY 1973.
       1      INFOSYSTEMS
              WITHINGTON, FG
              ARTHUR D. LITTLE, INC.
              TRADITIONALLY, LARGE ORGANIZATIONS HAVE DECENTRALIZED AUTHORITY
       TO ESTABLISH AND MANAGE COMPUTER CENTERS TO THE SAME DEGREE THAT THEY
       HAVE DECENTRALIZED AUTHORITY FOR CONTROLLING OPERATIONS.  EACH
       DIVISION HAS BEEN PERMITTED TO EVALUATE ITS DATA PROCESSING NEEDS AND
       ESTABLISH DATA PROCESSING CENTERS INDEPENDENTLY FROM ALL OTHERS.
       LARGE ORGANIZATIONS WITH MULTIPLE CENTERS ARE NOW TENDING TO CONSIDER
       CHANGES IN THEIR DATA PROCESSING ORGANIZATIONS, HOWEVER, FOR FOUR
       BASIC REASONS WHICH ARE UNIVERSALLY FELT.
              COST OF DUPLICATE SYSTEM DEVELOPMENT.  DESIRABILITY OF STANDARD
       EQUIPMENT.  DESIRE FOR UNIFORM MANAGEMENT REPORTING.  ECONOMY OF
       SCALE IN COMPUTERS.
              IT IS EVIDENT THAT EACH OF THESE FORCES TENDS TOWARD
       CENTRALIZATION.  TOWARD CENTRAL CORPORATE CONTROL OF THE ACQUISITION
       OF COMPUTERS AND OF THE DESIGN OF NEW INFOSYSTEMS.  SINCE THE FORCES
       ARE GENERALLY FELT, ONE WOULD EXPECT TO SEE A UNIVERSAL
       CENTRALIZATION PROCESS OCCURRING.  THIS IS NOT THE CASE, BECAUSE
       CORPORATE MANAGEMENT GENERALLY REALIZE THAT THERE ARE DRAWBACKS TO



730000214                            JOURNALS   04/13/73    687780

     EDPAA 01-73 P1-14.  THE EMERGING COMPUTER NETWORKS.  JANUARY 1973.
       4      EDP ANALYZER
              14P.  THIS REPORT, THE FIRST IN A SERIES ON TRENDS IN DATA
       COMMUNICATIONS, DEALS WITH AN IMPORTANT NEW ENTITY- THE COMPUTER
       NETWORK.  THERE ARE SOME NOVEL FEATURES OF THESE NETWORKS THAT MAKE
       THEM DIFFERENT FROM MOST OF THE OLDER DATA COMMUNICATIONS NETS-
       FEATURES SUCH AS AUTOMATIC ALTERNATE ROUTING AND SOPHISTICATED ERROR
       DETECTION.  COMPUTER NETWORKS USE EXISTING COMMON CARRIER FACILITIES
       BUT DELIVER AN ADDED VALUE TYPE OF SERVICE.  THEY CAN HANDLE A WIDE
       RANGE OF TERMINAL TYPES, FROM TELETYPEWRITERS TO REMOTE BATCH
       TERMINALS, AS WELL AS OTHER COMPUTERS.  AND IT APPEARS THAT EVEN THE
       SMALLER COMPUTER USERS WILL BE ABLE TO AVAIL THEMSELVES OF COMPUTER
       NETWORKS, THROUGH JOINT USE AGREEMENTS.  HERE IS A DEVELOPMENT THAT
       DESERVES THE ATTENTION OF DATA PROCESSING MANAGEMENT.
```

```
721302239                                          ENG INDEX 04/13/73    687780
       COMPUTERIZED DATA MANAGEMENT AND CONTROL SYSTEMS FOR RESEARCH AND
       TEST LABORATORIES.
  49         EIX721302239
             BOZICH, D. J.
             ARONE, R. A.
             INST ENVIRON SCI, PROC, 17TH ANNU TECH MEET, LIVING IN OUR
       ENVIRONMENT, LOS ANGELES, CALIF, APR 26-30 1971 P 475-483

             WYLE LAB
             THE IMPLEMENTATION OF A SYSTEM REQUIRES A THOROUGH
       UNDERSTANDING OF $LEFT DOUBLE QUOTE$ HARDWARE $RIGHT DOUBLE QUOTE$
       AND $LEFT DOUBLE QUOTE$ SOFTWARE $RIGHT DOUBLE QUOTE$ REQUIREMENTS
       AND PERSONNEL AND FISCAL LIMITATIONS SUCH THAT THE DATA MANAGEMENT
       SYSTEM CAN RESPOND TO CURRENT AND FUTURE TEST REQUIREMENTS IN A
       SERIES OF MODULAR TRANSITIONS INCLUDING MINI-, SMALL, AND/OR
       MEDIUM-SCALE ON-LINE COMPUTER SYSTEMS.  THIS PAPER PRESENTS A
       METHODOLOGY FOR DEVELOPING A DATA MANAGEMENT SYSTEM AND/OR CONTROL
       SYSTEM BY CONSIDERING FIVE MAJOR ELEMENTS  INSTRUMENTATION/DATA
       ACQUISITION   ON-LINE COMPUTERS   DATA ACCUMULATION, MONITORING AND
       CONTROL   DATA ANALYSIS AND INTERPRETATION   AND INFORMATION DISPLAY.


721302326                                          ENG INDEX 04/13/73    687780
       CONFERENCE ON DISPLAYS.
  50         EIX721302326
             HOPKIN, V. D.
             PARSON, J. F.
             HUDDART, K. W.
             CONFERENCE ON DISPLAYS, UNIVERSITY OF TECHNOLOGY, LOUGHBOROUGH,
       ENGL, SEP 7-10 1971, BY CONTROL AND AUTOMATION DIVISION, INST OF ELEC
       ENG, LONDON, ENGL, CONF PUBL N 80, 1971, 374 P




             FOLLOWING IS PART 4 OF THE LIST OF TITLES AND AUTHORS
       COMPUTER-GENERATED DISPLAYS FOR PSYCHOLOGICAL RESEARCH.  BY V. D.
       HOPKIN AND J. F. PARSONS.  ROAD TRAFFIC CONTROL $EM DASH$ EXAMPLES
       OF DISPLAY DESIGN.  BY K. W. HUDDART.  AN EVALUATION OF
       ALPHANUMERICS FOR A $ MULTIPLIED BY$ 7 MATRIX DISPLAY.  BY H. F.
       HUDDLESTON.  CRT DISPLAYS OF GRAPHS IN CEGB POWER STATIONS.  BY M. W.
       JERVIS.  EFFECTS OF SIGNAL-TO-NOISE RATIO, BANDWIDTH AND CONTRAST ON
       INFORMATION PROCESSING IN SIMULATED DIGITAL ENCODING TELEVISION


721304851                                          ENG INDEX 04/13/73    687780
       DU PONT INFORMATION FLOW SYSTEM.
  84         EIX721304851
             HOFFMAN, WARREN S.
             J CHEM DOC V 12 N 2 MAY 1972 P 116-124
             JCHDA
             E. I.  DU PONT DE NEMOURS + CO, INC, WILMINGTON, DEL
             THE INFORMATION FLOW SYSTEM IS A LARGE-SCALE INFORMATION
       RETRIEVAL SYSTEM DEVELOPED FOR PROCESSING OF DU PONT INFORMATION
       FILES.  AS CURRENTLY IMPLEMENTED, THE SYSTEM STORES AND RETRIEVES
       INFORMATION ON COMPANY TECHNICAL REPORTS.  IMPORTANT FEATURES OF THE
       SYSTEM INCLUDE THE USE OF THREADED LISTS IN ADDITION TO INVERTED
       FILES TO PERMIT OPTIMUM SEARCHING.  USERS PREPARE SEARCHES IN A FREE
       FORMAT QUERY LANGUAGE, WHICH IS THEN OPTIMIZED BY THE SYSTEM TO MAKE
       MOST EFFICIENT USE OF THE FILE STRUCTURE.  ANSWERS ARE IN THE FORM OF
       ACCESSION NUMBERS OF ABSTRACTS.  EXTENSIONS OF THE SYSTEM FOR
       HANDLING CHEMICAL STRUCTURE INFORMATION AND ON-LINE PROCESSING ARE
       ALSO DISCUSSED.  3 REFS.
```

Figure IIA4-3.   Computer printed abstracts of documents.

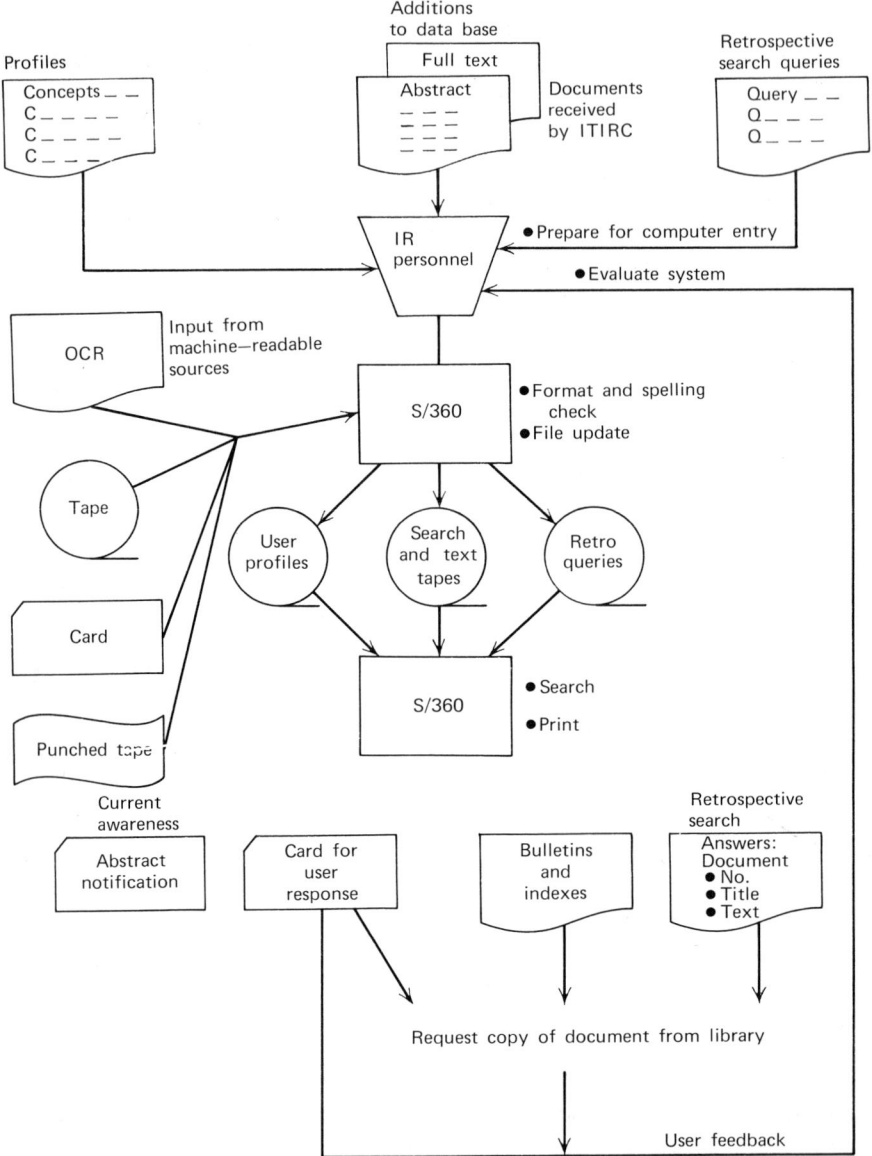

Figure IIA4-4. System Overview.

A. DATA COLLECTION

Because of the unique ITIRC System/360 programs, the unit cost for a search has already dropped to $14, and will continue to decrease as the volume of usage grows.

CIS Search

When a CIS search is to be run, the profiles are converted into memory loads, based on core storage space available. These memory loads are essentially logical tables related to the search logic specified. At search time each memory load (representing up to 120 users) is processed against the search tape as shown in Figure IIA4-4. Any match or "hit" is then sorted so that all document numbers relevant to a particular user profile are collected under that profile.

The Logic of the 360 Search

PROGRAMS. Each profile is designed to search any of the active data bases in the ITIRC system, currently as many as a thousand documents at a time. The entire entry in the computer file is searched, including title, author, publishing source, source codes, assigned index terms, and the full text of the abstract. Matching may occur within any of these document elements.

The tools of logic used to build the profiles are generally familiar.
The basic building blocks are:

1. Single words.
2. Adjacent words, or phrases, which must appear in identical sequence to be matched (symbol, ADJ).
3. Sentence or "with" logic, in which the two or more words must occur within a sentence unit to be matched (symbol, WITH).

The connectives or "operators" that join these elements together are:

1. Or logic, used to group single words or phrases or sentence logic appearing in an abstract, or to group single words the phrase or sentence units.
2. AND logic, which can be used for all the elements in a variety of ways. ANDing, of course, covers the entire text of an abstract.
3. ABSOLUTE logic is the imperative (symbol, ABS). Used with any of the building blocks, it indicates that a match will produce a hit regardless of any other logic in the profile.
4. NOT logic, as the name implies, indicates that the appearance of this particular element in a document cancels any other matching that may occur (except for ABSOLUTES).

References

1. David L., Hines, "User's Guide to the Computerized Literature Search Services of the IBM Technical Information Retrieval Center." Technical Report 07.450, Rochester, Minn., September 17, 1971.
2. Charles J., Meadow, "Information Retrieval," in *Man-Machine Communication,* Wiley, New York, 1970, pp. 145–181.
3. D. E., Walker, Ed., *Interactive Bibliographic Search,* AFIPS Press, Montvale, N. J., 1971.
4. Anonymous, "Searching Normal Text for Information Retrieval, Data Processing Application," E20-0335-0, May 1970.
5. Paul J., Nelson, "User Profiling for Normal Text Retrieval", *Proceedings of the American Documentation Institute,* 1967.
6. Robert V. Katter and Davis B., McCarn, "AIM-TWX-An Experimental On-Line Bibliographic Retrieval System," from Reference 3.
7. David A., Thompson, "Interface Design for an Interactive Information Retrieval System: A Literature Survey and a Research System Description," *Journal of ASIS,* November–December 1971, 361–373.

B. EXAMINATION

A crucial step in the solution of many scientific and technical problems is the examination of complex or voluminous data. As mentioned previously, the human has developed, over the ages, a magnificent ability to perceive and extract information from a two- or three-dimensional scene. Most attempts to develop fully automatic techniques that are competitive with humans in the execution of this function have been doomed to failure.

The success stories almost invariably have resulted from using the computer as a preprocessor whose function is to present information to the human in a more concise and/or more comprehensible form.

Basic operations performed in this preprocessing role include:

1. Selection of data samples of interest from many candidates, according to some known rule.
2. Normalization (e.g., Correction for baseline drift, correction for known or measurable distortion); scaling; alignment of time-shifted signals.
3. Transformation of the data from one format to another as befits the nature of the data or the preference of the viewer.

More sophisticated preprocessing operations include:

1. Juxtaposition of recent sample with historical samples which meet certain criteria.

2. Synthesis of an image from data recorded in various nonpictorial form.
3. Projection of multidimensional data into a two- or three-dimensional subspace which has been selected to preserve as much information as possible.

In this chapter we consider four examples in which the computer is used as a monitor and preprocessor, in each case serving primarily to present pertinent information to a human specialist for his examination at the right time in the most useful form.

First we consider a patient-monitoring application in a San Francisco medical center. Next, the generation of subsurface "pictures" from seismic data to assist geologists in locating petroleum deposits is described. Then, techniques are presented for examining consumer preference patterns, for use in market research. Finally, an application to the medical diagnosis of shock victims is described.

CASE STUDY 5   Patient Monitoring*

Introduction

One of the advantages of using a general-purpose computer in data acquisition is that the data being acquired can be screened, continuously or periodically, to identify conditions that warrant corrective action or human intervention. At such times, after giving an alarm, the computer can also provide summary data to assist the human in performing the proper corrective act.

Patient monitoring is one such application. This work is directed by Dr. John Osborn at the Pacific Medical Center in San Francisco.

Objectives

The amount of knowledge available in medicine is rapidly outrunning the means of making all that knowledge useful in the care of patients. We will describe an intensive-care-ward measuring and monitoring system that was developed to acquire, digest, and quickly present in useful form some important cardiac and respiratory data in very sick patients.

This system was designed with three major and quite separate aims:

1. First, to accumulate new and useful data of a kind that is normally not available to doctor and nurse and that might contribute directly to

---

* This case study has been exerpted from Osborn et al. (1).

the diagnosis and treatment of the patient. In other words, it was to extend the information available to the physician for his use in clinical care and in research.

2. Second, to speed up the acquisition, processing, and analysis of presently accepted clinical data (blood pressure, temperature, and other commonly measured parameters) and present these data in collated form that could be more effectively appreciated.

3. Third, to promote work simplification for nurse and doctor. It was planned to achieve this partly as described above by developing rapid methods of data compilation and partly by the provision of automated nurses' notes and the elimination of chores such as maintaining fluid-balance charts, etc., which might directly cut the manpower costs of illness. Further, the automation itself would have important effects in improving the quality of the data gathered. For instance, traditional methods of annotation by hand can be shown to be inaccurately time-related, and traditional notes are usually weakest during periods of crisis, when most needed. As planned, the system would make it possible to carry out sophisticated studies over long periods, without increasing the work load of nurses and doctors and with a precision superior to that of hand methods.

We also seriously considered allowing the system to execute therapeutic steps directly, such as replacing intravenous fluids lost; in other words, designing the system to "close the control loop." However, we made the tentative decision that, at least at this time, analysis plus control might be attended by instabilities that might harm the patient, so development of a control function was deferred.

Description of the Computer System

The physiological monitoring system consists of a number of different units in different locations, all connected to a central IBM 1800 computer and each doing basically the same types of data collection, computation and display. It has been partially described previously (4). It includes four bed-study units for intensive-care patients, a mobile respiratory analysis cart for use in isolation rooms or to reach less accessible locations, a treadmill exercise-study unit with special display capabilities, and a study unit for the catheterization laboratory. The functions and interrelations of these various units are shown in Figure IIB5-1. In an intensive-care ward now being completed, all of the 14 bed positions have wiring installed capable of carrying any analog signals obtained to the computer for processing. Modular bedside input/output terminals for each bed are being constructed. The original two-bed study ward is shown in Figure IIB5-2.

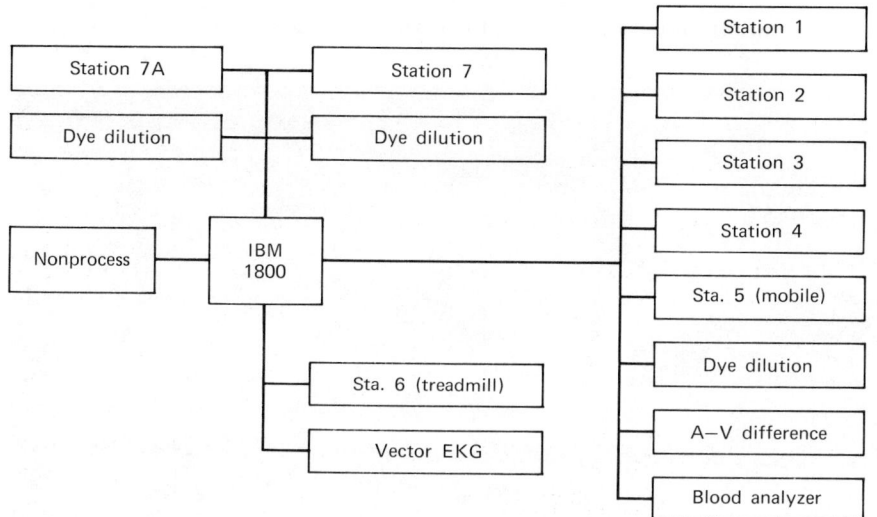

Figure IIB5-1. Organization of sensing and computing units.

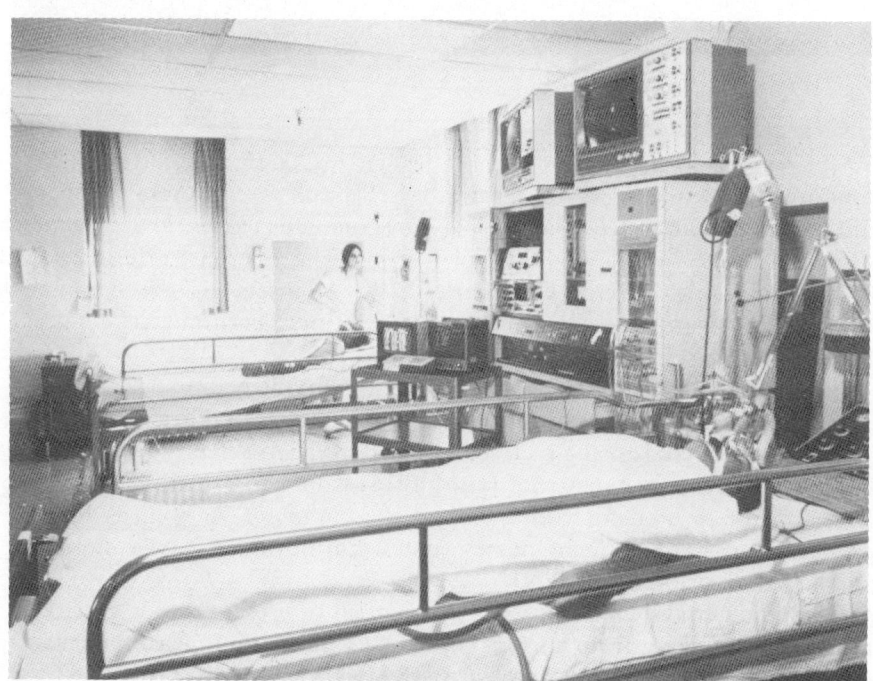

Figure IIB5-2. Original two-bed study ward.

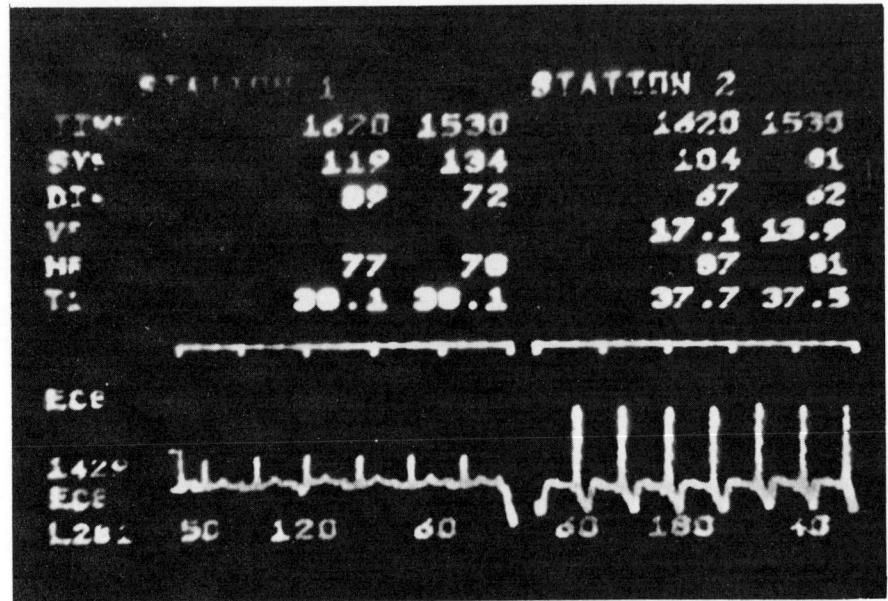

Figure IIB5-3. Display of digital information.

All have similar instrument capabilities, viz, ECG, three blood pressures, respiratory flow and pressure, respiratory P_{O_2} and P_{CO_2}, several temperatures, a closed-circuit television display for computer values, and a number of digital input switches and control buttons. The Eberhart arteriovenous oxygen analyzing cuvette (Eberhart, 1968) connects to the computer through one ward console, and a dye-dilution densitometer connects through any console.

The central console contains sensing and amplifying equipment and input and control panels for each patient, plus one analog oscilloscopic display for each patient and a single closed-circuit television screen for computed displays. A keyboard typewriter (IBM 1816) is in a recess in the corner of the ward and is used for commands to the computer, as well as for the generation of hard copy of nurses' notes, cardiovascular or respiratory computations, or other matters.

The computer system's display screen is used to present a wide variety of information, ranging from current computed values of all measurements to temporal logs of past events and warnings of various sorts. The displays are presented on a 14-in. closed-circuit television screen from information generated on the faces of one of a series (three, being expanded to five) of

Tektronix 564 oscilloscopes, each viewed by a TV camera. The information to be displayed is chosen as desired by manipulation of the switches or control buttons on the console or by typewriter entry.

Several typical displays are shown in Figures IIB5-3 and IIB5-4. The displays can be called or changed very rapidly or a series reviewed in sequence. The plots of variables against time can be shown for any number of hours from one to twenty four. In many of the standard numerical displays, several columns of data are presented showing changes over many hours. A heading on the screen always shows the appropriate bed number and the variables shown.

For permanent records, a 24-hour printout is made of all recorded data, and at the same time a graphic plot is derived using an IBM 1627 plotter, as illustrated in Figures IIB5-5 and IIB5-6. These plots have been particularly useful in demonstrating unexpected trends. For instance, the plots of Figure IIB5-6 (4) showed a malfunction of the respirator at about the 18th hour (near the right-hand side of the record), which resulted in severe hyperventilation, a dangerous drop in expired-carbon-dioxide concentration, a rise in heart rate, and a temporary deterioration in the patient's condition,

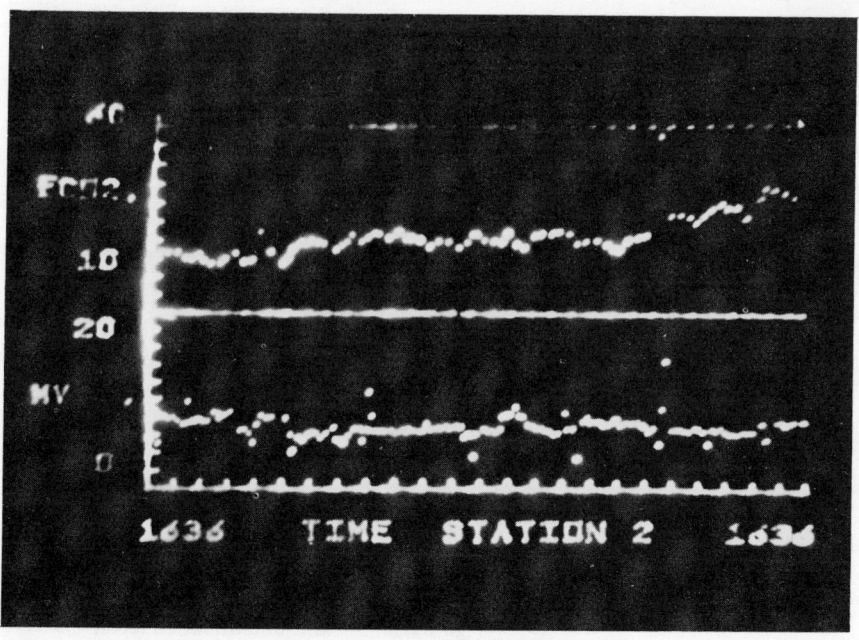

Figure IIB5-4. Twenty-four-hour plot.

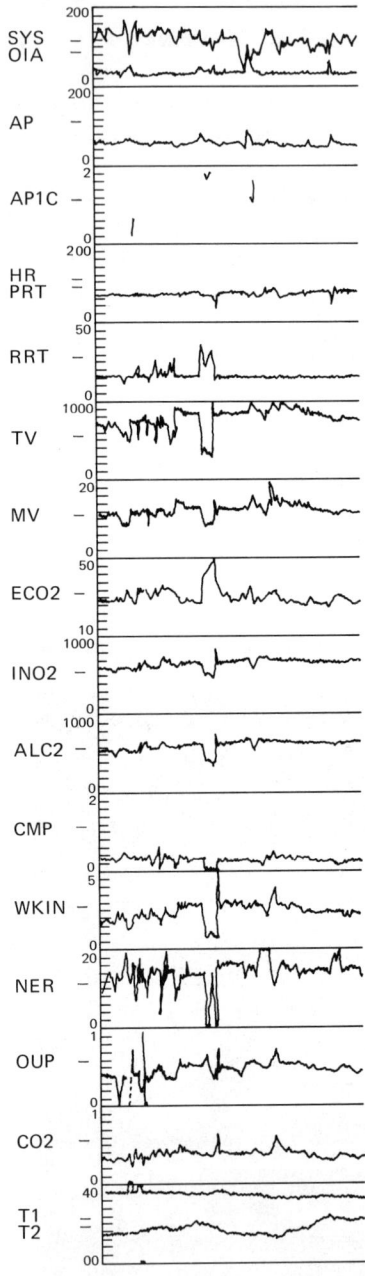

Figure IIB5-5. One of the daily data plots.

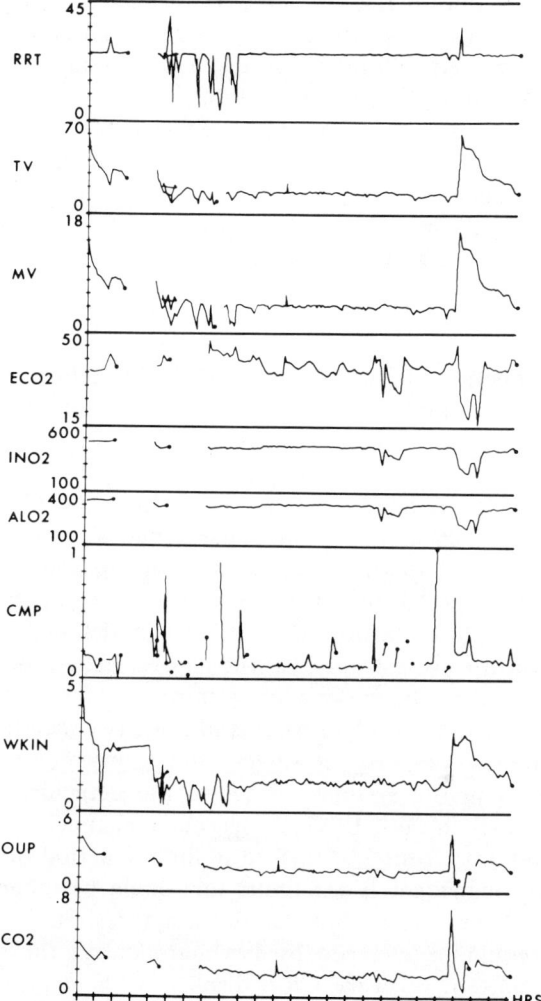

Figure IIB5-6. Part of a plot redrawn.

as noted by the nurse. Proper function of the respirator was restored and the respiratory values returned to normal.

All programs operate under the control of the IBM 1800 TSX (time-sharing executive) system. At this writing the operating system is being converted from TSX to MPX (multiprogramming executive), which allows multiple core loads to be in execution simultaneously. Alarm analysis programs operated 5 times per second on data that have been obtained during the preceding 200 msec. Routine analysis programs and display-generating programs are executed automatically every ten minutes and additionally upon request. An interrupt heirarchy establishes priority among the several programs. When no process program is being executed nor in queue, control is turned over to nonprocess jobs such as report and plot generation, compiling and assembling new programs, or totally unrelated background-data processing. In normal operation about two thirds of the computer's time is available for such nonprocess jobs.

Alarms

An important function of an on-line monitoring system must be to provide alarms when there are threatening changes in the parameters being measured.

The first alarms provided in the system were similar to limit alarms on commercial analog monitor systems (high and low ECG and arterial pressure values) which activated light and sound signals, together with a written explanation of the limit exceeded in the ICU display CRT. Both physiological channels provided the commonly experienced and unacceptable excess of false alarms from artifacts. A detailed study confirmed that all false alarms arose from extrinsic causes, patient or operator originated and not within the sensing or data-processing components of the system (2). Since this form of alarm is traditionally concerned with alerting staff to a cardiovascular crisis, it was possible to make use of the data-correlation function in the system to require the coincidence of exceeding alarm-limit settings in both ECG and vascular channels, which effectively reduced false alarms from 330 to 8 in a similar period of study. These 8 were caused by inadequately set limits and could be ignored. During the following year there were no failures due to nonoperation in critical situations. Limits could be changed by keyboard entry; the set values were shown at the bottom of every CRT display, with identification of those exceeded if an alarm situation arose.

Such a program is, however, extremely demanding of computer time. Without analog signal preprocessing, it requires continual analysis (in consecutive segments of 15 sec) of both arterial and ECG signals in this system, at high sampling rates, with a comparison procedure also continuously operating. This takes up to 20% of available computer time, observing only two beds, which might perhaps be considered in terms of $2000 monthly computer time rental. In a research study ward and during prototype development of a computer system, it is still considered necessary at this time to have a trained nurse for each acutely ill patient. In practice the few such critical cardiovascular emergencies have always been noted by the bedside nurse from traditional analog displays as early as the computer alarm operation. We have therefore, for the moment, abandoned the operation of this alarm system. Whether this would be a justifiable omission in any nonresearch scheme or whether it would be acceptable to other medical staff is debatable, but the economic implication should not be overlooked, compared with the cost of hiring additional trained observers. Use of signal preprocessing should greatly reduce cost, however.

Alarms, as so far described, can be considered the first grade of a series, progressively more complex, of diagnostic analyses. The second group of "alarms" are those occasioned by a change beyond alterable limits or of preset degree, usually in a single physiological parameter, either measured or calculated. They are of occurrences sensed by the system that should be made available for clinical consideration or that frustrate its own care-support ability or research accuracy. Output is by a text CRT display, and several appear in the hard-copy log in order to qualify the recorded data values, if they may be used in research. We report limit infringements of heart rate or mean arterial pressure in this cateogry of alarm. "Arterial line damped," signifying damping of the arterial waveform, is displayed if pulse pressure falls to less than 20% of mean arterial pressure, calling usually for flushing of the intravascular cannula.

The display "TV unbalanced" is shown if inspiratory and expiratory tidal volumes measured by the pneumotachograph differ by more than 10%. Such a difference calls for a review of airway connections for leaks and rejection of current respiratory data for research, although trend significance is often retained by such values as respiratory gas exchange when the tidal volume error observation is only slightly greater than the set limit. The following will be added: a fall in total chest compliance, a rise of maximum inspiratory pressure beyond preset value during mechanical ventilation (denotes airway obstruction), and the reporting of the patient's being out of phase with the mechanical ventilator (work of inspiration greatly increased with erratic changes in total compliance). This category is valuable for temporary use, in order to build up an experience of the significance of any particular degree of signal variance in relation to some noted or anticipated clinical change, with a view to incorporation of that alarm as a routine function or as part of a more complicated diagnostic program.

Evaluation of the System

In one of its primary functions (to provide new data for research purposes) the system has been very successful. New and interesting findings in the "natuaral history" of acute cardiac disease have developed and are being assembled for separate publication.

It second function, as a clinical monitoring and early warning device, has been highly successful in some ways and needs further modification in others. On the positive side there have been many examples of clinical understanding due to the computer system where the diagnosis would probably never have been known without it. Particularly, the incidence of "unexplained" cardiac arrest has diminished almost of zero during its use. Two short examples will show why.

In a 73-year-old man; sudden cardiac standstill without clinical warning signs was clearly shown (by study of the 1627 plot of variables) to have begun four hours earlier, when an improperly set respirator led to respiratory acidosis, voluntary respiratory movement with increased oxygen uptake, gradually increasing oxygen debt, and finally the "unexplained" standstill.

As a second example, in patient with cerebral edema, the decision was made to use whole-body hypothermia to reduce metabolic demand. When the cold blanket was turned on, the oxygen uptake rose from approximately 290 cc per minute to 650 cc per minute and his condition deteriorated precipitously. The patient had received sedation; there was no obvious shivering. Close inspection, however, after the increased oxygen uptake was observed, showed almost imperceptible fibrillatory movements of skeletal muscles, which might be called "subliminal shivering." With a much increased dosage of sedation, the oxygen uptake dropped back to below control levels.

In other patients, hemothorax has been diagnosed by the occurrence of a sudden fall in chest compliance before it was evident clinically. And finally, the "trend plots" on the display screen have certainly alerted the attending personnel to changes of one kind or another in a large number of patients, with results that are hard to document firmly, but which were certainly to the patient's benefit.

On the negative side, however, the very multiplicity of data available has caused problems in interpretation. We have discussed some of these in the section on alarms. It has become evident that important changes in one or more variables are often lost in the mass of information available. To make full clinical use of the system it will be necessary to implement a large number of what might be called "diagnostic programs," in which the computer senses changes in single variables or in patterns of variables and responds with appropriate diagnoses written in real language, identifying the specific changes as well as their possible meaning. A start in this direction has been described under "Alarms," but this type of function must be much expanded.

The impact on nursing staff has, in general, been favorable. Full impact on nursing cannot be evaluated until further progress is made in automating the information usually contained in nursing notes and, in general, reducing the work load of the nursing staff.

A final philosophical note: We try to think of the system not as a mechanical doctor or nurse competing with us, but as an extension of our senses and our memories. Thus it is not designed to take over our functions, but rather to provide us the means to function more intelligently for the benefit of the patient who, after all, pays the final bill.

References

1. J. J., Osborn, J. O., Beaumont, J. C. A. Raison, and R. P., Abbott, "Computation for Quantitative On-Line Measurements in an Intensive Care Ward," in *Computers in Biomedical Research*, Vol. III, R. W. Stacy and B. D. Waxman, Eds., Academic Press, New York, 1969.
2. J. C. A., Raison, J. O. Beaumont, J. A. G. Russell, J. J., Osborn, and F., Gerbode, "Alarms in an Intensive Care Unit: An Interim Compromise" in *Computers in Biomedical Research*, Vol. II, Academic Press, New York, 1968.
3. K. V., Martz, and J. O., Beaumont, "Computer-Based Monitoring in an Intensive Care Unit (ICU): Implications for Nursing Education, *Heart and Lung: The Journal of Critical Care*, **1,** 1 (January-February 1972), 90–98.
4. J. J., Osborn, J. O., Beaumont, J. C. A., Raison, J. Russell, and F., Gerbode, "Measurement and Monitoring of Acutely Ill Patients by Digital Computer," *Surgery*. **64,** 6, (December 1968), 1057–1070.

CASE STUDY 6   Petroleum Exploration*

The search for petroleum is one of the most competitive and technology-intensive fields in today's industrial world.

The technical problem is to pinpoint the locations of subterranean petroleum or natural gas accumulations with sufficient accuracy and confidence to justify exploratory drilling. This problem is solved by creating synthetic pictures or "sections" of the subsurface structure from which expert geologists can identify likely sites. These sections are generated by computer processing of vast quantities of seismic time signal data.

Figure IIB6-1 shows how this data originates, in the case of prospecting at sea. The ship generates a sharp sound periodically. The seismic disturbances travel down through the water and subsurface, sending back reflec-

---
* This case study is based on information kindly provided by Carl H. Savit, Western Geophysical Company of America, Houston, Texas.

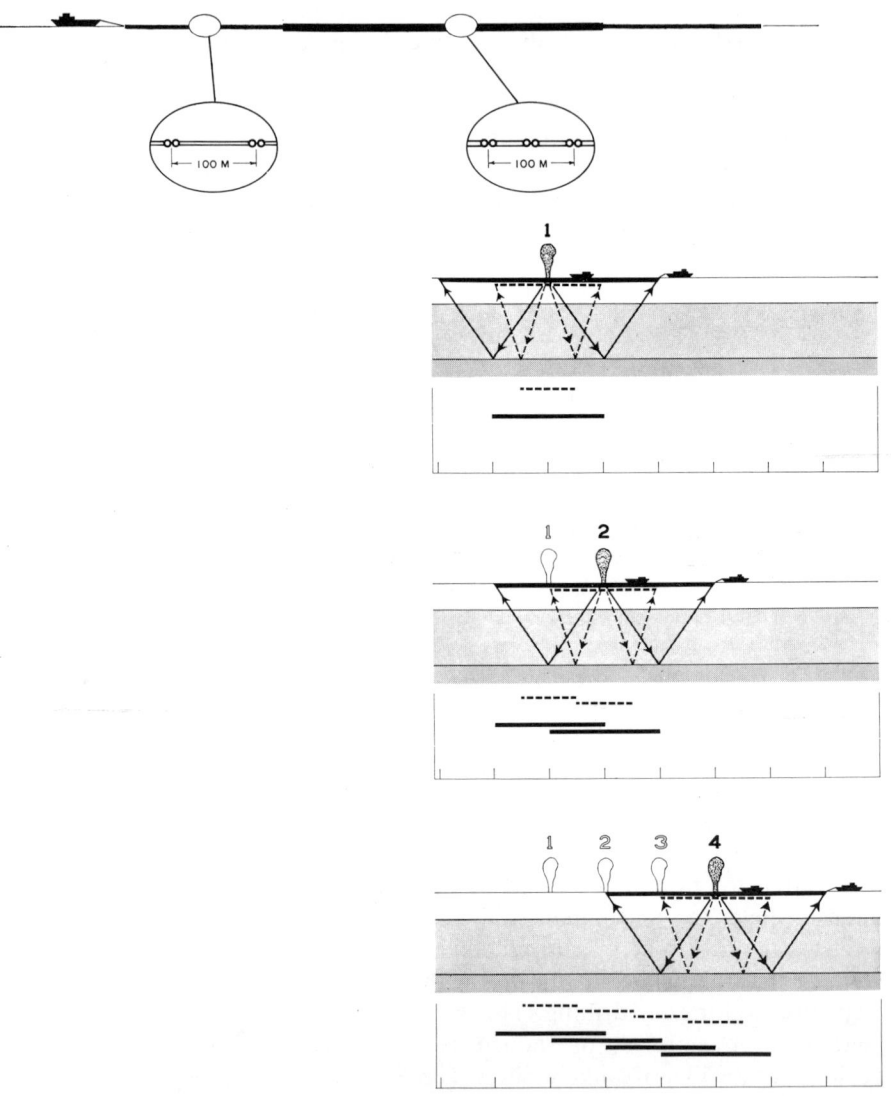

Figure IIB6-1. Schematic of dual marine cable and its use.

tions as various geologic layers are traversed. These complex reflected waves are detected by sensitive hydrophones contained in a cable which is towed behind the ship. The cable is characteristically two miles or more in length and contains several dozen groups of hydrophones. Each group is an array of detectors, the physical arrangement of which has been optimally designed by computer to reject horizontally travelling components of the seismic disturbance.

The time signals are sampled, converted to digital form for maximum fidelity, and recorded on magnetic tape aboardship. Figure IIB6-2 shows typical waveforms, as received.

The travel time of the reflected waves is a function of the depth of the rock layers and the propagation velocity of the intermediate media. The computer's role is to:

1. Align and enhance the time signal data.

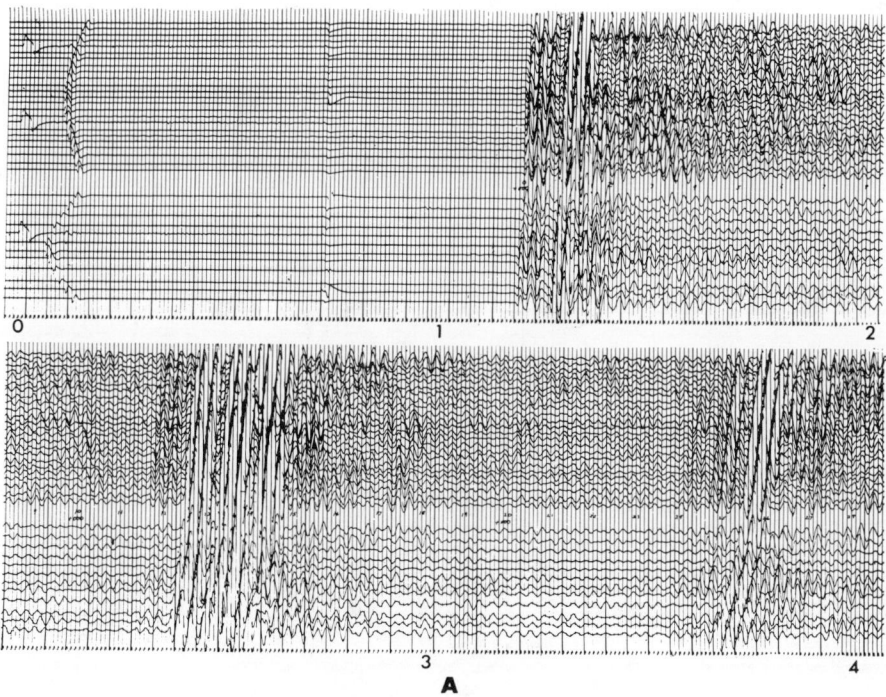

Figure IIB6-2. Typical seismic waveforms, as received.

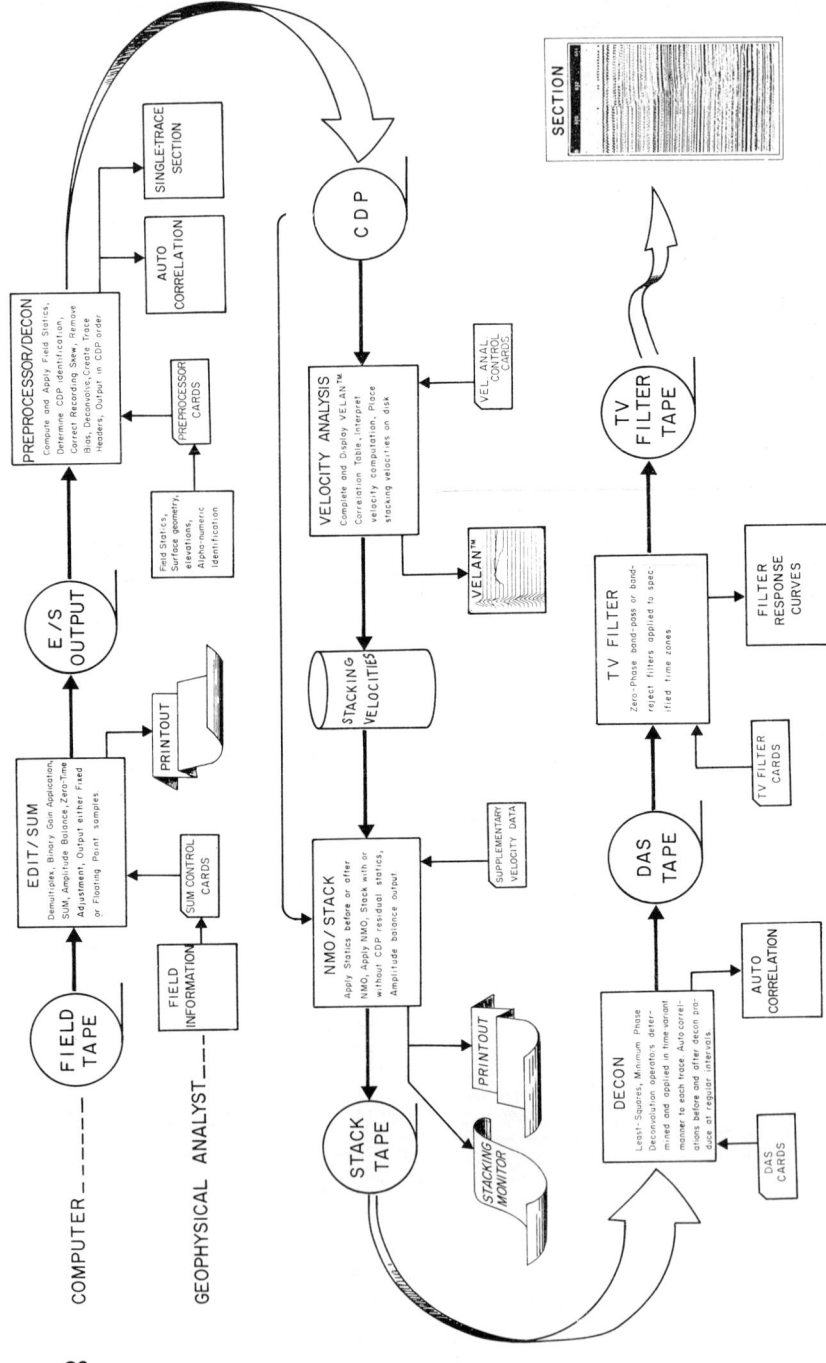

Figure IIB6-3. Digital processing flow chart.

2. To infer the propagation velocity through the various layers transversed.
3. To resolve ambiguities over location of reflecting interfaces.

The signal processing techniques employed in these operations are too elaborate to be described in detail here.* The flow chart shown in Figure IIB6-3 gives some indication of the extent of the basic operations involved.

Computationally, the basic operations are pulse shaping, deconvolution, time shifting, compositing, and cross-correlation. Pulse shaping, for example, is employed to correct the imperfection of the explosive source of seismic energy, as shown in Figure IIB6-4. Curve A is a typical pressure signature as recorded by a source monitor hydrophone, showing the initial explosion plus aftershocks caused by bubble implosions. Figure B illustrates the effectiveness of a 401-point symmetrical pulse shaping operator in collapsing the bubble energy of A into a single central pulse.

One product of the velocity analysis of seismic reflection data is illustrated in Figure IIB6-5. To a reflection time of approximately 1.8 seconds, the average velocity distribution is relatively uniform across the profile. Below this time there is a significant difference in the velocity gradients in the right and left portions of the section, the velocities being slower on the right. The vertical change in gradient on the right requires an interval velocity inversion, as displayed in the interval velocity section at the top.

Velocity sections derived from such vast quantities of observed data are being used to improve seismic interpretations. The velocity variations along this profile provide an insight into structural development prior to deposition of the section above the strong reflection near 1.8 seconds, help us to understand the faulting sequence, and provide useful information on gross lithologic variations. Average velocity from the surface to the indicated reflection time is automatically plotted in the center section. Dotted lines represent the contours of equal average velocity in increments of 100 feet per second, the 6 representing 6000 feet per second. Each plotted point along an isovelocity line represents the result of a separate calculation in

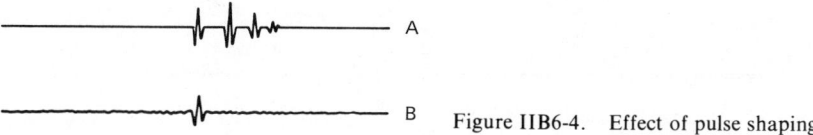

Figure IIB6-4. Effect of pulse shaping.

* For more detailed descriptions, see References 1 and 2.

82

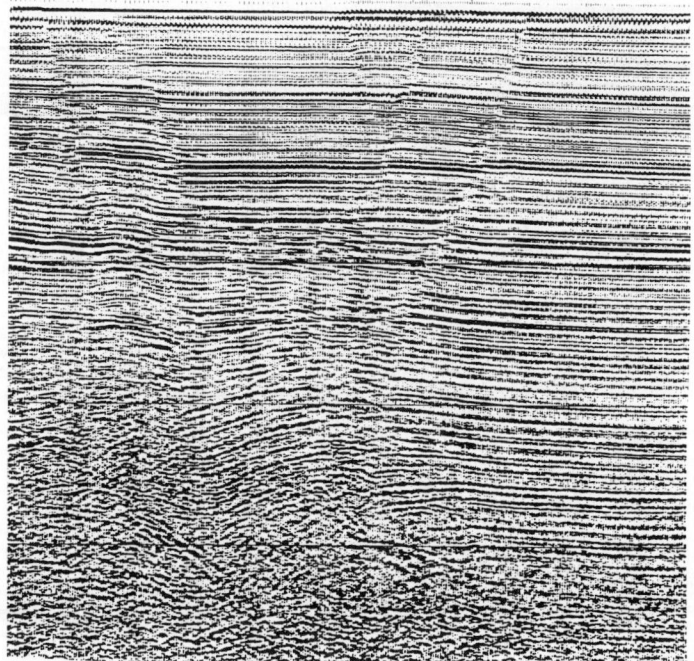

Figure IIB6-5. Velocity analysis.

which all possible shot-to-receiver distances are represented. In 12-fold CDP shooting, for example, one velocity analysis "trace" is computed for every two stacked reflection traces. The corresponding conventional reflection section in time is shown below.

The smoothed average data were converted to an interval velocity distribution at every twelfth plotted point as displayed in the top section. The vertical line through each interval velocity "curve" represents the velocity 9000 feet per second. The scale above each interval velocity set is incremented at 1000 feet per second.

All of these filtering and correlation processes require multiple-add operations, in great quantities. In order to perform these and related vector operations more rapidly and efficiently IBM, with the collaboration of Western Geophysical, developed a peripheral processor called the 2938 array processor.

To execute its seismic processing workload, Western Geophysical uses seven digital computers ranging in size from 360/44 to 370/165, each coupled with a 2938 array processor.

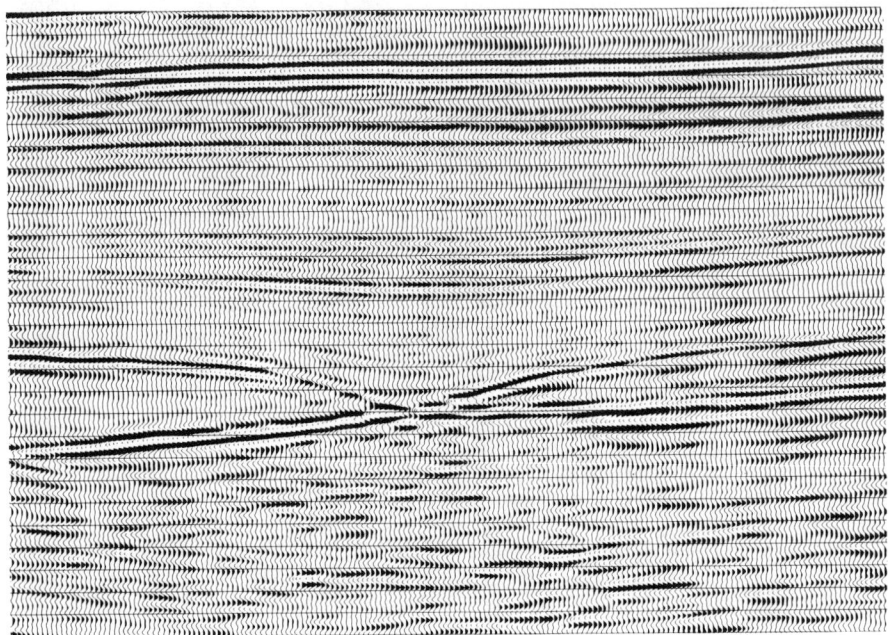

Figure IIB6-6. Display of subsurface structure.

The output sections are produced on a specially constructed oscillographic plotter. As seen in Figure IIB6-6, the image consists of closely spaced waveforms, with excursions beyond a specified magnitude filled in for optimal readability.

This application probably represents an ultimate in data reduction. The volume of seismic data collected by Western Geophysical amounts to 100,000 reels of magnetic tape per year. Digital processing transforms that volume of raw data to about 3000 reels of output numerical data which in turn is converted to visual information produced on the single output device described above.

Remarkable as is this sort of seismic processing, until recently it made use only of time and *velocity* information—to determine the *subsurface geometry*. Information conveyed in the amplitude of the reflected signal had not been exploited. Signal amplitudes are determined by a combination of geometric spreading, reflection coefficients, and attenuation losses in the medium (1). It is these last two parameters, the reflection coefficients and the attenuation, that allow us the completion of the partial lithographic (or material) picture afforded by velocity values. Recently the reflection coefficient information has permitted direct identification of hydrocarbon deposits in several parts of the world.

Within the last five years, exploration seismology has achieved the instrumentation needed to preserve all of the information in a seismic event. In June of 1966 the first operational use of binary gain-ranging amplifiers ushered in a new era. For the first time, instrument limitations no longer stood in the way of the ultimate goal—both acoustic velocity and acoustic attenuation values were inherently present within the seismic signals brought back from the field.

With the combined knowledge of the acoustic velocity and the acoustic attenuation constant, we can come quite close to identifying the lithologic character of a subsurface zone. For example, the combined knowledge of velocity and attenuation enables us to distinguish among sandstone, shale, and limestone. As Figure IIB6-7 shows, neither velocity nor attenuation is alone sufficient to resolve these lithologies, but the combination of the two values can distinguish among these kinds of sedimentary rocks. It can be expected that as experience is acquired, many lithologic distinctions will be made by means of these physical parameters. Indeed, it is theoretically possible to derive three independent (orthogonal) quantities such as the bulk modulus of elasticity, the density, and the attenuation coefficient from seismic reflection data. With three such parameters, sharp lithological distinctions will be possible and lithological distinctions are the answer to the question: "what?"

Since oil often collects in porous materials, even in the absence of structural anomalies, this extended mode of seismic processing promises the discovery of entire fields heretofore invisible. A complication is that ve-

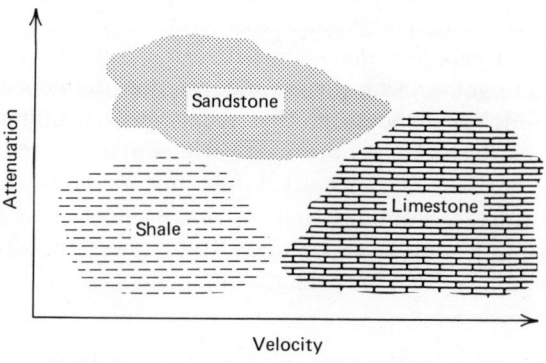

Figure IIB6-7. Combined use of velocity and attenuation.

locity variations cause only minute third order effects on the signals, so that even more sensitive and sophisticated processing techniques must be developed to achieve the required resolution.

References

1. C. H. Savit and E. J. Mataker, Jr., "From 'Where?' to 'What?'", Proceedings of the Eight World Petroleum Congress, pp. 95–104.
2. W. A. Schneider, "Developments in Seismic Data Processing and Analysis (1968–1970), *Geophysics,* **36**, 6, (December 1971), 1043–1073.
3. Anonymous, "IBM 2938 Array Processor," IBM Publication GA24-3519.
4. M. B. Dobrin, *Computer Processing of Seismic Reflections in Petroleum Exploration, from Computer Applications in the Earth Sciences—An International Symposium,* D. F. Merriam, Ed., Plenum Press, New York, 1969.

CASE STUDY 7   Data Analysis: Market Research*

Marketing research is a way to find patterns in the market place. These patterns may involve product preferences, consumer tastes, market dimensions, or similar factors. The computer is not absolutely essential, but over the last few years it has greatly extended the power of marketing research.

Computers are important for a number of reasons. They can store and manipulate large amounts of data, much more than would be feasible manually. Marketing research is based on sampling, and larger samples increase the researcher's confidence in the results. Complex calculations can be performed by computers, and repetitive computations can be performed rapidly even on large masses of data.

The primary targets for marketing research have been mass market items. Mistakes in going to market with consumer products can turn out to be multi-million dollar blunders, so that even expensive computer-based research can be cost-justified. As more powerful software becomes available, and computing costs decrease, market research methods are moving into new application areas. Political analysts and students of social problems are borrowing more and more of these techniques. Industrial and commercial marketing is becoming increasingly dependent on sophisticated methods.

* This case study has been exerpted from Valerie H. Free and Thomas E. Neman, Market Research Matches Products to Consumers, *Computer Decisions,* May 1972, p. 12, Copyright 1972, by Hayden Publishing Company.

B. EXAMINATION   87

Because of this expansion, managers in any field should be aware of marketing research progress.

How Marketing Research Happens

Normally marketing research is initiated by a product group. Research can help define the market for a new product or service. For an existing product, or an extension to a product line, it may be necessary to find out whether a new package, advertising strategy, or product improvement will be successful against the competition. The product group will take its problem either to an internal market research department or to an outside organization. The market research specialists will refine the problem definition and determine the analytic framework. One study may have multiple uses. An existing product might be examined for only one or two of the segments of the product cycle illustrated in the chart (see Figure IIB7-1 and Table IIB7-1), such as a test of a new package. A new product might go through most parts of the cycle.

Next a survey will be conducted using a sample from the target population. In the consumer field an outside survey organization normally does this. A field survey organization will coordinate interviewing in selected test cities. If this is done by phone it is normally conducted from a central location over WATS lines. A mail survey is also done from a central location.

Data reduction is also normally done outside. Even when the company doing the research has its own keypunching group, the work is usually sent to one of the numerous firms specializing in this area. These firms have special skills in such areas as pre-cleaning the data (checking that date of birth matches the age, that a woman is a housewife, that a question is not answered both yes and no, and so on). After this operation the data is coded and keypunched. Then tabulations of results and marginal values are prepared. Tabulations might include average scores for each product where several products are compared, or the total numbers of people who saw a TV commercial in different test cities, or similar data. They also might be statistical measures such as means, medians, standard deviations, proportions, and so on. This data will normally be returned to the marketing research department for further analysis and interpretation.

If a new product is an innovation, the first area for research might be a concept test to find out consumer's potential acceptance. The concept might be presented through a sample ad, a package, or a written description. The respondent may be asked to rate the concept as to purchase intent, utility (such as: "On what occasions would you serve it? How often

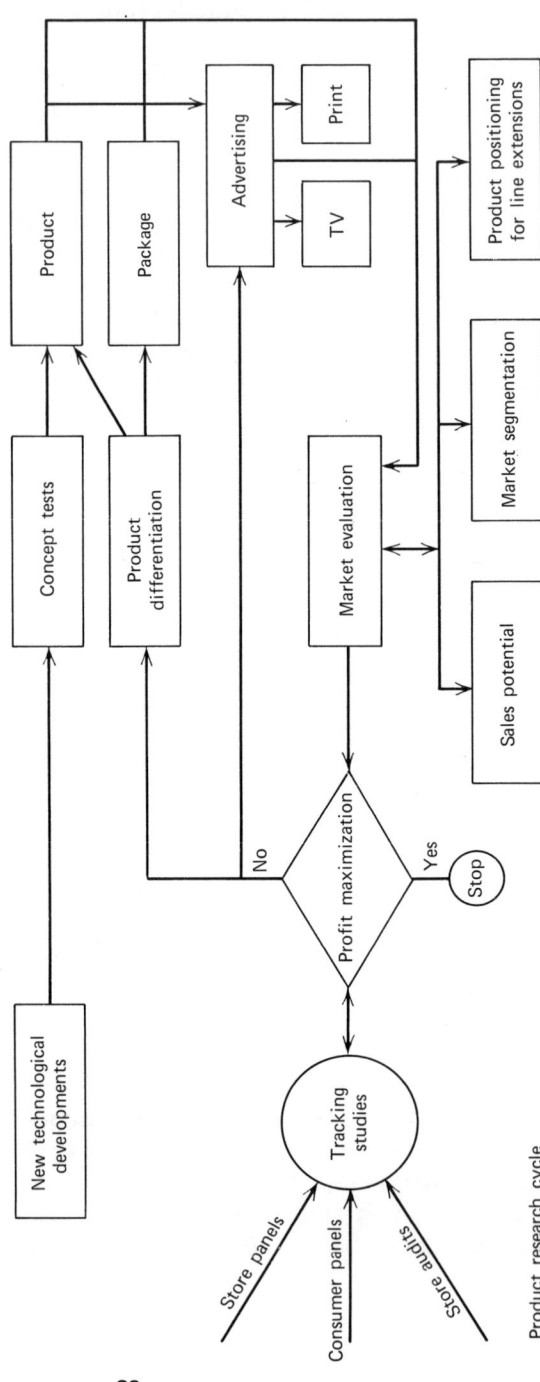

Figure IIB7-1. Product research cycle: targets for research studies.

Table IIB7-1 Targets for Research Studies

	New Product	Established Product — Reformulation	Established Product — New Image
Concept test	Is the product acceptable?		
Product test	Do the consumers like the taste/appearance/performance of the product?	Is the reformulated product better than the old product?	
Package test	Is the package appealing compared to similar products?	Does the package convey the improvements in the product? Is it more appealing than the old one?	Is the package consistent with the new image?
Advertising TV Print	Which advertisement creates the greatest recall and awareness of the product?		Are changes in perception of the product affected by new advertising campaign?
Market evaluation Product position	In the competitive framework of the market, where is the product positioned?		Has the product's positioning in the market been changed?
Market segmentation	What types of people are the potential consumers of this product?		Who is currently buying the product? Who are the market target segments for the new image?
Sales potential	What are the expected unit or dollar volumes forecasted?		What degree of market share change can be expected from the product's new image?
Tracking studies		Who is buying the product? In what type of outlets? How much are they buying? What is the rate of repeat purchase? Any out of stock conditions? What are the competitors' shares?	

would you use it?"), uniqueness, and other relevant measures. If the product itself is to be tested, it might be done in the respondent's own home (in-home testing) or at special facilities like a trailer or a testing laboratory (central-location testing).

For a new product the investigation of package designs or promotional strategy would be put aside until after a market evaluation and profit analysis. The sales potential for a product must be projected, and an estimate made of its possible impact on present products. The new product may turn out to have a potentially negative impact on profits! Or it may not, even with an optimistic forecast, meet the profit objectives of the firm.

If the product is new, it may be necessary to determine what types of products it will be close to in consumer perception. For example: Is lobster newburg closer to fish products or to beef stroganoff in the marketplace? Are cola products closer to coffee and tea than they are to other soft drinks in the perceptions of consumers? Intuition is not trustworthy in such cases. Studies show that lobster newburg is more closely related to food products like beef stroganoff than to fish, and that colas are closer to coffee and tea, then to ginger ale, which is perceived as closer to drink mixers.

Multidimensional scaling is used to reveal the major dimensions that shape the marketplace. For example, with lobster newburg these might prove to be factors like difficulty or ease of preparation, degree of acceptance by husbands or children, a woman's vanity (serving Continental cuisine), and cost. The aim in studies is to find separate factors that are most relevant to purchase behavior. Then products can be "positioned" in consumer perception so as to appeal to the largest group in as many of these critical factors as possible.

Market segmentation studies can help segment the market according to product perceptions, consumer attitudes and consumer behavior. If the product is a line extension, segmentation will help in estimating dollar size of potential consumer segments.

Psychographic studies allow another important type of segmentation of consumers into market groups. Personality, social roles and aspirations are explored in this type of testing. Attitudinal and life-style profiles can help identify characteristics of potential customers, suggesting ways to shape a product or promotional theme. In the past, demographic data was most widely used for this purpose. For example, the major purchasers of a certain type of product may prove to be young mothers in the 20 to 35 range. However psychographic studies may help to separate this group into distinctly different segments, each with individual product perceptions and buying habits. Some of them may be "child-oriented." Others may be "home-maker oriented." A third group may like to think of themselves as "swingers." Product or promotional appeals would then be tailored for one or more of these segments.

These studies can help determine strategy for positioning a product within an existing or a new marketplace. An example is illustrated for the cereal market in Figure IIB7-2. The important factors in this study turned out to be health/nutrition, child's taste acceptance, and ease of preparation. Some existing cereal products are placed along these three dimensions. Oatmeal, for example, is perceived as nutritious, but difficult to prepare and not so high in a child's taste acceptance.

Once these tests have been analyzed, and decisions are made on how to position the product in the marketplace for maximum profit potential, the product differentiation stage begins. Some features of the actual product may be modified, such as adding cinnamon flavor to instant oatmeal. Package design may emphasize some feature of the product, or may be tailored to have more appeal than competing packages that will be next to it in the store. Consumer tests may be done on alternative package designs, and also against competing packages. Some of the analytical techniques to

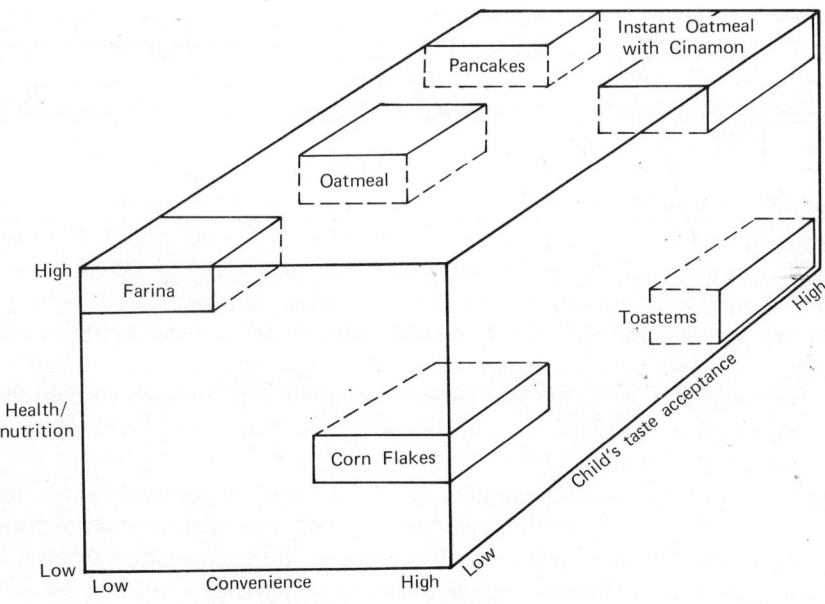

Figure IIB7-2. Multidimensional scaling for cereal market. Cereal market study reveals three main perceptual dimensions. Instant oatmeal with cinnamon should score high on all three.

be described later may be required to determine if differences are due to chance, or are statistically significant. Central location tests, or test marketing in selected areas, may be done to see if a new product actually does better than existing products in the marketplace.

At this point in the cycle, TV commercials and print advertising may be prepared and tested. Forced exposure is one approach. Tests are conducted in a laboratory or theater setting. Another approach is on-air copy testing. For example, two commercials might be tested in similar positions, such as on competing eleven-o'clock news programs. Telephone interviewing of the viewing audience is then conducted. Both methods measure recall of perceived product benefits or attributes, and intention to purchase. Forced exposure testing is also capable of recording both before and after exposure measures. Test print ads may be run in selected regions or on split runs of the same editions. Comparisons are made between two ads, or between a new ad and the norm of ads in that product group, to determine influence on consumers.

If an existing product is involved rather than a new one, research may begin with tracking studies. Consumer panels may be operated to track the types of people who are buying the product. The amount of brand switching will be tracked. Store audits may be used to observe actual volumes. These audits also track the effects of promotional activities by the competition. This data may help segment the market into groups of homogeneous consumer types.

Reducing and Analyzing the Data

Once the data has been keypunched, tabulations including marginal runs (totals, averages, etc.) can be printed out. Then, depending on whether the study was metric or non-metric, further data reduction may be performed to extract greater insight into the results. Data reduction normally starts with standard statistical measures on one variable at a time (univariate). Then two variables, or even two statistical distributions may be compared (bivariate), or analyses of several variables or distributions at once may be performed (multivariate).

Metric data are scaled responses. For example, respondents may be asked to rate products or attributes of some product on scales from 1 to 10. Non-metric data do not involve scaled values. These might be yes or no responses, or choices within categories such as which products are used for what purposes.

If the study was non-metric, the responses for various items or for various respondents may be broken into proportions or percentages. A variety of statistical techniques are available to find whether the differences between these groupings are statistically significant.

Distance matrices are a second type of non-metric measure. These matrices of scores or calculated values represent "distances" between products or between groups of subjects.

In hierarchical clustering objects or groups of objects are grouped on the basis of similarity or dissimilarity. First it will find the two objects or clusters that are closest to each other. On a graph an ellipse may be put around these two. Then the next closest will be found and a new loop drawn. Eventually clusters will become linked with other clusters, so that a loop can be drawn about pairs or groups of clusters.

In multidimensional scaling, the computer helps find not only which products are perceived as close to each other in the marketplace, but also what the major dimensions of this perception might be. A major dimension for mouthwash would be taste.

Three or more important dimensions may be discovered, so that the results can be graphically represented in space along the major dimensions.

Metric data analysis normally begins with finding means and standard deviations. The mean response for a particular attribute of a product might be 7.2 on a scale of 10, for example. This is obtained by adding all the scores and dividing by the number of responses. The standard deviation gives some idea of the scatter of responses around this central value.

The tests of hypotheses are used to examine differences between means or distributions. For example, the test may determine whether the responses to TV commercials in two markets are merely due to chance or are statistically significant. Bivariate tests make use of t tests, while F tests can be used for multivariate.

Another major group of analytical methods involves some sort of correlation between two or more items, groups of responses, types of consumers, and so on. In simple correlation analysis, one might be looking for the degree of association between items two at a time across a number of respondents. In multiple correlation, two or more items are correlated with a single item. The covariance is one measure of relationship. For example, how much of the variability in IQ scores can be attributed to the Head Start program. Regression analysis is used to measure the relationship of two or more independent variables on the basis of a dependent variable. For example, sales might be predicted on the basis of previous advertising expenditures, projected disposable income, and similar factors.

Canonical correlation is similar to multiple regression, except that several dependent variables might be involved. In the sales example, the dependent variables could be the sales of several products. This method is used to relate TV viewing habits and life-style factors.

Factor analysis is a way to reduce many data inputs into a few common groups, or factors. Such a factor is a composite of many variables. There are two major types, R and Q. In R-type factor analysis the underlying question is "Which items are responded to in a similar manner." For the Q-mode it is "Which people have the same response patterns?" The computer performs matrix algebra, the multiplication and inversion of matrices, to produce "loadings" of items on factors and factors on items. The analyst can see which items have the highest loadings on a factor, and then on the basis of these items can postulate some general characteristic or psychological dimension of these items.

Discriminate analysis is a method of assigning individuals to one group or another based on a set of observations for all the groups as shown in Figure IIB7-3. Each observation consists of scaled responses to a set of product ratings, imagery or psychological items. Other categorical and demographic data may also be used to help determine the groupings. A dis-

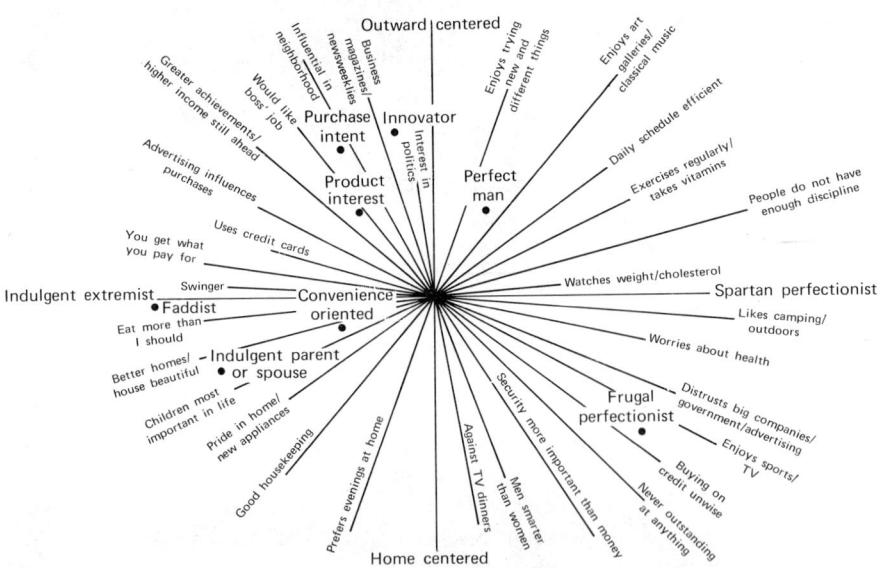

Figure IIB7-3. Discriminate map of six consumer groups. Six consumer groups are arrayed in discriminate map. The innovator, perfect man, convenience-oriented, and indulgent parent groups appear to be a promising market target. But adding another dimension, cost, reveals that the convenience-oriented group does not go with the others.

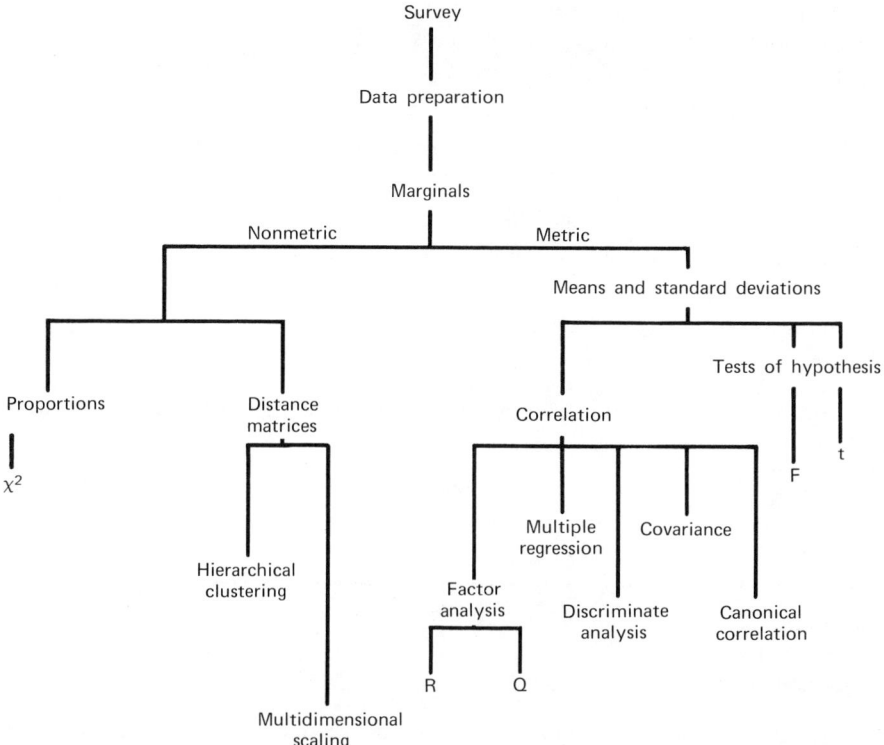

Figure IIB7-4. Tools of marketing research.

criminate function is computed, and probabilities of group membership determined, so that an individual can be clearly assigned to a group.

The tools of marketing research are continually changing. New and more powerful techniques are being developed to make the matching of products to consumers less of an art and more of a science. Figure IIB7-4 presents a taxonomy of several techniques currently used in marketing research.

Study for a Video-Cassette Console

An example of how marketing research might be used for a completely new product is a good way to illustrate some of the techniques. The product will be a video-cassette console, competitively priced with the more expensive color-TV consoles. It contains a play-back unit as well as a video recorder.

Several questions to be answered are:

Is there a sizeable potential market?

Who will buy the product?
What types of people are they?
How can we reach them?
How should the product be positioned?

To start the study, some tests are given and information collected about one thousand women. The data gathered was as follows:

- 150 product utility measures.
- 300 life-style and personality-agreement scales.
- 54 demographic factors.
- Concept acceptance and purchase interest data.
- Perceptions of product similarity to others.

Product utility attitudes were expressed on a five-point scale, as were life-style and personality questions. For example:

Statement	Agree Completely	Agree Somewhat	No Opinion	Disagree Somewhat	Disagree Completely
I avoid foods that are high in cholesterol.	5	4	3	2	1

For the perceptual similarities data, the respondents were given cards containing the names of some existing products or other items as well as the new product. They were asked to place the cards in piles according to the similarities of the products and then to rank each pile on its usefulness to the household.

A Q-mode factor analysis was done on the product utility data, resulting in six market segments and 75 unassigned individuals who did not match well with any of the six segments.

The psychological data on life style and personality were used to determine the segment profiles.

Segment	Number in Group	Identifying Label
1	225	Convenience oriented
2	140	Innovators
3	261	Indulgent parent or spouse
4	120	Frugal perfectionist
5	132	Perfect man
6	47	Faddists

The convenience-oriented types are home and gadget-oriented who buy many labor-saving devices, both practical and impractical. The innovators find excitement in change. They are self-confident, decisive and socially secure, and are leaders in organized change. The indulgent parent or spouse is also home-oriented, but toward people rather than gadgets. She seeks admiration from the family through gifts and services. The frugal perfectionist is a self-disciplined primarily about health and expenditures. They consider themselves shining stars in a world full of people doing the wrong things, such as buying on credit, believing advertising, eating TV dinners, etc. The perfect man is a model of self-discipline, careful about diet, appearance, and public image. Non-necessity items are only bought if they improve his image. The faddist is self-indulgent, highly susceptible to advertising, but will not try a new product until it is the "in" thing.

Next, an R-mode factor analysis was done on personality and life-style data to group the 300 items into 25 factors.

Using the factors that were developed, the Q segments were analyzed using F tests to determine the significance of the differences in the mean responses. For each segment, 75 of the highest loading items in each factor were used to perform a discriminate mapping. This helped visualize segment positioning.

As a result of the analysis it was decided to position the home entertainment center as a substitute for the "uninvolved" entertainment media of conventional color TV. However there would be a strong emphasis on educational facilities. The segments selected for marketing emphasis, (the innovators, perfect man, and indulgent parent or spouse groups) represented 30 percent of the sample. If the product was a success with these groups, the faddists would join.

CASE STUDY 8   Medical Data Analysis*

Today, the physician at a large modern hospital has at his service not only the disciplines of medicine, chemistry, physics and bacteriology, but an arsenal of precise instruments such as X-ray, electro-cardiograms and electroencephalograms. Yet even today, the physician confronted by a critical case relies primarily on professional experience—his own and that of colleagues—in identifying the particular physiological pattern of the illness and deciding how to treat it.

---

* From J. Brennan, "Computers and the Critically Ill", IBM Research Report, Vol. 7, No. 2, 1971.

For the physician without a well-developed clinical frame of reference, the management of a critical case imposes an awesome responsibility indeed. The vast amount of biomedical data made available by modern techniques frequently tends to confuse rather than enlighten.

Not only is the mortality rate in septic shock very high, but roughly half of the patients die within 48 hours. In the short time available to him, the doctor must make a diagnosis and initiate antibiotic or other therapy, frequently without waiting for the usual blood tests and sensitivity studies. Moreover, septic shock cases constitute a heterogeneous group with wide variations in cardiac output, blood pressure and other primary variables, and with some patients responding to certain types of drugs while others do not. Thus, septic shock represents a classic example of a diagnostic category urgently requiring therapy, yet so broad as to be of very little value to the therapist. The goal of the research group, simply stated, was to try to establish a frame of reference within which the different patterns of sepsis might be classified according to physiologic complications so that, hopefully, those indicating the onset of septic shock could be identified. Armed with such information, the physician would gain time in which to carry out his therapeutic strategy.

To assist physicians in such situations, Dr. John H. Siegel, Associate Professor of Surgery at the Albert Einstein College of Medicine in New York City, Roger M. Goldwyn and Martha Miller of IBM Research, and Herman P. Friedman of the IBM Systems Research Institute, joined forces in 1967 to investigate various areas of critical illness. They decided to explore the possibility of using large digital computers to combine the physician's unique ability to recognize patterns of critical illness with the computer's capacity for retrieving and mathematically manipulating biomedical information on great numbers of patients treated in the past. The investigators codified a large volume of historical patient records, stored the case material in a computer data bank, then used it to create a broad physiologic frame of reference within which various categories of critical illness could be studied. As its initial project, the group chose the category of shock resulting from sepsis (severe infection).

The material on which the research project is based consists of data collected over a period of years from 182 patients who were studied and treated at the Clinical Research Center-Acute of the Albert Einstein College of Medicine. These patients had in common the fact that the severity of their illnesses required the special monitoring and other intensive care and emergency facilities available at the Center.

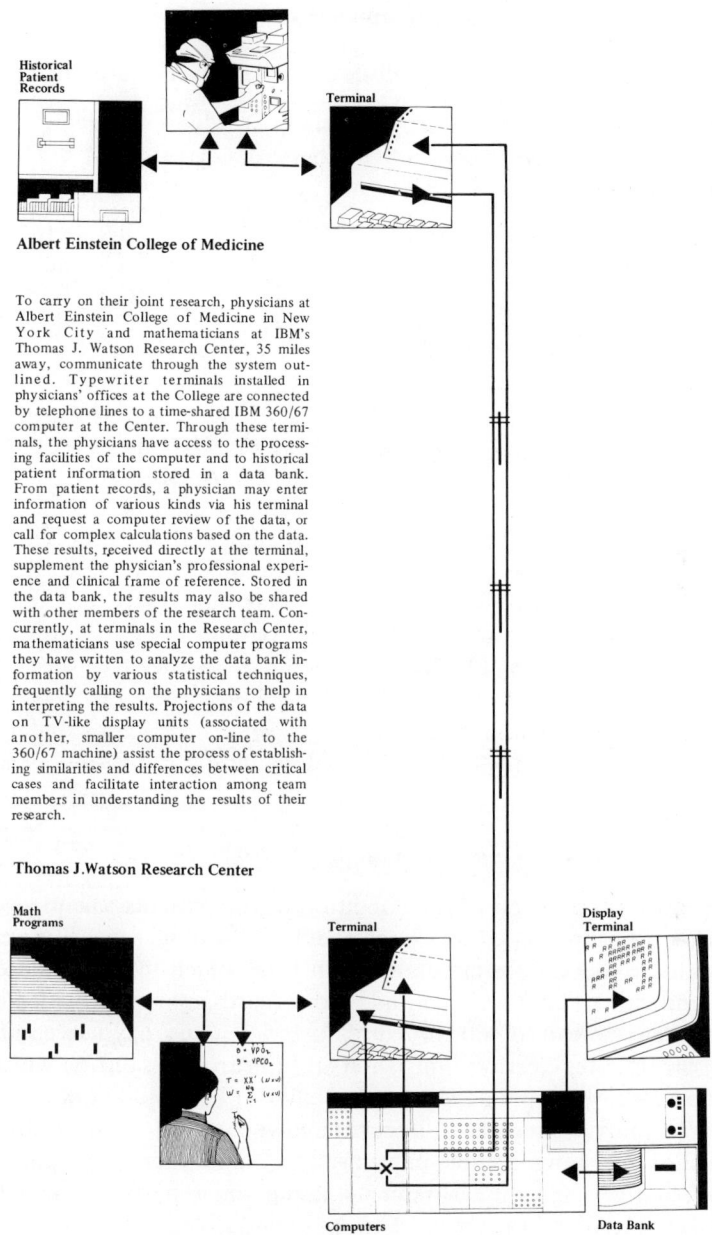

Albert Einstein College of Medicine

To carry on their joint research, physicians at Albert Einstein College of Medicine in New York City and mathematicians at IBM's Thomas J. Watson Research Center, 35 miles away, communicate through the system outlined. Typewriter terminals installed in physicians' offices at the College are connected by telephone lines to a time-shared IBM 360/67 computer at the Center. Through these terminals, the physicians have access to the processing facilities of the computer and to historical patient information stored in a data bank. From patient records, a physician may enter information of various kinds via his terminal and request a computer review of the data, or call for complex calculations based on the data. These results, received directly at the terminal, supplement the physician's professional experience and clinical frame of reference. Stored in the data bank, the results may also be shared with other members of the research team. Concurrently, at terminals in the Research Center, mathematicians use special computer programs they have written to analyze the data bank information by various statistical techniques, frequently calling on the physicians to help in interpreting the results. Projections of the data on TV-like display units (associated with another, smaller computer on-line to the 360/67 machine) assist the process of establishing similarities and differences between critical cases and facilitate interaction among team members in understanding the results of their research.

Thomas J. Watson Research Center

Figure IIB8-1.   System description.

System Description

To carry on their joint research, physicians at Albert Einstein College of Medicine in New York City and mathematicians at IBM's Thomas J. Watson Research Center, 35 miles away, communicate through the system outlined in Figure IIB8-1. Typewriter terminals installed in physicians' offices at the College are connected by telephone lines to a time-shared IBM 360/67 computer at the Center. Through these terminals, the physicians have access to the processing facilities of the computer and to historical patient information stored in a data bank. From patient records, a physician may enter information of various kinds via his terminal and request a computer review of the data, or call for complex calculations based on the data. These results, received directly at the terminal, supplement the physician's professional experience and clinical frame of reference. Stored in the data bank, the results may also be shared with other members of the research team. Concurrently, at terminals in the Research Center, mathematicians use special computer programs they have written to analyze the data bank information by various statistical techniques frequently calling on the physicians to help in interpreting the results. Projection of the data on TV-like display units (associated with another, smaller computer on-line to the 360/67 machine) assist the process of establishing similarities and differences between critical cases and facilitate interaction among team members in understanding the results of their research.

High-Dimensional Representations

To serve as an indication of the condition of the patients, the physicians in the research group singled out a set of nine physiologic measurements, relating cardiac function to circulatory function, which they considered to be most significant. These were: cardiac index (cardiac output divided by body surface area), mean blood pressure, arteriovenous oxygen content difference, heart rate, ejection time (interval of heart cycle during which blood is ejected), central venous pressure, venous pH (acid-alkaline balance), venous P_{O_2} (partial pressure of oxygen) and venous P_{CO_2} (partial pressure of carbon dioxide). Each sample entering into the mathematical analysis was reduced to these nine measurements taken on a particular person at a particular moment in time. The plan was to treat these samples mathematically as if they were points in nine-dimensional space to see if they tended to cluster or separate in ways that might make it possible to organize them into groups.

In the clustering procedure used by the mathematicians in the research group, the objective was to find groupings of the samples such that the average distance between samples within the groups was small compared to the average distance between samples in different groups. First, the computer plotted all the samples as points in space whose locations were determined by the nine parameters representing the physiological measurements. These points were then arbitrarily partitioned into trial groups and a 9-dimensional mean for each group was computed by dividing the sum of the measurements in each group by the number of samples in each group. Next, the distance of each sample from the mean of its group was measured. The sum of such measurements represented the dispersion, or "scatter," in each individual group. Finally, the sum of all these within-group dispersions provided the total within-group "scatter," W. By attempting various partitions of the samples into different numbers of groups, the researchers eventually succeeded in identifying four clusters that appeared—like galaxies in a miniature cosmos—to occupy different regions in a 9-dimensional space.

Returning to Three-Dimensions

In order to display the results of the cluster analysis in a way that would best illustrate the separation of the four clusters, the research group called on another statistical procedure known as linear discriminant analysis. In this process, the samples represented by the original 9 variables were reduced by linear combinations to three measurements, each of which was weighted sum of the original 9. The reduced samples in each of the four clusters were then plotted as points in 3-dimensional space, producing the pattern shown in the artist's rendition at top left of Figure IIB8-2. Next, the samples were identified as a reference group, R, and three septic groups, A, B and C. In the two-dimensional figure at bottom left, showing the actual distribution of the samples among the four groups, the A group appears to overlay the others. Drawing between shows how the three-dimensional representation is translated into two dimensions.

Interpreting the Results

Bringing all of these findings together, and reviewing the clinical data in light of the physiologic evidence, the investigators were able to make some tentative hypotheses. The reference group, while authenticated as a mainly basal population, contained septic samples indistinguishable from the basal samples, presumably because the septic data were taken at a time when the

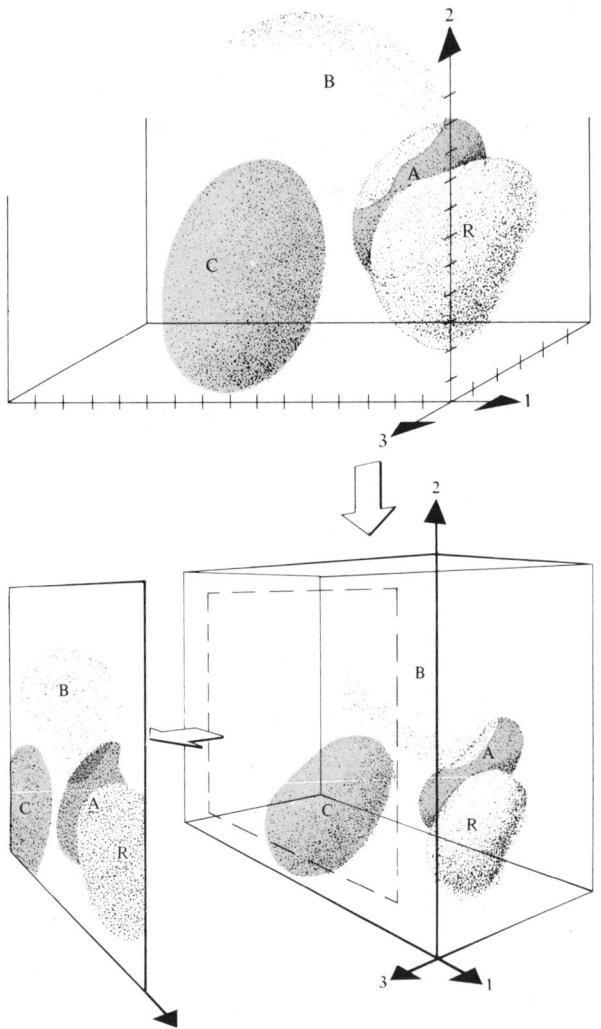

Figure IIB8-2. Cluster analysis.

particular patients were coping well with their infections. The group A patients, while showing moderately elevated heart action, appeared to have good basic cardiac function and a circulation at least adequate to supply body tissues. In other words, they were "holding their own." The basal samples in this group represented patients who had been exercising, or receiving exercise-simulating drugs, for the purpose of pre-operative

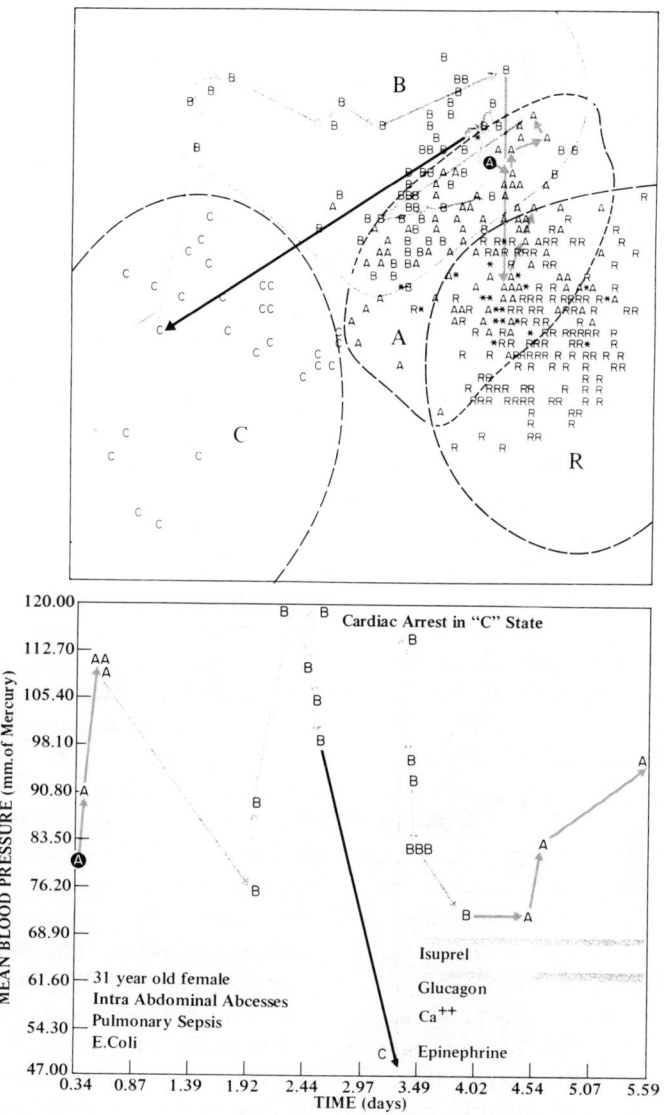

Figure IIB8-3. Transition of desperately ill patient.

evaluation. The B group patients reflected an exaggerated cardiac response in which the increased heart action was not accompanied by adequate circulatory function, and the body's metabolic needs were not being met. The few basal samples in the group reflected a hyperdynamic response to stress accompanying major operations. The C group patients presented the most abnormal pattern of all, revealing evidence of both heart and circulatory failure, repayment of a major oxygen debt, severe venous acidosis, and the release of large amounts of carbon dioxide. For these patients the equilibrium of life was unbalanced and death seemed near.

To help formulate a clearer clinical picture of these results, the investigators undertook to investigate the records of 81 patients who had shifted about as their condition changed. They found that although the patients moved around quite frequently, they tended to do so mainly within the confines of the same group. For example, the patients in the R group made 109 in-group transitions and only 24 to other groups. A to B group and B to A group transitions also occurred as well as frequent moves from A to R. There were, however, no patients moving directly from the R state to the preterminal C state and discouragingly few from C into other groups.

To explore how the results of their research might be useful to the physician managing a patient in crisis, the investigators obtained computer-generated projections of various individual patients in order to show, through their transitions, how they had responded to fateful developments in their illnesses and to changes in therapy. One such clinical trajectory is shown in Figure IIB8-3. The patient, a young woman with severe sepsis in the form of multiple intra-abdominal abcesses and also pulmonary infection, had been in the A group initially. Her condition grew worse and she passed into the B group, and then into the C group, where she went into shock and suffered a cardiac arrest. Emergency measures were taken to resuscitate her—heart massage, artificial respiration, the use of heart strengthening drugs—and her heart action was restored. The patient was given cardiovascular support by a continuous infusion of drugs to increase the force of heart contraction and to dilate the blood vessels to the peripheral tissues. On this therapy, she reverted back to the B group and then to the A group. By plotting these transitions and comparing them with the historical record, it could be seen that the shift of the patient from the A to the B to the C group very accurately represented her deteriorating condition, and then the shift back from C to B to A correctly indicated her response to the change in therapy. Clearly, it is possible for a physician in a real-life situation to take samples from a seriously ill patient and feed them to the computer for analysis and assignment to one of the four groups. Then by calling for a display of all samples in that group, the physician could obtain at a glance a broad physiologic frame of reference within which to assess the clinical status of his own patient and make his therapeutic decisions.

Some Wider Implications

While Dr. Siegel and the IBM researchers have concentrated thus far on the specific problem of septic shock, they are now extending their investigations in the nature of critical illness to include studies of cirrhotic liver disease and the shock state associated with a heart attack or a major hemorrhage. However, their work has wider implications as well. The computer methodology developed by the group is not only applicable to other areas of medicine, but also to a variety of problems involving the classification, identification and interpretation of data arising in the social and natural sciences.

Moreover, the system has interesting educational potential. Dr. Siegel has pointed out: "A most effective pedagogic technique in teaching a clinical discipline is still the case system, where the motivating stimulus to learning is having the responsibility for a patient's care. By focusing data retrieval techniques on the specific case for which the individual physician is responsible, the computer forms the basis of a teaching system which can permit a more relevant kind of continuing education in the care of the critically ill." Finally, an interactive computer system could greatly facilitate consultation among physicians themselves. As in the time of Herodotus, there is still no substitute for experience in the diagnosis and treatment of catastrophic illness, but the means now exist to quantify, interpret and transmit that experience on a scale heretofore impossible.

References

1. R. M. Goldwyn, M. Miller, H. P. Friedman, and J. H. Siegel, "The Evolution of a System for Complex Data Bank Analysis Using a General Purpose Time-Sharing System," IBM Research Report, RC-3178, December 10, 1970.
2. J. H. Siegel, R. M. Goldwyn, and H. P. Friedman, "Pattern and Process in the Evolution of Human Septic Shock," IBM Research Report, RC 3245, February 12, 1971.
3. Anonymous "Analyzing Patterns of Illness," *IBM Computing Report,* **IX.** 1 (Spring 1973).

C. PROBLEM FORMULATION

Once data have been collected and examined, the scientist's job is to formulate his problem broadly enough to admit the solutions of probable interest, but narrowly enough to avoid dissipation of energy and resources. This is of course an important phase of the scientific process, since it determines the extent and direction of subsequent efforts. However, it is an informal, free-wheeling phase of the scientific process in which computers will be supportive only if they are responsive—and natural—enough to help more than they hinder. We need tools that support and enhance the logical and intuitive skill of the individual in a very dynamic fashion. Delays of hours or even minutes while waiting for computer response are harmful, if not intolerable, disruptions to the flow of the intellectual and intuitive process. By the same token, any requirement that the problem be articulated either in an artificial, computer-oriented language, or to an intermediary programmer, is destructive to the creative process.

For these reasons, a number of special-purpose, problem-solving languages and systems have been developed. JOSS, developed at SDC, BASIC, developed at Dartmouth, and APL developed by Ken Iverson at Harvard and implemented at IBM are noteworthy examples of such systems.

The term special-purpose, applied to these systems, is only relative and does not imply that they are useful only for scientific problem solving. Indeed, over the years, a rapidly broadening spectrum of applications has been attacked through their use. The term special-purpose does imply that many functions were deliberately excluded from these systems so that they could be made easier to use.

Also, these systems are all "interpretive." That is, each instruction is interpreted and executed immediately after submission, rather than being collected and executed as a job-sized unit. This interpretive mode of execution reduces the efficiency of machine computation, but increases the efficiency of the human problem-solving process. This improvement results directly from the benefits of receiving responses from the system after each input instruction. This response may be the answer to a question or sample calculation, or it may be a diagnostic message, immediately calling attention to an input error or inconsistency.

CASE STUDY 9   Large Mathematical Problems, Meteorology*

The analysis of computer applications and the programming of unbuilt computers for such applications are elements of an uncertain art. A given application problem may be formulated in many different ways; there may

---

* This case study has been excerpted from H. G. Kolsky, "Problem Formulation Using APL," *IBM Systems Journal* November 3, 1969, p. 204–219.

be differing opinions even among experts in the same field: also, two different application programmers may cast the same numerical model in different ways on a new machine.

This paper proposes the use of a mathematical programming language, such as APL, for removing some of the arbitrariness from the problem-formulation stage. The purpose of the proposed approach is to eliminate errors in the logical formulation early in the design of a large scientific program. Using a mathematical programming language for expressing the overall program logic in an unambiguous, compact way prevents many of the logical errors that can creep into a program because of its sheer size. As an illustration of this approach to program design, the analysis of a numerical meteorological model is discussed. In our discussion we compare a general approach using FORTRAN alone during problem formulation with an approach in which APL augments FORTRAN in the problem formulation stage. Although a knowledge of APL is not required for an understanding of this paper, an interest in programming large mathematical problems is assumed.

The APL language is used here because it is a powerful and concise way of representing complex relationships and because it exists in the form of a time-sharing terminal language (2) that enables the testing of parts of the program as they are written. The main theme of this paper is to illustrate the power and utility of such a language as a mode of mathematical notation and expression for programming purposes.

Although the APL language may seem alien and difficult to read at first, the power of the notation is derived from such conventions and definitions as the right-to-left execution convention. Variables in APL equations need not be scalar quantities, but may also be vectors, matrices, and arrays of higher dimensions. The notation is highly consistent internally, whereas standard mathematical notation is a conglomerate of conventions that have developed over many years from many different sources. The structure of the monadic and dyadic functions (shown in the Appendix) is very general and applies to data arrays of many ranks and mixed types. (A monadic function is one that takes a single argument, and a dyadic function takes two arguments.) In APL one writes |A for the absolute value of A. The vertical bar is a monadic operator, whereas the bar in B|A means the residue of A modulo B. The standard mathematical notations are |A| and A mod B. In FORTRAN, on the other hand, one writes ABS (A) and MOD|(B,A).

From a machine architecture point of view, the most important aspect of APL is the large amount of freedom in the order of execution of the individual arithmetic steps. This can be very important in the allocation of resources of a multiprocessor or a vector processor. For example, when one writes $A = B + C$ in APL, where A, B, and C are three-dimensional matrices, this implies that a large number of additions of components of B and C yield the corresponding components of A. However, nothing is said concerning the order in which these additions take place or concerning the number that can take place simultaneously. A suitable compiler could use this freedom to avoid storage or other resource allocation conflicts when necessary. Thus, the APL formulation is very concise concerning the final results desired, but allows considerable intermediate freedom whereby the system achieves these results.

LARGE-PROBLEM FORMULATION. Since the meteorological application discussed in this paper exemplifies partial differential equations, some of the general considerations involved in their formulation for numerical solution are now presented. The first step is to understand the physical phenomena and the applicable fundamental physical laws.

From this understanding of the physical problem, a mathematical model is prepared, usually in the form of partial differential equations with approximations for subscale and superscale phenomena. These phenomena are physical effects that are either much smaller or much larger than those being studied. The differential equation model is then transformed into a difference equation form for computational purposes. The numerical meteorological simulation equations discussed later are concerned with numerically tracing the time development of large-scale cyclonic-motions in the atmosphere. Small-scale atmospheric motions, such as storm fronts and local thunderstorms, are considered subscale. Long-term phenomena, such as glacial formation during ice ages, are considered superscale in time for the model. However, some subscale motions in the meteorological model are of sufficient importance to be included in approximations that take into account average effects of turbulent and convective motions smaller than the grid size in the differnce equations. This is done by including diffusion terms in the model.

Difference equations are conventionally formulated using a notation involving the components of the variables. This formulation usually involves the use of subscripts to index spatial locations and superscripts for the time steps of a given variable. For example, $T_{k,l,m}^{n}$ implies the temperature at time step n at point indexed location $k,l,$ and m. When the differentials in the partial differential equations are replaced by finite differences, the subscripts and superscripts in some of these equations can become quite involved.

C. PROBLEM FORMULATION

The next step in the general procedure is to lay out storage and data flow for the model. It is here that the machine dependence of the calculation is strongest. Often, the number of points or the horizontal spacing in a meteorological model are determined largely on the basis of the storage size. A FORTRAN or PL/1 program is prepared using the difference equations, storage, layout, and data flow. Frequently, the difference equations and storage layout are modified during the writing of such a program, and the original mathematical model may be modified in this process. Finally, before making test experiments with the complete program, there is a debugging and checkout of the program parts.

The APL procedure starts with the same physical phenomena and mathematical model, but makes the transition to difference equations by using a "compact" notation. This notation is an extension of that which has been used by Shuman, Smagorinsky, and others in the field (3, 4). The aim of the procedure discussed here is toward an APL formulation in which the data arrays are considered as a whole and not as isolated components. After setting up the difference equations in compact notation, a layout and data flow analysis of the problem is made using the APL notation. The next step is to program the problem in APL and to check the logic of individual pieces using dummy data. The APL formulation is then transcribed into a higher-level language such as FORTRAN or PL/1, for execution. Even though additional errors may creep into the problem during the program transcription, such errors should be more "localized" and easily caught in checking out the FORTRAN program. Transcription is necessary because the current APL system cannot handle data arrays of the size required in the meteorological model and is presently available only as an interpretive time-shared system. Although program debugging, checkout, and the test experiments are conventionally performed, most of the logic and data flow of the program have been previously checked by using the APL procedure.

Of course, there is a class of errors for which segmentary debugging of the logic is not sufficient. Parts may work correctly, but the problem as a whole may be unstable. However, these errors really represent incorrect numerical modeling, not flaws in the logic or data flow. Research weather calculations have produced marked examples of such instability. Smagorinsky (4) found that certain types of neutral instabilities can require in the order of hundreds of time-steps to reveal themselves. This corresponds to advancing the weather model by as much as thirty days to verify the stability of the numerical method.

The size of a weather problem can be estimated by the number of mesh points used in the difference equations for the model. The length of a time step is determined by stability requirements. A number of physical quantities are stored for each atmospheric mesh point, and several special quantities are stored for each surface mesh point. In addition, several quantities that vary only with longitude or only with latitude are stored as one-dimensional vectors. A given physical parameter of the atmosphere is thus represented in the numerical model as a three-dimensional array of numbers (or, more precisely, as two three-dimensional arrays of numbers, one for each hemisphere).

Often in the logic of a problem, similar calcuations could be done on a particular physical parameter for all mesh points of the array. The nature of FORTRAN, however, is such that computations are done on one number at a time, that is, one scalar member of the multidimensional array at a time. Therefore, a three-dimensicnal array computation requires at least a triple DO-loop or equivalent to perform the computation. An advantage of the APL formation, in which the equations contain multi-dimensional arrays as their basic elements, is that many DO-loops are eliminated, thereby improving program logic. The remaining loops are those having to do with the actual program flow.

Two difficulties of large fluid dynamics problems are those of handling special and boundary cases. In APL, these cases can be represented by the sides and edges of three-dimensional data arrays. The APL statement of a problem can thus take the form of a general expression for the array as a whole, plus special statements for certain of the sides of edges of the array. The properties of APL have two significant effects. One is that the total length of a program written in APL is much shorter than that of FORTRAN. (Ratios of five or ten to one are not uncommon.) Also, special cases are stated explicitly and not obscured in the programming.

CONCLUDING REMARKS: The APL formulation of a large-scale scientific problem can specify the solution precisely, while allowing the system much freedom in producing computed results. The testing and debugging stages of such application programming can be carried out at a terminal. The simplicity of APL helps the programmer see the main design of the problem by reducing the program size. In the problem-formulation phase, the APL programmer is aided by the mathematical consistency of the language and by the inherent explicitness of APL program statements from a mathematical point of view.

APPENDIX

APL primitive mixed functions

Name	Sign[1]	Definition or example[2]
Size	⍴A	⍴P ↔ 4 ⍴E ↔ 3 4 ⍴5 ↔ ⍳0
Reshape	V⍴A	Reshape A to dimension V 3 4⍴⍳12 ↔ E 12⍴E ↔ ⍳12 0⍴E ↔ ⍳0
Ravel	,A	,A ↔ (×/⍴A)⍴A ,E ↔ ⍳12 ⍴,5 ↔ 1
Catenate	V,V	P,⍳2 ↔ 2 3 5 7 1 2 'T','HIS' ↔ 'THIS'

Index[3,4]	V[A]
	M[A;A]
	A[A;..
	..;A]
		P[2] ↔ 3 P[4 3 2 1] ↔ 7 5 3 2
		E[1 3;3 2 1] ↔ 3 2 1
		                            11 10 9
		E[1;] ↔ 1 2 3 4
		E[;1] ↔ 1 5 9 'ABCDEFGHIJKL'[E] ↔ ABCD
		                                              EFGH
		                                              IJKL

Index generator[3]	⍳S	First S integers ⍳4 ↔ 1 2 3 4 ⍳0 ↔ an empty vector
Index of[3]	V⍳A	Least index of A P⍳3 ↔ 2 in V, or 1+⍴V P⍳E ↔ 5 1 2 5 3 5 4 5 4 4⍳4 ↔ 1 5 5 5 5
Take Drop	V↑A V↓A	Take or drop |V[I]| first 2 3↑X ↔ ABC (V[I]≥0) or last (V[I]<0) EFG elements of coordinate I ⁻2↑P ↔ 5 7
Grade up[3,5] Grade down[3,5]	⍋A ⍒A	The permutation which ⍋3 5 3 2 ↔ 4 1 3 2 would order A (ascend- ing or descending) ⍒3 5 3 2 ↔ 2 1 3 4

Compress[5]	V/A	1 0 1 0/P ↔ 2 5 1 0 1 0/E ↔ 1 3
		                                              5 7
		                                              9 11
		1 0 1/[1]E ↔ 1 2 3 4 1 0 1/E
		              9 10 11 12

Expand[5]	V\A	1 0 1\⍳2 ↔ 1 0 2 1 0 1 1\X ↔ A BCD
		                                              E FGH
		                                              I JKL

Reverse[5]	⌽A	⌽X ↔ DCBA ⌽[1]X ↔ ⊖X ↔ IJKL
		      HGFE EFGH
		      LKJI ⌽P ↔ 7 5 3 2 ABCD

Rotate[5]	A⌽A	3⌽P ↔ 7 2 3 5 ↔ ⁻1⌽P 1 0 ⁻1⌽X ↔ BCDA
		                                                EFGH
		                                                LIJK

Transpose	V⍉A	Coordinate I of A AEI becomes coordinate 2 1⍉X ↔ BFJ V[I] of result 1 1⍉E ↔ 1 6 11 CGK DHL
	⍉A	Transpose last two coordinates ⍉E ↔ 2 1⍉E
Membership	A∊A	⍴W∊Y ↔ ⍴W E∊P ↔ 0 1 1 0 P∊⍳4 ↔ 1 1 0 0 1 0 1 0 0 0 0 0
Decode	V⊥V	10⊥1 7 7 6 ↔ 1776 24 60 60⊥1 2 3 ↔ 3723
Encode	V⊤S	24 60 60⊤3723 ↔ 1 2 3 60 60⊤3723 ↔ 2 3
Deal[3]	S?S	W?Y ↔ Random deal of W elements from ⍳Y

Notes:

1. Restrictions on argument ranks are indicated by: S for scalar, V for vector, M for matrix, A for Any. Except as the first argument of $S\iota A$ or $S[A]$, a scalar may be used instead of a vector. A one-element array may replace any scalar.

2. Arrays used in examples: $P \leftrightarrow 2\ 3\ 5\ 7$ $E \leftrightarrow \begin{matrix} 1 & 2 & 3 & 4 \\ 5 & 6 & 7 & 8 \\ 9 & 10 & 11 & 12 \end{matrix}$ $X \leftrightarrow \begin{matrix} ABCD \\ EFGH \\ IJKL \end{matrix}$

3. Function depends on index origin.

4. Elision of any index selects all along that coordinate.

5. The function is applied along the last coordinate; the symbols ⌿, ⍀, and ⊖ are equivalent to /, \, and ⌽, respectively, except that the function is applied along the first coordinate. If $[S]$ appears after any of the symbols, the relevant coordinate is determined by the scalar S.

APL primitive scalar functions

Monadic form fB		f	Dyadic form AfB	
Definition or example	Name		Name	Definition or example
$+B \leftrightarrow 0+B$	Plus	+	Plus	$2+3.2 \leftrightarrow 5.2$
$-B \leftrightarrow 0-B$	Negative	-	Minus	$2-3.2 \leftrightarrow {}^-1.2$
$\times B \leftrightarrow (B>0)-(B<0)$	Signum	×	Times	$2 \times 3.2 \leftrightarrow 6.4$
$\div B \leftrightarrow 1 \div B$	Reciprocal	÷	Divide	$2 \div 3.2 \leftrightarrow 0.625$
$\begin{array}{c\|c\|c} B & \lceil B & \lfloor B \\ \hline 3.14 & 4 & 3 \\ {}^-3.14 & {}^-3 & {}^-4 \end{array}$	Ceiling	⌈	Maximum	$3 \lceil 7 \leftrightarrow 7$
	Floor	⌊	Minimum	$3 \lfloor 7 \leftrightarrow 3$
$*B \leftrightarrow (2.71828..)*B$	Exponential	*	Power	$2*3 \leftrightarrow 8$
$\circledast N \leftrightarrow N \leftrightarrow *\circledast N$	Natural logarithm	⊛	Logarithm	$A \circledast B \leftrightarrow$ Log B base A $A \circledast B \leftrightarrow (\circledast B) \div \circledast A$
$\|{}^-3.14 \leftrightarrow 3.14$	Magnitude	|	Residue	$\begin{array}{l\|l} \text{Case} & A\|B \\ \hline A \neq 0 & B-(\|A) \times \lfloor B \div \|A \\ A=0, B \geq 0 & B \\ A=0, B<0 & \text{Domain error} \end{array}$
$!0 \leftrightarrow 1$ $!B \leftrightarrow B \times !B-1$ or $!B \leftrightarrow$ Gamma$(B+1)$	Factorial	!	Binomial coefficient	$A!B \leftrightarrow (!B) \div (!A) \times !B-A$ $2!5 \leftrightarrow 10 \quad 3!5 \leftrightarrow 10$
$?B \leftrightarrow$ Random choice from ιB	Roll	?	Deal	A Mixed Function
$\circ B \leftrightarrow B \times 3.14159\ldots$	Pi times	○	Circular	See Table at left
$\sim 1 \leftrightarrow 0 \quad \sim 0 \leftrightarrow 1$	Not	~		
		∧	And	$\begin{array}{c\|c\|c\|c\|c\|c} A & B & A \wedge B & A \vee B & A \barwedge B & A \veebar B \\ \hline 0 & 0 & 0 & 0 & 1 & 1 \\ 0 & 1 & 0 & 1 & 1 & 0 \\ 1 & 0 & 0 & 1 & 1 & 0 \\ 1 & 1 & 1 & 1 & 0 & 0 \end{array}$
		∨	Or	
		⊼	Nand	
		⊽	Nor	
		<	Less	Relations
		≤	Not greater	Result is 1 if the relation holds, 0 if it does not:
		=	Equal	$3 \leq 7 \leftrightarrow 1$
		≥	Not less	$7 \leq 3 \leftrightarrow 0$
		>	Greater	
		≠	Not Equal	

Table of Dyadic ○ Functions:

$(-A) \circ B$	A	$A \circ B$
$(1-B*2)*.5$	0	$(1-B*2)*.5$
Arcsin B	1	Sine B
Arccos B	2	Cosine B
Arctan B	3	Tangent B
$({}^-1+B*2)*.5$	4	$(1+B*2)*.5$
Arcsinh B	5	Sinh B
Arccosh B	6	Cosh B
Arctanh B	7	Tanh B

References

1. K. E. Iverson, "Programming Notation in System Design," *IBM Systems Journal,* **2** (June 1963), 117–128.
2. The APL/360 program, and the APL/360 User's Manual by A. D. Falkoff and K. E. Iverson may be obtained through any IBM branch office.
3. F. G. Shuman and J. B. Hovermale, "An Operational Six-Layer Primitive Equation Model," *Journal of Applied Meteorology,* **7**, 4 (August 968), 525–547.
4. Smagorinsky, S. Manabe, and J. L. Holloway, "Numerical Results from a Nine-Level General Circulation Model of the Atmosphere," *Monthly Weather Review,* **93**, 12 (December 1965) 727–768.
5. C. E. Leith, *Numerical Simulation of the Earth's Atmosphere*, University of California (Berkeley), Lawrence Radiation Laboratory Report, UCRL-7986-T, 1964.

C. PROBLEM FORMULATION

CASE STUDY 10 Data-Dependent Problem Formulation

A key characteristic of scientific activity is unpredictability. By definition, research is the process of observing and speculating about partially understood phenomena. Quite often our ignorance is such that not only are the data unpredictable, but, in addition, the approach, the choice and sequence of operations, cannot be determined in advance. This state of affairs is represented schematically in Figure IIC10-1, and is referred to as data-dependent problem formulation. In fact, under these conditions, the phases of data collection, examination, and problem formulation are practically inseparable, and usually are undertaken iteratively.

Clearly, the computer services supporting this sort of activity must be flexible and responsive if the processes of collection/examination/formulation are to proceed expeditiously. In IBM research, an extension of APL has been designed and widely used for several years.

The extension is called a Data Interface Adapter (DIA) and is, in effect, a switch box that permits experimental data obtained from various sensors to be stored in an APL file, just as though it had been keyed in on a typewriter terminal. See Figure IIC10-2.

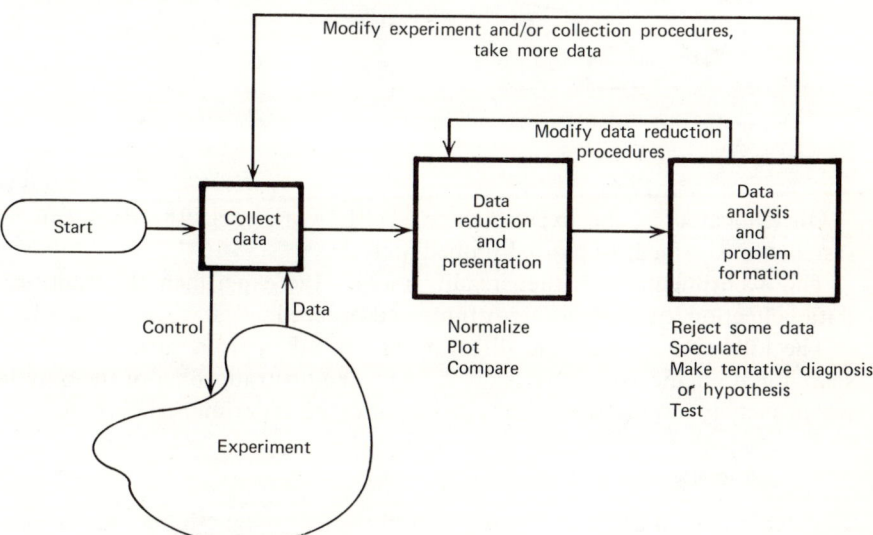

Figure IIC10-1. Interactive problem formulation.

114 CURRENT USAGE: CASE STUDIES AND CRITIQUES

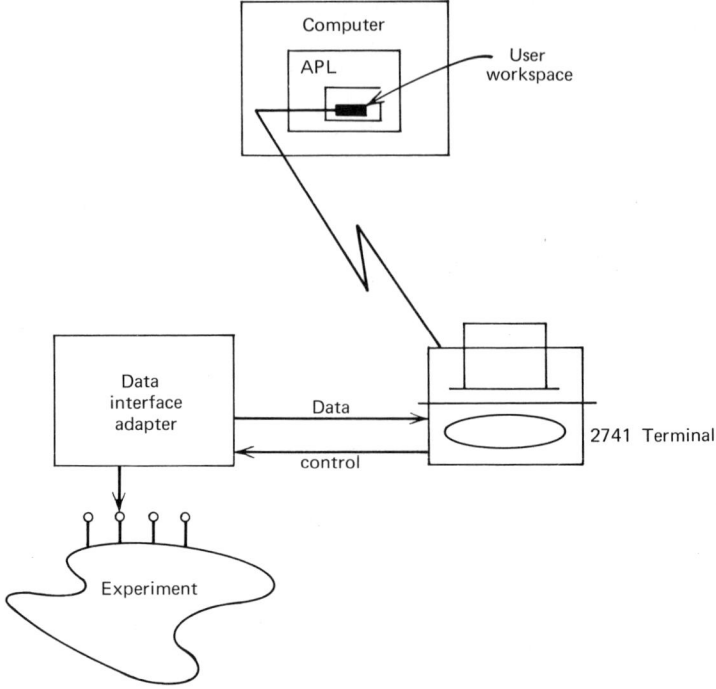

Figure IIC10-2. Data interface adapter.

Once located in the experimenter's APL workspace, the data can be tested, transformed, or plotted immediately.

The experimenter can then readily modify the experimental conditions, data collection, or analysis algorithms and proceed.

The following exerpts and illustrations are taken from various IBM research and engineering reports (1, 2, 3) to demonstrate some of the uses to which such an interactive system can be put in the experimental process.

Application (1)

The experimental apparatus was a pulsed nuclear magnetic resonance spectrometer, used to investigate various relazation times occurring in a sample of solid helium-3. Since the experiment involves cryogenic temperatures, which can be maintained only for limited times, there is a premium on obtaining the maximum possible amount of information in one run, usually of six hours duration.

C. PROBLEM FORMULATION

One datum consists of one measurement of the time interval between two pulses generated in a pulse transmitter, and two measurements of pulse heights, characteristic of the magnetism of the sample. The variation of magnetism with time generally follows a functional form consisting of a simple exponential, with sometimes the sum of two appearing. A set of data would then consist of say, 20 points along the relaxation curve, where the information of interest is the characteristic relaxation time, and several incidental instrumental parameters determined from the same curve.

Data words, upon being entered, are accumulated in a matrix. Upon receiving a predetermined number of points, or upon command, the matrix is stored externally to the program, and computation is performed. The first step in computation is examination of the data for out-of-range numbers, missing numbers, inconsistent data, exclusion of points that do not lie

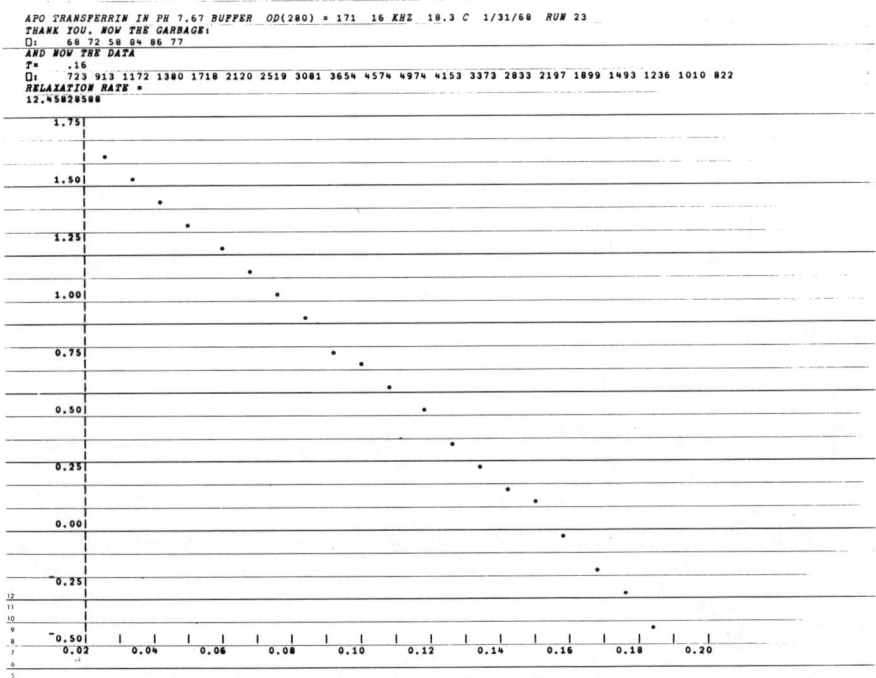

Figure 2. Typical plot of the decay of magnetization with time in a magnetic field of 4 Oe. Experimental parameters and echo heights typed into the computer, appear on the top of the page. The program then determines a least square value of the relaxation rate T_1^{-1} and plots the natural logarithm of the corrected echo height versus time on the same typewriter terminal. If some of the data points deviate from a good straight line, they may be discarded or the experiment may be immediately repeated.

Figure IIC10-3. Typewriter-drawn plot.

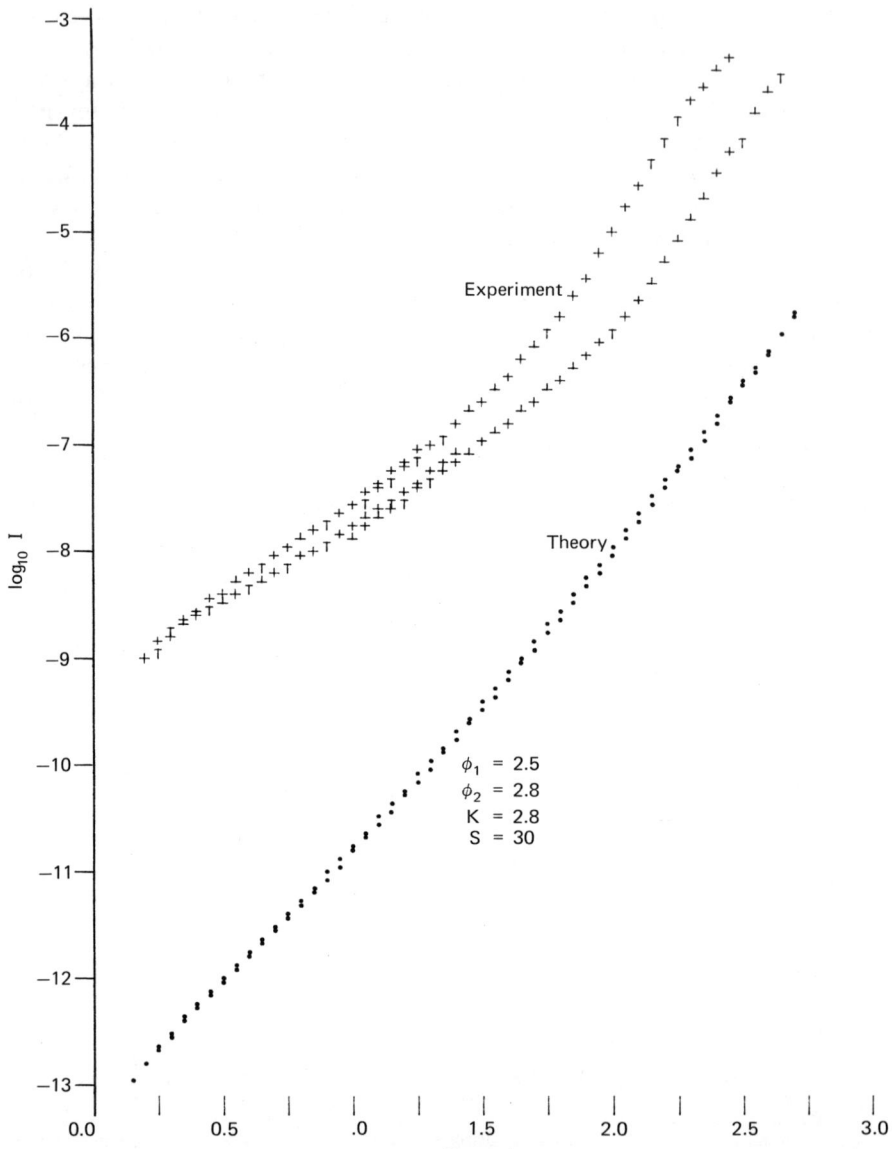

Figure IIC10-4a. Use of fine resolution typewriter plotter.

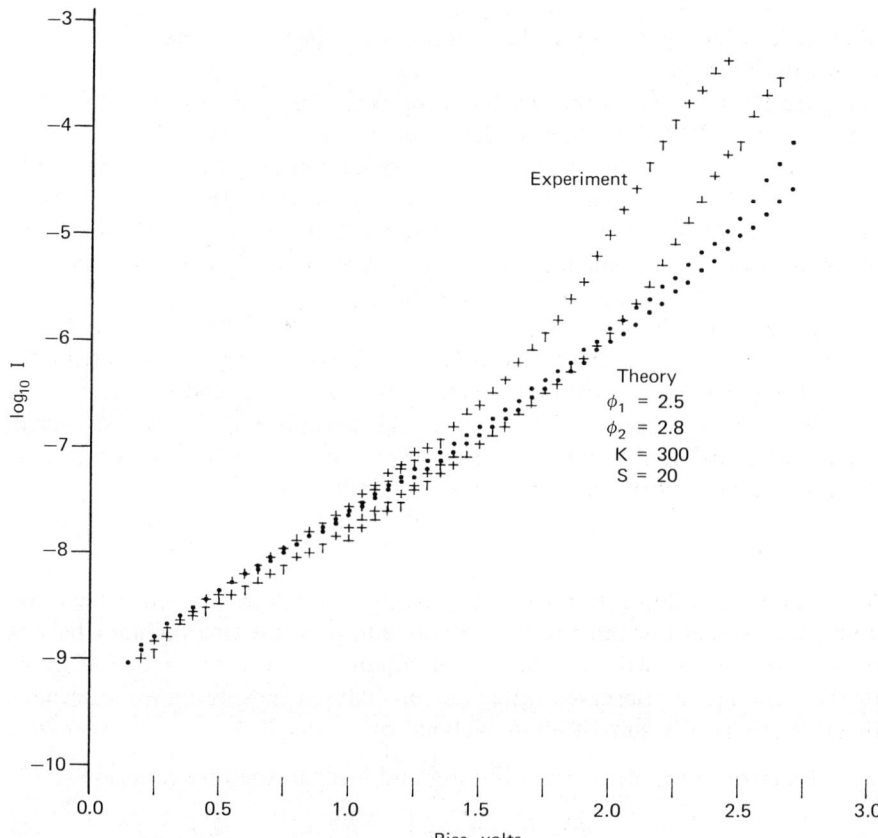

Figure IIC10-4b. Use of fine resolution typewriter plotter.

on an approximately smooth curve, etc. Use is made of all a priori knowledge about the data.

Least-square curve fitting is then done, using nonlinear iterative methods. After the "best" values of the parameters are determined, the program goes back and compares each residual with the average expected residual. If a point lies more than three RMS deviations away from the calculated curve, it is considered to be a mistake and is eliminated. The least-squares reduction is then repeated with the remaining points. After no more points are thrown out, a single line of output results. This output contains the values of the parameters, their standard error, the sum of the squares of the residuals, and a list of the points thrown out, together with an indication of why. The entire computation takes about 2 seconds on the

M44/44X, which is less than the time for the typewriter carriage to return the width of a page.

Figure IIC10-3 shows the results of an experiment of this type (2), plotted by an APL PLOT routine on the experimenter's 2741 terminal.

Figure IIC10-4a shows a plot of some experimental data compared with the relationship predicted by existing theory. Clearly there is a conflict between that theory and the experimental results. Figure IIC10-4b compares the same experimental data with predictions of a revised theory, formulated in an attempt to resolve the discrepancy.

FiguresIIC10-4 illustrate the use of a so-called "fine plot" feature. Ordinarily, the use of a typewriter terminal limits the resolution of plotting to the normal spacing between characters. However, a special selectric typeball has been designed which contains 15 periods and 15 crosses, each located at a different point in a three-by-five matrix. This makes possible the generation of fairly smooth curves, as can be seen.

Application

Most metals develop a thin oxide or tarnish film when exposed to reactive ambients, even at low temperatures relative to their melting points. Characteristically, the growth rate decreases rapidly in time so that almost no further change is observed after a few days exposure. Two alternate theories are usually submitted in explanation:

1) Electron transport is rate-limiting and leads to the rate equation

$$dX/dt = a \exp(-X/X_1), \tag{1}$$

where X is the oxide thickness, t the time, and a and X_1 are physical parameters of the theory to be calculated from the experimental data.

2) Charged lattice defect transport is rate-limiting and leads to the rate equation

$$dX/dt = 2a \sinh(X_1/X). \tag{2}$$

The solutions of Eqs. (1) and (2) are of a logarithmic type making graphical distinctions inconclusive. More precisely, the solution of Eq. (1) is easily seen to be

$$X_1/X = n a (t + \tau) X, \tag{1a}$$

where the offset τ depends on the initial film thickness X. The solution of Eq. (2) is asymptotically

$$X_1/X = -\ln(X_1/X) a(t + \tau)/X_1. \tag{2a}$$

```
        ∇FIT[☐]∇
      ∇ FIT;XX;TT;X0;N
[1]     'GIVE THICKNESSES'
[2]     XX←☐
[3]     'GIVE TIMES'
[4]     TT←☐
[5]     'GIVE X0'
[6]     X0←☐
[7]     'ARGUMENTS'
[8]     '         T              X           1/X          T/X2'
[9]     TT AND XX AND(÷XX) AND TT÷XX*2
[10]    N←ρXX
[11]    N;' OBSERVATIONS'
[12]    ''
[13]    FITDIR
[14]    FITMC
[15]    ''
[16]    ''
      ∇
        ∇FITDIR[☐]∇
      ∇ FITDIR; ALFA;X1;X;Y;ORD;RERX1;RERALFA;A;B;C;VARA;VARB;
          COVAB
[1]     ⍝ DX/DT = ALFA×EXP(−X/X1)
[2]     'DIRECT LOG'
[3]     X←⊕TT
[4]     Y←XX
[5]     LSF
[6]     X1←A
[7]     ALFA←A×*B÷A
[8]     C←1−B÷A
[9]     ORD←⌊XX[1],XX[⌊(ρXX)÷2],XX[ρXX]
[10]    'XFIT:  ';ORD
[11]    'TFIT:  ';(X1÷ALFA)×*ORD÷X1
[12]    RERX1←(VARA*0.5)÷A
[13]    RERALFA←(((VARA×(C*2))+VARB+2×COVAB×C)*0.5)÷A
[14]    'X1, LIM ERRX1:  ';X1,(X1×1+RERX1),X1×1−RERX1
[15]    'REL ERR, ERR X1:  ';RERX1,X1×RERX1
[16]    'ALFA, LIM ERRALFA:  ';ALFA,(ALFA×1+RERALFA),ALFA×1−
          RERALFA
[17]    'REL ERR, ERR ALFA:  ';RERALFA, ALFA×RERALFA
[18]    'OFFSET TAU ≤';(X1÷ALFA)×*X0÷X1
[19]    'LIMITING THICKNESS:  ';X1×⊕ALFA×1440
[20]    ''
      ∇
```

Figure IIC10-5*a*. APL program for problem formulation.

∇FITMC[☐]∇
∇ FITMC;ALFA;X1;X;Y;ORD;RERX1;RERALFA;A;B;C;VARA;VARB; COVAB
[1] ⍝ DX/DT = ALFA×EXP(X1/X)
[2] 'MOTT−CABRERA'
[3] X←●TT÷XX∗2
[4] Y←÷XX
[5] LSF
[6] X1←−÷A
[7] ALFA←(∗−B×X1)÷X1
[8] C←1−B÷A
[9] ORD←(÷100)×⌊100÷XX[1],XX[⌊(⍴XX)÷2],XX[⍴XX]
[10] '÷XFIT: ';ORD
[11] 'T÷X∗2FIT: ';(÷ALFA×X1)×∗−X1×ORD
[12] RERX1←(VARA∗0.5)÷|A
[13] RERALFA←(((VARA×(C∗2))+VARB+2×COVAB×C)∗0.5)÷|A
[14] 'X1, LIM ERRX1: ';X1,(X1×1+RERX1),X1×1−RERX1
[15] 'REL ERR, ERR X1: ';RERX1,X1×RERX1
[16] 'ALFA, LIM ERRALFA: ';ALFA,(ALFA×1+RERALFA),ALFA×1−RERALFA
[17] 'REL ERR, ERR ALFA: ';RERALFA,ALFA×RERALFA
[18] 'OFFSET TAU ≤';((X0∗2)÷ALFA×X1)×∗−X1÷X0
[19] 'LIMITING THICKNESS: ';X1÷(−5)0÷2×ALFA×1440
[20] ''
∇

∇LSF[☐]∇
∇ LSF;AVX;AVY;VARX;VARY;COV;R;VAR
[1] ⍝ LEAST SQUARE FIT Y = AX + B, Y ON X
[2] AVX←(+/X)÷N
[3] AVY←(+/Y)÷N
[4] VARX←+/(X−AVX)∗2
[5] VARY←+/(Y−AVY)∗2
[6] COV←+/(X−AVX)×(Y−AVY)
[7] A←COV÷VARX
[8] B←AVY−A×AVX
[9] R←COV÷(VARX×VARY)∗0.5
[10] VAR←(VARY×1−R∗2)÷N−2
[11] VARA←VAR÷VARX
[12] VARB←(VAR×+/X∗2)÷N×VARX
[13] COVAB←−AVX×VARA
[14] 'CORR COEFF: ';R
[15] →(1=|R)/GOODFIT
[16] 'T TEST FOR CORR: ';(R×(N−2)∗0.5)÷(1−R∗2)∗0.5
[17] →0
[18] GOODFIT:'|CORR|=1, NO T TEST'
∇

Figure IIC10-5b. APL program for problem formulation.

Equation (1a) is generally called the direct-logarithmic law; Eq. (2a) will be referred to as the Mott-Cabrera law.

The remainder of this report describes a simple APL program which asks for data, fits it according to Eqs. (1a) and (2a), and returns the physical parameters and X_1 as well as the estimated standard errors due to scatter in the data. The relative likelihood of these two theories is weighed on the basis of a Student t-test.

Description of the Program

Calling for the main program FIT (Figure IIC10-5a) activates the sub-programs, FITDIR and FITMC, corresponding to the two theories previously mentioned. Each sub-program calls for the least-squares fit procedure LSF.

LSF (Figure IIC10-5b) calculates the parameters (A,B) of a straight line, $Y = AX + B$, in the usual way. It also evaluates their variances (VARA, VARB, COVAB) as well as the correlation coefficient R and the value of the appropriate Student t-variable with $N - 2$ degrees of freedom, $R(N - 2)^{1/2} / (1 - R^2)^{1/2}$, where N is the number of observations. Student's t-variable tests the so-called null-hypothesis, i.e., the probability that linear correlation results from chance rather than from the physics of the situation. The larger the magnitude of t, the smaller this probability becomes. Probability tables are readily available.

FIT asks for thickness measurements and the corresponding observation times as well as an estimate of the initial thickness X_0. The data are entered as vectors. The arguments $t, X, 1/X,$ and t/X^2 are calculated and the sub-programs FITDIR and FITMC are then executed. RERX1 and RERALFA are the estimated relative errors on X and a as computed from the variance matrix of A and B. These errors can be used to calculate confidence limits for X and a.

This program has been used to analyze the oxidation kinetics of Ta, Pb, and In. A sample run from the analysis of Ta at 300°C shows, from the t-test, that the Mott-Cabrera law is much more probable than the direct-logarithmic law. The program has the obvious advantages of rapidity and precision over graphical methods, particularly when the latter yield inconclusive results as is often the case.

Conclusion

It is concluded that the use of interactive means of data collection, reduction, analysis, and problem formulation are feasible and helpful for experiments where the several-second computer response is not detrimental and the load is too light to justify the use of a local dedicated computer (4).

The advantages of on-line operation are greater than might appear just from the decrease of turnaround time. The terminal printer serves as the laboratory notebook, creating a record of all pertinent conditions, data and results computed.

The possibility of errors in transcription is eliminated. Errors in procedure become immediately apparent, so that they may be corrected during a run, before large amounts of useless data accumulate. Finally, the ability to relate data to physical concepts, such as the expected exponential behavior of some quantity with the reciprocal temperature, leads to immediate checks on theoretical understanding of phenomena. Novel or unexpected behavior may thus be immediately recognized and pursued.

The fact that data may be stored independently of the data reduction program gives rise to a further flexibility, in that if an unexpected functional relation is suspected, new analysis programs may be written, and data may be analyzed by someone else at another terminal simultaneously, and even remotely.

References

1. H. A. Reich, "An Experimental System for Time-Shared On-Line Data Acquisition," *IBM Journal of Research and Development,* **13,** 1 (January 1969), pp. 114–118.
2. S. H. Koenig and W. E. Schillinger, "Nuclear Magnetic Relaxation Dispersion and Dielectric Dispersion in Protein Solutions, IBM Research Report RW102, July 1968.
3. R. Ghez, "Data Fitting Thin Film Oxidation and Tarnishing Reactions with APL, "IBM Research Report RC 3817, April 1972.
4. K. L. Konnerth, "Use of a Terminal System for Data Acquisition," *IBM Journal of Research and Development,* **13,** 1 (January 1969), pp. 132–138.
5. A. L. Jones, "The Use of APL/360 in Mechanical Analysis," Proceedings IEEE International Computer Conference, Washington, D.C., June 1970.

D. DESIGN

Once a problem has been formulated, the design of solution concepts commences. Depending on the nature of the problem, design may require a creative or inventive solution, or may involve only the synthesis of existing components.

Synthesis, in many cases, is sufficiently well-defined to be preprogrammed. That is, satisfactory solutions can be derived deductively from the formulation of the problem. In such cases computerization of the process is feasible, and is often referred to as "design automation." Some phases of electrical circuit design, for example, are susceptible to such automation.

D. DESIGN

In most cases, however, design is *not* a rigorous, deductive exercise, but a creative process in which the human somehow associates a number of possible solutions with the stated problem, drawing on his experience and imagination. In this more general case, the solution is not preprogrammable, given the present state of the art of programming. Therefore, the computer's role is limited to aiding the human designer in various ways. This symbiotic mode is referred to as computer-aided-design.

The computer's roles in aiding the designer include the recall of relevant data (such as a history file of similar cases, or a data base of component parts available), and the calculation and/or display of the attributes or behavior of a proposed solution concept.

Three case studies are presented to illustrate the man-computer design process:

Case study 11, "Automotive Design," is interesting from a historical point of view. It reviews a development effort spanning more than a decade. It illustrates some of the complexities of computerizing the design process in cases in which aesthetic and other subjective criteria are important.

Case study 12, "Computer-Aided Circuit Design," illustrates a comparatively tidy problem. Circuit design is often a matter of synthesizing a functional entity from a limited variety of standardized components. These components, furthermore, were designed to facilitate the use of computer aids in subsequent stages of synthesis. This case study illustrates the manner in which successive stages in a complex process can be coordinated by means of an integrated set of computer programs.

Case study 13, "Architectural Design," describes a design problem involving functional, aesthetic, structural and economic factors being attacked via a flexible computer-aided approach.

CASE STUDY 11   Automotive Design*

This presentation will describe some of the development work performed on the use of Computer Graphics in Automotive Design within the General Motors Corporation. The discussion will outline some of the earlier work performed by GM Research Laboratories and cover in detail the present effort by the Manufacturing Development Staff, GM Technical Center in Warren, Michigan. Before getting too far into the presentation, a few

---

* This section has been exerpted from Gerhard W. Sood, "Computer Graphics in Automotive Design," presented at the American Society for Engineering Education, Annual Meeting, June 21–24, 1971.

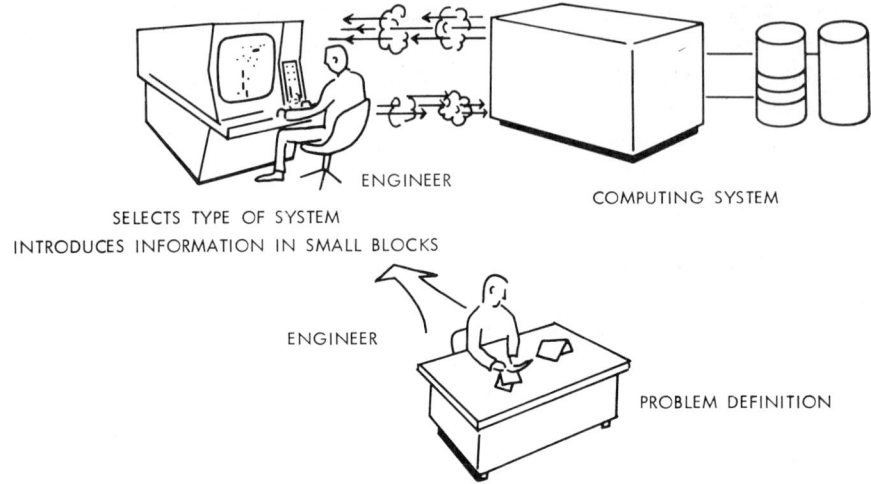

Figure IID11-1. Graphics man-computer communication loop.

words of explanation pertaining to what is meant by a computer graphic system and how it compares with the conventional man-computer communication loop is in order.

A computer graphic system must provide some form of man-computer interaction utilizing conversational graphics. Conversational graphics simply permits the operator to direct the work of a computer through the use of pictorial displays and allows the operator to review the computed results as new or modified pictorial displays. The total system must consist of many graphic console terminals, all connected to a large scale computer with almost unlimited memory and the necessary software to make the whole system practical. This can be shown in the first illustration. Once the engineer or designer defines his problem, he should be able to go to a graphic console to solve the problem in a minimum of time, as implied by Figure IID11-1. The user should be able to converse with the computer system through the graphic console in a language that has meaning to the engineer and his problem. In this way the engineer can make his decisions as they arise at the console, keeping an unbroken continuity of thought on the solution of his problem with a minimum of error, delay and paper work. The comparison of the computer graphic system with the conventional man-computer communication loop using the batch mode of operation clearly shows many advantages. The conventional batch-mode cycle time for a job is normally measured in hours, sometimes even days; it normally involves much more paper work together with its associated errors and delays. The engineer's thought process pertaining to the problem is broken during the interim time period and all decision making must always be done in advance of any computer run.

The teletype terminal computer system eliminates many of the weaknesses of the conventional computer system but it still lacks the important feature of interactive graphic communication.

The initial effort of using computer graphics in automotive design within General Motors was performed by the GM Research Laboratories in 1959, when they first demonstrated the feasibility of having a digital computer read a drawing, manipulate the graphic data, and reproduce new drawings as a product of the design process. The formal name given this project by Research was DAC-1 where the letters represented Design Augmented by Computer. The "1" indicated that this effort was just the beginning, for the goal of the project was to learn how to use the high speed of the computer as an aid in the design process with particular emphasis on the automotive body design area.

The basic hardware involved in the DAC-1 system consisted of an IBM 7094 digital computer, additional computer memory, a graphic console and an image processor. To make this system operate, special software had to be developed by the Research personnel. The special computer language developed for the designer was called the Descriptive Geometry Language. The designer used the Descriptive Geometry Language to define or construct points, lines and surfaces which defined his design, made corrections and/or modifications at the graphic console, and obtained 35 mm slides for later use in generating Xerox copies of his design. Once the design was acceptable, the designer working at the console could initiate the generation of the necessary tapes to guide numerically controlled drafting machines and/or machining equipment. This hardware was installed in the Research Laboratories in January of 1963, and was at that time the only man-machine image-processing system of that type anywhere in the world.

The DAC-1 Graphic Console included a 10×10 inch cathode ray tube, a set of function buttons, a voltage pencil, an alphanumeric keyboard and an IBM punched card reader. Comparing this equipment with today's IBM System/360 graphic console shows that the cathode ray tube has grown only a few inches larger, the voltage pencil has changed to a light pen and the card reader has disappeared.

The DAC-1 system was never released as a full production tool but during its development life many production items were designed using this equipment. Personnel from Fisher Body, Styling, Chevrolet, the former Ternstedt and Saginaw Steering Gear Division participated by using some of their plant design problems in the development of the system. The experience gained in using the DAC-1 system clearly illustrated the immediate accessibility of design information between different design groups. No sooner had the Styling group finished their work on a windshield design when the Fisher Body group could reference the resulting data to start their activity. Another advantage of the DAC-1 system was its fast recovery from any last minute styling change which would normally create a major problem at Fisher Body in the conventional design process. This system also showed a time saving of one-third as compared to the conventional methods while the costs were approximately the same. All of the experience clearly illustrated the great potential of Computer Graphics in the automotive body design activity.

The arrival of the next generation of computer hardware in the form of the IBM System/360 and the availability of newer computer languages caused the end of the development work on DAC-1. Since the computer software in DAC-1 was not compatible to the newer systems, the question arose as to whether to reprogram the DAC-1 systems programs to operate on the new computer systems or to start fresh. The decision was to start fresh using all of the experience gained in DAC-1 and to make full use of the greater power available in the new computer systems and languages. Thus, in 1966 the CADANCE System was started when a group of Research personnel from the DAC-1 project started to write the specifications. In 1967, a CADANCE group was set up at Manufacturing Development Staff and the actual work on the application system was started. Starting in 1968, people from Fisher Body, Styling and Chevrolet Motor Division were assigned to work with the people at Manufacturing Development Staff in the development of the CADANCE System. Although the present CADANCE System is not ready for full production use, some production activities have been performed during this development period and examples of these will be covered in this presentation. So now the question is, what is the CADANCE System?

The CADANCE System is the application of conversational computer graphics to automotive body and general engineering design. The basic objectives for the CADANCE system are:

1. Lower Design Costs
2. Reduce Lead Time.
3. Provide Faster Implementation Programming Means at a Low Cost.
4. Provide Ways to Reduce the Conversion Costs When New Operating Systems are Introduced.

The word CADANCE is the acronym for *C*omputer *A*ided *D*esign *a*nd *N*umerical *C*ontrol *E*ffort. It is a large scale application of the GM Re-

D. DESIGN

search Laboratories' developed Interim Time-Sharing System (ITSS) which is available only on their IBM System/360 Model 67 Computer. The memory capacity of the system consists of one million bytes of high speed computer core, two IBM 2314 Disc Drives and two IBM 2301 Drum Units which through the use of the paging technique, makes available to each user a virtual memory of 16 million bytes. The time sharing system operates under conventional batch-mode at the Research Laboratories and through seven IBM 2250 Model III Graphic Console terminals located at Research, Manufacturing Development and GM Styling. Figure IID11-2 shows the new graphic console.

The software package developed by Manufacturing Development personnel is written in the PL/1 language, the Associative Programming Language (APL) and uses the Graphic Codes needed to handle the graphic displays on the IBM 2250 terminals. The PL/1 language is the full F-level Compiler, Release 19, Version 5 available through IBM. The Associative Programming Language and the Graphic Codes were both developed by Research personnel for the general use of the total computer system. Al-

Figure IID11-2. Picture of CADANCE graphic console.

though different groups within the Corporation are using the computer system for special projects, the CADANCE group is by far the largest user of the system.

One important problem that exists in any large scale computer system is the data management problem. A computer graphic system for automotive design requires the ability to handle millions of pieces of data efficiently. Therefore, the ability to store, search, delete, modify and retrieve data efficiently is of primary importance. The Associative Programming Language (APL)* was designed especially to effectively handle the data management problem. Information can be stored within a computer system in either an array or ring structure. APL makes use of the basic ring structure and adds the feature of data association. Each type of data item is defined as an entity whose attributes describe the individual data item. Each entity has the ability to own other entities as well as be owned by other entities. In this way there is an association between a given entity and the entities it owns as well as between the entities that own it. A simple example of this would show that all of the point entities that describe a line belong to the line entity, all of the line entities that describe the surface belong to the surface entity, all of the surfaces that make up the automotive hood belong to the hood entity, etc. In this approach to data management, each data entity is stored only once and it can be owned by any number of other entities and the association among the different data entities are all built in. The use of unique names for each entity is not needed in this arrangement for the desired entity can always be located through its proper association to other entities.

The APL language is available to create, delete, find, insert and remove various entities within the data structure. The person working in CADANCE also has the full power of the PL/1 language which together with the APL language is used to write the computer programs for the system. The CADANCE application type computer programs can be written either as conventional PL/1 procedures or as special CADANCE operators. The special feature of a CADANCE operator is that it will receive part or all of its input data through the man-machine communication at the graphic console. For each CADANCE operator, there is at least one or more operator pictures which will present sufficient instruction to the user for the proper execution of the CADANCE operator.

To accurately illustrate the total CADANCE System in some pictorial form is a very difficult task. Therefore, an attempt has been made to show

---

* The term APL is used in this case to refer to an Associative Programming Language, and *not* to the interpretive system described in case studies 9 and 10.

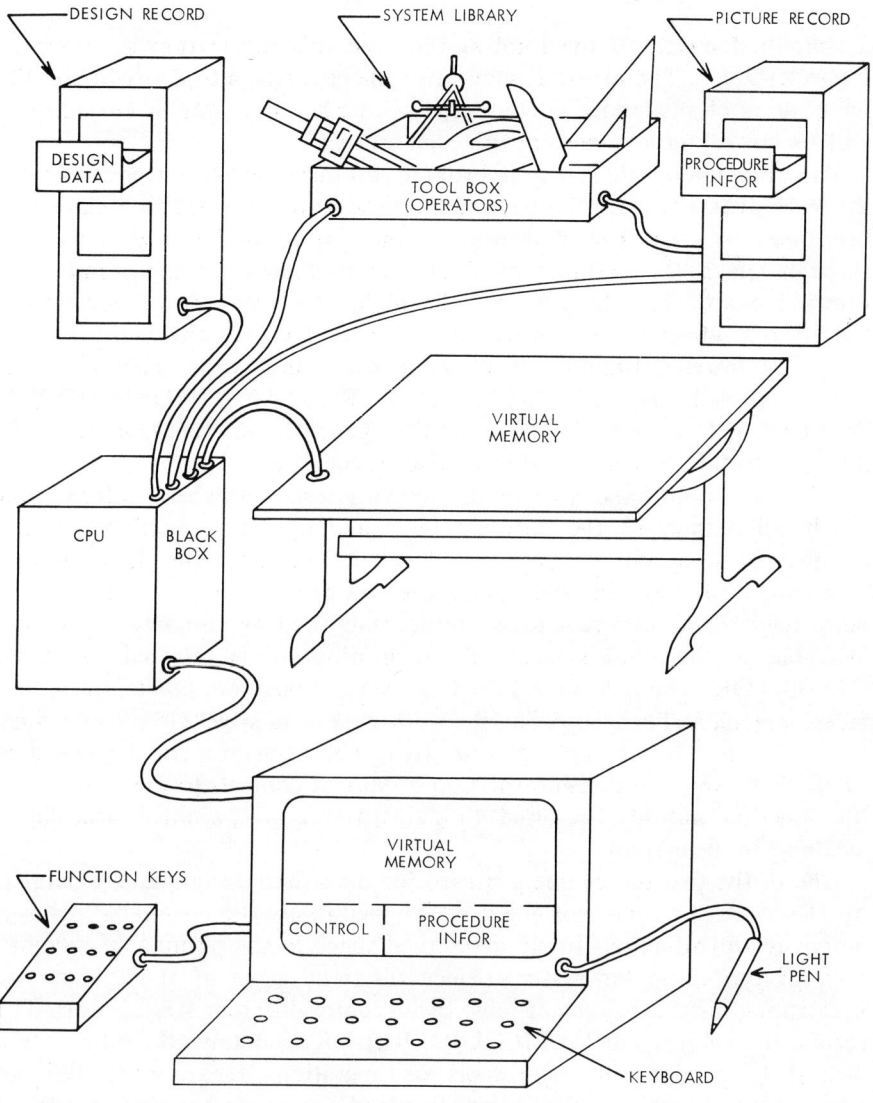

Figure IID11-3. Computer-aided design tools.

a simplified model of the total system and this illustration is shown in Figure IID11-3. The pictorial shows two file cabinets, a tool box full of different design tools, an infinitely large drafting board, a graphic console and a black box all interconnected with each other.

The graphic console screen is broken into three separate areas; namely, the work area, the control area, and the procedure information area or picture operator area. The work area on the console is the viewing window through which the designer examines selected areas of an infinite size drawing board. The designer has the ability to create new information, modify old information, and delete information viewed through the work area. The lower left-hand area of the screen contains the general control functions such as PROCEED, OUT, RESTART, PUSH-DOWN, SCALE, VIEW, RECORD, etc. The general control functions are available to the console user throughout his run at the console.

The lower right-hand area of the screen is used to present information which will either list the different tools and operation available to the designer or if a tool or operation has been selected, the displayed information will explain and guide the designer in its use. The tasks performed by the different tools are accomplished by computer programs available in the total system and each program is referred to as an OPERATOR. The light pen is used to select or position, points, lines, surfaces, scalers, and characters on the work area or to select character strings on the control or operator picture area. The alphanumeric keyboard is available to key in either information or special controls to the system and the function buttons are used to perform pre-programmed procedures available in the system.

One of the two file cabinets is used for the stored design data generated by a user. Each designer or engineer assigned to use the system has his own design record which is simply a reserved space in the permanent memory area of the computer system. Since different users of the system are performing different types of jobs, they require different sets of tools. The second file cabinet labeled PICTURE RECORD contains the information needed to properly use the tools or operations for a given type of engineering. Therefore, the automotive body engineer has his own set of design tools which are quite different from the safety engineer who is performing vehicle crash studies. Some tools used by the different engineers are the same but the manner and terminology involved may be different. The difference between the automotive stylist and the hood hinge designer using the same line generator is handled by the use of different PICTURE RECORD files. In this way the designers of completely different areas of engineering may use the same basic tool but the CADANCE System will permit them to communicate in their own language.

The infinitely large drawing board schematically represents the large virtual memory available in the system and the black box labeled CPU represents the computational power of the computer system.

Automotive Body Design

Although the CADANCE System is capable of handling both automotive body design as well as general engineering design, the present development work by GM Styling has been directed primarily to the automotive body area. Before getting too involved in the GM Styling activity using CADANCE, it must be recognized that this activity is only a part of the total Styling effort. The stylist creates his ideas by means of artistic sketches and special renderings which slowly develop into a full scale blackboard drawing of the vehicle. This activity continues in the form of numerous models of interior and exterior features of the vehicle which finally results in a full scale clay model of the complete vehicle. A great deal of fine tuning of the overall design is performed on the clay model which normally involves more sketching, renderings and blackboard drawing work. Once the clay model is acceptable to management, data is taken from the model and developed into accurate Engineering Release Drawings describing the interior and exterior surfaces of the vehicle. The acquisition of digital data from the clay model is a separate problem in itself but the important part to recognize is that the clay model is not accurate enough to directly produce the Engineering Drawings. Therefore, the recorded raw data has to be sweetened to produce smooth lines that blend together to produce aesthetic surfaces that also blend together into the total vehicles described in the Engineering Release Drawings.

The last activity is the work that GM Styling is developing using the CADANCE System. The basic needs of the styling designer to convert the recorded raw data points from the clay model into the finished Engineering Release Drawings are as follows:

1. Exercise control over the aesthetic quality of the key lines.
2. Controlled adjustment of raw point data.
3. Practical line smoothing techniques.
4. Generate surfaces.
5. Evaluate all results.
6. Manipulate views for drawing composition.
7. Speed—ease of operation—economy.

132 CURRENT USAGE: CASE STUDIES AND CRITIQUES

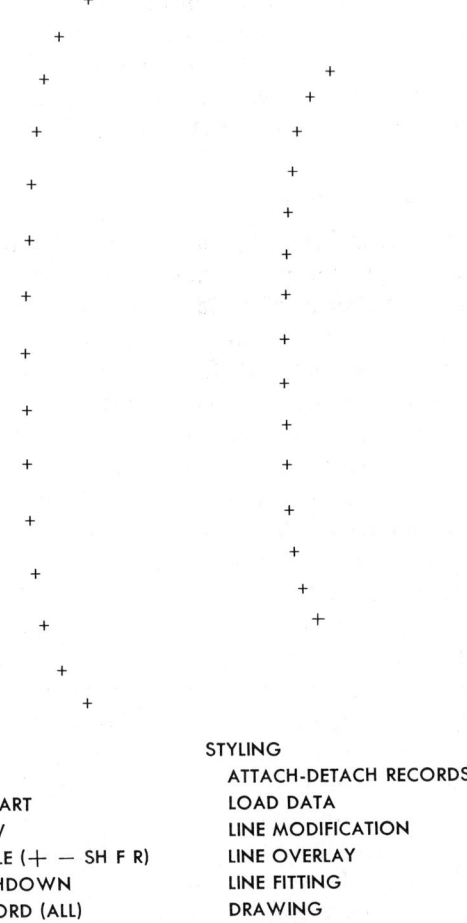

	STYLING
OUT	ATTACH-DETACH RECORDS
RESTART	LOAD DATA
VIEW	LINE MODIFICATION
SCALE (+ — SH F R)	LINE OVERLAY
PUSHDOWN	LINE FITTING
+RECORD (ALL)	DRAWING
	TYPE IN OTHER: (CH)

Figure IID11-4. Graphic use in styling design.

To date, the Styling development effort within CADANCE has been successful in producing a line conditioning package and a drawing composition package. Mr. E. Norton from the Computer Graphics Department of Styling has been successful in developing a practical drawing composition program with which the styling designer can perform his job. Mr. J. Jones, also from the same department of Styling, has developed a line conditioning program which includes line modification, line smoothing and line evaluation.

The Styling effort to date includes the training of some of the designers to use the line conditioning and drawing composition packates in their work. The body surfacing development work clearly shows the potential to produce the Engineering Release Drawing for a given body panel but more experience working with the system is required before the complete task can be economically performed. The CADANCE System can accomplish a large percentage of the work involved in producing the Engineering Release Drawing but some surfaces must still be added to the Release Drawing using the conventional drafting methods. This is also true for all drawing

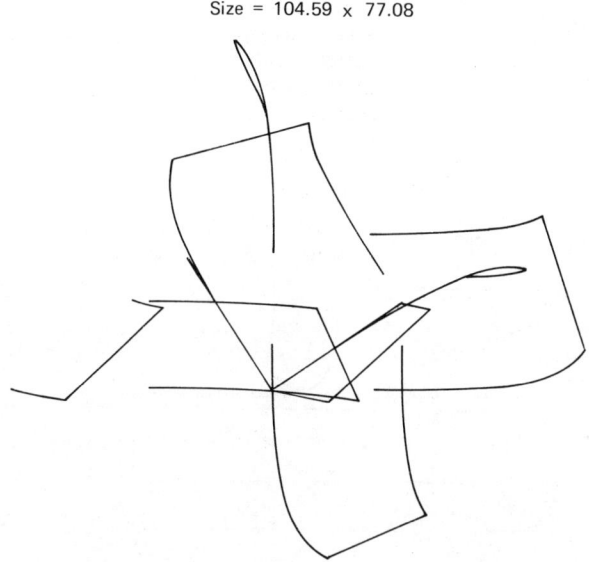

PROCEED		DRAWING CONTROL	
OUT			*BUILD NEW PICTURE
RESTART			ADD TO EXISTING PICTURE
VIEW			DELETE GROUP FROM PICTURE
SCALE (+ − SH F R)		DISPLAY DATA	DELETE ENTIRE PICTURE
PUSHDOWN		SIDE	AUX1 AUX5 AUX9 INPUT
+RECORD (ALL)		PLAN	AUX2 AUX6 AUX10 WKLNS
		FRONT	AUX3 AUX7 AUX11 FTLNS
		REAR	AUX4 AUX8* AUX12 GRID
			RETURN HERE

Figure IID11-5. Graphic use in styling design.

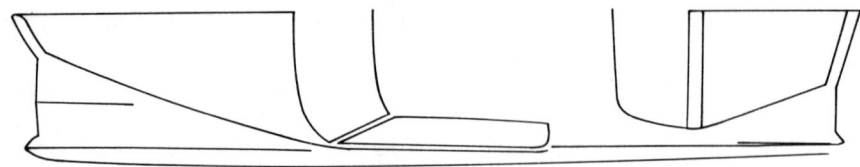

	DRAWING CONTROL	
OUT	INITIALIZE DATA	PERMUTE
RESTART	GROUP DATA	REBUILD INPUT
VIEW	DEFINE AUX VIEW	CONVT MATH LNS
SCALE (+ − SH F R)	DISPLAY DATA	IDENTIFY GROUPS
PUSHDOWN	SHIFT	
+RECORD (ALL)	GRID	
	DEINITIALIZE DATA	
	SPREAD REFERENCE	
	PUNCH CARDS	
	DELETE MATH LNS	
	MIRROR-ROTATE	
	DUPL	

Figure IID11-6. Graphic use in styling design.

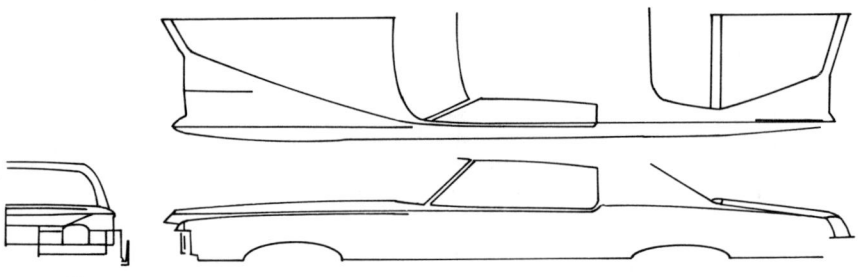

	STYLING LINE DESIGN	
OUT	SELECT CURVE	VIEWS
RESTART		PLAN-SIDE
VIEW	CURVATURE PLOT	SIDE-FRONT
SCALE (+ − SH F R)	RAW PLOT	FRONT-PLAN
PUSHDOWN	AVERAGED PLOT	SKEW-CHORD
+RECORD (ALL)	APPROXIMATION FIRST	1ST VIEW OK
		2ND VIEW OK
	COMPARE TO FIT LINE	SPACE CURVE
		PLANE CURVE

Figure IID11-7. Graphic use in styling design.

D. DESIGN   135

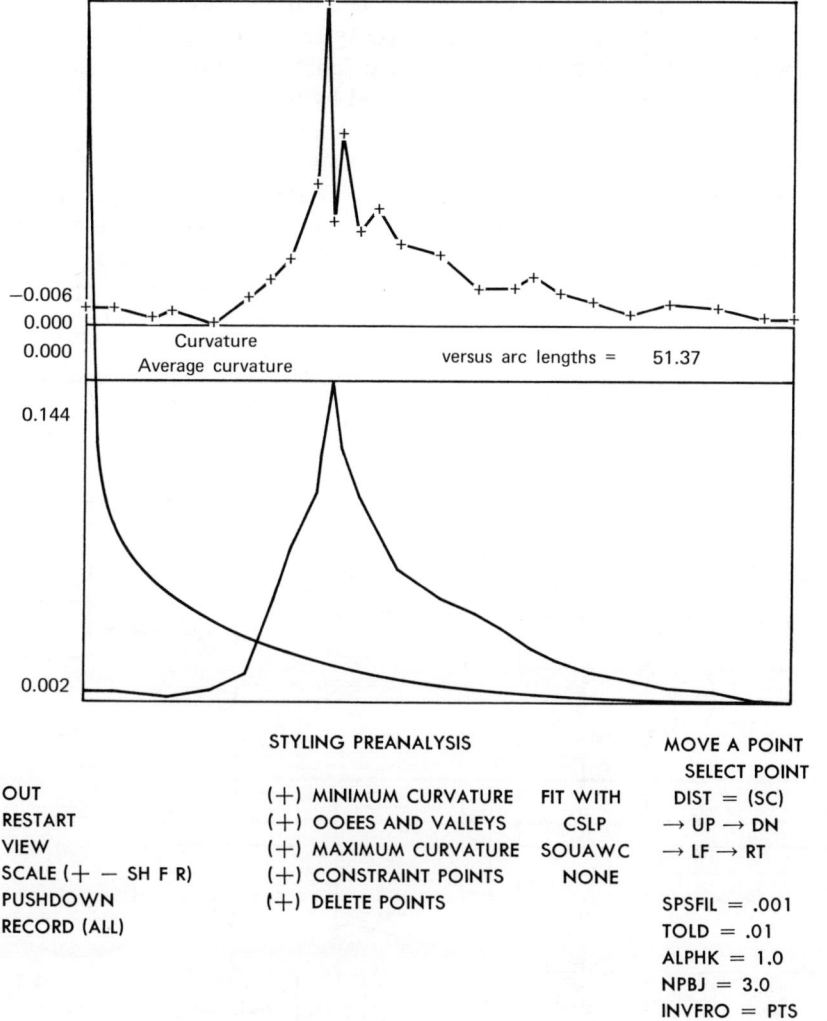

Figure IID11-8. Graphic use in styling design.

notes and dimensions because this work can be performed more economically by hand.

Illustrations

Figures IID11-4 through IID11-8 illustrate the environment of the styling designer working at the graphic console screen.

CASE STUDY 12 Computer-Aided Circuit Design*

The first step in the use of an ideal CAD system is for the designer to state his performance specification (e.g., logic function, transfer characteristics, etc.). This specification is then interpreted by the computer program to determine what physical units must be interconnected to provide the desired performance. The physical units may be individual resistors and transistors or complete functional units (e.g., a NAND gate). The designer then controls a simulation to be performed by the computer. The computer outputs an indication of the simulated performance which the designer examines. If the simulated performance is not what he wants he must change his

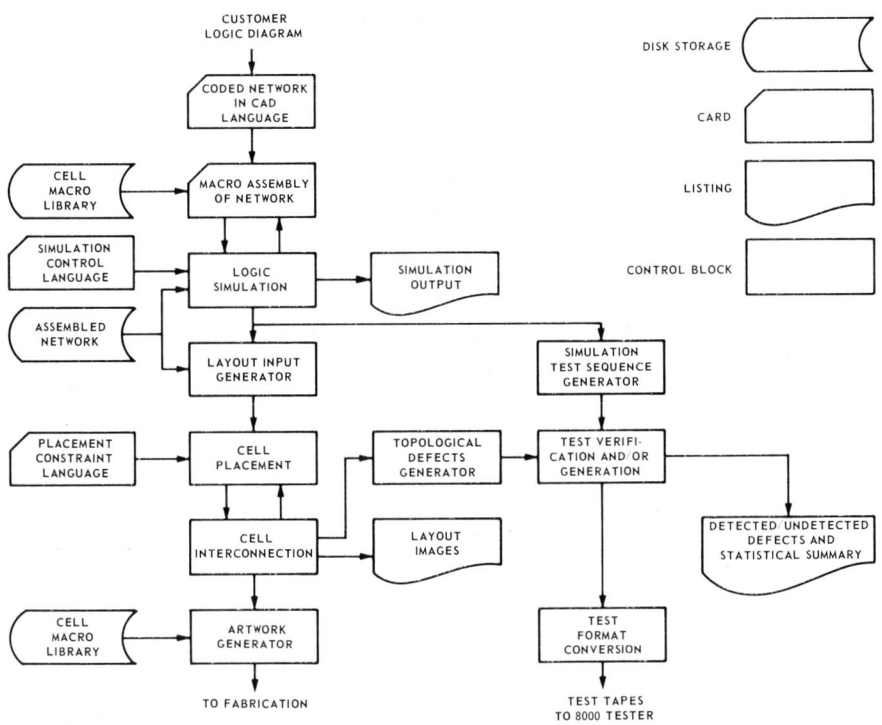

Figure IID12-1. CAD flow chart for micromosaic subsystem design, test generation, simulation, and artwork generation.

* This case study has been exerpted from References 1, 2, 3, which were provided by James Koford of Fairchild Semiconductor, a Division of Fairchild Camera and Instrument Corporation. Some of the material appeared in the *IEE TRANSACTIONS on Circuit Theory*, **CT-18**, 1 (January 1971), 10–13.

primary specification. After a satisfactory performance has been simulated, the computer is started on the actual layout of the chip. Once a final layout has been established, the computer produces a set of instructions for artwork generation. The artwork generator might be an x-y plotter for drawing the mask, a light head exposing a photographic plate, or an electron beam exposing the wafer directly.

The ideal CAD system is seldom realized, and the computer is used as a design aid rather than as a fully automatic tool. The basic reason is that it is more economical to let the designer interact with the computer than it is to make the programs fully automatic.

The complete LSI program is shown in Figure IID12-1. A proposed LSI design is coded into FAIRSIM language along with a test sequence. After simulation, the FAIRSIM data becomes the basis for computer aided cell placement, interconnection, and acceptance test generation programs.

Logic Simulation

FAIRSIM, Fairchild's logic simulation program, provides for the computer simulation of digital systems containing up to 3,000 basic logic gates. The power of FAIRSIM is derived from the compact languages that the program makes available for the specification of logic networks and simulation procedures. Logic networks may be described by statements specifying the individual logic gates, or portions of a network may be specified using macro statements, where each macro statement can cause many logic gates to be assembled into a predefined logical function. Once assembled, the network is simulated through the use of a Simulation Control Language that provides many different types of control statements for the execution of complex simulations.

The simulation algorithm used by FAIRSIM permits the simulation of logic gates with a range of gate delay from 0 to 63 simulated time units. Different rise and fall delays may be specified for any of the standard gate functions. Special elements, such as wired-AND gates, wired-OR gates, read-only memories, or simple flip-flops are available as basic logic simulation elements. All logical functions are simulated with an algorithms that allows logical signals to take on any one of three values: the usual logical 0 and 1, plus an additional "undefined" state. The inclusion of the undefined state is very helpful in keeping track of network states during initialization, and in flagging unspecified or anomalous logic conditions to the user.

The logic simulator can be used for any logic and is not limited to MOS micromosaic. The library of existing logic cells corresponds to our physically available cells in the micromosaic families; however, it would be possible for users to define any logic circuit by using primitive blocks such as NAND or NOR. The advantage of our cell set to the customer is that he needs fewer statements to describe his circuits; the advantage to Fairchild is that we could implement his circuit in MOS micromasaic.

Fairchild Test Verification and Generation

The Fairchild Test System is used in the production of functional tests for digital logic. The system considers certain specific classes of defects in a logical circuit. These are:

1. Defective outputs of logic blocks,
2. Defective inputs of logic blocks,
3. Shorts between pairs of signals, and
4. Opens in signal leads.

The Test Verification program determines which defects are detected by a given test sequence. This is done by simulating the logic network, first in its original form, then in the presence of a particular defect. The output signals resulting from these two simulations are compared and, if different, the defect is considered detected. This is done for all defects selected by the user.

The Fairchild Test Generation program (FAIRGEN) is an automated system for generation of functional tests for digital logic. It is designed to relieve much of the engineering burden of test generation by performing many routine tasks automatically. The user provides the FAIRGEN system with a description of the digital machine to be tested, in the same format as used by the FAIRSIM simulation program. An initial test sequence is also provided by the user. Under control of user supplied options and control information, the program then attempts to augment this user-supplied sequence to form a complete functional test.

During the test generation process, the program determines which defects are detected by the test sequence so far. It then attempts to synthesize a test for an undetected defect. The user may obtain a wide variety of listings and other output from the program which aid in the effective generation of functional tests.

While the results of the program's use at Fairchild have been very good in general, certain types of logic, particularly highly sequential counters and shift registers, present a more difficult test generation problem. In such cases, the percentage of defects detected may be reduced, but the program is still considerable value. In any case, the combination of verification and test generation capability provides a powerful tool for functional test synthesis.

D. DESIGN

Layout Program

The Fairchild Integrated Circuit Layout Programs provide extensive computer aids for the cell placement and interconnection of large scale integrated circuit (LSI) chips. These programs enable a designer to modify cell locations, orientations, terminal assignments, or interconnections on a partially interconnected chip. In addition, automatic cell orientations, interconnection, and checking are provided. Two versions of the program exist at presesnt, one for metal gate MOS and one for silicon gate MOS.

The functions of the layout programs may be divided into five major categories: 1) data input, 2) cell manipulation, 3) interconnection, 4) information production, and 5) checking. The data input function consists of reading in either a description of the network and cells to be used or changes to be made in an existing network description. The cell manipulation function includes the location, orientation, and terminal assignment of cells, or groups of cells. The interconnection function involves the signal and power interconnection of cells using both automatic algorithms and manual interaction. The purpose of the information function is to provide information about the network on the chip layout. Included in this function are the production of maps and charts. Finally the function of checking is diffused throughout the entire program.

Circuit Simulation

FAIRCIRC is derived from the University of California CANCER program (Computer Analysis of Nonlinear Circuits Excluding Radiation). It is designed for the complete simulation of integrated electronic circuits. The following are the principal features of FAIRCIRC:

1. Nonlinear dc analysis for obtaining the quiescent operating point, linearized small signal values, transient analysis initial conditions, and static transfer characteristics.
2. Small signal ac analysis to obtain the frequency response with nonlinear devices replaced by linearized equivalents at the quiscent operating point.
3. Frequency domain noise analysis to determine the overall and individual contributions of thermal noise sources, which are again dependent on the quiescent operating point.
4. Large signal transient analysis to determine the time domain response starting with a set of initial conditions calculated in the dc analysis.

FAIRCIRC can presently accommodate linear resistors, capacitors, inductors, voltage dependent current sources, independent current sources, grounded independent voltage sources, junction diodes and bipolar transistors. Work is under way to incorporate models for MOS transistors.

Input to FAIRCIRC consists of a network description, input stimulus description, and specification of quantities to be output. The input language is free-format, and permits the use of the customary engineering notation in specifying input parameters. For example, a 5000 ohm resistor can be specified as "5k." For modeled non-linear devices (transistors and diodes), the specification of the device parameters is separated from the specification of device interconnections, simplifying the description of a circuit which uses a number of similar devices.

Fairchild Automated Graphics System

The Fairchild Automated Graphics System was constructed for the purpose of increasing the speed, accuracy and ease of modification in making drawings and rubylith masks for large scale integrated circuits. The system is composed of four basic subsystems. They are an interactive graphics display system, an automatic plotting and cutting system, a digitizer system, and a computer oriented graphics language.

The interactive display system consists of a specially designed Sanders 960/201 indicator and logic unit with 16,000 16 bit words of external refresh memory. It has a 21 inch CRT with a drawing rate of one-half inch per microsecond and a fixed frame rate of 45 frames per second. The system is controlled by 16,000 word IBM 1130. The following three main programs are used in design work; a program for layout, one for editing, and one for library maintenance. By use of a light pen an operator can draw lines and rectangles, delete lines or sides of rectangles, move figures or sides of figures, etc., in order to form cells. He can also place, call, group, rotate, reflect, copy, delete, etc., any cell or group of cells he wishes. Other features include variable scaling, windowing and plane selection.

The plotting and cutting system consists of a Cal Comp 718 plotter used with its own IBM 1130. Either a knife head or pen head can be mounted on the plotter. Software was written to increase the efficiency in plotting through use of a sorting algorithm.

The digitizer is an Auto-Trol 3800A connected to an IBM keypunch. It is programmed to punch specially formatted cards. A grid calibration program along with a line straightening algorithm is used to remove some of the digitizing errors.

System Description

The programmers and design engineers at Fairchild use the CP-67/CMS time-sharing system to achieve a virtual machine environment. This makes it possible to simulate functionally a central-processing unit and its associated I/0 devices.

The Control Program CP-67, builds and maintains for each user a virtual System/360 machine from a predescribed configuration. It is not distinguishable to the user and his programs from the real System/360, although it is only one of many that CP-67 is managing. Resources of the real machine are allocated to each virtual machine in turn for a short "slice" of time before moving on to the next virtual machine.

"We have achieved significant savings with this system," said Dr. C. Hugh Mays, manager of computer-aided design and topography, at the Fairchild Semi-conductor Division of Fairchild Camera and Instrument Corporation. "We would be faced with a higher investment in programming and our design engineers would spend more time on design work without this capability of interacting with the computer."

On an average day, the Model 67 is used about 20 percent of the time in the terminal-oriented mode. The terminals are used primarily for development of computer-aided design programs in FORTRAN and Assembler languages. Most of the batch workload is done with multiple CMS batch systems, although OS, DOS and Programming System/44 are also run in the virtual machine.

References

1. C. H. Mays, "A Brief Survey of Computer-Aided Integrated Circuit Layout," *IEEE Transactions on Circuit Theory*, **CT-18**, 1 (January 1971), 10–13.
2. C. H. Mays, "Fairchild Semiconductor CAD Programs," Fairchild Camera and Instrument Corporation, May 25, 1971.
3. J. Koford and R. Walker, "Fairsim II User's Manual," Fairchild Camera and Instrument Corporation, October 1969.
4. Charles W. Beardsley, "Computer Aids for IC Design, Artwork and Mask Generations," *IEEE Spectrum*, September 1971.

CASE STUDY 13   Architectural Design*

Introduction

Why have Architects wanted to become involved with computers? To some Architects the computer is not a future development, but is now an integral

---

* The material in this case study has been exerpted from papers written by Clifford Stewart or Kaiman Lee, and provided by John Nilsson, all of Perry, Dean and Stewart, Architects, Boston, Massachusetts.

part of practice. Although the majority of Architects in the United States may not believe in the computer, many architectural firms in the United States are utilizing computers to their advantage in many phases of their work. Perry, Dean and Stewart is a medium sized architectural firm in Boston which has integrated the use of the computer in all stages of its professional services.

Today's Architect practices in an extremely sophisticated atmosphere. He is faced with an enormous amount of available information on each project and is pressed to complete the design process in the least amount of time. He is now involved in the design of elements such as hospital automatic cart delivery devices which require special movement spaces and assembly line technique, and in all things is very much involved in technology. In the design process the Architect must communicate information accurately and comprehensively to his client, to public agencies and to the members of the design team.

Buildings have become more and more complex. The Architect must constantly make decisions, but often does not have the necessary information and often does not have time to analyze the tremendous amount of available information in making those decisions. We feel that the computer is the most promising tool readily available and adaptable to assist the Architect in these areas. The computer aided professional service that we offer to the client is called ARK/TWO computer system. It includes computer programs applicable to problems in all stages of architectural design; architectural programming, schematic design, design development, working drawings, contract documents, project control and office management. The following description of the use of this system is in lay rather than technical terms.

The Process

At the outset of a project the client retains an Architect and describes his problem, for instance, the building he wants to build. The Architect, in turn, tries to advise the client whether the project is feasible. The Architect's advice may be rough assumptions based on his own experience. But with the aid of the computer, the Architect's experience can be broken down into subject matters, codified and stored in the computer memory. He can then retrieve any information he needs from the computer at any time. For example, a survey of 100 hospitals which includes their space utilization and space characteristics has been stored in the computer. COMPROGRAM can analyze the statistics and output meaningful figures such as minimum and average patient unit areas for various types of hos-

COMPROGRAM: data base information on over 75 existing hospitals and 12 PDS optimized models

COMPROGRAM SUMMARY REPORT
PERRY, DEAN AND STEWART   ARK-2 SYSTEM

VALLEJO GENERAL HOSPITAL
601 TENNESSEE STREET VALLEJO, CALIFORNIA 94590

BEDS IN NURSING	92
BEDS IN INTENS. CARE UNITS	5
BEDS IN SURGERY	7
OPERATING ROOMS	4
DELIVERY ROOMS	2
LABOR ROOMS	4

TOTAL

TYPES OF AREA	NET AREA	GROSS AREA	% OF GROSS	NET-GROSS CON. FAC.	NET AREA/BED	GROSS AREA/BED
GROSS AREA		81531.				841
NET ASSIGNABLE AREA	47740.		58.55	1.71	492	
MECHANICAL AREA	5262.		6.45		54	
CIRCULATION AREA	17447.		21.40		179	
EXTERIOR BUILDING AREA	0.		0.00		0	
UNFINISHED UNAS. AREA	0.		0.00		0	
CONSTRUCTION AREA	11082.		13.59		114	
OTHER	0.		0.00		0	

BY DEPARTMENT

	NET AREA	GROSS AREA	% OF GROSS	NET-GROSS CON. FAC.	NET AREA/BED	GROSS AREA/BED
ADMINISTRATION						
ADMINISTRATION	4643.	6464.	71.83	1.39	48	67
DIAGNOSTIC & TREATMENT						
EMERGENCY	1434.	1724.	83.18	1.20	15	18
OUTPATIENTS	264.	264.	100.00	1.00	3	3
PATHOLOGY	1444.	1728.	83.56	1.20	15	18
RADIOLOGY	1990.	2538.	78.41	1.28	21	26
SURGERY	3597.	4583.	78.49	1.27	37	47
PHYSICAL THERAPY	597.	597.	100.00	1.00	6	6
SERVICES						
CENTRAL STERILE SUPPLY	1860.	1860.	100.00	1.00	19	19
DIETARY	4413.	4413.	100.00	1.00	45	45
PHARMACY	324.	324.	100.00	1.00	3	3
GENERAL STORAGE	2092.	2092.	100.00	1.00	22	22
HOUSEKEEPING	1154.	1154.	100.00	1.00	12	12
LOCKER ROOMS	592.	592.	100.00	1.00	6	6
MAINTENANCE	365.	365.	100.00	1.00	4	4
NURSING						
INTENSIVE CARE	557.	557.	100.00	1.00	6	6
NURSERY	1545.	1633.	94.61	1.06	16	17
NURSING	18778.	24789.	75.75	1.32	194	256
OBSTETRICS	2091.	2707.	77.24	1.29	22	28

Figure IID13-1.   COMPROGRAM: data base information.

```
PERRY, DEAN, AND STEWART
ARCHITECTS AND PLANNERS
ARK2 SYSTEM - COMPROPLAN


NAME   LENGTH  WIDTH

ENTER    0       0
CASH    10       8
INTRC   10      35
INTRR   10      12
ADMWT   15      45
SOCAL    8      12
CLERK   25      25
DIRCT   12      12
CONFC   12      12




RELATIONSHIP MATRIX

        - ENTER -
CASH    -   1
        - ENTER - CASH   -
INTRC   -   1       1
        - ENTER - CASH   - INTRC -
INTRR   -   2       6        1
        - ENTER - CASH   - INTRC - INTRR -
ADMWT   -   1       3        1       5
        - ENTER - CASH   - INTRC - INTRR - ADMWT -
SOCAL   -   5       2        3       6       5
        - ENTER - CASH   - INTRC - INTRR - ADMWT - SOCAL -
CLERK   -   5       5        2       2       6       2
        - ENTER - CASH   - INTRC - INTRR - ADMWT - SOCAL - CLERK -
DIRCT   -   4       6        6       1       6       5'      2
        - ENTER - CASH   - INTRC - INTRR - ADMWT - SOCAL - CLERK - DIRCT -
CONFC   -   5       6        6       6       6       1       2       4
```

Figure IID13-2. **COMPROPLAN** matrix.

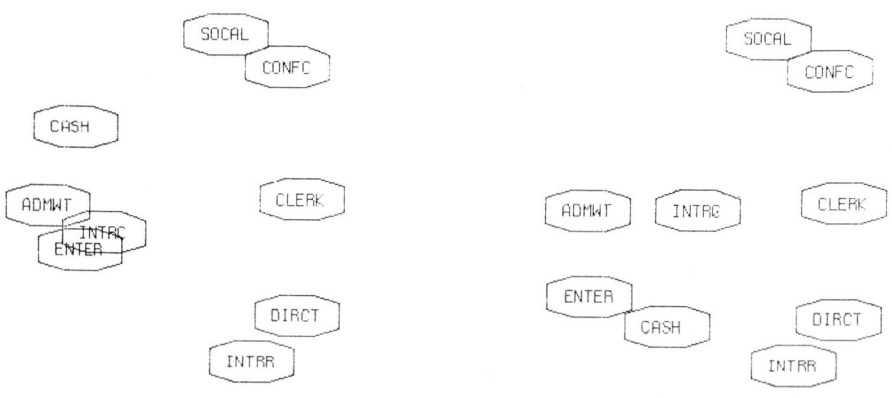

created from matrix automatically   adjusted by designer for clarity

Figure IID13-3. **COMPROPLAN** bubble diagram.

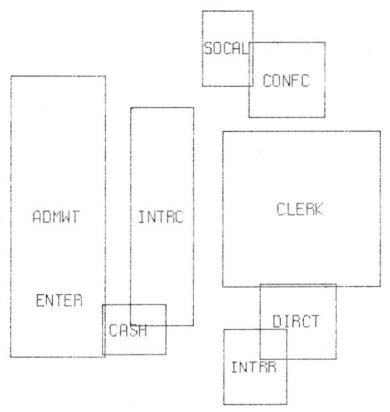
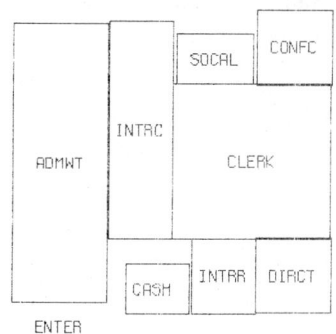

created from bubble diagram automatically

adjusted by designer to
fit gross area envelope

Figure IID13-4. COMPROPLAN block diagram.

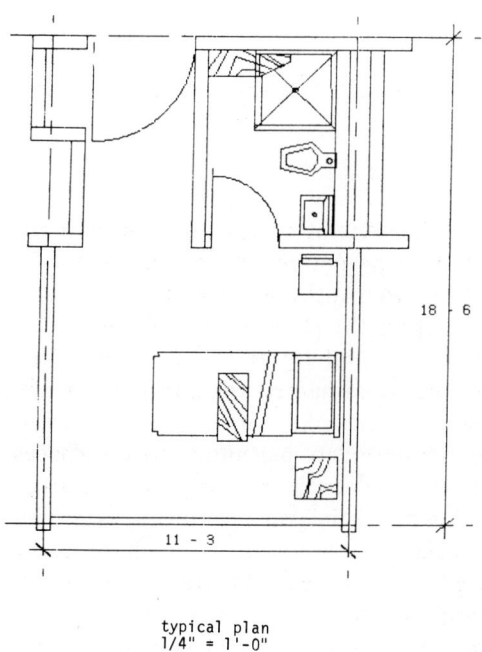
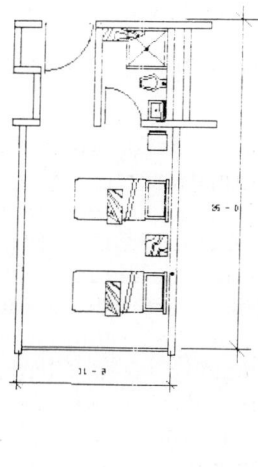

typical plan
1/4" = 1'-0"

same plan edited
and displayed
1/8" = 1'-0"

Figure IID13-5. COMPROSPACE floor plans.

145

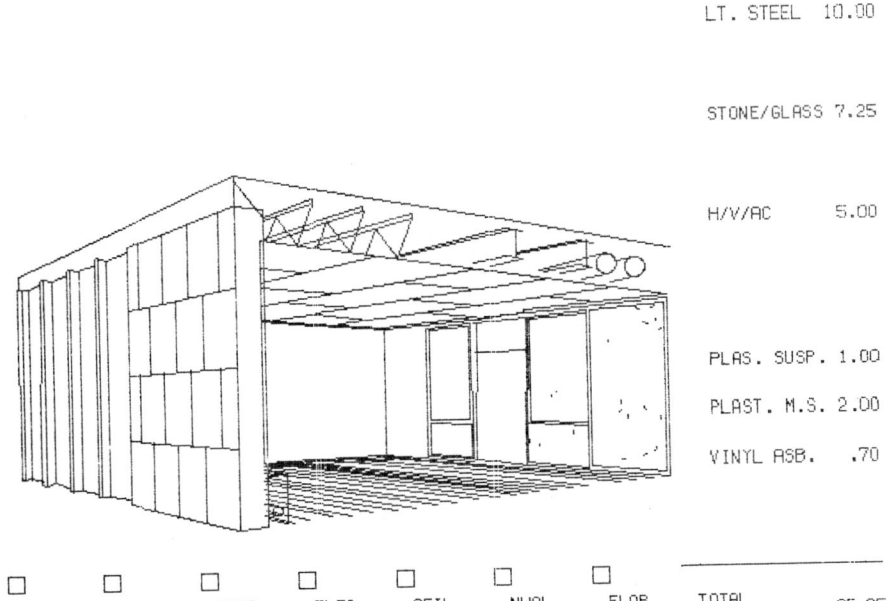

Figure IID13-6. COMPROSYSTEM.

pitals, as shown in Figure IID13-1. The Architect can then retrieve information relating to that type of project and make feasibility studies including the services needed, spatial requirements and estimated costs.

COMPROGRAPH is used to assist in the development of an architectural program to determine the current and future space needs of the client. Entered into the program are the room names, the number of each, room dimension, cost per square foot and the phase in which they should be constructed. Characteristics and requirements pertaining to the spaces may also be entered. The computer will tabulate the running totals of areas and costs. The graphic version of this program will also draw rectangles proportional to their areas and tone them according to their phase in the total program. Of course, one may go back and edit the area and cost factors and obtain new totals for the entire project.

One of the serious design problems that an Architect faces is space allocation, or relationships between spaces and supply values that represent how the spaces should ideally relate to each other. The COMPROPLAN program will at first generate a basic relationship diagram resulting from the input matrix as shown in Figure IID13-2. The designer can edit this by

```
CRIT. NO.     NO. OF ALTERN.     FACTOR
    1                4               1
    2                3               1
    3                5               1
    4                5               1
    5                3               1
    6                4               1
  TOTOAL NO. OF ALTERNATIVES
```

program to score the compatibility of subsolutions

```
101   ICU BED         01
102   ICU BED         02
103   ICU BED         03
104   ICU BED         04
201   INTERM BED      01
202   INTERM BED      02
203   INTERM BED      03
301   ICU STRUCT      01
302   ICU STRUCT      02
303   ICU STRUCT      03
304   ICU STRUCT      04
305   ICU STRUCT      05
401   INTER STRUCT    01
402   INTER STRUCT    02
403   INTER STRUCT    03
404   INTER STRUCT    04
405   INTER STRUCT    05
501   INFORMN         01
502   INFORMN         02
503   INFORMN         03
601   ANCILLARY       01
602   ANCILLARY       02
603   ANCILLARY       03
604   ANCILLARY       04
```

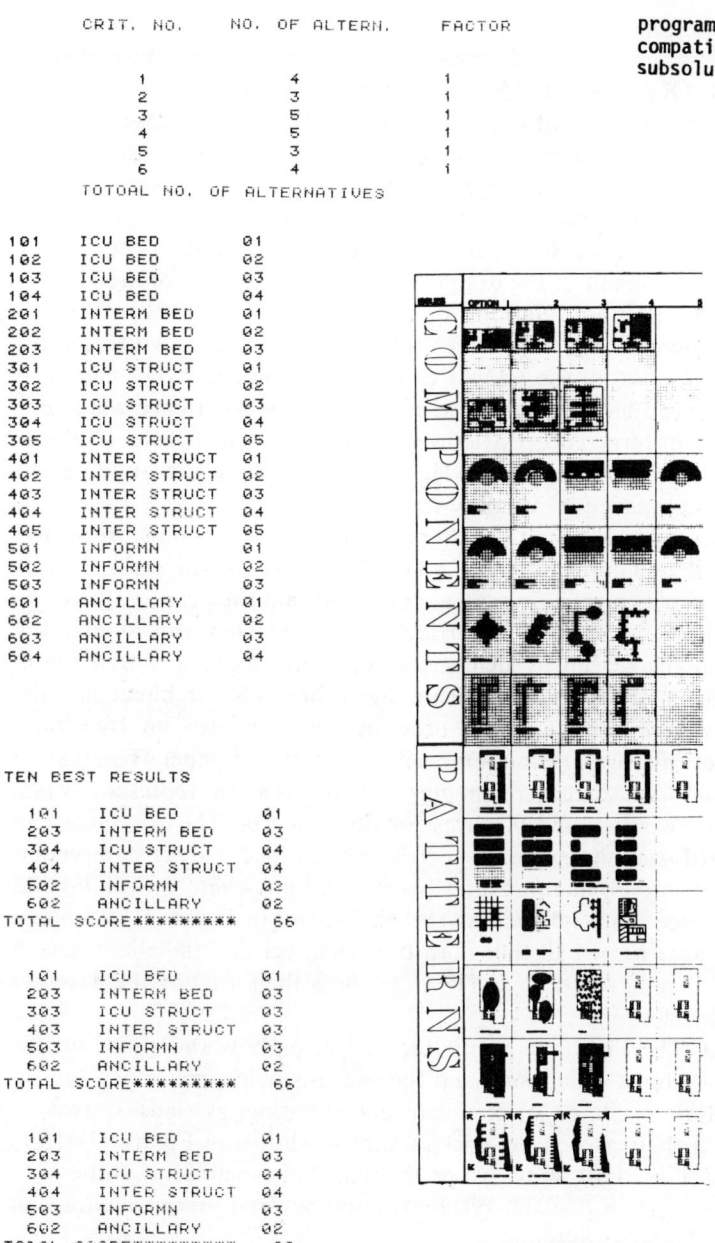

```
TEN BEST RESULTS

   101    ICU BED          01
   203    INTERM BED       03
   304    ICU STRUCT       04
   404    INTER STRUCT     04
   502    INFORMN          02
   602    ANCILLARY        02
TOTAL SCORE*********      66

   101    ICU BED          01
   203    INTERM BED       03
   303    ICU STRUCT       03
   403    INTER STRUCT     03
   503    INFORMN          03
   602    ANCILLARY        02
TOTAL SCORE*********      66

   101    ICU BED          01
   203    INTERM BED       03
   304    ICU STRUCT       04
   404    INTER STRUCT     04
   503    INFORMN          03
   602    ANCILLARY        02
TOTAL SCORE*********      66
```

Figure IID13-7. COMPROLINK.

changing the relationship ratings if he discovers he has made a mistake, and a completely new bubble diagram will be generated as illustrated in Figure IID13-3. Of course, the Architect can learn with this until he gets the diagram which satisfies all requirements. But the real purpose is to put in factural data which he then will analyze on a nonsubjective base and obtain a useful diagram. The computer output serves only as a basic diagram upon which the designer can improve. If there is anything absurd about the bubble diagram, it is because he entered something absurd in the matrix which may well be a result of the designer dealing with preconceptions.

Based on these optimum relationship diagrams, COMPROPLAN draws on the screen schematic plans in which all the rooms are drawn to the dimensions decided upon in the COMPROGRAPH. The designer can then manipulate the basic block diagram with input of his experience which encompasses other criteria and restrictions, as indicated in Figure IID13-4. He may move or rotate the spaces. He can also draw in the building envelope and provide space for circulation.

Typical spaces such as hospital patient rooms and classrooms are stored graphically in the computer memory. COMPROSPACE will assist the Architect and the client to retrieve typical spaces so that they can evaluate the suitability of those spaces to the particular project. They can modify the space shown on the screen by deleting a line here, moving a wall there, changing furniture or equipment within the room. The architect has the choice of drawing circles, variable arcs, etc. or can also do free hand drawings—practically everything done with a pencil and paper. To create a patient room on the screen, rectangles can be used to represent walls, straight lines for window and 90° arcs for door swings. The Architect can retrieve standard graphic elements such as chairs, beds, x-ray equipment, etc. from the computer memory and place them anywhere on the layout. The resulting space diagram such as the one shown in Figure IID13-5 can be printed out as a record so that both the Architect and the client have a record of what they have decided. The printout is then used by the designer as a guide for his design.

In COMPROSYSTEM the computer will also show the client on the screen the sub-systems which make up the spaces; such as exterior wall, interior wall, floor, ceiling, mechanical and lighting systems drawn in perspective with their associated cost factors as shown in Figure IID13-6. Alternative total systems may be generated. This enables the client to understand the effect of one sub-system on another and on the square foot cost of the space he is specifying.

With the layout and building systems tentatively established the designer can then develop elevations. The computer can take over much of the te-

Figure IID13-8. COMPROVIEW.

dium of the job of drawing out the various alternatives and does so in much less time than a draftsman. The main advantage of using the computer in this aspect is to accommodate the repetition involved. A module can be drawn once and repeated as many times as needed without involving any manual effort. This not only creates more complete basic drawings, but also frees the designer for more creative work.

COMPROLINK is an alternative scoring system. It assists the designer to select the best alternative design schemes by rating and connecting the compatible subsets of solutions. This program is integral part of the P.D.S. design methodology. An example is shown in Figure IID13-7.

The computer has the ability to draw perspectives of a space on the screen and to take the viewer on a walk into it, to look at it from any side. The input to COMPROVIEW consists of digitized points described as three dimensional coordinates, and information on whether or not a point is connected to another by a line. The computer can generate any number of perspectives from different station points using the same data. The designer may choose several perspective drawings from an infinite number possible and obtain hard copies which he can take back to his desk and render. It is also possible to specify a continuing series of viewing points in order to simulate the view of a person walking around a building or entering a building. It is useful to help the client and the designer see an accurate representation of what he will get in the future. Examples are given in Figure IID13-8 and IID13-9.

The computer is also used for estimating purposes. COMPROAREA can make area calculations for a schematic design. Preliminary estimates are obtained when the areas are multiplied by respective square foot costs. If areas are taken off from working drawings and multiplied by detailed cost factors, including labor and material, detailed quantity take off cost estimates can be projected.

With COMPRODRAFT the computer can store a vast number of standard working drawing details. A selected drawing can be retrieved by coded commands scaled and displayed on the screen. Elements of the drawing can be deleted, moved, rotated, redrawn or replaced with other parts previously stored in the computer. Standard graphic elements such as concrete block or brick with appropriate hatchings can be called up and repeated at any location. The finished drawing will be the one that fits the particular requirements of a project. It can be stored in the computer memory and can be retrieved at a later data if new situation demands changes in this detail. The same drawing can be plotted to produce actual working drawings on vellum.

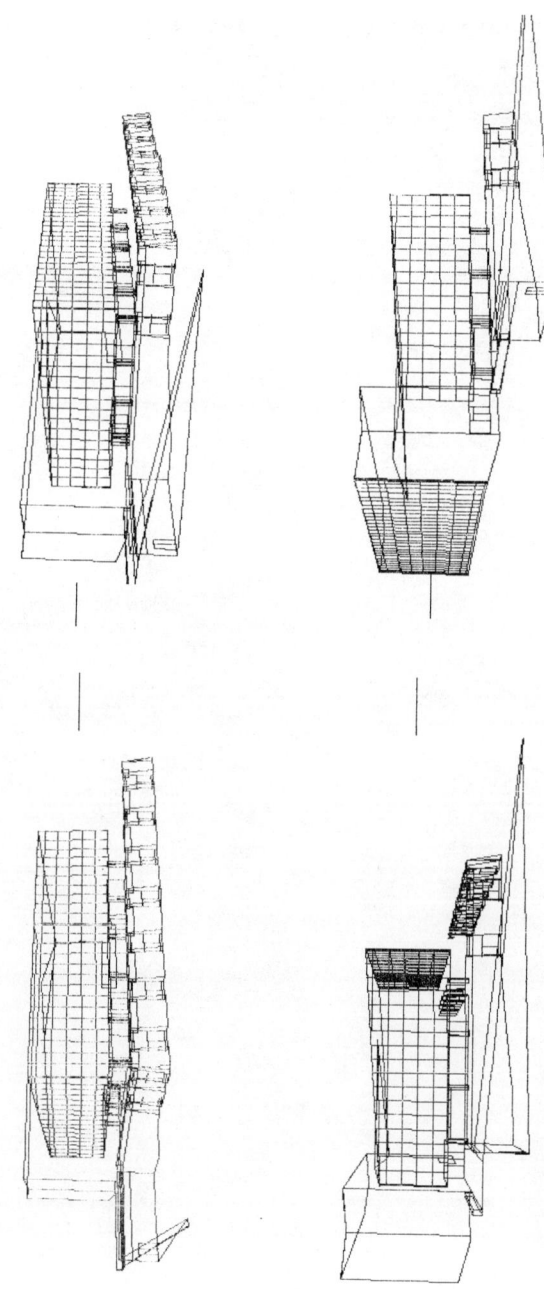

Figure IID13-9. Perspectives.

ARK 2 software

	Special					Manipulate/Manage						Collect/Sort			Draw			
COMPROGRAM	COMPROSIGN	COMPROPARK	COMPRORATE	COMPROSTAIR	COMPROSPEC	COMPROCOST	COMPROAREA	COMPRONET	COMPROMAN	COMPROWORK	COMPROPLAN	COMPRORELATE	COMPROGRAPH	COMPROVIEW	COMPROSPACE	Task	Phase
●		●			●	●	●						●		●	Check similar projects	Predesign
								●		●						Estimate schedules	Predesign
									●	●						Estimate manpower needs	Predesign
●							●						●		●	Review similar room types	Programming
●							●						●			Model area program	Programming
												●				Work out relationships	Programming
●		●			●				●	●				●	●	Establish parameters	Programming
										●	●	●	●		●	Develop plan layouts	Schem. des
		●											●			3-dimensional studies	Schem. des
	●				●	●	●									Establish cost goals	Schem. des
					●				●				●		●	Start outline spec	des development
						●				●	●	●	●		●	Review room details	des development
		●												●		Mech studies	des development
														●		3-dimensional studies	des development
	●				●	●	●									Revise cost goals	des development
					●				●							Redo outline specs	des development
				●						●	●	●	●		●	Plans sections elev.	Working drgs.
		●											●			Mech. studies	Working drgs.
					●			●								Construction network	Working drgs.
					●	●	●	●								Estimate	Working drgs.
					●	●				●			●			Edit master spec	Specs
					●				●	●					●	Print specifications	Specs
					●	●	●		●	●					●	Cost review	Bid
								●	●							Construction monitor	Construct
					●	●										Cost monitor	Construct
		●														Shop drawing monitor	Construct

Figure IID13-10. ARK 2 software.

A master specification is stored in the computer memory. COMPROSPEC allows it to be retrieved, edited and manipulated to produce new project specifications. The project specification can be updated and changes can be integrated without rewriting or retyping the entire specification. The final specification is printed out in upper and lower case at the rate of one page every two seconds.

COMPRONET is a development of the Critical Path Method or project scheduling known to clients and Architects for many years. It is used to schedule design and construction activities. COMPROWORK is a special program to predict and allocate manpower for each office project based upon normal work flow and to tell the project Architect as well as the management how many people will be performing what tasks during a certain week. COMPROMAN gives management weekly and monthly reports on the progress of each project in the office.

ARK 2 software, shown in Figure IID13-10, runs on a DEC PDP 15/20 computer system, equipped with a Computek display system, a Gould-Clevite printer, and an Autotrol digitizer.

Conclusion

The main idea behind the ARK/TWO system is interaction; the client is urged to participate in the entire process so that he knows exactly what the economic and aesthetic results will be when the project is finished and whether the design will suit his particular needs. It is hoped that the ultimate result of this commitment will be better architecture, with less drudgery, more control and more depth of involvement by the Architect and client. We feel that time is running out on our profession. We can no longer practice architecture in the same old way. The world is our problem, we should really start to look at the world in much broader ways. We feel, perhaps, our ARK/TWO system has opened the door just a little bit to a whole new world of a computer aided architectural profession.

References

1. C. Stewart and K. Lee. "The ARK 2 System—Can a 54-Year-Old Architectural Firm Find Romance and Happiness with an Interactive Computer System?, reprints from *Progressive Architecture,* July 1971.
2. C. Stewart and K. Lee. Troika for Architectural Planning, reprints from Association for Computing Machinery, National Conference, 1971, Chicago.

3. K. Lee, Computer Aided Professional Services, *Bulletin of Computer Aided Architectural Design,* March 1971.
4. K. Lee and R. Correira, "A Mental Health Project Programmed and Designed with the Aid of Interactive Computer Graphics," Proceedings ACM, IEEE Design Automation Workshop, June 26–28, 1972.

E. ANALYSIS AND OPTIMIZATION

The phases of analysis and optimization are markedly more susceptible to computerization than are problem formulation or design. By this point in the process, invention has given way to the more formal and rigorous activities of: (1) deducing the logical consequences of the proposed ideas, and (2) determining the best parameter settings and operating points of the various designs.

These activities usually are describable in logical and mathematical terms, and the computational power of digital systems can be applied to great advantage.

Three case studies are presented to demonstrate the power both of the computer and of the mathematical tools of analysis and optimization.

Case study 14, "Election District Delineation," describes an attempt to determine election district boundaries in Missouri that are equitable with respect to voter influence, and impartial with respect to political interest. The advantage of using the computer here, in addition to computational speed of course, is the machine's lack of political bias (as far as we know).

Case study 15, "Structural Analysis," describes a field that has been radically transformed by the computer. Matrix methods of analysis and so-called "finite-element methods" have been developed by which physical structures can be simulated by a complex lattice of small members, the finite-elements. The structural behavior of this lattice (deflections, stresses, etc.) is readily computable and, by analogy, describes the behavior of the original physical structure. The case study describes a general-purpose application package called NASTRAN, which is widely used in the aerospace industry.

Case study 16, "Circuit Optimization and Sensitivity Analysis," illustrates the application of powerful matrix and variational methods. This approach allows one to examine the simultaneous and interdependent effects of all the parameters of a complex device.

E. ANALYSIS AND OPTIMIZATION

CASE STUDY 14 Election District Delineation*

Introduction

Political redistricting is the means by which a geographic area is divided into districts. In the past, redistricting has been done by state legislatures, but this tends to introduce partisan political considerations into the final district plans. In many cases, redistricting becomes a battle to protect incumbents, or an attempt to reorganize districts to benefit a specific party or special interest group. Political expediency is a dominant factor, and the result is often a gerrymander. This in turn can lead to legal intervention and eventually to an imposed solution, like that established in Baker vs. Carr (12, 13, and 14). Thus rigorous and well-defined approaches to redistricting need to be formulated and documented for future use.

We attempted a nonpartisan computer-based algorithm to systematically eliminate the inequities of present redistricting practices. We then applied the algorithm to the specific problems of redistricting the state of Missouri into ten congressional districts and St. Louis County into seven County Council seats.

Initial Considerations

Ideally, a formal method of redistricting would consider each dwelling (e.g. house or apartment building) separately. Since this is not practicable, dwellings are grouped into larger units called population units. Population units are assigned to one, and only one, district.

If the population units chosen have too large a population, it may be impossible to formulate a plan which assigns all units successfully; or the algorithm may be forced to overlook solutions which could be superior. Even if a solution falls within an acceptable population tolerance, it may well be possible to form another, more desirable, plan which would produce a further subdivision of the population units. Thus for most algorithms a major consideration is the number of population units that can be handled by the algorithm in a reasonable amount of computer time and storage.

A major drawback of the redistricting process is the means of grouping by which population units are formed. A partisan political bias can be introduced (either consciously or unconsciously) in this initial phase. This is of particularly great concern in large urban areas where, for instance, the

---

* From Robert E. Helbig, Patrick K. Orr, and Robert R. Roediger, "Political Redistricting by Computer," *Communications of the ACM,* **15,** 8 (August 1972).

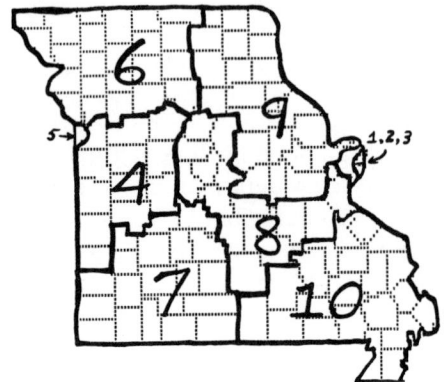

Figure IIE14-1. Ten current congressional districts.

method of assigning a ghetto area may deprive a minority group of a representative.

Data made available by the U.S. Census Bureau group population in several ways, including block groups or enumeration districts (the smallest units available), census tracts, townships, and counties. Population units are chosen from these data in such a way that acceptable solutions may be obtained without incurring prohibitive costs (e.g. in computer time and storage). This choice is based on the relative population size and density given in the various population data available, as well as on the particular redistricting algorithm.

Criteria

The following criteria could be considered in the development of nonpartisan computer-based methods for political redistricting.

1. Population Equality. This criterion is based on Westbury vs. Sanders (22), "... one man's vote in a congressional election is to be worth as much as another's." Population equality should be the prime concern of any redistricting plan. There are three common measures of equality. One is the ratio of the largest district to the smallest. Specifically, in Drum vs. Seawell (15). "... the aim should be to come as close as possible to a one-to-one ratio." Another measure of equality is the smallest percentage of voters controlling the majority of representatives. Thus for the ten Missouri congressional districts this is the percentage of voters living in the five smallest districts. (This figure should be nearly 50 percent.) A third measure of population equality is the deviation of the size of the population of each

district from that of an ideal district. For the current congressional districts for Missouri (Fig. IIE14-1) these values are given in Table IIE14-1.
2. Compactness. A district is said to be geographically compact if it is nearly convex. A district is said to be compact in terms of population if the population center is close to the geographic center of the district. Hess (6) suggests that a measure which takes into account the distance of the population from the center of the district (e.g. population compactness) is more reasonable. However, no quantitative definition of compactness has yet been accepted.
3. Contiguity. A district is said to be contiguous if its area is not divided into two (or more) geographically separate entities.
4. Preservation of Existing Boundaries. It is desired that districts cross predefined or predetermined boundaries (e.g. rivers, major highways, county lines, etc.) as infrequently as possible. Maintenance of these boundaries simplifies the mechanics of the election procedure by providing a uniform ballot within each political unit. Maintenance of such boundaries also tends to reduce the number of alternative solutions produced by an algorithm although it could preclude solutions

Table IIE14-1 Statistics for the Current Congressional Districts for the State of Missouri (1970 Census Figures)

District Number	Population	Deviation from Ideal (467,650)
1	382,673	−84,977
2	510,683	+43,033
3	390,606	−77,044
4	515,497	+47,847
5	378,874	−88,776
6	452,764	−14,886
7	484,495	+16,845
8	613,491	+145,841
9	546,058	+78,408
10	401,380	−66,270
	4,676,501	

Ratio of largest to smallest district: 1.62.
Minimum percent to control the majority: 42.90%.

that are potentially superior in terms of population deviation, compartness, or other criteria.

The redistricting solutions presented below should not be interpreted as "the only possible" solutions satisfying the above criteria. Rather these plans are solutions satisfying the criteria imposed by the method. Obviously, with the same criteria weighted differently, different solutions could result.

Our objective was to obtain solutions that would satisfy Supreme Court criteria for redistricting plans; this objective can be achieved by considering the minimal set of criteria mentioned above. Strong arguments can be given for and against the inclusion of other criteria. For example, one might consider the heterogeneity or homogeneity of cultural backgrounds of the population. Additional considerations could include voting histories, projected population shifts, party affiliations, protection of incumbents, and others of a more partisan nature. Obviously there is no such thing as a "best solution" to a particular redistricting problem.

Transportation Approach

This approach treats political redistricting like a classical linear programming transportation problem. The transportation problem seeks to minimize the cost of transporting quantities of a given product from m different origins to n different destinations. Constraints exist for the availability of the product at each origin and the demand for the product at each destination. Our approach is to consider population units as the product. We intend to ship these units to the districts while minimizing an objective function designed to achieve population compactness.

Let D_j be the jth district ($j = 1, \cdots, n$) and U_i be the ith population unit ($i = 1, \cdots, m$). Let (u_i, v_i) be the cartesian coordinates of the population centroid of the ith population unit. For units small enough in area, this centroid can be approximated effectively by the geographic center of the unit. Let p_i be the population of the ith population unit. Our iterative scheme is to improve compactness with each pass through the transportation algorithm. We continue to generate redistricting plans until successive plans differ insignificantly. Following is an outline of the method.

1. Guess the centroids, (a_j, b_j), of D_j ($j = 1, \cdots, n$). To avoid undesirable results, some care should be taken in their selection. A possible initial solution would be the centers of the current districts. It may be possible to generate different redistricting plans by considering different initial solutions. Thus several alternative sets of these starting points should be tried.

E. ANALYSIS AND OPTIMIZATION

2. Compute

$$d_{ij} = [(u_i - a_j)^2 + (v_i - b_j)^2]^{1/2}, \qquad i = 1, \ldots, m; j = 1, \ldots, n,$$

the distances from the centers of the D to the centers of the U.

3. Using the transportation algorithm, solve the following subproblem for the x_{ij}'s to obtain a new redistricting plan. Define.

$$x_{ij} = 1 \qquad \text{if } U_i \text{ is in } D$$
$$\phantom{x_{ij}} = 0 \qquad \text{if } U_i \text{ is not in } D.$$

Then we minimize (1)

$$z = \sum_{j=1}^{n} \sum_{i=1}^{m} x_{ij} d_{ij} p_i \tag{1}$$

subject to (2)

$$\sum_{j=1}^{n} x_{ij} = 1, \qquad i = 1, \ldots, m \tag{2}$$

$$\sum_{i=1}^{m} x_{ij} = g_j, \qquad j = 1, \ldots, n. \tag{3}$$

Equation (2) is used to quarantee that each population unit is assigned to one, and only one, district. Since $\sum_i \sum_j x_{ij} = m$, we are guaranteed that each population unit will be assigned to a district. Therefore, it is not possible for enclaves to be formed.

Equation (3) determines the number of population units g_j to be assigned to district j. If the population units are relatively equal in number of people, then we can choose $g_j = m/n$ for all j. Therefore, the same number of population units would be shipped to each legislative district and the condition of population equality would be reasonably satisfied. Since we require each initial x to be either 0 or 1, the elements of the solution matrix (x_{ij}) will be integers if m, the number of population units chosen, is a multiple of n, the number of districts to be formed (5).

In general, it is impractial to find population units that are relatively equal in population so that it is not necessarily true that each $g_j = m/n$, an integer. Even if m equal population units can be found, it may not be true that m is a multiple of n. Therefore, the g_j are computed iteratively. Any choice for the g_j could be used to start the procedure, although some thought should be given to selection so that computer time will not be wasted. The method we found to be effective for iteratively modifying the g_j is outlined in step 6.

If Eq. (1) is minimized, reasonably compact districts will result. Although no explicit provisions are made for contiguity, it is believed that a reasonably compact district will be contiguous. In our application of this procedure noncontiguous districts have not resulted.

4. Calculate the centroids, $(\bar{a}_j, \bar{b}_j)$, of the districts generated in step 3 as follows:

$$\bar{a}_j = \sum_{i=1}^{m} u_i p_i x_{ij} \bigg/ \sum_{i=1}^{m} p_i x_{ij}, \quad j = 1, \ldots, n$$

$$\bar{b}_j = \sum_{i=1}^{m} v_i p_i x_{ij} \bigg/ \sum_{i=1}^{m} p_i x_{ij}, \quad j = 1, \ldots, n$$

5. Check to see if the new solution is significantly different by computing $|\bar{a}_j - a_j|$ and $|\bar{b}_j - b_j|$. If these differences are less than a predefined tolerance (e.g., $|\bar{a}_j - a_j| < \epsilon \wedge |\bar{b}_j - b| < \epsilon$) proceed to step 6. If not, go to step 2 and repeat the above process using $(\bar{a}_j, \bar{b}_j)$, as the new values for $(a_j, b_j), j = 1, \cdots n$. The redistricting plan just generated is represented by the x_{ij}. When $x_{ij} = 1$, then U_i is in D_j.

6. Modify the g_j $(j = 1, \cdots, n)$ as follows:

a. Find the district with the largest population and call this district l. Likewise, find the district with the smallest population and call this district s.

b. Calculate the ratio of largest to smallest districts (ratio = p_l/p_s).

c. Compare this new ratio with the lowest ratio obtained thus far. The first time step 6 is executed, this comparison is ignored. Instead proceed with the modification outlined in (i) below.

(i) If the new ratio is less than the previous ratio, then subtracted one from g_l and add one to g_s. All other g_j will remain the same. Retain this new ratio as the best ratio obtained thus far and set $r = 0$. Then proceed to step 2.

(ii) Otherwise add one to r. If this new value of r is equal to h (h is a predefined constant that specifies the number of consecutive times this part is allowed to be executed) then terminate. Otherwise subtract one from g_l and add one to g_s. All other g_js will remain the same. Proceed to step 2.

Although one may consider a more complex scheme for modifying the g_j (e.g. changing more than two of the g_j's at a time) we have found the above method sufficient.

Hess (7) also considers solving the redistricting problem by using mathematical programming techniques. He formulates this problem as a warehouse location problem that assigns people to a specific warehouse (political district). Solving the problem in this matter forces each resulting district to have the same ideal population. In general, this will require population units to be split between political districts. This solution is aceptable only if political or natural boundaries are not to be preserved. Even when such solutions are acceptable, one does not know the precise boundaries of split population units. In an extreme case, households may be split districts. To avoid these problems, Hess regroups so that no population units are split between districts. He uses the solution obtained from regrouping as a starting point for continuing as before. However, there is no guarantee that these solutions are monotonically converging.

Hess (7) also formulates the political redistricting problem as an integer programming problem, one that he admits cannot be solved at present. Our formulation is also an integer programming problem, but it is one that can be solved efficiently using the transportation algorithm (5). In our formulation we chose to assign population units rather than individual people as in the warehouse approach. This choice allowed us to preserve the integrity of the population units and consequently avoid the regrouping problem.

Results

We applied our procedure to the problem of generating ten congressional districts in the state of Missouri. Our choice of population units was counties and census tracts. Because of differing population densities, counties were used in rural areas of the state while census tracts were used in metropolitan areas. Since the average population of a rural county in

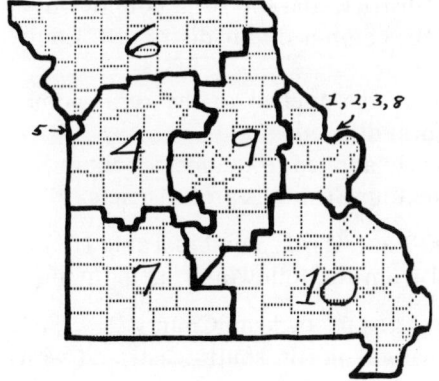

Figure IIE14-2. Districting plan generated by transportation method.

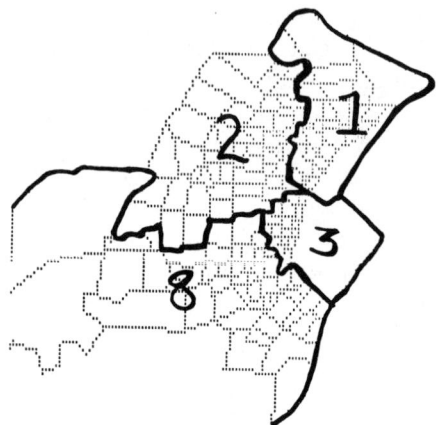

Figure IIE14-3. Detail of congressional districting plan.

Missouri is approximately 18,000 and the population of an average urban census tract is 6,500, it was necessary to combine urban census tracts to form population units of approximately equal population. Similarly, smaller rural counties were combined. This produced 200 population units for the entire state.

Initial attempts were made to determine ten districts in a single application of the algorithm. Problems arose in finding a complete solution because of the large differences in population density between outstate and metropolitan areas. Results indicated the following sequential development of districts:

1. The St. Louis metropolitan area should have four districts, Kansas City (within Jackson County) one district, and the rural counties five districts. The precise boundary of the combined four-district St. Louis area was also defined.
2. The transportation procedure above was applied to the rural population units to determine the five rural districts.
3. The same procedure was subsequently applied to the metropolitan St. Louis population units to obtain the four St. Louis area districts.

These results appear in Figures II14E-2 and II14E-3 and in Table IIE14-2. The districting plans were generated from the following starting points:

1. Rural districts-four corners of the state and Jackson County.
2. Metropolitan St. Louis districts—as far north, south, east, and west as possible within the area considered.

Note that in Figure IIE14-2 two rural counties (Wright and Clay) were each split between two districts. These divisions were necessary in order

E. ANALYSIS AND OPTIMIZATION

Table IIE14-2 Statistics for the Plan Generated by the Transportation Method for Ten Congressional Districts for the State of Missouri

District Number	Population	Deviation from Ideal (467,650)
1	467,960	+310
2	468,324	+674
3	467,823	+173
4	468,324	+674
5	467,542	−108
6	467,649	−1
7	467,065	−585
8	467,468	−182
9	467,173	−477
10	467,173	−477
	4,676,501	

Ratio of largest to smallest district: 1.002.
Percent to control the majority: 49.96%.

to obtain a desirable ratio of largest to smallest district. Other sets of starting values were tried, but the ratios of largest to smallest district in these attempts did not yield as low a value as the plans presented. The ratio for this plan (1.002) is well within the bounds specified in U.S. Supreme Court decisions.

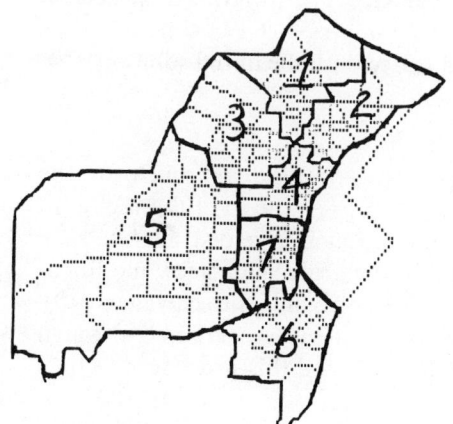

Figure IIE14-4. Districting plan for seven county council seats.

Table IIE14-3 Statistics for the Plan Generated by the Transportation Method for the Seven County Council Seats for St. Louis County

Seat Number	Population	Deviation from Ideal (135,907)
1	136,486	+579
2	137,347	+1,440
3	136,820	+913
4	136,534	+627
5	133,551	−2,336
6	135,841	−66
7	134,774	−1,133
	955,353	

Ratio of largest to smallest district: 1.0284.
Percent to control majority: 56.82%.
(Based on four smallest divisions—ideally 57.14%.

Seven St. Louis County Council seats were also determined by the above procedure. The 147 census tracts for St. Louis County were used as the population units. It was not necessary to sequentially develop these districts, as it was for state districts, since the population is more uniformly distributed. The starting points were generated randomly. These results appear on Figure IIE14-4 and Table IIE14-3.

The redistricting algorithm that produced the above results was written in PL/1 and run on an IBM 360/50 under OS. The program required on the average 65K bytes and ran from 3 to 7 minutes of CPU time in 2.5μ s core. The times and storage requirements varied with the initial solution.

Other Approaches

Thoreson and Littschwager (10) present a grid-type approach to the political redistricting problem. A grid is placed over a map of the region to be redistricted to obtain the population units. Legislative districts are then formed by successively grouping the cells of the grid. With a few modifications we implemented Method 2 of Thoreson and Littschwager (10). Results from using this method can be found in Figures IIE14-5 through IIE14-7, and Tables IIE14-4 and IIE14-5. We found this procedure to be a

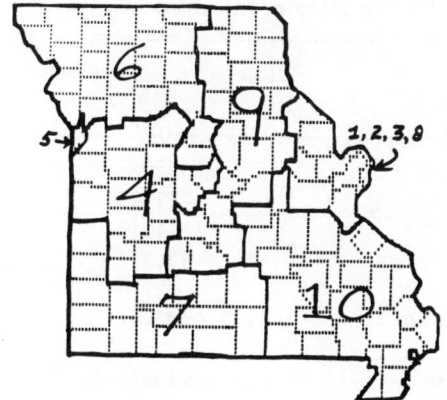

Figure IIE14-5. Plan generated by modified grid approach.

fast (approximately 30 seconds CPU time) method for obtaining a good initial solution for our transportation algorithm.

Another method is the implicit enumeration technique presented by Garfinkel (2, 3). This method generates all possible districts based on his constraints. From this set he determines acceptable redistricting plans. With the data for St. Louis County, this program* required excessive computer time.

Figure IIE14-6. Congressional plan by modified grid approach.

* The program for Garfinkel's algorithm was obtained from Nelson Heller of the St. Louis Police Department.

Table IIE14-4 Statistics for the Plan Generated by the Modified Grid Approach for Ten Congressional Districts for the State of Missouri

District Number	Population	Deviation from Ideal (467,650)
1	466,677	−973
2	466,505	−1,145
3	468,790	+1,140
4	454,293	−13,357
5	467,542	−108
6	478,057	+10,407
7	476,349	+8,699
8	469,603	+1,953
9	461,245	−6,405
10	467,440	−210
	4,676,501	

Ratio of largest to smallest district: 1.05.
Minimum percent to control the majority: 49.52%.

Table IIE14-5 Statistics for the Plan Generated by the Modified Grid Approach for the Seven County Council Seats for St. Louis County

County Council Number	Population	Deviation from Ideal (135,907)
1	140,223	+4,316
2	141,429	+5,522
3	135,039	−868
4	134,444	−1,463
5	132,033	−3,874
6	137,537	+1,630
7	130,648	+5,259
	951,353	

Ratio of largest to smallest district: 1.08.
Smallest percent of people controlling the majority: 56.66%.
(Based on four smallest divisions—ideally 57.14%).

E. ANALYSIS AND OPTIMIZATION

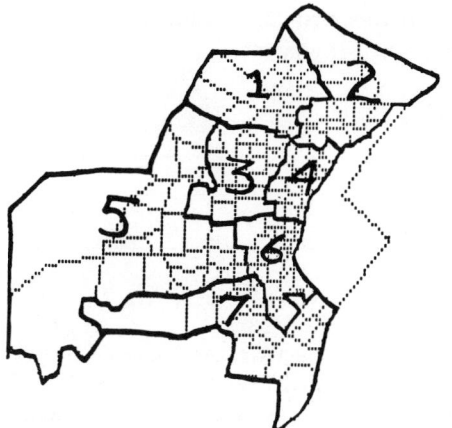

Figure IIE14-7. Modified grid approach for seven county council seats.

Conclusions

A suit is now pending to allow the courts to reapportion the ten congressional districts for the state of Missouri (21). We have submitted our solutions to the court for consideration (4). The Office of the Attorney General of the State of Missouri has recommended to the federal panel that it use computers in accomplishing the task of redistricting the state of Missouri. An editorial in the *St. Louis Post-Dispatch* (8) has made public our efforts to redraw Missouri congressional districts. However, it is not our intent to try to impose these solutions or to actively lobby for their adoption, but rather to demonstrate the feasibility of accomplishing political redistricting with the aid of a computer.

Political redistricting, and its consequences, should not be taken lightly. For a political system such as that in the United States to function properly, popular representation must truly be as equal as possible, for, "No state legislature can unnecessarily abridge one's right to an equal vote in a congressional election any more than it may constitutionally deny his right to trial by jury, his right of free speech, his right to freedom of religion, his right to peaceful assemblage, or any one of his many other rights guaranteed by the Constitution of the United States." [17]

Acknowledgment

This project was supervised by Dr. David I. Steinberg, Assistant Professor of Applied Mathematics and Computer Science at Washington

University. Other people who worked on this project include Richard P. Berger, Gerald L. Hansberger, and Joseph S. Maynard.

References

1. A. F., Castillon, Jr. "Political Apportionment by Computer. *Brown University Computer Review,* **1** (1967), 5–24.
2. Robert S. Garfinkel, "Optimal Political Districting," Working paper #6812, College of Business Administration University of Rochester, October 1968.
3. Robert S. Garfinkel, and George L. Nemhause, "Optimal Political Districting by Implicit Enumeration Techniques." *Management Science* **16** (April 1970), 495–508.
4. Floyd R. Gibson, Letter to him (October 29, 1971) and corresponding reply (November 5, 1971).
5. G. Hadley, *Linear Programming,* Addison-Wesley, Reading, Mass., 1963.
6. S. Hess, "Compactness—What size and shape?" Workshop on Computer Application to Legislative Districting, 73rd National Conference on Government, National Municipal League, New York, 1967.
7. S. Hess, J. Weaver, H. Siegfeldt, J. Whelan, and R. Zitlau, "Nonpartisan Political Redistricting by Computer," *Operations Research,* **13** (November 6, 1965), 998–1006.
8. Fred W. Lindecke, "Students Let a Computer Offer Redistricting Plan," *St. Louis Post-Dispatch,* September 20, 1971, 1B, 4B.
9. James Munkres, "Algorithms for the Assignment and Transportation Problems," *Journal of the Society for Industrial and Applied Mathematics,* **5** (March 1957), 32–38.
10. J. Thoresor, and J. Littschwager, "Legislative Districting by Computer Simulation," *Behavioral Science,* **12** (1967), 237–247.
11. James B. Weaver, "Fair and Equal Districts: A How-to-do-it Manual on Computer Use." National Municipal League, New York, 1970. Court Cases
12. Baker vs. Cass, 179 F. Supp. 824, 1959.
13. Baker vs. Carr, 369 U.S. 186, 1962.
14. Baker vs. Carr, 206 F. Supp. 341, 1962.
15. Drum vs. Seawell, 250 F. Supp. 922, 1965.
16. Kirkpatrick vs. Preisler, 385 U.S. 450, 1967.
17. Kirkpatrick vs. Preisler, 279 F. Supp. 952, 1968.
18. Kirkpatrick vs. Preisler, 395 U.S. 917, 1969.
19. Preisler vs. Secretary of State, 238 F. Supp. 187, 1965.
20. Preisler vs. Secretary of State, 257 F. Supp. 953, 1966.
21. Paul W. Preisler et al. vs. the Secretary of Missouri, et al., Civil Action No. 1716 in the U.S. District Court for the Western District of Missouri, Central Division (now pending).
22. Westbury vs. Sanders, 376 U.S. 1, 1964.

E. ANALYSIS AND OPTIMIZATION

CASE STUDY 15 Structural Analysis*

NASTRAN had its beginning in 1964 when a committee within NASA surveyed the existing structural computer programs in the aerospace industry with a view toward seeking a program to be used as a standard at NASA centers. Since no existing single program met all their requirements, the committee recommended the development of a new program. After a period of preliminary analysis and technical evaluation, detailed development of NASTRAN was begun in July 1966 by an industry team consisting of Computer Sciences Corp., the Baltimore Division of Martin-Marietta, and The MacNeal-Schwendler Corp., all under the management supervision of a group at Goddard Space Flight Center. Later, some important contributions to the list of structural elements were made by Bell Aerosystems.

A preliminary version of the statics portion of the program became operational early in 1968 and was delivered to several NASA centers. Delivery of the completed program to NASA centers began in April 1969.

It is the intention of NASA to maintain a standard version of the program for use on three third-generation computers (IBM 360, UNIVAC 1108, and CDC 6600) and one second generation computer (IBM 7094/7040 Direct Coupled), and to sponsor continued development.

Design Objectives

Since NASTRAN is intended for general use, it must answer to a wide spectrum of requirements. In order to compete with other general and special purpose programs, it must be efficient, versatile, and convenient to use. It must be standardized to permit interchange of input and output among different users. It must be structured to permit future modification and extension to new problem areas and to new computer configurations without major redevelopment.

The range of application of the program extends to almost every kind of structure and to almost every type of construction. Structural elements are provided for the specific representation of the more common types of construction, including rods, beams, shear panels, plates, and shells of revolution. More general types of construction are treated by combinations of

---

* This section has been exerpted from R. H. Neal and C. W. McCormick, "The NASTRAN Computer Program for Structural Analysis," presented at the National Aeronautic and Space Engineering and Manufacturing Meeting, Los Angeles, Calif., October 6–10, 1969. In complete form it is available as SAE 690612.

these elements and by the use of "general" elements. Control systems, aerodynamic transfer functions, and other nonstructural features can be incorporated into the structural problem.

The range of analysis in the program includes: static response to concentrated and distributed loads, to thermal expansion and to enforced deformation; dynamic response to transient loads, to steady-state sinusoidal loads, and to random excitation; determination of real and complex eigenvalues for use in vibration analysis, dynamic stability analysis, and elastic stability analysis. The program includes a limited capability for the solution of nonlinear problems, including piecewise linear analysis of nonlinear static response and transient analysis of nonlinear dynamic response.

NASTRAN has been specifically designed to treat large problems with many degrees of freedom. The only limitations on problem size are those imposed by practical considerations of running time and by the ultimate capacity of auxiliary storage devices. The program is decidedly not a core program. Computational procedures have been selected to provide the maximum obtainable efficiency for large problems.

Research was conducted during the design of the program in order to ensure that the methods used were consistent with current advances in technology. The areas of computer program design that are most sensitive to state-of-the-art considerations are program organization and numerical analysis. The organizational demands on the program design are severe in view of the multiplicity of problem types and user conveniences, the multiplicity of operating computer configurations, the requirement for large problem capability, the requirement for future modification, and the requirement for responsiveness to improvements in programming systems and computer hardware.

The organizational problems have been solved by applying techniques that are standard in the design of computer operating systems but which have not, as yet, been extensively used in the design of scientific applications programs. The main instrument of program organization in the program is an executive system that schedules the operating sequence of functional modules and which plans and allocates the storage of files.

Most difficulties in numerical analysis arise in connection with three basic implicit operations: matrix decomposition (or inversion), eigenvalue extraction, and integration of differential equations. The major difficulties that occur in the application of these operations to large problems are excessive computing time, error accumulation, and instability. Many methods that work well with small or moderate sized problems are not acceptable for large problems. The method employed for matrix decomposition is especially important because of its extensive use as a base for the other two implicit operations. The method employed in the program takes maximum advantage of matrix sparsity and bandedness. The latter aspect is particularly important, owing to the enormous gain in efficiency that accrues when banding techniques are properly employed by the user in setting up problems for the displacement method.

The needs of the analyst must be considered in all aspects of the design of a general purpose computer program. The first thing to be remembered is that, in view of the wide range of possible applications of NASTRAN, we do not know exactly what these needs may be. For this reason a high degree of flexibility and generality has been incorporated into certain areas of the program. For example, in addition to the usual list of structural elements that refer to specific types of construction, the user is provided with more general elements that may be used to construct any type of special element, to represent part of a structure by deflection influence coefficients, or to represent part of a structure by its vibration modes. For the more conventional types of structural analysis, the user is presented with a large number of convenience features, including automatic generation of loads and plotting routines.

Functional Capability

The problems that can be solved by NASTRAN include the following general classes:

1. Static structural problems.
2. Elastic stability problems.
3. Dynamic structural problems.
4. General matrix problems.

Each general problem class is further subdivided into case types that differ with regard to the type of information desired, the environmental factors considered, or the method of analysis. The mathematical computations required to solve problems are performed by subprogram units called "functional modules." Each case type requires a distinct sequence of functional module calls that are scheduled by the Executive System.

A flexible procedure is provided for the solution of general matrix problems. All matrix operations (such as addition, multiplication, triangular decomposition, and eigenvalue extraction) used in the program can be directly addressed by the user according to a system of macro instructions called DMAP (for Direct Matrix Abstraction Program). The user constructs a chain of DMAP instructions in order to effect the solution of general matrix problems.

Table IIE15-1 Rigid Formats Currently Available in NASTRAN

A. Static analysis
   1. Basic static analysis.
   2. Static analysis with inertia relief.
   3. Static analysis with differential stiffness.
   4. Piecewise linear analysis.
B. Elastic stability analysis
   5. Buckling.
C. Dynamic analysis
   6. Normal modes analysis.
   7. Direct complex eigenvalue analysis.
   8. Direct frequency and random response analysis.
   9. Direct transient response analysis.
   10. Modal complex eigenvalue analysis.
   11. Modal frequency and random response analysis.
   12. Modal transient response analysis.

For structural problem types, the sequence of module calls, and hence the general method of solution is established internally for each case type according to a rigid format stored in the Executive System. Execution of a structural problem proceeds in one run to final solution or, at the option of the user, to a desired intermediate point. Twelve rigid formats are currently available in NASTRAN, each corresponding to a different problem type as shown in Table IIE15-1.

At present all static problems are solved in NASTRAN by the matrix displacement method, for which the governing equation is

$$[K] \{u\} = \{p\}, \tag{1}$$

where $\{u\}$ is a vector of unknown displacement components at grid points, $\{p\}$ is a vector of loads applied to grid points, and $[K]$ is the stiffness matrix generated from the properties of structural elements connected between grid points. The capability to solve problems by the matrix force method will be added at a later date. Figure IIE15-1 illustrates the problem flow for basic static analysis. Each block in the flow diagram represents a number of functional modules. The actual number of modules called is approximately equal to 30. Briefly, the functions performed in the various blocks of Figure IIE15-1 are as follows:

1. The input file processor, as the name implies, scans the input data cards and creates data blocks consisting of lists of similar quantities.

E. ANALYSIS AND OPTIMIZATION

2. The geometry processor generates coordinate system transformation matrices, tables of grid point locations, a table defining the structural elements connected to each grid point, and other miscellaneous tables such as those that define static loads and temperature at grid points.
3. The structures plotter generates tape output for an automatic plotter that will plot the structure (that is, the location of grid points and the

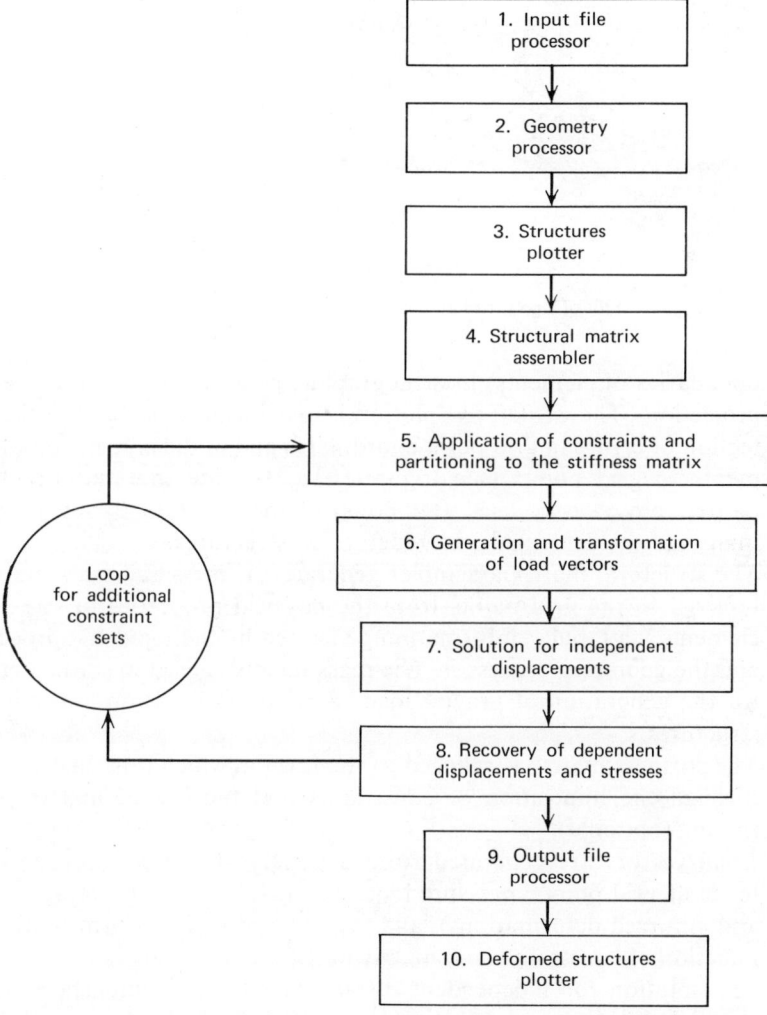

Figure IIE15-1. Simplified flow diagram for basic static analysis.

174 CURRENT USAGE: CASE STUDIES AND CRITIQUES

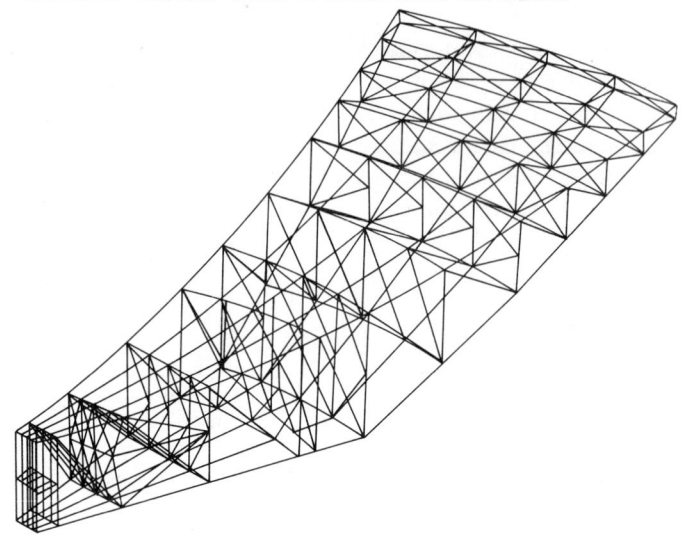

Figure IIE15-2. Plot of a sector of an antenna.

boundaries of elements) in orthographic, perspective, or stereographic projection. The structures plotter is particularly useful for the detection of errors in grid point coordinates and in the connection of elements to grid points (see FigureIIE15-2). Note that the structures plotter may also be used at the end of the program to superimpose images of the deformed and undeformed structures.

4. The structural matrix assembler generates stiffness and mass matrices referred to the grid points from the physical properties of structural elements via tabular information generated by the input file processor and the geometry processor. The mass matrix is used in static analysis for the generation of gravity loads and inertia loads on unsupported structures.

5. The stiffness matrix is reduced to the form in which it is finally solved through the imposition of constraints and the use of matrix partitioning (optional).

6. Load vectors are generated from a variety of sources (concentrated loads at grid points, pressure loads on surfaces, gravity, temperature, and enforced deformations), and are reduced to final form by the application of constraints and matrix partitioning.

7. The solution for independent displacements is accomplished in two steps: decomposition of the stiffness matrix $[K]$ into upper and lower triangular factors; and a solution for $\{u\}$ for specific load vectors $\{p\}$ by means of successive substitution into the equations

E. ANALYSIS AND OPTIMIZATION 175

represented by the triangular factors of $[K]$ (the so-called forward and backward passes). All load vectors are processed before proceeding to the next functional block.

8. Dependent displacements are determined from the independent displacements by means of the equations of constraint. The internal forces and stresses in each element are then computed from

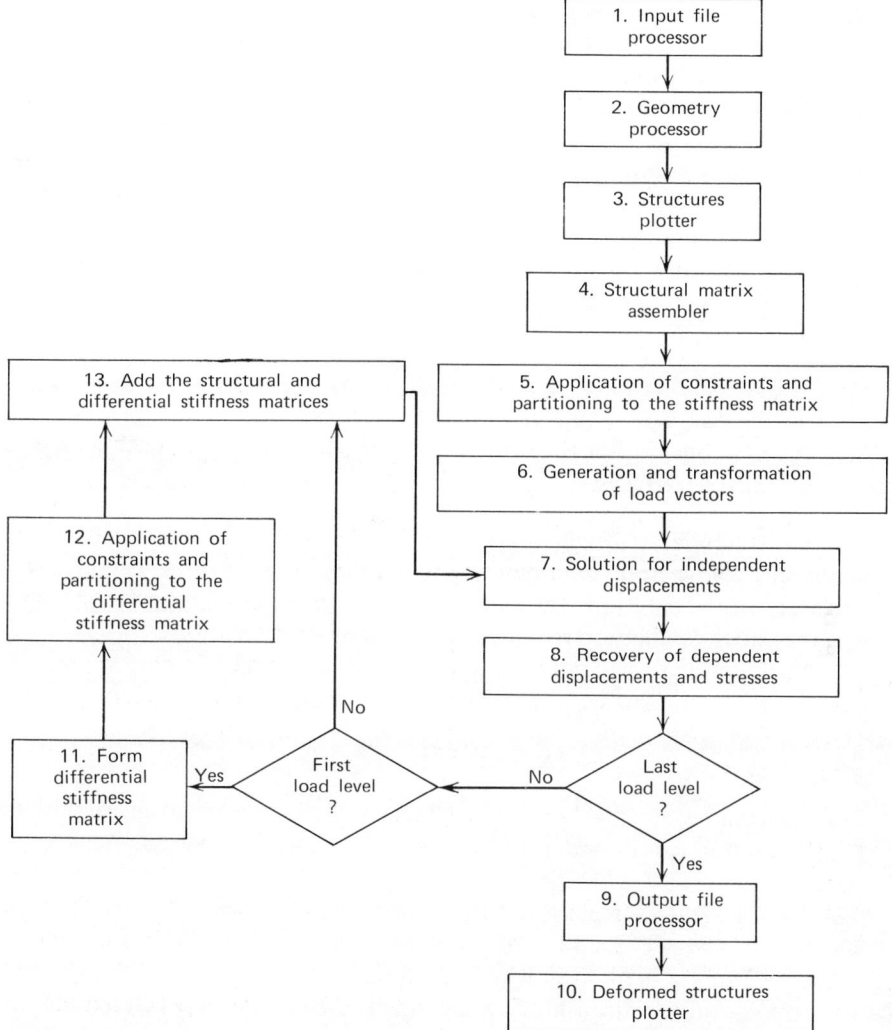

Figure IIE15-3. Simplified flow diagram for static analysis with differential stiffness.

knowledge of the displacement components at the corners of the elements and of the intrinsic structural equations of the element.
9. The output file processor prepares the results of the analysis for printing according to format options selected by the user.

The loop for additional constraint sets, shown in Figure IIC15-1, is introduced to facilitate solutions for different boundary conditions, which are applied by means of constraints. In particular, the symmetric and antisymmetric responses of a symmetric structure are treated in this manner.

The flow diagram for static analysis with differential stiffness is illustrated in Figure IIE15-3. The term "differential stiffness" refers to the stiffening effects that result from the presence of a static load such as may occur in beam columns and in centrifugally loaded structures. The differential stiffness effect is represented by a separate stiffness matrix $[K^d]$, which is calculated from the geometry and the internal loads in structural elements. The solution of a problem with differential stiffness effects included consists of two passes through the solution generating part of the program:

1. A first pass in which a solution with elastic stiffness only is obtained for the purposes of calculating differential stiffness.
2. A second pass after the differential stiffness matrix has been added to the elastic stiffness.

The differential stiffness matrix is assumed to be proportional to the magnitude of the static loading condition so that the first pass becomes unnecessary in the solutions for additional load levels. It is important to note that the entire calculation may be performed in one execution.

In buckling analysis (rigid format 5, Table IIE15-1), the elastic and differential stiffness matrices are used to form the eigenvalue problem

$$[K + \lambda \ K^d] \ \{u\} = 0 \qquad (2)$$

The eigenvalues are the factors by which the load level used in calculating $[K^d]$ is multiplied in order to produce the various modes of elastic instability.

A flow diagram for piecewise linear analysis is shown in Figure IIE15-4. This rigid format is used to solve nonlinear problems with plastic material behavior, using a method in which the load level is incrementally increased. The stress-strain relationships are assumed to be linear between load levels, resulting in an equivalent linear stiffness matrix that is recalculated after each increment.

In dynamic analysis, information regarding the structure is generated in

E. ANALYSIS AND OPTIMIZATION

the statics portion of the program, blocks 1–5 in Figure IIC15-1. Figure IIE15-5 shows the additional major operations performed in the solution of dynamic problems. Three basic types of analysis are performed (eigenvalue extraction, frequency response analysis, and transient response analysis) according to either of two methods of problem formulation (direct or modal). In all, there are seven different paths through the flow diagram of Figure

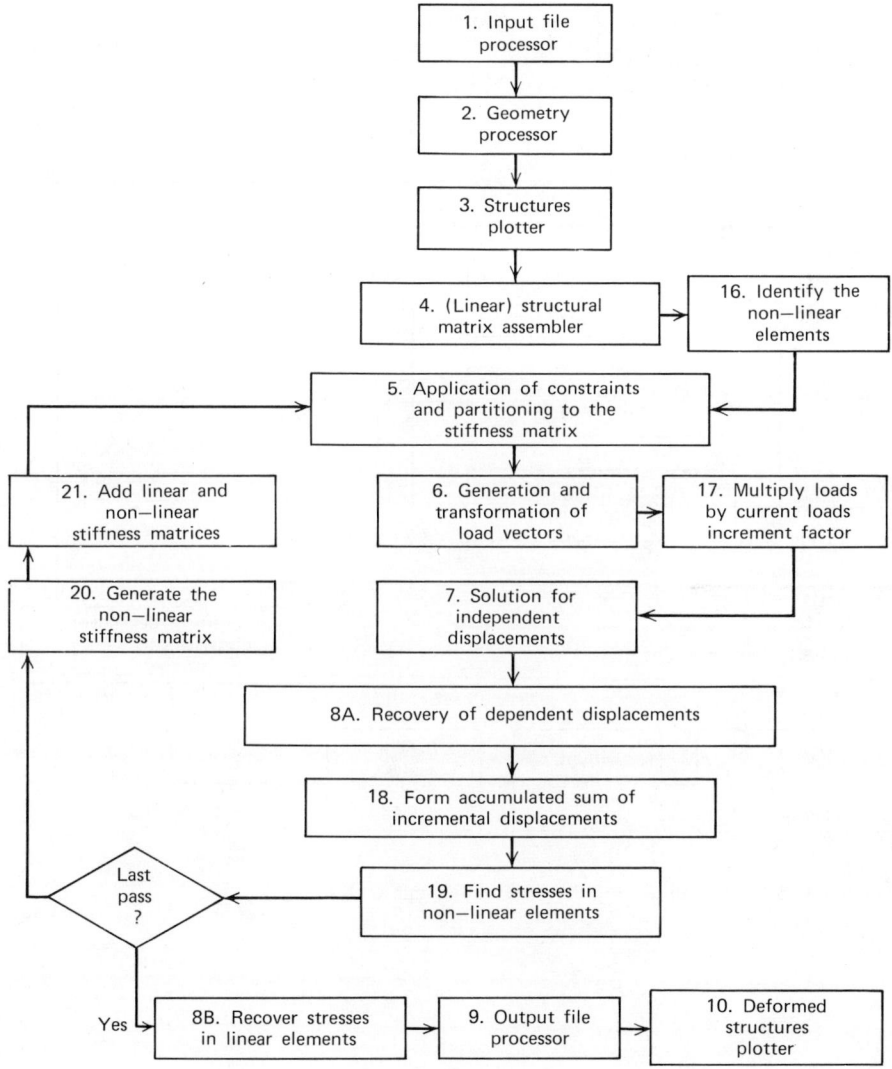

Figure IIE15-4. Simplified flow diagram for piecewise linear analysis.

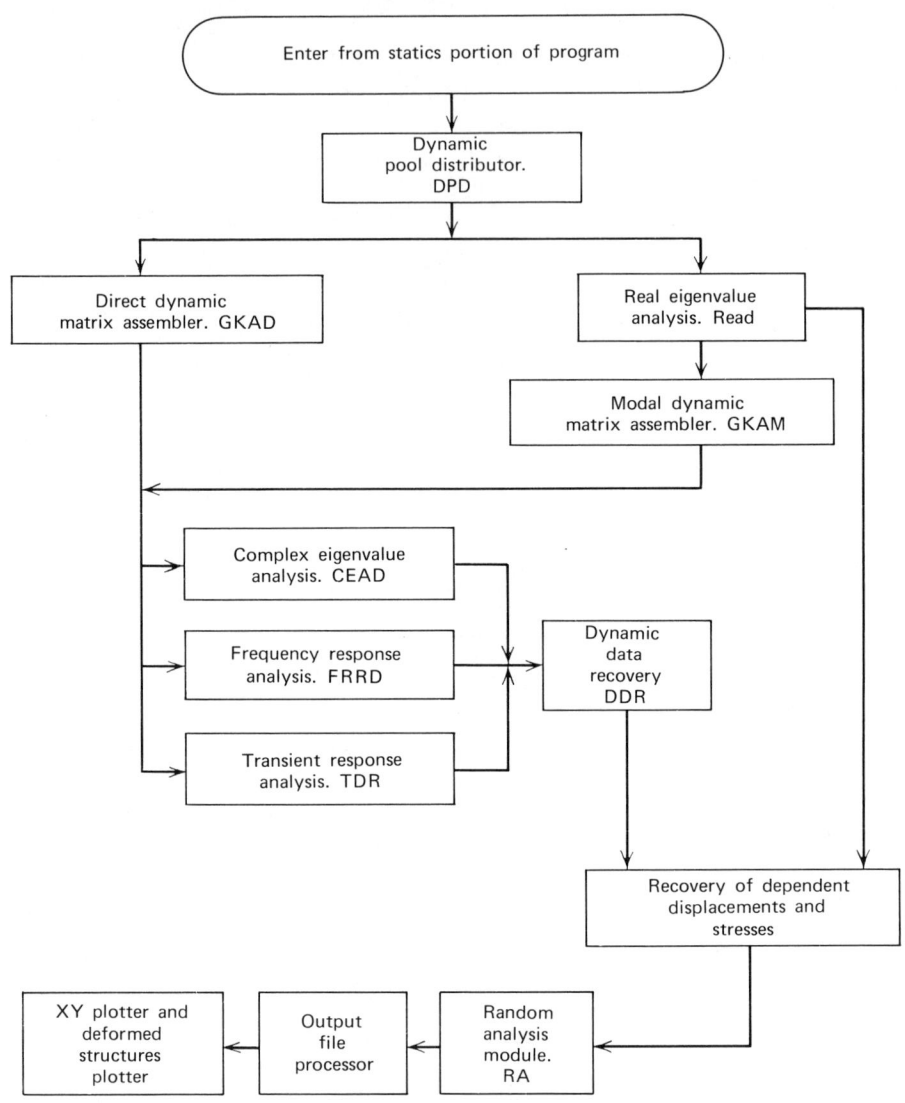

Figure IIE15-5. Simplified flow diagram for dynamic analysis.

IIE15-5, corresponding to the seven rigid formats for dynamic analysis listed in Table IIE15-1.

In the modal method of dynamic problem formulation, the vibration modes of the structure in a selected frequency range are used as degrees of freedom, thereby reducing the number of degrees of freedom while maintaining accuracy in the selected frequency range. In the direct method, the degrees of freedom are simply the displacements at grid points.

It is important to have both direct and modal methods of dynamic problem formulation in order to maximize efficiency in different situations. The modal method will usually be more efficient in problems where a small fraction of all modes are sufficient to produce the desired accuracy, provided the band width of the direct stiffness matrix is large. The direct method will usually be more efficient for problems in which the band width of the direct stiffness matrix is small and for problems in which a large fraction of the vibration modes are required to produce the desired accuracy. For problems in which matrices of the modal formulation are diagonal, the modal method will frequently be more efficient, even though a large fraction of the modes are needed. The choice of method is left to the user.

The matrix properties of the dynamic system are assembled in three different modules, as shown in Figure IIE15-5. The dynamic pool distributor performs a number of preliminary bookkeeping chores such as organizing tables for dynamic loads and nonlinear functions. The direct dynamic matrix assembler collects and superimposes contributions from various sources to the mass, damping, and stiffness matrices in terms of displacements at grid points. The modal dynamic matrix assembler applies a modal transformation (based on orthogonal modes calculated in the real eigenvalue analysis module) to the mass, damping, and stiffness matrices.

In NASTRAN, dynamic analysis is performed via a basic quadratic format:

$$[Mp^2 + Ep + K] \{u\} = \{F\}, \qquad (3)$$

wherein "p" is interpreted as: an unspecified parameter in complex eigenvalue extraction; a known parameter, $p = i\omega$, in frequency response analysis; and the time derivative operator, $p = d/dt$, in transient analysis. The matrices $[M]$, $[B]$, and $[K]$ are assembled in part from the properties of structural elements generated by the statics portion of the program and in part from additional (direct input) terms supplied by the user. Direct input terms may be used to simulate a control system, a fluid environment, or any other nonstructural influence. The means whereby nonstructural

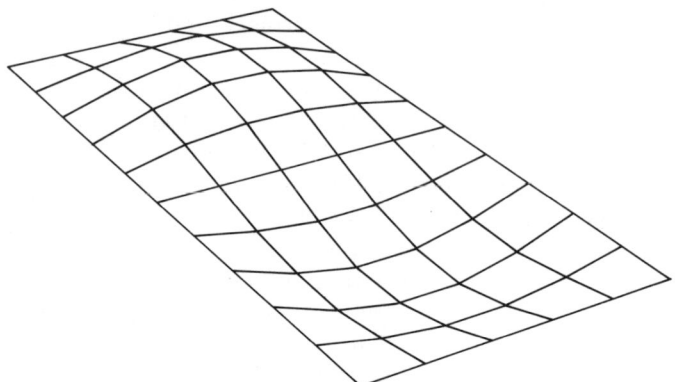

Figure IIE15-6. Perspective plot of vibrating plate.

properties may be expressed in the basic quadratic format, Eq. 3 are discussed later. Terms in the damping matrix $[B]$ are obtained from viscous dampers, from material damping specified as a property of elastic elements, and from direct input matrices.

The modules for complex eigenvalue analysis, frequency response analysis, and transient analysis produce solution vectors consisting of displacement components (in the case of a direct formulation) or of generalized modal coordinates (in the case of a modal formulation). The additional operations in the data recovery chain are indicated in Figure IIE15-5. The solution vector is partitioned, transformed, and augmented in various ways to obtain the complete vectors of grid point displacements from which the stresses in structural elements are computed.

Use of the mode acceleration method of solution improvement (1)* is optionally available in the dynamic data recovery module. Subsequent data recovery operations utilize the same modules as those used in static analysis. Calculation of the response to random excitation is performed as a data reduction task on the results of frequency response analysis. The power spectral density and autocorrelation function for any output quantity (displacement, stress, and so forth) may be requested.

The results of normal modes analysis and of transient response analysis may be represented in deformed structures plots (see Figure IIE15-6). The results of frequency response analysis and transient analysis may also be represented in XY plots.

* Numbers in parentheses designate References at end of paper.

E. ANALYSIS AND OPTIMIZATION

Special Engineering Features

STRUCTURAL ELEMENTS. Much of the individuality of a structures program is exhibited in the structural elements that it employs. Since the intended range of applications of NASTRAN is broad, the number of different structural elements is large and their properties are less specialized than in most other programs. In addition, the modular design of NASTRAN facilitates the addition of new elements. The structural elements that are currently available in NASTRAN are the following:

1. Beam and Rod Elements. A number of special features are included, such as the ability to offset the neutral axis of a beam from the grip points to which it is attached, and the ability to remove the connections between the grid points and any of the six motions at either end of the beam.
2. Shear Panels. The shear panel may have a general quadrilateral shape and its corners need not lie in a plane, Garvey's formulation (2) is used.
3. Plates. A total of nine different plate elements include: those with triangular and general quadrilateral shapes; with solid and sandwich

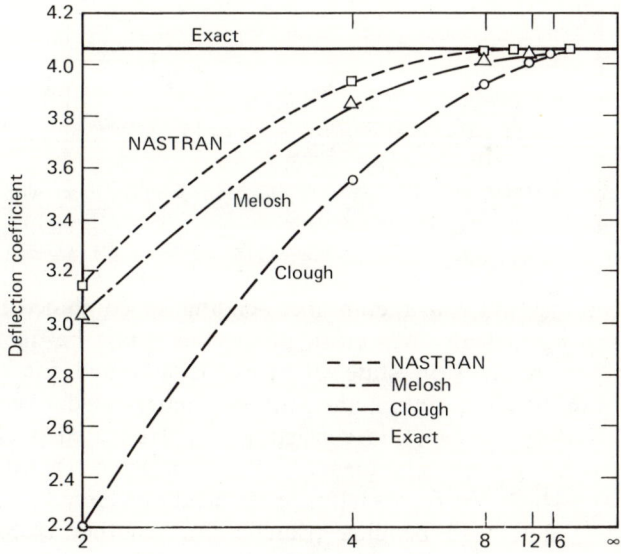

Figure IIE15-7. Central deflection of a uniformly loaded square plate with simple supports.

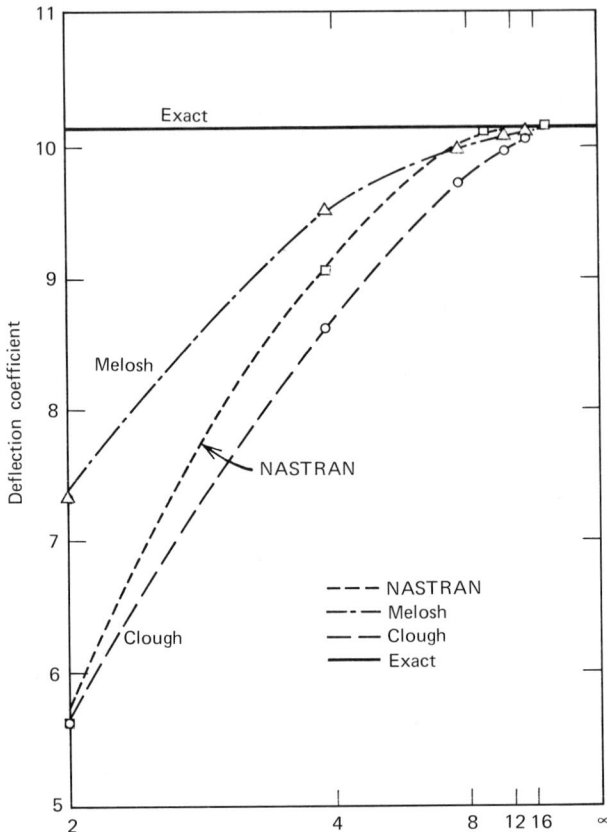

Figure IIE15-8. Central deflection of a uniformly loaded rectangular plate with simple supports, aspect ratio = 2.

cross sections; and with membrane, bending, or combined membrane and bending action. Material properties may be isotropic or anisotropic. A uniform state of stress is assumed for membrane action. For bending action, the stiffness matrix is derived from an assumed deflection function consisting of a truncated double power series expansion in the planform (X, Y) coordinates. Transverse shear flexibility is included (optionally) in all bending elements. One of the forms is the Clough bending triangle (3). Another is the simpler "basic" bending triangle, which has a linear variation of normal slope along one edge only.

The quadrilateral bending element consists of four basic bending triangles arranges so that each is connected to a different set of three corner points, and so that the edge of each triangle with the linear variation of normal slope lies along a diagonal of the quadrilateral. Since the surface area of the quadrilateral is covered twice by the triangles, the resulting stiffness matrix is divided by 2. Comparisons are made in Figures IIE15-7 and IIE15-8 of results obtained with the Clough triangle, the NASTRAN quadrilateral, and the Melcsh rectangle (4), which is an excellent element but which is restricted to rectangular shapes. It is not included in NASTRAN.

4. Axisymmetric Conical Shell. The axisymmetric conical shell element includes transverse shear flexibility and orthotropic material properties, and permits nonaxisymmetric bending.
5. Doubly Curved (Toroidal) Shell. The toroidal shell element (5) includes higher-order displacement functions that are accommodated by adding the first derivative of tangential displacement and the second derivative of normal displacement along the meridian as degrees of freedom at grid points. The loading must be axisymmetric.
6. Solid of Revolution Elements. The solid of revolution elements (6 and 7) are rings with triangular and trapezoidal cross sections. They are used in the analysis of axisymmetric solids with axisymmetric loads.
7. Scalar Elements. The scaler spring and the scaler damper can be conected between a single degree of freedom and "ground," or between any pair of degrees of freedom.
8. General Element. The general element can be connected to any number of degrees of freedom. Its properties are defined by deflection influence coefficients rather than by stiffness coefficients because the former are more directly related to test results and because the latter require extremely accurate values to avoid violation of free body properties.

References

1. Bisplinghoff, Ashley, and Halfman, *Aeroelasticity,* Addison-Wesley, Cambridge, Mass., 1955, p. 642.
2. S. J. Garvey, "The Quadrilateral Shear Panel," *Aircraft Engineering,* (May 1951), 134.
3. R. W. Clough and J. L. Tocher, "Finite Element Stiffness Matrices for Analysis of Plate Bending," Proceedings of the Conference on Matrix Methods in Structural Mechanics, Air Force Flight Dynamics Laboratory Report AFFDL-TR-66-80, December 1965.

4. R. J. Melosh, "A Stiffness Matrix for the Analysis of Thin Plates in Bending," *Journal Aeronautical Science,* **28** (1961), 34.
5. R. H. Mallett and E. Helle, "Formulation and Evaluation of a Toroidal Ring Discrete Element," Bell Aerosystems Corporation Report No. 9500–941001, May 1966.
6. E. Helle, "Formulation and Evaluation of a Triangular Cross-Section Ring Discrete Element," Bell Aerosystems Corporation Report No. 9500-941-003, June 1966.
7. R. H. Mallett and S. Jordon, "Formulation and Evaluation of a Trapezoidal Cross-Section Ring Discrete Element," Bell Aerosystems Corporation Report No. 9500-941-004, November 1966.
8. R. Khol, "Super Program Spells Doom for Cut-and-Try Design," *Machine Design,* (February 24, 1972), 72–77.

CASE STUDY 16 Circuit Optimization and Sensitivity Analysis*

Introduction

Fortunately, power and availability of "package" circuit analysis programs has increased (1, 3) rapidly in response to the impact of integrated circuit technology on circuit design problem (4). Ultimately, however, the emphasis in computer-aided circuit design must turn from analysis—the necessary first step in design—to design optimization. To effect this transition, package programs would ideally be designed from the outset with the optimal design procedures clearly in mind. Optimization procedures must, therefore, be found which are compatible with the inherent realities of automated circuit analysis.

We propose, in the following, a variational approach to optimum switching circuit design which satisfies both of the above requirements. The approach is treated in the context of high-speed switching circuit design, but is easily applicable to other design problems such as those of low-power or large-scale integrated switching circuit design. Specifically, the class of problems addressed is that in which the dependence of the performance functional to be extremized on the set of design parameters is known only through the solution of nonlinear differential equations. This problem class has in the past necessitated the use of "step-and-repeat" methods for computing sensitivity of network performance to parameter variation. (1, 2, 5) The variational methods reported here provide an M-fold computational advantage over step-and-repeat methods in calculating the sensitivity of M designable parameters.

It turns out that the task of "dc" design—typically carried out by worst-case or Monte Carlo methods (6)—is necessarily included in the reported

* This case study is exerpted from G. D. Hachtel and R. A. Rohrer, "Techniques for the Optimal Design and Synthesis of Switching Circuits", *Proceedings of the IEEE,* **55,** 11 (November 1967), 1864–1877.

procedure for time domain optimization. The procedure is basically one of design parameter value synthesis and is specifically directed toward device design as well as circuit design. Thus, the design parameters are not elements of the circuit model themselves but physical parameters (e.g. base width) which indirectly influence several of the circuit elements simultaneously. In such cases, it is not meaningful to vary one circuit element and hold the others constant. The procedure assumes that the circuit configuration (e.g. emitter-follower-current switch) is given and is thus distinct from the configuration synthesis procedures recently reported (7).

The design procedure is based upon an expression for the vector sensitivity of a scalar performance function (e.g., delay, rise time, total dissipation, etc.) to variations in the set of design parameters. The expression is derived from the variational calculus (8) and both applies and extends the variational techniques of classical mechanics (9) and control theory (10). These techniques have been notably successful in the design problems of aerospace (11) and industrial (12) control. These techniques are applicable to switching problems; nevertheless, it has been found that an exclusively control-theoretic approach based on Pontryagin's Maximum Principle (13) strains the interfacial context of the presentation. Thus, a self-contained development based on the calculus of variations has been employed. Variational techniques have already been applied to circuit design problems by Rohrer (14) who achieved the synthesis of linear, distributed, lossy transmission lines.

Gradient methods (15) are employed in the procedure to use the scalar performance function and its vector sensitivity to iterate to an optimum set of design parameters. It is shown that if the parameter set is bounded, at least a local optimum exists. The problems of uniqueness and attainability of an optimum in this class of problems remain theoretically outstanding, but straightforward applications of the well-known steepest descent (16) and conjugate gradient (15) methods have worked well on model problems.

The High-Speed Switching Circuit Design Problem

The instantaneous state of the switching circuit to be optimized is assumed to be characterized by a state vector of N components.

$$x \equiv \text{col}(x_1, x_2, x_3, \cdots x_N), \qquad (1)$$

where N is the number of independent degrees of freedom in the circuit. The state vector x is constrained to satisfy the set of N first-order ordinary differential equations

$$\dot{x} = F(x, p, t), \qquad (2)$$

which will be referred to as the state equations. The symbol p in (2) represents a vector of M designable parameters; that is,

$$p \equiv \text{col}(p_1, p_2, \cdots p_M), \tag{3}$$

where the vector p is bounded by parameter bounding vectors pu and pl, so that

$$pl \le p \le pu; \tag{4}$$

pl and pu are determined by economic or technological limitations. The components of p are regarded as the design variables of the circuit. In an integrated circuit, for example, these parameters would ideally be mask dimensions, starting resistivities, diffusion and epitaxial concentrations, time and temperatures. In a conventional lumped circuit it would be appropriate for p to be a vector of actual circuit element values, i.e., resistances, capacitances, etc. In general, however, a model must intervene between the actual structure of the circuit and its analytical representation. Note that the relationship of model to circuit is such that it would be possible for one circuit parameter to affect the value of every element in the circuit model.

By definition, the components of p are constrained to remain constant as the transient response evolves. That is,

$$\dot{p} = 0. \tag{5}$$

The above circuit design problem is formulated mathematically as follows:

Choose the design vector p so that the integral scalar performance functional

$$P(p) = \int_0^{t_f} h(x(p, t), p, t)\, dt$$

of the instantaneous performance function $h(x(p,t),p,t)$, is minimum.

The minimization is to be accomplished iteratively, with decisions on updating p made in terms of the scalar performance function $p(p)$ and the vector gradient

$$\frac{\partial P}{\partial p} = \frac{\partial}{\partial p} \int_0^{t_f} h(x, p, t)\, dt$$

of P in the M-dimensional Cartesian space of designable parameters.

The difficulty in obtaining the gradient

$$\frac{\partial P}{\partial p} = \frac{\partial}{\partial p} \int_0^{t_f} h(x(t, p)p, t)\, dt$$

E. ANALYSIS AND OPTIMIZATION

is that the value of the state vector x at time t depends on p. However $\partial x(p, t)/\partial p$ may not be obtained analytically because the functional dependence of x on p and t is known only through solution of the state differential equations (2). This difficulty is overcome by the introduction of a Lagrangian function

$$L(x, p, \lambda, \mu, t) \equiv h(x, p, t) + \lambda^T(\dot{x} - F(x, p, t)) + \mu^T \dot{p},$$

where $\lambda^T \equiv (\lambda_1, \lambda_2 \ldots \lambda_N)$ is a row vector of the same dimension (N) as x, and $\mu^T \equiv (\mu_1, \mu_2 \ldots \mu_M)$ is a row vector of the same dimension (M) as p. Thus, $\lambda^T(\dot{x} - F)$ and $\mu^T \dot{p}$ are scalar, or inner, products. The λ-vector will be referred to as the adjoint state vector and the μ-vector as the adjoint parameter vector.

It is recognized that the Lagrangian function $L(x, p, t)$ is identically equal to the differential performance function $h(x, p, t)$ if the constraints (2) and (5) are satisfied (i.e., if $\dot{p} = 0$ and $\dot{x} = F(x, p, t)$, so that

$$P(p) = \int_0^{t_f} L(x, \dot{x}, p, \dot{p}, t, \lambda, \mu) \, dt.$$

Computational Procedure

The calculation required for gradient determination may be appreciated by reference to the flow chart of Figure IIE16-1. Newton-Raphson type iterative solution of the equibibrium equation $\dot{x}_0 = F(x_0, p) = 0$ is required. Second, the non-linear state equation (2) must be solved in forward time and the x-vector saved as a function of time. The final (initial in backward time) value of the adjoint state vector is then obtained. Third, the linear time-varying adjoint state equations must be solved with time running backwards in the integration, and the adjoint state vector being saved as a function of time. Finally, the saved x- and λ-vectors are used to determine the integrand

$$\frac{\partial h(x[t], p)}{\partial p} - \lambda^T(t) \frac{\partial F(x[t], p, t)}{\partial p}$$

of the gradient integral-summation (actually, the gradient integral-summation may be included in the backward time) adjoint state equation integration loop of Figure IIE16-1). For a limited number of cases this process may be carried out analytically, but, in general, gradient calculation is suited primarily to digital computation.

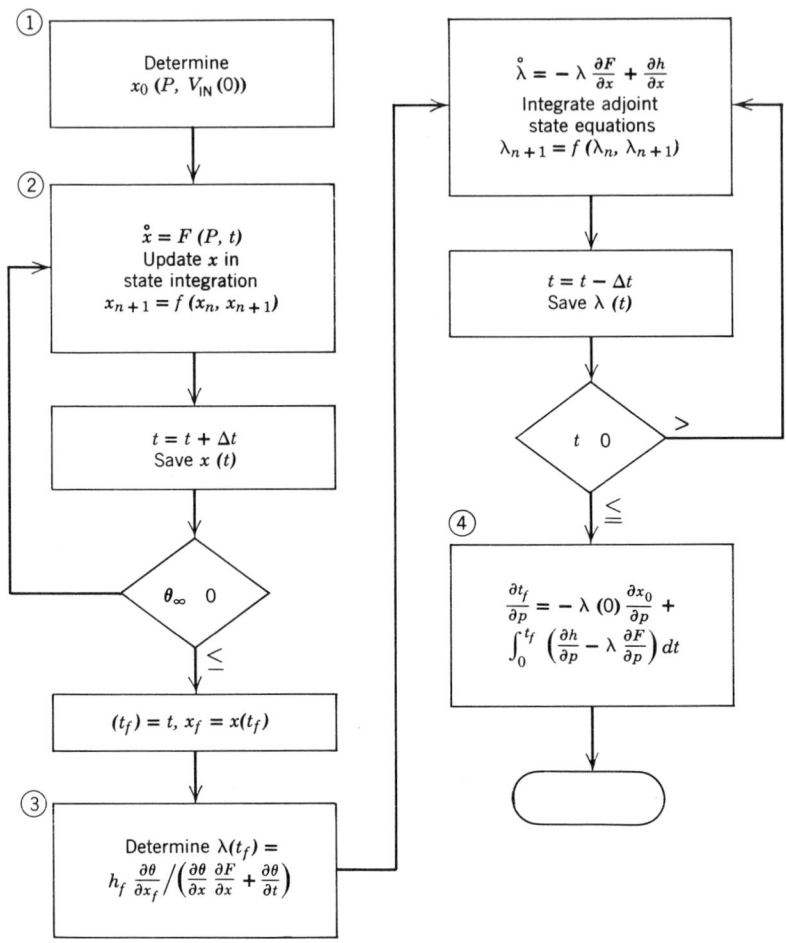

Figure IIE16-1. Flow chart for performance gradient calculation.

Optimal Design Examples

We now treat two examples of two-parameter optimization—for simplicity, a series RLC circuit, and for reality, a current switch with nonlinear, Ebers-Moll, transistor models. The step-driven series RIC circuit is shown in Figure IIE16-2a. The circuit is to synthesize the response (Figure IIE16-2b)

$$V_D(t) = 1 - e^{-t} \cos \pi t$$

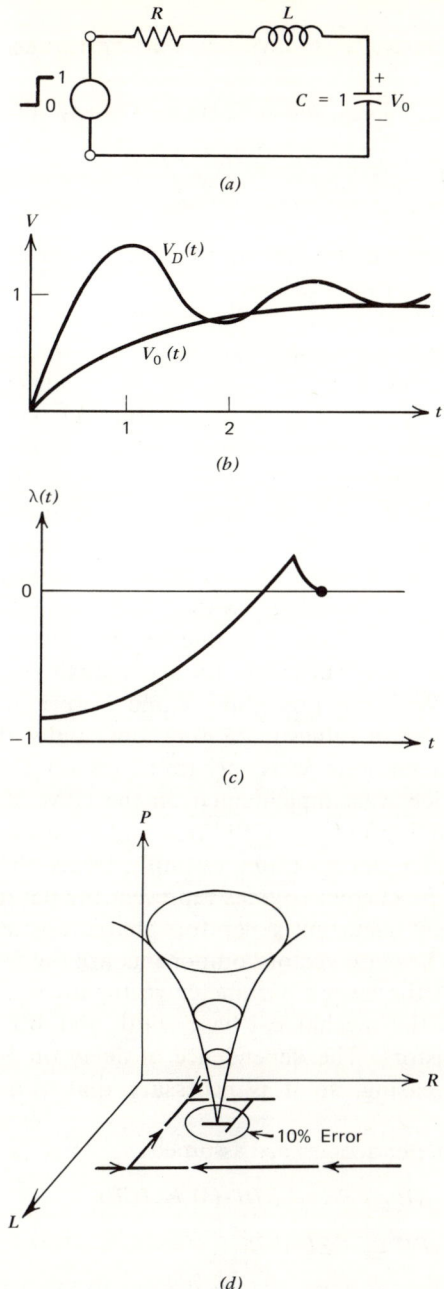

Figure IIE16-2. Series RLC parameter synthesis. (*a*) RLC circuit. (*b*) Specified and calculated voltages. (*c*) Adjoint state variable. (*d*) Iteration to vicinity of optimum.

over the interval (0,2). Thus, the performance function is chosen to be

$$P = \int_0^2 \sqrt{(V_D(t) - V_0(t))^2} \Big/ (V_D(\infty) - V_D(0)) \, dt$$

In this contrived example, it is known that the answer is $R = 2L$, $C = 1$, $L = (1 + \pi^2)^{-1}$. The starting guess ($R = 2$, $L = 2$, $C = 1$), solution 1, is labeled $V_0{}^{(1)}$ in Figure IIC16-2b.

The adjoint variable $\lambda_0(t)$ is shown in Figure IIC16-2c. The cusp is due to the fact that the driving function $2h/2x$ of the adjoint equation jumps discontinuously from -1 to $+1$ as V_0 passes through V_D. The existence of such cusps complicates the integration procedure considerably.

A conjugate gradient type of integration procedure was employed. Shown in Figure IIE16-2d is the concave, flaired-conical surface of the performance function in the P, L, R space. The projection of the performance function point onto the $P = 0$ plane is marked by arrows which denote the search for optimum R (with L fixed) or vice versa. Each one-parameter search first brackets the value which minimizes P. It was found that five iterations were sufficient to accomplish each successive one-parameter search. With this procedure R and L were brought to within 10 percent of their optimum values in 23 iterations, and within 1 percent in 72 iterations. The calculations were programmed on the APL 360 time-sharing system which was implemented on the IBM 360, Model 50 computer. This required 3 minutes of CPU (Central Processing Unit) time.

The current switch optimization example treats the circuit shown in Figure IIE16-3a. The current sources represent the parallel combination of diodes and dependent α-current generators characteristic of the Ebers-Moll transistor model. The state vector components are the 5 capacitor voltages. The components of the design parameter vector are chosen to be WB and WE, where WB is the mechanical base width and WE the emitter stripe width of the transistors. The dependence of delay on WE is known to be monotonically increasing, so it is necessary that WE be given a lower bound.

The following dependencies are assumed:

$$RB \triangleq RS + RBI \cdot (WE/WB)$$

$$TE \triangleq TEI \cdot WB^2$$

$$I_{E1,2} \triangleq IESI(WE/WB)(e^{QV_{CE1,2}/KT} - 1)$$

$$C_{E1,2} \triangleq CJEI \cdot WE + \frac{Q}{KT} I_{E1,2} \cdot TE.$$

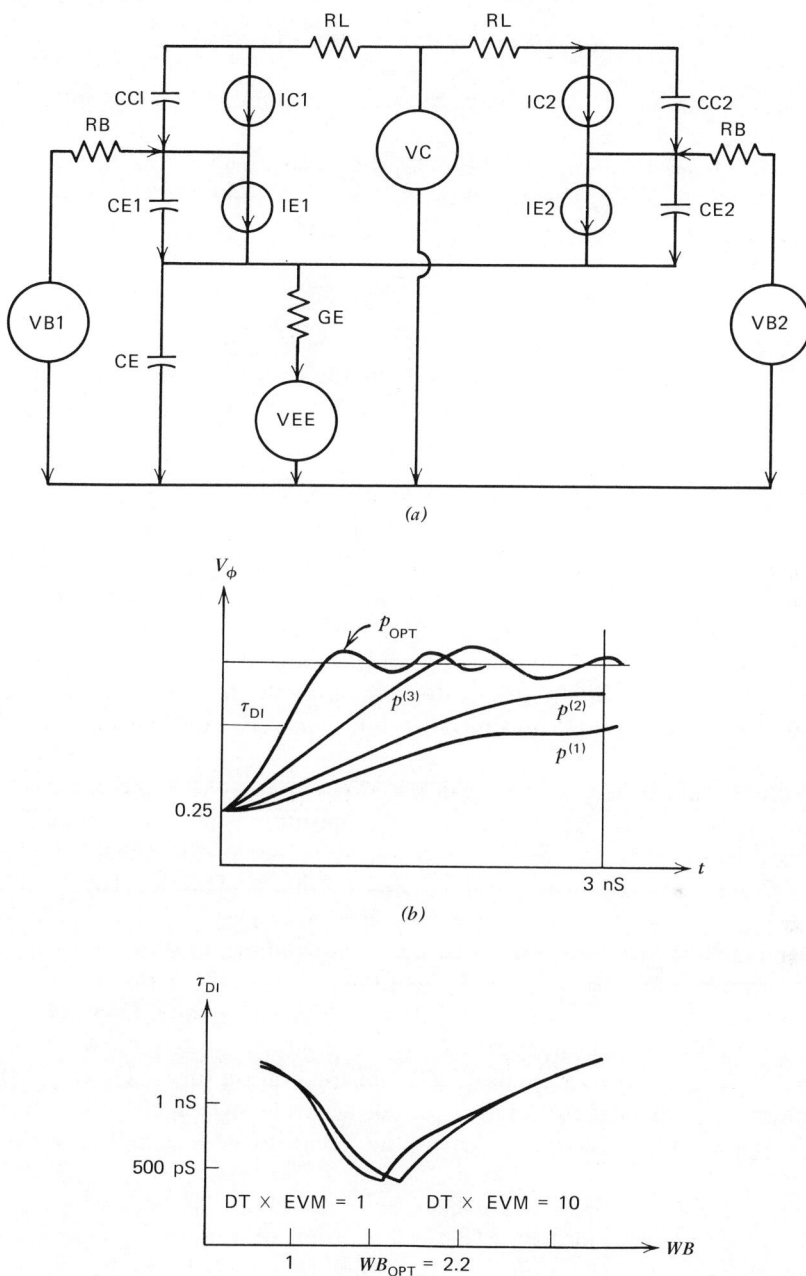

Figure IIE16-3. Current switch optimization. (*a*) Current switch circuit. (*b*) Ideal and calculated in-phase outputs. (*c*) Ideal delay versus base width.

The parameter values were normalized to a nominal corresponding to $RBI = 50\ \Omega$, $TEI = 30$ ps.

It was desired to minimize the delay between an ideal in-phase output voltage step from $V_{\min} = 0.25$ volt to $V_{\max} = 1$ volt, and the actual in-phase output voltage (Figure IIE16-3b). Thus, the performance function was chosen to be

$$P = \int_0^{t_f} \frac{\sqrt{(V_{ID}(t) - V_\phi(t))^2}}{(V_{\max} - V_{\min})}\, dt$$

with t_f chosen to be 3 ns. Steps 1)–4) of the procedure were carried out modifying the only initial state. The radius ϵ of the (circular) initial target set θ_0 was chosen to be 5 mV. Starting with $WE = 1$, $WE = 1$, this set was attained in 7 Newton-like iterations.

A steepest descent minimization technique was employed. WE reached its lower bound in 11 iterations; condition (19) remained satisfied at $WE = pl_2 = 0.1$ as WE was iterated in 12 further steps to an interior optimum of $WE = 2.2$. The minimum ideal delay was ~ 500 ps. Note that increaing WB and decreasing WE from the nominal has the effect of trading off (profitably) increased transit time TE for decreased base resistance.

The 33 iterations required 66 integrations of the 5 × 5 systems of differential equations. This consumed 1.5 hours of APL 360, IBM Model 50 CPU time.

The variation of C_{Dt} with WE in the $WE = pl_2 = 0.1$ plane is shown in Figure IIE16-3c. The apparent cusp at the optimum is not understood. Two curves are shown, which demonstrate the influence of the integration step size DT on the location of the predicted optimum. The quantity EVM is defined as the modulus of the eigenvalue of largest modulus, and corresponds to the linearized circuit at the final equilibrium state. For explicit integration schemes (e.g. Runge-Kutta) the product $DT \cdot EVM$ must be on the order of unity. With the implicit integration algorithms employed, numerical stability is obtained for $DT \cdot EVM$ products ten to a hundred times larger. The larger time step allows shorter integration times. However, this economy is traded off for a slight loss of accuracy, which could be serious whenever it is necessary to know the location of the optimum very precisely.

More recent implementations have been run under the operating system OS/360, rather than in APL. The optimization procedures have been carried out on the 360/91 for circuits containing over 1000 elements.

Conclusions

The variational, time domain methods presented constitute a basis for a radical, but increasingly necessary, departure in the design and synthesis of switching circuits and other nonlinear networks. These methods reduce the time domain optimization problem to that of minimizing the magnitude of a function given its value and the value of its gradient in the space of its arguments. The variational methods are computationally efficient, in that they provide an M-fold computational advantage and are designed for the exploitation of spareseness. The mathematical framework embodied in the flow chart of Figure IIE16-1 is well suited (even the differentiation required for forming the arrays $2h/2p$, $2F/2p$, and $s/2p$ may be done symbolically) for incorporation into a package program for automated circuit analysis.

Fast convergence to an optimum has been demonstrated for simple problems (the APL 360 system is 10 to 50 times slower than FORTRAN on the IBM 7094). This should prompt designers to use the method on more complex problems. It is therefore foreseen that performance function and gradient determination may take so long on very large problems that significant future research will be required on fast integration methods and strategies for descending down the gradient toward an optimum.

In general, it is concluded that the variational method will be most useful in cases where complicated trade-offs prevent the designer from securing reliable intuition about design criteria, and most necessary in situations like repetitive switching circuits where a highly designed basic building block is profitable.

Acknowledgement

The authors are indebted to R. A. Willoughby, D. Chazan, W. L. Miranker, and N. L. Wong for the interchange of ideas and stimulating discussion. The numerical results owe a special debt to discussions with R. A. Willoughby.

References

1. "1620 Electronic Circuit Analysis Program (ECAP)," Application Program 1620-EE-C2X, IBM Corporation, Data Processing Division, White Plains, N.Y.
2. "Automated Digital Computer Program for Determining Responses of Electronic Systems to Transient Nuclear Radiation," Vol. 11, IBM Space Guidance Center, Oswego, N.Y., Technical Report AFWI-TR-66-126.
3. F. F. Kuc, "Network Analysis by Digital Computer," *Proceedings of the IEEE*, **54**, (June 1966), 820–829.
4. F. H. Eranin, Jr., "Computer Methods of Network Analysis," *Proceedings of the IEEE*, November 1967, 1787.
5. A. F. Malmberg, F. I. Cornwell, and F. N. Hofer, "Net-1 Network Analysis Program," Los Alamos, N. Mex., Rept. LA-31119, 1964.

6. A. G. Kennard, "ASAP—An Automated Statistical Analysis Program," IBM Corporation, Technical Report, 1142, June 1964.
7. R. A. Rohrer, "Fully Automated Network Design by Digital Computer: Preliminary Considerations," *Proceedings of the IEEE*, November 1967, 1929.
   L. C. Hill, D. C. Pederson, and R. S. Pepper, "Synthesis of Electronic Bistable Circuits," *IEEE Transactions Circuit Theory*, **CT-10,** (March 1963), (25–35.)
8. L. E. Elsgole, *Calculus of Variations*, Addison-Wesley, Reading, Mass., 1962.
9. H. Goldstein, *Classical Mechanics*, Addison-Wesley, Reading, Mass, 1962.
10. R. E. Kalman, "The Theory of Optimal Control and the Calculus of Variations," Research Institute for Advanced Studies, Baltimore, Md., RIAS Rept. G1-3, 1961.
11. R. E. Bellman, I. Glicksberg, and O. A. Gross, "On the Bang-Bang Control Problem," *Quarterly of Applied Mathematics,* **14,** (1956), 11–18. Also, "Numerical Techniques in Optimization," *IEEE International Convention Digest,* 1967, 26–31.
12. M. Athens and P. L. Falb, *Optimal Control*, McGraw-Hill, New York, 1966.
13. L. S. Pontryagin, V. G. Boltyanski, R. B. Gamkredlidge, and E. F. Mischenke, *The Mathematical Theory of Optimal Processes*, Interscience, New York, 1962.
14. R. A. Rohrer, "Synthesis of Arbitrarily Tapered Lossy Transmission Lines," presented at Symposium on Generalized Networks, Polytechnic Institute of Brooklyn, April 1966.
15. G. Leitmann, *Optimization Techniques*, Academic Press, New York, 1962.
16. A. E. Eryson and W. Denham, "A Steepest-Ascent Method for Solving Optimum Programming Problems," *Journal Applied Mechanics Transactions ASME,* **84,** ser. E. June 1962, 247–257m.
17. N. L. Wong, "Switching Circuit optimization," Master's thesis, Department of Electrical Engineering, University of California, Berkeley, May 1967.
18. G. D. Hachtel and R. A. Willoughby, "On the Computational Use of the Jacobian in Circuit Analysis," presented at Asilomar Conference on Circuit and System Theory, Asilomar, Calif., November 1967.
19. N. Sato, and W. F. Tinney, "Techniques for Exploiting the Sparsity of the Network Admittance Matrix," *IEEE Transactions Power and Apparatus,* **82,** (December 1963) 944–950.
   W. F. Tinney and J. W. Walker, "Direct Solutions of Sparse Network Equations by Optimally Ordered Triangular Factorization," *Proceedings of the IEEE,* (November 1967), p. 1801.
20. P. D. Crout, "A Short Method for Evaluating Determinants and Solving Systems of Linear Equations with Real or Complex Coefficients," *Transactions AIEE,* **60,** (1941), 1235–1241.
21. E. S. Kuh and R. A. Rohrer, "The State-Variable Approach to Network Analysis," *Proceedings of the IEEE,* **53,** (July 1965), 672–686.
22. C. G. Broyden, "A Class of Methods for Solving Nonlinear Simulataneous Equations," *Mathematical Computation,* **19,** (October 1965), 577–593.
23. A. D. Falkoff and K. E. Iverson, "The APL Terminal System: Instructions for Operations," IBM Thomas J. Watson Research Center, Yorktown Heights, N.Y.
24. F. Gustavson, W. Liniger, and R. Willoughby, "Symbolic Generation at an Optimal Crout Algorithm for Sparse Systems of Linear Algebraic Equations," to be published.

F. EXPERIMENTATION

While the formulation of a problem has led to the design of various solution concepts and to the analysis and optimization of these competing designs, it also leads, through the definition of requirements and specifications, to the execution of certain experiments and tests. The intent of these tests is to determine the feasibility of the various designs and to determine which design best meets the requirements.

The main role of the computer in this phase is the control of experiments, testers, and prototype processes. Three case studies have been selected to demonstrate these functions.

Case study 17, "Automobile Traffic Control," describes the monitoring and controlling of traffic in the Lincoln Tunnel, on an experimental basis, from a computer in a research laboratory 40 miles distant.

Case study 18, "Controlling Manufacturing Processes" describes some of the direct and indirect consequences of using a computer, rather than special hardware, for controlling manufacturing processes, with emphasis on the testing of components and assemblies. This case study introduces the notion of hierarchical computer systems, a topic to be discussed at length in subsequent sections.

Case study 19, "Control of Thermonuclear Experiments," describes the control of large-scale, extremely important and potentially hazardous experiments. The ideas of ultrareliability and fail-safe design are introduced.

CASE STUDY 17 Automobile Traffic Control—The Lincoln Tunnel*

Introduction

Digital computers were first introduced for the control of urban traffic lights in Toronto, in 1959. An IBM 650 computer, one of the earliest general purpose digital computers, was adapted for the control of nine traffic lights using a variety of mixes of traffic control strategies (2). The experiment demonstrated the flexibility of a computerized system in responding to a wide variety of traffic situations. In the early 1960s, the city of Toronto obtained a large computer system built around a Univac 1107 computer, for the control of some 1000 intersections. Since then,

---

* This case study has been excerpted from Gazis (1).

CURRENT USAGE: CASE STUDIES AND CRITIQUES

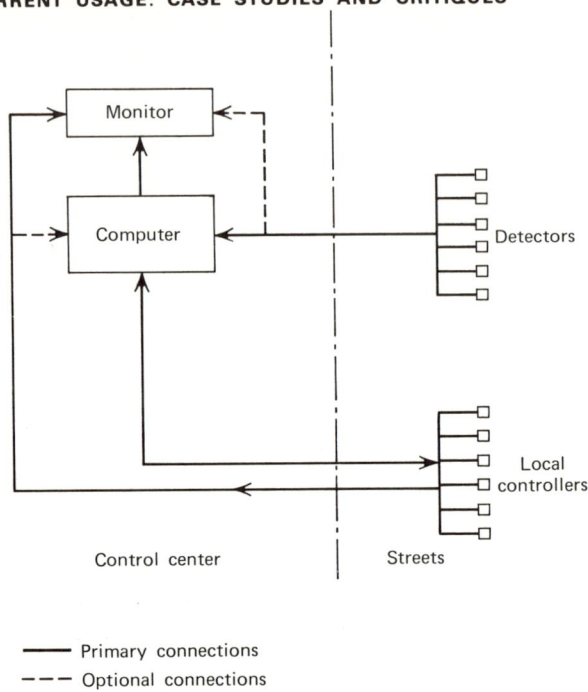

Figure IIF17-1. The basic elements of a computerized traffic control system.

other studies have been undertaken for the purpose of developing computer-based hardware configurations and control methodologies. Among these are the study (3) undertaken by the city of San Jose, Calif., and IBM, in 1964, and two studies in Great Britain undertaken by the British Ministry of Transport, one being carried out in West London (4) and one in Glasgow (5,6). Today, there are several systems in operation, both in this country and abroad, and the computerization of traffic control is a clearly established trend. I shall divide the discussion of such systems into a discussion of hardware and software.

All computerized traffic control systems contain the basic elements shown in Figure IIF17-1. There is a detection system that measures traffic, a central computer which houses the control logic, a system of local controllers which operate the traffic lights, and monitoring equipment.

Radar, sonar, treadles, and magnetic loops have been the most widely used detectors, with the magnetic loops holding an edge in reliability and low maintenance costs. Exotic methods of detection such as processing of a TV signal sweep have not gone past the conceptual stage.

Reports on computerized traffic control systems have been plentiful, and generally laudatory. The intent of some of these reports has been not only to evaluate the performance of the systems according to some objectives, but also to provide justification for these systems in terms of cost effectiveness arguments. Generally speaking, the measured reduction of delay, converted into dollars, appears to pay for the system within something of the order of a year. While some economists may argue with an economic analysis which considers only two alternatives, something or nothing, the cost effectiveness computations appear to be convincingly in favor of a computerized system. There is, however, one weakness in most of these analyses: more often than not, the improvements quoted are due to a new synchronization scheme, made on the basis of better traffic date. Thus the true contribution of the computer systems has been lumped together with the effectiveness of a new synchronization technique, a fact not overlooked by some critics. A reasonably accurate assessment of the experience with computerized systems, in broad terms, might be the following.

The computer makes the collection and updating of traffic data easy, and hence facilitates the design of a good synchronization scheme. Although the implementation of this scheme may be possible with hardware that predates computers, the computer allows easy implementation, updating, and multiple choice of synchronization schemes through software changes. Perhaps the greatest asset of a computerized system is exactly the fact that it allows maximum flexibility for implementation of current or future control algorithms. Moreover, computerized systems have become increasingly acceptable as their cost, per traffic light, has become comparable to that of noncomputerized multi-dial systems.

The Lincoln Tunnel

The Lincoln Tunnel of New York City is a unique traffic facility in many respects. Its six lanes, in three tubes, are subject to heavy demand in both directions, eastbound and westbound, during the rush periods. Some balancing of the demand is achieved by reversing the direction of traffic on one or both of the lanes of the center tube. The optimum allocation of reversible lanes is an interesting problem in itself and has been the subject of a previous paper (8). The tunnel also displays dramatically the degradation of service due to congestion. When densities exceed about 55 cars/mi. the throughput of the tunnel falls from an observed average of 1200 cars/lane/h to about 1100 cars/lane/h. Starting in 1959, the Port of New York Authority which operates the tunnel, experimented with the idea of controlling the input into the tunnel in order to prevent its jamming. Some

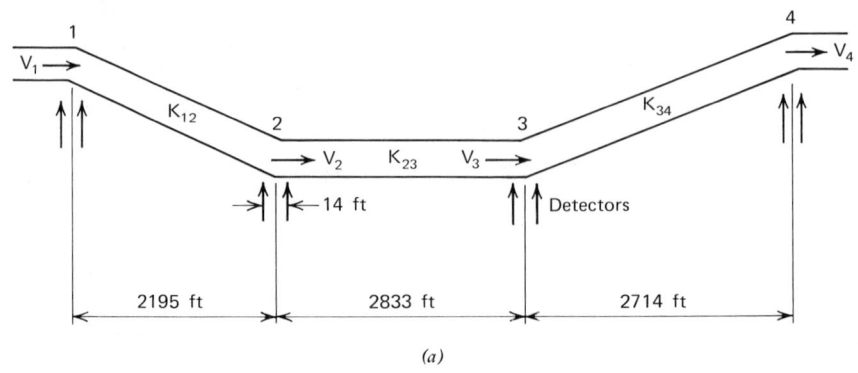

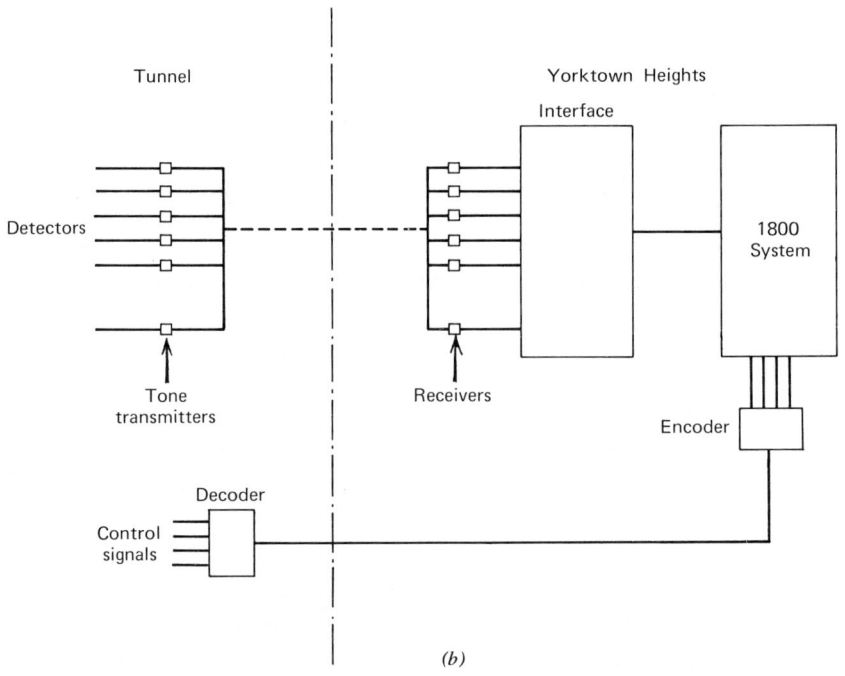

Figure IIF17-2. The south tube, Lincoln Tunnel. (a) Geometric configuration of the South Tube of Lincoln Tunnel. (b) Geometric and hardware configurations of the experimental traffic control system used at the Lincoln Tunnel.

early experiments (8-10) proved the idea fruitful. However, in those experiments the effectiveness of input control was limited by the inability to measure and respond to the actual traffic conditions inside the tunnel.

In 1966 the Port of New York Authority and IBM initiated a joint study aiming at the development of computer-based control methodology for the Tunnel. In the course of this study, two main system configurations were used. Both comprised tunnel instrumentation, a communication link, and a computer installation located at the IBM Research Center, about forty miles away from the tunnel. I shall describe only the final configuration of the system which was in use until the end of the joint study, in June 1969. A more detailed discussion of the systems used, the control methodologies and the experimental results have been given in (11, 12).

The geometric and hardware configuration of the experimental control system are shown in Figure IIF17-2. Eight pairs of photocell detectors, 14 ft. apart, were placed at four locations along both lanes of the eastbound South tube. The four locations were the entrance, foot of the downgrade, foot of the upgrade, and exit. The signals from these detectors were multiplexed by means of tone transmitters and transmitted via a telephone line to Yorktown Heights. There, they were "unscrambled" by matching receivers, converted into machine words by an interface, and then processed on-line by an 1800 computer. The processing produced, in successive stages, the following information:

1. It yielded accurate computation of the speed and length of each vehicle passing over a pair of dectors.
2. It made possible the determination of the exact number of cars in each section of the tunnel lane between pairs of detectors. This was done by recognizing the pattern of successive lengths of cars over two consecutive pairs of detectors. It was the most accurate determination of traffic density accomplished anywhere.
3. It produced a control command, which was encoded and transmitted from Yorktown Heights to the tunnel over another telephone line. The control command regulated control devices at the entrance of both lanes of the South tube. These devices comprised traffic lights and special signs which had the overall effect of reducing the input rate into the tunnel by about 30 percent. The decision whether such control was necessary or not was made by the computer on the basis of an adaptive control algorithm developed through analysis of extensive measurements of the performance of the tunnel. Briefly, the algorithm defines domains in state space, where the state variables are the densities in different sections of the tunnel, corresponding to dif-

ferent control requirements. The boundaries between domains may be shifted by the use of a scaling factor which depends on the speed at the foot of the upgrade which is the most frequently observed bottleneck of the system. This particular adaptive feature had the effect of accounting for unobservable influences, mostly outside the tunnel. It tended to impose input control more frequently when the observed speeds did not quite "jibe" with the observed densities.

4. Finally, the computer printed monitoring information on the on-line printer, and stored records of the traffic and control data for future off-line study.

The results of the experiment were consistently satisfactory. Throughput during controlled conditions was about 10 percent higher than during uncontrolled conditions. In addition, the smooth flow of traffic reduced car breakdown due to overheating and the ventilation requirements of the tunnel. Currently, all of the lanes of the Lincoln and Holland Tunnels are being instrumented along similar lines, with two Hewlett-Packard computers of the mini range at each of these two sites providing the heart of the control system.

References

1. D. C. Gazis, "Traffic Control: From Hand Signals to Computers," *Proceedings of the IEEE*, July 1971, and IBM Research Report RC3194, December 22, 1970.
2. S. Cass and L. Casciato, "Centralized Traffic Signal Control by a General Purpose Computer," *Proceedings of the Institute of Traffic Engineering*, 1960, 203–211.
3. "San Jose Traffic Control Project—Final Report," IBM Corporation, Data Processing Report, San Jose, Calif., December 1966; see also D. C. Gazis and O. Bermant, "Dynamic Traffic Control Systems and the San Jose Experiment," *Proceedings 8th International Study Week in Traffic Engineering*, Barcelona, Spain, 1966, Vol. V. 1–9.
4. A. B. Williams, "Area Traffic Control in West London Assessment of First Experiment," *Traffic Engineering and Control*, **10** (1969) 125–134.
5. J. A. Hillier, "Glasgow's Experiment in Area Traffic Control," *Traffic Engineering and Control*, **8** (1965) 502–509.
6. J. A. Hillier, "Area Traffic Control by Computer—Equipment in the Glasgow Experiment," *Traffic Engineering and Control*, **9** (1968), 496–498.
7. D. C. Gazis and C. H. Knapp, "On-line Estimation of traffic densities from Time series of flow and speed data," IBM Research Report, RC2997, August 1970, submitted for publication.
8. H. Greenberg and A. Daou, "The Control of Traffic Flow to Increase the Flow," *Operations Research*, **8** (1960) 524–532.

9. W. Crowley and I. Greenberg, "Holland Tunnel Study Aids Efficient Increase of Tube's Use," *Traffic Engineering*, **35** 20 (March 1965).
10. R. S. Foote, "Instruments for Road Transportation," *High Speed Ground Transport Journal*, May 1968.
11. B. T. Bennett, D. C. Gazis, L. C. Edie, and R. S. Foote, "Control of the Lincoln Tunnel Traffic by an On-Line Digital Computer," *Proceedings 4th International Symposium Traffic Theory*, Bonn, Germany, 1969, pp. 48–56.
12. D. C. Gazis and R. S. Foote, "Surveillance and Control of Tunnel Traffic by an On-Line Digital Computer," *Transportation Science*, **3** (1959) 255–275.
13. D. C. Gazis, "Estimation of Traffic Densities at the Lincoln Tunnel from Time Series of Flow and Speed Data," IBM Research Report, RC 3500, July 30, 1971.
14. D. C. Gazis, "Traffic Control: Theory and Application," IBM Research Report, RC 3720, February 4, 1972.

CASE STUDY 18 Controlling Manufacturing Processes*

Abstract

Historically, control functions for "make" and "test" operations in discrete manufacturing processes have been satisfied with special purpose hardware. In recent years, computers have replaced much of this special purpose hardware. The initial reasons for employing computers were to decrease capital and development costs while providing greater flexibility in responding to process changes. It now appears that the greatest benefits of applying computers in discrete manufacturing processes are the increased process yields and decreased rework through the use of Process Control Data. The process information which computers have easy access to can be used in a variety of ways to assist in controlling discrete processes.

This paper gives examples and discusses aspects of Process Control Data acquisition, analysis, and report techniques, and how these techniques are used to improve discrete processes. Also discussed are some of the more important requirements for evolving toward an integrated process control system such as production traceability, systems architecture, data collection and data management.

Introduction.

A discrete manufacturing process consists of the following operations: 1. Receiving inspection where parts or raw materials enter a process; 2.

---

* This case study has been excerpted from R. A. Bradford and J. E. Stuehler, "The Role of Process Data in Controlling and Optimizing Manufacturing Processes,", *IEEE Transactions on Manufacturing Technology*, June 1972, Vol. MFT-1, No. 1, pp. 5–9.

Process, fabrication and assembly operations such as plating, etching, casting, joining or machining; 3. "In process" measurement and test where process and product characteristics and parameters are monitored; and 4. Final test or inspection which is the last step in a discrete process where the product is measured against specifications and design criteria.

Traditionally, the complex test and process control operations in such discrete processes have been performed by sophisticated custom hardware. Such equipment lacks versatility since it must be modified to react to process changes and scrapped in cases of product evolution. The impact of process or product changes can be minimized with the use of computer control systems. In the application of such systems, control functions are executed by software which is relatively easy to modify in order to react to process and product changes. Functions performed by hardware can be limited to that necessary to interface a computer to the product or process (e.g., channel interfaces and signal conditioning). In addition to controlling testers and process equipment, the computer can be programmed to perform application data analysis. Product measurement data and process parameters can be obtained and translated for communication to operators. Such information can be compared to constants in order to make accept/reject decisions, establish process set points and qualify measurements for later engineering analysis. In addition to handling control information, the computer control system can report tester and process equipment behavior in order to determine maintenance and calibration requirements. Quality and Production Control data such as defects per units, in process inventory, and yields can also be extracted from information collected by the computer.

Figure IIF18-1 is an illustration of a discrete process where dedicated data processing systems interface to process operations. As shown, the receiving inspection, in process and final testers are independently controlled by computers. The input/output devices (I/0) attached to the computer are used to contain test programs and accumulate and report process behavior and test results.

A current trend in industries employing such control computers is a movement from dedicated computer applications (Fig. IIF18-1) to hierarchical computer configurations as illustrated in Figure IIF18-2. The primary characteristic of the hierarchical system is the connection of multiple satellite control computers applied in the process, to a larger central system. As illustrated, several test and process operation computers are connected to a central computer system. The computing power of the central system reduces the size requirements of the satellite control computers by providing processing capabilities for program assemblies, process data analysis and reporting.

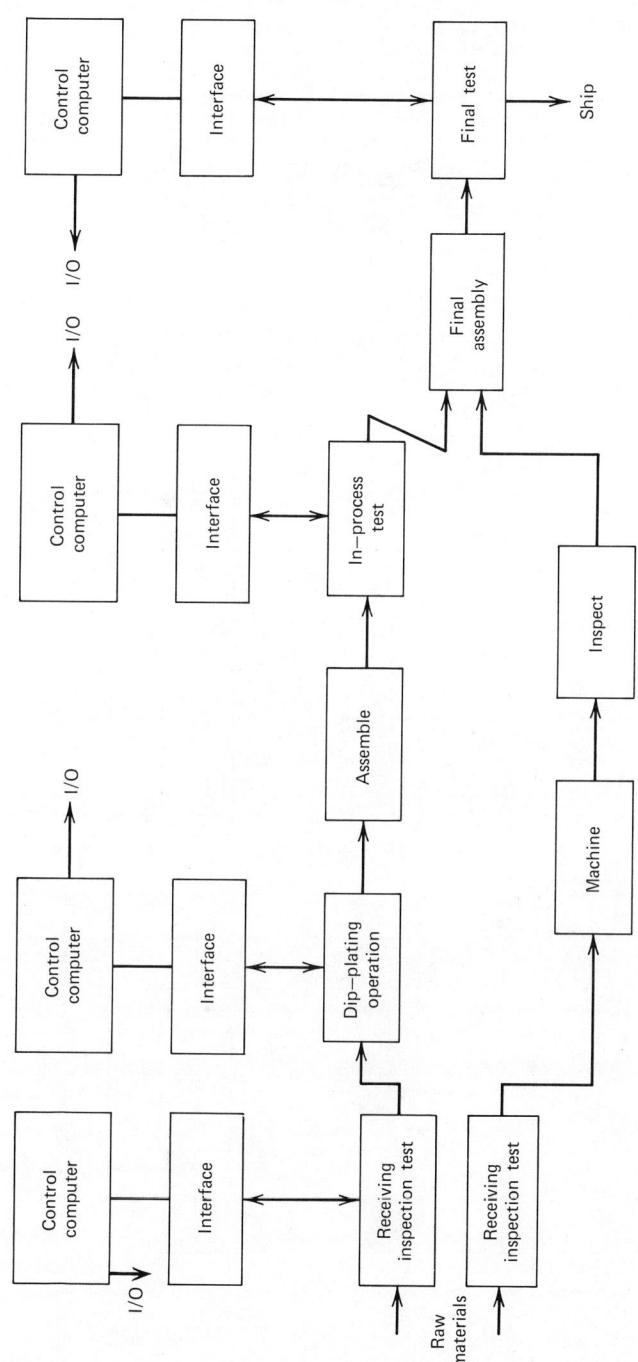

Figure IIF18-1. Stand-alone process control system.

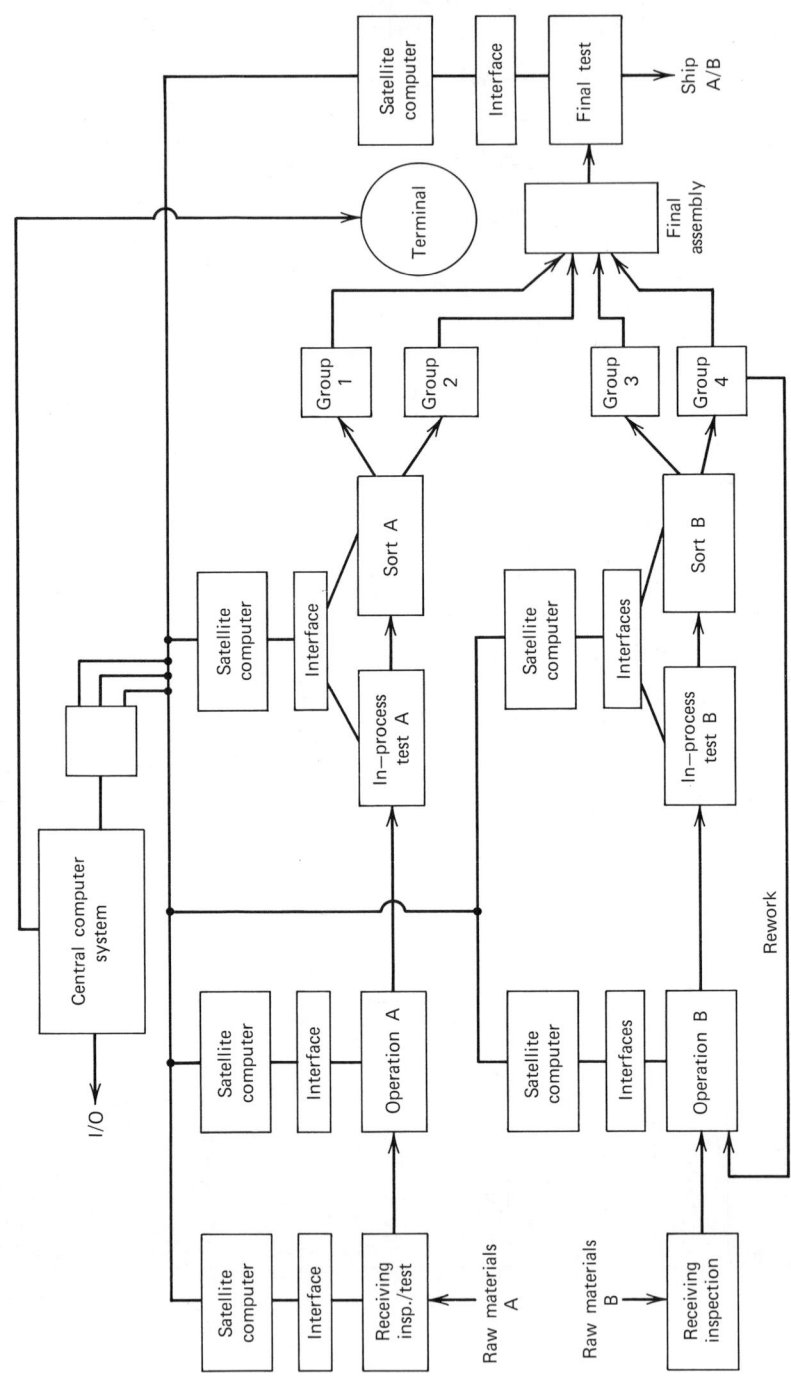

Figure IIF18-2. Hierarchical process control system.

The central system provides the main data base thus saving the need for I/0 at the satellite level. Significant data processing equipment cost savings can be realized by reducing satellite system size and I/0. In addition to providing data base facilities for collection of process information, the central system also is the common source for satellite control programs, test and calibration sub-routines and process control constants. This data can be shared by multiple satellites and is easily updated to compensate for process changes. The central system must be able to quickly service requests from satellite controllers on a real time basis in order to prevent process operations from "waiting" for communication transactions. Central systems subroutines operating in real time to service specific requests such as satellite program load, can also be shared by multiple satellite controllers. Besides satellite support, the central system can also support other real time applications such as terminal data collection hardware which may be required to satisfy additional process and man/machine information requirements.

The most important benefit of the hierarchical system configuration is that all data collected from satellite systems is combined at a central point. This facilitates either real time or batch data analysis to interrelate process and product parameters obtained throughout a discrete process. This interrelation of data between process steps is vital in gaining higher levels of process/product knowledge in order to improve discrete processes.

Using Process Control Data

Once computers have been installed in a discrete manufacturing process, reliable process information may be easily collected. The analysis of such data is now becoming the most significant aspect of applying computers in manufacturing. The collection and analysis of this data is essential in helping Process Engineers to better understand and control complex discrete processes. Development of collection and analysis techniques can be evolutionary. The experience gained through setting up one process control analysis project will be invaluable since techniques learned can be applied to other production processes. The first step in the evolutionary use of process data is to allow the central computer system to be used to collect and record raw process and product data from satellites. This data is used to report current product/process measurements and may be used as history to compare newer data when process problems occur. Examples of this raw data are: mechanical and electrical measurements taken from automatic testers and measurement devices, and process information such as chemical bath chacteristics or oven temperatures.

As a next step, the central computer of a hierarchical system can be used for data analysis. Programs may be developed which generate histograms to plot the distribution of data. With this tool, Process Engineers can define process capabilities and identify process shifts when comparing current data against history. Correlation programs can be employed to identify significant process parameters. In a complex, discrete process, it is important to establish specifications for product components as they are being manufactured in order to control process parameters. Histogram and correlation studies may be used to compare product parameters from one point in the discrete process to those at another point in order to determine interaction, significance and tolerance. For instance, if electrical components are tested prior to assembly in a complex circuit, it is possible to relate final circuit performance to the component characteristics. Key components and their tolerance requirements can be identified by correlating the distribution of component measurements to the distribution of final test readings. There are three approaches that can be used here. The first is to examine the current process data for parameter interrelationships. The second is to examine historical data in the same way. The third and best approach is to experiment with the current process by introducing experimental parts or modifying the process at certain points under controlled conditions in order to determine product/process results. Once significant process parameters and limits are identified, the third evolutionary use of process data is to control the process. Trend analysis software is used to predict process or product shifts. Engineers can use population study and trend analysis data as a basis for making process adjustments. Process drifts can be compensated for by re-establishing "in-process" set points, measurement qualifications, and accept/reject criteria. Analysis software can be set up to generate process behavior reports on an exception basis. The generation of control charts would only occur when process parameters exceed predetermined limits.

A key to being able to effectively use process data is the application of "in process" tests. Such tests save costs in irreversible production applications by rejecting marginal parts, or compensating for them early in the process rather than detecting failures due to tolerance build up at final test where product cost is highest. The three basic approaches to controlling a process employ "in process" tests. "Feed forward control" is using information to adjust the process ahead to compensate for detected differences in product components. For example, if it has been found (by correlation analysis) that the heat applied at the final stage of a chemical process is a significant factor in determining ultimate product characteristics, then that parameter might be controlled to compensate for a raw material difference detected at the input to the process. "Feed backward control" is when information is used to adjust the process behind the point where a product deviation is detected. For example, if at the final test station of a transistor production line a population shift of frequency response is detected, then key parameters of a previous diffusion process may be altered to compensate for this. Selective assembly is a combination of both feed forward and feed backward control since both "in process" and final process measurements are used. Once significant process/product parameters have been identified, population studies will allow the classification or grouping of "in process" parts. With algorithms supplied by Process Engineers, the process control system can generate best fit part combinations to optimize final production characteristics and yields. The part combinations or assembly instructions can be communicated to the production line automatically via terminal or satellite fabrication equipment.

In the example shown in Figure IIF18-2, parts are tested and sorted by "in process" test stations under satellite computer control. Product measurements from these tests can also determine control functions for the previous process steps. The satellite "in process" test computers reject or sort parts into groups according to parameter characteristics and quantities, and on final yield and product specification requirements.

Both electronic and mechanical parts can be selectively assembled under computer control to achieve uniformly high quality and yield. Analysis software makes it possible for Process Engineers to experiment with a process in order to further understand process variables and effect controls. The goals are to decrease product cost and increase product quality by implementing controls to narrow the population distribution of a given process (build uniform parts) in order to increase final yields and reduce or eliminate controls such as selective assembly. Process control can be carried to a further step by ultimately removing the Process Engineer from the loop by introducing feedback software and equipment to make necessary process adjustments automatically.

In order to control a discrete process through the utilization of data, the following three criteria must be met: product traceability, data integrity and data management. Product traceability is the ability of being able to trace parts through a process by identifying the parts uniquely at each process operation where a computer collects product/process data. Traceability is essential in performing correlation analysis. For instance, to determine the effect of components on a final assembly, it is necessary to correlate the component variables, measured early in the process, to the final assembly parameters. Thus, the components in the final assembly must be traceable back to an early component test. Several forms of traceability are possible. Components may be traced by sequence or time in a very simple process. Components may be traced in lots or batches if time and sequence tracing are not adequate. Or, components may be uniquely identified by serial number. At any rate, whenever the central computer receives information concerning product/process parameters, additional information must be sent which associates that information with specific parts. Since process and part identification is just as important as measurement information, this data should be entered into the system and combined with measurement data at the same point, the satellite computer.

The second criterion is insuring the accuracy or integrity of the data which the computer collects. If parameter data is not repeatable, or if parameter data cannot be associated with specific parts, then correlation between process operations is not possible. The best way to insure accuracy of data is to let the computer obtain it directly through sensors or other automatic equipment. This includes process parameter and identification information. Product identification information may be input to the computer through a terminal which reads relevant information from a card or badge that travels with the product. Where product/process information is manually entered into the system through a terminal or keyboard, attention must be given to developing critical and effective editing techniques in the computer to minimize the probability of entering faulty data.

The third important criterion for using data to control a scheme must be used when it becomes necessary to handle large amounts of data and to provide fast accss. It is important that data collected from various process points, and from various processes, be consistently formatted in order that common programs may operate on the data. Real time and background process control software should be standardized in order to decrease development costs, as well as to facilitate product/process transfer, expansion and product/process evolutions. Once a process is stabilized, then the amount of data collected can be reduced to the absolutely necessary to maintain control. Data processing resources can then be reallocated to other problem processes. In a data management system, a simple control interface between engineers and the system must be provided so that Process Engineers can have easy access to data and analysis programs. Through the use of macro statements, the engineer can easily select specific data and specific programs to perform data analysis.

A decision to employ real time data analysis in the central system should be considered carefully. Real time analysis is more costly since data processing resources must be reserved full time. Process control data analysis software should be executed in batch mode except in cases where output is required immediately for time dependent applications. The proper choice of a data management scheme can ease the transition from batch to real time analysis.

A trade off must be established relative to the storage of raw data at the central system. A tendency might be to pass all raw process data to the central system for storage and analysis. A determination of on-line data storage requirements must be made. Insignificant, or out-dated data must be discarded or dumped to history tape in order to conserve central system I/0 facilities.

The analysis of process control data has application in various industries such as aircraft, automotive, electronic and chemical where the control of discrete processes is essential in reducing costs and maintaining quality. Some of the techniques discussed in this paper have been used in the production of multi-track magnetic tape heads in IBM and have netted yield increases of up to 40%. Through empirical modeling techniques, process engineers are able to qualify process variables without contaminating actual production processes. It is possible to look ahead into some of the process control requirements for new technologies to be employed in future processes. Valuable process and product information can be obtained from laboratory experimentation. Many modeling and simulating techniques are available, which can assist Process Engineers in determining some of the control requirements which will be necessary when the actual production facility is established.

Summary

Control of discrete manufacturing processes is possible by using the data being collected by computers which are used to control test and process equipment in those processes. An evolutionary use of the data is to first acquire, record and report. Next, data analysis and trend prediction capabilities can be implemented. Finally, correlation of data between various operations in the discrete process will allow feed forward and feed backward process control. In order to utilize the acquired data, considerations must be given to product traceability, data integrity and data management.

References

1. J. E. Stuehler. "An Integrated Manufacturing Process Control System: Implementation in IBM Manufacturing," *IBM Journal of Research and Development*, November 1970.
2. R. B. Fisher, C. M. Cox, and C. Holdinski. "Computer Aided Testing and Fabrication of Magnetic Tape Heads," *IBM Journal of Research and Development*, November 1970.

CASE STUDY 19 Control of Thermonuclear Fusion Experiments*

For two decades, scientists have sought to harness the thermonuclear power of the hydrogen bomb and make its energy available for peaceful purposes. Within another decade, they hope to demonstrate the feasibility of controlled thermonuclear fusion as a step toward accomplishing that goal.

In a hydrogen bomb, the mechanism for releasing fusion energy is simple enough: an implosion slams hydrogen nuclei into one another to initiate a nuclear reaction. But it is much more complicated to produce a controlled and sustained fusion reaction. Theoretically the reaction can take place when the hydrogen is heated to form an ionized gas, or plasma, with a temperature greater than 10^8 degrees Kelvin.

A magnetic field of extremely high intensity provides the only known means for confining such high-energy plasma long enough to sustain the reaction. Much of today's research centers on creating a hot enough plasma and confining it long enough within a toroidal (doughnut-shaped) chamber by means of a toroidal magnetic field as shown in Figure IIF19-1.

The Plasma Physics Laboratory at Princeton University is one of four major facilities supported by the United States Atomic Energy Commission for conducting research in controlled nuclear fusion. Other nations support such research as well. For example, in 1969 Russian scientists announced significant progress in lengthening the time that a hot, dense plasma could be confined in their pioneering Tokamak T-3 plasma device. When British scientists went to Moscow's Kurchatov Institute to check the experiments, they confirmed the results that the Russians had obtained.

Meanwhile, Princeton scientists were creating their own version of the Tokamak (the name is a Russian acronym for toroidal chamber machine). Dubbed the ST for Symmetric Tokamak, the Princeton device became operational in the spring of 1970. In most respects similar to the T-3 device, the ST has yielded results that broadly parallel the T-3 results. The ST is much more prolific, however, producing experimental data 10 to 30 times faster than the T-3.

"There are two main reasons for our greater output," explains Dr. Donald J. Grove, the physicist who heads the ST program at Princeton. "First, the ST has a superior cooling technology which permits more frequent generation and observation of the hot plasma. Second, we use an IBM 1800 to gather and analyze data. The Russians still do that

---

* This case study has been exerpted from References 1 and 2, which were kindly provided by Ellis Simon of Princeton University. This work was performed under the auspices of the U.S. Atomic Energy Commission, Contract AT(30)-1238.

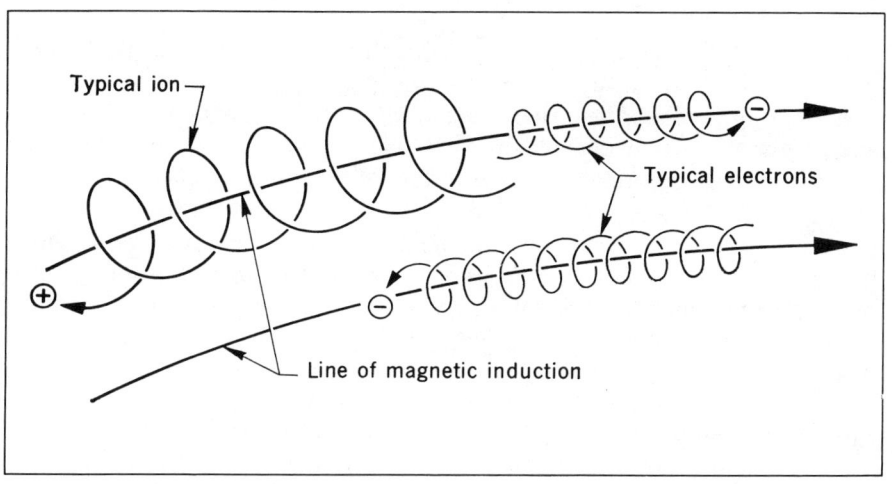

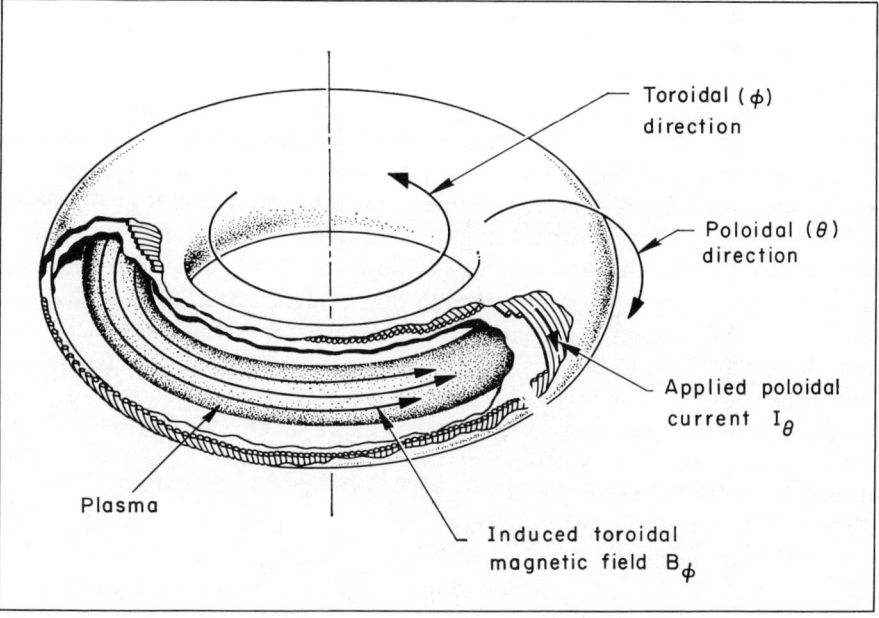

Figure IIF19-1. Confining effects.

manually." In the manual procedures used at Kurchatov, data from an experiment is obtained by photographing an oscilloscope on which are presented, in graphic form, the values of the currents and voltages recorded within the blue-glowing plasma. Measurements are taken from the photograph, calculations are made to determine plasma temperatures, and the results are plotted by hand.

Information about the plasma's ionization and temperature is provided by spectroscope, laser-beam scattering, microwave interferometry, and other observational methods. With the 1800, much of the data reduction is accomplished automatically by digital/analog communication with the ST. About five seconds after a set of observations has been made, analysis of the data is complete and a plasma temperature curve is displayed on a cathode-ray tube.

The display is used for reference in setting the parameters of the next observation set-for example, adjusting the electric currents that control the heating of the plasma and the intensity of the retaining magnetic field. Other independent variables include the amount and type of gas that is injected to form the plasma.

The temperature, degree of ionization, density, and confinement time of the plasma are determined by the parameter settings decided on by the experimenter. On-line output of this information shows whether an experiment is running as expected. (Unless this information were available in real time, a lengthy experiment might be run only to discover that the data was useless.) Later, the data from many observation sets can be analyzed in detail to determine relationships among the variables. A single-sheet report of each observation set is prepared automatically for further reference. It is not clear why Tokamak devices such as the ST can confine plasmas for longer periods than other types of devices. Information on the question will soon be forthcoming, however, from an experimental program now underway using Princeton's newest plasma device, known as the FM-1. The design of the FM-1 permits further exploration of the principles underlying Tokamak behavior because the intensity and shape of the retaining magnetic field are more nearly independent of the heating of the plasma than is possible with a Tokamak device. Figure IIF19-2 shows the structure of Tokamak and FM-1 devices.

A basic feature of the FM-1 is a 60-inch, 500-pound superconducting ring of niobium tin which floats freely in the toroidal chamber during an observation. It must float freely because mechanical support would disturb the plasma and distort the data obtained. The ring is levitated by a system of magnetic fields, and to keep the ring from falling in case the levitation system fails, the FM-1 is equipped with mechanical catchers which can be

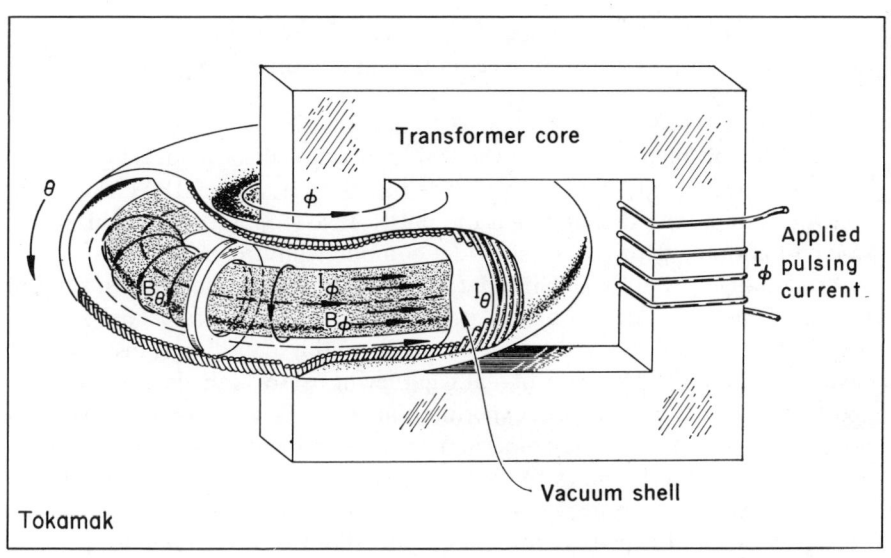
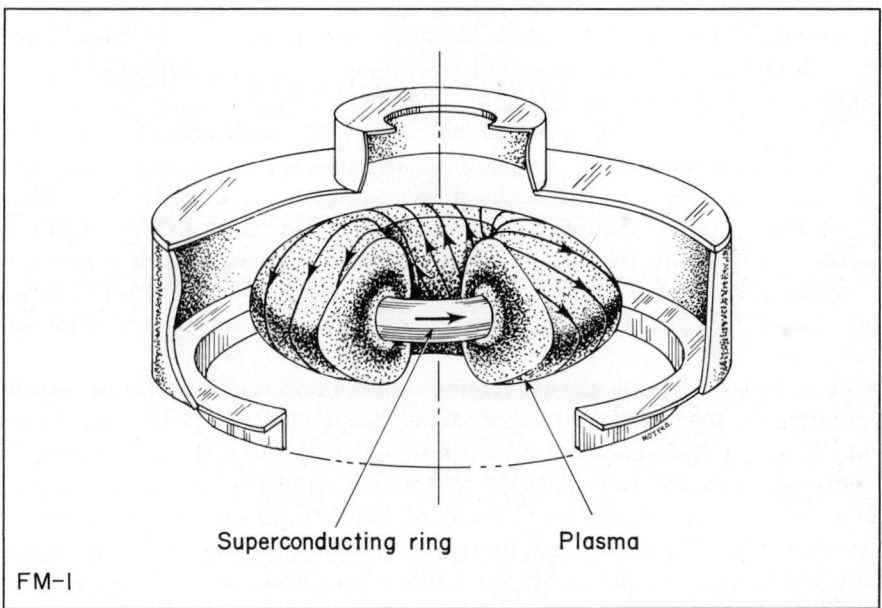

Figure IIF19-2. Controlled fusion devices.

slammed into place by high-speed air valves. The catchers confine the ring to no more than a half-inch of free motion in any direction.

Fail-Safe Control

The control problems posed by the levitated ring led to the development of a system for fail-safe control, which is based on a second IBM 1800. The control system would shut down the entire FM-1 operation should an unsafe condition be detected, or should a computer failure occur.

As explained by Ellis D. Simon, the engineer in charge of system support for the FM-1, the decision was made to install a separate computer to handle the control system because of two major considerations: "First," says Mr. Simon, "The rate of data gathering is so high that a dedicated 1800 is required during an experimental run. The physicist must have unhampered use of the machine and freedom to tinker with its programming. On the other hand, a failure in the data-gathering system should not be permitted to interfere with the control computer, which is responsible for a great deal of expensive and potentially dangerous equipment."

The control system handles more than 1,000 input signals from contact switches that monitor currents that create the magnetic fields. This data comes from many points in three buildings; one houses the FM-1 itself, one houses electrical generators, and one contains large, fast capacitors which supply power to the plasma heating equipment.

The 1800 scans the input signals every 80 milliseconds and, after analyzing the data, sends control signals to some 500 switches and five analog devices which control the power sources. If the analysis indicates anything amiss, the computer initiates appropriate action within a tenth of a second. It might, for instance, print a message stating that a noncritical door is open. For a more serious condition it might shut down the entire operation, first firing the catchers to secure the ring and then shutting off all power.

The FM-1 research device requires the simultaneous operation of approximately twenty separate subsystems. Some of these systems are shown in Figure IIF19-3. Each subsystem interacts with the FM-1 device, and in most cases a subsystem must interact with a number of other subsystems. An obvious example of this is the need for removal of coil current in the event of loss of water flow, followed by removal of other fields due to the loss of the first, and the cutoff of heating due to field loss.

This subsystem interdependence creates the necessity of having an overall system that can accomplish the following objectives:

1. Supervise all interactions between subsystems.
2. Cause subsystems to operate in a manner that will not permit undesirable interactions.

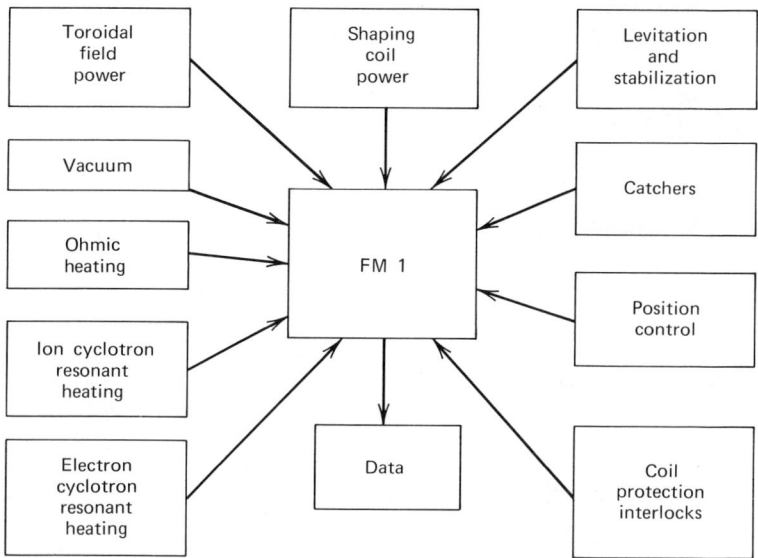

Figure IIF19-3. Major systems on FM-1.

3. Protect operators and equipment from injury.
4. Survey itself and revert to a safe condition in the event that it is unable to continue the above tasks.
5. Convey to the experimenter information about the subsystems.

It is important at this point to emphasize that if the experiment is to be an organized efficient, coordinated operation, the control system must be treated as an integrated system, separate and distinct from the subsystems. Bringing together a dozen remote control boxes does not in itself create a central control system.

Levels of Operation

The FM-1 subsystems contain energy sources that can be dangerous to equipment and personnel. For this reason control action is taken according to the following priority schedule:

1. Personnel safety.
2. Equipment safety.
3. Experiment parameter requirements.
4. Sequence timing.

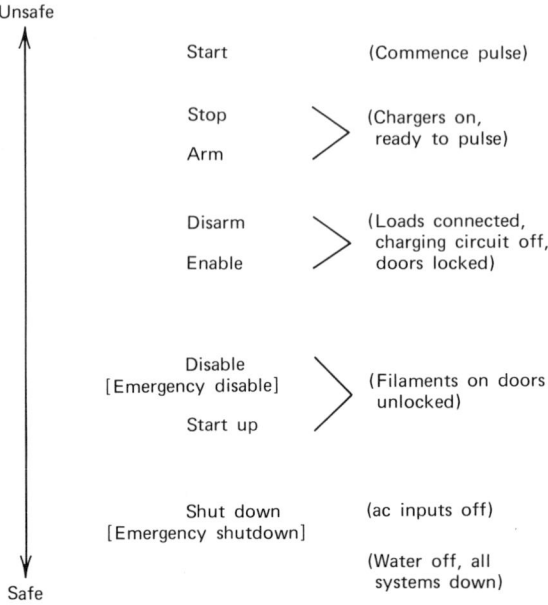

Figure IIF19-4. Possible levels of system operation.

The following levels of operation are standard on large research devices at the Plasma Physics Laboratory:

1. *Shutdown.* At this level, all ac power sources are disconnected from a subsystem, access may be had to all areas, and there is no connection to the loads.
2. *Startup, but Disabled.* AC power is connected, auxiliaries are energized, but operating access is not permitted to a subsystem. However, no connection exists from subsystem to load and access may be had to the FM-1 device. All high-voltage equipment is deenergized. This is the normal access state when an experimental run is made.
3. *Enabled, but not Armed.* The subsystem is now connected to the load. Access to the FM-1 device is NOT permitted.
4. *Armed, but not Started.* All high voltage sources are energized, energy storage banks are ready, and generator fields are energized. System requires only timer pulse to deliver energy.
5. *Start.* All steady-state fields come on; sequence timer begins its operation.

F. EXPERIMENTATION

The system may be placed in each successive level of operation if, and only if, all requirements for that level have been met. It is also required that increasing levels of operation be taken one at a time. The ascending levels of operation are shown in Figure IIF19-4.

Digital vs Relay

Two approaches may be taken to plasma device control systems. Hardware, such as relays, gates, etc., can be used to produce the required logic of wire connections between elements, or, one can utilize a computer to produce the logic via programming. The relay system is inflexible, requiring hardware changes to effect a change in logic. The digital approach is very flexible, since all logic is incorporated in the programming. Since the logic is programmed, the changes take less manpower and less overall time to complete. A digital system also permits one output device to convey detailed information on all aspects of the control system.

Unfortunately, the initial cost of a digital system is so high that at first glance it may appear to be prohibitive. However, a plasma device is a research device and research demands change-requiring changes in controls as well as in experiments. A large relay system may demand the full-time services of a draftsman and a technician to make these alterations. Over a period of years these changes will cost more than the initial cost of the digital system. Further, the time required to make a needed change operational on a relay system seldom is less than a month, whereas a digital system can be changed in days, including debugging.

For the above reasons the FM-1 control system is based on a programable digital computer.

System Description

The controller is an IBM 1800 data acquisition and control system. The control processor has a 16,000-word random-access memory. Instruction execution takes 2 microseconds. The core memory is augmented with a 512,000-word disk storage unit. Programming input and output is done via a card reader-punch which reads at 300 cards per minute and punches.

Process inputs include 416 binary points in 16-point groups and 128 binary interrupts in 16-point groups. Analog inputs include 45 analog points multiplexed through one analog to digital converter, which has a conversion rate of 20,000 conversions per second.

Process outputs consist of 480 binary points in 16-point groups and 12 digital-to-analog converters.

Supporting software of the system includes an executive system which permits programs to be transferred into the core from the disk and executed without external intervention. Time sharing with non-process programs is also implemented.

Since this processor is responsible for preventing injury to people or equipment, the following steps have been taken. The cpu and the disk unit are equipped with two extra bits on every stored word—one is a parity bit and the other is a storage protect bit. Each is checked by the hardware. There is an operations monitor which must be reset every 5 seconds or an alarm is tripped. All outputs are pulse type, with a duration of 80 milliseconds. The processor must update at the end of 80 milliseconds or the output reverts to a fail-safe condition. All inputs are scanned at the same rate. Thus, any failure of cpu, disk, or program causes a system shutdown.

Control System Operation

In order to avoid problems in training operators to be proficient typists, and in order to make the FM-1 controls similar to existing systems, the processor-operator interface is a console with lighted push buttons. Each button lights when it can be pressed and contains a micro instruction such as "Push to Enable." When pressed, the button goes dark and another button lights saying "Push to Disable." Thus, in a darkened control room, all useful buttons are lighted. Further, someone not intimately familiar with the system can be led through the operation by the push buttons themselves.

The push buttons are augmented by storage oscilloscopes on which system status information is written.

Parameter settings (such as field levels, timer settings, and voltage settings) may be entered via a ten-button data entry panel (see Figure IIF19-5). The operator enters a 2-digital number, followed by a 5-digital variable. Confirmation of the input appears at the bottom of the scope face. When the operator is satisfied that the data is correct, he presses "ENTER" and the system updates that parameter. A portable version of this terminal may be plugged in right at the FM-1 device for on-the-spot debugging of the interlocks.

"The FM-1 control system gives the computer an unusual degree of direct control," says Mr. Simon. "Most control systems are really supervisory, with the main control functions handled by hardware. A pump, for example, might have an overload detection device and a water-flow switch wired directly to the pump's power supply so that the pump can be shut down independently of the computer. But in the FM-1 control system, any

F. EXPERIMENTATION   219

Figure IIF19-5.   FM-1 and control room.

overload signal goes to the 1800. The computer then determines whether to shut down the pump."

The advantage of this approach is flexibility of the control system itself. Previously, changes could be made in the control system only by altering the control circuitry. Now must such changes can be effected simply by recoding part of the 1800's FORTRAN program.

"The control system," points out Dr. Shoichi Yoshikawa, physicist in charge of the FM-1 research effort, "is really designed as the interface between the FM-1 and the experimenter. Without good controls, it is very difficult to perform incisive experiments. By providing continuous information on all systems, the 1800 helps insure a maximum experimental yield from the brief productive period. Also, by putting the entire FM-1 operation directly under the control of the computer, we can more easily change the experimental setup as we get more experience and as new needs occur."

References

1. E. D. Simon, S. P. Duritt and M. Pelovitz, "Digital Control of a Research Device," MATT-726, Plasma Physics Laboratory, Princeton University, Princeton, N.J.,

presented at the May 1969 Symposium on Engineering Problems of Controlled Thermonuclear Research.
2. Anonymous, "Thermonuclear Fusion—Energy Source of the Future," *Computing Report,* December 1971, pp. 4–8.
3. E. D. Simon and S. P. Duritt, "Process Controlling a Research Device," *IEEE Transactions on Nuclear Science,* **NS-18**, 4, (August 1971), 351–356.

G. MODELING, SIMULATION

One of the glories of the scientific process is the use of models, or analogs, of real-world devices or phenomena. Simulation is the process of experimenting with such models in lieu of the real thing.

Simulation is used, justifiably, either because it is cheaper, faster, safer, more controllable or measurable, more humane, or in any other respect more advantageous or feasible than experimenting with the real article.

The big question is validity. Do the particular results obtained from simulation accurately portray the behavior of the real thing? The validity of simulation results must always be questioned.

The three case studies in this chapter have been chosen to illustrate the advantages of simulation and the means of validation.

Case study 20, "Simulation of Automobile Dynamics," demonstrates clearly the advantage of simulation, rather than real experimentation, in studying automobile collisions. The means of validating is also shown.

Case study 21, "Simulated Chemical Reactions," describes the possibilities of obtaining through simulation a more detailed and quantitative understanding of transient and other hard-to-measure phenomena.

Case study 22, "Calculation of Radiation Treatment Dosage," describes a widely used program for predicting the detailed dosage densities resulting from a proposed treatment protocol. This case study demonstrates the practicality of providing such a service over great distances from a single "center of excellence."

CASE STUDY 20 Simulation of Automobile Dynamics[*]

INTRODUCTION

Evaluations of geometric design features of highways and roadsides, with regard to the dynamic behavior of vehicles traversing them, are pre-

---

[*] This section has been exerpted from Raymond R. McHenry, Norman J. DeLeys, and John P. Eicher, "Analysis of the Effects of Highway and Roadside Geometries on Motor Vehicle Behavior" presented at the Fifty-Seventh Annual Meeting, American Association of State Highway Officials, Miami Beach, Florida, December 6–10, 1971.

dominantly experimental at the present time. Such experiments require the selection of specific test conditions to represent the wide distributions of variables that actually exist (e.g., vehicle sizes and characteristics, operating conditions, and driver control inputs). In accident situations, the ranges of vehicle operating conditions and evasive control inputs are, of course, greatly increased. The total number of tests of a given design feature is generally limited by costs, and the extrapolation test results is made difficult, if not impossible, by the prevalence of nonlinearities.

The computer program that is described in this paper (Highway-Vehicle-Obstacle Simulation Model, or HVOSM) has been aimed at supplementing experiments related to physical criteria for highway and roadside design. The technical approach consists of an application of nonlinear mathematical modeling techniques to the dynamics of highway vehicles in general, three-dimensional motions.

This research has been sponsored by the Office of Research of the Federal Highway Administration (FHWA) as part of an overall research program aimed at the development of improved roadside protective systems to enhance occupant survivability in single vehicle accidents.

Description of HVOSM Computer Program

A digital form of computer program, in the Fortran IV language, was selected for ease of transfer to other computer facilities. In this form, the operating cost of the program has been found to be quite moderate for most applications, and the relative ease of adaptation to a variety of computers has led to the distribution, by FHWA, of forty copies of the program to other research organizations to date (1).

Geometric and surface details of the terrain profile are introduced as tabular inputs to the program. Likewise, open-loop control parameters in the form of the steer angle at the front wheels, the throttle setting, the hydraulic pressure in the brake system, and the transmission ratio are entered as tabular functions of time. There is also a provision in one version of the model to simulate closed-loop (driver) control inputs (2).

The vehicle is treated as an assembly of four rigid masses, as depicted in in Figure IIG 20-1, with a total of fifteen degrees of freedom. These consist of the six degrees of freedom associated with three-dimensional, rigid-body motions of the spring mass; a total of five degrees of freedom associated with motions of the unsprung masses (wheel assemblies) relative to the sprung mass (i.e., suspension deflections and front wheel steer); and the four rotational degrees of freedom of the wheels. The steer mode degree of freedom, for which are inertial coupling effects are neglected, is introduced at the front wheels when rigid obstacles (e.g., curbs) are encountered by

Figure IIG20-1. Analytical representation of vehicle.

either or both of those wheels. The rotational degrees of freedom of the four wheels have been incorporated in order that the effects on tire forces of rotational wheel slip, in braking or traction, can be approximated. Inertial properties, suspension and tire characteristics, and the detailed brake system are represented (3).

Validation of Predictions

A high degree of correlation has been achieved between the responses of the vehicle as predicted by the computer model and as measured experimentally in a rigorous investigation of validity that included both separate and combined cornering and ride motions (4). A sampling of these response comparisons may be seen in Figures IIG 20-2 and IIG 20-3. Preliminary comparisons of collision predictions with experimental results for certain classes of fixed obstacles also exhibit generally close agreement (5, 6).

One of the objectives in this research program has been to apply each item of the vehicle parameters in a directly measurable form. Since it is a common practice in mathematical modeling to define "equivalent" parameters and to adjust the values to achieve correlation with experimental data, it is well to distinguish the present approach. A subcontract was let to the Ford Motor Company for measurement of the vehicle parameters, and the results of their measurements have been used directly. The tire properties were measured by the General Motors Engineering Staff and were also applied directly.

Because of the direct use of parameters as measured by disinterested individuals, it should be very clear that the correlation with experimental responses is genuine, involving no "tune-up" of the simulated vehicle properties.

Within the CAL validation program, repeated runs of all but one of the ten test conditions were performed. It is unfortunate that most other experimental efforts that have been performed in relation to vehicle dynamics and to automobile collisions have not included measures of the variability of the experimental responses. Without such measures, the accuracy of analytical predictions cannot be properly evaluated.

In Figures IIG 20-2 and IIG 20-3, the high degree of repeatability of the experimental responses reflects the use of closely controlled experimental procedures. The performance of repeated experiments enables the quantification of statistical reliability and comparison of mean test results with analytic predictions.

The required extent of the total validation effort is determined by the nature of specific intended applications. For example, a primary interest in

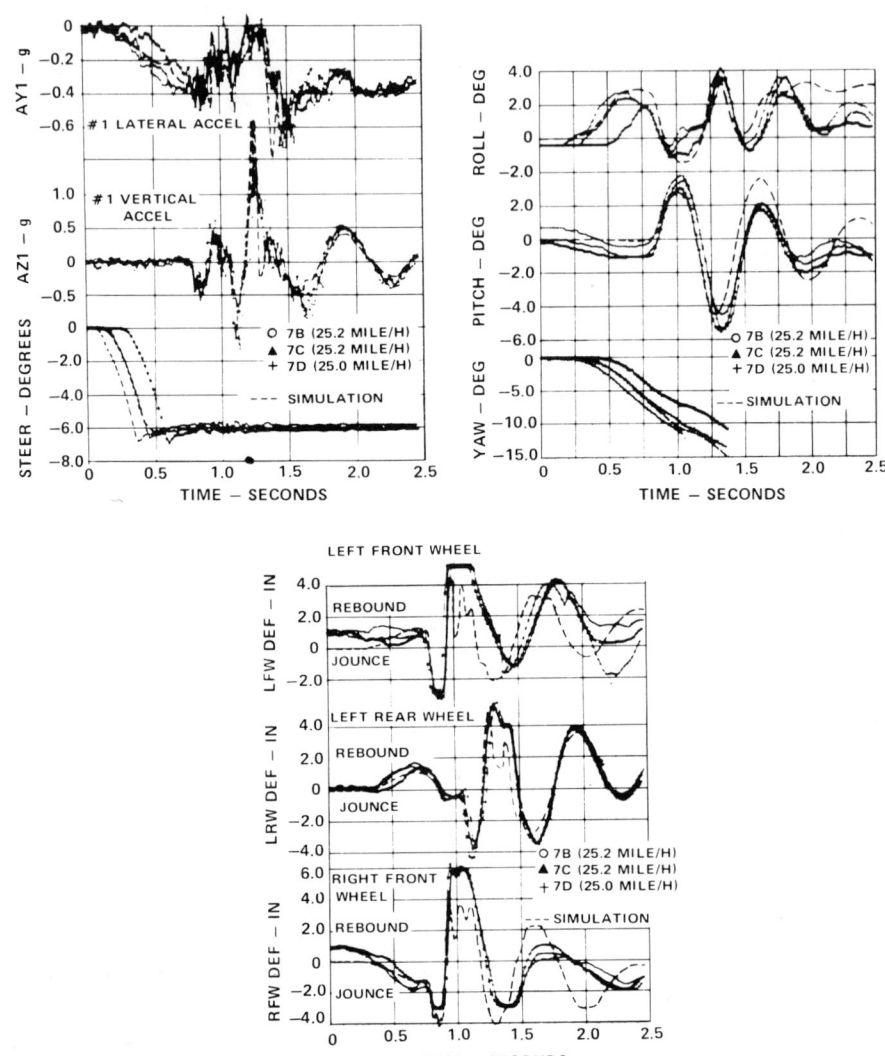

Figure IIG20-2. Measured and simulated responses of vehicle traversing ramp.

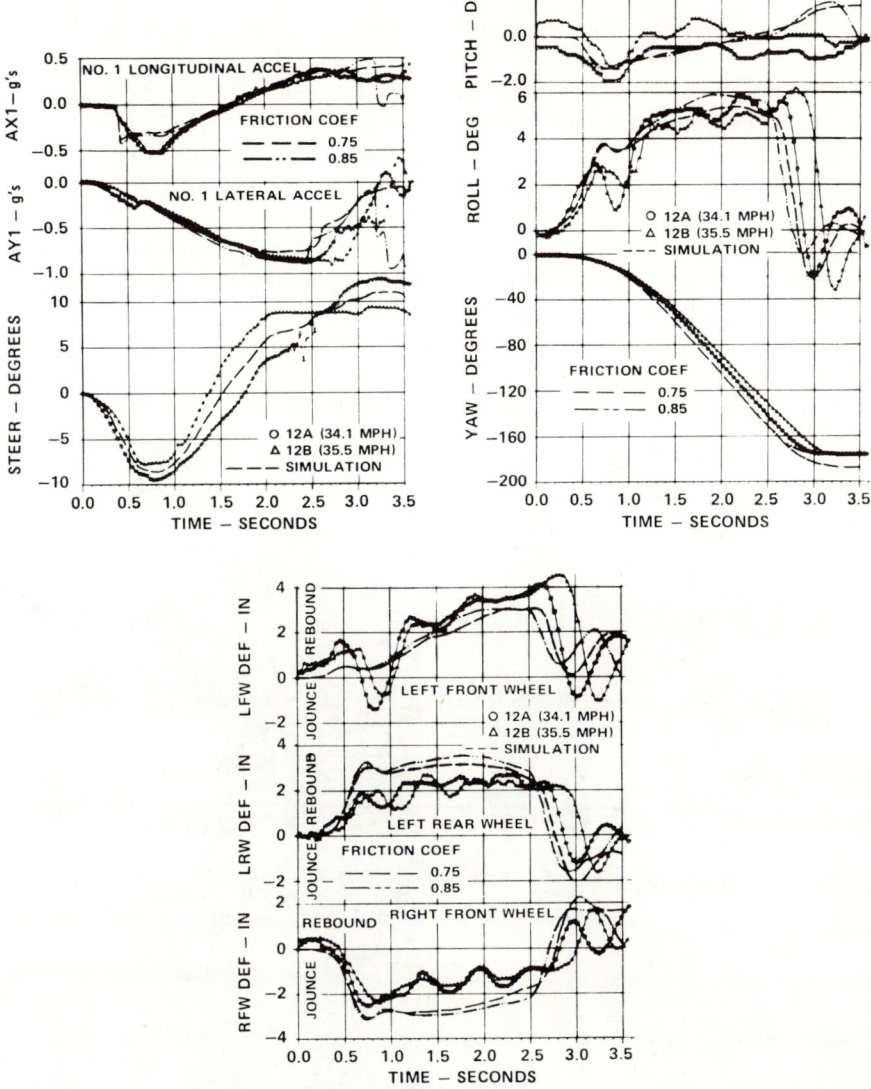

Figure IIG20-3. Measured and predicted responses of vehicle in foreward skid on dry pavement.

226 CURRENT USAGE: CASE STUDIES AND CRITIQUES

kinematics (i.e., the trajectory of the vehicle), as opposed to the detailed time history of acceleration, could be satisfied with a less extensive validation effort, in view of the direct measurements that can be made (i.e., no instrumentation response problems) and the "smoothing" or "filtering" effect of double integration of the simulated acceleration. On the other hand, a primary interest in acceleration waveform and peak accelerations generally requires a greater validation effort.

As a supplement to the conventional time-history form of simulation outputs, an auxiliary computer-graphics program has been developed within the CAL research program to produce perspecitve drawings of the simulated vehicle as seen from selected viewing positions and at selected times during a predicted event (7).

Figure IIG20-4. Sequence photos of test no. 1 impact.

G. MODELING, SIMULATION 227

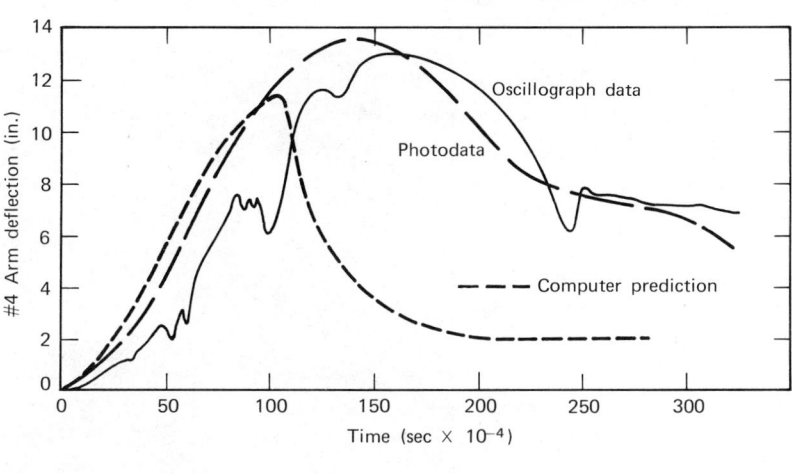

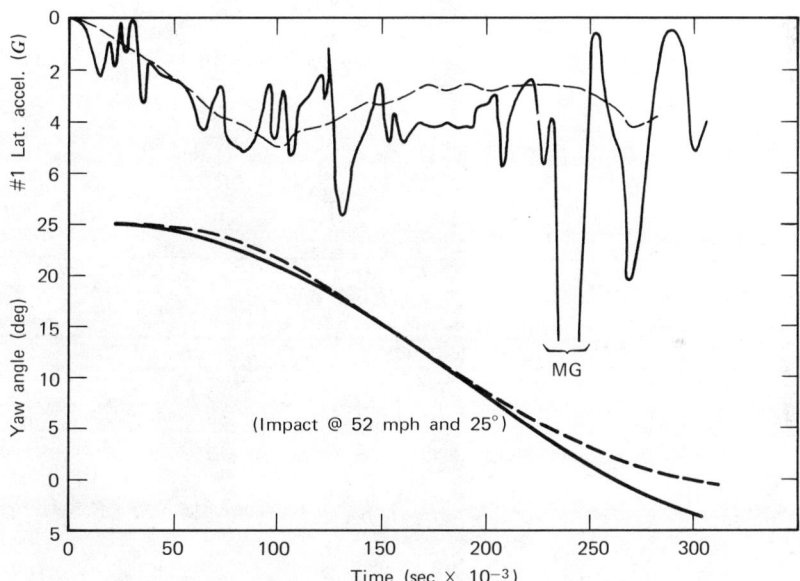

Figure IIG20-5. Vehicle and bridge railing responses—test no. 1.

Torsion-Post Bridge Rail (6)

The capability of the BPR-CAL computer model for simulating vehicle impacts with roadside structures was used in a recent application of the simulation in a research program to evaluate a new type of bridge railing conceived by the District of Columbia Department of Highways and Traf-

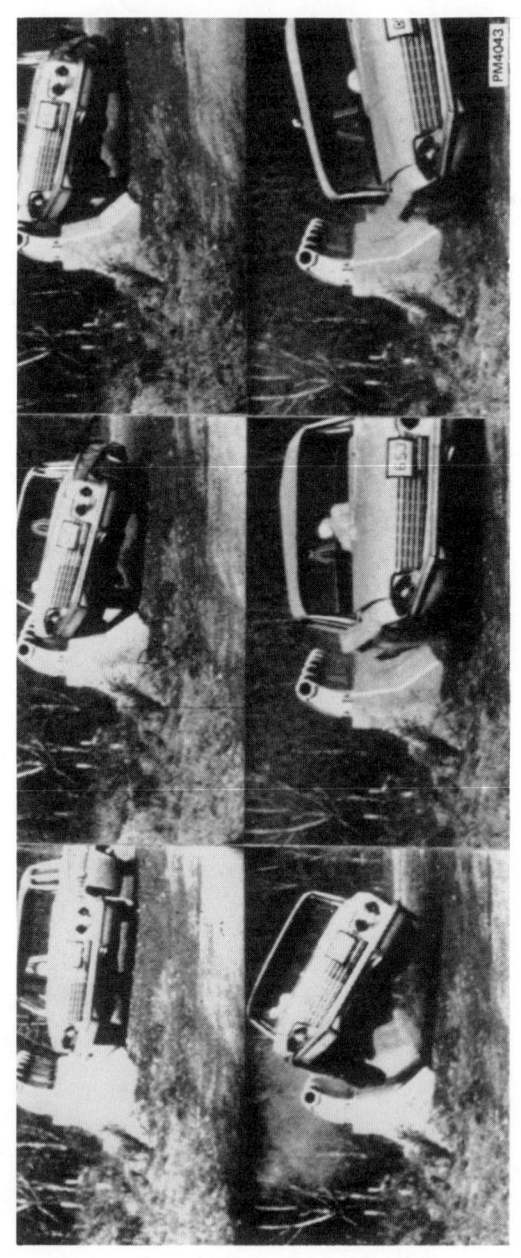

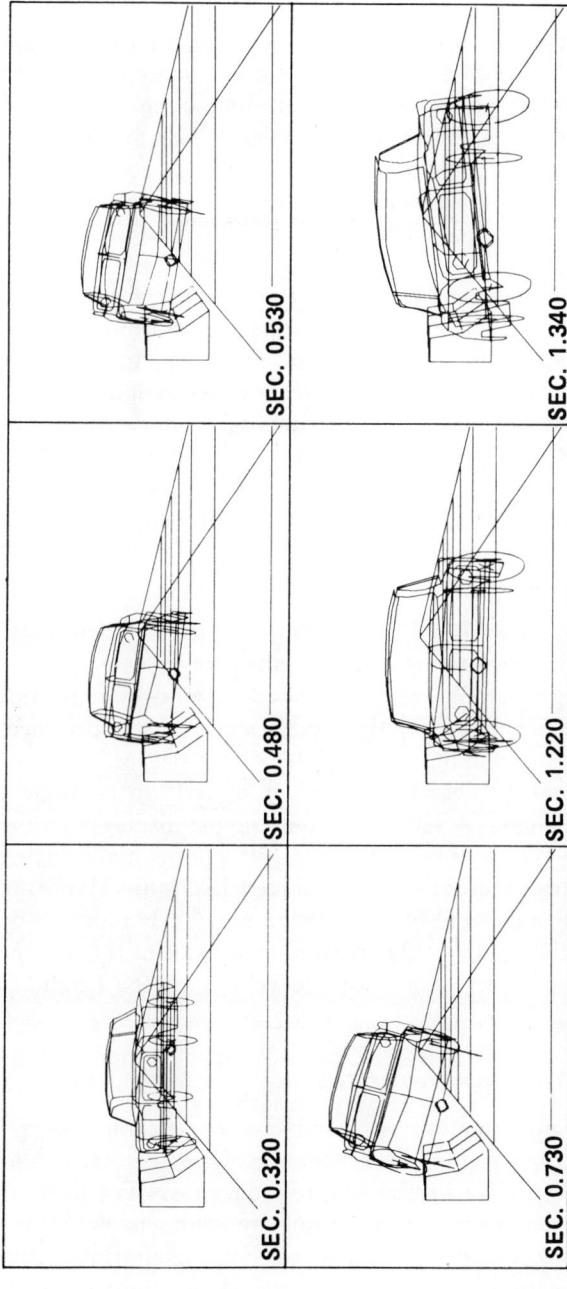

Figure IIG20-6. Experimental and predicted vehicle responses for collision with bridge parapet.

fic. A primary feature of the concept was the use of torsion posts for supporting the rails to provide flexibility of the structure and to absorb and subsequently release energy transferred from an impacting vehicle by operating within the elastic range of the post material. It was hypothesized that good redirection characteristics might result from a configuration having a larger inertia that would effectively delay release of the energy stored in the torsion posts until the vehicle had already departed from the impacted area.

The computer simulation was used to predict the dynamic responses of the vehicle and bridge railing under various impact conditions and to provide guidance in the selection and design of prototype torsion post bridge railing configurations for subsequent full-scale experimental testing.

Sequence photos of a test of one of the experimental bridge railings are presented in Figure IIG 20-4. Figure IIG 20-5 shows a comparison of the predicted and measured responses of the vehicle and bridge rail for the test impact conditions of 52 MPH and 25 degree angle of approach.

Bridge Parapet Investigation (1)

The computer simulation was applied in a brief investigation to determine how the response of a vehicle impacting a rigid, redirecting barrier such as the General Motors bridge parapet or the New Jersey median barrier would be affected by variations of the friction coefficient of the sloped face. Simulation runs of vehicles impacting at 30 MPH and 5 degrees angle of approach and 50 MPH and 12 degrees for values of friction coefficient between 0.25 and 0.7 were made. A representative graphic display showing the predicted response of a vehicle for comparison with photos made during a test performed by General Motors (9) is presented in Figure IIG 20-6. The results of the study substantiated the conclusion previously reported by Lundstrom et al. (9) that the value of the friction coefficient of the surface does not significantly affect the response of the vehicle or the height of climb up the wall.

Railroad Grade Crossing Topography (10)

An exploratory analytical investigation was conducted to determine speed-topography combinations for which vehicle responses when traversing railroad grade crossings may be sufficiently violent to induce loss of control.

It was found that neither steer effects from tire contacts with rails protruding above the highway surface nor "wheel hop" excitations from protruding rails or other terrain irregularities constitute a significant control problem at grade crossings. Crossings situated on crest vertical curves were concluded to be potentially prone to loss of vehicle control contingent,

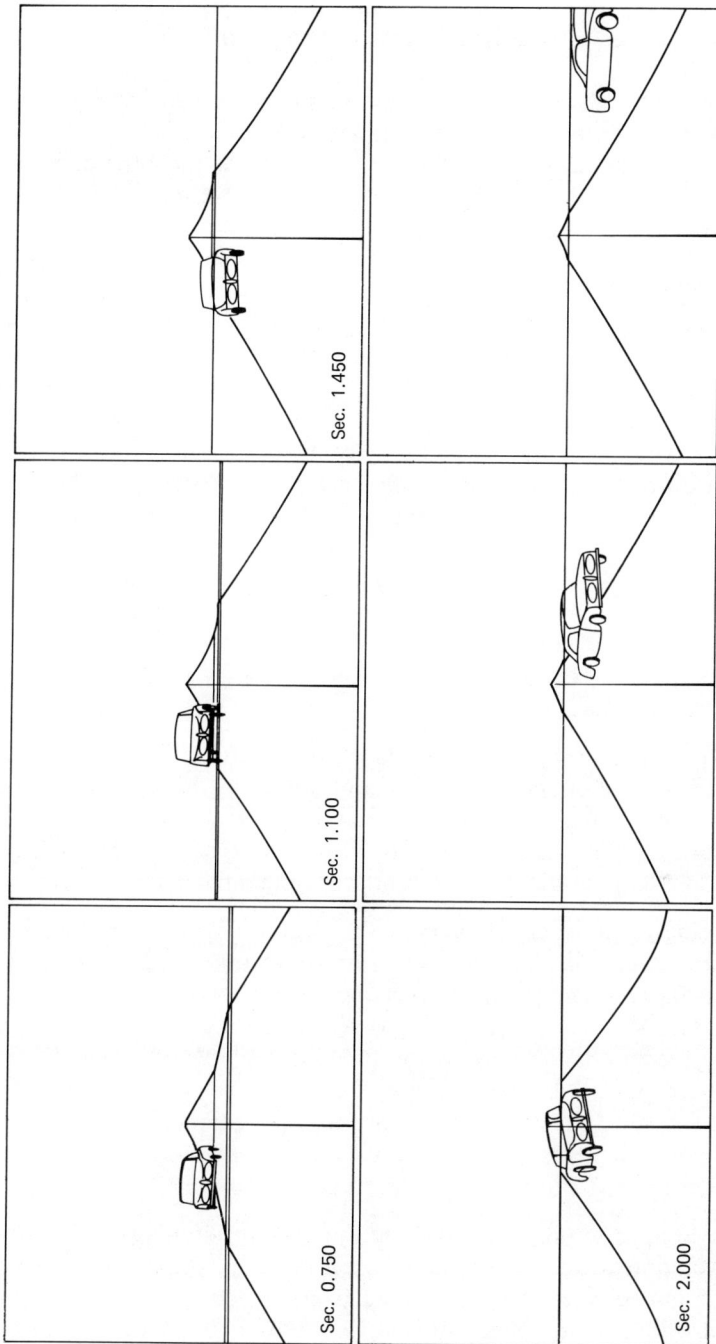

Figure IIG20-7. Simulated traversal of railroad crossing.

of course, upon the specifics of the cross section. The exploratory analysis demonstrated most importantly that dimensional tolerances for highway-railroad grade crossings may be objectively defined on the basis of dynamic vehicular responses assessed through the BPR-CAL model for a representative family of highway vehicles.

Figure IIG 20-7 shows a computer-graphics display of a simulation run for an actual railroad crossing with a crest vertical curve in the Buffalo, New York area where loss of vehicle control resulted in a ran-off-roadway fatal accident. To exaggerate potential loss of control effects, a speed of 70 MPH was selected, and a steer input of 3° (at the front wheels) was entered while the front wheels were off the ground.

In Figure IIG 20-7 the simulated event is viewed from a constant distance ahead of the vehicle, along the center line of the road. The simulated vehicle went up on its two right side wheels and then departed from the opposite side of the roadway. Such a driver maneuver conceivably could have been made in an attempt to avoid encroaching on the ditch on the right side of the roadway, with an excessive steer input applied while the front wheels are off the ground.

Potential Future Applications

The HVOSM computer program in its *present* status of development and validation is capable of addressing a host of questions that are of interest to the highway safety community with implications for new highway construction projects as well as safety improvement programs such as TOPICS.

Typical applications which are now addressable include the efficacy of—

1. Roadside terrain details such as the degree of side slope flattening, configuration and placement of drainage channels and the geometric and surface characteristics of curbing;
2. Protective structures such as rigid redirective barriers (e.g., the New Jersey median barrier design and the GM bridge parapet) and limited classes of guardrail type structures;
3. Highway design practices such as the geometric and surface interactive elements of horizontal curvature and superelevation and consideration of transition and spiral connections.

With the application of a relatively minor amount of additional effort on related development and validation, those aspects of the model associated with interaction between the vehicle and fixed objects will have progressed to the point where greater generality can be accommodated in the treatment of roadside structures.

The capability of this analytical aid to represent a cross section of vehicles and driver evasive maneuvers affords a unique opportunity for definitive analyses. The potential of the HVOSM program for objective evaluation of highway design practices and for rational development of warrants and specifications for roadside safety is virtually untapped. It also has an important potential as an aid in the analytical reconstruction of highway accidents.

Concluding Remarks

This paper has presented a brief review of the status and capabilities of the HVOSM computer simulation program. Copies of this program have been widely distributed by FHWA with the objective of contributing to a general elevation of the state of the art of highway vehicle dynamics.

The exisiting capabilities of the computer model can and are being exploited by a number of research organizations to converge on improved roadway and roadside geometrics and protective devices. The present version of the model represents, with confidence, the motions and responses of a motor vehicle on the roadway or in contact with the terrain irregularities of the roadside. This research effort, at full fruition, will also provide analytic procedures for evaluating the performance of a variety of roadside structural concepts in their ability to "protect" the vehicle and its occupants in the collision environment.

The acceptance of computer simulations such as the HVOSM program has been found to be greatly enhanced by the use of computer graphics. Some researchers in the field of highway safety have a tendency to view experiments, whether part or full scale, as being more real and believable than analyses. At least part of this tendency stems from the fact that physical experiments can be seen and photographed. The computer graphics displays help in allowing the direct observation of computer experiments.

In actuality, many physical experiments are poorly defined and controlled. Instrumentation errors sometimes yield individual items of response that are not compatible with each other. For example, in the series of physical experiments that were performed to validate the described vehicle simulation, a number of instrumentation difficulties were revealed by the comparisons with analytically predicted results. It is not intended to suggest that computer simulation can ever eliminate the need for physical experiments. Rather, the intention is merely to point out the fact that computer simulations can serve as valuable aids for interpreting the results of physical experiments with nonlinear systems, as well as for interpolation and extrapolation to other combinations of test conditions.

References

1. R. R. McHenry, and N. J. DeLeys, "Development of Analytical Aids for Minimization of Single Vehicle Accidents," CAL Report No. VJ-2251-V-10, July 1971.
2. C. V. Kroll, "A Preview-Predictor Model of Driver Behavior in Emergency Situations," technical paper presented at the 50th Annual Meeting of the Highway Research Board, Washington, D.C., January 1971.
3. R. R. McHenry and N. J. DeLeys, "Automobile Dynamics—A Computer Simulation of Three-Dimensional Motions for Use in Studies of Braking Systems and of the Driving Task," CAL Report No. VJ-2251-V-7, August 1970.
4. R. R. McHenry, and N. J. DeLeys, "Vehicle Dynamics in Single Vehicle Accidents—Validation and Extensions of a Computer Simulation," CAL Report No. VJ-2251-V-3, December 1968.
5. R. R. McHenry, D. J. Segal, N. J. DeLeys, "Computer Simulation of Single Vehicle Accidents," Proceedings of the 11th Stapp Car Crash Conference, Anaheim, California, October 1967.
6. N. J. DeLeys, "Investigation of a Torsion Post-Beam Rail Type of Bridge Railing," CAL Report No. VJ-2363-V-1, November 1970.
7. C. M. Theiss, "Computer Graphics Displays of Simulated Automobile Dynamics," The Spring Joint Computer Conference, Boston, May 1969.
8. R. R. McHenry, "A Preliminary Analytical Investigation of the BRIG Road Safety Edge Concept," CAL Report No. VJ-2251-V-8, October 1970.
9. L. C. Lundstrom, P. C. Skeels, B. R. Englund, R. A. Rogers, "A Bridge Parapet Designed for Safety," Highway Research Record No. 83, National Academy of Sciences—National Research Council, Washington, D.C., 1965.
10. "Automobile Accidents Related to Railroad Grade Crossings—A Study of the Effects of Topography and a Computer-Graphics Display of Traffic Flow," CAL Report No. VJ-2251-V-4, March 1969.

CASE STUDY 21   Simulated Chemical Reactions*

Chemistry has traditionally been considered a laboratory science, that is, one which relies heavily on experimental data rather than on theoretical calculations. In the last few years, however, with the advent of high speed computers theoretical calculations are becoming increasingly more important, so important in fact, that they may well revolutionize the entire study of chemistry.

To understand how this "revolution" is coming about, it is necessary to review some of the basic theory of quantum chemistry. It is an awesome

---

* This case study has been exerpted from Alex Malozemoff, "Chemistry by Computer," IBM Research Report, Vol. 4, No. 2, 1968.

fact that all of chemistry, no matter how complex, can in principle be derived from a single simple-looking equation $H\psi = E\psi$. This is of course the famous Schrödinger equation. It was first published by Erwin Schrödinger in 1926, and it forms the basis of his famous theory of quantum mechanics. Today, there is little or no doubt that this theory is entirely correct for all chemical purposes.

It is not difficult to see how the Schrödinger equation works. Imagine some system one is interested in, say with a couple of nuclei and a couple of electrons. Now ψ is called the "wavefunction" for the system, that is, it is a function of the positions of all the nuclei and electrons in the system and describes their distribution in space. E is the energy of this distribution. And finally, H is a differential operator called the Hamiltonian, which is characteristic of the system of nuclei and electrons and which is described in Figure IIG21-1.* It has a series of terms which correspond to all the energies in the problem: the kinetic energies of the nuclei and the electrons, and the potential energies of the interactions between the nuclei and the electrons, as well as other smaller interactions.

Now, to use the Schrödinger equation, one starts out by writing the Hamiltonian operator of the problem according to Schrödinger's prescription, as given in Figure IIG21-1. For example, if the system has only one

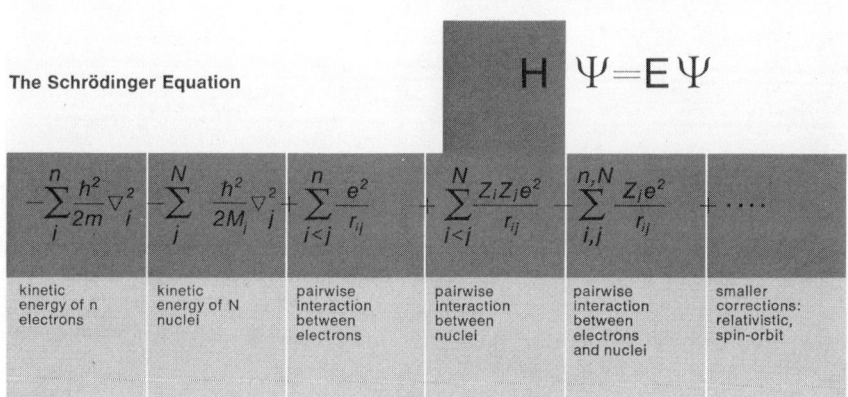

Figure IIG21-1. The Schrödinger equation.

* Respectively, M_j and Z_j are the mass and charge of the jth nucleus. The wavefunction ψ is a function of r_i and r_j, the positions of all the electrons and nuclei. The distance between particles i and j is represented by r_{ij}. $\hbar$ is $\frac{1}{2}\pi$ times Planck's constant (6.62×10^{-27}), e the electronic charge (1.6×10^{-10}), and ∇_i^2 the Laplacian operator with respect to the ith coordinate.

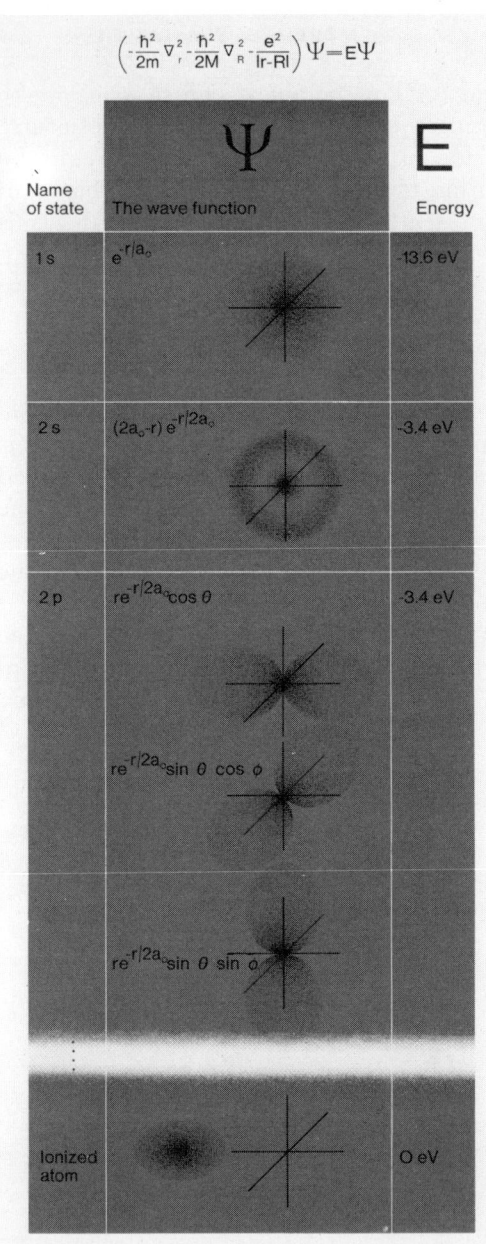

Figure IIG21-2. Wavefunctions of the hydrogen atom.

electron and only one nucleus (a proton), one gets the fairly simple looking equation shown in Figure IIG21-2. Initially one knows neither E nor ψ. Then one can solve for E and ψ, and because of the form of the equation and its boundary conditions, it turns out that solutions are only possible for certain values of E. All in all, one gets a discrete list of ψ-functions—or electron distributions—and an energy for each of them as shown in Figure IIG21-2, and these solutions, according to Schrödinger, are the only states in which the system can exist: a series of discrete states called "quantum states."

But this is a remarkable result. First off, as one examines the list of Figure IIG21-2, one can immediately see that in any of these states, the wavefunction is continuous. That is, a typical distribution function or "state" does not just have a nucleus at one point and an electron at another. Rather, the electron—and to some extent the nucleus also—is a smear; it is spread out over space. This smear can be understood as a probability distribution of the electron as it zips about in its orbit. Actually, the precise path of the orbit can never be known and is, in fact, a meaningless concept, as explained by Heisenberg's uncertainty principle.

In addition, as one further examines the list, one finds a state with the lowest energy (-13.6 eV) in which the electron distribution closely surrounds the nucleus; this is the stable state of the hydrogen atom. One finds other states with higher energy; these are the excited states of the hydrogen atom, and the energy differences between these states correspond to the well-known spectral lines of hydrogen. One finds states of even higher energy in which the nucleus and the electron are entirely separated; this is the ionized hydrogen atom. If one had a more complicated system with several nuclei and several electrons, one would have similarly found states with all the nuclei close together and surrounded by electrons; this would be a molecule. One would have found distributions with a higher energy in which the nuclei were far apart and a few electrons were around each one; this would be a state involving separated atoms.

Schrödinger's theory goes on to say that once one knows the possible states of the system in terms of their wavefunctions and energies, one may proceed to use certain formulas to calculate all the observable properties of the system.

The One-Electron Approximation

A powerful technique for making conceptual progress in chemistry is something called the "one-electron approximation." Precisely because of the fact that one-electron problems are so easy to visualize and understand, it was natural for the early workers to try to apply these concepts to the

238 CURRENT USAGE: CASE STUDIES AND CRITIQUES

many-electron case, and even today no one has devised a really successful alternative to this approach.

The Hartree-Fock Approximation

A much better one-electron type of approximation is the famous Hartree-Fock approximation which solves the problem of inter-electron correlation effects by taking an average of all the $(N - 1)$-particle distribution functions and assuming that the particular electron interacts with this averaged electron cloud (Figure IIG21-3d). Since H is now independent of the position of the electron, hence independent of $\dot{\psi}$, the approximation has yielded a one-electron problem, which, while leaving out correlation, includes a large part of the electron interactions and thus gives a reasonably accurate one-electron distribution function of "orbital" for the particular electron in question.

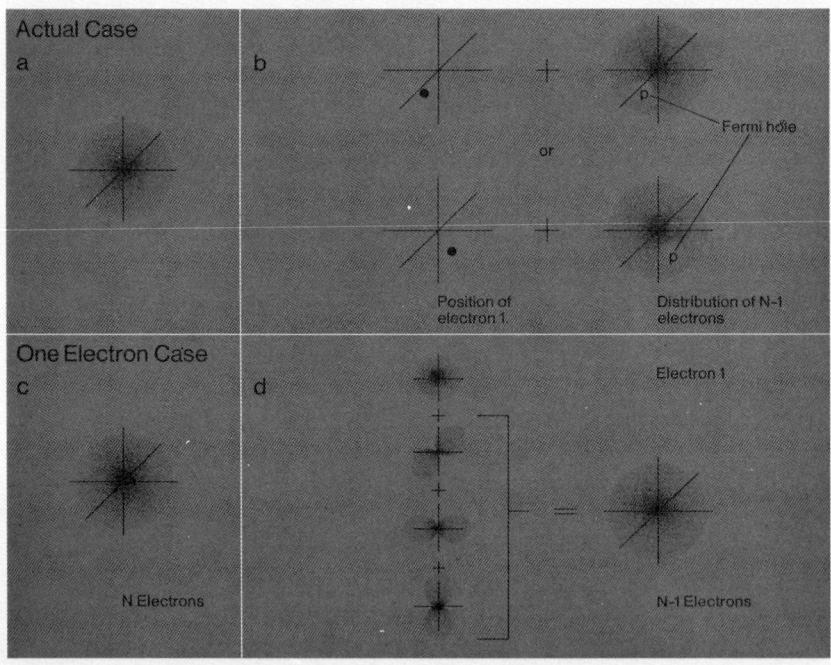

Figure IIG21-3. Approximations of electron distribution functions.

In fact, the method can be used in a systematic fashion to get all of the orbitals. First one guesses a series of orbitals. Then one goes through taking one out at a time and using the others to give the (N - 1)-particle distribution function and to calculate a new orbital. In this way one can obtain an entire new series of orbitals and then start over, recycling until (hopefully) the series gradually begins to reproduce itself. Thus one finally obtains a series of "self-consistent orbitals," that is, ones which are consistent with the last set and which solve the Schrödinger equation in the one-electron approximation. It is a common misconception that the Hartree-Fock method works only for atoms; in actual fact it is equally applicable to molecules also, although in this case, of course, it is more complicated.

In Figure IIG21-3 an actual many-electron wavefunction (for N electrons) is shown very schematically in (a), the orbits of the electrons are inextricably interdependent. Thus, if one specifies the location of electron 1 at point P, as in (b), the distribution of the remaining N-1 electrons depends on where P is. This is the phenomenon of correlation.

In the so-called one-electron approximation, although the total distribution function (c) may look like the distribution in (a), it is actually just a sum or superposition of the independent electron distributions shown in (d); so if one takes out electron 1, the distribution of the remaining electrons is not dependent on where electron 1 is.

In the Hartree-Fock type of one-electron approximation, the (N-1) electron distribution function of (d) is taken to be the average of the actual (N-1) electron distribution functions of (b).

The impact of this approximation was—and still is—very great, but it was primarily a conceptual one. Above all, it provided a model which justified thinking about atoms and molecules in terms of the easily-visualized one-electron orbitals. Furthermore, results of the Hartree-Fock method, though very laborious to obtain, gave a good first estimate of what total electron distributions looked like; total energy values for these distributions in simple systems came out roughly 1% from experimental values. This accuracy is especially impressive when one realizes that these are "ab initio" calculations, that is, calculations from first principles, and that they involve no empirical parameters. Nevertheless, this kind of 1% accuracy, which is inherent in the one-electron approximation, cannot be called quantitative for the purposes of chemistry. For instance, one of the most important chemical quantities is the bond energy, but usually it is only 1% or less of the total energy, so that it lies entirely within the range of the error of the approximation. That is, bond energies cannot be computed in the one-electron approximation.

Such then was the state of the art of quantum chemistry before the advent of computers. Except for the hydrogen atom, the Schrödinger equation for any chemical problem could not be solved analytically and the only accurate many-body results were obtained through laborious calculations which provided very little conceptual insight as well as very few quantitative results. Instead, group theory and the one-electron approximation were providing the basic framework for understanding atoms and molecules. By the late 1950's, however, the computer was already beginning to modify this situation.

Enter the Computer

Mulliken and Roothaan at the University of Chicago, Slater at MIT, Coulson at Oxford, and Boys at Cambridge were among the first to sense the potential revolution that the computer would bring about in quantum chemistry. From among their students and associates, a number have come to the IBM laboratory in San Jose, which is now becoming one of the major centers for computational chemistry.

Needless to say, the basic impact of the computer has been in doing tedious calculations at high speeds and thus in making possible calculations of a complexity heretofore unimaginable. One of the most common applications of the computer has been in doing Hartree-Fock calculations on bigger systems than had ever been done before. For instance, Clementi at IBM has recently done such calculations on a series of aromatic compounds such as pyridine and pyrazine which have as many as fifty electrons.

In addition, using the computer it has been possible for the first time to do extensive calculations beyond the limits of the one-electron Hartree-Fock approximation and thus to include the correlation effects of large systems in a quantitative way. Nesbet at IBM, for instance, has been able to compute correlation effects in atoms as large as neon involving ten electrons, using a method based on the "Bethe-Goldstone formalism." Actually methods which use the one-electron approximation as a starting point appear to be closest to overcoming the correlation problem in a systematic and quantitative way. One such method is called the "configuration interaction" or the "multi-configuration technique." It was introduced long ago by Frankel, Hartree, Slater, Yutsis, and others, but is only currently in the process of being programmed for actual use in molecules, in particular at IBM. In simplest terms, the "configuration" expansion is like a Fourier expansion or any other expansion in an infinite series of orthogonal functions. That is, a true many-body wave functions

G. MODELING, SIMULATION

can always be expanded in an infinite series of products of one electron orbitals. The Hartree-Fock result is only the first term of the expansion, in effect, and by adding configurations with excited orbitals, one gets further terms in the expansion.

Ethane's Rotation Barrier

Without going any further into the details of the computer calculations, which are very much the province of the specialist, one can easily see that computers have made the Schrödinger equation a quantitative tool in chemistry whereas before it was almost entirely qualitative. A typical example of specific quantitative information that the computer can supply is the calculation of the barrier to rotation caused by the difference in energy between the "staggered" and "eclipsed" forms of ethane. This molecule has two methyl groups which rotate around the central bond between the carbons like two wheels with three spokes each. It is easy to see, as in Figure IIG21-4, that since electrons repel each other, the energy of this system will be lowest when the spokes of the two wheels are misaligned or "staggered" and highest when the methyl groups line up with—or "eclipse"—each other. It was an intriguing challenge in quantum calculations to see if one could compute the energy difference between these

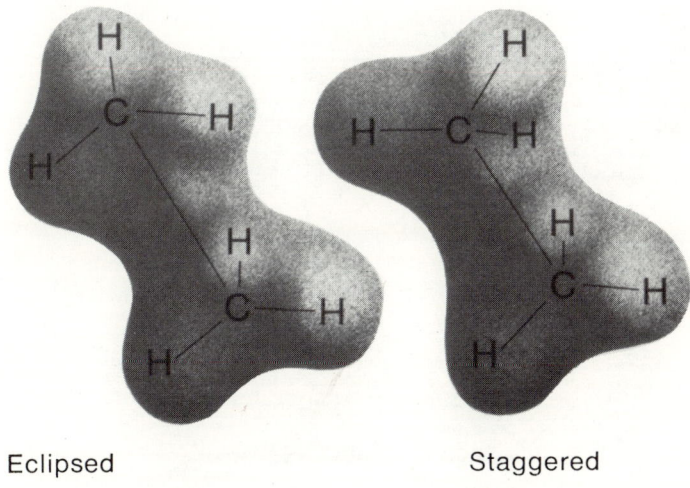

Figure IIG21-4. Ethene molecule.

two forms, minute though it is, and check with Lide's experimental value of 3.0 ± 0.3 kcal/mole. Among several calculations, one of the most thorough was that of Clementi and Davis at IBM, who got an answer of 3.6 kcal/mole. Although this is only accurate to 20%, it must be remembered that this is an "ab initio" calculation, with no empirical parameters. Perhaps the real impact of this calculation however will be in the future, when such "rotational barriers" will be calculable in cases more complicated than ethane, cases in which the barrier cannot be found in any way through experiment.

Reaction of NH_3 and HCl

Perhaps the most spectacular calculation so far has been Clementi's calculation of the system NH_3 and HCl reacting to form NH_4Cl. This work introduces one of the most exciting prospects for quantum chemistry, namely that of getting a detailed and quantitative understanding of "transitional states" and hence also of the entire field of kinetics. By their very nature, these transitional states, or intermediate steps in a chemical process, do not last very long and as a result are difficult to study by experiment. Yet they are obviously key in explaining how the reaction comes

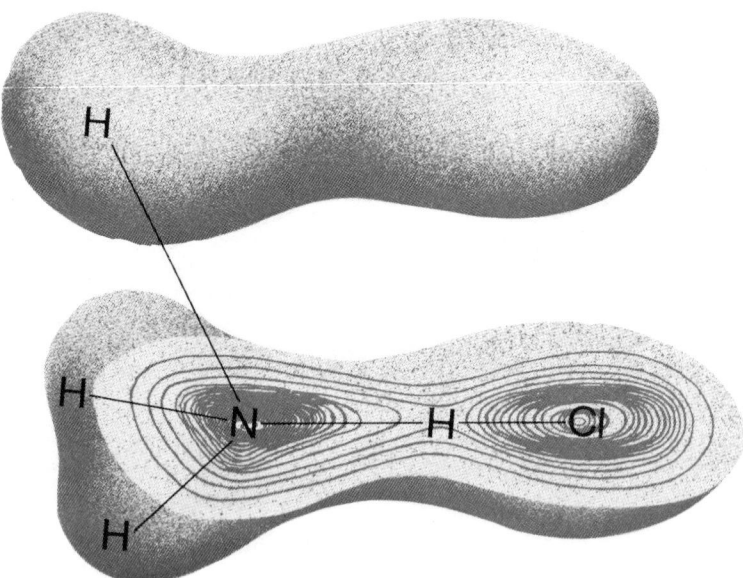

Figure IIG21-5. Computer results for $NH_3 + HCl \rightarrow NH_4Cl$.

a

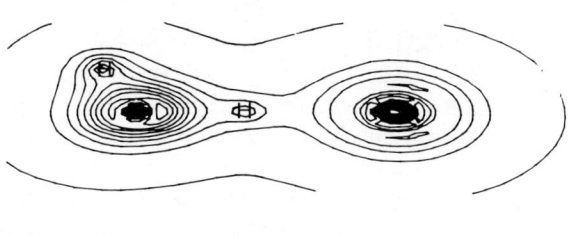

b

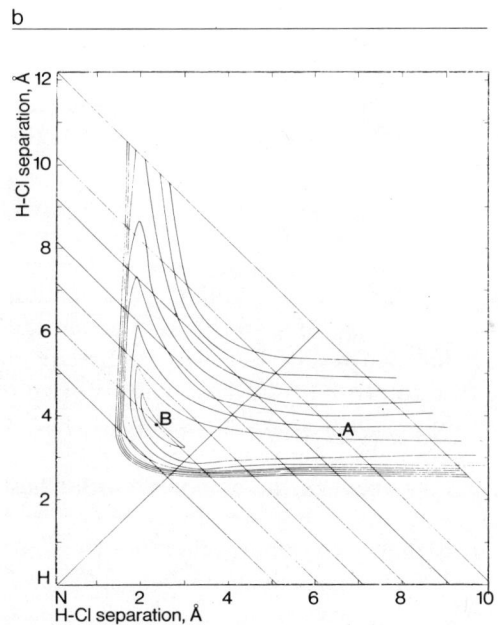

243

about. In the case of NH_4Cl, Clementi was able to calculate from first principles an entire "reaction surface" which describes the process of forming the hydrogen bond in the compound. Figure IIG21-5 gives computer-produced maps of electron density which show what happens to an electron distribution at two stages of the process: while the molecule is in the process of reaction, and after it has completed the reaction. The electron density maps a and b are taken on a plane along the N-Cl axis, as illustrated schematically in the drawing on the left, and show clearly how the electron density changes during the reaction. The configurations in a and b correspond to points on the energy contour map shown below. Such an energy contour map is variously known as a "reaction surface" or an "interaction potential," and is a key element in any quantitative theory of kinetics. The possible courses for a reaction follow the valleys in this map. (Each energy contour represents a step of 0.68 eV). Clementi was also able to predict that there would be no activation energy, and that NH_4Cl would be stable by 17 kcal/mole. Although these results disagreed with old experimental data, recent experiments by Goldfinger and Verhaegen have since found that NH_4Cl is indeed stable and by roughly $14 \pm$ kcal/mole. Furthermore, knowledge of the exact "interaction potential" between two molecules, as illustrated for NH_3 and HCl in Figure IIG21-5, is crucial to the entire theory of gases and liquids.

Conceptual Insights

We have been talking so far primarily about the quantitative impact of computers in chemistry. A further important point is that the computer has provided not just quantitative results but also qualitative results, that is, conceptual or theoretical improvements. This point is often overlooked because the computer is envisioned as a "brute-force" calculator that rides rough-shod, as it were, over clean conceptual insights. In fact, it is probably fair to say that the main impact of the computer so far has actually been conceptual.

One reason for this is that a large portion of the work to date has been done with the Hartree-Fock approximation, which, as we have already noted, ignores the key effect of correlation and hence cannot be considered truly "quantitative" for many purposes. On the other hand, these same calculations have made it possible for chemists to visualize clearly and to have a good feel for molecular orbitals in large molecules. For instance, the calculations by Clementi on NH_4Cl provide a graphic demonstration of how one-electron orbitals can add up to a total electron distribution. Thus in Figure IIG21-6 one can see how two orbitals in this molecule add up to the usual symmetrical distribution. Two such orbitals, the π_x and π_y orbitals,

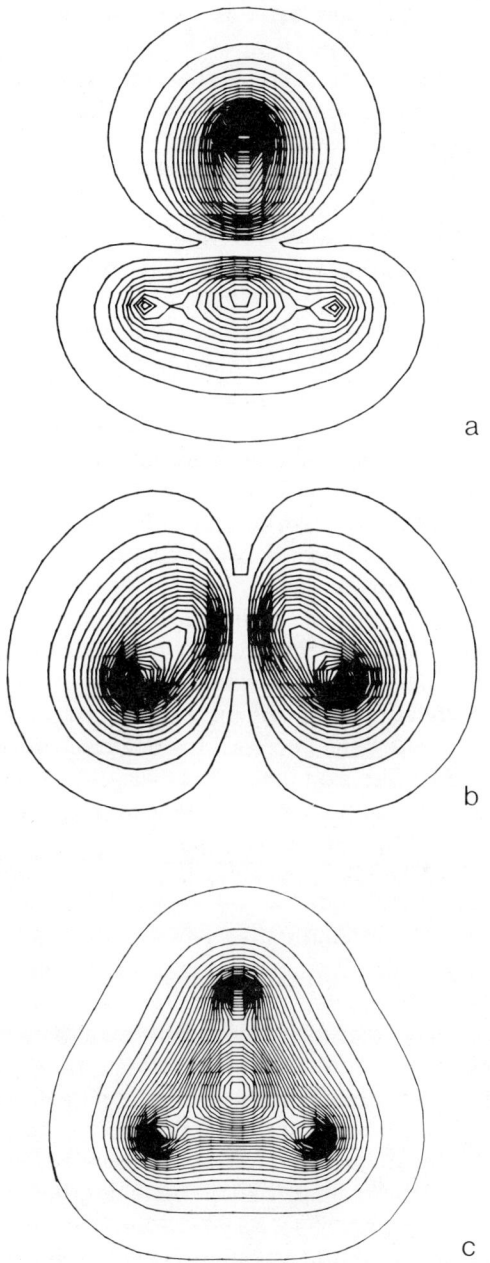

Figure IIG21-6. Cross section of orbitals, NH$_4$Cl Molecule.

are shown in cross section perpendicular to the N-Cl axis (in the plane of the three hydrogens) of the stable NH_4Cl molecule shown in Figure IIG21-5. When superimposed the two π orbitals add up to a symmetrical distribution shown in the third part of the picture.

Strange though it might seem, Hartree-Fock calculations have also given a great conceptual insight into correlation. For instance, merely by comparing Hartree-Fock results, which leave out correlation, to experimental results, which of course include it, Clementi has been able to formulate a very simple pairing model which accounts for many of the effects of correlation. That is, if one considers all the one-electron orbitals two by two, one can deduce, in crude terms, that there is a large correlation effect between orbitals that are concentrated in the same region of space like $2p$ and $2s$ orbitals of atoms, but a smaller correlation between orbitals that are concentrated in different regions of space, like the $1s$ and $2s$ orbitals. Furthermore, he finds a large correlation effect between orbitals with opposite spins, but a smaller effect between orbitals with parallel spins since roughly the exclusion principle already provides some correlation by keeping electrons with the same spin out of the same orbital. Even more interesting, he finds enhanced correlation effects in molecules. This fact indicates that a large part of the energy stabilization of a chemical bond is due precisely to correlation and explains—or at least gives a rationale for—why one cannot compute bond energies in a one-electron approximation.

However successful the computer has been in providing quantitative results or qualitative insights, it is important to keep such achievements in perspective. Although computers have pushed up the limit on the size of systems which can be handled, the limit is still finite. In fact, with present computers, it is probably fair to say that calculations will never solve systems with more than a hundred electrons. This is so because the length of the calculation goes up as a high power of the number of electrons: thus if a calculation with fifty electrons takes several hours or so, one with a hundred electrons, only twice as many, might take many days.

At the same time, one must not underestimate the significance of being able to do exact calculations on systems of up to a hundred electrons. Much of the chemistry of even more complex systems, especially organic or biological ones, can be understood in terms of the smaller chemical units of which they are made up, units like a methyl group which has only 9 electrons, or a benzene ring which has 42. An especially interesting case of combining smaller units into larger ones is that of polymers, and calculations of this type are being planned at IBM. There are of course fine effects which arise precisely when one combines these smaller units into larger ones and which will probably long be inaccessible to ab initio computations. Nevertheless when one realizes that before the advent of computers not even a single one of these smaller units was quantitatively understood, one can appreciate the magnitude of the improvement the computer has made.

And the method of using computer calculations to do this study is so versatile that in some cases it may actually be cheaper and better than the sophisticated experimental equipment needed in the modern laboratory.

In sum then, the techniques of quantum chemistry, that is, the computer solution of the Schrödinger equations, have brought about a major breakthrough in the many-body problem of quantum mechanics. They have provided both important conceptual insights and a vast amount of quantitative data, which is bound to get more and more accurate as time goes by, on a host of important chemical systems. In fact, as these calculations get more and more sophisticated, they will begin to compete both scientifically and financially with experimental techniques for getting physical information.

References

1. E. Clementi, "Ab Initio Computations in Atoms and Molecules," *IBM Journal of Research and Development,* **9** (1965), 2.
2. E. Clementi, "Study of the Electronic Structure of Molecules, Wavefunctions for the $NH_4 + HCl\ NH_4Cl$ Reaction, *Journal of Chemical Physics,* **46** (1967), 3851.
3. A. D. McLean and M. Yoshimine, "Computation of Molecular Properties and Structure," *IBM Journal of Research and Development,* **12** (1968), 206.
4. R. S. Mulliken, "Spectroscopy, Molecular Orbitals, and Chemical Bonding," *Science,* **157** (1967), 13.
5. J. C. Slater, "The Current State of Solid State and Molecular Theory," *International Journal of Quantum Chemistry,* **1** (1967), 37-103.

CASE STUDY 22 Calculation of Radiation Treatment Dosage*

Interest in radiation therapy is excited by the demonstrated ability of x-rays as well as other radiations to cause lesions to regress or to disappear and to achieve cures in many patients. Aside from surgery, radiation therapy is the only reliable method of cancer treatment with substantial

---

* This case study has been exerpted from References 1-3, kindly provided by John S. Laughlin, Memorial Hospital for Cancer and Allied Diseases, New York, N.Y.

cure rates. Statistics in the literature demonstrate the substantial role that proper radiation therapy has in curative as well as palliative cancer therapy. It is not competitive but complementary to surgery, since radiation is inherently capable of reaching where the surgical knife cannot.

Inherent Difficulties in Radiation Treatment

As contrasted with other methods of treatment, use of radiation is made more difficult because:

1. X-rays and other therapeutic radiations are invisible—the human eye is unable to follow their path as it can that of the knife or needle;
2. the biologic action often takes place within the patient, below the surface in areas which are not open for visual examination; and
3. the biologic effect is delayed-reaction or lack of it is not immediately apparent as in the case of the use of the scalpel or other direct methods.

As a consequence of these three inherent difficulties in the use of radiation, the evaluation of treatment methods is apt to be difficult and subjective.

Limitations in the Use of Radiation Treatment

Limitations in the use of radiation in man have included such side effects as the production of erythema, nausea, depression of blood count, necrosis in adjoining healthy tissue, etc. To a large extent these effects result from the irradiation of healthy tissue in the path of radiation beams reaching the target volume. The limitation of these effects requires concentration of the radiation dose as much as possible on the lesion and illustrates the importance of radiation dose distribution. Previously, radiation treatment in given cases was often seriously limited by one or more of these various undesirable side effects.

A major factor that must be considered in treatment planning is that of the different absorbing properties of the different structures in the body. For instance, in the plan for Co rotation treatment of an esophageal lesion (Figure IIG22-1), correction for the decreased absorption of the lungs has been included. The lack of absorption by the lungs causes the actual dose in the esophagus to be appreciably higher than would have been calculated on the basis of unit density considerations. The planned dose to the lesion was 6000 rads; if correction had not been made for the presence of lung, the delivered dose would have been in excess of 6800 rads. Such comprehensive

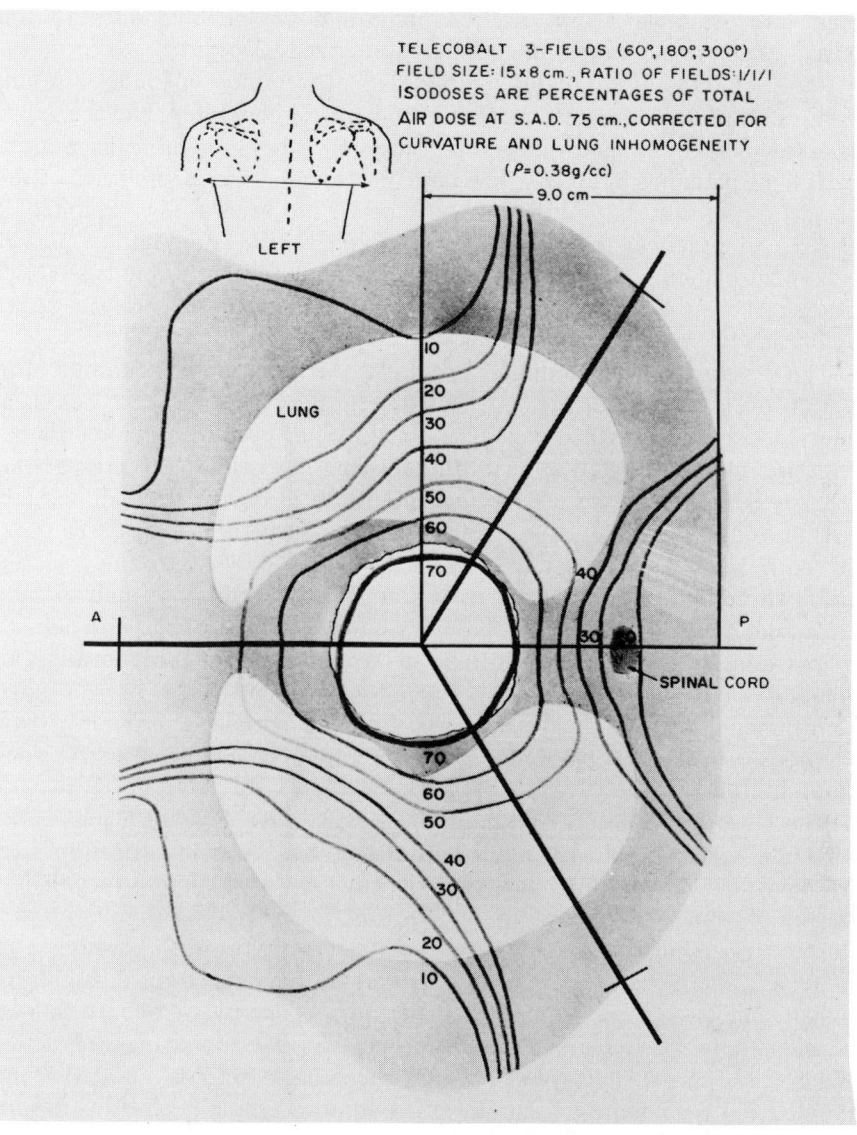

Figure IIG22-1. Treatment plan for esophageal lesion.

250 CURRENT USAGE: CASE STUDIES AND CRITIQUES

plans are available in any desired plane and are possible on a routine basis because of the development of computerized procedures.

The usefulness of computerized methods of treatment planning has long been established. However, because of the cost of computers and the extent of associated staff and programs necessary, they are used in routine treatment planning by only a few large centers and the possibilities of this powerful tool in radiation therapy have so far not been widely exploited. A cheap and practical linkage system that makes the computation part of treatment planning available at low cost to collaborating hospitals has been developed by the staff of Memorial Hospital, and the experience gained with this system is described below.

The development of computer programs for radiation dose computation began over a decade ago at Sloan-Kettering Institute and has been continuously refined since then. The objective has been to provide dose distribution plans for external beam therapy and interstitial and intracavitary therapy. Computer-assisted dose computations in two or three dimensions permit consideration of the effects of surface curvature, lung tissue, bony structure, and external obstructions in the radiation beam on the radiation field within the patient. While it is possible to produce an approximate treatment plan without a computer, a comprehensive treatment plan requires considerable design effort, and the number of computations are frequently beyond the scope of practicality. To facilitate the rapid production of individualized treatment plans for each patient, computer-assisted methods of treatment planning have been developed and are used routinely in Memorial Hospital.

The Dose Distribution Computation Service (DDCS), which makes this methodology available to other institutions, has been in operation since March 1967. An ordinary teletypewriter is used as a remote terminal by means of which all input/output data are transmitted to a collaborating hospital via regular telephone lines. The teletypewriter was chosen as a remote terminal because it is readily available, most economical, highly reliable, and easy to operate. Reliability and economy of operation were considered to be the most important factors in establishing a practical linkage system. A teletypewriter may be rented for less than $100 per month, and the cost per computation is nominal. Initially, five institutions collaborated with Memorial Hospital in the computation network. Other hospitals were added within a few months. Indicated in Figure IIG22-2 is the distribution of more than 40 of the hospitals now serviced on a regular basis by this system.

To date the policy has been to offer the service only to radiation therapists and only for use with high-energy x-ray and electron equipment

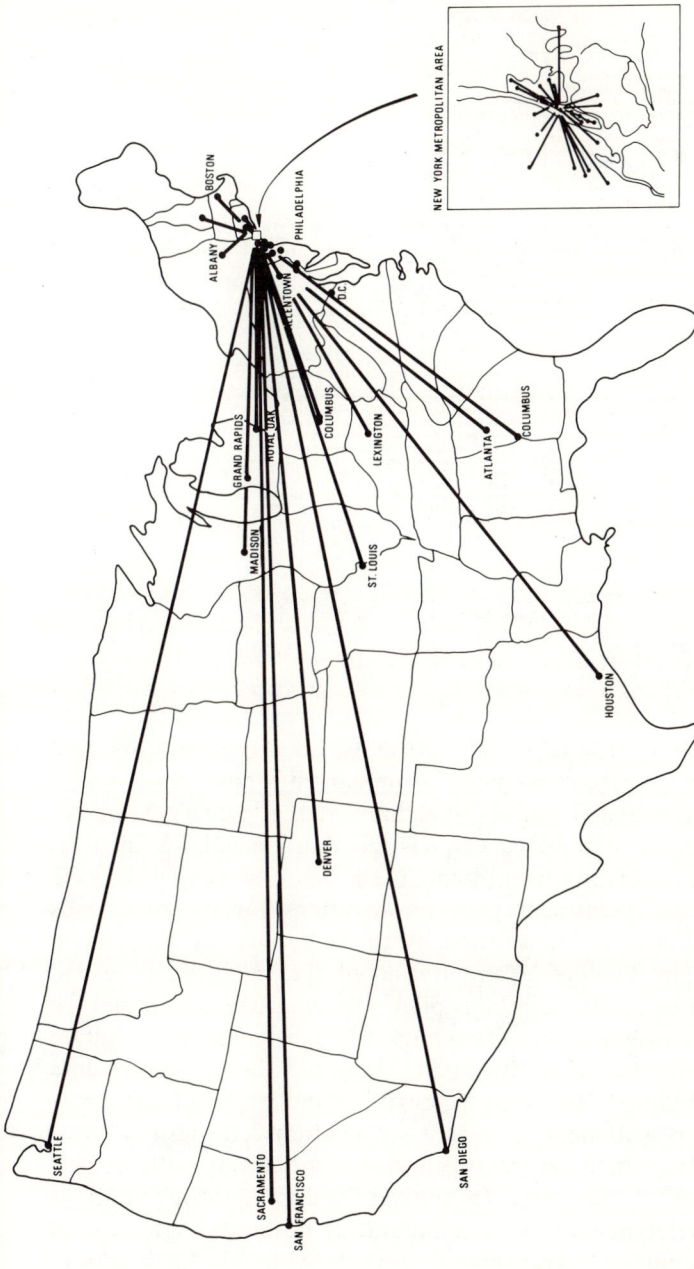

Figure IIG22-2. Memorial dose distribution computation service.

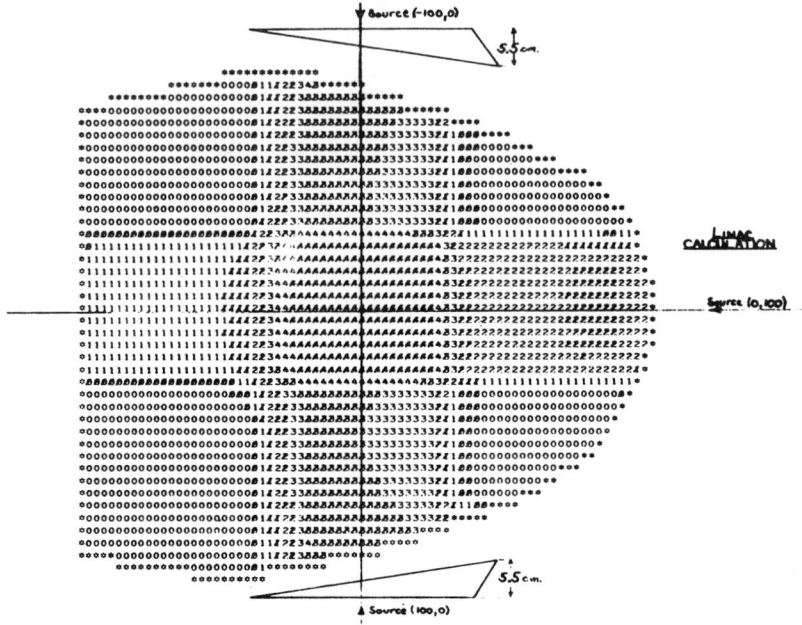

Figure IIG22-3. Isodose contour map; pituitary adenoma.

for external irradiation, including cobalt-60 units, linear accelerators, and betatrons. The system is also convenient for implanted radionuclides and is programmed for encapsulated sources of radium, radon, cobalt-60, iodine-125, iridium-192, etc. It should be emphasized that the DDCS involves computation only, with the treatment plan being designed by the collaborating hospital. Treatment plan specifications for external fields and/or internal sources are transmitted by the collaborating hospital to Memorial Hospital by teletype. Computation of the radiation dose distribution that would be produced by this plan is done at Memorial, and the resulting dose distribution is transmitted back to the originating institution via teletypewriter over telephone lines. At Memorial the computed dose distribution is punched. Normally a turn-around time of 24 hr is guaranteed, which is sufficient for most applications. If desired, it is possible to return the completed treatment plan computation within a few hours. Figure IIG22-3 illustrates a typical isodose contour map as transmitted over a teletypewriter to a collaborating hospital. In the case of large contour, the contour is transmitted in parts with fiducial marks to permit reconstruction by taping the separate parts together. Similar dose distributions are transmitted for intracavitary or interstitial implantations of radioactive sources.

The experience of the collaborating hospitals and our staff has demonstrated the feasibility of a practical linkage system for establishing a computation network. At present there is a nationwide need to make computer facilities of large centers available to qualified hospitals. The American College of Radiology has obtained some government support for the funding and the development of computation centers (PHS Grant No. 55042A67). Partial support for our program, which so far operates at less than its cost to Memorial Hospital, has been obtained through the American College of Radiology. The general aim of the computer centers is to promote better treatment planning and to serve large communities. It is expected that an increasing number of community hospitals will participate in a computation network for treatment planning. This development appears to be consistent with that of the Regional Cancer Centers within the Heart, Stroke and Cancer Regional Medical Program, and regional planning might very well include participation in such computation networks.

References

1. J. S. Laughlin, "Realistic Treatment Planning," *Cancer,* **22,** 4 (October 1968), 716–729.
2. J. G. Holt, S. Balter, A. Baker, J. S. Laughlin and R. F. Phillips, "Experience with a Dose Distribution Treatment Planning," *Annals of the N.Y. Academy of Sciences,* **161** (July 3, 1969), Article 1, pp. 344, 347.
3. G. Randall, S. Balter, J. G. Holt and J. S. Laughlin, "The Memorial Implant Dosimetry Automated System," *Computer Programs in Biomedicine,* **2** 3 (April 1972), 137–152.

H. DOCUMENTATION

The final formal phase in the scientific process is the documentation of the results and their distribution.

Case study 23 describes the documentation process as it has been developed in a large engineering environment, the Chevrolet Total Specifications Information System.

Case study 24 describes the Washington State Legislative Information System. Although legislators and lawyers are not thought of as scientists, it is interesting to observe the similarity between their activities and the phases of the scientific process described earlier.

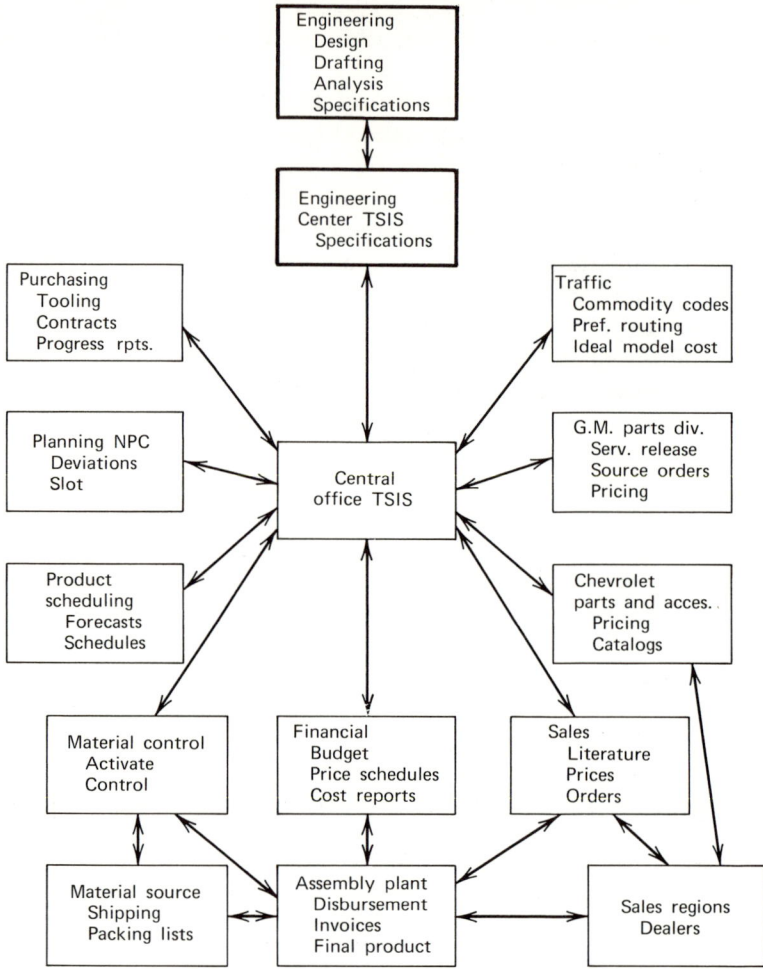

Figure IIH23-1. Chevrolet total specification information system.

CASE STUDY 23 Chevrolet
Total Specifications Information System*

Chevrolet is now using a new procedure for disseminating specification-type information. The new Total Specification Information System (TSIS)

* This case study has been exerpted from Milton R. Freivogel, "Total Specifications Information System," Automotive Engineering Congress, Detroit, Michigan, January 10–14, 1972.

is an on-line terminal system featuring immediate response and a common data base. This paper is concerned with the Engineering Dept.'s role in the implementation of this new system.

The distribution of information necessary to build our products is primarily a function of Engineering. The need to distribute and coordinate this information speedily and efficiently with all concerned activities—manufacturing, distribution, sales, etc.—is obvious. We will examine the efficiency of our new system, which will be completely effective during the 1972 model year, as well as previous methods. Some of the decisions, statistics, successes, and failures involved in the development of TSIS will be enumerated. Also, the future of TSIS will be explored.

The chart shown in Figure IIH23-1 depicts a Total Specification Information System for the Chevrolet Motor Div. Only Engineering Dept. activities are currently encompassed by TSIS. Briefly, TSIS is an on-line terminal system featuring immediate response and a common data base. The individual desiring information formulates an inquiry, and enters it through a remote terminal. The current status is returned either to his terminal or to an output (Data 100 printer) station nearby. The user has immediate access to information that is current, complete, accurate, and in usable form.

A significant feature of TSIS is the use of common Engineering Center files. Because of the frequency of use, not all data are retained on-line. When there is need to transfer information from the on-line files to the off-line files, it is accomplished automatically without reentering the information. TSIS is designed to operate in a large computer terminal network. In this environment, information can be passed readily from computer to computer. TSIS uses IMS/360 (Information Management System) for terminal and data base support.

A review of the following topics will set the stage for a detailed description of TSIS:

1. A description of how specifications functions and what is accomplished by this activity.
2. A description of how this same function was accomplished prior to TSIS.
3. History of TSIS development.
4. IMS/360

Functions of a Specifications Department

The Specifications Department has the responsibility of coordinating the publication of engineering documents. In performing this function, it has the task of converting drawings and layouts into a language understood by

256 CURRENT USAGE: CASE STUDIES AND CRITIQUES

Table IIH23-1 Document Volume Processed in 1970

	Documents	Reproduced and Distributed
ECR	10,396	814,712
Release notice	205,684	12,428,885
Parts list pages	174,863	8,912,169

nonengineering personnel guiding the activities of the central office and field departments (Figure IIH23-1).

In carrying out this function, the Specifications Department makes use of some basic tools. Let's define a few of these.

1. Engineering Change Recommendation (ECR)—The ECR is the authority to incorporate additions, deletions, or revisions into a Chevrolet product. The ECR describes in a general way the change to be made; it can vary in scope from a simple change to a single part, to an entire carryover program.
2. Release Notice—The release notice is a part number related document providing information for a single part number. A single ECR can cause one or many release notices to be issued. Various sub-breakdowns or part usage can occur requiring multiple release notices

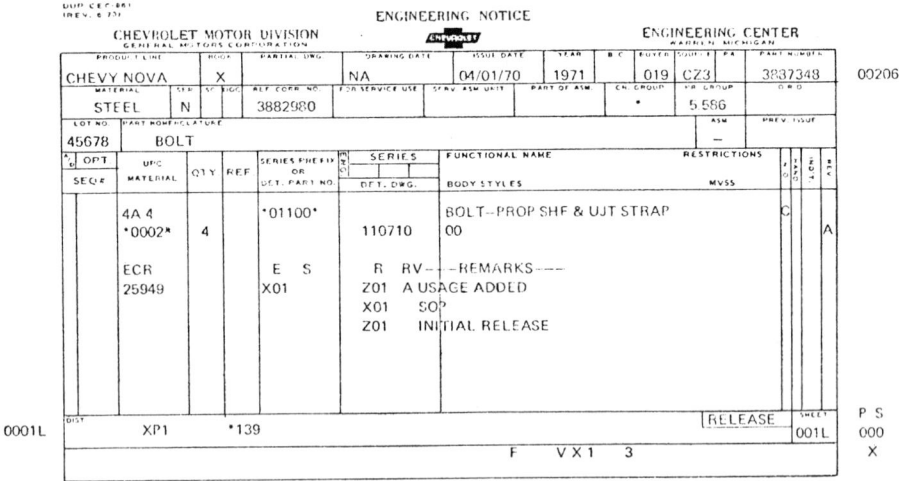

Figure IIH23-2. Release notice.

CHEVROLET MOTOR DIVISION — GENERAL MOTORS CORPORATION

ENGINEERING PARTS LIST

ENGINEERING CENTER — WARREN MICHIGAN

ENG USE	ASM	ON	PART NAME	HAND	PART NUMBER	CODE B C	REF	QTY	REV	PREFIX CHASSIS	PREFIX ENGINE	SERIES	ALL	27	BODY STYLES	REPLACED PART NUMBER	E.C.R NUMBER
01000 0002		O	PLATE-VEHICLE IDENT NO		3929909		D	1			110	710	X				17831
01020 0002		O	RIV-VEHICLE IDENT PLT		9423220			2			110	710	X				17831
01040 0002		O	REINF-VEH IDENT PLT		3929911			1			110	710	X				17831
01060 0002		O	LABEL-VEHICLE CERTIFICATION		3975433			1			110	710	X				17831
01080 0002		O	OVERLAY-VEHICLE CERTIFICATION LABEL		3983908			1			110	710	X				17831
01100 0017	—	O	LABEL-GM PRODUCTS TO BE ATTACHED TO FDR SK ADJACENT TO OIL LEVEL GAGE		734791			1	R			710	X				3K395
J05112																	
01440 0002		O	CEMENT-SPL ADHES AS REQD APPROX 3.75 GALS PER 1000 JOBS USED TO CMT PRICE LABELS		3764800			*	BM		110	710	X				3K395

CAR NUMBER AND IDENTIFICATION PLATES AND COMPLIANCE
PLATES

D—DOCUMENTATION REQUIRED
W—DOMESTIC ONLY
X—EXPORT ONLY

Y—FOR SHIPPING PURPOSES ONLY
Z—FOR ADDTL. INFO. SEE INSTR. MANUAL
*—SEE BELOW

R—AS REQUIRED
δ—PURCH. LOCALLY
√—PURCH. LOCALLY AGAINST CO. CONTRACT

A—ADDED
F—PART NAME REV.
G—NOTE REV.
(RELOCATED)

H—OPTIONAL NOTE REV.
K—HAND REV.
M—REFERENCE REV.

N—QUANTITY REV.
R—MODELS REV.
S—GENERAL REV.

DATE	REV. NO.	ENG USE	MODEL YR	BOOK	UPC	SHT NO
07/31/70	002	SOP	1971	X CHEVY NOVA	14F	1L PARTS LIST

Figure IIH23-3. Parts list.

for the same part. One of these is a breakdown by "BOOK" (Figure IIH23-2).
3. Book—Each carline produced by Chevrolet is assigned a book identifier—Chevrolet is book B, Chevelle is book A, Camaro is book F, etc. If the same part is used on Chevrolet, Chevelle, and Camaro, three release notices would be issued, one for each book.
4. Parts Lists—The parts list records all parts which have been published by release notices, and groups these parts by build conditions. The parts list is also controlled by BOOK and is the document used to determine the complete listing of parts required to build a specific Chevrolet product. Figure IIH23-3 is a sample parts list page.

The volume of documents processed during the 1970 calendar year are shown in Table IIH23-1. Specifications supplies processed documents to approximately 60 different recipients.

Procedure Before TSIS

Any engineering revision requires an ECR. Most changes affecting design involve various stages of layout, detailing, and checking before final drawings result. During that period when detail parts are in layout form only, a drafting analyst, using a drafting job sheet, would name, assign part numbers, determine quantity, and establish use—all recorded manually. Copies of the drafting job sheet were then sent to the Specifications Department for review and translation onto Specifications Department forms—parts list sheets and release notice forms. Because of inadequate or incomplete information at the drafting analyst level, a complete rewrite was generally required. The Specifications forms were then sent to data processing for keypunching and batch update of computer files, and for periodic publication of release notices. A review of the release notice mat before printing and distribution was made to ensure accuracy.

A complete set of release notices were retained and controlled by a group within the Specifications Department. This group had to properly accumulate the individual part releases and package them for the parts list. Chevrolet procedure dictated that all parts used on a base model car must be grouped in a base-car parts list, and all parts required for optional equipment grouped by option. The packaging of release notices, therefore, into parts lists was not a simple task; it was accomplished by marking up another set of forms, keypunching the same revision to update a parts list file, and finally printing the parts list.

The printed documents, after review by the Specifications Dept., were forwarded to the Distribution Dept. where the reproduction and mailing

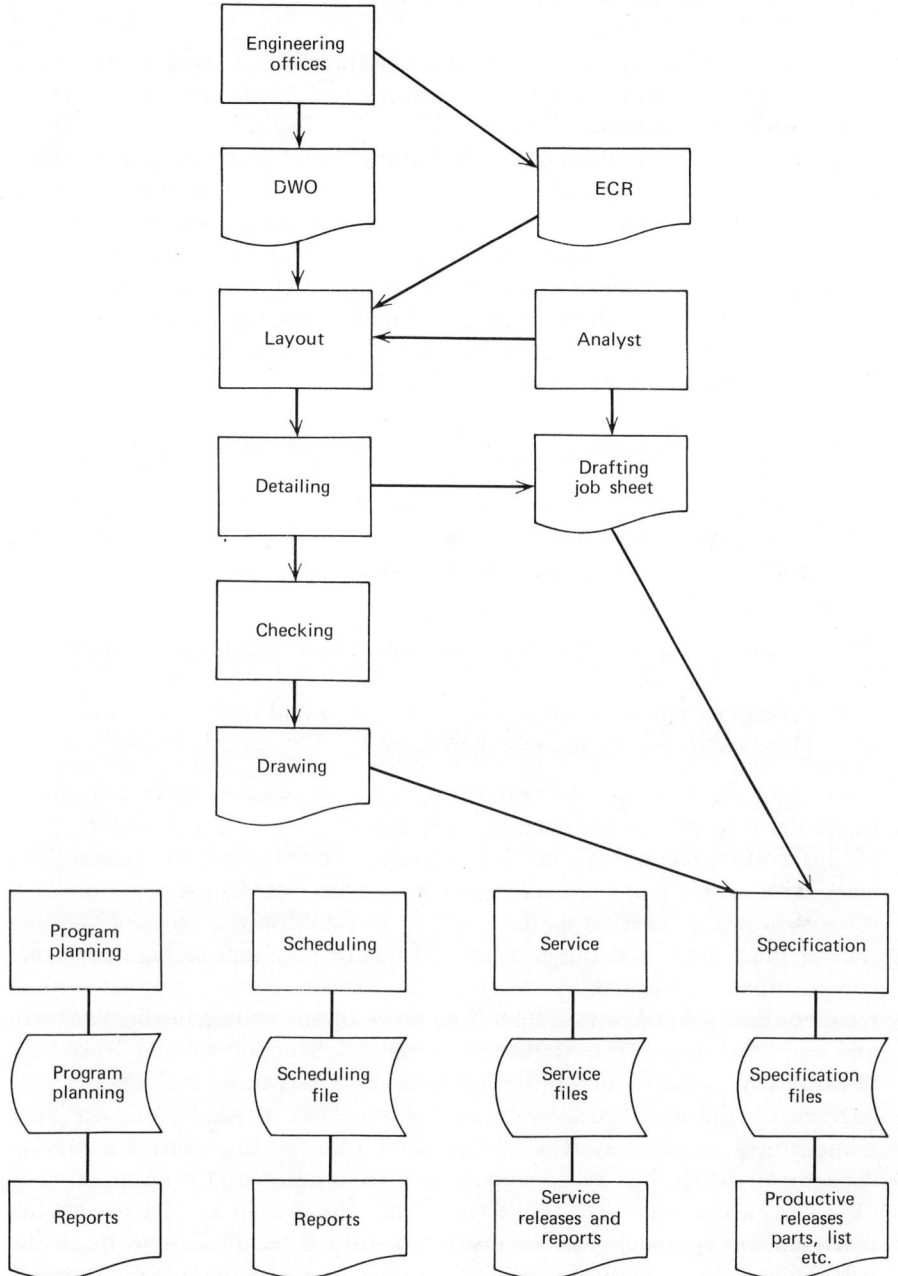

Figure IIH23-4. 1971 specification system.

progress began. Because of volume, mailing time, etc., a week elapsed time from receipt of mats in distribution to receipt of the document in the field was considered creditable.

The receipt of documents in the field started another round of keypunching and updating of material, order processing, costs, and related files.

Figure IIH23-4 shows our previous specifications system. Each department within Engineering had its own files, created its own input and distributed its own reports within Engineering, and, in many cases, outside of Engineering. Each recipient went through the same motions. The fact that there are no connecting links between the various files is symbolic of the lack of coordination between the files.

History of TSIS Development

TSIS began with management realization that processing of Engineering releases within Chevrolet needed to be expedited, clarified, and made much more automatic to satisfy increasing product complexity. This conclusion was arrived at because:

1. Releasing information was invariably late reaching all interested parties.
2. Personnel requirements to handle the job would need to be increased.
3. The incidence of errors was increasing.

In 1966, a committee of Engineering personnel was established to investigate the possibilities of alleviating these problems. The first major action of this committee was to involve employees from other departments to work with a newly created information systems activity. A full-time task force then began work in the fall of 1967 to establish the areas of jurisdiction of the system and the early definitions of potential techniques of accomplishment. The task force consisted of one systems analyst with a recipient background; one systems analyst with an engineering background; and representatives from Drafting, Program Scheduling, and Specifications. Early results were the agreement that larger, more sophisticated hardware configurations were necessary, that a genuine data base management software system was required, that the Engineering computer department needed to be expanded both in systems and programming in order to accomplish this objective, and, finally, that a true project management approach was necessary to involve technicians from all departments associated with releasing engineering specifications. By 1968, agreement had been reached on hardware and software, the implementation of a schedule (Figure IIH23-5), and the initial manning of the

H. DOCUMENTATION

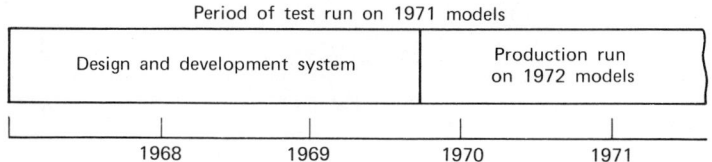

Figure IIH23-5. TSIS implementation.

group. Several false starts were generated and the full establishment of personnel took a great deal longer than at first anticipated. By 1969, enough of the total problem had been defined so that programming was able to begin in earnest, in the early months of that year. By early 1970, some 44 man-years of programming effort and 12 man-years of systems effort had been expended along with a great deal of user participation. By mid-1970 the decision was reached to actually begin the release of the 1972 product, employing TSIS as the releasing mechanism. The last and probably the most traumatic hurdle was the conversion of data permitting the establishment of initial files. When this was accomplished, official releasing via TSIS was started in 1970, leading to the use of the two systems: the final release of the 1971 specifications employing the historical system, and the release of the 1972 specifications using TSIS. All specifications within the engineering department are now released using TSIS.

Information Management System (IMS)

We required a software system which would allow flexibility, support on-line activity, and free the programmer from the task of file management. We had basically two alternatives:

1. Develop and program the software system ourselves.
2. Find a software package meeting all of the requirements including the IBM 360/65.

If we were to meet the established implementation schedule, it was evident that we had better find something to fit the second alternative.

We were able to get IMS, a beta test version, to evaluate it before full implementation of TSIS. The features of IMS which made it an attractive system were its data base support, its teleprocessing support, and its overall system capabilities.

In the data base area the following points were considered significant (Figure IIH23-6).

CURRENT USAGE: CASE STUDIES AND CRITIQUES

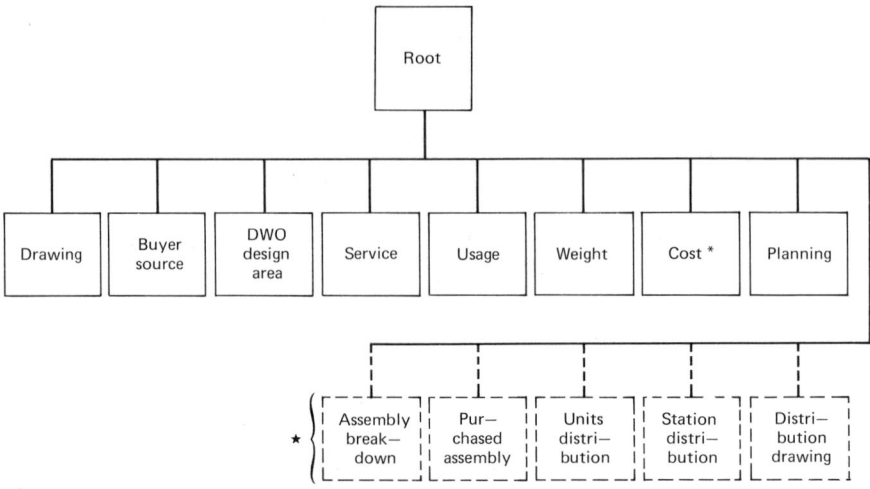

*Segments added without affecting existing segments
*Because of sensitivity only cost program has access to this data

Figure IIH23-6. Part number master.

1. Hierarchial structures allowed the TSIS data bases to be defined in a relatively straightforward manner.
2. New data definitions could be added to the structure without the necessity of reorganizing the data base, and without the necessity of rewriting the application programs.
3. Application programs could be defined to access from the data structure only that data which was of interest to them, thereby providing a measure of security.

In the teleprocessing area the following points were considered significant:

1. Security features provided that only valid, previously defined transaction codes were accepted by the system; and transaction code could have a password assigned to it; and transaction codes could be restricted to entry from certain terminals.
2. The output from an application program is normally returned to the invoking terminal. If that terminal was to fail, terminal independence allows the output to be redirected to a different terminal.
3. The system included a fairly rich command language which allowed the master terminal operator to monitor system activity and modify system operational parameters where desirable.

H. DOCUMENTATION 263

System capabilities which were of interest included the following:

1. The application scheduling facility allows priorities to be assigned to each application program, and when there is a backlog of programs to be executed, the programs are scheduled based on these priorities. The scheduling system also allows dynamic modification of scheduling priorities based on queue lengths.
2. Data base integrity is accomplished by controlled scheduling of application programs to prevent concurrent scheduling of programs which modify the same data base.
3. Checkpoint/restart facilities were included for taking checkpoints and restarting the IMS system following various kinds of failures without loss of message queues. The checkpoint/restart capability is also used to bring the system down at the end of the day and up on the following day.
4. Data base recovery utilizes a journal tape and software for restoring the data bases from backup and automatically rerunning activity after a data base failure.
5. The system had the capability for running multiprogrammed application programs, as well as multiprogramming IMS with standard operating system (OS) batch work.
6. A remote batch capability to address the on-line data bases was available (batch and teleprocessing refers to the ability of IMS to run programs entered via remote terminals and local batch).

The first version of IMS supported the 2740 typewriter terminal and promised support of cathode ray tubes in the future.

The normal concept of on-line processing involves a quick response to the terminal and IMS supported this type processing.

In TSIS, a simply inquiry could result in lengthy response. The inquiry was to come from a typewriter terminal and the response go to a medium-speed printer. IMS did not support this type of processing, but our software programmers developed the necessary interface to do the job.

Total Specifications Information System

The method of operation prior to TSIS is shown in Figure IIG23-4 in a single concise manner. There was no attempt to coordinate the various files; in some instances the same basic information was manually written and keypunched several times to update the various files. The existing system did not provide normal progression and control of data from plan-

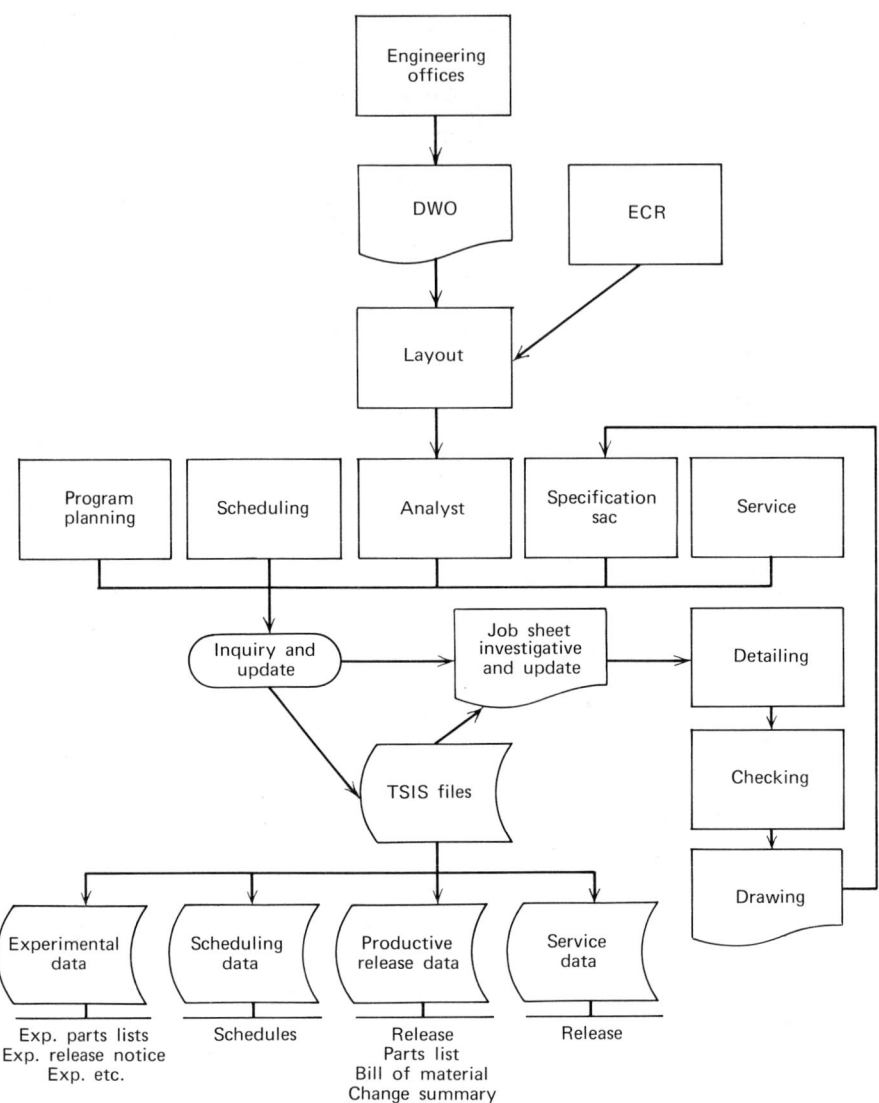

Figure IIH23-7. General flow of information in TSIS.

H. DOCUMENTATION   265

ning through productive release and then into service release. TSIS was designed with this procedure as a prime target.

Figure 11H23-7 illustrates the general flow of information in TSIS. The same operations are external to the computer as in the prior system except the job sheet. In TSIS the job sheet is printed from the computer files based on an inquiry, and will always contain the latest information. There is one common master file available to program scheduling, analyst, specifications, service, etc.

As we progressed in the development of TSIS, it became apparent that we could not meet the target date of productive use by October 1970, if we attempted to include all functions. The decision was to concentrate on the

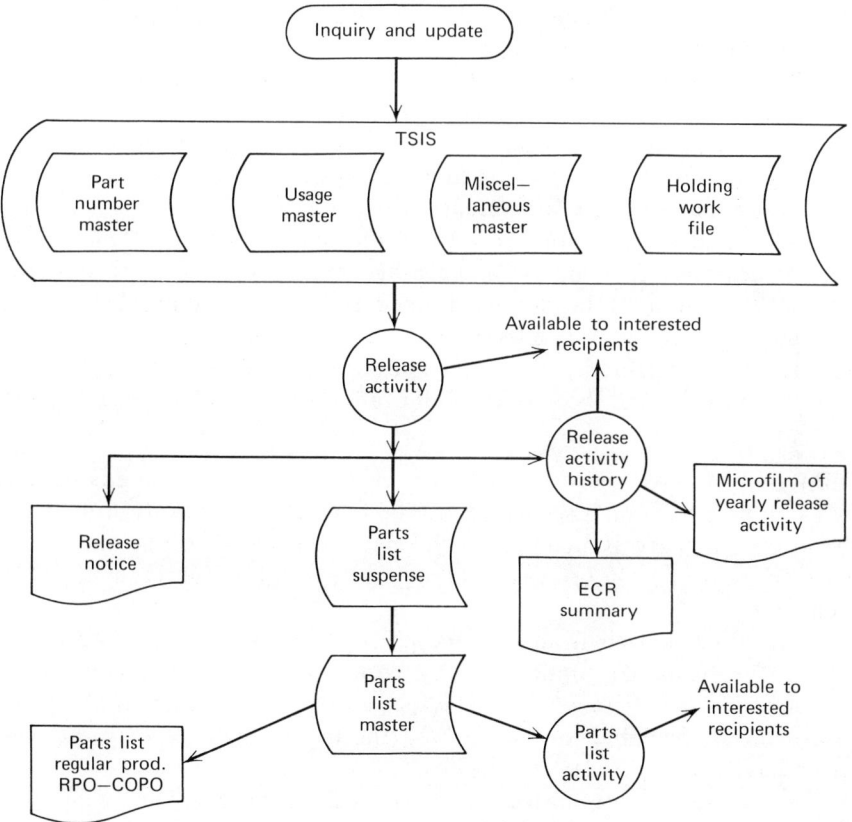

Figure IIH23-8. TSIS file finer breakdown.

productive release functions and the operation of the analyst and specification departments, but to organize the master files to facilitate all engineering specifications functions.

It is impractical to store all data required by the various departments in the on-line files; therefore, activity records generated from the on-line files; are used to automatically update related off-line files and produce the desired reports and transmittals to outlying locations.

Figure IIH23-8 illustrates a finer breakdown of the TSIS files, and shows how the on-line update and inquiry is subsequently processed through the system to produce the end product of release notices and parts lists.

Note the TSIS file is actually four major on-line files.

1. The part number master contains all data which is related to the part number and which is independent of the usage.
2. The usage master contains the latest release notice data for the current model year and an unlimited number of future model years.
3. The miscellaneous master is the dictionary used to interpret the many codes on the other TSIS on-line files as well as to prepare the release notice, parts list, ECR summary, etc.
4. The holding work file (HWF) is the audit segment of the release processing. All updates to the usage master must pass through the HWF and must be double-checked to ensure that proper revisions have been made. When the manual review is complete, the mechanical review is triggered and many edits are made before the usage master is updated and before the data are approved for release notice processing.

Data which have been approved for release notice processing is handled by batch programs on a second shift. The release notice mat is printed, and the release activity is updated to the parts list suspense and the release activity history. The release activity is available for transmittal to recipients.

Also, in a batch environment, the parts list suspense is used to update selected years, books, options, etc., to the parts list master and publish associated parts lists. The parts list activity record created in this processing is available for transmittal (the record includes only the parts which have been revised).

The release activity history will be used to produce an engineering change summary. The Specifications Department will submit parameters including the ECR (or ECRs) to be summarized. All release activity referring to these ECRs will be selected from the history file to prepare the summary.

H. DOCUMENTATION

The same release activity history will be used at the completion of each model year to microfilm the entire year's activity.

The brief definition of the major on-line files and the quick run through of the batch activity gives an overview of TSIS processing. Before describing the details of the normal job flow, some of the concepts embodied in TSIS, will be elaborated.

1. Data Filing—All data are entered into files by the dapartment responsible for the data; they then become available to all users. This concept is partly responsible for the split in the TSIS master file. Part number data are entered only once against the part number, and the same information is used on every release notice printed for the part. For example, part 103321 (WA LK-MED SPR LK 0.375-washer, lock—medium spring lock 0.375 diameter) has over 1000 usages in the usage masters; it will appear on approximately 1000 release notices; however, the name is entered only once for recording on all 1000 release notices. Not only does this concept greatly reduce the number of entries, it ensures that the name is identical on all documents.

2. Coding—Coding techniques are used whenever possible to reduce file size, reduce the possibility of introducing errors, facilitate user update, and simplify computer processing.

   Examples of our coding technique are shown in Figure IIH23-9. The codes are included in the part number master, usage master, holding work file, release activity, parts list master, etc. However, the meaning is contained only once (concept 1) in the miscellaneous master.

   The model code (1A0202) can be stored on the many records which use it in a much more efficient manner than the seven-line usage statement it represents. The possibility of error is greatly reduced if the user can reference 1A0202 rather than the complicated usage statement. Also, it is much easier and quicker for the user to enter 1A0202 rather than the usage statements.

   Decoding occurs only when necessary; it is normally associated with

	UPC	BOOK	FUNCTIONAL NAME	CLASS	OPTION	MODEL CODE	PART #	QTY
DECODED	ENGINE	NOVA	ENGINE ASM 350 CID/ AS SHIPPED	REGULAR PRODUCTION OPTION	ENGINE V8/350 CID	114 714 27	9399735	1
CODED	6	X	00400	B	L48	0119	9399735	1

Figure IIH23-9. Decoded versus coded record.

the printing of a document or report. Figure IIH23-10 shows a comparison of a coded record as opposed to a decoded one, and visually illustrates some of the advantages of coding from a file and update point of view.

There is another significant advantage to coding—the association of the Federal Motor Vehicle Safety Standard (MVSS) codes with the functional name address can be achieved to ensure that all parts used on our vehicles for safety related functions will have the same MVSS. A careful audit of the functional name address one time eliminates many repetitious updates and audits of each individual part number record and guarantees consistency.

3. Use of Existing Data and Records—As shown in Figure IIH23-8, the release activity prints the release notice and parts lists, and updates the release activity history used to print the ECB summary and microfilm the years release activity. This would have required much duplication of effort in the past. In fact, the method used to microfilm from the hard copy release notice is approximately 4 years behind right now. This concept will allow us to have 1972 activity microfilm before 1969, 1970, and 1971.

4. Use of Model Codes—A single model code for each usage statement within a book, and the model code, is computer assigned. For example model code B0001 will always mean series and model 15435 (Brookwood two-seat station wagon); all parts indicating a usage of model code 001 in book B (which included the Brookwood) are used in the production of a 15435 wagon. An example of a coded versus decoded record is shown in Figure IIH23-9.

No other model code will have that same meaning. The procedure to obtain a new model code is to ask the question: "What is the model code for the usage statement 15435?" The TSIS transaction at the terminal would be as follows:

TZ11 YEAR = 1, ECK = B, MAN = JCE;
15435 (END OF TRANSMITTAL)

The model code program takes over and makes many edits of the related files in the miscellaneous master, and checks every existing model code for BOOK "B" to see if there is one exactly the same as requested. If the answer is yes, then the response back to the terminal is the model code number or, in this example, B0001 equals 15435. If the model code did not previously exist, then the next sequential model code number is used and the response is B1000 equals 15435, but please confirm that this is exactly what you wanted. Another entry is required to confirm and establish B1000 equals 15435.

H. DOCUMENTATION

The concept of one model code for each unique usage statement has been used as the cornerstone in developing many of the new systems to be implemented by Chevrolet in the 1973 and future model years.

5. Importance of Functional Name Address—As shown in Figure IIH23-10 the functional name address (FNA) consists of the uniform parts classification (UPC) number plus a five-position name number which is manually assigned to properly locate the function in the parts list. "Properly locate" implies that the major functional part is listed first followed by all attaching parts and fasteners. The Functional Name Address is not restricted to a particular car line but rather is used for all car lines. Any time a part is used for a function of body assembly-radiator, it will be assembled in UPC 13A and will carry FNA 00150. The FNA is used to sequence the parts list; therefore, all car line parts lists will show the body assembly-radiator in the same relative location. This concept allows an inquiry by functional name to produce a listing of all parts used for that function throughout the system, and will greatly aid in the deproliferation of parts.

The user has at his fingertips 75 programs which operate through the terminals in an on-line environment. Some are inquiry, some are update, some access a single segment of one of the files, some access many segments of all the files. Each ECR is unique and will require one or more of the 75 on-line programs to handle the ECB to completion. There is no single way that a job must be processed through the system and there is no need to handle programs in a strict sequential order. Some job steps do require that prior

TYPE CODE	CODE KEY		MEANING
	BOOK	CODE NO.	

MODEL CODE	1A	0202	132134534 00
			136 36 39 46 49
			138 36 46
			         &LS3#
			136
			    536 00 6780
			    &LS3,LS5#

	MODEL YEAR	CODE NO.	
BOOK CODE	1	1A	CHEVELLE SECOND LEVEL SEGMENT WILL CONTAIN ALL BODY STYLES FOR THE 1971 CHEVELLE
	UPC	CODE NO.	
FUNCTIONAL NAME ADDRESS	13A	00150	BODY ASSEMBLY—RADIATOR SECOND LEVEL SEGMENT WILL CONTAIN ALL MOTOR VEHICLE SAFETY STANDARD CODES

Figure IIH23-10. Coding technique examples.

270 CURRENT USAGE: CASE STUDIES AND CRITIQUES

```
                                                    JOB # 05000   ECR 12345
 RECORD IN HWF                  STEP 1              MAN  JOE

                           C
              B            L
         U  O  FUNCTIONAL  A
         P  O  NAME        S                          MODEL              CANCEL AND
  REC #  C  K  ADDRESS     S  OPTION  PART #  QUANTITY  CODE  REVISION  REPLACES PART #
• M0001  6  X  00400       B    L48   9399735     1     0119   ——           ——

 • M INDICATES THIS IS A RECORD FROM THE USAGE MASTER
```

```
                                 STEP 2
         ENGINEERING CHANGE RECOMMENDATION IS REPLACE 9399735 WITH 5379939
 TERMINAL INPUT IS— TZ27 JOB=G5000, MAN=JOE, UDC=C, REC=0001, PTN=5379939;
```

```
 RESULTS                        STEP 3
                           C
              B            L
         U  O  FUNCTIONAL  A
         P  O  NAME        S                          MODEL              CANCEL AND
  REC #  C  K  ADDRESS     S  OPTION  PART #  QUANTITY  CODE  REVISION  REPLACES PART #
  M0001  6  X  00400       B    L48   9399735     1     0119  T=CANCELED    5379939
• U0001  6  X  00400       B    L48   5379939     1     0119  A=ADDED       9399735

 • U INDICATES THIS IS AN UPDATED RECORD — WHEN THE JOB IS COMPLETE,
   THE (U) RECORD WILL REPLACE THE (M) RECORD IN THE USAGE MASTER
```

Figure IIH23-11. Procedure for updating in HWF.

action has taken place—a record cannot be revised in the holding work file unless it has previously been placed into the holding work file. In general, the user has the tools and the flexibility to process an ECR in the manner which he deems most efficient.

Upon receipt of an ECR in the Specifications Department, much of the groundwork will be accomplished prior to any analyst activity in the design areas. If, for example, a new model, body style, option, or UPC group is required, it will be added to the TSIS files by the individual releasing groups in specifications.

As layouts are completed in design or have sufficient information to involve the analyst, inquiries are made specifying the data in question. Inquiries can be by UPC or part number, with many combinations of qualifiers (year, book, functional name address, etc.). The job sheet generated reflects the latest release information and is designed for use by the analyst as a worksheet to indicate what revisions, additions, or deletions are necessary as indicated by the ECR. All information to mark up a job sheet satisfactorily is at the analyst's immediate disposal with two exceptions. New addresses for functional names and optional and item notes, still have to be requested by the analyst from a central control group in Specifications. It is the responsibility of this central control group to load the proper functional names and/or notes to the file, and to furnish the analyst with the appropriate address. This control is necessary to eliminate duplication and provide a uniform method of sequencing usages in the parts list.

H. DOCUMENTATION 271

Secondly, new model codes, if required, are furnished to the analyst by the respective releasing groups or the analyst coordinators upon request.

When the job sheet has been completely marked up, loading and updating the holding work file can be accomplished. The size of the job and amount of updating required will determine the terminal operator. Experienced typists or keypunch operators are located throughout the design areas for the purpose of mass updating. Relatively small jobs can be handled by the individual analyst responsible. The operator requests a job number using the analyst's initials, and the ECR number associated with the job. After receiving a job number, the operator will proceed to load the holding work file (HWF). The extent of the load is dependent upon the nature of the changes reflected on the marked up Job Sheet. Records can be moved to the HWF, one at a time or in bunches.

After loading the HWF and having received a printout reflecting those records which were loaded, the operator can begin updating. To identify the item requiring change, only the record number is required. In the actual update, only those fields reflecting a change are required (Figure IIH23-11).

New part numbers must be added to the Part Number Master File. Entering the new part numbers on the files as soon as possible is given the utmost consideration.

Upon completion of the update, a finalized job sheet is requested. The result is a printout on job sheet form, showing only those usages in an update state. Any usages initially loaded to the HWF, which were not updated will be bypassed.

The analyst reviews the job to insure that it is accurate and complete. Any corrections must be accomplished using the maintenance program. If any corrections or additional updates are required, another request for a finalized job sheet is submitted. When the job is considered complete by the analyst responsible, it is forwarded to an audit group in Specifications.

The audit groups in Specifications will coordinate releasing all jobs from the various design groups for a given ECR. They will again insure accuracy, completeness, and uniformity for the total job. They have the ability to use the same update and maintenance programs available to the analyst or terminal operator if alterations become necessary.

The audit group will then finalize the ECR control information by adding the correct effective point, stock disposition, and reason. A single entry for effective point, stock disposition, and reason for the ECR is applied to all records associated with the ECR, unless specific data have been entered to the contrary on individual records.

Assuming all previous steps have transpired satisfactorily, the job is ready to be released. The releasing program, among its many edits, checks all codes on each record to be released against the miscellaneous master to insure that all codes have a meaning. If any information pertaining to the job does not pass the edits or is missing, the entire job will be held up until necessary corrections are made, with one exception: the absence of a drawing date on a new drawing will not restrict the release of a job. It will, however, prevent a notice from being issued on those parts requiring drawing information. The subsequent addition of drawing information to the part number master will trigger the Release Notice.

All of the above transactions take place during the prime 8 h shift. They are accomplished on-line using the 2740 typewriter terminal, and at sometime or other, all of the 75 on-line programs. The net result is that a number of records in the HWF are coded in such a manner that the nightly batch processing will print the Release Notice, create the release activity, update the release activity history, etc.

Two-hundred programs have been developed for use in the batch-processing environment.

Educational Requirements

Switching from a completely batch-oriented system (cne in which everyone maintained his own files for his own use) to a terminal-oriented system with a unified data base concept, required an enormous amount of education. The IMS requirement of transaction codes proved to be a big assistance in the education. The various segments of the files are updated and inquired by particuar departments. Each segment has its own unique transaction code.

A user's manual was prepared for each transaction code; it describes the objective of the program, all key words assocated with the program, and gives examples of inquiries and responses. Figure IIH23-12 is the terminal guide for the general part number inquiry. By reviewing the user's manual, a novice can use the terminal productively within a few minutes. Although the entire system can be viewed as complicated, each individual program is simple to use and understand. Knowledge of the interaction of the programs, and choice of the shortest route to obtain a correct answer, is necessary for efficient operation. "Hands on" experience is our best education.

Initially, a class giving approximately 25 h of instruction was set up for all Specifications people. Because the subject matter was completely new and further, we lacked training aids or real examples, much of the program was not absorbed by our employees. Realizing this, another education program was established with a smaller group of employees. We included supervisors, coordinators, and employees who would be responsible for

H. DOCUMENTATION

```
TRANSACTION CODE:      TA13                    PROGRAM NAME:   GENERAL PART NO. INQUIRY
DATE:                  10-1-70
DATA KEY DELIMITER:    (COMMA)
END OF MESSAGE DELIMITER:  (SEMI-COLON)                        SHEET 1 OF 1
DESCRIPTION                        KEYWORD = CODE              CODE EXPLANATION
     TRANSACTION CODE              *TA13b
     MAN NUMBER                    MAN = A/N                   3 POS.
     SEGMENT KEYS                  *SEK = A                    5 POS. (MAX.)
                                                                 A = ANALYST
                                                                 D = DRAWING
                                                                 K = COPS
                                                                 P = RELEASE
                                                                 R = PART ROOT
                                                                 S = SERVICE
                                                                 W = WEIGHT

                                                                 U = USAGE (MUST BE ALONE)
                                                                 X = ALL OF THE ABOVE
                                                                     EXCEPT USAGE

     PART NO.                      *PIN = A/N                  5 POS. (MIN.)
                                                               8 POS. (MAX.)
                                                                 SEPARATE PART NOS
                                                                 WITH ONE (1) BLANK

     RECORD TYPE (WGTS. ONLY)      **TYP = A                   3 POS. (MAX.)
                                                                 A = CURRENT WGT. - ROOT
                                                                 B = MATL SPEC - ROOT
                                                                 C = CARD, STG DETAIL
                                                                 E = EST WGT ROOT
                                                                 X = ALL OF ABOVE

*REQUIRED INPUT
**A MAXIMUM OF THREE (3) WEIGHT SEGMENT TYPES MAY BE INQUIRED AT ONE TIME,
  OR ALL IF 'X' IS USED.

REMARKS:  A MAXIMUM OF FIVE (5) SEGMENTS MAY BE REQUESTED AT ONE TIME
          OR ALL EXCEPT USAGE IF 'X' IS USED.

          A MAXIMUM OF EIGHT (8) PART NOS. CAN BE INPUT IN ONE INQUIRY.
```

Figure IIH23-12. TSIS terminal guide.

modification to the data base; approximately 90 people were involved. The approach in these classes was to review each program as to its function during 2 h scheduled each week over a 3 1/2 month period. The time required to educate those in the user department, with an on-line system, appears to be a minimum of 1–2 months per man. The total time has exceeded 22 man-years for the Specifications Dept. to date; when all educational requirements are met, with all phases of the system operational, the time expended, may exceed 40 man-years.

Statistics

Many determinations are involved in evaluating any set of statistics; indeed a single set of figures will cause varied reactions. For this reason the following statistics will include a few "attaching" comments.

The part number master is contained on two 2316 disc packs; it includes 74,000 unique part numbers. An average of nine segments of data are associated with each unique part number for a total of 640,000 segments. The size of this file will continue to grow because the file will become his-

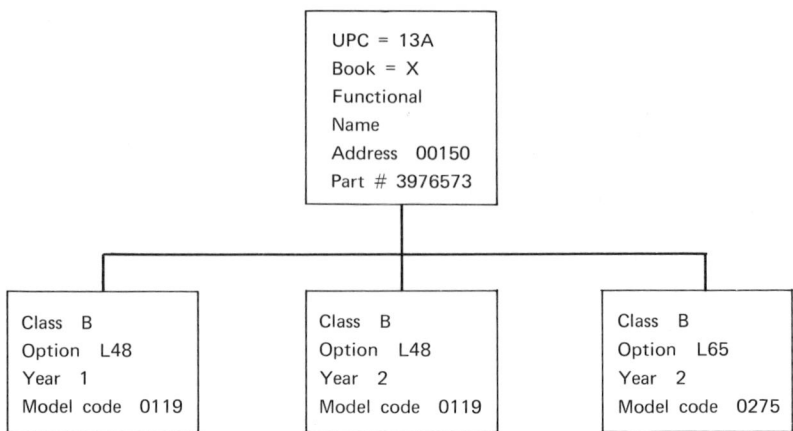

Figure IIH23-13. Usage master.

tory when the usage of the part is inactive, and additional segments will be added with future development.

The usage master uses one and one-half 2316 disc packs, and contains 68,000 prime usage records; each prime record in turn contains between two and three segments. Separate segments are required when the same functional usage of a part number is used for two different model years, two different options, or two different model codes (Figure IIH23-13). The counts in this file represent model years 1971 and 1972, and a little of 1973. When TSIS becomes fully operational, the number of records will approximately double and will include five model years at most times. When a model year is complete, the records will be removed from the active on-line file.

The HWF can hold 500–10,500 jobs, and is contained on three-quarters of a 2316 disc pack. It is significant to note that, in theory at least, jobs are established on the HWF and completely processed to produce release notices in a short span of time. Consequently, this file is reorganized frequently to remove completed jobs and make room for the next day's activity. During normal operations there will be about 450–500 open jobs in the HWF at one time. These jobs are active.

The miscellaneous master, or the "TSIS dictionary," contains 70,000 prime records with 130,000 segment records. This file remains relatively constant as only a small portion of the total file is affected by multiple years. For example, a single functional name dictionary covers all years in the related files. The same is true for model codes, option names, UPC names, etc.

The present terminal system consists of twenty-five 2740 terminals scattered throughout the Engineering Center and adjacent buildings. Four Data 100s are strategically located so that all users of the job sheet have one within easy reach.

Since beginning productive use of ISIS in October, 1970, our biggest day of activity involved better than 5000 inquiries and updates into on-line files. Of the inquiries, approximately 500 were requests for job sheets and involved a response at the Data 100 as well as at the terminal.

One last statistic—an on-line system such as this is not cheap. Figure IIH23-14 shows a breakdown of the 3072K core in our 370/165 computer. Please note that the TSIS requirement is 886K including the IMS nucleus, which is also available for any other IMS application.

Appraisal of System

Once the initial fear of the terminal was overcome, and the system became familiar, it was readily accepted. There are shortcomings. For instance, some of the data should be moved from one file to another to simplify processing. Some jobs require multiple steps when only a single step should be required. Some of the original ground rules used to develop TSIS are outdated. We were forced to drop planning and scheduling functions in order to use TSIS for the 1972 model. The improvement of existing pro-

OS NUCLEUS	136K
SYSTEM QUEUE AREA	142K
FREE SPACE: NORMAL JOBS	1092K
TSIS TYPE 2 (3)	270K
*TSIS MESSAGE REGIONS (2)	180K
*IMS NUCLEUS	352K
*IMSRDR	20K
*TPWTR (4)	64K
CRBE	106K
CRBEWTR	8K
TCAM	60K
TSO CONTROL REGION	122K
TSO FOREGROUND REGION	128K
CUE	14K
RDR	22K
WTR (4)	48K
PTWTR	20K
TV	12K
MASTER SCHEDULER & LINK PACK AREA	276K
TOTAL	3072K
*TOTAL TSIS REQUIREMENTS	886K

Figure IIH23-14. 370/165 core layout.

grams and files, and the inclusion of new functions, will be a continuing requirement.

The flexibility of TSIS will allow the Engineering Center to convert to a new releasing concept with a minimum of effort and program rewrite. Termed "total modular," it will be effective for the 1973 model year. Also, the establishment of a single model code for a book is very instrumental in enabling Chevrolet to convert downstream systems for the total modular concept.

The use of machine-readable records is more and more requested by recipients of engineering data. We are much closer to the day when the millions of hard copies now used can be reduced or eliminated. Further, the replacement of some 2740 terminals with CRTs will greatly increase the efficiency of the system, as well as the efficiency of the girls who process the job sheet updates.

Long lists of advantages are always prepared to help sell a system; the ones that really count, however, are those which attest to its success long after the system is operational. Such TSIS advantages were prepared by people who used the system after it was operational and, therefore, serve as the best appraisal of the system

These TSIS advantages are:

1. One programming system.
2. Reduce education requirements.
3. Increase manpower flexibility.
4. Standardize engineering output formats.
5. Eliminate duplication.
6. Complete and latest information.
7. Information available as required.
8. Functional names standard for all books.
9. Uniform parts list sequence.
10. Standard model codes.
11. Preprinted job sheet.
12. Carryover a complete UPC with one transaction.
13. Audit information before release.
14. More complete obsolete list.
15. Provide better check point ability.
16. Reduce release cycle.
17. Reduce number of release notices.

Summary

Although many new concepts were introduced with TSIS, they were not revolutionary, and thus they did not completely upset the method of operation familiar to the user departments. The use of TSIS during the past year, and the flexibility contained in the TSIS files and programs will greatly aid us in incorporating the revolutionary change to a "Total Modular Releasing System in 1973."

If we were starting another project such as TSIS with our present experience behind us, three improvements would be sought:

1. Involve more participation of the ultimate user at an earlier time.
2. Involve a higher level of management in approving and supporting new concepts.
3. Get the downstream departments interested in joining the project at its inception.

CASE STUDY 24   Washington State Legislative Information System*

Introduction

For the past several years the Legislative Information System in the State of Washington has been engaged in developing a group of automated information services for the benefit of several major areas of state government. The chief beneficiary of these services is the State Legislature, which has had designed for it an online inquiry and update system and a series of daily, weekly, and as-required reports published and distributed while the legislature is in session. These data processing systems have been instrumental in providing the legislature and the citizenry with timely reporting of the process and substance of current legislation. Another major endeavor consists of the development of a computer search system for Washington's statutory, administrative, and decisional law. This task will eventually have a profound effect on legal research methods in the state. The third major application development is the processing, correction, and/or manipulation of text materials for a variety of users, the major users being the Code Reviser's Office in the process of drafting legislation, the House and Senate workrooms in the process of engrossing amendments into bills and enrolling bills, and the Code Reviser's Office in publishing the session laws (Acts of the Legislature). Future data processing projects contemplate the extensive use of the computer in the process of publishing the Revised Code of Washington and the Washington Administrative Code and in the creation and maintenance of various indexes related to these

---

* This case study has been exerpted from IBM Application Description GE 20-0389, which was written by the Code Reviser's Office of the State of Washington for publication by IBM. Only the sections involving documentation are included here.

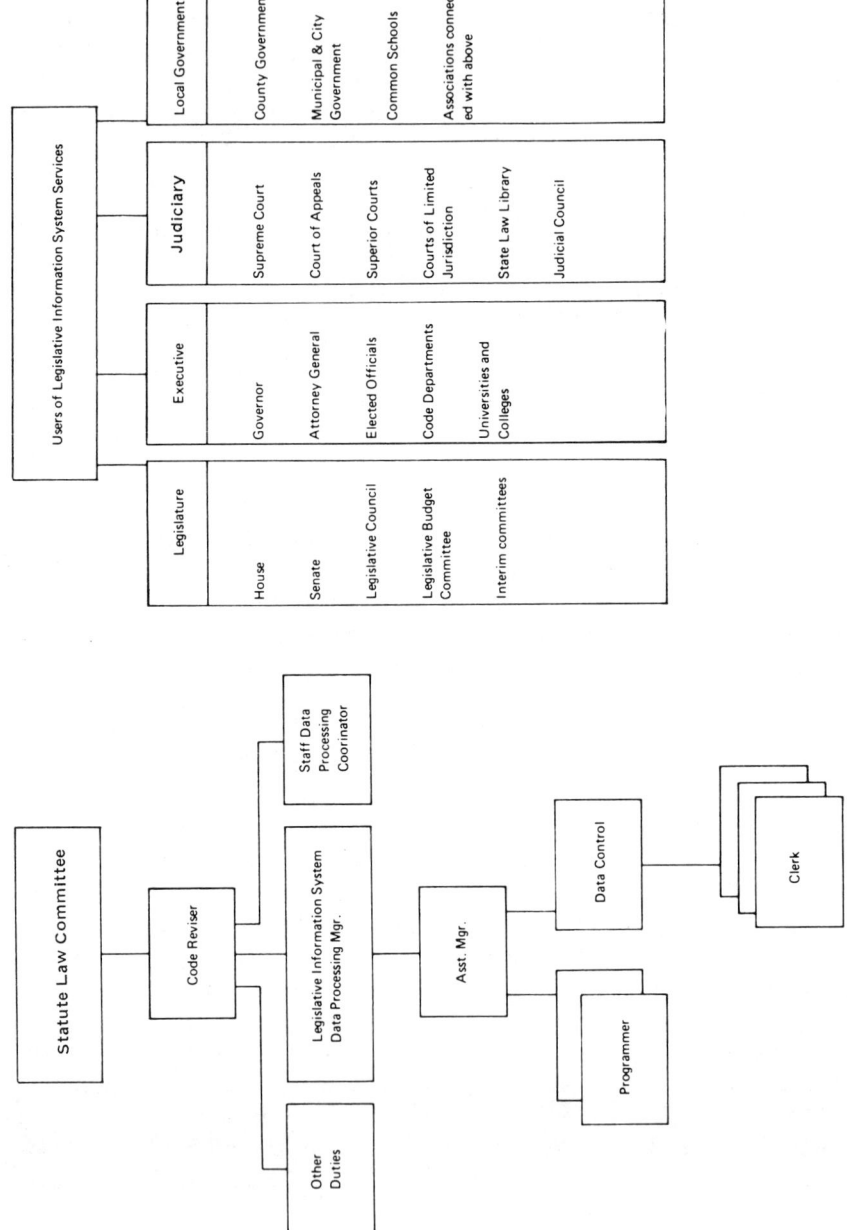

Figure IIH24-1. Legislative information system services.

legal materials. The structure of these functional and user groups is shown in Figure IIH24-1.

History

In 1967 several events took place which contributed significantly toward the development of the legislative and legal applications described in this publication:

1. Chapter 115, Laws of 1967 extraordinary session created the Data Processing Advisory Committee and made funds available to the Central Budget Agency (Office of Program Planning and Fiscal Management) to make possible the creation of a system planning staff.
2. The Department of Institutions inaugurated a keypunch training program for women inmates at the Walla Walla state penitentiary and made its services available as source for the creation of a law-oriented information retrieval data base.
3. Comprehensive programming in support of ADP information retrieval was made generally available from vendor sources (IBM's Document Processing).
4. A comprehensive system for applying data processing techniques to legislative status reporting and other legislative record keeping was developed by the Commonwealth of Pennsylvania and was offered for use in the State of Washington.

Text Processing

The State of Washington has implemented an electronic data processing system to aid in the bill drafting process. The system was developed in-house by the data processing manager in consultation with the many users. This generalized text processing system may be used in a number of ways in processing, manipulating, updating, and correcting the text materials of the users and of the legal search data bases.

Permanent Storage

During the 1971 legislative sessions, a data cell was used for the bulk of the permanent storage needs. After November 1, 1971, all of the permanent storage was placed on IBM 3330 disk drives as part of the new hardware configuration. The concept of permanent storage allowed for multiple files in the data cell assigned to various users; thus each user has a file security to protect the integrity of the file along with an optional document security. None of the users, other than the Code Reviser's Office, availed themselves of the document security feature. The Code Reviser's Office used the document security on the redistricting and reapportionment bill requests and on drafts of the operating budget bill during the 1971 legislative sessions.

From a Bill Request to a Code Section (Statute)

Initially, prior to and during the 1971 legislative sessions, the bill requests were keystroked via 2741 Communication Terminals into the Code Reviser's terminal operator's working storages and then stored in permanent storage in the Code Reviser's file. All this transpired before introduction in either the House or Senate. By an informal agreement between the two legislative houses, each bill must be perused for technical accuracy by the Code Reviser's Office prior to introduction, even though it be an executive or departmental request. In practice the other bill drafting attorneys welcome the technical criticisms set forth by the Code Reviser's bill drafting attorneys since they make for better legislation. Various drafts of the request may be made to adjust the legislation to the sponsor's desires. Typographical corrections and revised drafts are processed by manipulating and revising the original draft of the text in the text processing system. The final copy of the request is sent out by the Code Reviser's Office to the legislator for a sponsor signature or signatures. The sponsor sheet is returned to the Code Reviser's Office along with the copy of the bill, and then the bill is formally readied for introduction. (See Figure IIH24-2.)

Upon introduction the Code Reviser's Office sends multiple copies of the bill up to the house of introduction for use by the workrooms, the press, and the legislative personnel involved in the digesting and indexing of the bills. Personnel in both the House workroom and the Senate workroom transfer a copy of the machine-readable form of the bill from the Code Reviser's request file to their working storage, and then they redefine the bill request as a bill and store the text in either the House or Senate permanent storage files. As the House and Senate personnel store the bill in the permanent storage files, the earlier mentioned storage process is being performed upon the bill title information to aid in building several tables relating either the bills to the statutes or the statutes to the bills.

Amendments to a bill are made in the various standing committees and on the House and Senate floors. These amendments are prepared on a manual typewriter and copies are appended to the bill books as slip amendments. Once these amendments are adopted, they must be engrossed into the previous draft of the bill. The workrooms of the respective bodies integrate the amendments into the bill and print out a new copy of the bill for sending to the opposite legislative body and, if desired, for reprinting in bulk form by the State Printer. The Code Reviser's Office prepared many amendments and keystroked the larger amendments into the computer, permitting the usage of this captured text of the amendment in the engrossing process by the workrooms without rekeystroking.

Amendments made by the opposite house are engrossed into the bill by the workroom of the house of origin after the final passage of the measure.

```
1   AN ACT Relating to education, including the transportation of    H -0
2          students or pupils therefor; adding a new section to chapter  0535;
3          223, Laws of 1969 ex. sess. and to chapter 28A.24 RCW; and   001
4          declaring an emergency.                                      PARTA
5   BE IT ENACTED BY THE LEGISLATURE OF THE STATE OF WASHINGTON:        ;001
6          NEW SECTION. Section 1. There is added to chapter 223, Laws   6
7   of 1969 ex. sess. and to chapter 28A.24 RCW a new section to read as  7
8   follows:                                                              7
9          Notwithstanding any other provision of law, after the         8
10  effective date of this 1971 amendatory act, no school district board  9
11  of directors shall require any student or pupil to be transported for  9
12  any purpose or for any reason without the written permission of the   10
13  parent or guardian.                                                   10
14         NEW SECTION. Sec. 2. If any provision of this 1971            11
15  amendatory act, or its application to any person or circumstance is   12
16  held invalid, the remainder of the act, or the application of the    12'
17  provision to other persons or circumstances is not affected.          13
18         NEW SECTION. Sec. 3. This 1971 amendatory act is necessary    14
19  for the immediate preservation of the public peace, health, and      15
20  safety, the support of the state government and its existing public  16
21  institutions, and shall take effect immediately.                      16
```

Figure IIH24-2. Copy of code reviser's bill drafting request.

IN THE LEGISLATURE
of the

CERTIFICATION OF ENROLLED ENACTMENT

HOUSE BILL NO. 27

CHARTER 14

LAWS OF 1971

EFFECTIVE DATE: June 10, 1971

Passed the House January 29, 1971
 Yeas 98   Nays 0

Passed the Senate February 20, 1971
 Yeas 39   Nays 0

CERTIFICATE

I, Malcolm McBeath, Chief Clerk of the House of Representatives of the State of Washington, do hereby certify that the attached is enrolled House Bill No. 27 as passed by the House of Representatives and the Senate on the dates hereon set forth.

Malcolm McBeath
Chief Clerk

DWC:vg HB-27/71 p--1

HOUSE BILL NO. 27

State of Washington by Representatives Chatalas,
42nd Regular Session Wolf and Kilbury
  (by State Treasurer request)

Filed with the Chief Clerk of the House of Representatives December 22, 1970, for introduction January 11, 1971. Referred to Committee on State Government.

1 AN ACT Relating to state government; increasing the state treasurer's
2   faithful performance bond; and amending section 43.08.020,
3   chapter 8, Laws of 1965 and RCW 43.08.020.
4 BE IT ENACTED BY THE LEGISLATURE OF THE STATE OF WASHINGTON:
5   Section 1. Section 43.08.020, chapter 8, Laws of 1965 and RCW
6 43.08.020 are each amended to read as follows:
7   The state treasurer shall reside and keep his office at the
8 seat of government. Before entering upon his duties, he shall
9 execute and deliver to the secretary of state a bond to the state in
10 ((the)) a sum of ((two hundred and fifty)) not less than five hundred
11 thousand dollars, to be approved by the secretary of state and one of
12 the judges of the supreme court, conditioned to pay all moneys at
13 such times as required by law, and for the faithful performance of
14 all duties required of him by law. He shall take an oath of office,
15 to be indorsed on his commission, and file a copy thereof, together
16 with the bond, in the office of the secretary of state.

Passed the House January 29, 1971.

Speaker of the House.

Passed the Senate February 20, 1971.

President of the Senate.

Approved February 26, 1971

Governor of the State of Washington

Figure IIH24-3. Copy of enrolled bill.

WASHINGTON LAWS 1971   Ch. 7

CHAPTER 7
[House Bill No. 93]
PROBATE--
CODE CORRECTIONS

AN ACT Relating to probate law and procedure; amending section 11.24.010, chapter 145, Laws of 1965 as amended by section 6, chapter 168, Laws of 1967 and RCW 11.24.010; and declaring an emergency.

BE IT ENACTED BY THE LEGISLATURE OF THE STATE OF WASHINGTON:

Section 1. Section 11.24.010, chapter 145, Laws of 1965 as amended by section 6, chapter 168, Laws of 1967 and RCW 11.24.010 are each amended to read as follows:

If any person interested in any will shall appear within four months immediately following the probate or rejection thereof, and by petition to the court having jurisdiction contest the validity of said will, or appear to have the will proven which has been rejected, he shall file a petition containing his objections and exceptions to said will, or to the rejection thereof. Issue shall be made up, tried and determined in said court respecting the competency of the deceased to make a last will and testament, or respecting the execution by a deceased of such last will and testament under restraint or undue influence or fraudulent representations, or for any other cause affecting the validity of such will.

If no person shall appear within the time aforesaid, the probate or rejection of such will shall be binding and final.

NEW SECTION. Sec. 2. This act is necessary for the immediate preservation of the public peace, health and safety, the support of the state government and its existing public institutions, and shall take effect immediately.

EXPLANATORY NOTE

The last paragraph of RCW 11.24.010 was omitted, but not indicated as deleted, in the amendment of the section by section 6, chapter 168, Laws of 1967. The apparently inadvertent omission is corrected in this bill by the restoration of the omitted material.

Passed the House January 29, 1971.
Passed the Senate February 17, 1971.
Approved by the Governor February 26, 1971.
Filed in Office of Secretary of State February 27, 1971.

CHAPTER 8
[House Bill No. 94]
EDUCATION--
CODE CORRECTIONS

AN ACT Relating to education; reenacting section 28B.10.465, chapter 223, Laws of 1969 ex. sess. as last amended by section 6, chapter 35, Laws of 1970 ex. sess. and by section 4, chapter 53, Laws of 1970 ex. sess., and RCW 28B.10.465; reenacting section 19, chapter 15, Laws of 1970 ex. sess. as amended by section 32, chapter 56, Laws of 1970 ex. sess. and by section 2, chapter 59, Laws of 1970 ex. sess., and RCW 28B.50.350; reenacting section 28A.58.420, chapter 223, Laws of 1969 ex. sess. as amended by section 3, chapter 237, Laws of 1969 ex. sess. and RCW 28A.58.420; reenacting section 1, chapter 29, Laws of 1945 and adding the same to chapter 223, Laws of 1969 ex. sess.; reenacting section 1, chapter 220, Laws of 1967 and

[21]

Figure IIH24-4.   Copy of session law page.

The workrooms of the opposite house used the text processing system at times to prepare their copy of the amendments to the bill by either entering the new text of the amendment into the storage files or taking a previously existing amendment and revising it. This saved keystrokes by the original house in engrossing the bills. The original house prepares an enrolled copy of the bill with signature places for the Speaker of the House and for the President of the Senate. These signature forms were put in place by the text processing system. After the presiding officers sign the bill, it is transmitted to the Governor. (See Figure IIH24-3.)

The Code Reviser's Office publishes the session laws (Acts of the Legislature) and utilizes the previously keystroked text. A copy of the passed bill is brought from either the House or Senate permanent storage files into the working storage of our personnel working with the session law publication. After adding new text materials necessary for the session law publication format, the chapter of the session laws is stored in a new storage file for session laws. Groups of several hundred pages of session laws are prepared for final printout. A special high-density print train carbon ribbon is used on the high-speed printer and it supplies a photo-offset ready copy for the State Printer. (See Figure IIH24-4.)

The Code Reviser's Office publishes the official version of the Revised Code of Washington and must periodically publish code supplements and also updates its Revised Code of Washington information retrieval file for automated law searches. The present version of the Code is manually codified and hot-lead set. The text processing system will allow the computerization of the codification processes and will lead us into the use of the photocomposition process in publishing the Code. The primary goal of our efforts in the codification process is to accomplish the menial tasks of codification by computer, freeing the codification personnel to concentrate on tasks involving human judgment.

The codifiers will use a copy of the session law printout to get an overall view of each act. The specific code section will be brought into working storage from the session law file by clerical personnel working with the codifiers. The section number, caption, and history note will be brought into working storage along with the section of the session law. The history note will be updated and the new code section will be stored via a key which will place it in code section sequence when listing out part of the permanent storage file. All the sections in the session laws will be processed in this fashion. A printout of each title or chapter will be obtained on which the codifiers will specify text changes to shape the materials in form for printing. The title or chapter printout with specified changes will be given to a terminal operator who will make the indicated codification changes along with adding embedded typographical codes to be used in the photocomposition process. The title or chapter will be printed out again for proofing and correction, if necessary. Further correction cycles will be used to perfect the code text.

Once a correct copy of the code section is obtained, it will be stored in the Revised Code of Washington permanent storage file under the correct code section number. At this point photocomposition can proceed along with search file updating and any other operations, such as drafting a bill using a new statute as the base or building a new Revised Code of Washington Inverse Cross Reference Table.

Other Uses of Text Processing System

The Legislative Budget Committee used the text processing and manipulation system to prepare cumulative commentary notes relating to the State operating budget bill.

The text processing system was used to prepare a bill number to request number table for utilization by the State Code Reviser's bill-drafting staff. Additional uses include letter writing and preparation of various pamphlets and manuals.

The 1971 Legislative Session Text Processing Evaluation

As far as change was concerned, the clerical personnel of the Code Reviser's Office and the House and Senate workrooms adapted readily to the new process, and at times our 15 terminals (in the Code Reviser's Office and the House and Senate workrooms) all had operators pounding away at them. The 1971 volume of bills was up 25%, but the Code Reviser's clerical staff was one less. In addition, we took two members of Code Reviser's clerical staff and had them do full-time line checking and proofing of bills. Overall, the Code Reviser's bill-drafting staff felt that they had a somewhat better break on hours than in past years. The system was not as efficient as it will be in future years due to (1) the new learning process, (2) the fact that we had no carry-over data bank from previous sessions, and (3) the fact that we did not have a routine from which to enter our present statutes. The reaction of the House and Senate workrooms was quite favorable, and they felt that the text processing system saved them time, especially with the short bills. The House workroom felt that the system reduced the time they used both in engrossing and in proofing the bills. They also reported that staff reductions would be possible in future years.

Other Applications

ROLL CALL VOTE REPORTS. The Legislative Information System offers other services to aid the workrooms in preparing various reports. Late in the summer of 1971, the 1971 roll call votes on all measures were placed in the data files by the workroom personnel utilizing the text processing system. Daily roll call vote transcripts were assembled from the stored data. Final tabulations of the roll call vote as related to a particular measure or to a particular member will be prepared by special programs on the data files. Our eyes are on the future when we will use this roll call vote data in the House and Senate Journal preparations.

INDEX TO JOURNALS. The basis for the construction of the indexes for the Senate Journal and the House Journal is provided by the Legislative Information System. These indexes are derived by a program using the data file of the Topical Index to the Legislative Digest and History of Bills and the legislative action file. The House and Senate Journal indexers insert additional entries in the computer printouts, and this copy is then used for typesetting by the State Printer.

REVISED CODE OF WASHINGTON INDEX PROJECT. A venture being undertaken at present is to capture the Index to the Revised Code of Washington, which is approximately 2300 pages. This index was originally published in 1961 and has been cumulatively supplemented in 1963, 1965, 1967, 1969, and 1970. At present we are keystroking the index into a permanent storage file in the text processing system. The alphabetic index will then be sorted down by statute cites, Washington Constitution cites, internal cross-reference cites, and Rules of Court cites for verification of the currency of the various index entries. The index will be maintained in inverse entry order and programs will be written to aid in indexing future session laws. The final step involves a program which will prepare the index for publication in 1973 and periodic republication thereafter.

CENSUS POPULATION INFORMATION. During the 1971 regular session an online census population information retrieval and manipulation system was developed to aid in the redistricting and reapportioning efforts. Retrieval was made upon the census units of population, that is, by state, county, census tract, enumeration district, or block group. Addition and subtraction commands were provided to aid the legislative staff personnel in checking out the various redistricting and reapportioning plans set forth by the legislature.

ADDRESS LABELS. An address label file and printing service is provided to the Code Reviser's Office for the distribution of the Washington Administrative Code and for the publicizing of the Automated Law Search system to state and local government.

J. FOLLOW-UP, CONTINUING RESPONSIBILITY

The scientist's or engineer's responsibility does not completely terminate at any point in time or in the product cycle. As the complexity and influence of technological developments increase, it becomes more essential that the innovator maintain awareness—during the subsequent stages of manufacturing, distribution, and use—and maintains the ability to participate in corrective action when necessary. Since years may pass between innovation and subsequent problem, the need for a continuing process of monitoring and analysis is evident.

The following, and final, case study is a description of such a "product assurance" system, developed by General Dynamics at Forth Worth as part of the F-111 program.

CASE STUDY 25   Quality Assurance System*

When the F-111 program began in 1964, a new quality control system for reporting and correcting product discrepancies was inaugurated. Designed to provide machine documented information for management and all the support organizations requiring discrepancy data, the system provided a means for monitoring reliability and maintainability growth, analyzing failed parts and reviewing and correcting quality discrepancies.

By the fall of 1968, problem areas directly related to acceleration and growth of the F-111 program were becoming apparent in this initial system. Indications were that data processing and attendant corrective action programs were becoming cumbersome and untimely and failing to keep pace with company goals. Thousands of quality assurance forms that required processing were being generated each month. A backlog was accumulating. Consequently, a project was established in October, 1968:

- Modernize and upgrade quality assurance data collection and processing through adaptation of the latest electronic data processing facilities.

* This case study was exerpted from J. Y. McClure, "General Dynamics PAAC Program—A Coalition of Minds and Machines for Quality," Reprinted by permission of the American Society for Quality Control, Inc., and J. W. McClure, General Dynamics Corporation.

J. FOLLOW-UP, CONTINUING RESPONSIBILITY

- Improve the responsiveness of all departments and functions to produce discrepancies regardless of responsibility.

The project was assigned to a task force of quality assurance and business data center personnel for study and recommendations.

Birth of a New Concept

After examining all weaknesses in the existing system and brainstorming for possible remedies, the team evolved a concept that is still a focal point of excitement and enthusiasm at the Fort Worth Division. The concept called for a new system, labeled PAAC for Product Assurance Action Center, that would consist of (1) a centralized staff of product-oriented, problem-solving specialists operating from a modern communications and display center and (2) a decentralized, or on-line, computer system that would be installed to support the specialists, management and other people who need access to quality assurance information.

Figure IIJ25-1 is an artist's interpretation of PAAC as conceived and visualized by the task force.

A time-phased implementation plan was prepared detailing each major action to be taken:

1. Redesign quality assurance forms.
2. Revise and coordinate operating procedures.
3. Determine equipment needs and place orders.
4. Activate a physical action center.
5. Establish computer output requirements.
6. Program the computer for input, update and output.
7. Convert the old data bank to a new format.
8. Train some 1,500 employees (new procedures/techniques).
9. Hire and train 33 terminal operators.
10. Reassign and train quality/factory liaison personnel.
11. Obtain corporation and customer approvals.

The equipment selected was available from IBM Corp. Major components peculiar to the new system are:

1. Two IBM Model 2314 Disc Storage Units.
2. Twenty-three IBM Model 2740 Terminals (Selectric Typewriters).
3. One IBM Model 2703 Terminal Control.
4. One IBM Model 2701 Terminal Control.

The 23 terminals are located at selected points throughout the facility where quality assurance rejection and complaint forms are initiated or

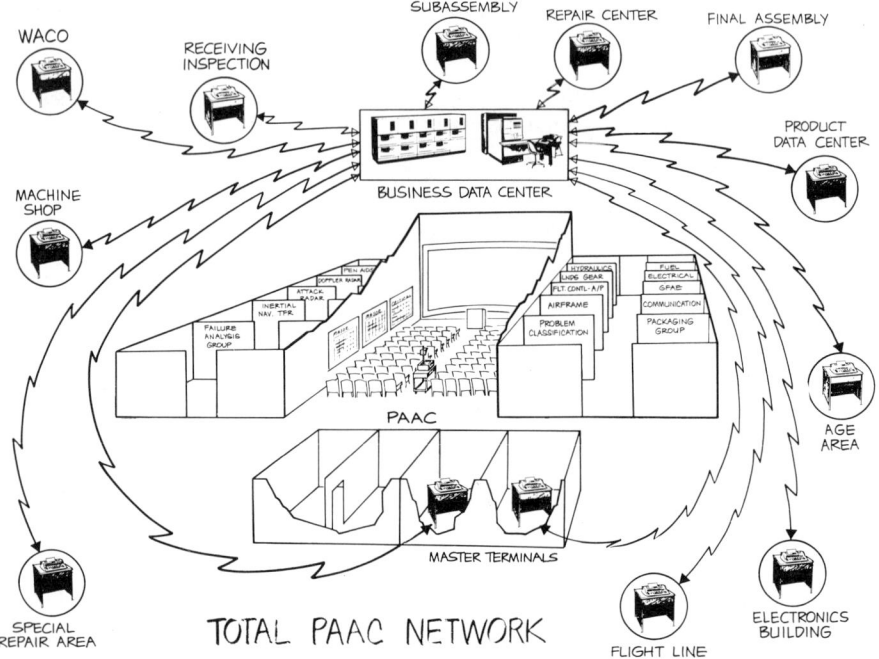

Figure IIJ25-1. Total PAAC network.

processed. These remote terminals are linked by telephone lines to an IBM Model 360/65 computer in the computer center. Data transmitted to the computer are received and processed in a background mode while other nonrelated batch jobs are being performed. The computer stores information sent from the terminals on magnetic discs.

As data are transmitted to the computer, records are immediately updated in a master file and three minifiles structured for automatic and immediate response to inquiries. The master file containing all data is maintained by document serial number. The minifiles are maintained in numerical sequences, resident on the two 2314 disc storage units which have a combined storage capacity of 414 million characters. Backup files are maintained on magnetic tapes as a safeguard against equipment malfunctions or human errors that might inadvertently destroy portions of the disc-stored records.

Quality assurance procedures designed for the new PAAC system call for immediate processing of discrepancy information. The source of this data is

J. FOLLOW-UP, CONTINUING RESPONSIBILITY

a battery of quality control documents (forms) consisting of inspection completion orders, standard repair authorizations, quality assurance data reports and discrepancy reports. Customer field complaints also are included in the system by converting the complaints to parts failure and service difficulties reports. Each document is designed to allow identification of data by individual item or groups of items. Individual items are identified by block numbers while groups are identified by alphabetical line designators.

Within minutes after initiation, updating or disposition of any report, rejection data are manually proofed by trained employees, transmitted from the remote terminals, computer edited upon input and transferred to disc storage. Integrity of the data is monitored by a PAAC liaison man; one is assigned to each remote terminal. The liaison man not only monitors the data but also approves inquiries and provides guidance in filling out rejection documents. The prime data input levels are:

1. When the discrepancy occurs.
2. When it is dispositioned.
3. When preventive action is taken.
4. When rework is planned.
5. When the form is coded and microfilmed.
6. When repair work is accepted.

"One of the finer sideline benefits of the PAAC system," says J. Weare, chief of the PAAC liaison and material survey functions, "is the computer's capability to detect overlooked data errors as the forms are input."

It never ceases to startle an operator when she depresses the return key for input of the next line of data to get back a message that reads something like, "Invalid Input-Field Size Error in Block 301." The computer is actually programmed, in every way practical, to aid in battling "Gigo" (garbage in = garbage out). Computer edits are applied to each block and line of data as they are typed over the terminals.

Prior to microfilming and storing original copies of discrepancy forms, a comprehensive check is made of each form by quality control analysts in the product data center. The discrepancy narrative is summarized in code to provide a method for automatic computer selection of recurrences. An abbreviated alpha code is used to summarize airframe manufacturing defects. Numeric "how malfunction" codes are used to describe systems discrepancies.

One analyst is stationed on the flight line to assure rapid input of the "how malfunction" codes from this vital area. Code input is kept timely by working from an advance copy or tear-off section of the forms. Just prior to archive storage, forms are final-checked for completeness and then microfilmed.

PAAC gives everyone with a need-to-know (certainly, this includes the customer representatives) direct access to the computer. Managers, quality engineers, inspectors, foremen and shop workmen have, in effect, a complete data bank at their fingertips. Within minutes after rejection data are input through a remote terminal, the data can be recalled by any or all the terminals. Instant response capabilities of the on-line system are even better than the original optimistic estimates. Answers to difficult questions can be obtained within seconds. Formerly, it took days and weeks, or it was discovered to be impractical to pursue certain answers.

The design of the Quality Inquiry Document (QID—Figures IIJ25-2 and IIJ25-3) proved to be a major breakthrough in the development of PAAC. This document is the key to extracting answers from the computer. It allows anyone with basic knowledge of the rejection forms to construct questions in a format the computer will recognize and answer. An inquirer

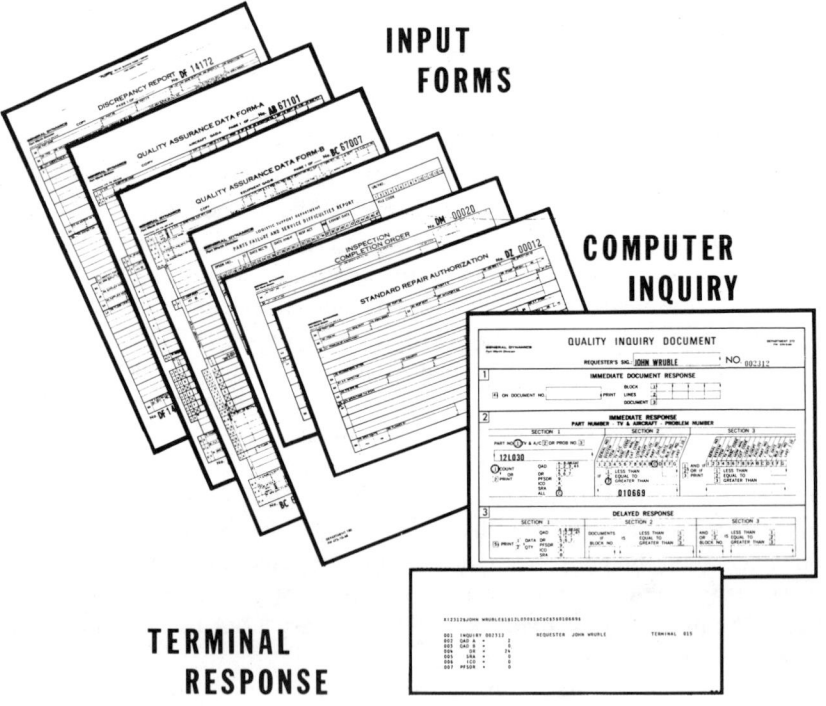

Figure IIJ25-2. Forms.

J. FOLLOW-UP, CONTINUING RESPONSIBILITY

Figure IIJ25-3. Quality inquiry document.

simply circles a few preprinted blocks of the QID, enters a data element or two and presents it to one of the terminal stations for input.

A PAAC liaison man gave this testimony on data inquiries: "The day I authorized my terminal operator to put in our first inquiry, the thought that flashed through my mind was what the instructor had said in PAAC school. His statement was, 'Fellows, you have to be careful in the way you fill out these inquiry forms. One little slip and you're liable to bury yourself in paper.' But I got my courage up and we pumped in the question. That typewriter talked back to us for about ten seconds and we had our answer." Four types of computer responses are provided to meet the special needs of all using groups: Immediate, Delayed, Periodic, Automatic.

Immediate Responses

Immediate responses, which make the computer seem conversational, are programmed for the frequently asked questions. These questions usually relate to the preprinted items shown on the QID, e.g., document, part and aircraft numbers, responsible departments and dates.

The QID's Part 1 alone can be used to construct some 439 million questions, i.e., possible combinations of data blocks and lines that can be designated on the form. Questions may be qualified in many ways, e.g., over a time span, by a group of airplanes, by a range of part numbers or according to specific discrepancy codes. An important point is that employees can ask for exactly what they need and receive only what they request. Formerly, it frequently was necessary to sift through volumes of machine listings to obtain the information desired.

Immediate response to inquiries can be obtained from any remote terminal location. However, practical limitations require that the terminal not be tied up for long periods to print long messages. Therefore, requests for immediate response are controlled and approved by PAAC liaison personnel stationed at each terminal. The PAAC liaison representatives frequently review and approve for input such questions as:

- How many rejections are open against airplane XXX? Identify them and print their status.
- What is the name of the inspector who accepted standard repair number XXX?
- Have there been customer complaints against part number XXX in the last 60 days?
- Print a copy of discrepancy form number XXX.
- Are there any material review board rejection documents without approved preventive action on airplaine XXX?
- How many rejections were charged to my department Friday? What are the accrued rework and scrap costs on the rejections?
- How many times has part number XXX been rejected?
- Who is the preventive action follow-up man on discrepancy report number XXX?
- What repair method was used on part number XXX that was rejected about three months ago?
- Print the discrepancies recorded against part number XXX bought from supplier number XXX.
- List all forms written against part number XXX in system XXX with a "how malfunction" code of XXX.
- Identify all discrepancy forms associated with PAAC problem number XXX.

Delayed Responses

The delayed response mode is programmed to handle complex and nonroutine questions overnight. Inquiries are made by filling out Section 3

J. FOLLOW-UP, CONTINUING RESPONSIBILITY

Recurring Conditions Report   Week Ending XXX

DEPARTMENT RESP.	ORIG.	PART NO.	DISC CODE H/M CODE	CAUSE OP.STP.	OPERATION NUMBER	P/A STATUS	DOC. NO.	INITIATION DATE	PROBLEM NUMBER
030	030	12A14501-101	HLELG	020		9	DG90123	30 08 69	
030	033	12A12501-101	HLELG	020		9	DG31129	25 08 69	
030	078	12A12501-101	HLELG	025		0	DF80981	27 08 69	
150	150	12L560-1	CNINR	045	2610	0	DF50126	29 08 69	3500-006
150	156	12L560-1	CNINR	045	2610	0	DF49988	02 08 69	3500-006
150	156	12L560-1	CNINR	055	2610	9	DF50012	15 08 69	
VEND	175	342665	290			I	BC60006	30 08 69	
VEND	175	342665	290			I	BC59680	24 08 69	
VEND	175	342665	290			I	BC58995	17 08 69	
VEND	175	342665	290			I	BC58601	15 08 69	
VEND	178	342665	290			I		(6)	
VEND	178	342665	290						
VEND	178	342							

(1) (2) (3) SORT SEQUENCES (5) (4)

PURPOSE
THIS COMPREHENSIVE TABULATION REPORT IS COMPILED WEEKLY AGAINST ALL RECURRING CONDITIONS DURING THE PAST 90 DAYS AS A "FAIL SAFE" DOUBLE CHECK AGAINST DAILY BELL RINGERS OCCURRING IN PAAC

Figure IIJ25-4.   Weekly computer report on recurring conditions.

of the QID (Figure III25-3). Answers to these queries usually involve considerable printing time and, therefore, are serviced overnight at the central computer center on a high speed printer.

Periodic response is available through regularly scheduled reports. The computer is programmed to issue periodic reports from data that have been computer edited, sorted and selected for a prescribed time period. After the given time span—a week, a month, a day—the computer prints out a summary of the required data on the high speed printer. Periodic reports are especially useful when detailed analyses of trends are needed and when voluminous information from a long time span is needed. A variety of periodic reports is prepared on this basis.

Microfilm indexes, supplier quality ratings, departmental and division quality performance and aircraft malfunction summaries are prominent among the routine reports published. An example PAAC printout is the weekly computer report (Figure IIJ25-4) on recurring conditions. This follow-up report is published to support the automatic responses.

Automatic Responses

A significant feature of the system is that the computer is programmed to provide automatic, or bell-ringer, responses. This printout is received in

296 CURRENT USAGE: CASE STUDIES AND CRITIQUES

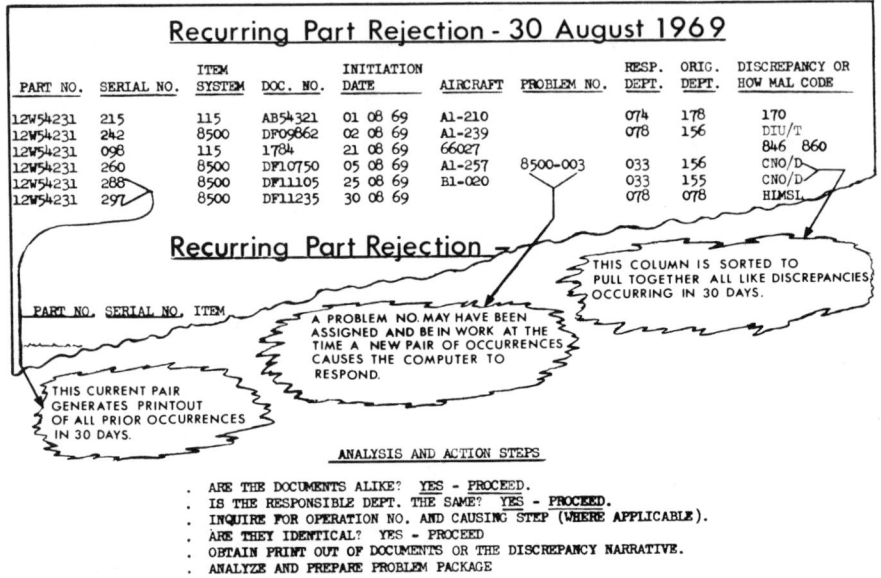

Figure IIJ25-5. Automatic computer printout on recurrences.

PAAC headquarters on an unattended terminal. The computer continuously compiles and scans information on part numbers and discrepancy, or "how malfunction," codes. When two like discrepancies are recorded on a part number within 30 days, preselected data are printed. When a part number falls within the prescribed parameters, rejection data for all defects reported during the prior 30 days are included in the printout. High cost rejections also are selected for automatic printout.

These data alert the PAAC problem packaging specialists to a recurrence, and an investigation is initiated to determine what action is necessary. Figure IIJ25-5 illustrates the automatic response procedure. Probably the most significant point about this feature is that because the computer continuously tracks rejections, the company is kept constantly alert to problems or potential problems as they develop.

The Action Center

The action center operations are composed of five major tasks:

1. Data Packaging. A problem packaging and classification group assembles data packages on discrepant conditions requiring investigation.

J. FOLLOW-UP, CONTINUING RESPONSIBILITY

2. System Specialist Activity. This group consists of personnel responsible for major aircraft systems. Responsibilities include the definition, investigations and resolution of repetitive and singular significant discrepant equipment conditions.
3. Failure Analysis Control. A group of specialists control a failure analysis program to obtain timely vital analyses of significant equipment failures.
4. Unsatisfactory Report Exhibit Status. A log is maintained to provide management visibility into the status of unsatisfactory exhibits received from the customer.
5. Displays. Current status charts of all items in work by action center personnel are kept in the display room.

Problem Packaging

When a rejection fits the "twice-in-thirty-days" category, the computer automatically transmits a message. The message is sent through a preselected unmanned terminal to the action center problem classification and packaging group which then obtains all data pertinent to the problem. This includes transmitting inquiries to the computer to obtain additional information, and researching failure analysis and data history files to obtain any other information that would benefit the system specialist in his investigation. When all data have been gathered, a preliminary PAAC resolution sheet (a status record) is initiated by the data packaging group, put with the package and given to the action center specialist responsible for that particular piece of equipment. Complete records of all PAAC resolution sheets in work are maintained in the action center.

The equipment specialist investigates to determine if corrective action is warranted. If not, results of the investigation are documented on the preliminary PAAC resolution sheet which is filed for future reference. If action is justified, an action center reference control number is assigned to the resolution sheet, the number is input to the computer records and an investigation is undertaken to determine the problem's cause. Problems requiring investigation are defined by General Dynamics' people at Fort Worth as any condition or occurence that has an immediate or major impact on cost, schedule, airworthiness, serviceability, reliability or quality of the aircraft or support equipment.

During the course of problem investigation, the equipment specialist can call together an ad hoc team from affected departments. The specialist is authorized to solicit assistance from any person or group that can aid in resolving the problem. For instace, the specialist might call a meeting of representatives from manufacturing, design engineering, material and manufacturing engineering, or the ad hoc team could consist only of the PAAC specialist and a member from any one of the affected groups.

The team reviews hardware and operating procedures, witnesses tests, requests a failure analysis of anything else required in the investigation. Vendor and customer participation in the investigation is utilized as necessary. The equipment specialist from the action center is team chairman and is responsible for documentation of the investigation.

The team must agree on the cause of the problem. Once this is determined and agreed upon, a course of action is formulated. The team and affected departments coordinate to determine the most workable solution. For instance, the group might decide that a new tool needs to be designed, that another material might be better, that the engineering drawing should be revised or that an additional inspection point needs to be called out in operation planning.

Once the problem has been analyzed and a decision has been made, the team reports its findings to the departments responsible for corrective action. The team also obtains commitments to accomplish the required action from affected departments, vendors or the customer. The problem-solving team establishes schedules and determines the airplanes to be affected. Any major change is reviewed by the director of the F-111 program so that he and his staff will be cognizant of the impact of the change on the total program.

The team then maintains surveillance over the implementation of their solution. They must verify resolution of the problem in the hardware at the scheduled effectivity point. Only when this is accomplished can the team close out an item under action center surveillance. The last step is documentation on the resolution sheet of the verified solution. Complete records of all problems in work are resolved, verified, and maintained in action center files.

Failure Analysis

The failure analysis control group was activated to provide a more effective and more closely controlled failure analysis program. Its specialty is pinpointing the exact causes of failures. Requests for failure analyses originate primarily from equipment test and repair areas throughout the Fort Worth facility, but a request for analysis also may originate from other concerned agencies and departments or from another group in the action center.

Upon receipt of a failure analysis request, the group reviews records for prior analysis on the same type failure and coordinates this with the affected design, quality assurance and action center personnel. The originator of the analysis request is informed of the decision to process or reject the request.

If the request is honored, the analysis control group selects a laboratory to perform the analysis. They have various company laboratories at their disposal or they can send failed samples to suppliers for analysis. This selection is determined by considering time required to perform the analysis, technical capability, quality of past work performed, work load of the laboratory and cost of analysis. If company or supplier laboratories are unavailable when needed or the required technical level is unavailable, the group has authority to use independent laboratories.

The costs of all analyses are closely monitored by the failure analysis control group. It assigns estimated labor costs to implant failure analysis job orders to control and authorize man-hour expenditures. It also coordinates the transfer of funds for interdivision budget realignment. It initiates and maintains a system to receive and review expenditures for planning and control purposes and prepares periodic reports for management on all expenditure categories. Control charts maintained in failure analysis control areas depict status of outstanding failure analyses. Periodic status reports are sent to management for review.

After diagnostic analysis is complete and laboratory results are received, copies of the analysis report are distributed to the originator, concerned action center groups and other affected departments responsible for obtaining corrective action. At this point, the failure analysis group helps the concerned parties evaluate results and decide a course of action. Complete records of all requests, analysis results and costs are maintained by this group.

Another important part of the problem-solving network is the PAAC liaison representatives who manage the remote terminals. Liaison representatives may secure and hold parts that require failure analysis when directed to do so by the failure analysis group. PAAC liaison personnel also notify the appropriate specialists in the PAAC office of serious, singular rejections occurring on the floor. This makes PAAC personnel alert to important rejections not classified as problems by the computer.

UR Exhibit Status

A UR (unsatisfactory report) exhibit is a part that has failed during service and has been sent from the customer (Air Force) to the contractor for corrective action. UR exhibits receive immediate attention to avoid recurrences. Analyses and corrective actions are handled in a manner similar to in-house failure problems.

Action center personnel maintain a cumulative UR exhibit status log for management's use. This log lists the receipt date, personnel assigned for resolution, location of exhibit, target disposal date, etc. The log is updated from a weekly electronic data processing printout supplied by the logistics department and copies of that department's internal and external communications.

The status log identifies delinquent UR exhibits and provides information needed for follow-up action. The log also is the source of statistics for compiling special charts and graphs depicting the length of time required to receive UR exhibits after they have been requested and the length of time the exhibits remain at Forth Worth or vendors before final disposal and acceptance.

Displays

To assure adequate management and customer visibility into the status of quality problems, a display room is provided in the action center. The room contains two types of charts-system status charts and significant item charts. The system status charts depict the current standing of each subsystem and equipment item under investigation. The item charts display those active items from each system status chart that are considered to be

Table IIJ25-1. The Problem Solving Approach.

BEFORE PAAC	WITH PAAC
• Many splinter groups working to identify and correct problems	• Action center organizes effort into an efficient centralized function for identifying and solving problems
• Part-time problem solving as a secondary assignment	• Action center specialists head problem solving teams, utilize ad hoc talent as required
• Every interested party kept their own problem status-- and seldom were two the same	• One centralized display of status of system problems and solutions, including verification of hardware
• Quality control attempted to obtain preventive action from shop on workmanship errors	• Factory specialists--familiar with and responsible for workmanship errors--carry the ball in resolving

Table IIJ25-2. Data Handling and Processing Approach.

BEFORE PAAC	WITH PAAC
• Manual file of each department's rejections	• Computer file of rejections from all areas
• Manual file search	• Terminal inquiry and immediate response
• Keypunch and verification of cards on rejections	• Terminal (selectric typewriter) input and visual verification
• Daily update of computer bank	• Instant update of computer bank
• Documents misfiled or not returned	• Computer storage
• Massive searches for lost documents	• Immediate response from terminal
• Rejection documents edited in data center and returned if incorrect	• PAAC liaison makes on-the-spot edit and obtains corrections before the story is cold
• Data requests for copies could not always be met	• Terminal prints exact information needed (not entire form)
• Labor hours mismatched to rejection form serial numbers	• Immediate input to computer thereby eliminating mismatch
• Manual labor adjustments	• Eliminated
• Status reporting not current	• Immediate computer update
• Extensive search of voluminous data listings to find information	• Immediate response

significant problems. Continual updating pinpoints the exact status of each item on the charts.

System specialists provide the information and display specialists maintain the charts. The display specialists also maintain weekly numerical summaries of items in work.

Action center personnel maintain close liaison with program managers and other members of top management not only through these charts but also through meetings held to inform managers of new problems and to establish priorities for investigations. Impromptu presentations and briefings are provided for management and customer personnel to apprise them of the status of items under action under investigation.

PAAC, with its on-line computer terminals and action center staff, may become the most powerful quality assurance tool the Fort Worth Division has ever known. (Tables IIJ25-1 and IIJ25-2 highlight some of the system's advantages.) Of course, PAAC can't be considered a panacea, but it is expected to help our people avoid multiple confrontations with the same problem.

The problem-solving functions once handled by numerous groups are now centralized in the action center. Specialists concentrate full time on the causes of and solutions to problems while other job functions are freed of this task. Communication is simpler with the centralized staff, and gathering information to report on the total picture is easier. Duplication of effort has been alleviated and responsibilities are more clearly defined by using this coordinated staff to collaborate on reducing discrepancies.

Building quality airplanes in this technological era has become linked with generating a lot of important and necessary paper. There is so much paper that old processing methods could not keep up with the flow. Too much time was devoted to traveling to and from the central data office to obtain needed data.

Decentralization accomplished by the remote computer terminals has decreased this travel time, and new disc storage and computer response capabilities have cut short the data searches. Now employees only need to take a few steps to transmit or receive information and most of their inquiries are answered immediately, saving money as well as time.

The on-line computer helps many people do their jobs more effectively. Some of the job roles assisted by the new computer system are managers, shop foremen, factory supervisors, purchasing agents, accountants, inspectors, flight crews, logistics representatives, Air Force inspectors and flight line personnel.

Even with the benefits now available, we know that the usefulness of this computer system is far from saturated. We are now exploring the possibility of adapting statistical analysis, traceability, configuration verification and vendor rating programs to allow fuller use of the on-line computer's potential.

Through the PAAC system, employees have gained significant benefits; instant data retrieval for tracking status, product-oriented specialists to analyze problems, up-to-the-minute summaries and displays for management decisions and automatic alert for quickly identifying problems. A functional coalition of minds and machines has been attained with the development of PAAC, and we at the Fort Worth Division now have a remarkably responsive system for guarding product integrity.

SECTION THREE
Issues of Management

INTRODUCTION

Section II dealt with the use of computer-based systems in support of scientific activities, presented from the point of view of the user. Section III is concerned with the planning and management of such service systems and, necessarily, must be viewed from a larger perspective than that of the individual user.

Referring to Figure III-1, we are concerned with the functions indicated within the dotted box, that is, the providing of in-house computer services. (Note that we exclude consideration of the interesting but separable problems of system acquisition and external purchase of services.)

Our study of in-house computer services, then, is represented as a dynamic relationship between three groups: general management, computer operations, and users.

The intersection between scientific process and computers that interests us here—is the application of quantitative, scientific methods to the problems of planning, managing, and justifying computer service systems.

We take the position that management of computing resources is *not* fundamentally different from the management of other phases of business activity, that, therefore, well-established principles of resource management can and should be applied to computer service systems. (Although few people argue this point of manageability, it appears that in many organizations computer services are the least-managed parts of the business. This state of affairs is probably due to the newness and strangeness of computers—encouraging management just to leave it alone.)

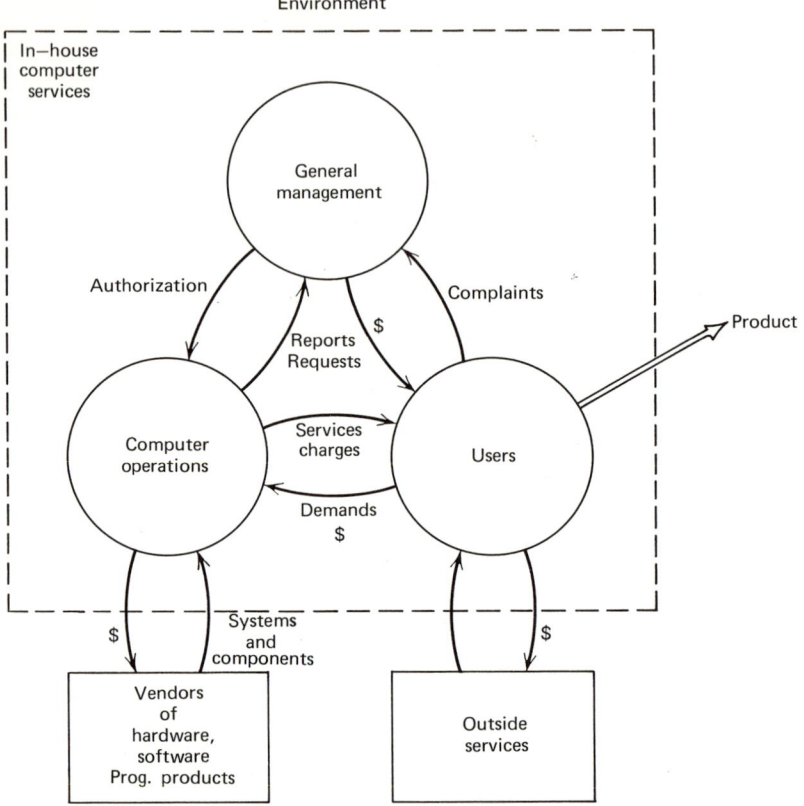

Figure III-1. ENVIRONMENT—computing services.

The philosophical structure that underlines Section III, therefore, is quite orthodox and briefly is as follows:

A. The first step is the definition of objectives. The objectives should be based on future user requirements. The objectives should be characterized by attributes which are measureable and which will provide the basis for evaluation of the computing function. The objectives, attributes and measures should be mutually determined by and agreeable to all three forces (general management, computer operations and users).
B. Decisions on the extent and form of computer services should be based on the value of the services provided, as well as on equipment

costs and utilization. This dependence on service value necessitates the articulation and quantification of factors and influences which often are ignored or sensed only intuitively and subjectively. This process of articulation and quantification is not exact, but is subject to the usual surveying and sampling errors and to errors arising from our ignorance of many facets of information technology. Our position is that:

- Value judgments must be made in order to manage computer services sensibly.
- Value analyses can be conducted competently enough to provide a favorable alternative to wholly intuitive or ad hoc decision making.
- The limited accuracy of such value analyses must always be considered—to avoid misuse or overuse of the results.

C. Attention must be given to the distribution of computing facilities within an organization. The maturing of data communication technology—along with the emergence of minicomputers, intelligent terminals, and functionally specific subsystems—has created many alternative arrangements of service facilities. Some of these arrangements offer substantial improvements in quality and economy of performance. Resource location/allocation programs have been used by operations researchers for some years to locate plants and warehouses. These techniques are applicable to computer service systems.

D. The performance of the computing function should be evaluated continuously. The evaluation should be based on the objectives described above. The resulting performance reports should be *usable* by general management and users, as well as by computer center personnel. Usable implies that the reports are understandable, concise, and reliable.

E. Control policies and mechanisms should be established to assure that the service objectives are met. These policies must cover: Who makes which decisions? How are the resources to be allocated? How are priorities to be assigned? Are charges to be employed as a control mechanism rather than simply to recover costs? And so on.

F. The *quality* of the man-system interface must be actively considered in all planning and management decisions. The short- and long-term effects of computing systems on the individual will require more attention as their use becomes a greater part of the workday experience. In particular, thought must be devoted to the problems of privacy, ease of learning and intermittent use, personalization in choice of mode and style of usage.

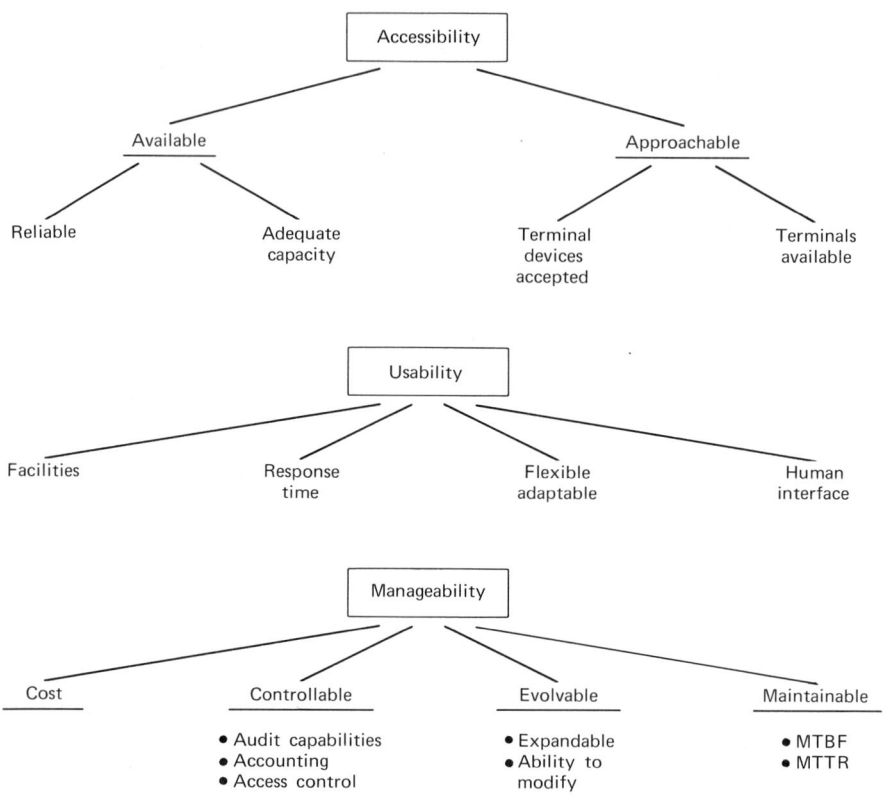

Figure IIIA-1. Criteria for time-sharing system assessment.

A. DEFINITION OF OBJECTIVES, ATTRIBUTES AND MEASURES

The starting point for the management of computer-based service systems is the articulation of objectives. Objectives, as we shall use the term, are broadly stated goals or aims which usually originate from higher management, sometimes as part of the charter of the service organization, sometimes as generally understood, unwritten policy. Some examples of service objectives are: "Use computers so as to minimize engineering task costs, considering equipment, human, and delay costs," or "Develop and provide computer services that are as good as those of our competitors," or "Shorten the product design cycle time by 20%," and so on.

To be constructive and measurable, such broad objectives must be translated into specific *attributes,* or characteristics, of the services provided.

A. DEFINITION OF OBJECTIVES

Variety of services offered
  (Suitability and completeness for supporting tasks of organization)
Capacity
- Number of access ports and devices
- Compute power
- Information reach

Responsiveness
- Mean and variability

Availability
- Scheduled—at all hours?
- Unscheduled—freedom from interruptions
- Geographic—access from all locations?

Human interface
- Ease of learning and use
- Flexibility, adaptability

Growth potential
- In size
- Functionally—open-endedness, generality

Cost
- Cost per job or transaction

Security, integrity, auditability
Precision, accuracy, freedom from errors

Figure IIIA-2. Attributes of computing services.

Also, *measures* (quantitative targets) must be established for the various attributes. There should be general awareness and agreement among general management, computer operations, and users that the specified attributes and measures are properly chosen to make meeting of the general objectives possible.

These attributes and measures, then, provide a basis for evaluation of the computing service systems. The output of these evaluations should be periodic reports that are accessable to, and useful to, general management, operations, and users alike.

Figure IIIA-1 shows an unusually complete taxonomy of the attributes of time-sharing systems developed by Jerrold Growchow, then of MIT (1, 2).

The following set of service attributes has been selected by Texas Instruments (3) to provide the basis of evaluation and reporting of their computer service systems:

Batch job turnaround
On-time delivery production jobs, (%)

Inquiry up-time
Inquiry response time
System availability
Unscheduled bombouts
Cost

Typical reports showing performance as compared to established targets or measures are presented in the section on evaluation.

Other characterizations of service attributes are given in References 4 and 5.

A fairly complete tabulation of computing service attributes, drawn from these and other sources, is given in Figure IIIA-2.

The choice of attributes to be monitored in any particular organization depends on the answers to the following questions.

What information is needed to:

- Predict success in meeting objectives?
- Resolve conflicts between users, operations, management?
- Make choices between alternative plans or policies?
- Determine cost/effective tradeoffs between equipment, personnel and time delay costs?

References

1. J. M. Grochow, "Utility Functions for Time-Sharing System Performance Evaluation," *Computer,* September–October 1972, 16–19.
2. J. M. Grochow, "On Managing Interactive Remote Access Computing," 3rd Annual SIGCOSIM Symposium, October 1972, Gaithersburg, Md.
3. G. Fischer, Unpublished memoranda.
4. B. Beizer, *The Architecture and Engineering of Digital Computer Complexes,* 2 vols., Plenum Press, New York, 1971.
5. R. M. Rutledge, "Installation Management—The Next Ten Years," *Proceedings SJCC* (1972), 833–839.

B. QUANTIFICATION OF VALUE OF SERVICES

One of the barriers to a more systematic management of computing services is the difficulty in quantifying the benefits of usage. As mentioned in the introduction to this section, we believe that value analyses are necessary, and that they can be conducted competently enough to provide an improvement over wholly intuitive or ad hoc decision making.

B. QUANTIFICATION OF VALUE OF SERVICES

The most direct benefits of computer services result from increases in user productivity and/or reductions in elapsed time to complete given tasks. These benefits are the basis for the analyses described in this chapter.

Other benefits deriving from improved quality of work are even more difficult to quantify, although in some cases management does make explicit tradeoffs between cost savings and product quality—by varying the number of design or testing iterations.

The first article in this section, "Cost Benefits of Computing Services," is based on usage in a research laboratory. In this case, users operate more or less autonomously and the predominant benefits relate to personnel productivity.

The second article, "Cost-Effective Matching of Task and Computing Device," results from a study of a highly structured product development environment—in the aerospace industry. In this case the predominant benefits are related to reducing time delays. Figure IIIB-1 shows the means of mapping time delays into product cost increments, based on experience with previous development cycles.

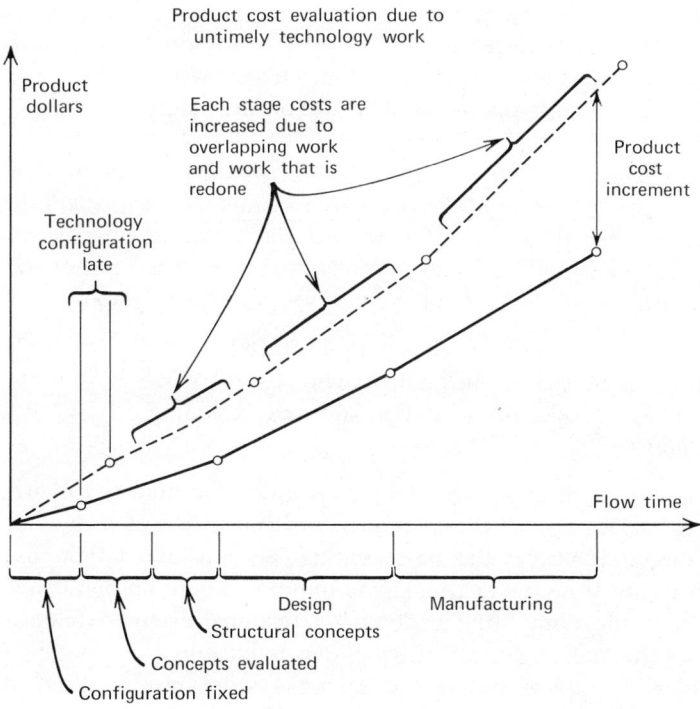

Figure IIIB-1. Product cost education due to untimely technology work.

Cost Benefits of Computing Services*

Computing services and their management have developed to a state that demands better tools of economic appraisal. Underlying this need is the increasing range of available system options, that is, the variety of computing services from which users can choose to solve their problems, and the diversity of facilities among which operations managers can choose for the services they provide (1).

In the field of scientific computing, there has been an apparent tendency to neglect economic considerations, and—more generally—service-related aspects of operations management. This tendency may derive from the fact that many computing center managers have a scientific or technical background, and therefore do not feel comfortable using the subjective data of value estimates used in this article. An example of this tendency is seen in the formulation of computing service objectives which are usually stated in terms of system characteristics (such as throughput or turnaround time), rather than the value of service delivered (2).

This article describes experience gained over the past several years in providing a variety of computing services to staff members at the IBM Thomas J. Watson Research Center. It reviews attempts to understand and quantify the effects of various services on the researcher and his work. Our intention is to stimulate interest and debate on the inherent concepts, rather than to claim hard, transferable results.

The following information is provided to give an insight into the magnitude of computer usage at the Research Center and forms the basis for this study. (These data do not represent the total usage, since a heavy external teleprocessing load and administrative services are not included.) The computing center consists of the following primary systems:

- System/360 Model 67 Simplex with TSS/360
- System/360 Model 67 Half Duplex with CP-67/CMS
- System/360 Model 91 with OS/360 and including LASP, RJE, and APL/360

There is a total of about 700 individual users, the majority of whom are professional scientists. Of these, about 75 are classified as heavy users, and 225 are moderate users; the balance may be considered light users. All personnel in the study work in a single building where no one is more than 300 yd from the computing center. All terminal-oriented teleprocessing service uses the dial-up system of telephone extensions.

A single-job-stream batch processing system model illustrates the

* This section appeared in IBM Systems Journal, 11, 3.

increasing system response time with system utilization. This is termed the system capacity characteristic. Also introduced is the observation that the relative value of a computation to an experimenter decreases with time. Maximum relative value is obtained for this model. A two-job-stream model illustrates the effect of priorities both on value to the user and on system capacity. Using a test program, these factors are evaluated for a variety of systems, including time-shared systems. Emphasizing time-shared systems, we evaluate system cost and user benefit tradeoffs for three modes of usage. By way of method of differential costs and benefits in a time-shared environment, productivity estimates are made. Also compared are the relative values of a spectrum of services that a large research establishment might offer.

A Conceptual Model

ONE JOB STREAM. Arguments supporting the choice of net value of a service as the operational objective function to be maximized, for example, are discussed by Sharpe (3). Based on this analysis, a conceptual model for

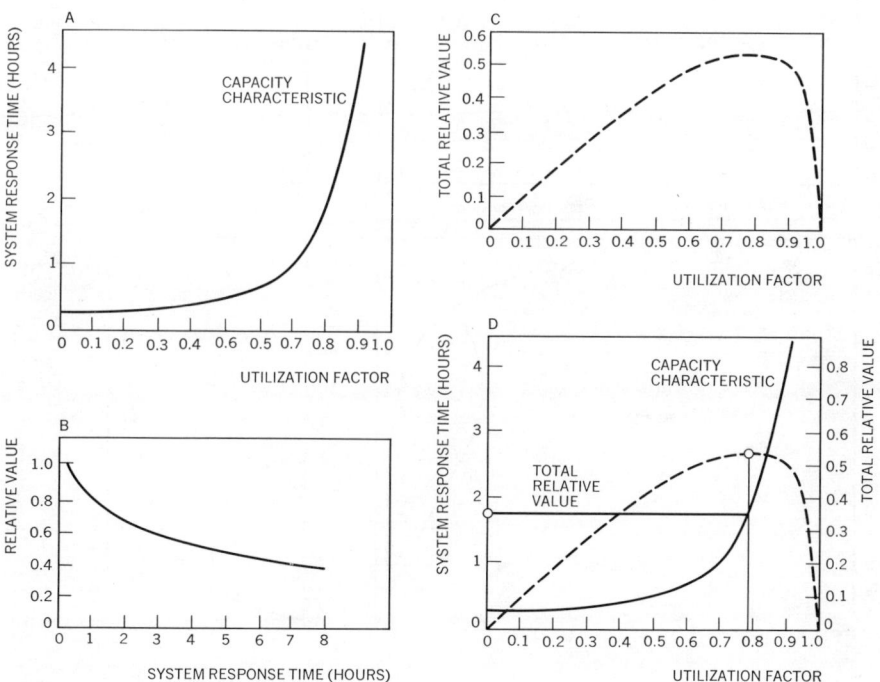

Figure IIIB-2. Single-stream batch processing.

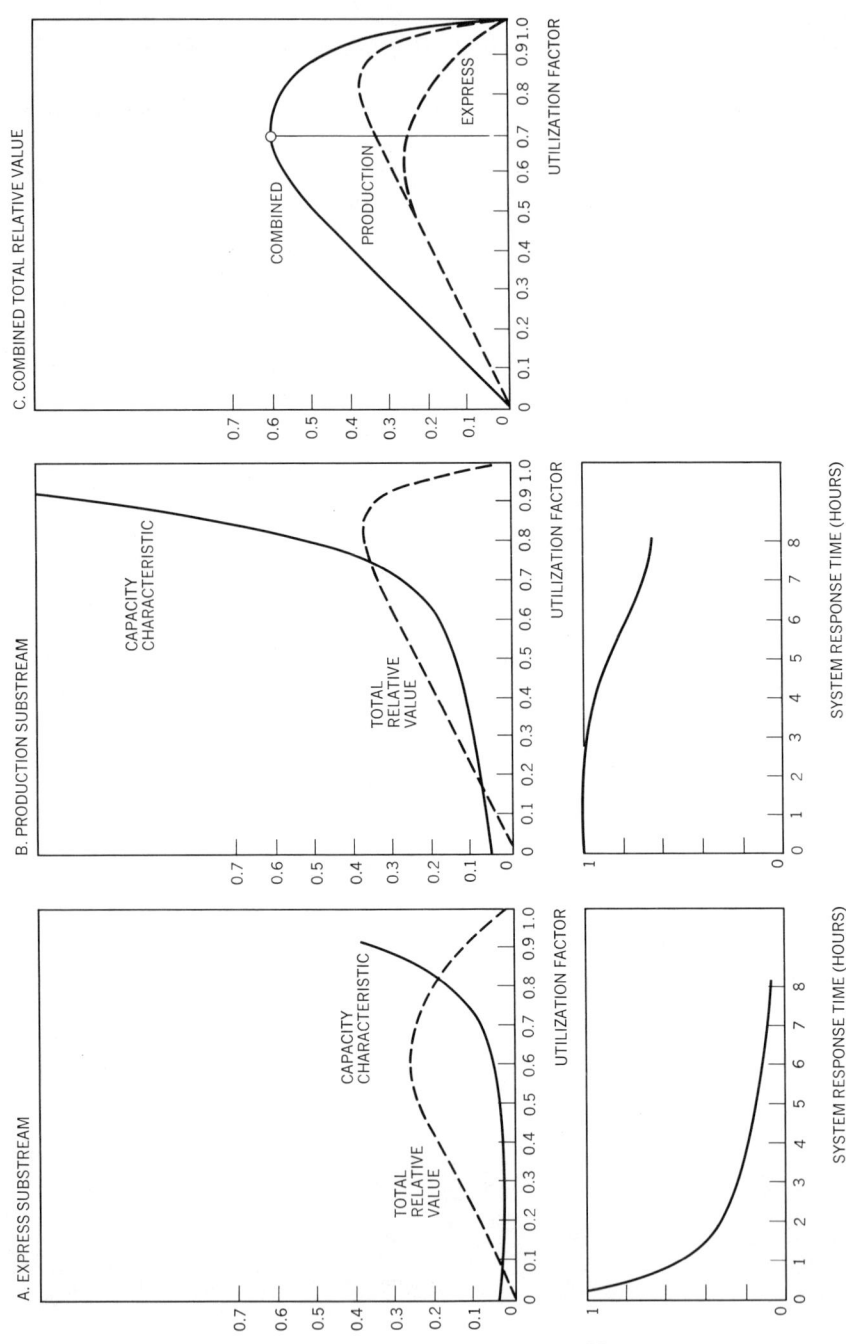

Figure IIIB-3. Dual-stream batch processing.

visualizing batch operations is shown in Figures IIIB-2 and IIIB-3. In Figure IIIB-2a, the curve represents the *capacity characteristic* of a system, which shows the effect of system utilization on system response time. The capacity characteristic curve here relates the *utilization factor* (the ratio of actual throughput to system throughput capacity) to system response or job turnaround time. The form of this curve can be derived from queuing theoretic considerations discussed in Reference 3, but it is more often determined empirically from observations of turnaround time under different levels of loading. The first model to be discussed is a single-stream batch processing system. Other models that use this characteristic are discussed later in this article.

The curve shown in Figure IIIB-2b represents the averaged quantification of subjective judgments of the diminution of the *relative value* of a job to the user as a function of system response time (with a 15-min response taken equal to unity). This curve has been determined primarily from responses to interviews or questionnaires submitted to users. Because the results have been independently checked in several ways, assume for now that such a curve can be determined with reasonable accuracy. Using the relative value curve in Figure IIIB-2b and the utilization characteristics curve in Figure IIIB-2a, the *total relative value* can be directly determined as shown in Figure IIIB-2c. Then, by overlaying Figures IIIB-2a and IIIB-2c, one can see in Figure IIIB-2d that operating the system at about 80% utilization maximizes the value of this system to this user population, assuming all jobs are given equal priority, in a single job stream. Correspondingly, we have observed that maximum value occurs when system response is just under 2 hr.

TWO JOB STREAMS. Consider now the operational alternative of dividing the job stream into two substreams, based on stated job urgency, and giving priority to one substream called the *express substream*. The rationale for doing this derives from user interviews, wherein respondents who experience difficulty articulating the single relative-value curve in Figure IIIB-2b usually agree to the dual curves—*production* and *express*—as shown by the relative values of turnaround time in the lower boxes of Figures IIIB-3a and IIIB-3b.

When a user's problem requires the output of one job before he can enter the next job, speedy results are of greatest value to him. Such *sequentially organized* jobs benefit most from the short turnaround time of the express substream. This sequential mode is usually required during exploratory phases of research, and during program development or debugging. At such times, the user's research progress relates directly to the number of runs he makes per day. Thus the total relative value curve for the express mode approximates a hyperbola, as shown in Figure III-3.

The complementary mode or substream is referred to as the *production substream*. Here one's program is essentially stable, but requires execution with new data or parameter settings and generally involves less need for fast turnaround. One run a day is often sufficient, and, if more results are needed, several copies of the program can be run in parallel with different data adjoined. The relative-value curve for the production substream, shown in the lower box of Figure IIIB-3*b* tends to be flatter than that for the express substream. Although the instantaneous form of such a curve may change with time of day depending on the user's work habits, these relative-value curves have been averaged over time of day as well as user population. Capacity characteristics are shown in Figures IIB-3*a* and IIIB-3*b* without ordinate scales simply for the purpose of comparison. For simplicity, the substreams are assumed equal in size. Therefore, the two capacity characteristics in Figures IIIB-3*a* and IIIB-3*b* average to the capacity characteristic in Figure IIIB-2*a*. Similarly, the relative-value curves in Figure IIIB-3 average to the relative value in Figure IIIB-2*b*.

Figures IIIB-2*a* and IIIB-2*b* effectively show batch-processing subtotals for the two substreams. The express total relative value is maximized by running with the system lightly loaded to keep the turnaround time short. Production total relative value, however, is maximized by running the system at a high utilization. The value of the total work load, thus partitioned, realizes maximum total relative value at about 70% utilization as shown in Figure IIIB-3*c*. The main point of interest demonstrated by this example is that a two-stream system, running at about 10% lower utilization than in the single-stream case, delivers about 10% greater value to the user population.

Several comments are perhaps called for in connection with the preceding and subsequent analyses. It is necessary to establish communication between operations management and the user community so that meanings and measures of "values" and benefits" can be ascertained. Communication channels employed include questionnaires and departmental user representatives. Perhaps more effective soundings could be taken during frequent conversations with a carefully selected small panel of users. Users and operations people should appreciate the necessity for articulating their thoughts and basing analyses and decisions on these subjective data. The nature and limited precision of these data should be kept in mind so that results of analyses are not exaggerated or misused. Concerning this last point, one should bear in mind that the examples given in this article are drawn from our experience in a research environment and require the special assumptions used here.

B. QUANTIFICATION OF VALUE OF SERVICES

Three Classes of Interactive Service

The foregoing discussion dealt with batch processing services. We now define and include the following three classes of interactive service: (1) computation only; (2) programming, debugging, and computation; and (3) problem formulation, programming, debugging, and computation. These definitions are intended to clarify and add structure to the succeeding analyses of the costs of various services.

CLASS 1: COMPUTATION ONLY. The computation-only class is the most straightforward, and it is included in the succeeding two classes. Nevertheless, there is considerable difficulty in defining a cost function that includes all significant costs associated with the solving of a computation problem. In this definition, we attempt to assess costs from the point of view of the management of the organization that employs the users and rents the computing and communications equipment. Thus it is reasonable to include in the cost function human and other costs as well as that of equipment costs. Also included in the costs should be a charge for time the scientist personally spends in solving a problem, charges for auxiliary services (keypunching, for example), and a delay penalty charge. A total cost formula that includes these charges may be expressed as:

$$T = S + C + U + D + A$$

where

T = total problem-solving cost
S = computing system costs (CPU time × CPU charge rate)
C = communications costs (connect time × communication charge rate)
U = cost of user's time
D = cost of delay (elapsed time × delay penalty charge)
A = auxiliary charges

Results of applying this cost formula to a specific problem are shown in Table IIIB-1. The problem used—ETEST—is a FORTRAN IV program which calculates the value of the base of natural logarithms e to 2500 decimal places. This problem places a fairly heavy computation load on the tested system, while remaining relatively insensitive to human response factors. Briefly, the program loops through 25 thousand iterations per line of output (or 2.5 million iterations for the complete problem). No penalty is imposed on machines without floating-point hardware, since the entire computation is made in integer arithmetic. For the same reason the problem is small enough to run on nearly any machine, while at the same time imposing a fairly realistic computational burden on it. These limitations often create some bias against the cost-effectiveness of larger ma-

Table IIIB-1 Options and Costs for the ETEST Program

	System 360/91/OS	System 360/67/TSS	System 360/67/CP/CMS	System IBM 1130	System 360/67/191 TSS/OS	System 360/67 Batch
CPU time @ $/min = system charge	0.25 min @ $15/min 3.75	2.56 min @ $10/min 25.60	2.26 min @ $10/min 22.60	21 min @ $0.40/min 8.40	0.25 min @ $15/min 3.75	0.71 min @ $10/min 7.10
Connect time @ $.06/min = connect charge	—	22 min 1.32	13 min 0.78	—	10 min 0.60	—
User's time @ $.50/min = user time cost	21 min 10.50	10 min 5.00	8 min 4.00	35 min 17.50	16 min 8.00	21 min 10.50
Elapsed time @ $.10/min = delay cost	120 min 12.00	22 min 2.20	13 min 1.30	155 min 15.50	85 min 8.50	120 min 12.00
Auxillary charges	(Keypunching) 2.00	—	—	—*	—	(Keypunching) 2.00
Total cost	$28.25	$34.12	$28.68	$41.40	$20.85	$31.60

* Assumes 2-hr wait for 1130 availability.

chines which have more comprehensive facilities. This bias, however, does not seriously affect our present use.

ETEST has been used informally in the industry as a basis for comparing the cost of using various systems. The extension here is to consider the other costs—in addition to the computer and communication system costs—when running the problem on several systems. The source program consists of 25 FORTRAN statements entered via cards on batch systems and via IBM 2741 terminals on time-sharing systems.

Some comments on the charge rates are in order. System charges are based on the rule of thumb of $5 or $6 per hour for each $1000 of monthly rental (4). The $30 per hour user time cost is calculated with an unusually heavy overhead burden placed on the scientist, first, because he is the sole source of output from the laboratory. Also, the corporation obtains only value received from its research division; that is, the division is not defined as a profit center. Therefore the nominal utility of a scientist equals the budget divided by the number of professional staff members.

The delay penalty rate is elicited from user-panel estimates of the average lowering of productivity that results from not having the solution to the problem of greatest current importance. On the average, this is estimated to be about a 20% reduction in productivity.

We can now make a few observations on the results shown in Table IIIB-1. First, the total cost of solving the ETEST problem is roughly the same whether the System/360 Model 91 with the System/360 Operating System (OS/360), or the System/360 Model 67 with the Time-Sharing System (TSS/360), or the Model 67 with CP-67/CMS time-sharing facilities is used. The fractions of the totals that are used for system and communication charges vary widely, however. They range from 13% for the Model 91 to 79% for CP-67/CMS terminal I/O. The batch user time consists of three walks to the computing center, and the elapsed time includes keypunching and batch turnaround time. The IBM 1130 CPU cost is in the medium range for the group. Note, however, the total cost includes 35 min of user time to punch the cards and compile and execute the program. An important factor in this case is the delay cost, which can become high when such a hands-on machine is used extensively.

The most economical service for the job is the coupled TSS/360–OS/360 computer network (5), which allows for terminal input via the Model 67 and TSS/360, program and data transmission, and then execution on the System/360 Model 91 with OS/360. Here programs are executed in the batch mode, and results are transmitted back to the user's terminal via the Model 67. Such a hybrid operation acquires some of the advantages of both interactive and batch modes.

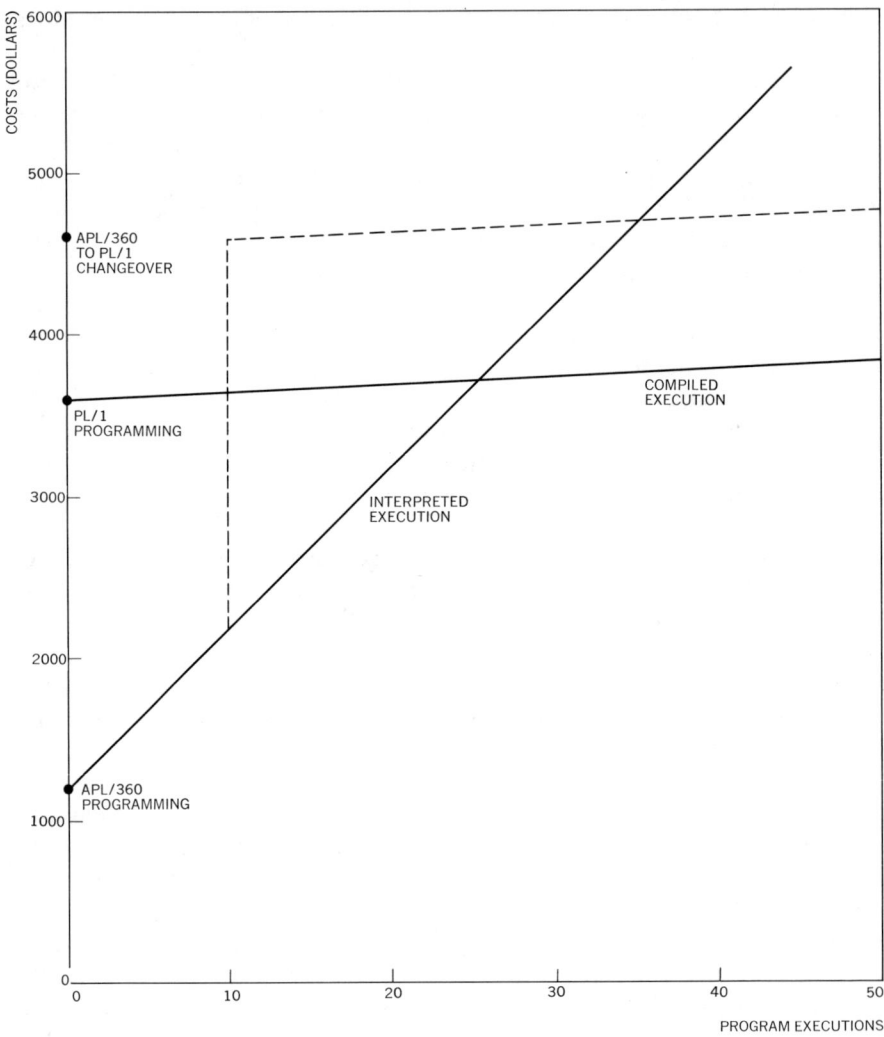

Figure IIIB-4. Hypothetical programming and execution cost comparison.

CLASS 2: PROGRAMMING, DEBUGGING, AND COMPUTATION. The analysis, when extended to include the programming and debugging functions, becomes more difficult, primarily because of greater variability in programming styles and proficiency. It is possible, however, to make a few observations about the choice of services at this level. The program considered here is whether to use an interpretive or a compiling language processor on a given problem. The Research Center provides APL/360 as an interpretive facility, and FORTRAN and PL/1 as compiling systems.

On several problems that have been coded both in APL/360 and in either FORTRAN or PL/1, experience shows that it takes about three times as long to program and debug a problem using FORTRAN or PL/1 as it does when APL/360 is used. However, the interpreted execution of the APL/360 program usually costs a factor of 10 to 100 more than the execution time to obtain a solution to the same problem using a compiled program. Figure IIIB-4 shows graphically the costs of programming plus execution for the two hypothetical programs, as a function of the number of executions. In this example (based on a factor of 3 difference), it is assumed that the programming costs are $1200 for APL/360 and $3600 for PL/1. The execution cost is $5 per run for PL/1 and $100 per run for APL/360.

If these assumptions are used, and factors other than programming and execution costs are neglected, the following conclusions emerge. The choice of a compiling or an interpreting processor should be based on the expected number of runs of the program. In a research laboratory, the evolving nature of many projects dooms most programs to a relatively short life span. This perhaps favors the use of an interpretive processor more than other environments would. If, however, the program life expectancy is not known until after development begins and then appears lengthy, reprogramming should be encouraged and facilitated. The dashed line in Figure IIIB-4 shows such a path, assuming the PL/1 programming time is reduced by one-third as a consequence of the APL/360 experience.

CLASS 3: PROBLEM FORMULATION, PROGRAMMING, DEBUGGING, AND COMPUTATION. We now come to the most comprehensive and difficult class of computer utilization for a research organization. This class involves the entire problem-solving process. Here we consider a means of quantifying benefits of using time-sharing services in the problem-solving process. Before presenting our findings at the Research Center, we summarize the results of an experiment conducted by Gold (6), who compared problem-solving cost and effectiveness using time-sharing and batch processing com-

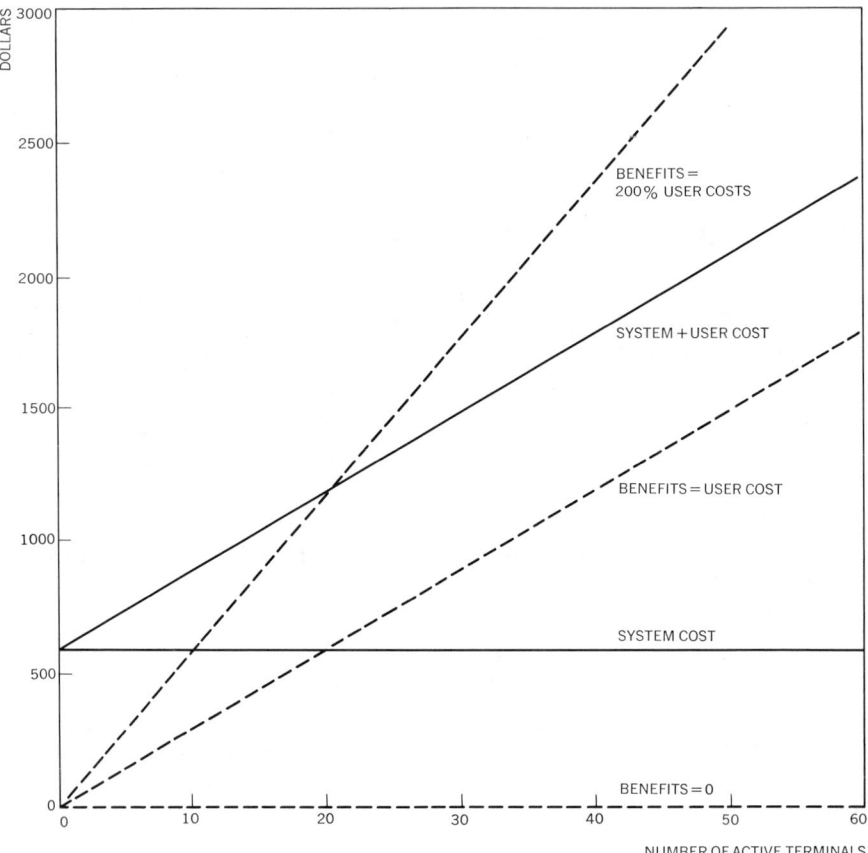

Figure IIIB-5. Benefits and costs in a time-shared system.

puter services. Gold's subjects were a class of 66 graduate students who were seeking ways of improving a business operation through a programmed simulation model of the business. Half of the students used time-sharing, and the other half used batch processing. All other factors, such as language skill and hardware, were assumed to be equal.

The salient findings of Gold's research are the following. Time-sharing users required five times as much computer time as the batch processing group. The average man time required by the users of the time-shared computer system was 16.0 hr, whereas users of the batch system expended 19.2 hr. Therefore, at the given system charging rates, the total cost of solving the problem was less when time-sharing was used, under the assumption that user time is worth more than $11.83 per hour. An average of 6.5 hr of man time was expended before the most successful decision rule for the time-sharing user was found, as compared with 12.0 hr for the batch user. For the batch user, the average increase in simulated profit was $244, whereas the corresponding increase was $444 for time-sharing users. This was greater than an 80% improvement in performance. Gold's analysis "of the students' perceptiveness and understanding of the problem" showed significantly higher grades assigned to the users of the time-sharing system.

TIME-SHARING COST-BENEFITS. Gold's findings correlate strongly with experience in time-sharing usage at the Research Center. In Gold's study the students repeated solutions of the same problem made possible a controlled experiment. Such an opportunity for control does not arise in a research laboratory where each user works on a different problem.

In referring to Figure IIIB-5, it is feasible to analyze the time-sharing usage costs in a statistical sense. Here the utilization factor is expressed in terms of number of active terminals. The system cost (rental) is independent of utilization, as is the case for a single-function, in-house system, and is represented by the flat rental curve in Figure IIIB-5. The value of the user's time is a $30 per hour nominal utility figure. From the representation in Figure IIIB-5, we can identify the following three simple cases.

- For users who are doing no useful work (benefits equal zero), the system-plus-user cost curve represents the combined cost of system and user time, which merely increases with the number of users without any possibility of justification.
- For users who are doing only as much work as they would without the assistance of the time-sharing system (benefits equal user costs), the user costs vanish—as shown by the system-plus-user cost curve—but leave the system rental as an unjustified cost.
- Users doing more work by using time-sharing increase the total (system-user) utility, resulting from a positive increment in productivity, which becomes a benefit. If, for example, the average user's productivity is doubled, the benefits-equal-100% cost curve shown in Figure IIIB-5 represents the benefit realized.

Consider now the more complete representation shown in Figure IIIB-6, into which the following refinements have been introduced. System costs are shown here as the differential cost between the time-sharing service and some alternative service to which it is compared (e.g., slide rules or batch computing). The differential system cost is assumed here to be $400 per

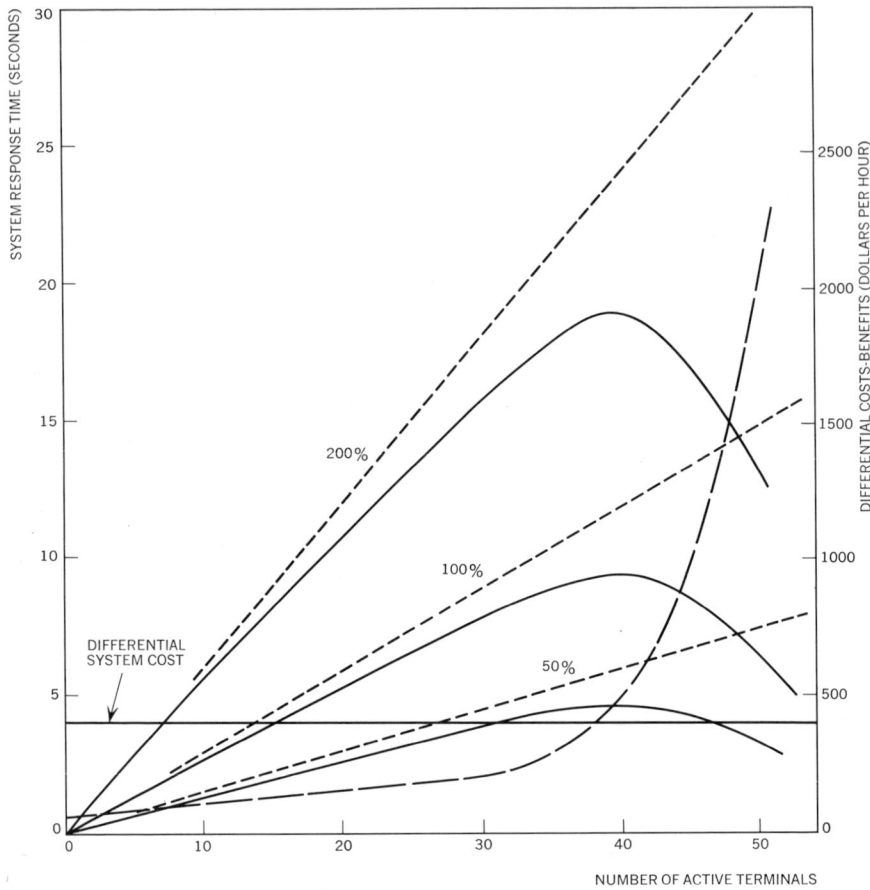

Figure IIIB-6. Differential system cost and productivity benefits.

hour. The cost-benefit curves are labeled with differential productivities that would be achieved on an instantaneously responsive system. That user productivity degrades as the system becomes more heavily loaded and slows down is shown by the saturation and decline of the cost-benefit curves. The magnitude of performance degradation takes into account the fact that user productivity is proportional to the number of interactions per unit time, where

$$\text{Interactions per hour} = \frac{3600 \text{ (sec/hr)}}{I \text{ (sec/interaction)}} = \frac{3600}{T_S + T_U}.$$

B. QUANTIFICATION OF VALUE OF SERVICES

Here

T_S = mean system response time from Figure IIIB-6
T_U = mean user response time (assumed to be 15 sec)

We conclude from this analysis that a time-sharing system is justified where the differential productivity benefits exceed the differential system cost for the average level of loading on that system. Note here that the family of percentage lines represents positive differential productivity based on instantaneous system responsiveness. Thus in Figure IIIB-6 the system is barely profitable where the average differential productivity is 50% and the average number of active users is between 32 and 46.

At the Research Center we generally estimate the differential productivity of users whose work requires interaction to range between 100 and 300%. We attempt to encourage discriminating use of available services, both by allocation and by pricing policies. Also encouraged is use of the computer network, which facilitates the shipment of jobs that do not require interaction (such as compilations, assemblies, and executions) to the batch processor.

A SPECTRUM OF SERVICES. We now compare relative values of three services on a continuous spectrum of system responsiveness as illustrated in Figure IIIB-7. Batch service with a turnaround time of 1 hr has a normalized value of 1. The resubmission time for a batch job is assumed to be 30 min. The reduction in value of batch service with a longer turnaround time is illustrated in Figure IIIB-7 by the falling off of the relative value curve as response time increases. The curves in Figure IIIB-7 are calculated by the following formula:

$$\text{Relative value} = \text{peak value} \times \frac{T_U + T_{so}}{T_S + T_U}$$

$$= \text{peak value} \times \left(\frac{1 + T_{so}/T_U}{1 + T_S/T_U}\right),$$

where T_{so} is the nominal system responsiveness associated with the peak value (which is 60 min in the batch case).

Similar curves are shown for high-speed batch and interactive services. For high-speed batch, we assume that the user waits for his output, scans it quickly, and resubmits his job in 5 min. The more responsive the system is, the more valuable is its service to users who require many turnarounds. Again, the value falls off sharply with increasing system response time T_S

324   ISSUES OF MANAGEMENT

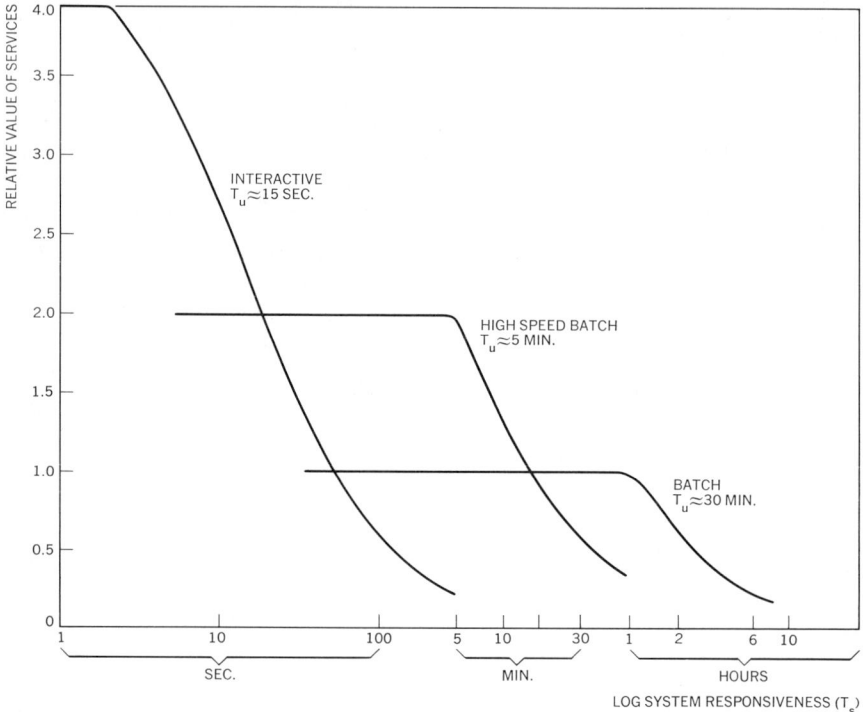

Figure IIIB-7.   Spectrum of relative values of computing service.

as the user waits for his output. This sensitivity is reflected in the above formula by the critical ratio T_S/T_U. Similarly, for interactive services there is also a characteristic user response time (about 15 sec), and a potentially high service value which degrades rapidly as users waste time at the terminal waiting for the system to respond.

To summarize these comparative cost-benefit considerations, there are several types of computing services that can be roughly characterized by a nominal system responsiveness or peak value of the service and by a characteristic user responsiveness in that mode. The value of each type of service quantitatively degrades as a function of the ratio of system responsiveness to user responsiveness.

Concluding Remarks

Evaluation techniques for measuring computing system efficiency continue to be refined as the variety of systems and their applications expand.

System measures often tacitly assume that the highest overall efficiency is achieved when a certain critical system parameter, such as throughput, is optimized. Recognizing that these measures may be quite valid when the computing system essentially models the business, this paper does not differ with such criteria. Used in a research environment for supporting individual research workers, however, system measures and policies should attempt to be more flexible, and should strongly consider the human costs and benefits involved. The reason for this is that research projects are so varied that a single system policy may not effectively model the "business" of research. Therefore, we attempt to evaluate and compare system costs and user benefits under a variety of user policies.

For batch systems, we have studied a two-substream policy—express and production—depending on the value of speedy results to the user. On a two-substream basis, we have found that there can be an increased relative value of the system output to users at an overall system utilization lower than that resulting from a single-stream policy.

In the case of interactive systems, we show the effects of several user policies. Here we conclude that such policies should encourage the use of interactive systems where the user benefits exceed the sum of all cost factors at least by an amount that the manager establishes as minimum.

The immediate advantage of policies that encourage the right choice of computing service is the more effective use of equipment. Still larger is the advantage of helping people become more effective and productive. The importance of achieving improvements has been pointed out by Peter Drucker (6), who wrote: "Productivity will . . . be a major challenge and a major concern of the next ten years. . . . The 'cost-squeeze' of today, on governments, universities, and business, is the first warning—it is really a productivity squeeze. The bulk of tomorrow's employment will be in the service trades, knowledge jobs—in health care, teaching, government management, research and the like. And no one knows much about the productivity of knowledge work, let alone how to improve it."

Acknowledgments

The authors wishes to thank Professor Bernard Galler of the University of Michigan for providing the ETEST program, which is the work of Steven Lundstrom.

References

1. H. Sackman, "*Man-Computer Problem Solving; Experimental Evaluation of Time Sharing and Batch Processing*, Auerbach, New York, 1970.

2. S. Stimler, *Real-Time Data Processing Systems*, McGraw-Hill, New York, 1969.
3. W. F. Sharpe, *The Economics of Computers*, Columbia University Press, New York, 1969.
4. W. P. Hegan, "Buying and Selling Computer Time," *Computers and Automation* **17**, 9 (September 1968), 32–40.
5. W. S. Hobgood, "Evaluation of an Interactive-Batch System Network," *IBM Systems Journal* **11**, 1 (1972), 2–15.
6. M. M. Gold, "Time-Sharing and Batch-Processing: An Experimental Comparison of Their Values in a Problem-Solving Situation," *Communications of the ACM* **12**, 5 (May 1969), 249–259.
7. P. F. Drucker, "The Surprising Seventies," *Harper's Magazine*, July 1971, 35–39.

Cost-Effective Matching of Task and Computing Device[*]
Ralph E. Miller, Jr.[†] *and John McCaslin*[‡]

Introduction

The primary goal of this investigation was to provide policy guidance to organizations which must decide the proportions of resources to be spent on men and computing devices to accomplish engineering tasks. The secondary goal was to develop an analysis for quantitatively evaluating the cost of performing a spectrum of engineering tasks on a spectrum of devices, and thereby determine: (1) The most cost-effective match of tasks and devices and cost improvements possible over current methodology; and (2) the cost penalty for utilizing a less cost-effective device spectrum.

Background

Several experimental studies (1–3) have dealt with the problem of economic trade-offs between batch computing and time-sharing. These studies describe from one to four tasks in depth, and experimentally assess the performance thereof in the two different environments. An attempt to parameterize the task descriptions and then to analytically model the computational environments will be made herein. This modeling is then applied

---

[*] Presented at the ASCE Fifth Conference on Electronic Computation, Purdue University Lafayette, Ind., August 31–September 2, 1970, and published in the *Proceedings of the American Society of Civil Engineers, Journal of the Structural Division,* January 1971, 329–337.
[†] Head-Stress Analysis Research, Structures Technology, Commercial Airplane Group, The Boeing Company, Renton, Wash.
[‡] Systems Analyst, Computing Staff, Commercial Airplane Group, The Boeing Company, Renton, Wash.

to a large number of tasks to optimally match the tasks with various facility configurations which contain a broad spectrum of types of computing devices.

Strategy for Analysis

The strategy for analysis development covered four points:

1. The choice of a set of computing devices and the description of the task performance attributes of each device.
2. The choice of a set of current engineering tasks and the description of each task in terms suitable to the computing devices selected.
3. The analysis of task cost for each task on each computing device to determine the least-cost device.
4. The display of engineering task total cost against computing cost for various spectrums of computing devices.

Classification and Simulation of Computing Devices

Seven types of devices were chosen to represent a spectrum of devices which could be available for use on engineering tasks. These were: (1) Slide rule; (2) mechanical desk calculator; (3) stored-program desk calculator; (4) small time-sharing system; (5) large time-sharing system; (6) small, local, dedicated batch computer; and (7) large, centralized, batch computer. These devices were simulated in terms of task input man-time, computation man-time, output man-time, man waiting time, machine time, and keypunch time. These terms were defined as follows (not all items, of course, are applicable to a given device):

1. Task Input Man-Time—Program writing, submission to keypunch, initial loading, debugging, spot corrections and reloading. Data transfer to coding forms, submission to keypunch, deck stacking, job submission, interactive input, interactive think time delays.
2. Computation Man-Time—Hand computation and table lookup; program compilation, loading, and execution for debugging and production runs if the task performers monitor the program as it runs. Time includes running time for plotting subroutines.
3. Output Man-Time—Monitoring intermediate (temporary) results, recording numbers for latter re-entry, time consumed by computer printout of intermediate results, writing down final results, typing up handwritten results, time consumed by final computer printout and cardpunching. These times are counted only if the output processing is monitored by task performers. Additionally included are plotting by

hand- or man-monitored mechanical plotters and transferring output to coding forms for further computer processing.

4. Waiting Time—For task performers, this includes keypunch turnaround for all input, and large batch computer turnaround time. For users of task results, waiting time is equal to all time spent by performers on input, computation, output, and waiting; plus turnaround delays for punched and plotted output; minus "minimum useable flowtime" as specified in the questionnaire. User waiting time thus calculated is then multiplied by the ratio of users to performers, to account for the downstream leverage exerted when a small group delays a large group.

5. Machine Time—Includes all activities which require machine residency: program and data input (from punched cards or prepunched tape, where possible), debugging, computation, temporary output, and other forms of output, to the extent that they are produced directly by the machine or are copied down before all answers are obtained. (e.g., mechanical calculator; residency time includes time to write down answers, but not the time to type the report, draw plots, or prepare coding forms for punched output). Plotters are included only during the time they are used, on an hourly-rental or per-frame basis.

6. Keypunch Time—Manpower costs for keypunching program, input, data, or output cards (not including keypunching for program corrections; this is assumed to be done by the performers and is included under "input man-time."

A brief synopsis of the model for each device is given in Table IIIB-2. An example of a detailed model of task simulation is given for the small time-sharing system:

Input Man-Time (on-line).

1. New program of specified length plus 10 extra statements per plot, 60 sec to write, 30 sec to punch tape, 3 sec to read.
2. 10% of program de-bugged, 120 sec per statement.
3. Repeat tasks loaded, 3 sec per statement.
4. Data 12 sec/values per line for each run.
5. Idle 20% of input time for overhead.

Computation Man-time (for each run).

1. Compilation and loading 20 sec.
2. Execution 0.02 sec per statement.

Output Man-time.

1. Printed, 2.4 sec per value.
2. Plotted, 3 min per plot.
3. Punched, 15 min per run.

Waiting Man-time.

1. Perfomers none.
2. Users task time + 2 hr for keypunch.

Machine.

1. Time available 84 hr per month, residency + (program and data input + computation + printed or plotted output).
2. Cost 15 terminal system, $271 per terminal month.

Keypunch

1. Cost, $0.01 per value; 4 values per card.

Device Disqualification.

1. Compute volume up to 220 program statements.
2. Accuracy up to 8 decimal digits.

Choice of Set of Engineering Tasks

A sample of 20% of the management of a 3,000 man engineering organization was made for typical small computational tasks that were currently (1968) being performed. The scope of the data obtained on each task is as follows:

1. Task number.
2. Airplane project code.
3. Plant location code.
4. Number professional task performers.
5. Number sub-professional task performers.
6. Number supervisory users of task results.
7. Number professional users of task results.
8. Number sub-professional users of task results.
9. Current device type code.
10. Number of data input values for task.
11. Number of individual computation steps.
12. Number of fortran program statements.
13. Accuracy Req'd (digits).

Table IIIB-2 Device Simulation Summary

(1)	Slide Rule (2)	Mechanical Calculation (3)	Program Calculation (4)	Small Time Sharing (5)	Large Time Sharing (6)	Small Batch (7)	Large Batch (8)
Program input man-time	None	None	35 sec per step	125 sec per statement	Same as small	100 sec per statement	Same as small batch
Data input man-time	Include with computation	Include with computation	10 sec per value	14 sec per value	12 sec per value	15 sec per value	
Compute man-time	30 sec per operation	25 sec per operation	20 program steps per sec	20 sec compile, 0.02 sec	10 sec compile, 0.01 sec per statement execution	30 sec compile, 0.0025	None
Printed output man-time	10 sec per value	10 sec per value	10 sec per value	3 sec per value	2 sec per value	1–5 sec per value	10 min to get output
Doer man-wait-time	None	None	None	None	None	Keypunch 2 hr	Keypunch 2-hr-old job 8-hr new–16 hr
User man-wait-time	(Task time)— (minute useful time)	(Task time)— (minute useful time)	(Task time)— (minute useful time)	(Task time)— (minute useful time)	(Task time)— (minute useful time)	Same as doer	Task time + 8 hr for plots

Machine time	Includes compute and output	Includes compute and output	Includes input compute and output	Includes input compute and output	Includes input compute and output	Same as task simulation	Central processor unit (C.P.U.) time Input 2×10^{-3} sec per value Compute 3×10^{-3} sec per statement Output 1×10^{-3} sec per line
Machine cost[a]	None	$0.40 per hr	$1.35 per hr	$3.20 per hr	$12.70 per hr	$24.00 per hr	$900.00 per cp hr
Keypunch	$0.04 per output card	$0.04 per output card	$0.04 per output card	$0.04 per output card	$0.04 per output card	$0.04 per program statement	$0.04 per program statement

[a] Industry average.

14. Number of temporary output data values.
15. Number of permanent printed output data values.
16. Code for short or long output format.
17. Number of plots required.
18. Average number of points per plot.
19. Code for rough or finished plots.
20. Number of punched output data values.
21. Number of nonredundant output data values (all type).
22. Minimum useable task flow time.
23. Number of repeated tasks per month.
24. Number of new tasks per month.

Data on 143 tasks were obtained for analysis.

Each task in this set of tasks was evaluated for each of the computing device types. Summary analyses were made for the entire task set on various device systems.

Engineering Task-Computing Device Analysis

A specific work flow pattern was assumed for each simulated task/device combination; this pattern is a function of the task description and the device type. Six cost components are calculated for each combination: (1) Man-time to input program (if any) and data; (2) man-time to perform (or monitor) computations; (3) man-time to produce all forms of output; (4) unproductive man-time spent waiting for delays in the problem solving process; (5) machine costs (if any); and (6) keypunch costs (if any). Task performance is assumed to start when a set of problem-oriented formulas and the input data are available, i.e., written down on paper. Time required for media conversion and for program debugging is also included in task costs where applicable. Finally, task costs are totaled for each device type, and the lowest-cost device type is identified, subject to constraints on computation volume and accuracy requirements.

Analysis information was obtained for each task and for the entire task set. For each task; the analysis summarizes as follows:

1. Current Data—Device type currently used; task frequency and location, and program size and accuracy requirements.
2. Data on Recommended (Lowest-Cost) Device—Device type recommended; number of devices needed; total monthly cost; and net cost savings over currently used device.
3. Data on Each Device Type—Name of device; number of devices needed; cost components preceding items 1 through 6; total monthly cost; net cost savings over current device; and reasons for disqualification of device (if any).

B. QUANTIFICATION OF VALUE OF SERVICES

Table IIIB-3 Device System Definition

Device (1)	Current System (2)	7 Device System (3)	6 Device System (4)	5 Device System (5)
Slide rule	•	•	•	•
Mechanical desk calculator	•	•	•	•
Programmable desk calculator	—	•	•	•
Small time-share system	—	•	•	—
Large time-share system	—	•	•	•
Small batch computer	—	•	—	—
Large batch computer	•	•	•	•

Table IIIB-4 Task Distribution by Device Type, as a Percentage (Survey Data)

Device (1)	Current System (2)	7 Device System (3)	6 Device System (4)	5 Device System (5)
Slide rule	13	0	0	0
Mechanical desk calculator	41	15	15	15
Programmable desk calculator	6	33	36	36
Small time-share system	—	7	13	0
Large time-share system	—	10	22	35
Small batch computer	—	30	0	0
Large batch computer	40	5	14	14

Table IIIB-5 Cost-Effective Number of Engineers per Device

Device (1)	Current System (2)	7 Device System (3)	6 Device System (4)	5 Device System (5)
Slide rule	—	—	—	—
Mechanical desk calculator	—	5.0	5.0	5.0
Programmable desk calculator	—	2.6	—	2.7
Small time-share system	—	4.2	1.8	0
Large time-share system	—	3.3	1.9	2.0
Small batch computer	—	12.2	0	0
Large batch computer	—	—	—	—

FOR ENTIRE SET OF TASKS. After simulating the entire task set, the program produces a totalization and summary for each device type, which assumes that each task would be transferred to the device type recommended for it. The summary shows: (1) Number of devices needed; (2) total monthly cost for all tasks which should use the device type; (3) net cost savings over currently-used devices, for these tasks; (4) list of tasks for which the device type is best, together with current device type; and (5) a list of tasks which currently use the device type.

Analysis Results and Evaluation

Four systems of devices, as defined in Table IIIB-3 were used to analyze the task data. The results of the analysis are given in Tables IIIB-4 and IIIB-5. Table IIIB-4 shows that the particular device system strongly influences the cost-effective distribution of the tasks. When the "current system" is expanded, as in the "5 device system," to include the programmable desk calculator and a large time-share system, then less tasks are

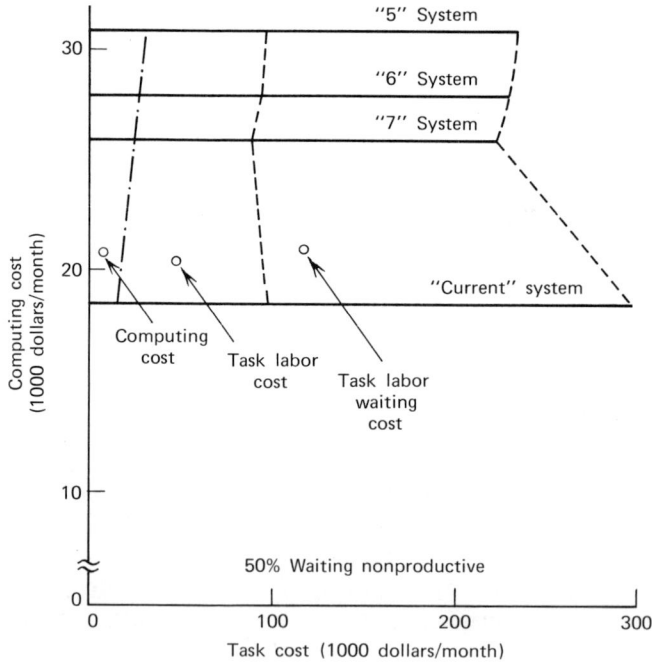

Figure IIIB-8. Task cost versus device system.

B. QUANTIFICATION OF VALUE OF SERVICES

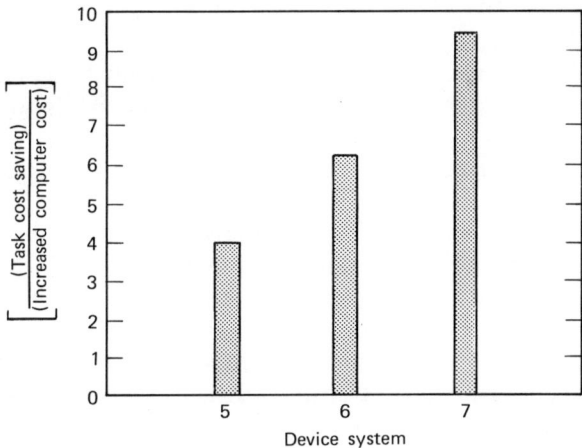

Figure IIIB-9. Device system benefit.

done on the mechanical calculator and large batch to achieve the least cost for this task set.

As a consequence of cost-effective matching of tasks to computing device, the number of devices and the number of task engineers required are shown in Table IIIB-5. This table gives some management guidance as to the desirable number of engineers per device, which will ensure that the device is not over-loaded and can still deliver cost-effective processing on its tasks. The cost results are summarized in Fig. IIIB-8, where it is seen that the task total cost is composed of approximately 10% computing equipment cost, 30% engineer performing cost, and 60% engineer waiting cost. It is readily seen that waiting is the significant portion of the task total cost. The major findings from comparing the different device systems in Fig. IIIB-8 are:

1. The current system has minimized the cost of computing equipment but this has unfortunately resulted in a task maximum total cost.
2. The 5, 6, and 7 device systems require that more money be spent on computing equipment than the current system; nevertheless, these alternate device systems drastically reduce the task total cost.

Fig. IIIB-9 displays the cost benefit to the task organization if processing is performed on different device systems. The task cost saving and increase in computer cost are referenced to the current system. Thus, a computer dollar spent on using a different device system will generate $4 to $9 in savings on the task total cost.

Conclusions

For the task data and computing services investigated, the current system of devices is not task cost effective. The current system is typical of many highly centralized, batch processing organizations wherein, as the analysis shows, the computer costs are minimized, however, this suboptimization has maximized the engineering task total cost.

Task cost reduction can only significantly come about through utilizing computing equipment in a manner that reduces "waiting time" to the minimum, useful level. The cost-effectiveness of the 7 device system is typically achieved by: (1) Transferring tasks from highly mechanical processing, e.g., slide rule and mechanical calculator, to programmable electronic calculators; and (2) transferring tasks from the large batch computer to a smaller electronic computer which the engineer can directly access while continuously pursuing his current task to completion. This implies that the current system must change.

As most task organizations operate at a fixed resource level and divide these resources between the various organizational elements, it is usually difficult for one organizational element to increase its cost-effectiveness if it is constrained by another organizational element.

Nevertheless, for situations as analyzed here, the manpower resources of the task organization could be reduced slightly and these savings could be used to revise the current device system so as to achieve a reduction in the task total cost.

References

1. H. Sackman, "Time-Sharing versus Batch Processing: The Experimental Evidence," Proceedings of American Federation of Information Processing Services Spring Joint Computer Conference, 1968.
2. H. Sackman, W. J. Erikson, and E. E. Grant, "Exploratory Experimental Studies Comparing On-Line and Off-Line Programming Performance," Systems Development Corporations Report SP-2687, December 1966.
3. M. Schatzoff, R. Tsao, and R. Wiig, "An Experimental Comparison of Time-Sharing and Batch Processing," *Communications of the Association for Computing Machinery*, May 1967.

C. LOCATION/ALLOCATION PROBLEMS

The growing and changing role of computer usage makes necessary a frequent reexamination of the distribution and arrangement of computing facilities within an organization. Such examinations often show that a system configuration that was eminently sensible several years ago is unsatisfactory today. Having made this discovery, management is confronted with the problems of determining a more appropriate system arrangement, and then persuading the parties involved—users, operations personnel, and management—that the change is desirable.

An examination of the location of computing facilities must take into account the following dynamic and, to some degree, countervailing tendencies:

Technology

- Modern data communications hardware and software make it possible to deliver many computing services over great distances.
- The development of intelligent terminals, minicomputers, and microprogramming offer new opportunities for the dispersion of certain computing service functions—from general-purpose systems to functionally specific subsystems.
- At the same time these technological developments make possible a greater dispersion of computing facilities, there is a growing need for integration of the information produced.
- The growing dependence of an organization on timely information and on-line services increases the pressure for assured continuity of service. "Robustness"—the ability to continue services despite component malfunction—is becoming a dominant criterion in determining configuration.

In this section we attempt to put these factors into a common framework and suggest methodologies for studying tradeoffs in making location/allocation decisions.

The first section, "Centralization versus Dispersion," considers the problem of consolidation at a multiinstallation level. This is the question facing an organization that has several, or many, computing centers, each of which provides the same set of services to people at its location. Should these existing centers be replaced by fewer, larger, generally accessible centers?

The second section, "Networks," examines the interconnection of computers in a network—so that users have access to the resources of several systems. A computer network can offer many of the economic and functional benefits of large consolidated installations and therefore should be considered as an alternative or supplement to a consolidation plan.

The third section, "Internal Organizational—Distribution of Function," surveys the possibilities for dispersion of computing function within a typical location, and reviews the factors to be weighed in determining the best location for particular functions—within a general-purpose system, within a functionally specific system or subsystem, or in an intelligent terminal.

Centralization or Dispersion of Computing Facilities

This article examines several of the relationships and tendencies that influence centralization-dispersion judgments. Some guidelines for determining an appropriate distribution of computing resources are developed and illustrated by example. The goal is to devise a strategy for centralization versus decentralization, and to develop a methodology for decision. The general conclusion of this examination is that at least some of the computer services in a large, widely dispersed organization can be provided economically out of relatively few centers.

The Tendency toward Centralization [*]

Quite understandably, the use of computers in many organizations has grown, not in accordance with an overall plan, but as the sum total of the plans of several, or many, more-or-less autonomous computer centers. At some point, it becomes clear that a review of the consequences of this fragmentation is in order—that substantial benefits might result from a greater centralization of the data processing function. The term "centralization" may refer to equipment and operations, or may be limited to a merger of some of the following ancillary functions.

- Strategic planning.
- Personnel selection and education.
- Measurement and evaluation.
- Systems support.
- Consulting and applications support.
- Charging, accounting, and control.

When operational consolidation is indicated, the concentration of systems in fewer—but larger—centers may be required. Alternatively, consolidation may be accomplished by interconnecting the existing centers in a suitably designed network.

ADVANTAGES OF CENTRALIZATION. This section concentrates on reasons in favor of physically consolidating general-purpose computing centers. Let us first consider some of the advantages of centralization.

[*] This section appeared in IBM Systems Journal 12, 3.

Economies of scale are possible with adequate processing volume. The larger and more cost-effective systems required may result in reduced cost per computation (provided the larger systems can be obtained).

Other economies are possible through reductions in record storage duplication and program preparation and maintenance. Site preparation and protection costs may similarly be reduced, since fewer sites are involved.

Fuller utilization of processing capability may result from the assignment of priorities over a larger and more diverse population of users, and offer better opportunities for around-the-clock utilization. For example, engineering and research demands tend to peak on the first shift, whereas manufacturing and administrative demands frequently peak during off-shifts. Operation costs for the third and fourth shifts are reduced, relative to benefits realized, in a large multisystem installation.

Certain personnel efficiencies may be possible by concentrating skilled programmers and technicians at a central site, thus making more effective use of their talents. A larger operation may appeal more to highly qualified computer specialists because of broader career opportunities.

Improved quality of services is the result of reduced mean and variance of turnaround time in larger centers, as we demonstrate later in this article. Also, a greater variety of services and programs can be offered to users of larger computing centers. As previously indicated, a larger and more expert pool of consultant services is available. There is less disruption to a computer user who transfers from one location to another when both sites use the same computer facility.

Integration of other functions, such as many administrative and technical services, may be considered for consolidation after a data communication network and common computational procedures are in place. Increasingly, there are functional and managerial advantages in centralizing a company's data base.

Some of the advantages of centralization just cited are difficult to quantify. It is possible, however, to evaluate several major considerations, at least to a first approximation.

ECONOMIES OF SCALE. In most cases, the primary motivation of computing resources is to realize economies of scale. It has long been noted that—up to a point—larger units tend to be more efficient in producing and distributing goods and services than smaller units. For example, operations research procedures have been developed to determine an appropriate number and location of manufacturing plants (1) or warehouses, (2), taking into account their economies of scale. "Appropriate" since optimum-determining algorithms have not been developed for most practical situations, although heuristic procedures have been found which apparently yield near-optimal solutions.

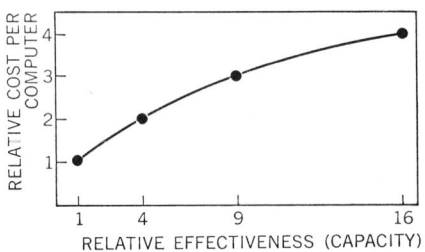

Figure IIIC-1. Quadratic effect of scale.

In the case of computing equipment, an economy of scale has been observed, wherein system effectiveness E is a quadratic function of system cost C. This quadratic effect of computer system scale may be expressed as:

$$E = KC^2 \qquad (1)$$

where K is a constant of proportionality between the selected measure of effectiveness (performance, speed, throughput, etc.) and cost.

Today the relationship cannot be so simply conceived. For example, throughput increases may be more directly related to larger and faster storage and data channels. However, personnel costs, which show very steep economies of scale (3), absorb a larger fraction of the total equipment operation costs. The user may select the parameters he believes most aptly characterize his system. The observed effect of scale may be somewhat greater or somewhat less than quadratic. For the analysis in this article, we assume a quadratic effect as shown in Figure IIIC-1 as an example expression. Illustrative of the quadratic relationships is a fourfold increase in effectiveness for a doubling of cost. A review of this subject—including several attempts at corroboration with third-generation price-performance data—is given by Sharpe (4).

Economy of scale is most obvious with respect to equipment costs, but it also obtains for other components of the total operational cost including floor space costs, number of operational and support personnel, and number of software packages to be maintained.

Figure IIIC-2 shows the quadratic economies of scale on the cost of executing 16 units of computational workload in a given time on various computer sizes, ranging from a single 16-unit-capacity computer to 16 single-unit computers.

Analytically, this is expressed as $K_o N^{1/2}$, where N is the number of installations and K_o is the constant of proportionality between costs and multiplicity of installations. The analysis assumes a single computer system per installation.

C. LOCATION/ALLOCATION PROBLEMS

DUPLICATION OF DATA BASE MAINTENANCE. Duplication of data base maintenance is another efficiency consideration that increasingly encourages the consolidation of computing services. In the trend toward data base systems, references are often made by many application programs to a common information pool or data base. Thus multiple-installation data base systems frequently maintain multiple copies of the data base and must transmit modifications of the data base reciprocally.

In the limiting case, in which all installations communicate directly with one another—as in a fully connected network—the total number of interinstallation *communication links* is given by:

$$L = \frac{N(N-1)}{2}. \qquad (2)$$

Here, N is the number of installations, and L is the number of interconnecting links. Each file modification must be transmitted to the $N - 1$ other installations. Therefore the total volume of interinstallation communication increases linearly with N.

Similarly, the volume of *traffic per link* decreases with increasing number of interconnected installations N according to:

$$\text{Traffic per link} = \frac{\text{total traffic}}{\text{total links}} = \frac{N-1}{N(N-1)/2} = \frac{2}{N}. \qquad (3)$$

Economics of scale similarly apply to communication charges. Therefore, if we assume the quadratic relation (1) to apply to the cost of

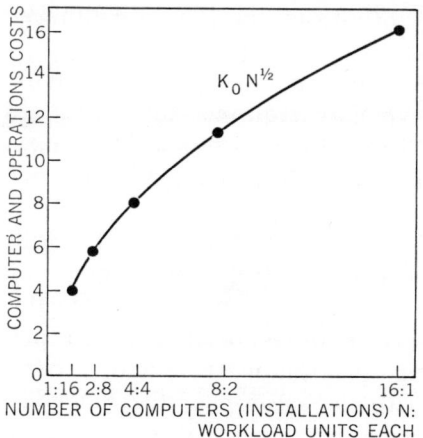

Figure IIIC-2. Quadratic economies of scale for assumed 16 units of workload.

interinstallation traffic, we obtain the relationship:

$$\text{Relative cost per link} = K_1\sqrt{2/N}, \tag{4}$$

where K_1 is a constant of proportionality. The *total cost of the interinstallation communications* is given as:

Total linkage cost = relative cost per link × total links

$$= K_1 \sqrt{2/N} \, [N(N-1)/2]$$
$$= K_1 \sqrt{N/2}(N-1).$$

The relations in Eq. (2) through (5) are shown as functions of N in Figure IIIC-3.

Thus the quadratic effects of relative costs of computing equipment and operations and interinstallation communication costs, respectively, as a function of the number of installations, tend to motivate consolidation. If these were the only factors involved, the motivation to centralize the computing resources of an organization down to a single large installation would be very strong indeed. In the following section, we consider some of the countervailing arguments.

The Tendency toward Decentralization

Let us begin by reviewing some of the arguments for decentralized computational operations. The following ideas are often advanced as advantages of decentralization.

Greater interest and motivation at local levels, combined with greater knowledge of local conditions, are often said to produce information of higher quality and value. This is believed to be advantageous even though unit processing costs may be higher.

Decentralization is also believed to permit tailoring to local requirements. The system standardization typically required for centralized processing may not be equally suitable for all divisions. With decentralization, special programs and services can be tailored to meet differing divisional needs.

Flexibility in coping with crises or changes in plan is more easily managed locally. When local management is in control of its computers, it may be able to take more immediate or preemptive action in reallocating resources than would a centralized service. With regard to operations personnel in a decentralized data processing organization, there may be benefits from a feeling of identification with the mission of the functional division to which center employees belong, rather than to a service organiza-

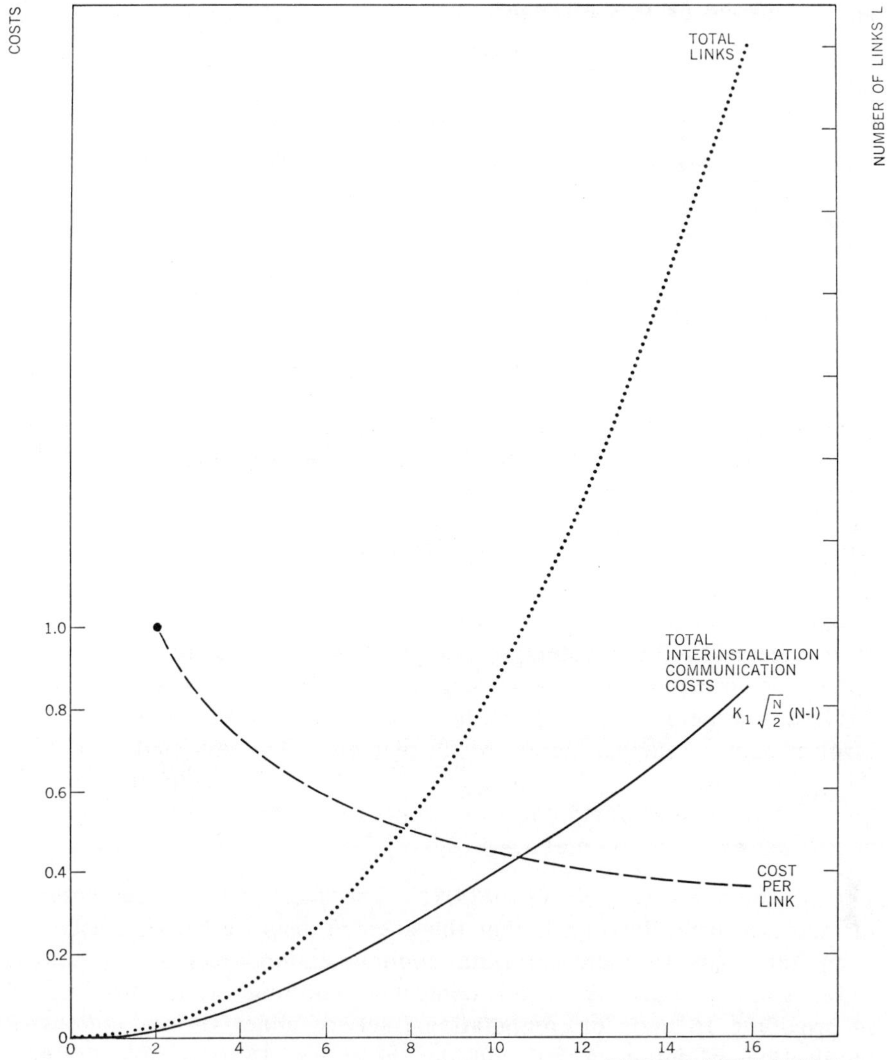

Figure IIIC-3. Relationships among costs and links for a range of network sizes.

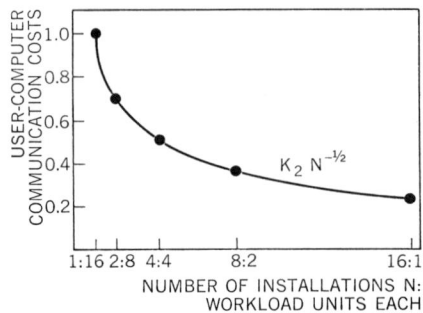

Figure IIIC-4. User-computer communication costs.

tion. Data processing personnel may also have more opportunities to communicate with, and transfer into, the line operations of the division, for example, sales, research and development, or management.

In a decentralized data processing organization, certain communication costs, errors, and interruptions are avoided. These communications are those that occur between users and computers, rather than the interinstallation communications previously discussed. Arguments for retaining some decentralized computers include psychological and showcase effects, and hands-on requirements for educational and testing purposes.

These considerations, like those favoring centralization described earlier, involve many intangible factors which that must be considered in making the final decisions. Again, however, it is helpful to make approximate quantifications of the major factors so as to provide aid in the final, more comprehensive, decision-making process.

USER-COMPUTER COMMUNICATION COST. The most obvious consequence of increased centralization is that the average distance between user and computer tends to increase. Data communication costs and problems increase commensurately. In this context we continue the idealized model of providing 16 units of computational service under various options of physical consolidation. Again, consider the case of 16 units of service provided in various ratios of installations (N) to units of workload.

User-computer communication costs for such a distribution are shown in Figure IIIC-4. We may ignore the irregularities of subregion shape that result from some multiples, and assume that users and computers are uniformly distributed geographically. Under these conditions it is evident that the average user-computer distance varies inversely with the square root of the number of installations. The user-computer communication cost curve in Figure IIC-4 assumes costs to be a linear function of distance.

C. LOCATION/ALLOCATION PROBLEMS

COST OF SERVICE INTERRUPTION. The cost of service interruption provides an argument against putting all an organization's computing capability into a single system or a single installation. The loss caused by a disruption in computing services varies according to the nature of the application, duration of the interruption, time of day, and amount of warning provided. The trend, however, is that the cost of service interruptions becomes a more dominant consideration as users become more dependent on computer services—especially with the growth of conversational and real-time usage.

For the first approximation analysis, assume that service interruptions at the various installations are mutually and statistically independent, and that the cost of service interruption is proportional to the probability that all systems are disabled. Therefore

Cost of service interruption = $K_3 (P)^N$,

where P is the probability that the system will be disabled, and K_3 is a constant of proportionality.

CENTRALIZATION OR DISPERSION COSTS. We now define a *cost of centralization for N installations, Cost (N)*, as consisting of the sum of equipment and operations costs, interinstallation communications costs, user-computer communications costs, and cost of service interruptions:

$$\text{Cost }(N) = K_0 N^{1/2} + K_1 \sqrt{\frac{N}{2}}(N - 1) + K_2 N^{-1/2} + K_3(P)^N. \qquad (6)$$

A hypothetical case is given in Figure IIIC-5 which shows *Cost (N)* and its components for $K_0 = K_2 = 4$, $K_1 = 0.5$, and $K_3 = 60$. Also assumed is a service interruption probability $P = 0.1$. These values of K_0, K_1, K_2, and K_3 are typical of computing centers, and they have been chosen here for illustrative purposes. The analysis for an actual organization is based on analysis of costs at the existing level of centralization. In the hypothetical case (under the assumptions given), the optimal number of installations is seen to be $N = 2$.

To examine the effect of the relative magnitude of K_0, K_1, K_2, K_3 on the optimal number of installations N, let us rewrite Eq. 6 as follows:

$$\text{Cost }(N) = K_0 \left[N^{1/2} + \frac{K_1}{K_0} \sqrt{\frac{N}{2}} (N - 1) + \frac{K_2}{K_0} N^{-1/2} + \frac{K_3}{K_0} (P)^N \right]$$

$$= K_0 \left[N^{1/2} + C_1 \sqrt{\frac{N}{2}} (N - 1) + C_2 N^{-1/2} + C_3 (P)^N \right]$$

ISSUES OF MANAGEMENT

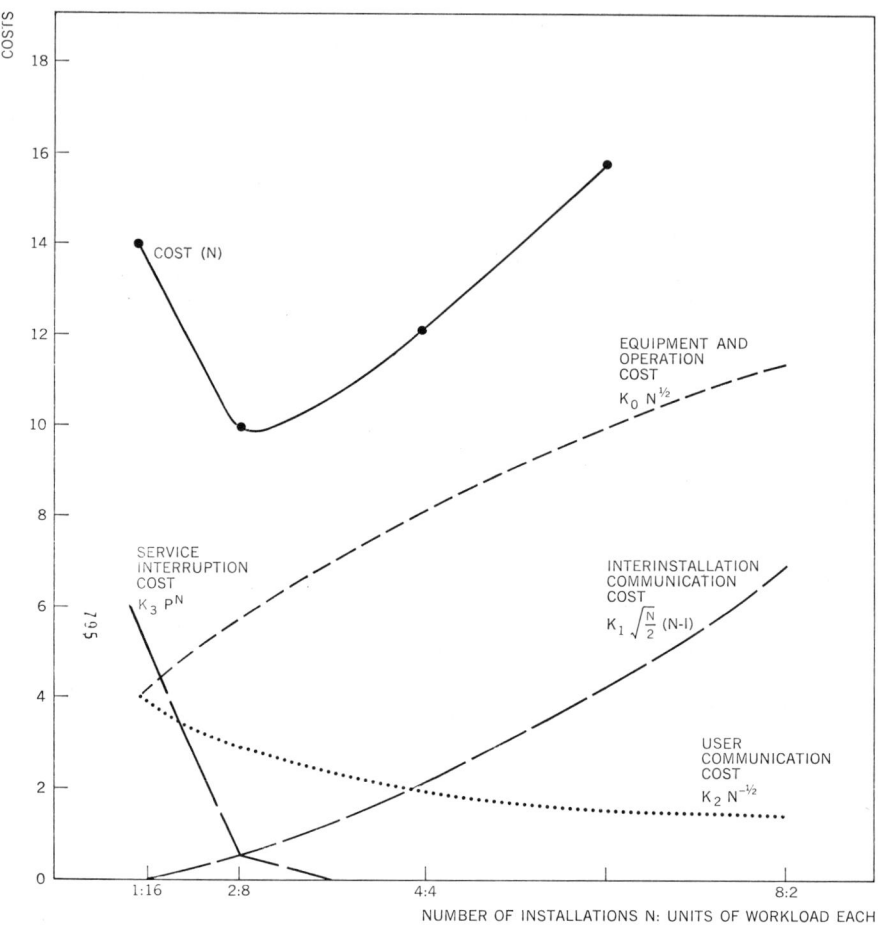

Figure IIIC-5. Minimization of centralization or dispersion costs.

Now we can study regions in a three-dimensional space of the parameters C_1, C_2, C_3 where

$C_1 = \dfrac{K_1}{K_0}$ = ratio of interinstallation communication to computing costs,

$C_2 = \dfrac{K_2}{K_0}$ = ratio of user-communication to computing costs,

$C_3 = \dfrac{K_3}{K_0}$ = ratio of service interruption to computing costs (sometimes referred to as availability insurance factor).

C. LOCATION/ALLOCATION PROBLEMS 347

Figure IIIB-6 shows the volume of this C-parameter space where

$$0 < C_1 < 1, \ 0 < C_2 < 2, \quad \text{and} \quad 0 < C_3 < 20.$$

This range of parameters has been chosen to include the feasible relative costs of providing general-purpose, nonmilitary computing services over a region of about 1000 mi radius, given current United States computer, personnel, and communication costs.

Within this feasible space can be seen three regions. These are the regions in which one, two, and three installations comprise the optimal solution to the cost equation.

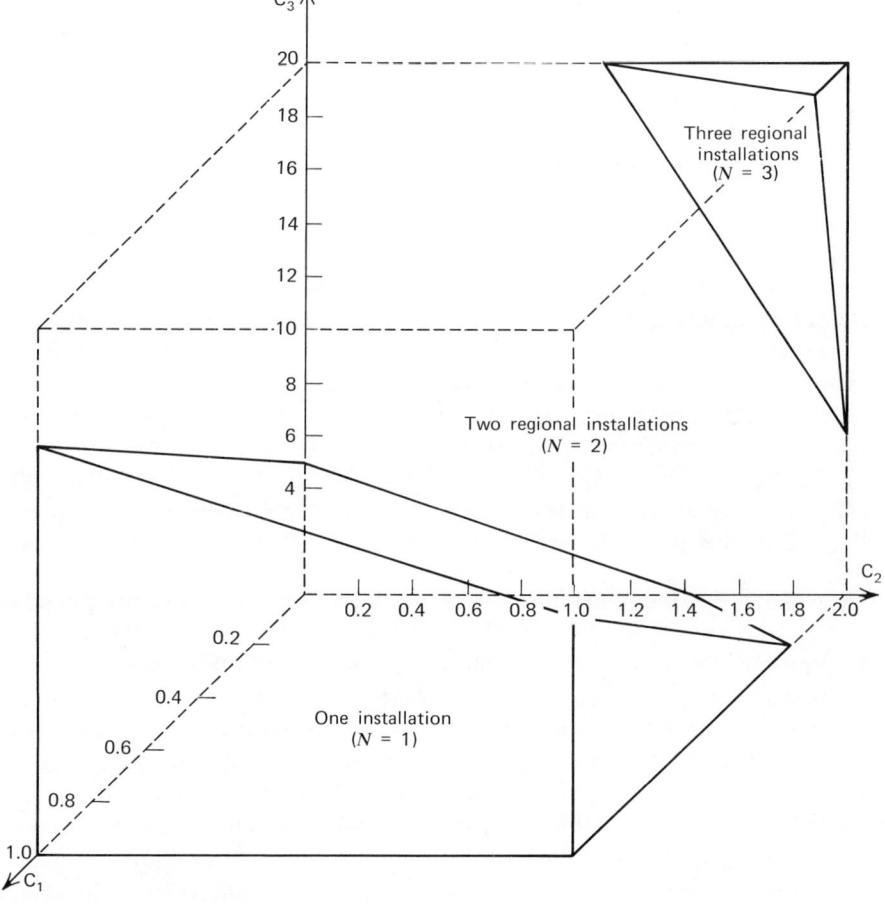

Figure IIIC-6. Relative cost space for centralization-dispersion decision.

Using the conditions and analysis given in this article, one would base his decision to consolidate into one, two, or three regional installations on the following observations from Figure IIIC-6.

- In the vicinity the origin, equipment and operating costs dominate, thus suggesting the optimal strategy of a single installation ($N = 1$) for all cases.
- Higher values of C_1 (higher interinstallation communication costs) increase the desirability of single-installation operation ($N = 1$).
- Higher values of C_2 (higher user-computer communication costs) and/or higher values of C_3 (higher service interruption costs) increase the desirability of multiple installations.
- No economic basis is indicated for operating more than three general-purpose computing installations ($N = 3$) within an organization in a region about half the size of the United States, under the simplifying assumptions and limitations of this analysis. (The assumption that economies of scale still prevail at this level of centralization should be verified in each case).

The following section outlines several refinements to the *Cost (N)* model and indicates the general effect of these modifications on our conclusions. Before proceeding, however, let it again be noted that, even with the subsequent refinements, our study represents only a first-approximation analysis of some of the factors. Clearly, other subjective factors must also be weighed in any particular case. It should also be understood that a reduction in the number of general-purpose centralized installations does not preclude the existence of many limited-function local facilities. Perhaps the following hypothetical example of a satellite central-network can clarify this distinction.

EXAMPLE. A given company has an autonomous, general-purpose computing installation at each of 10 locations. Each installation is responsible for satisfying the computing needs of all employees at its particular location. The following strategy for regional integration of computing services is proposed. (1) Concentrate widely used, general-purpose services and data bases at one, two, or three regional service centers as indicated in the foregoing analysis. The centers are connected by broadband links as shown in Figure IIIC-7. Standard production services, such as batch, time-sharing (TSO), information management (IMS), and text processing (ATS) may be provided from such centers. (2) Maintain processing capability and file residence at each of the original locations as required to satisfy the following needs.

- To send work to and receive work from the large regional centers via remote job entry (RJE). These locations are thus satellite to one or more of the large regional centers.
- To provide services and major applications used only at one site or which are in a state of development.
- To provide host support for local intelligent terminals and controllers.

Such a division of computing service responsibility permits an organization to enjoy many of the advantages of centralization, and at the same time avoid many of the disadvantages that sometimes follow complete consolidation.

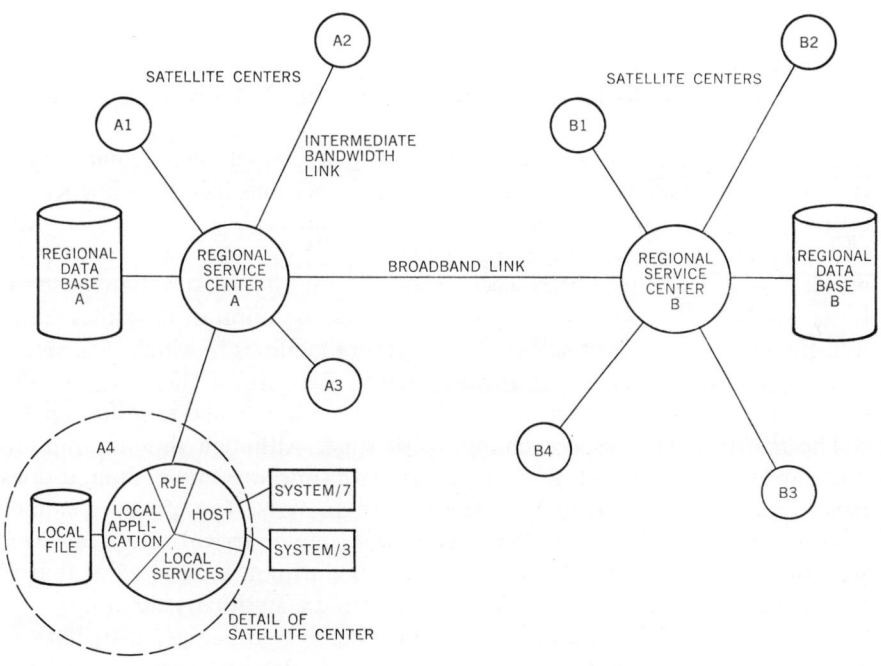

Figure IIIC-7. Regionalization of computing services.

Centralization-Dispersion Effects on Service Quality

Previous sections have concentrated on costs of centralization or dispersion of computing facilities. Let us now examine some effects on the quality of the services provided, using system turnaround time as the indicator of performance. The effect of scaling on system turnaround time is well known in queuing theory, but otherwise is not widely appreciated.

The scaling effect in queuing can be described briefly as follows. Assume customers arrive randomly at a service facility with an average *arrival rate* of λ customers per hour. Also, the system has the capacity to service customers at an average *service rate* of μ customers per hour (with $\mu > \lambda$, otherwise the waiting line grows indefinitely). Under these conditions a waiting line develops, and an average waiting time T_W is experienced by customers before they receive service.

QUEUING MODEL. The scaling effect is such that doubling both the service rate ($\mu \to 2\mu$) and the arrival rate ($\lambda \to 2\lambda$) results in reducing the waiting time by half. This effect is a factor to be considered in studies of potential centralization, if actual computer service systems behave as does this simple queuing model of turnaround time. Therefore, let us examine the model and its underlying assumptions, which are those generally made in elementary queuing theory (5).

The arrival traffic is assumed to be Poissonian, which means that the arrival of a customer is independent of past events and has no influence on future arrivals. Also, simultaneous arrivals are freak events with a negligibly small chance of happening. This assumption rules out situations in which customers arrive either with periodic regularity, or simultaneously in large batches. It is generally agreed that this assumption describes quite well the situation in most scientific computing facilities in which jobs arrive from many customers acting independently. Because of their lack of dependence, arrivals with Poisson distribution are often called random inputs.

The traffic load does not change with time. Although this assumption does not preclude our analyzing a system with time-varying loading, it does mean that we are performing a steady-state analysis. Therefore we cannot obtain a movie of transient effects after a change in arrival rate. However, we can obtain a picture of the system status during a time interval that is long enough for the arrival rate to be considered a stationary quantity.

Service times vary according to the exponential probability distribution. This assumption is similar to the assumption of Poisson arrivals in that it requires the service time to fluctuate randomly from customer to customer. The assumption is also one of convenience, for it leads to great simplification in the form of the solution. If computer service times are in fact distributed according to some other density function, a suitable correction can often be applied after the analysis based on the random service time assumption. In our simple case, in which we seek only the mean of the waiting times, the results depend only on the mean and variance of service times. Therefore the exponential service time assumption need not hold.

Proceeding now on these assumptions, consider again the case of a single queue with Poisson arrivals and a single server with exponential service times. The queue is serviced on a first-come-first-served basis. If the queue is not empty, the server finishes service of one customers and immediately begins to service the next. Under these conditions,

Service rate $\mu = \dfrac{1}{T_s}$

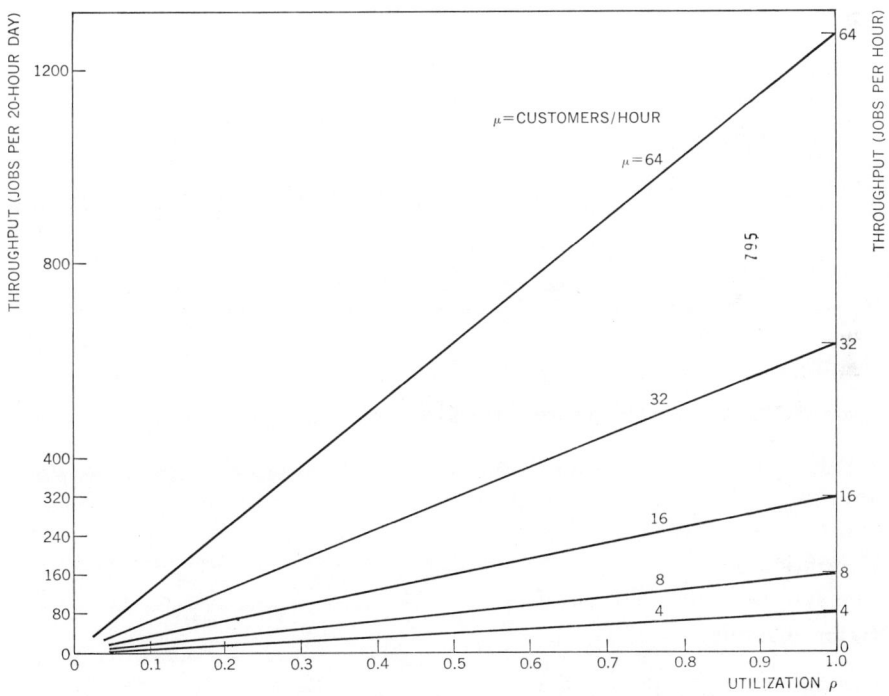

Figure IIIC-8. Relationships among utilization, service rate, and throughput.

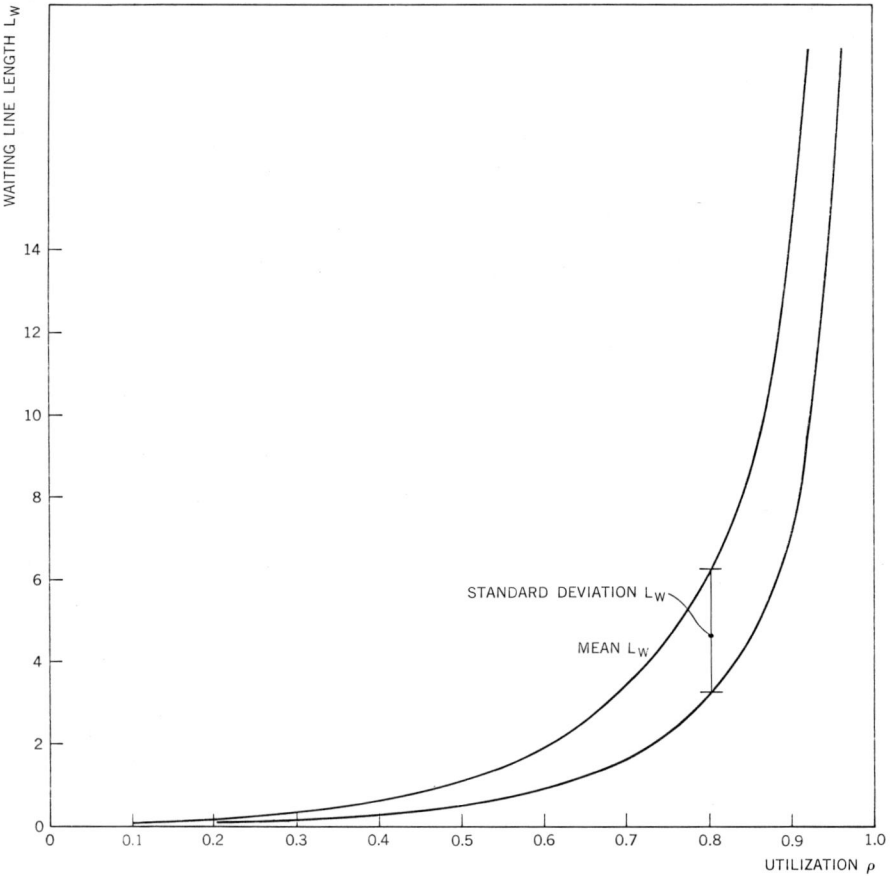

Figure IIIC-9. Effect of utilization on waiting line length.

and

Utilization $\rho = \dfrac{\lambda}{\mu}$

If, for example,

$\lambda = 3.2$ customers per hour

and

$\mu = 4.0$ customers per hour,

C. LOCATION/ALLOCATION PROBLEMS

then

$$\rho = \frac{3.2}{4.0} = 0.8.$$

Figure IIIC-8 shows the relation between ρ, μ, and throughput. The mean length of the waiting line is:

$$L_W = \frac{\lambda^2}{\mu(\mu - \lambda)} = \frac{\rho^2}{1 - \rho}.$$

Figure IIIC-9 shows the effect of utilization on line length. The mean and variance of line length increase sharply as utilization approaches 100%. The mean wating time is

$$T_W = \frac{L_W}{\lambda} = \frac{\lambda}{\mu(\mu - \lambda)}.$$

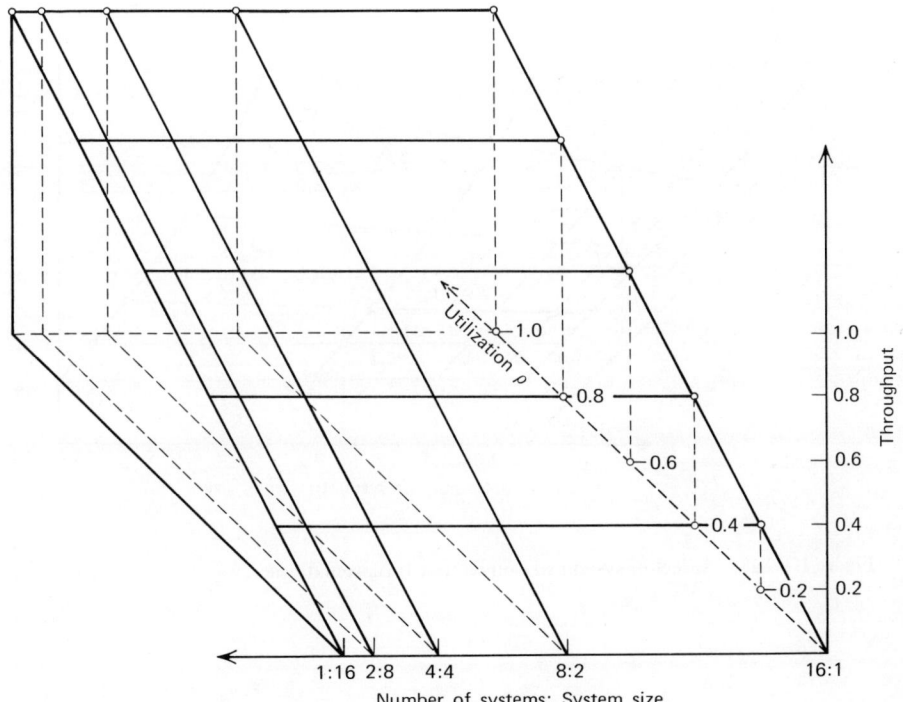

Figure IIIC-10. Throughput as a linear function of utilization.

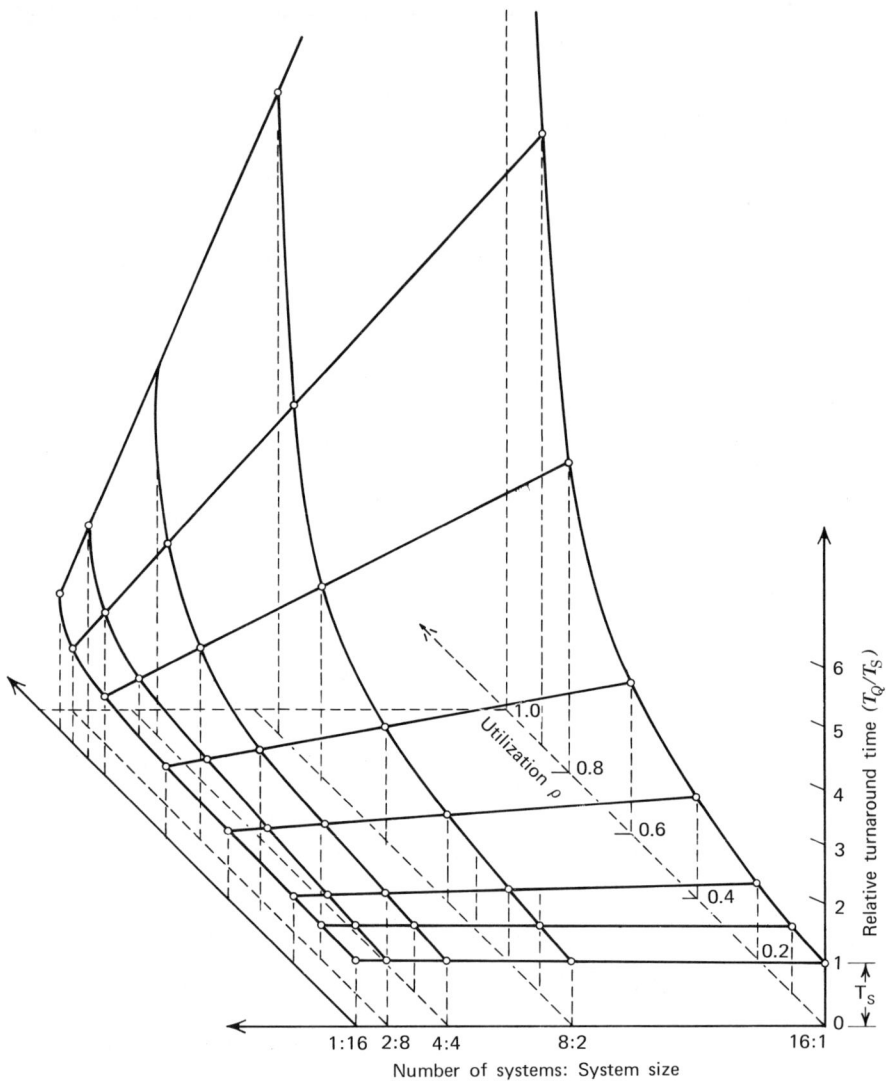

Figure IIIC-11. Effect of system size on relative turnaround time.

C. LOCATION/ALLOCATION PROBLEMS

Now suppose we use a larger-capacity service system that is, the service and arrival rates are $m\mu$ and $m\lambda$ customers per second. Substituting these rates in the Eq. (7) and (8) we obtain the new waiting line length:

$$(L_W)_m = \frac{m^2\lambda^2}{m\mu(m\mu - m\lambda)} = \frac{\lambda^2}{\mu(\mu - \lambda)} = L_W.$$

The mean line length does not change, as the service and arrival rates are scaled up proportionately. However, the waiting time varies inversely with the system capacity indicated by the service rate $m\mu$:

$$(T_W)_m = \frac{L_W}{m\lambda} = \frac{m\lambda}{m\mu(m\mu - m\lambda)} = \frac{1}{m}(T_W).$$

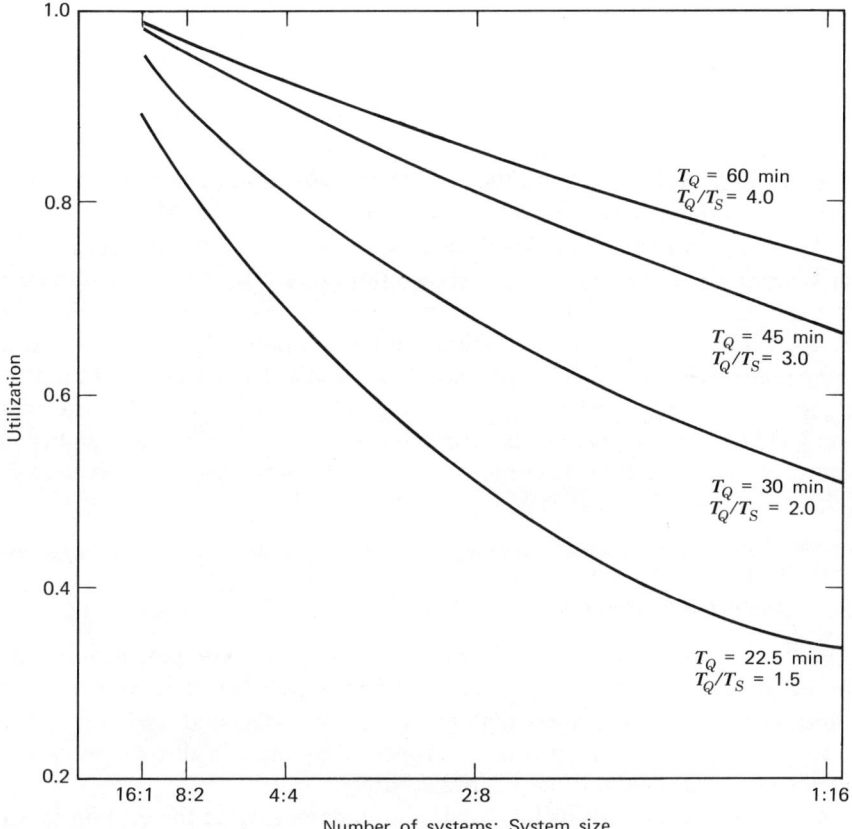

Figure IIIC-12. Contours of equal turnaround time.

This can also be understood intuitively since, despite the fact that the line length remains the same, it moves faster, that is, in direct proportion to system capacity.

Now let us apply these results to the hypothetical situation used earlier in this article, which involves 16 units of computational workload to be executed on systems of various sizes. Figure IIIC-10 combines the relationships between system utilization and throughput illustrated in Figure IIIC-8 with the concept of system size and number of systems wherein each combination has the capacity of 16 units of work. Throughput is shown as a linear function of the utilization in each case.

Figure IIIC-11, however, shows the effect of system size on the relative turnaround time T_Q/T_S which is the ratio of the turnaround time $T_Q = T_W + T_S$ to the service time T_S. This effect is quite dramatic as utilization increases. One way of interpreting Figure IIIC-10 is that, if all processors are loaded to a certain utilization, say $\rho = 0.8$, the turnaround time is significantly greater when smaller systems are used. Another way of viewing this phenomenon is to draw contours of equal turnaround time on the surface in Figure IIIC-11. These contours are shown in a plan view of the surface in Figure IIIC-12. Note the increased utilization achievable in larger systems, at comparable system responsiveness.

If a relative value is associated with the computer service as a function of turnaround time, then the surface shown in Figure IIIC-13 can be obtained. The difference between the value obtainable at the optimal condition of centralization and the existing operating point can be viewed as a "cost of compartmentalization." This is a cost that results from barriers within the organization, which restrict access to the total resources of the organization. This analysis permits determination of the cost of the quality of service that can be used, in conjunction with the previously defined costs, to guide decisions of centralization versus dispersion.

Concluding Remarks

We have presented several considerations which are pertinent to the degree of centralization or dispersion of computing facilities within an organization. We have argued that costs can be associated with the major factors involved so that effects of proposed changes in dispersion can be assessed quantitatively, if only approximately.

A dimensionless analysis has been used to demonstrate the economic feasibility of providing general production computing services over a large geographic region with relatively few large computer centers.

C. LOCATION/ALLOCATION PROBLEMS

A strategy for regional integration of computing services has been proposed, the goal of which is to allow economies of scale and other advantages of centralization, without losing the variety and quality of services provided by a small local facility. The success of this strategy depends on making a distinction between standard production services, which can be adequately delivered from a large remote center, and locally anomalous, personalized or evolving services which may still be better provided on site.

This division of workload permits proper exploitation of two different types of operating systems. The first, as exemplified by OS/360, is well suited for production and supplying of standard, stable services and ap-

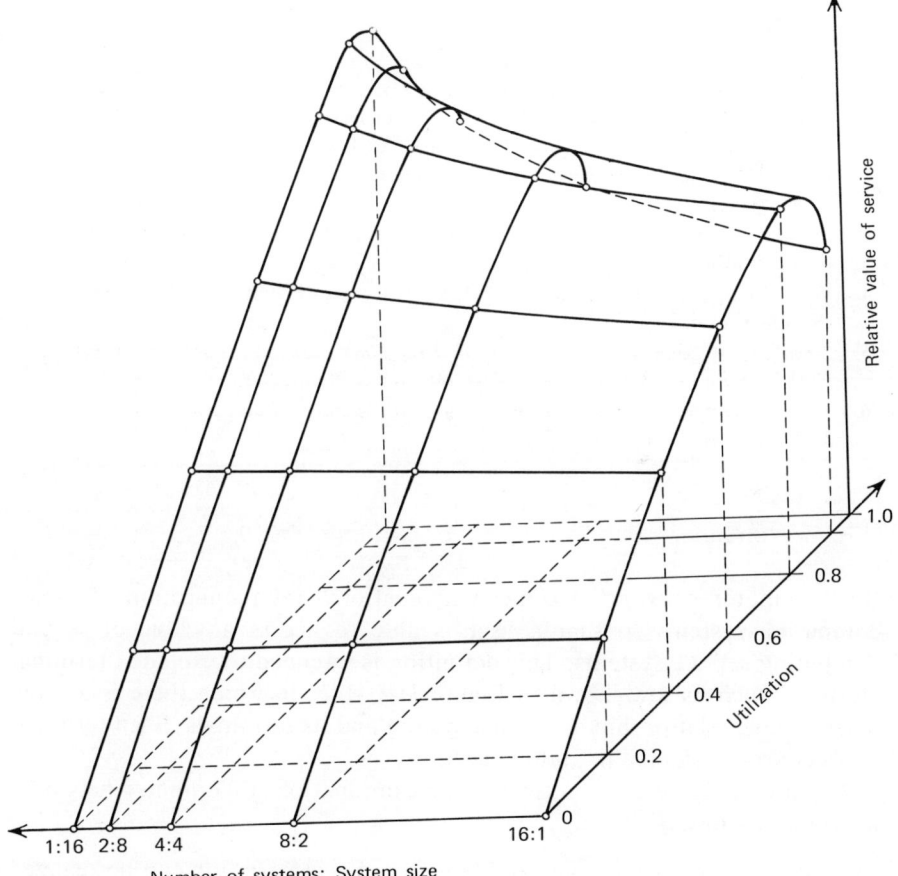

Figure IIIC-13. Relative value of computer service.

plications. The second type, as exemplified by CP/67 or VMS/370, provides diversity, protective application autonomy, and facilities for growth.

The effect of centralization on service responsiveness was determined and used in conjunction with the notion of value of responsive services to determine another cost—the "cost of compartmentalization." This is represented as the cost of barriers within an organization that prevent free access to the resources of that organization.

References

1. A. S. Manne, "Plant Location under Economics of Scale-Recentralization and Computation," *Management Science* **11**, 2 (November 1964), 213–235.
2. E. Feldman, F. A. Lehrer, and T. I. Ray, "Warehouse Location under Continuous Economies of Scale," *Management Science* **12**, 9 (May 1966), 670–684.
3. L. L. Selwyn, "Competition and Structure in the Computer Service Industry," *Proceedings of the Second Annual ACM SIGCOSIM Symposium,* (October 26, 1971), pp. 48–56, Gaithersburg, Md.
4. W. F. Sharpe, *The Economics of Computers,* Columbia University Press, New York, 1964, pp. 314–322.
5. *"Analysis of Some Queuing Models in Real-Time Systems,"* Form No. GF20-0007, IBM Corporation, Data Processing Division, White Plains, N.Y.
6. D. N. Streeter, "Cost-Benefit Evaluation of Scientific Computing Services," *IBM Systems Journal* **11**, 3 (1972), 219–233.

Networks

By "computer network" we mean a functional interconnection of major computing systems so that a user is able to access any one of several computing service systems. This definition is intended to exclude "terminal clusters" such as are shown in Figure IIIC-14*b*, in which there is a fixed master-slave relationship between a system and its terminals. Such terminal clusters are considered in another section.

The preceding section motivates our examination of computer networks for three reasons:

1. Many of the economies and benefits of centralization can be realized without physical consolidation, if the computing resources can be interconnected in a network to provide general accessability.

C. LOCATION/ALLOCATION PROBLEMS   359

2. Rather than providing the entire spectrum of services from each center, it may be more manageable to create centers of functional specialization.
3. Whatever strategy of centralization is embraced by an organization, some distribution of data will probably persist, partitioned on a geographic or functional basis. As the need for timely comprehensive data increases, a network will be required for the occasions when the data stored at one location are needed for processing or use at another location.

When computers are linked together into general-purpose networks, the user can avail himself of services from more than one system.*

We are speaking here of linkage among more-or-less independent systems, each with its own mission(s) in life but with a certain willingness to swap services with the others. The linkage, in current practice, is most likely to be via telephone lines or private wires (but higher-capacity links exist). Physical remoteness between the systems is possible, but is not a necessary part of the concept; there may be perfectly good reasons to link computers within the same building.

Essentially, the kind of networks we have in mind attempt to make the services of a variety of systems available, in whole or in part, to the general

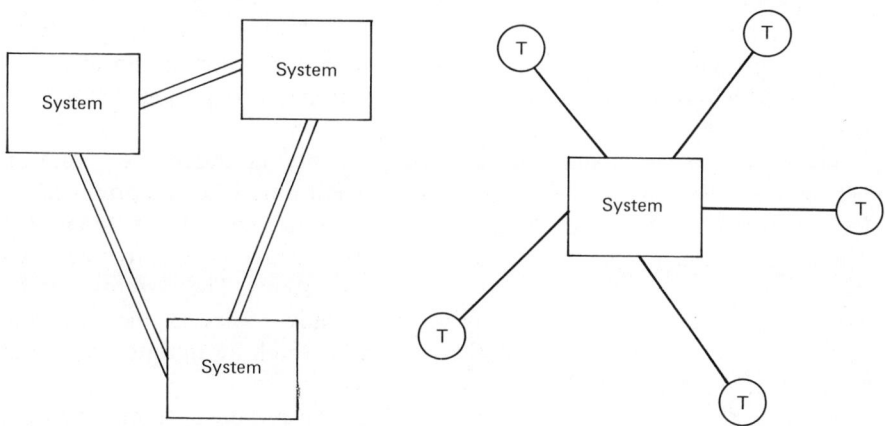

Figure IIIC-14. (*a*) Computer network. (*b*) Terminal cluster.

* The remainder of this section has been excerpted from D. H. Frederickson, "Describing Data in Computer Networks," *IBM Systems Journal*, **12**, 3 (1973).

run of users at each of the systems—without, however, tying the whole complex into a tightly knit supersystem. They are not oriented toward any specialized application, but aim to pool the facilities for all purposes that the ingenuity of programmers and systems engineers may suggest.

The participating systems in such a network may be look-alikes, but more commonly they are a rather diverse assortment. Access to "more of the same" might motivate the pooling of systems through a communications network, even if the systems are all identical; but the incentive is stronger when each has a specialty or two that the others lack. For example, one might be a paging system, especially advantageous for operations such as text editing and on-line debugging; another might be a batch system with a massive core storage, more economical for production runs. Linked into a network, they offer the combined clientele the advantages of both worlds.

Thus the differentness of the systems participating in a network is one of the incentives for its existence. At the same time it is a source of complications—just as the desire to be more and more things to more and more people introduces growing complexity into an operating system.

The Network Environment

A "REMOTE JOB ENTRY" NETWORK. Now let us look at some progressively more ambitious types of linkages among computers, working up to a network in which arbitrary collections of data can be moved about among the member systems.

To keep the discussion simple, we generally consider the situation between two systems, mentioning a third system only when its presence affects a principle. We speak of a "remote" system and a user's "own" (or "home") system, but this is just a matter of arbitrary perspective adopted for convenience in distinguishing between two systems. The systems may be physically close, and the user may have as ready access to one as to the other. The user's own system is the one from which he initiates whatever transaction we happen to be discussing.

Suppose the user wants to submit a job to the remote system. Then the (operating system) program that schedules jobs at the remote system must "listen" to a communications line, as well as to its local sources of input (card readers, etc.). And the job image sent must include whatever job control cards are usual at the remote system.

This much is fairly obvious, but if the user's own system is also a batch operating system, he is involved in writing job control cards for two jobs:

the one at his own system, which transmits the remote job, and the remote job itself.

Typically, that does not end the matter. When the job is completed at the remote system, the user will wish to receive output for printing or punching. For example, it may be that the remote system was merely asked to assemble a program later to be executed by the user's own system. It would be handy to receive the punched-card output, at least, without actually punching the cards, mailing them, or putting them through a card reader at the home system.

But this brings still more system programs into play, both remotely and locally. At the remote system a program which would normally do the punching must redirect its efforts and send the card images over a communications line. And some program(s) must stand ready at the user's side to receive the card images and see that they become accessible to the user.

The user may not want all his output transmitted to his home system; or he may want copies at both systems. He may even wish to direct copies to a third system. In short, he needs a means to indicate his intentions—and this, as always, implies further control cards or further parameters on existing ones.

Remote job entry, such as described above, is today a fairly commonplace facility (1, 2). For example, the *A*ttached *S*upport *P*rocessor (ASP) system, used with the MVT level of Operating System/360, offers such a facility (1, 3). Briefly, various modules of ASP collect job input from various sources—card readers, communication lines, or whatever—perform some scheduling functions over and above those of OS/360, and then feed the jobs to the OS system tasks which normally handle job input.

Similarly, ASP modules intercept any output the user has designated "system" output to be printed or punched by system routines. Other ASP routines can then either output the data locally, or send one or more copies to other systems via communication lines.

The situation can be envisioned as in Figure IIIC-15*a*. ASP (considered here only as a communication interface) is interposed between the regular operating system and the communication line(s). It gives outside systems a pathway to the local job input stream, and it gives the local job output stream a pathway to outside systems.

This takes care of entry and egress at the remote system, but what about the situation at the user's own system? How does he reach the outside world? What program stands ready to receive the returning output of his remote jobs? A small but useful network, which is in operation at the IBM T. J. Watson Research Center in Yorktown Heights, New York, may prove illuminating in this regard (4).

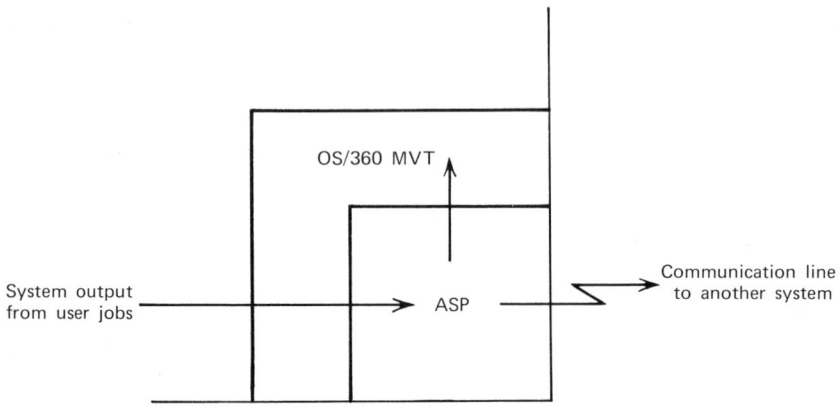

Figure IIIC-15a. Relationship of System/360 to ASP.

The Research Center has three major computer systems: an IBM System/360 Model 91, running under OS/360 with ASP (in the local mode); a Model 67 which runs under the System/360 Time-Sharing System (TSS); and another Model 67 which runs under Control Program-67/Cambridge Monitor System (CP/CMS). Each system has its own advantages, and there is every incentive to parcel out the stages of a job to the systems that will do them best. A particularly useful operation is to edit program source decks at one of the time-shared systems (TSS or CP/CMS), and then ship them for assembly to the Model 91 (which does that sort of thing more cheaply). The resulting object decks can be run on the Model 91 or, in the case of CP/CMS, returned to the time-shared system for on-line debugging runs.

However, the ASP system at the Model 91 does not stand ready to accept input from just any source; a communications line must be available, and ASP must be notified by the system operator to start a reader program which will read from that line. This is scarcely a convenient operation to repeat once for each remote job that comes in, nor can each user afford to keep a private wire open all day for jobs he might submit. The answer of course is that there has to be a communications interface at each of the time-shared systems, serving communications purposes comparable to those of ASP.

Such is indeed the case; a program called RJE91 operates all day at each of the time-shared systems. The implementation is different at the two systems, conforming to the different structures of TSS and CP/CMS, but the basic function is the same; RJE91 serves as a funnel from all the users into the communication lines, and from the outside world back to the users.

C. LOCATION/ALLOCATION PROBLEMS 363

Thus source "cards" can be sent to the Model 91, and object "decks" sent back, with never a hole being punched. Prospective printouts, too, can be sent back and—incidentally—edited at the time-shared system before or after being printed.

In schematic form Figure IIIC-15b shows this elaboration of the situation. At each system there is a "communication interface": ASP at the Model 91, RJE91 at the TSS and CP/CMS systems. Things are not symmetric, however, between the Model 91 on the one hand, and the time-shared systems on the other. While traffic flows in both directions, the user at the time-shared system can contact the batch system only for purposes of submitting jobs; a job running at the Model 91 can contact one of the time-shared systems only to forward job output (after the job has completed) to a user. No contact is possible between a user and his remote job while it is running, nor between user programs running simultaneously on two systems.

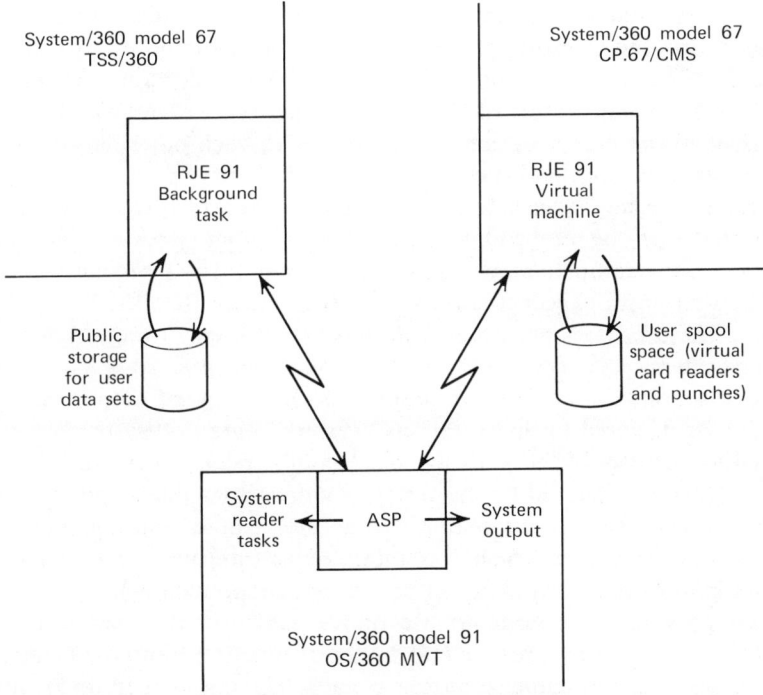

Figure IIIC-15b.   Remote job entry network.

REASONS FOR WANTING A MORE GENERALIZED FACILITY THAN "REMOTE JOB ENTRY". The principal motivation for the above network is that it capitalizes upon the differences among three operating systems. By this criterion the limitations are harmless; it normally makes no sense to move a job from a batch system to a time-shared system, and one does not wish a job in the batch system to tarry while interacting with a remote user.

There are other promising network applications, however, for which such limitations are more serious. Suppose, for example, that the principal attraction at another system is not its operating system, but a program that has to be run there. (Why? Perhaps because it uses a device that is not available at the home system. Perhaps because it is proprietary. Perhaps because it would require costly revisions to run on the user's own system.) With this for motivation one is impelled to look for a more comprehensive facility than remote job entry (RJE).

First, one might wish to invoke the program as a sort of "remote subroutine" from a program running on one's own system. That is, one might like to run the job on the opposite system, and then communicate input values from a program running on the home system, receive output values from the remote program, and proceed from there—perhaps repeating the exchange many times and making decisions in one's program based on the values returned. For this one needs a communications interface that allows user programs to interact with each other as well as with the remote program that takes in jobs.

Second, one might wish to forward more arbitrary forms of input than those that can be embedded in the "job" input stream. The remote program, for example, may require data saved from a previous run, and may be written to expect it from some other source than the "input" deck proper. The user does not necessarily have permanent storage rights at the remote system.

Likewise, one likes to receive more arbitrary forms of output than those that can be declared to the system as "system" output. "System" output is normally stored only temporarily, on "spool" space; there are limitations upon its format, dictated by the system routines available to postprocess it. One may wish to retrieve material that the remote program put out to permanent storage, or which was intended as intermediate output (hence put out in a format no system postprocessor accommodates).

With growing experience in use of the network, the user is likely to spread his operations over several systems, availing himself of particular advantages and particular resources at each. Having worked up his data at several systems, he may then have to gather it together for a new job at any one of them.

"Load leveling" and system backup are two further network applications that reinforce the wish to transmit arbitrary data sets from system to system. In load leveling a job is shunted from a busy system to one whose current load is lighter—say, from one in New York at 11:00 a.m., to one in California where it is 8:00 a.m. and people are just arriving for work. Naturally, any data sets used by the job must accompany it. The same is true when jobs are sent to remote systems because the home system is down. (The latter application of course presupposes that some subsystem that can access both the data and the communication line is still functioning.)

Any collection of data can be broken into 80-character records, perhaps interspersed with control records which tell how to reassemble it, and put out as punched-card output of a job. In this manner one could in principle have all necessary data sets moved from system to system, using one job to acquire each data set. It would be a clumsy mode of operation, however, and would require that several different programs be written to cope with different types of data sets.

For all these reasons one is impelled to seek a communications interface that offers either or both of two new services: (1) access from a user program on one system to a user program on another; programs that produce output other than "system" output can then in many cases redirect it to their correspondents at remote systems; and (2) transmission of data sets by the communications interface itself, or by programs that it invokes by itself, without further intervention by the user.

References

1. D. W. Barron, *Computer Operating Systems,* 23 and 105–106, Chapman and Hall, Ltd., London.
2. The Comtre Corporation, A. P. Sayers, Ed., *Operating Systems Survey,* Auerbach Publishers, New York, 1971, pp. 79–80.
3. *IBM System/360 and Systems/370 Attached Support Processor System (ASP), Version 2, System Programmer's Manual,* Form GH20-0323-8, 9th ed., International Business Machines Corporation, Data Processing Division, White Plains, N.Y., March 1971.
4. W. S. Hobgood, "Evaluation of an interactive-batch system network," *IBM Systems Journal* **11,** 1 (1972), 2–15.
5. R. A. Meyer and L. H. Seawright, "A Virtual Machine Time-Sharing System," *IBM Systems Journal* **9,** 3 (1970), 199–218.
6. D. Fredericksen, L. Loveless, J. Rooney, R. Ryniker, S. Seroussi, and A. Weis, *OS/360 Network Interface User's Guide,* IBM Research Report RA 23 (#15638), IBM Thomas J. Watson Research Center, Yorktown Heights, N.Y., 1971.

7. D. B. McKay and D. P. Karp, "Protocol for a computer network," *IBM Systems Journal* **12,** 3 (1973).
8. *The MERIT Computer Network: Progress Report for the Period July 1969–March 1971,* Publication 0571-PR-4, Reproduced by the National Technical Information Service, PB 200 674.
9. M. Donaldson, S. Robinovitz, and B. Wolfe, *Preliminary Draft: Proposed MICIS Standard for Data Description*, Michigan Interuniversity Committee on Information Systems (December 1970).
10. R. Rustin, Ed., *Computer Networks*, Prentice-Hall, Englewood Cliffs, N.J., 1972.

Internal Organization—Distribution of Function

The previous sections have considered the problems of location and allocation of computing resources on a gross level—how computing installations should be located and interconnected within a corporation. Now let us examine the internal organization of computing resources at a typical location. Here again, we consider various alternatives: centralization versus dispersion of function on a local level, and stand-alone versus interconnected structures.

Throughout our study we try to keep in mind the entire spectrum of services required and to make provision for future growth of usage and new technologies.

As a point of departure let us consider the two extreme cases shown in Figure IIIC-16.

In the first case, shown in Figure IIIC-16*a*, all computing and storage capability is assumed to be concentrated in a single, centralized installation; the only equipment located outside the computer installation consists of terminals which serve only an input/output function, without processing or storage.

Many of the advantages of this sort of centralized local facility are similar to those cited earlier when centralization on a higher level was considered; that is, economies of scale, elimination of redundant equipment and effort, and so on. Other advantages of such a shared "utility" were cited by Fano (9) in describing MIT's MAC System: " . . . by placing at his fingertips a variety of services in the form of public procedures, *data* and programming aids, and by allowing him to store and retrieve his own private files of data and programs, a computer utility could provide customers having common interests with convenient means for collaboration. For instance, designers who are working together on a complex system would be in a position to check continually the status of the complete, overall design as each of them develops and modifies his own contribution."

C. LOCATION/ALLOCATION PROBLEMS

Despite these advantages, a completely centralized service facility imposes serious penalties on some of its users. These penalties, or limitations, generally fall into one of four categories:

1. *Responsiveness.* A large system shared among many users may not respond rapidly or consistently enough for many real-time and some conversational applications.
2. *Reliability.* Unscheduled service interruptions, especially from software crashes, occur more frequently in multiusage systems.
3. *Overhead.* A fixed cost of task initiation is high for large systems and cannot be economically written off if the task is very simple.
4. *Regimentation.* To make use of the centralized facility, one must conform to the procedures, languages, time schedules, and so on, of the computing center.

As a reaction against these limitations of the centralized facility, and in response to a generalized desire to have a machine all to oneself, there has been a trend toward the distributed stand-alone environment represented in Figure IIIC-16b.* In this arrangement various midi-, mini-, and microcomputers are operated autonomously by various individuals or groups to satisfy their several particular needs.

The great attractiveness of this arrangement is independence from the computing center: the freedom to change, personalize, and specialize the machine to suit individual requirements. Another advantage is the relatively high reliability of a machine with a narrower spectrum of usage, a lower utilization factor, and fewer components.

The disadvantages of such a stand-alone arrangement are primarily:

1. *Human effort required.* Some of the systems, applications, and maintenance effort heretofore provided by the computing center staff

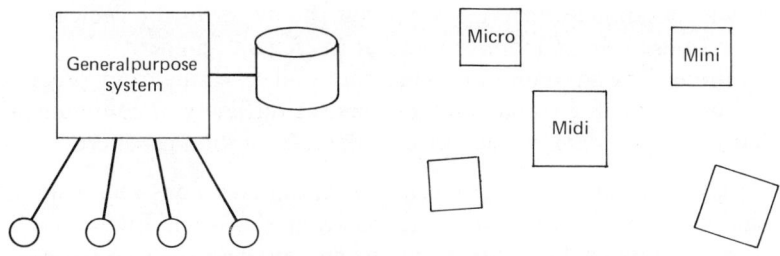

Figure IIIC-16. Extreme cases—internal organization.

* There is a rapidly growing body of literature on mini- and microcomputers. See, for example, References 5, 6, 10, and 12.

368 ISSUES OF MANAGEMENT

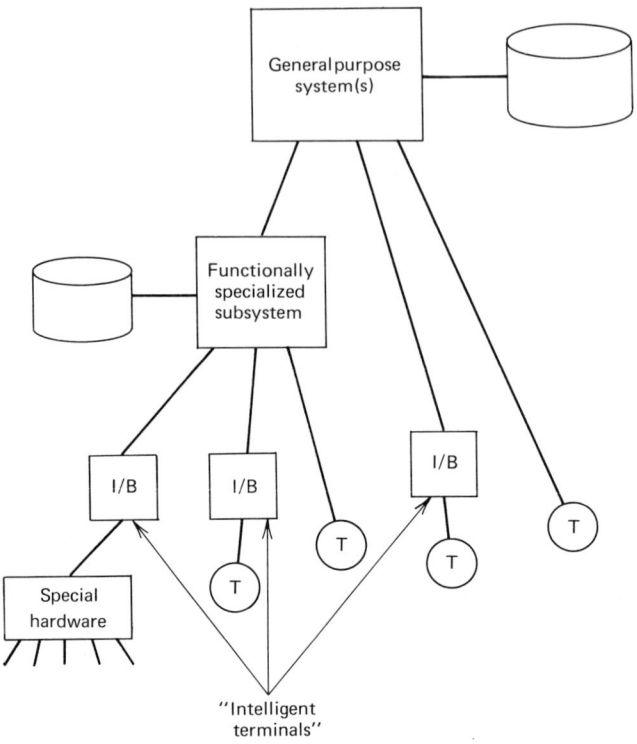

Figure IIIC-17. Hierarchic distribution of function.

are usually assumed by the functional group obtaining the minicomputer.
2. *Limited facilities.* Limitations of memory size, processing capability, utility and applications software, and so on, may serve to limit the growth of computer services or tempt the owner of the dedicated machine to use it in an inappropriate or inefficient manner.
3. *Isolation.* The autonomy of machines and freedom from procedural and programming standards increases the difficulty of communicating and sharing of data, procedures, or the information produced.

A compromise between totally centralized organizations and distributed organizations is the hierarchical organization shown in Figure IIIC-17. This treelike organization has some of the processing and storage capability retained in a central general-purpose center, some located in intermediate nodes in functionally specific subsystems, and some distributed in the tips of the branches in so-called intelligent terminals.

It is argued that this hierarchical organization—with distributed processing and storage capability but with comprehensive interconnection—is generally superior to either of the "pure" organizations described earlier.

The treelike topology of the interconnection shown is not the only, or necessarily the best, topology; some "ring" and "wheel" topologies, for example, have certain attractive features, especially with respect to availability. However, the tree structure is used here because it shows most clearly the functional relation between the various components.

The major advantages of the hierarchical organization follow from the fact that it offers choices to the user. Functionally, the user has an opportunity to execute some tasks locally and some centrally, as best suits his needs, with intermediate results readily transferable within the hierarchy. With respect to reliability, the distribution of intelligence and storage makes it possible to devise fallback strategies so that service can be continued despite the failure of some components.

The intelligent terminals can handle rapidly and efficiently the interruptions and transactions arising from event-driven real-time applications or from data entry, editing, or inquiry applications. Within the limitations imposed by response-time requirements, the terminal can buffer and collect a number of transactions into blocks. This "blocking" of transactions, by reducing the frequency and total cost of task initiation, makes it feasible to process many applications in larger processors than otherwise would be possible.

Finally, the presence of intelligence in the terminal provides some insulation from the constraints and publicity of the central system. For example, a person can compose, edit, and review sensitive material before transmitting it. Another attractive possibility is to use the terminal as an instrument of personalization, transforming the standardized symbols and syntax of the system into a form more natural and useful to the individual.

The major drawback of hierarchical organization is its complexity. Development and maintenance of a hierarchical system requires cooperation between the central and functional departments, and a collaboration of hardware, software, communication, and application skills.

Considerations in Locating Function within the Hierarchy

Assuming the existence of a treelike distribution of computing and storage capability within an organization, what guidelines indicate where a particular function should be located?

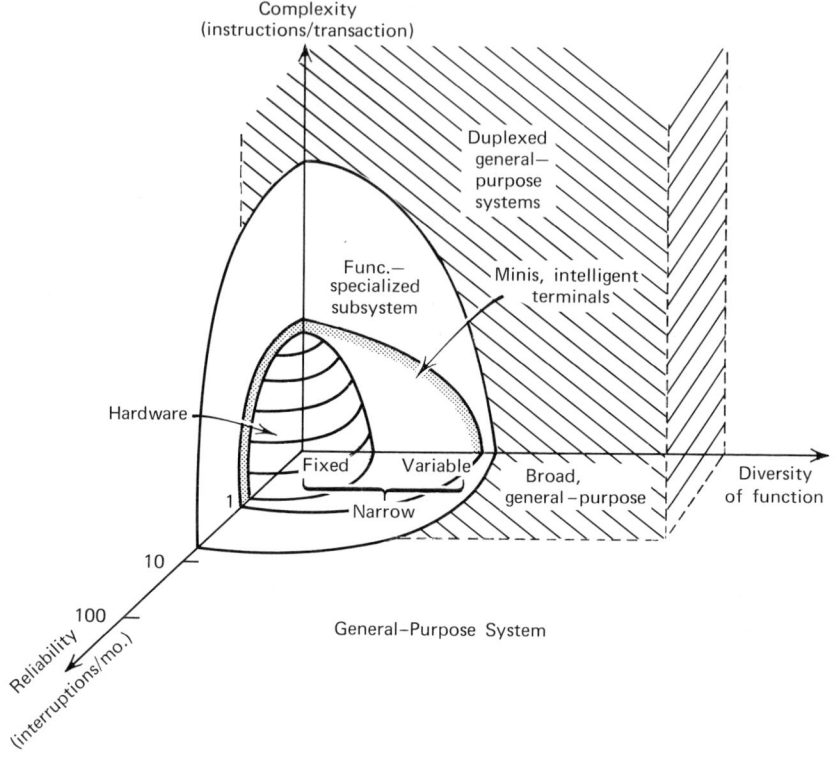

Figure IIIC-18. Considerations: location of function.

Figure IIIC-17 shows four possible locations: (1) within a central general-purpose system, (2) in an intermediate-sized functionally specialized subsystem, (3) in a relatively small intelligent terminal, and (4) in special-purpose hardware.

Figure IIIC-18 indicates schematically the influence of several key factors on the location of function within a hierarchy of function. These factors are diversity, required reliability, and complexity of the function under consideration.

If the function is logically narrow and specialized, and the transactions quite simple (i.e., few instructions per transaction), or if exceedingly high reliability is required, then intelligent terminals, dedicated minicomputers, or special-purpose hardware are likely means of execution. The choice between special-purpose hardware and a small programmable device is largely determined by the likelihood that the function will be modified, the

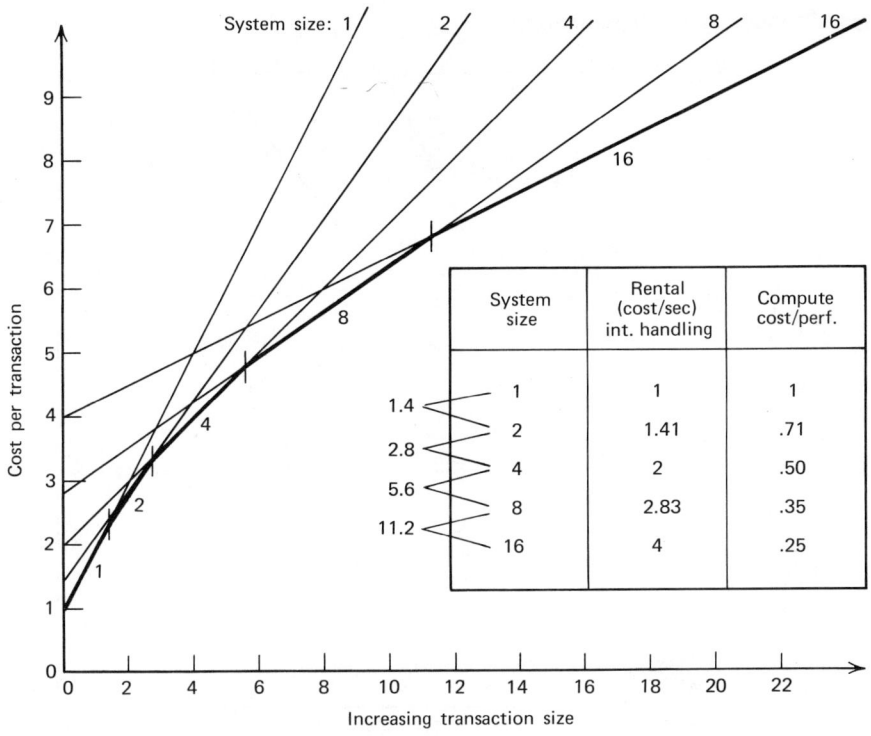
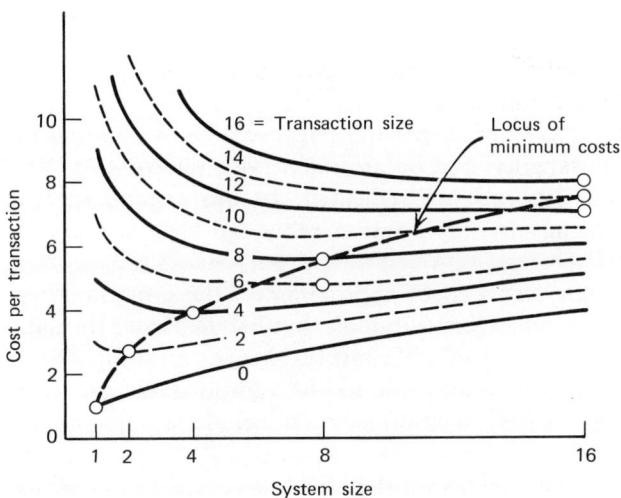

Figure IIIC-19. System and transaction size.

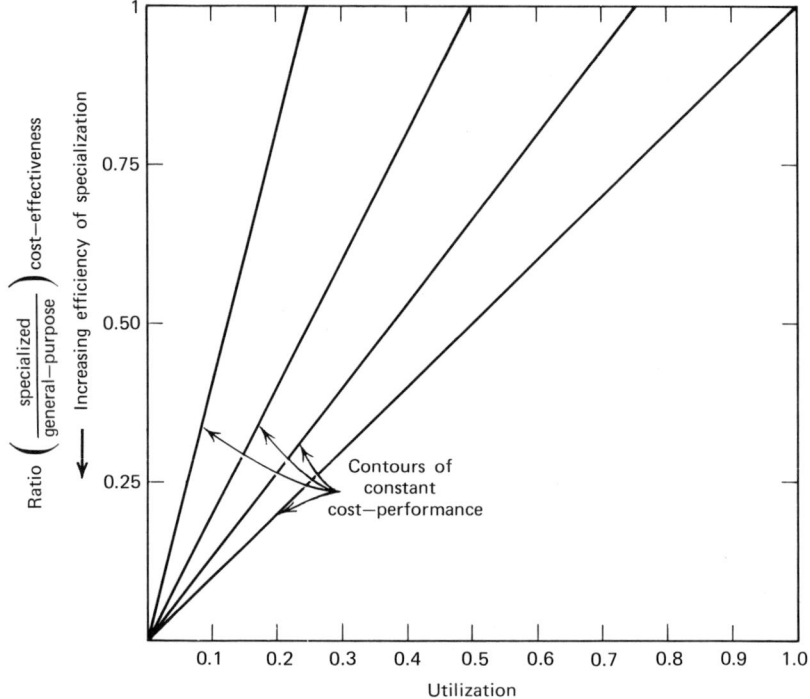

Figure IIIC-20. Effects of specialization.

relative ease and speed of altering a program rather than hardware favoring the latter for changeable applications.

At the other extreme, where broad, general-purpose logic is required or the transactions are quite lengthy, and occasional service interruptions are tolerable, general-purpose systems are indicated. In this region, service interruptions are avoided only by duplexing or other fall-back stratagems employing redundancy.

Functionally specific subsystems cover approximately the same range of diversity in this space as the intelligent terminals, but handle larger transactions and larger user populations. Examples are communications processors, terminal support processors, and so on. Additional factors to be considered in determining the best function location include responsiveness, cost, and ease of use.

Perhaps some additional comments on the effect of function complexity are in order. The economy of scale of a large processor can be realized only on transactions large enough to exploit the processor's full power. The higher speed of the large processor does not help it get underway much faster than the small processor—in fact, given the increased complexity of its housekeeping tasks, the larger processor may consume *more* time than the small processor in task initiation.

Figure IIIC-19 shows the effect of system size on the cost of executing various size transactions, assuming (1) quadratic economies of scale to prevail once the processing is underway, but (2) equal times required to initiate the transaction. Figure IIIC-19 makes evident the advantage of matching system size to transaction size.

Another factor affecting the economic distribution of function is the balance between the efficiency of specialization of subsystems and the lower utilization often experienced by such specialized systems. Figure IIIC-20 shows the compensating effect of these tendencies.

References

1. L. C. Hobbs, "The Rationale for Smart Terminals," *Computer,* November–December 1971, 33–35.
2. "360/370—Compatible Terminals," *Modern Data,* September 1972, 38–46.
3. J. S. Sobolewski, "Programmable Communication Terminals," Proceedings of the 1st International Conference on Computer Communications, October 1972, pp. 380–389.
4. V. K. M. Whitney, "Comparison of Network Topology Optimization Algorithms," Proceedings of the 1st Conference on Computer Communications, October 1972, pp. 332–337.
5. F. F. Coury, Ed., *A Practical Guide to Minicomputer Applications*, IEEE Press, New York, 1972.
6. Anonymous, "A Capability Study on the HP—35 Pocket Calculator," Hewlett Packard Advanced Products.
7. Robert E. Blue, "Organizing Multiple Computers for On-Line Control," *ISA Transactions,* **10,** 2 (1971), 151–158.
8. M. M. Lehman, and G. Waldbaum, "An Analytical Model for Upper Bounds on the Performance of Event Driven, Hierarchical Computer Systems," *Information Processing (IFIPS Proceedings)* (1971), 570–576.
9. R. M. Fano, The MAC System: The Computer Utility Approach, *IEEE Spectrum,* January 1965, 56–64.
10. H. S. Kleiman, Expanding the Role of Small Computers, *Automation,* August 1971, 46–48.
11. P. M. Grant, T. R. Lusebrink, and D. G. Taupin, Hosted-Satellite Computers in Laboratory Automation," IBM Research Report RJ 1113, October 1972.
12. J. D. Schoeffler, and R. H. Temple, Eds., *Minicomputers: Hardware, Software and Applications*, IEEE Press, New York, 1972.

D. EVALUATION

In this section we are concerned with evaluation of the computing function within an organization. We do not consider measurement and analysis of the internal condition and balancing of system components, important as that subject is. (References 1–3 are available for those who want information on that topic.)

Instead we focus on evaluation of the overall performance of the computing function in meeting its objectives. As mentioned previously, computer service objectives should be mutually determined by and agreed to by general management, computer operations, and users. Similarly, evaluation reports should be usable by all three groups.

Each of the four sections that follow uses an existing evaluation system to illustrate the feasibility of evaluating some aspect of the computing service function:

1. The generation of usable evaluation reports.
2. The use of a query system to answer questions about service quality.
3. The prediction of service performance attainable via system or procedural changes.
4. The evaluation of *user* performance.

The Generation of Usable Evaluation Reports

Figures IIID-1 through IIID-5 show some usable evaluation reports, as generated by the Corporate Information Center of Texas Instruments. These reports are more remarkable and unusual than one would suppose. Their existence presupposes:

1. That service objectives have been defined.
2. That quality goals have been set (see Figures IIID-2 and IIID-3.)
3. That evaluations are conducted consistently enough that trends can be detected over periods of months and years.

Unfortunately, relatively few computing installations maintain the discipline necessary to generate reports of this quality. According to Glenn Fischer, manager of this computing center, these reports are carefully read by upper management at Texas Instruments, which may help to explain the high quality.

D. EVALUATION   375

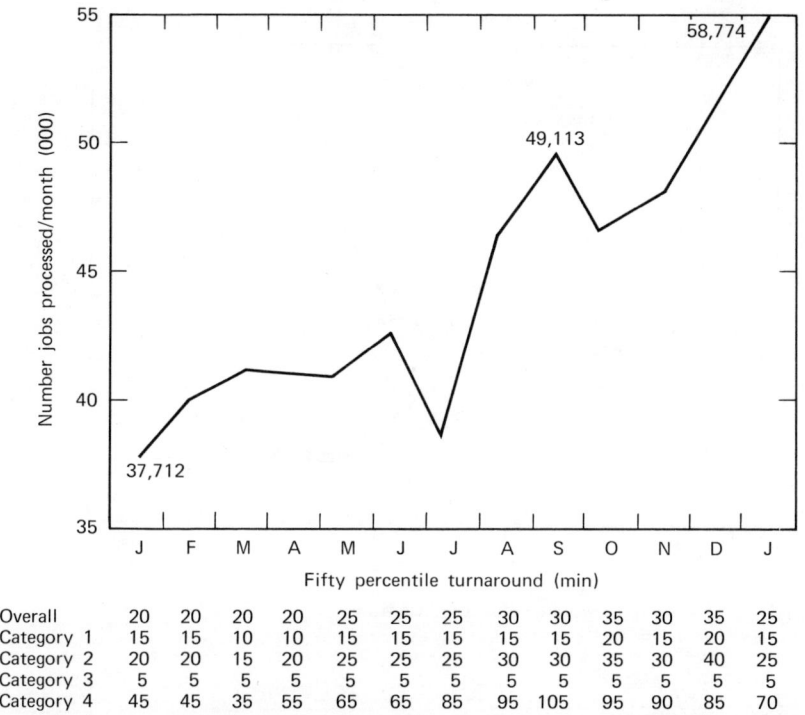

	J	F	M	A	M	J	J	A	S	O	N	D	J
Overall	20	20	20	20	25	25	25	30	30	35	30	35	25
Category 1	15	15	10	10	15	15	15	15	15	20	15	20	15
Category 2	20	20	15	20	25	25	25	30	30	35	30	40	25
Category 3	5	5	5	5	5	5	5	5	5	5	5	5	5
Category 4	45	45	35	55	65	65	85	95	105	95	90	85	70

Figure IIID-1. Job volumes and turnaround.

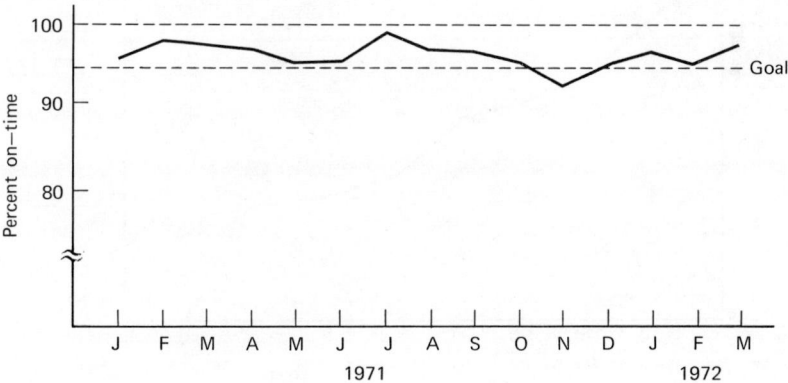

Figure IIID-2. Overall production performance.

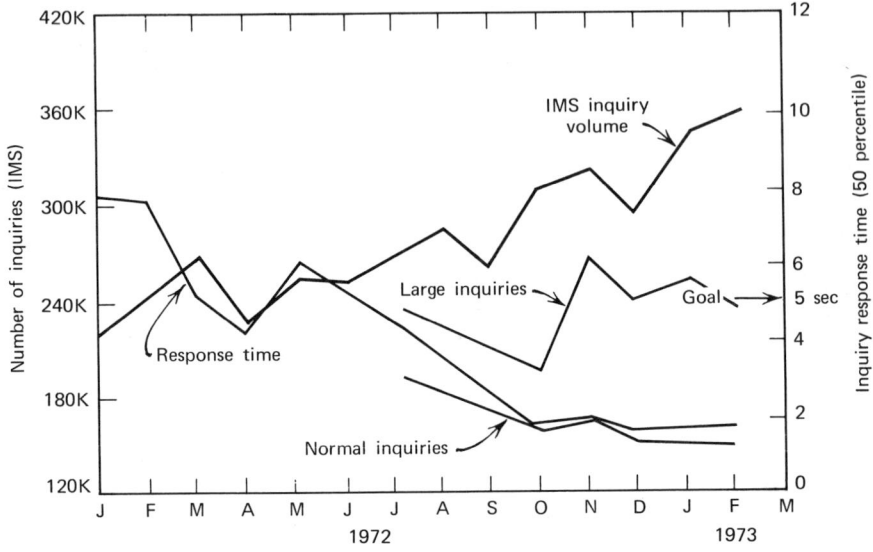

Figure IIID-3. IMS inquiry volume and response time.

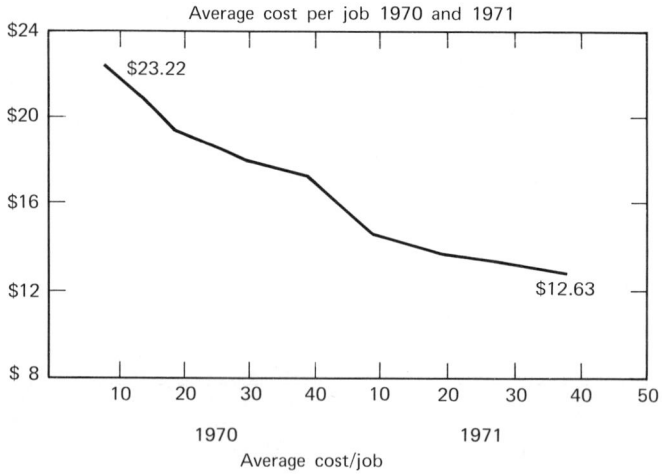

Figure IIID-4. Average cost per job.

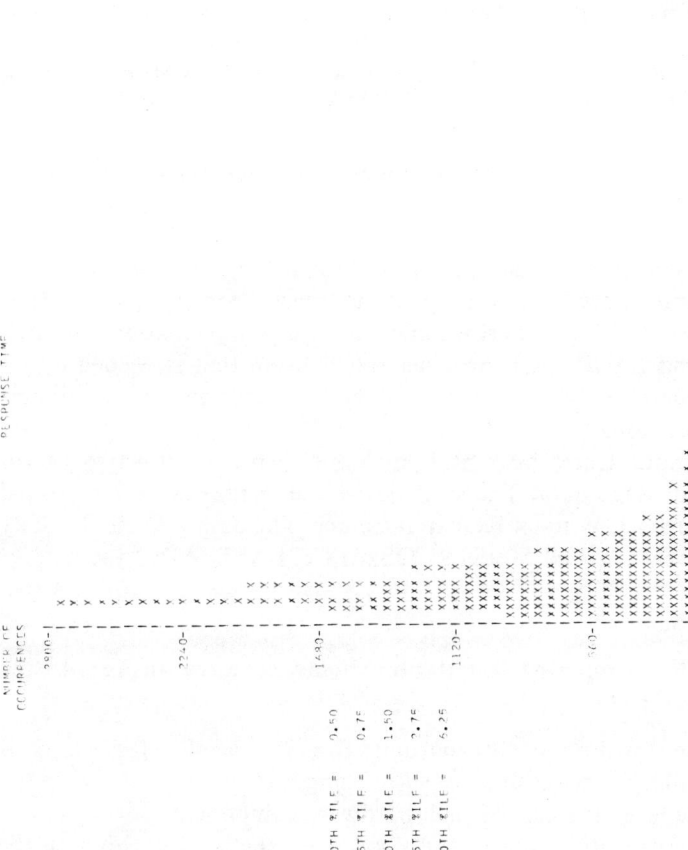

Figure IIID-5. Responsiveness histogram.

An interesting sidelight is that the histogram program that generates plots such as Figure IIID-5 is available to users. Therefore they can, and do, evaluate the quality of the service they or their departments have received—and compare it with overall statistics.

References

1. H. C. Lucas, Jr., "Performance Evaluation and Monitoring," *Computing Surveys,* **3**, 3 (September 1971), 79–91.
2. W. Freiberger, Ed., *Statistical Computer Performance Evaluation,* Academic Press, New York, 1972.
3. *Performance Evaluation Review,* a quarterly publication of the ACM special interest group on measurement and evaluation. ACM, 1133 Avenue of the Americas, New York.

The Use of a Query System to Answer Questions about Service Quality*

The Statistics Gathering Package, SGP, is an information retrieval program supplemented with a variety of summarization techniques. It is used to access a data base of performance and usage information collected by OS, SMF, and LASP. SGP provides information that is needed by installation management, system programmers, consultants and computer users to make decisions.

This paper demonstrates how SGP makes possible an effective use of performance and usage data. The statistics in the examples were collected at the IBM Thomas J. Watson Research Center. The data reflects the daily workload on the System 360 Model 91 OS/MVT/LASP/APL system.

Introduction

The manager of a computing installation should have the answers to the following questions:

1. What is the distribution of turnaround time for specific classes of jobs or users? Which service objectives are being met?
2. What is the level of usage of each hardware component?
3. Which departments, projects and users place the heaviest load on the system?

* This section has been exerpted from J. A. Cooperman, H. W. Lynch and W. H. Tetzlaff, "SGP: An Effective Use of Performance and Usage Data," IBM Research Report RC3756, March 1972, and in *Computer,* September–October 1972.

4. Which programs place the heaviest load on the systems?
5. What is the error rate of programs?
6. Who is receiving exceptionally good or poor service and why?

Today more and more computer installations collect daily information on the usage and performance of their systems. This information should be sufficient to answer these questions. The problem is how to effectively manage and use this voluminous amount of data.

Installation managers, project managers, system programmers, consultants and computer users require some of the information as input to their decision making processes. The information can be used to evaluate service, to establish priorities and evaluate changes in the system, to determine what users are doing so that better ways can be suggested, to identify users having problems and to assess users' future needs. If the daily information is collected and maintained in a data base, then the people requiring information can address their specific questions to the common data base. The historical nature of the base will make it invaluable in detecting trends in performance and usage.

What approach should be taken to providing access to the data base? A common but often inefficient approach is described below:

1. Determine who the users of the data base will be.
2. Determine which questions each user will want answered.
3. Assign priorities to the questions.
4. Define output formats.
5. Produce programs aimed at answering one or more questions.

Since this agenda can be executed in a reasonable period of time, the approach will initially seem fruitful. However a treadmill effect is then likely to follow: a) Completed programs will have to be changed because on using the output you discover the need for additional data items or the advantages of a different output sorting, b) Other more important questions will arise based on initial answers, and c) Other users of the data base will be identified.

A better approach to providing access to the data base is to develop a general query system that will allow individual users to frame questions relevant to their evolving needs. With this approach particular users and specific questions need not be anticipated. The system would allow users to specify which records they wished to select and which data items in the records they wished to print. This involves specifying a query language and implementing one program to function as an information retrieval system. Since answers should not contain extraneous data, the query system should

Reduction request:

Require dev address = 'OC4';
Set tape used = dev requests > 0;

Report   Count device, count tape used,
         total dev time, total channel time,
         total dev requests;

Reduction output:

Requests for tape	Count tape used	Total device time	Total channel time	Total excp count
437	134	1110	1108	68,321

Figure IIID-6. Plot Tape Use.

be capable of summarizing information as well as listing records. The system the authors have developed has extensive summarization features.

Statistics Gathering Package (SGP)

At the IBM Thomas J. Watson Research Center, information describing the performance and usage of the S/360 model 91 OS/MVT/LASP/APL system is maintained in a historical data base. The Statistics Gathering Package (SGP) is used to access the data base and to answer questions including those listed above. A SGP user states a question in a PL/I-like query language which SGP translates into a PL/I program and passes to the PL/I compiler. The output is a program which accesses the data base to answer the specific questions. SGP enables a user to specify a subset of the data base and the format of his output. In addition SGP provides a variety of summarization options which result in questions being answered with a minimum of output. The examples below illustrate the language, the summarization features, and the use of SGP.

SUBSETTING. Last year it was observed that the turnaround time of plot jobs was becoming quite long. At that time plot jobs wrote to a seven track tape drive. The tape was then taken to the plotter for off line plotting. A particular seven track tape drive (OC4) was reserved for this purpose. We wished to determine the effect of having LASP spool plot instructions to a disk and later drive the plotter directly.

Figure IIID-6 shows how brief a request for reduction can be. The "REQUIRE" statement caused a subset of the data base to be created which included only references to the dedicated tape drive. The "REPORT" statement caused the counting of the number of times the device was

Reduction request:

Report Copy programmer name,
        Total job CPU time,
        Mean turnaround time,
        Count jobs,
        Percents turnaround time (20, 60, 180),
   Print on programmer name;

Reduction output:

Programmer name	Total CPU seconds	Mean turnaround minutes	Count jobs	Percents turnaround minutes <= 20	<= 60	<= 180	> 180
John Smith	4	8.03	5	100.0	0.0	0.0	0.0
Edgar Smith	2,348	19.86	107	60.7	34.6	4.7	0.0
Ezekiel Smith	2,733	23.21	188	67.6	25.0	5.8	1.6
Bob Zeke	913	131.76	29	6.9	17.2	48.3	27.6

Figure IIID-7. Grouping by User.

allocated and several other counts and totals. SGP took over all of the details of the file processing, selection, summarization, headings and formats.

Note that only 31 percent of the requests for the tape actually used the tape. The solution to this particular turnaround problem was to spool the input for the plotter to disk. This also relieved the operator of a large and unnecessary tape mounting load.

SUMMARIZATION BY USER. It is frequently useful to sort the data base in order to gather together information with common characteristics. We sort the data base by user name in order to monitor individual service.

The "REPORT" statement shown in Figure IIID-7 caused a summary line to be printed for each user. The summarization included individual cu-

Name	Count of steps	Mean Core residence minutes	Percents core residence minutes <= 0.5	<= 1.0	<= 4.0	<= 10	> 10
Assembler	1014	0.54	67.3	21.5	9.5	1.6	0.1
Fortran G	1579	0.43	76.1	15.8	7.5	0.6	0.0
Fortran H	2239	0.64	58.2	25.4	15.7	0.7	0.0
Link edit	6143	0.77	67.6	21.4	10.4	0.5	0.0
PL/1	1631	1.24	29.5	36.4	29.7	3.2	1.2

Figure IIID-8. Sort by Program Name.

Trace through time

Time of day	Multi-prog level	Core in use
14.33.05	6	674K
14.33.38	5	680K
14.34.56	5	770K
14.35.15	7	1000K
14.35.29	7	994K
14.37.55	7	914K
14.38.44	6	780K
14.39.39	5	570K

First shift summary

Mean core in use	Percents Core in use					
	$<= 500$	$<= 600$	$<= 700$	$<= 800$	$<= 900$	> 900
655K	20.1	19.7	16.6	16.4	14.8	12.4

Figure IIID-9. Multi-Programming Level and Core in Use.

mulative distributions of turnaround time. For example it shows that all of John Smith's jobs were run in less than or equal to 20 minutes. Again SGP took over all of the details of file processing, selection, summarization, headings and formats for the user.

SUMMARIZATION BY PROGRAM. The data base can be sorted by any data item in order to create an appropriate grouping. For example we sort by program name in order to gather together references to each program. We are then able to summarize the resources used by each program. Figure IIID-8 gives an example showing the use of main storage by various program names.

Summarizing the resource demands by program name may point out a program that makes large use of an important resource. Knowledge of the resource demands and frequency of use of individual programs identifies which programs should be considered for performance improvements.

TRACE. SGP is used to observe the utilization of a particular resource, such as main storage. We can either trace the use of a resource or summarize its use over some time period. In the example below we examined main storage use by considering the multi-programming level and the storage assigned to regions. The first part of Figure IIID-9 shows both measures traced through several minutes of time. A convenient summary of core storage use for a shift is shown after the trace data. Notice that 52.7 percent of the time more than 500K and less than or equal to 800K are in use. "CORE IN USE" represents the total size of the regions allocated for batch work. The multi-programming level is the number of regions currently resident in core storage.

Conclusion

SGP is used to provide needed information for installation management, system programmers, consultants and users. The information can be used to evaluate service, to establish priorities and evalute changes in the system, to determine what users are doing so that better ways can be suggested, to identify users having problems and to assess users future needs. The appendix contains a case study which demonstrates how we have used SGP to evaluate turnaround time.

An increasing number of people at this installation are discovering that the data they need to make decisions is easily accessible via SGP from the common data base. The approach to data reduction embodied in SGP is applicable to many data bases. In fact, the particular implementation of SGP described here has been used to query several data bases. Our experience shows there is an advantage in cost and time of developing a query system over implementing a set of programs to answer a specific set of questions.

Appendix

CASE STUDY: Turnaround Time

The figures that follow show the evolution of our use of SGP to gain a better understanding of the service provided at our installation. Typically the answer to one question leads to another question. Our look at turnaround time began with the question "What is the quality of service that the users are getting?" Figures IIID-10 and IIID-11 show the answers for the entire user population and Figure IIID-12 analyzes the results by department.

In our study of turnaround time at our installation we were able to discover some of the significant factors in turnaround time and to evaluate the service provided. Figures IIID-13 through IIID-16, respectively, show the effect of setup requirements, priority assignment, memory region size re-

Average turnaround time = 69 minutes

Is there a wide range in the quality of the service provided?

Figure IIID-10. Mean turnaround for all users.

384 ISSUES OF MANAGEMENT

	Percents turnaround minutes				
< = 30	< = 60	< = 90	< = 120	< = 180	> 180
38.6	29.2	11.2	6.8	4.3	9.9

Although average turnaround time was 69 minutes, almost 10 percent of the jobs experienced turnaround times in excess of 3 hours.

What is the quality of service provided to the various departments?

Figure IIID-11. Distribution of turnaround time.

Dept. numb.	Average turnaround	Percents turnaround minutes		
		< = 60	< = 180	> 180
001	78	78	19	3
002	67	68	19	13
003	54	76	18	6
004	77	74	14	12
005	60	74	17	9
006	66	66	23	11
007	57	73	20	7

We find no significant difference in the service given in the different departments.

How does the requirement for setup devices affect a job's turnaround?

Figure IIID-12. Service by Department.

	Setup jobs	Non-setup	All jobs
Count of jobs	1176	1294	2470
Average turnaround (minutes)	80	59	69
LASP input queue (minutes)	51	24	37
OS/360 time (minutes)	8	7	7
LASP output queue (minutes)	21	28	25

We observe a significant difference in service provided to setup and non-setup jobs. We see that the difference is in the time spent in the LASP input queue waiting for a device to become available.

What is the effect of priority on service?

Figure IIID-13. Effect of Setup Devices.

D. EVALUATION

LASP prty	Mean turn-around Minutes	Number of jobs	Percents turnaround minutes					
			$<=20$	$<=40$	$<=60$	$<=120$	$<=180$	>180
8	93.5	46	4.3	17.3	13.0	28.1	21.7	15.1
9	82.7	108	7.4	19.4	15.7	35.1	7.4	14.7
10	76.1	24	0.0	12.5	12.5	45.7	25.0	4.1
11	82.5	357	9.5	18.2	19.6	25.0	12.0	15.3
12	70.0	130	12.3	19.2	20.7	25.2	12.3	9.9
13	66.3	1673	25.5	21.7	15.7	15.4	9.3	11.9
14	53.3	69	34.7	30.4	24.6	4.2	2.8	2.8
15	54.0	63	30.1	31.7	14.2	12.5	6.3	4.7

Regardless of priority there is a significant tail of jobs that get poor service (greater than three hour turnaround time).

What are the resource demands that could result in poor service?

Figure IIID-14. Service by LASP priority.

Programmer name	Job name	Program name	Region size	Core used	Unused core
USER1	WTCJAP1	SIX11001	300	124	176
USER2	REVTEST	DJLEXEX	300	68	232
USER3	LKSORT1	SPSS	380	190	190
USER4	KAHNSORT	SELECT	228	86	142

Use of large regions was found to be a frequent cause of long turnaround time. In some cases the region was not being fully used by the program. In such cases the programmers are told how to reduce their region sizes and increase the probability of better service.

What are the I/O characteristics of jobs that get poor service?

Figure IIID-15. Effect of Large Regions.

Programmer name	Job name	Program name	Excp count	Average block size
USERA	LMPSG	MAIN	11,772	1771
USERB	BRID658	DAG01V	17,736	1850
USERC	OUTP1	TASK01	14,641	1140

It was determined that some steps ran for an excessively long time because they did a great deal of I/O while using a small block size. When this is observed the users are contacted and a larger block size is suggested.

Figure IIID-16. I/O Information For Jobs With Long Service.

quirements, and I/O requirements. In addition we were able to develop selection criteria for locating jobs and users that received poor service. We are now able to contact the users and advise them about such things as region sizes and blocking factors. This is done on a regular basis in order to provide better service to the users and also to make more efficient use of the computing resources.

References

1. J. A. Cooperman, "The Statistics Gathering Package Collector," RC 3065, IBM Thomas J. Watson Research Center, September 24, 1970.
2. Jerome A. Cooperman, and William H. Tetzlaff, "Analysis in an OS User Environment," RC 3161, IBM Thomas J. Watson Research Center, September 3, 1970.
3. William H. Tetzlaff, "Statistics Gathering Package Reduction Program," RC 3483, IBM Thomas J. Watson Research Center, August 4, 1971.

The Prediction of Service Performance Attainable via System or Procedural Changes*

Introduction

This paper deals with one possible way of determining the changes which should be made to a system in order to improve or even optimize its performance. In particular, it describes a simulation model of a computing system and how this model can be used to provide such a capability.

Simulation is not the only method for determining the changes which should be made to a computer system. Experiments on the real system offer an alternative approach. However, if a simulation model can be built which is a valid representation of a computer system and the time to perform such a simulation can be made small enough, then simulation has the advantage that it is susceptible to experimentation to a degree otherwise impossible. Moreover, only simulation permits experimentation on non-existent hardware. Without the help of simulation, the only way to evaluate the effect of adding hardware is to extrapolate results from experiments with less hardware (1).

The availability of a performance optimizer does not eliminate the need for both a performance objective function and a method for evaluating

---

* This section has been excerpted from G. Waldbaum and H. Beilner, "Soul: A Simulation of OS under LASP, IBM Research Report RC3810, March 10, 1972.

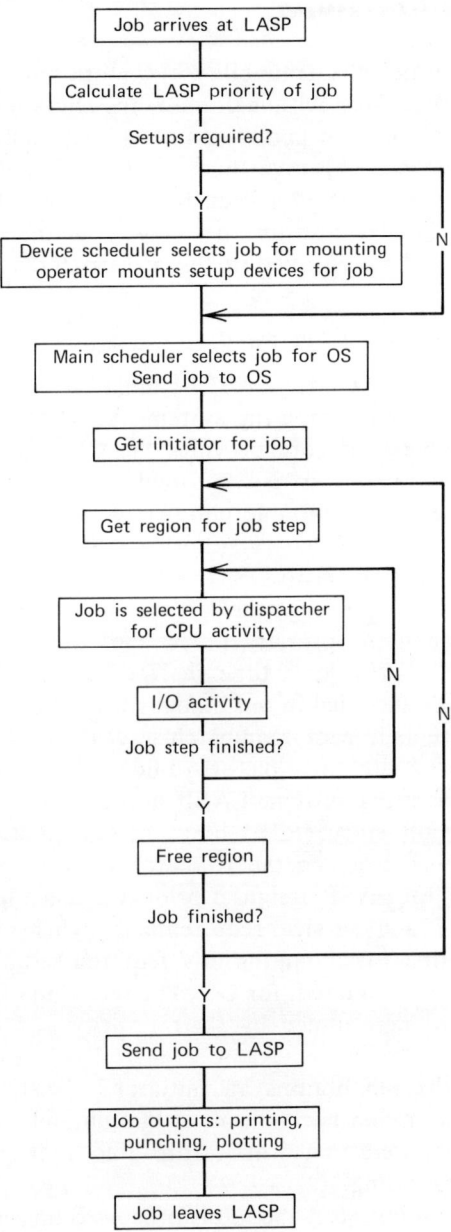

Figure IIID-17. Job flow in research center's batch system.

system changes. In fact, the availability of the optimizer even increases the need for these prerequisites. Although many installations have attempted it, one can not really optimize performance without first specifying the installation's performance objective function. Likewise, the availability of a performance optimizer creates a need for evaluating changes on the real system since the decisive test for the validity of the optimizer's recommendations can only be performed on the real system.

The System which is Simulated

Soul (Simulation of OS Under LASP) simulates the Thomas J. Watson Research Center's batch computing system. An IBM System/360 Model 91 with two megabytes of core provides the CPU power for this batch system. Its software power is obtained by running OS/MVT (2) (multiprogramming with a variable number of tasks) under the control of the Research Center's modified version of LASP (3) (local attached support processor), a supplement to OS. In this dual operating system, LASP manages the flow of jobs through the system while OS concentrates on executing jobs. Although the primary purpose of this system is to provide batch service, it also provides a time sharing service, APL (4). However, APL is not explicitly included in our model since APL's design (5) and current usage minimize its impact upon batch service.

Figure IIID-17 is a simplified picture of how a job flows through the Research Center's operating system. LASP accepts jobs from local readers, about 20 remote job entry (RJE) lines, and a computer network that permits time sharing users on the Research Center's two model 67's to submit batch jobs (6). LASP assigns a priority to each job depending upon the job's resource and service requirements. This priority is used in queueing the job first for mounting any required setup devices and then, once these devices are mounted, for OS. The selection of jobs by LASP for execution on OS is determined by their priority and the availability of resources on OS.

Once on OS, the job obtains an initiator, a system program which manages the initiation and termination of the job and its steps on OS. The number of initiators, determined at startup time, represents the maximum level of multiprogramming.

After obtaining an initiator, the job is processed on a job step basis until every step in the job has been completed. Each step first queues for the region (amount of core) that it needs. After the job step has obtained its region, the step generally oscillates between three states: CPU execution, I/O execution and wait, and CPU wait. In the CPU wait state, a job is ready to use the CPU but has to wait because the CPU is allocated to another ready job with a higher OS dispatching priority. Any output to be printed, punched, and plotted is intercepted during I/O execution by LASP (without OS's knowledge) and spooled on disk. At the end of the job step, the region is released.

Once a job is finished on OS, it returns to LASP. LASP transmits the job's spooled outputs from disk to the destinations which the job actually designated (i.e., printer, punch, RJE line, model 67) according to the job's output priority. After this has been done, the job is purged from the system.

During a typical day at the Research Center, about 700 OS jobs, containing a total of about 2200 job steps, are executed on this system. These jobs exhibit a wide range of job characteristics because of the wide range of work performed at the Research Center and at the locations which submit jobs via RJE lines.

Simulation Objectives

SOUL was developed to provide a means for determining the changes which should be made to the Research Center's batch computing system in order to improve the service provided to the users of this system. SOUL should provide the groundwork for a computing system optimizer, a facility which would permit an installation to tune its hardware, software, and operating procedures with respect to its workload and the measures used by the installation's management for rating the quality of service obtained by the jobs in this workload.

Properties of Soul

SOUL has several significant properties. Although some of these are possessed by other computer systems simulators, SOUL appears to be the first simulator to possess all of these properties:

1. In essence, SOUL simulates a total system: hardware, software, workload, hardware and software reliability, and operator actions. SOUL is able, for example, to simulate the loss of recovery of certain hardware components (e.g., printers, setup devices) and software facilities (e.g., initiators) as well as various levels of operator performance in mounting setup devices.
2. SOUL simulates most of the events that really happened in an entire day's operations. Many managers and programmers are skeptical of computer systems simulations which are driven by probabilistic data

since these data have frequently been improperly calculated from real data. In order to avoid this difficulty and to make SOUL more convincing, it was decided to simulate the real workload amidst the real system's reliability problems. As a result, SOUL, unlike certain other computing system simulators (e.g., AMAP (7)), is able to simulate a real day's uncontrolled environment instead of just a short and carefully selected batch system.

3. SOUL simulates a whole day's computer activities in less than one minute of CPU time on the same computer. This permits SOUL to be used in an interactive optimizing procedure.
4. SOUL simulates the real world at a level of detail that permits a reasonable match between the behaviour of most jobs in the real and simulated worlds. SOUL is a macro model. Initially, only those parts of the total system were simulated which seemed most important for obtaining the desired match. Detail has only been added where the calibration process has determined serious model inadequacies.

Overall Structure of Soul

Figure IIID-18 depicts the overall structure of SOUL partitioned into:

- The pre-processor. The purpose of the pre-processor is to provide, via a single run, all the necessary job data for performing multiple simulations of some period during a single day's activities.
- The simulator. The simulator models the flow of jobs through OS and LASP. The simulator's inputs consist of job information provided by the pre-processor and control information provided by the user of SOUL.
- The post-processor. The post-processor is designed to aid in the calibration of the simulator as well as in using the simulator for improving the performance of the system being simulated.

During normal batch operations, data describing certain characteristics of every job (such as arrival time and resource requirements) are collected by SGP, a Statistics Gathering Package (8) developed at the Research Center. These (historical) trace data form the main (driving) input for the simulator.

The primary purpose of the pre-processor is to provide an abstraction of the actual workload. This information, consisting of all the necessary job data, is stored in a data set on disk. Thus, a single pre-processor run produces the information required for performing multiple simulations of a single day's activity. Figure IIID-19 lists the job data provided by the pre-processor as input to the simulator. Note that a significant part of this side information is not collected by SGP. Instead, the pre-processor calculates estimates for these missing data from the the SGP data which is available. This, of course, directly introduces error into SOUL's input data and indirectly into its output.

In addition to the job data provided by the pre-processor, the simulator also accepts certain control information as input. Control information provides most of the historical data that is missing in the SGP trace. It is specified by parameters and "external events," data describing what these events are and when they occur. In particular, there are five types of control information:

1. Hardware configuration control information. This control in-

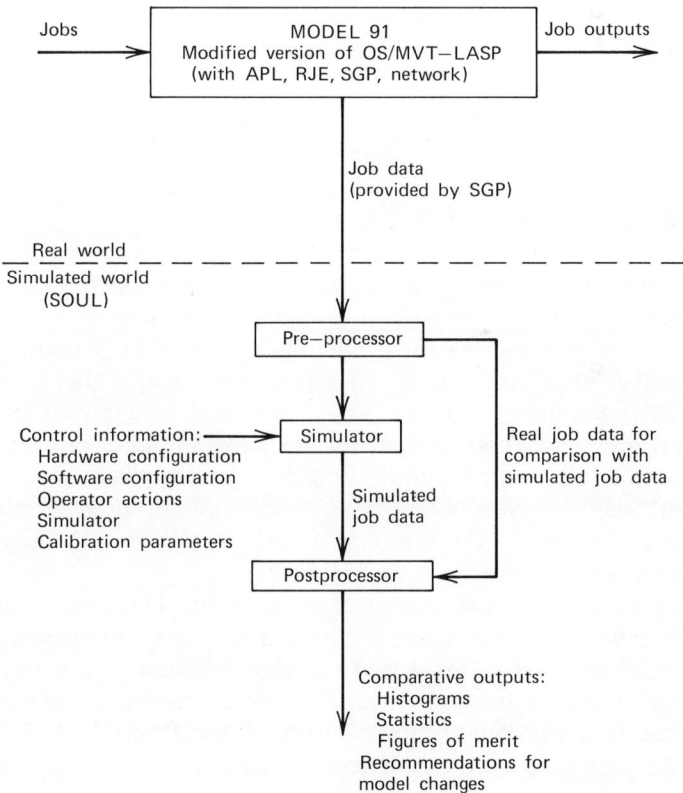

Figure IIID-18. Overall structure of SOUL.

Data per Job

- LASP number
- Job name
- User's estimate of CPU time
- User's estimate of lines to be printed.
- LASP's estimate of maximum region size*
- Arrival time at LASP
- Number of 7 track tape setups*
- Number of 7 track tape setups used for plotting*
- Number of 9 track tape setups*
- Number of 2314 disk setups*
- Time for printing
- LASP's estimate of the number of lines to be printed*
- Location where job is printed*
- Initial priority of job on OS
- Research Center's shift parameter

Data per Job Step

- Size of region used
- Amount of CPU time used
- Number of EXCPs (i.e., number of executed channel programs) for non-overlapped I/O*
- Amount of non-overlapped I/O time (from issuance of an EXCP to recognition of the final device-end)*

Figure IIID-19. Job data used by SOUL.

formation describes an initial hardware configuration (e.g., amount of core available for all batch jobs, number of setup devices of different types, scaling factors for simulating various CPU's and I/O devices, number of printers). It also describes any changes that later occurred in this configuration such as the loss and recovery of devices (i.e., RJE lines, printers, setup devices). Changes in hardware configuration control information permit simulation experiments to be conducted with the same workload on hardware configurations. It also permits an evaluation of the effect of certain hardware reliability problems upon performance.

2. Software configuration control information. This control information describes an initial software configuration (e.g., number of initiators, LASP parameters for device and OS scheduling, priority tables used by LASP, parameters which determine whether or not to simulate various LASP modifications made at the RESEARCH Center). It also permits simulation of the loss and recovery of various software facilities (e.g., initiators). Changes in software configuration control

---

* Estimates of these items are calculated by the pre-processor.

information permit simulation experiments to be conducted with the same workload on different software configurations. It also permits an evaluation of the effect of certain software reliability problems upon performance.
3. Operator control information. This control information permits the simulation of various operator commands (e.g., change priority of job, hold or release a job, hold or release main, initiate or terminate certain modifications to LASP). By omitting these data, one can determine whether or not operator actions were detrimental to system performance.
4. Simulator control information. This control information is useful during debugging, calibration, validation, and experimentation. It permits the user, for example, to limit his output to what he really needs, such as certain statistics required during calibration and experimentation or certain snaps and event traces required when studying system phenomena in greater detail.
5. Calibration parameters. These parameters, described in the following section, are used for calibrating the model.

At present, the creation of control information is very time consuming and error-prone since it requires the examination of several hundred pages of console listings. However, future listings will be put on tape to permit the pre-processor to automatically generate most of the control information.

In order to aid in the manual creation of control information, the pre-processor also provides time maps which indicate the availability of various system resources. These maps are used to construct external events for simulating the unavailability of system resources. Figure IIID-20, for example, shows a time map for the initiators on a particular day. This map shows that eight initiators were used for batch jobs, but the initiator associated with protect key 13 was used only for job number 1011. Whatever caused the real world to stop using this initiator, the initiator was not available for any other job during the rest of the day. Thus, an external event had to be created to remove an initiator from service at the time when job 1011 finished using it. Similarly, the initiator associated with protect key 12 appears to have been lost between 11:00 and 11:30 and an appropriate external event was created for it too.

The Simulator

SOUL was written in PL/I since this language appeared to provide a flexibility which is not currently available in any simulation language. This

ISSUES OF MANAGEMENT

IN THE TIME INTERVAL BEGINNING AT HH:MM	THESE PROTECT KEYS HAVE BEEN USED							
	6	7	8	9	10	12	13	14
8:30	* 4	* 2	* 5	* 2	* 5	*3	1011	1015
9:00	* 2	* 5	* 6	* 2	* 2	*4		* 6
9:30	* 7	* 6	* 3	* 7	* 4	*5		* 7
10:00	* 3	* 2	* 6	* 5	* 5	*5		* 2
10:30	* 6	* 6	* 4	* 6	* 5	*4		* 5
11:00	* 6	* 4	*10	* 3	* 7	*7		* 4
11:30	* 2	* 2	* 4	* 3	* 3			* 2
12:00	* 4	*10	* 4	* 7	*11			* 6
12:30	* 6	*16	* 6	* 6	* 6			* 6
13:00	1124	* 8	* 9	* 8	* 6			* 2
13:30	1124	* 6	* 7	*10	* 8			* 8
14:00	* 9	* 6	* 6	*10	*10			* 3
14:30	*10	* 4	*11	* 4	* 5			1481
15:00	* 9	*10	* 6	* 5	* 7			* 4
15:30	* 2	1530	* 7	* 6	* 9			* 9
16:00	*13	* 8	* 8	* 4	* 7			* 9
16:30	* 5	* 8	*10	* 8	* 5			* 7
17:00	* 5	*10	* 4	1729	* 9			* 2
17:30	* 3	* 7	* 3	* 7	* 9			* 5
18:00	* 5	* 5	* 3	* 6	* 7			* 6
18:30	* 6	* 3	* 5	* 4	* 6			* 6
19:00	* 3	1228	* 4	1238	* 3			* 5
19:30	1872	* 3	1435	* 4	* 3			* 3
20:00	1872			1871	1869			
20:30								

Figure IIID-20. Time map for initiators.

especially appeared to be the case in the area of I/O. Moreover, it was hoped that the simulator could be modularized in such a way that certain modules from the real system could be incorporated in SOUL. Not only would the use of such a capability increase SOUL's accuracy, but it would increase the utility of SOUL by making it even more receptive to system debugging.

In retrospect, the use of PL/I does not appear to have hampered the development of SOUL in any way, not even while coding the standard features which simulation languages typically offer. In fact, the capabilities of PL/I proved more than adequate for satisfying all of our programming requirements (although no attempt has yet been made to incorporate real OS/LASP modules in SOUL). The simulator, approximately 2000 PL/I statements, was written and debugged in less than three man-months. Its execution time is excellent, even without having optimized the object code.

D. EVALUATION 395

Most of the functions shown in Figure IIID-17 (e.g., calculation of LASP priority and main scheduling) are modelled at the micro-level. CPU and I/O activities, however, are simulated at the macro-level since:

1. The frequency of their occurrence is almost two orders of magnitude greater than the frequency of occurrence of all other events combined. Thus, the greatest potential for savings in simulation time is in the simulation of CPU and I/O activities.
2. Detailed information about the duration of each CPU and I/O activity is not available. For each job step, only the total CPU time and the total I/O time, as well as the number of I/O activities, is collected by SGP.

The method of simulating CPU and I/O activities is illustrated in Figure IIID-21. Assuming that CPU and I/O activities for some real job step are shown in Figure IIID-21a then Figures IIID-21b and IIID-21c indicate the levels of abstraction at which SOUL may simulate this job step. (The number in each box represents the duration of the activity in some arbitrary time unit.) Note that the total I/O time and the total CPU time per job step remains unchanged. Only the number of CPU and I/O activities and their durations change.

Figure IIID-21b represents a kind of micro-modelling since the number of simulated CPU (I/O) activities is equal to the number of real CPU

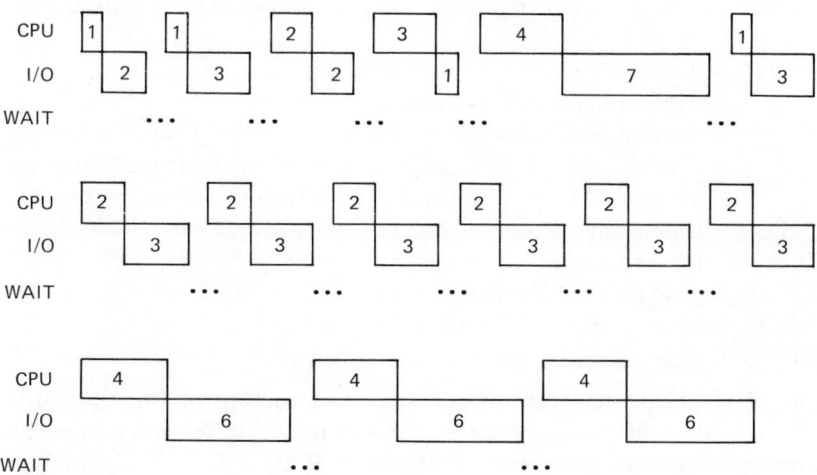

Figure IIID-21. Simulating CPU and I/O activities via the reduction factor method. (a) The real world. (b) The simulated world (PEDE = 1). (c) The simulated world (PEDE = 2).

(I/O) activities. In order to reduce the number of activities to be simulated, SOUL employs a control parameter called the reduction factor, REDF, which can be assigned integral values greater than or equal to 1. In particular, the number of simulated I/O (CPU) activities is approximately equal to the number of real I/O (CPU) activities divided by REDF while the duration of each such I/O (CPU) activity is approximately equal to the product of the average duration of each real I/O (CPU) activity and REDF. When a REDF greater than 1 is used (e.g., see Figure IIID-21c), we say that SOUL models CPU and I/O activities at the macro-level.

As expected, experiments show that simulation time is very sensitive to changes in the value of REDF. For example, a simulation may take a half-hour of model 91 time when running with an REDF of 1 while less than half a minute when running with an REDF of 5000. Since experiments indicate that the variation in the accuracy of the model due to changes in REDF is negligible compared to other errors in the model, simulators can be performed with large values of REDF and therefore consume little CPU time.

SOUL employs another macro-modelling approach. All time intervals whose durations are unknown, but considered significant, are modelled by analytic functions of the job's characteristics. The parameters in these analytic functions are the so-called calibration parameters whose values are adjusted at calibration time:

DELMAIN = time between request for main or device scheduler and the start of the scheduler
MINSTIM = fixed amount of I/O overhead per job step
OV0 = fixed amount of CPU overhead per job step
OV1 = amount of CPU overhead per msec of CPU time in job step
OV2 = amount of I/O overhead per msec of I/O time in job step
OV3 = amount of CPU overhead per I/O operation in job step
TIMNTOT = time to mount a tape drive
TIMNTOD = time to mount a disk drive
TIMOSFJ = time for OS to finish a job
TIMSLOS = time to send a job from LASP to OS
TIMSOSL = time to send a job from OS to LASP

Figure IIID-22 depicts the overall internal structure of the simulator. SOUL has two event chains, one for jobs and the other for external events (e.g., operator actions and hardware changes). Both chains are ordered according to the time of the next event. A control routine selects the event which must occur first from the top of the two chains and branches to the appropriate routine for that event. This technique permits events to be

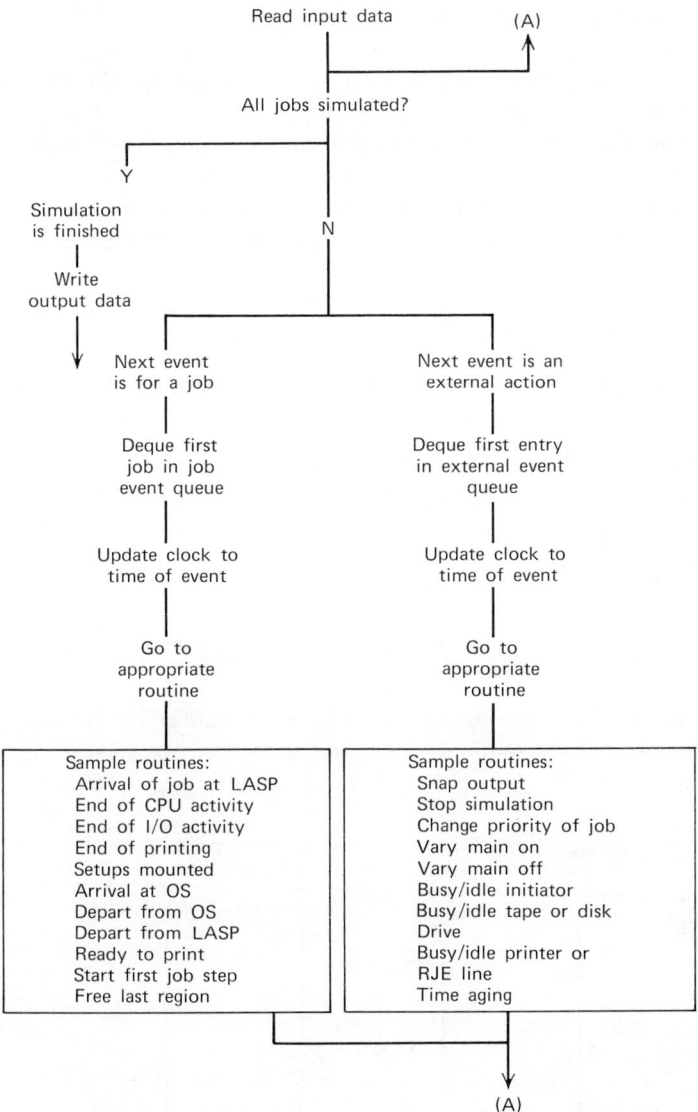

Figure IIID-22. Overall internal structure of simulator.

processed very rapidly. It also makes it easy to change the simulator for simulating a new type of event.

The simulator is designed to permit many different types of experiments to be conducted just be changing parameters. SOUL is also designed to make it easy to change the simulator, whether it be for the purpose of modelling the real world more accurately or for experimenting with system changes.

The Simulator's Outputs

The simulator's primary output consists of three simulated event times for each job:

- The time the job leaves LASP for OS.
- The time the job returns to LASP from OS.
- The time the job departs LASP.

and two simulated event times for each job step:

- The time the step starts.
- The time the step finishes.

The user of SOUL also has the capability of displaying some histograms and statistics which provide a feel about the degree of success of the calibration or optimization process. These histograms and statistics may be

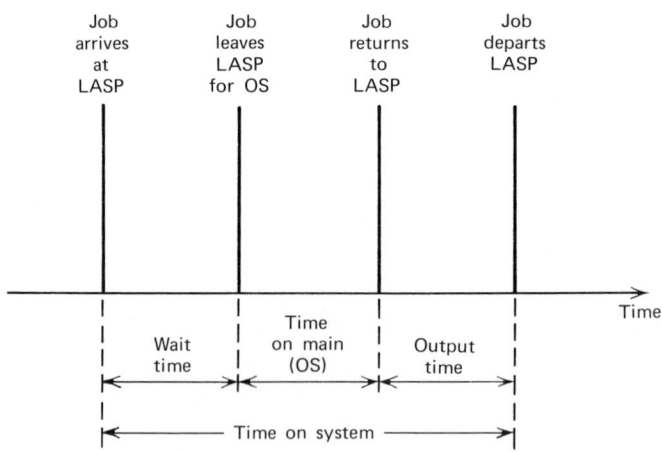

Figure IIID-23.   Phases which comprise time on system.

D. EVALUATION

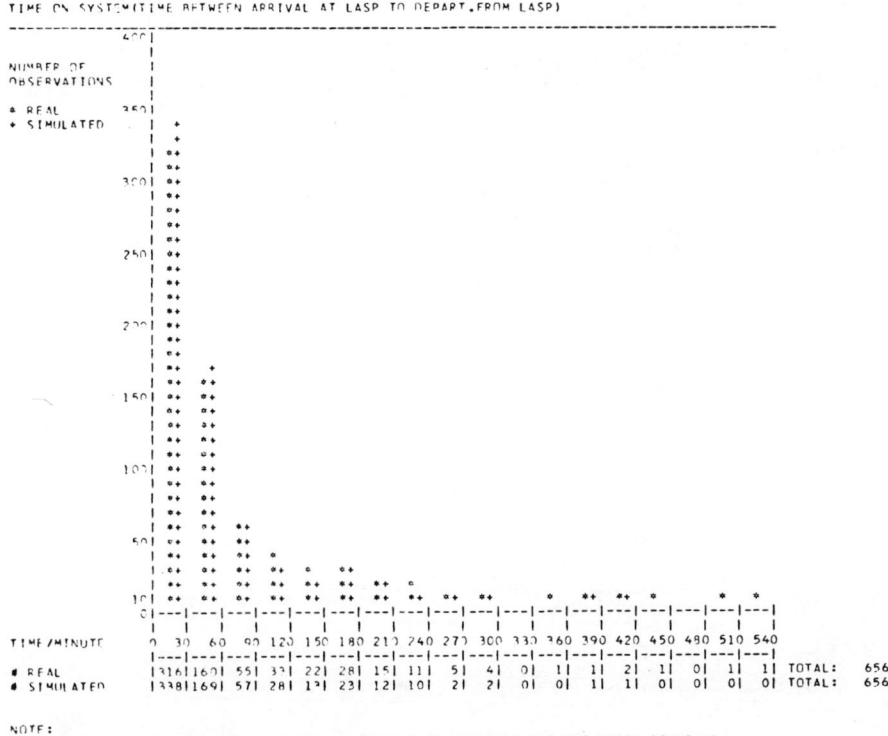

Figure IIID-24. Histogram for time on system.

produced for the time on system (i.e., the time between the arrival of a job at LASP and its departure) as well as for each of the three phases, shown in Figure IIID-23, which comprise the time on system.

Three types of histograms may be printed:

1. Sample distributions for both the real and simulated times that a job spends in a particular phase. For example, Figures IIID-24 and IIID-25 show the real and simulated sample distributions for the time on system and the time on main.
2. Sample distributions for the difference between the real and simulated times that a job spends in a particular phase. During calibration and validation, this time difference represents the error in simulating a job. Figure IIID-26 depicts such a histogram for the time on main.

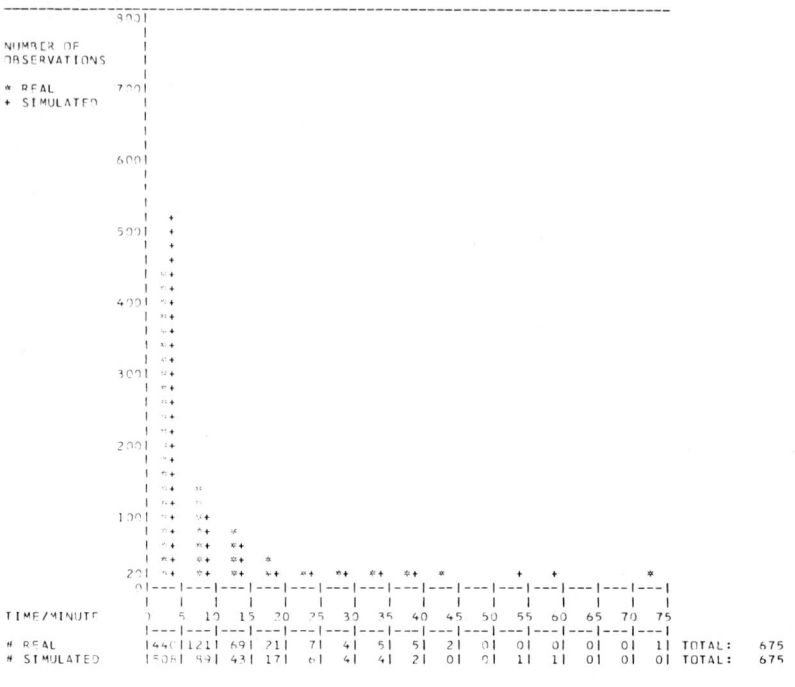

STATISTICS:

	AVERAGE VALUE (SAMPLE MEAN) TIME/MIN	AVERAGE ABSOLUTE VALUE TIME/MIN	AVERAGE SQUARED VALUE	SAMPLE STANDARD DEVIATION TIME/MIN	RANGE FROM TIME/MIN	(JOB #)	TO TIME/MIN	(JOB #)
REAL	5.52	5.52	79.67	7.02	0.05	(619)	70.30	(104)
SIMULATED	4.10	4.10	53.79	6.08	0.20	(17)	55.83	(8)

INTERESTING INTERVAL(S):

BETWEEN	AND	# REAL	# SIMULATED
0.000	1.000	132	241
1.001	2.000	140	113
2.001	3.000	66	72
3.001	4.000	62	50
4.001	5.000	40	32

Figure IIID-25. Histogram for time on main.

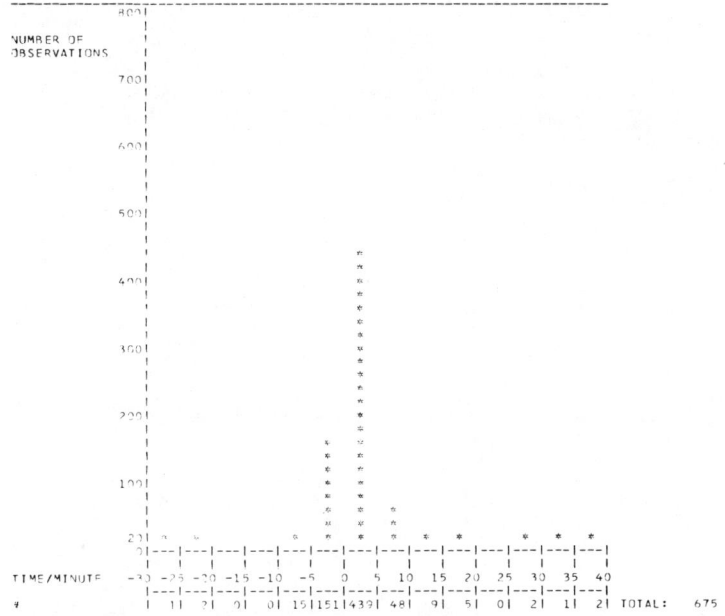

Figure IIID-26. Histogram for error in time on main.

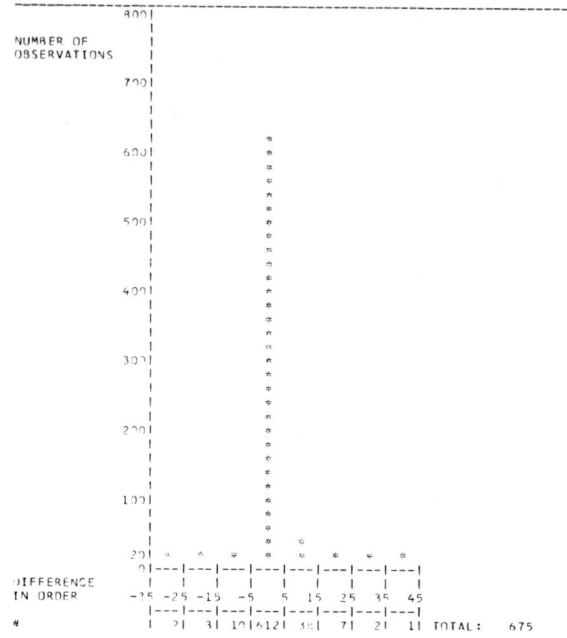

Figure IIID-27. Histogram for error in order of departure from OS.

D. EVALUATION

3. Sample distributions for the difference between the real and simulated ordering of events of a certain type (e.g., order of arrival at OS, order of departure from OS, and order of departure from LASP). Figure IIID-27 depicts such a histogram for the order of departure from OS.

Each type of histogram may be produced for all jobs or just for those jobs having certain characteristics. For example, SOUL can produce histograms on the time in the output phase for each RJE line or the time on the system for jobs whose region sizes fall within a specified range.

The Post-Processor's Outputs

A more refined analysis of every simulation run may be obtained by running the post-processor. This program maintains and uses an extensive data-base on disk containing, in condensed form, information about all previous calibration, validation, and experimentation processes performed

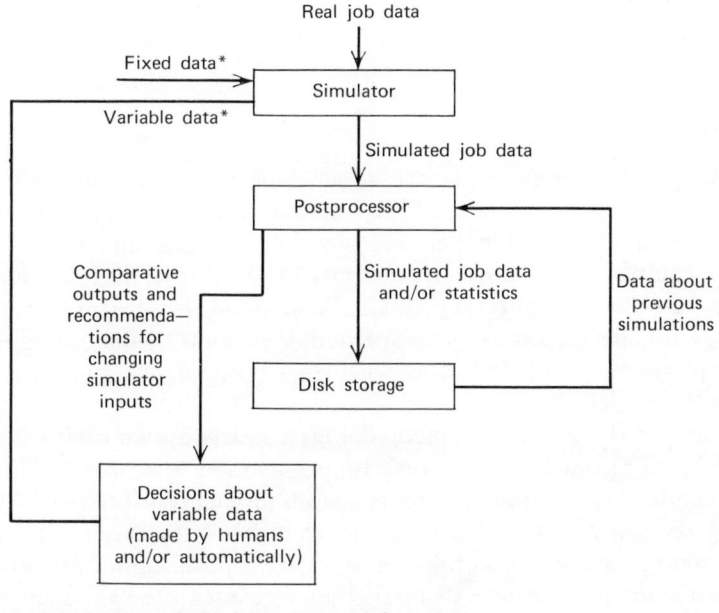

* Variable data + fixed data = control information

Variable data = { hardware configuration (when experimenting)
software configuration (when experimenting)
operator actions (when experimenting)
calibration parameters (when calibrating) }

Figure IIID-28. The calibration/experimentation process.

with SOUL. The post-processor optionally provides:

- Statistics including average values, average absolute values, and average squared values of both the difference and the percent between real and simulated times for the jobs or job steps in any phase.
- Statistical decisions stating whether or not the present simulation run, as measured by one of several possible figures of merit, is significantly better than some previous run or each individual run in the series of continuously improved runs.
- Multiple linear regression analyses with any difference variable as the dependent variable and any subset of the job or job step characteristics as independent variables.
- Multiple linear regression analyses with any figure of merit as dependent variable and any subset of the calibration (or experimentation) parameters as independent variables.

via these options, the post-processor offers a capability, as shown in Figure IIID-28, to control semi-automated calibration, validation, and experimentation processes.

Calibration

Calibration of a simulator is the process of tuning certain calibration parameters and changing parts of the simulator's structure so as to yield, in some sense, a good match between simulator output and some desired simulator output (e.g., real world output) for a selected set of input data. For the purpose of calibrating SOUL, a semi-automated calibration methodology was developed (9). This methodology controls the tuning of calibration parameters and indicates whether structural changes have to be made to the model.

The basis of the calibration methodology consists of two tuning methods and one decision method. The first tuning method attempts to eliminate any dependencies of model errors upon job characteristics, thereby reducing the sensitivity of the model to changes in the driving input. The second tuning method controls an iterative optimization process with respect to some given figure of merit that measures the "goodness of fit" between the behaviour of real and simulated jobs (e.g., the mean square error, the average absolute error, the average absolute percent error). A decision method is a necessary prerequisite when optimizing under uncertainty. Such a method decides whether or not an improvement in some figure of merit is statistically significant.

D. EVALUATION

Several objectives have been used during calibration. One objective, for example, has been to minimize the average absolute percent error of the jobs' turnaround times, subject to (nearly) zero average percent error for the turnaround times. However, we have never chosen an objective of the (frequently used) type: Minimize the average error (or average percent error). Although such an objective can easily be achieved by SOUL, it is of little use because of the always existent compensating errors.

UNCALIBRATED STATE			CALIBRATED STATE		
VALUES OF PARAMETERS AFFECTING MAIN:			VALUES OF PARAMETERS AFFECTING MAIN:		
TIMSLOS =0			TIMSLOS =10000		
TIMOSSJ =0			TIMOSSJ = 0		
MINSTIM =0			MINSTIM = 1000		
OV0 =0			OV0 = 1000		
OV1 =0			OV1 = 0.05		
OV2 =0			OV2 = 0.04		
OV3 =0			OV3 = 6.00		
TIMOSFJ =0			TIMOSFJ = 0		
TIMSOSL =0			TIMSOSL = 0		
DAY	1/11/71	1/12/71	DAY	1/11/71	1/12/71
AVERAGE % ERROR ON MAIN	60.7%	59.7%	AVERAGE % ERROR ON MAIN	11.6%	13.3%
AVERAGE ABSOLUTE % ERROR ON MAIN	66.3%	71.9%	AVERAGE ABSOLUTE % ERROR ON MAIN	49.9%	58.7%
X	PERCENTAGE OF JOBS WHOSE ABSOLUTE PERCENT ERRORS ARE LESS THAN X		X	PERCENTAGE OF JOBS WHOSE ABSOLUTE PERCENT ERRORS ARE LESS THAN X	
10%	2%	2%	10%	12%	10%
20%	5%	4%	20%	25%	22%
30%	10%	9%	30%	37%	41%
40%	17%	16%	40%	51%	55%
50%	27%	29%	50%	64%	68%

Figure IIID-29. Calibration results for the main phase-obtained, using two days' data, when the objective was to minimize the average absolute percent error for time on main.

The calibration process can be performed with respect to one or more days. Figure IIID-29 gives calibration results obtained from two days' data. In this case, the calibration objective was to minimize the average absolute percent error for the jobs' turnaround times subject to nearly zero average percent error for the turnaround times.

Validation

In a very general sense, validation of a simulator can be defined as determining the domain of situations for which the simulator yields valid results once calibration has been established (10).
Validation of a trace-driven simulator such as SOUL has two different aspects (9):

- A validation of the calibrated model is necessary in order to ensure that the simulator is a valid representation of the real system for more than just the particular set of traces used during calibration. This type of validation can be achieved by confirming the validity of the simulator for sets of input data which were not used during calibration. Figure IIID-30 indicates the degree of the validity of SOUL for two days that occurred nine months after the two days which were used for calibration.
- It is also necessary to assure that the simulator is a valid representation of certain unreal systems which could be real. Since the purpose of SOUL is to permit controlled experiments on different hardware and software configurations for the purpose of improving system performance, SOUL must be capable of simulating these unreal systems as well as the real system. In particular, any experimentation with SOUL should aim to find an unreal system with a significantly better performance than that of the real system. The validity of the simulation of such an unreal system can only be confirmed by making the proposed changes to the system and then checking whether the simulator's forecasts are valid.
- It is not reasonable to expect that a simulator is valid for every imaginable system. However, the invalid as well as the valid forecasts determine the domain of SOUL's validity and thus establish the basis for continued and intelligent use of the simulator.

EXPERIMENTATION METHODOLOGY. A methodology similar to the one used for calibration can be used for experimentation. In particular, improvements in the system's performance can be achieved in a controlled process by adjusting our methodology (10) in the following way:

- Whereas in calibrating we try to obtain a model which behaves, in some sense, as closely as possible from the real world. In this case, we can measure the distance between real and simulated worlds by job improvements (i.e., differences in job phase durations between reality and model) and try to maximize certain functions of these job improvements.
- Whereas one important part of the calibration process consists of tuning certain calibration parameters, one important part of the experimentation process consists of tuning certain system parameters.

METHOD: DETERMINE WHETHER THE DISTRIBUTIONS OF THE AVERAGE ABSOLUTE PERCENT ERROR FOR BLOCKS OF 30 JOBS ARE THE SAME FOR THE DAYS TO BE VALIDATED AS THEY ARE FOR THE CALIBRATED DAYS.

AVERAGE ABSOLUTE PERCENT ERRORS FOR BLOCKS:

DAY:	1/11/71	1/12/71	10/14/71	10/15/71
	45.5%	69.5%	50.7%	33.7%
	53.1%	56.6%	44.2%	40.9%
	72.7%	55.7%	48.1%	71.9%
	49.6%	61.9%	68.5%	45.0%
	34.6%	44.1%	60.4%	54.8%
	40.7%	49.5%	63.7%	68.0%
	38.8%	45.3%	60.3%	50.4%
	42.8%	36.4%	66.4%	52.6%
	61.2%	61.3%	52.3%	55.5%
	54.3%	63.3%	52.2%	65.9%
	53.3%	46.5%	49.2%	45.9%
	44.3%	53.5%	48.6%	64.1%
	42.3%	82.0%	55.1%	63.6%
	62.6%	53.9%	45.3%	58.3%
	42.1%	51.4%	51.2%	49.2%
	44.0%	43.6%	66.6%	56.7%
	47.0%	67.2%	38.5%	41.6%
	51.7%	46.0%		32.7%
	70.9%	35.7%		
	34.2%	49.4%		
	70.2%			

RESULT: THE MANN-WHITNEY-U-TEST DOES NOT REJECT THE HYPOTHESIS THAT THE TWO SAMPLES (1/11+1/12 AND 10/14+10/15) HAVE BEEN DRAWN FROM THE SAME POPULATION AT A SIGNIFICANCE LEVEL OF 0.25.

Figure IIID-30. Statistical validation of the calibrated main phase for two traces not used during calibration.

Status of Soul

At present, SOUL appears to provide a reasonable match between the behaviour of most jobs in the real and simulated worlds. However, SOUL's accuracy can be improved by extending SOUL to model certain activities which it does not presently model such as I/O contention, device sharing, waiting for a volume or a data set which is not shared, "borrowing of core" by LASP, automatic holding and releasing of jobs, and variability in operator procedures during the mounting of setup devices.

SOUL has already been used to discover and correct weaknesses in the Research Center's batch system and to answer some questions posed by management.

Experiments conducted to date include determining the effect on performance of:

- Number of printers.
- New Scheduling algorithms.
- Cancelling jobs which perform excessive I/O.
- Core fragmentation.

References

1. G. Waldbaum, "Large Capacity Storage and Time Sharing System/360," IBM RC 2698, November 11, 1969.
2. "IBM System/360 Operating System: Concepts and Facilities," Form GC28-6535.
3. "IBM System/360 Attached Support Processor System (ASP): System Programmer's Manual," Form GH20-0323.
4. "APL/360/OS and APL/360-DOS User's Manual," Program number 5734-XM6 (OS), IBM.
5. C. R. Attanasio, P. W. Markstein, and C. E. Shanesy, "A Dispatching Algorithm for a Conversational, High-Capacity Computational Subsystem for OS/360, MVT," IBM RC 2483, May 23, 1969.
6. W. S., Hobgood, "Evaluation of an Interactive-Batch System Network," *IBM Systems Journal*, 11, 1, (1972).
7. "Advanced Multiprogramming Analysis Procedure (AMAP) Service Description Manual," Form GH20-0725, IBM.
8. J. A. Cooperman, and W. H. Tetzlaff, "Analysis in an OS User Environment," IBM RC 3161, September 3, 1970.
9. H. Beilner, and G. Waldbaum, "Statistical Methodology for Calibrating a Trace-Driven Simulator of a Batch Computer System," Conference on Statistical Methods for the Evaluation of Computer Systems Performance," Brown University, November 22–23, 1971.
10. W. A. Ernst, "Problems in Computing Systems Performance Modelling: Characterization, Calibration and Validation," IBM RC 3319, April 6, 1971.

The Measurement and Evaluation of Usage Performance

The measurement of *system* performance shows only half of the computer service picture. The measurement of *usage* performance completes the picture and, for the first time, provides the data and the perspective to evaluate the reciprocal effects and interdependence of system and usage behavior.

The importance of having this perspective increases with the growth of on-line interactive services. Fortunately, it becomes easier to monitor usage behavior with interactive systems, since the users are totally engaged while using the system. This means that there are fewer ambiguities and uncertainties about resubmission rates and nonrelated activities.

The following illustrations are of time-sharing usage measurements made at IBM research laboratories. These measurements were made of TSS/360 usage. However, the same measurement concepts and techniques could be applied to any interactive system. This section was excerpted from two IBM research reports (1, 2) which are available if more detail is desired.

The basic data collection tool is an event recording program called SIPE (3). SIPE was used in such a way as to keep the CPU measurement overhead to less than one percent.

The SIPE data is subsequently processed by a TSS USAGE ANALYSIS PROGRAM, which is an installation management tool developed at the Research Center. Its outputs are in the form of graphical load descriptions and itemized abnormality descriptions.

The output of the TSS USAGE ANALYSIS program shown in Figure IIID-31 makes evident the variation over time of the load on TSS, in terms of number of users, on a given day. The time interval was chosen as five minutes. The two columns following time show the number of users on the system and the number active during each five minute period. If a user submits an input during a period, he is considered active during the period. The histogram uses O's and *'s to show the number of active users and the number of inactive users during each interval. Note the occurrence of a system crash shortly before noon. The load was relatively constant on the given day.

Figures IIID-32 and IIID-33 show distributions of system and user response time, respectively. Taken together, these characteristics permit the calculation of user productivity as a function of system responsiveness and consequently, determination of optimal level of system loading (as described in Chapter III.B).

Figures IIID-34 and IIID-35 show the time histories of system and user response times during a given work day. Each bar indicates the mean of all responses that ended in the particular five minute interval.

```
TIME            N.USERS ON  N.ACTIVE
 7:35 (     0)      4          4    0000
 7:40 (   300)      5          5    00000
 7:45 (   600)      7          7    0000000
 7:50 (   900)      7          7    0000000
 7:55 ( 1200)      7          7    0000000
 8: 0 ( 1500)      7          7    0000000
 8: 5 ( 1800)      8          8    00000000
 8:10 ( 2100)     10         10    0000000000
 8:15 ( 2400)      9          8    00000000*
 8:20 ( 2700)     11         10    0000000000*
 8:25 ( 3000)     15         13    0000000000000**
 8:30 ( 3300)     20         16    0000000000000000****
 8:35 ( 3600)     22         20    00000000000000000000**
 8:40 ( 3900)     26         17    00000000000000000*********
 8:45 ( 4200)     27         20    00000000000000000000*******
 8:50 ( 4500)     28         23    00000000000000000000000*****
 8:55 ( 4800)     27         25    0000000000000000000000000**
 9: 0 ( 5100)     28         25    0000000000000000000000000***
 9: 5 ( 5400)     29         25    0000000000000000000000000****
 9:10 ( 5700)     30         27    000000000000000000000000000***
 9:15 ( 6000)     31         26    00000000000000000000000000*****
 9:20 ( 6300)     31         24    000000000000000000000000*******
 9:25 ( 6600)     31         27    000000000000000000000000000****
 9:30 ( 6900)     30         23    00000000000000000000000*******
 9:35 ( 7200)     32         23    00000000000000000000000*********
 9:40 ( 7500)     31         24    000000000000000000000000*******
 9:45 ( 7800)     31         26    00000000000000000000000000*****
 9:50 ( 8100)     32         25    0000000000000000000000000*******
 9:55 ( 8400)     32         26    00000000000000000000000000******
10: 0 ( 8700)     32         25    0000000000000000000000000*******
10: 5 ( 9000)     31         24    000000000000000000000000*******
10:10 ( 9300)     31         22    0000000000000000000000*********
10:15 ( 9600)     32         21    000000000000000000000***********
10:20 ( 9900)     31         24    000000000000000000000000*******
10:25 (10200)     28         20    00000000000000000000********
10:30 (10500)     26         18    000000000000000000********
10:35 (10800)     25         20    00000000000000000000*****
10:40 (11100)     28         24    000000000000000000000000****
10:45 (11400)     27         23    00000000000000000000000****
10:50 (11700)     29         25    0000000000000000000000000****
10:55 (12000)     28         24    000000000000000000000000****
11: 0 (12300)     29         25    0000000000000000000000000****
11: 5 (12600)     28         24    000000000000000000000000****
11:10 (12900)     25         22    0000000000000000000000***
11:15 (13200)     25         22    0000000000000000000000***
11:20 (13500)     23         22    0000000000000000000000*
11:25 (13800)     15         15    000000000000000
11:30 (14100)      0          0    0
11:35 (14400)      0          0    0
11:40 (14700)     11          8    00000000***
11:45 (15000)     16         14    00000000000000**
11:50 (15300)     17         15    000000000000000**
11:55 (15600)     19         15    000000000000000****
12: 0 (15900)     19         13    0000000000000******
12: 5 (16200)     20         14    00000000000000******
12:10 (16500)     22         16    0000000000000000******
12:15 (16800)     25         17    00000000000000000********
12:20 (17100)     23         15    000000000000000********
12:25 (17400)     24         16    0000000000000000********
12:30 (17700)     25         19    0000000000000000000******
12:35 (18000)     26         19    0000000000000000000*******
12:40 (18300)     25         20    00000000000000000000*****
12:45 (18600)     24         20    00000000000000000000****
12:50 (18900)     27         23    00000000000000000000000****
12:55 (19200)     27         21    000000000000000000000******
13: 0 (19500)     28         20    00000000000000000000********
13: 5 (19800)     27         22    0000000000000000000000*****
13:10 (20100)     27         22    0000000000000000000000*****
13:15 (20400)     27         21    000000000000000000000******
13:20 (20700)     29         23    00000000000000000000000******
13:25 (21000)     27         20    00000000000000000000*******
13:30 (21300)     27         18    000000000000000000*********
13:35 (21600)     27         20    00000000000000000000*******
13:40 (21900)     26         19    0000000000000000000*******
13:45 (22200)     28         22    0000000000000000000000******
13:50 (22500)     29         19    0000000000000000000**********
13:55 (22800)     28         18    000000000000000000**********
14: 0 (23100)     30         18    000000000000000000************
14: 5 (23400)     29         18    000000000000000000***********
14:10 (23700)     29         19    0000000000000000000**********
14:15 (24000)     29         18    000000000000000000***********
14:20 (24300)     30         19    0000000000000000000***********
14:25 (24600)     30         18    000000000000000000************
14:30 (24900)     30         24    000000000000000000000000******
14:35 (25200)     29         23    00000000000000000000000******
14:40 (25500)     29         22    0000000000000000000000*******
14:45 (25800)     29         20    00000000000000000000*********
14:50 (26100)     29         21    000000000000000000000********
14:55 (26400)     28         19    0000000000000000000*********
15: 0 (26700)     27         17    00000000000000000**********
15: 5 (27000)     27         16    0000000000000000***********
15:10 (27300)     29         19    0000000000000000000**********
15:15 (27600)     29         20    00000000000000000000*********
15:20 (27900)     29         20    00000000000000000000*********
15:25 (28200)     28         22    0000000000000000000000******
15:30 (28500)     28         19    0000000000000000000*********
15:35 (28800)     28         22    0000000000000000000000******
15:40 (29100)     28         22    0000000000000000000000******
15:45 (29400)     28         20    00000000000000000000********
15:50 (29700)     28         24    000000000000000000000000****
15:55 (30000)     28         21    000000000000000000000*******
16: 0 (30300)     27         19    0000000000000000000********
16: 5 (30600)     25         18    000000000000000000*******
16:10 (30900)     27         19    0000000000000000000********
16:15 (31200)     29         18    000000000000000000***********
16:20 (31500)     29         20    00000000000000000000*********
16:25 (31800)     32         24    000000000000000000000000********
16:30 (32100)     32         26    00000000000000000000000000******
16:35 (32400)     31         23    00000000000000000000000********
16:40 (32700)     29         23    00000000000000000000000******
16:45 (33000)     30         22    0000000000000000000000********
16:50 (33300)     28         21    000000000000000000000*******
16:55 (33600)     25         19    0000000000000000000******
17: 0 (33900)     24         17    00000000000000000*******
17: 5 (34200)     22         18    000000000000000000****
17:10 (34500)     20         15    000000000000000*****
17:15 (34800)     18         13    0000000000000*****
17:20 (35100)     15          9    000000000******
17:25 (35400)     13          9    000000000****
17:30 (35700)     11          9    000000000***
17:35 (36000)     10          8    00000000**
17:40 (36300)     10          9    000000000*
17:45 (36600)      9          8    00000000*
17:50 (36900)      8          4    0000
17:55 (37200)      4          4    0000
18: 0 (37500)      1          1    0
18: 5 (37800)      0          0    0
```

Figure IIID-31. Number of users.

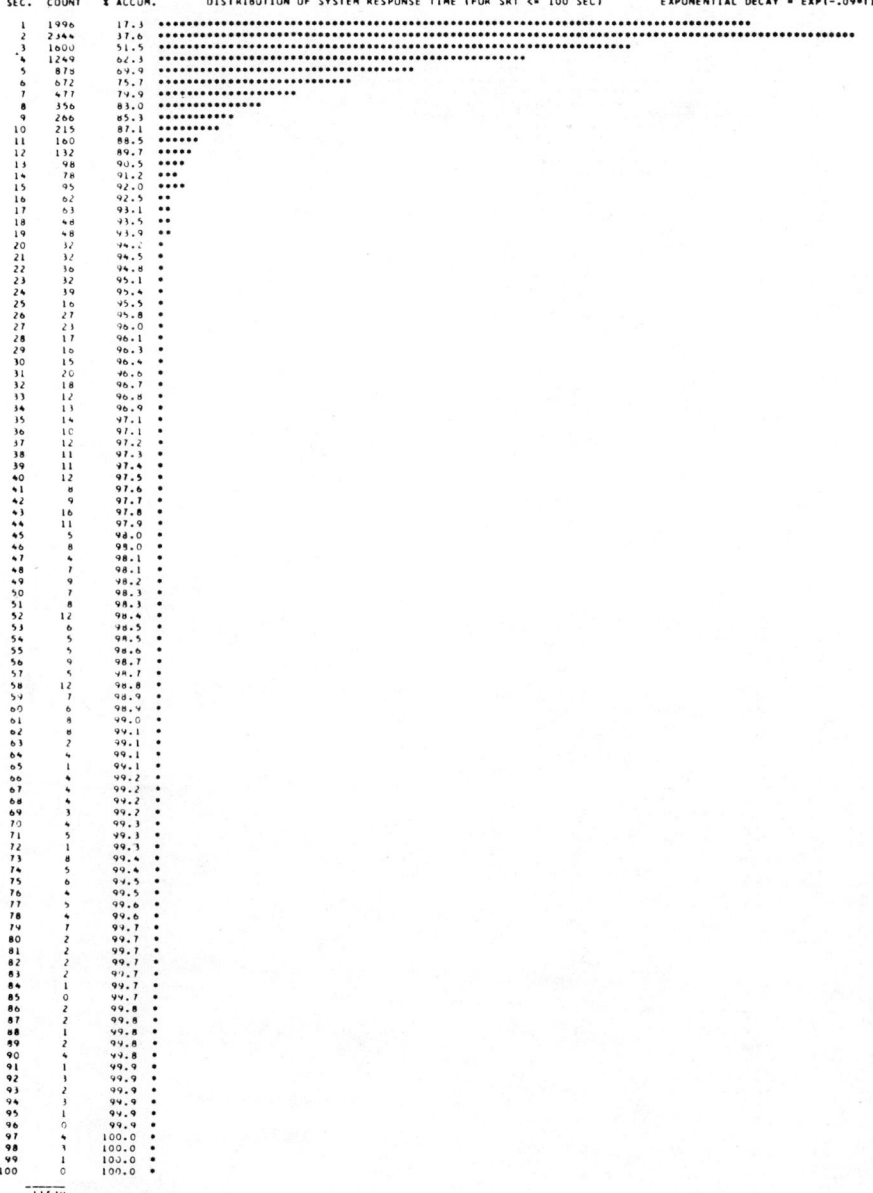

Figure IIID-32. Frequency of system response time.

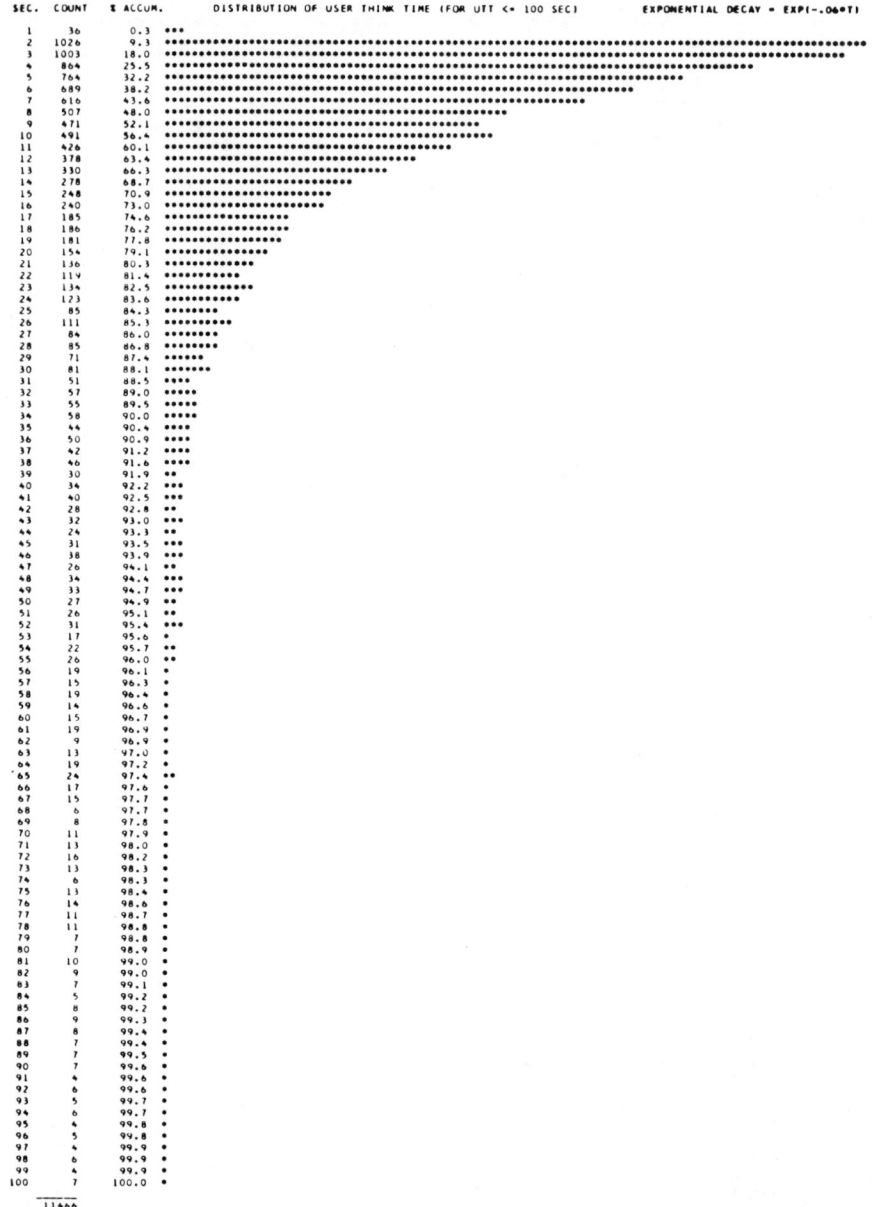

Figure IIID-33. Frequency of user response time.

```
TIME         SYSTEM RESPONSE TIME    AVERAGE FOR THE SESSION=   9.7    (FOR SAT STEP AVG <= 100 SEC)
7:35 (    0)    -1.9  *
7:40 (  300)    42.4  ******************************************
7:45 (  600)     0.7  *
7:50 (  900)     1.6  *
7:55 ( 1200)     0.9  *
8: 0 ( 1500)     0.6  *
8: 5 ( 1800)     1.4  *
8:10 ( 2100)     2.4  **
8:15 ( 2400)     1.2  *
8:20 ( 2700)    10.4  ***********
8:25 ( 3000)     2.9  ***
8:30 ( 3300)     2.2  **
8:35 ( 3600)     6.3  *******
8:40 ( 3900)     3.7  ****
8:45 ( 4200)     4.3  ****
8:50 ( 4500)     2.8  ***
8:55 ( 4800)     7.0  *******
9: 0 ( 5100)     3.7  ****
9: 5 ( 5400)     6.0  ******
9:10 ( 5700)     4.8  *****
9:15 ( 6000)     7.6  ********
9:20 ( 6300)    11.5  ************
9:25 ( 6600)    11.4  ************
9:30 ( 6900)     7.1  ********
9:35 ( 7200)     6.7  *******
9:40 ( 7500)     6.4  *******
9:45 ( 7800)     8.0  ********
9:50 ( 8100)    10.3  ***********
9:55 ( 8400)    20.6  *********************
10: 0 ( 8700)   32.1  *********************************
10: 5 ( 9000)    8.9  *********
10:10 ( 9300)   12.2  *************
10:15 ( 9600)   23.7  ************************
10:20 ( 9900)    7.0  *******
10:25 (10200)   10.8  ***********
10:30 (10500)   15.9  ****************
10:35 (10800)   11.2  ************
10:40 (11100)   12.9  *************
10:45 (11400)    8.2  *********
10:50 (11700)    9.8  **********
10:55 (12000)    9.2  **********
11: 0 (12300)   14.0  ***************
11: 5 (12600)   11.3  ************
11:10 (12900)   11.3  ************
11:15 (13200)   15.9  ****************
11:20 (13500)   29.7  ******************************
11:25 (13800)   13.4  **************
11:30 (14100)    0.0  *
11:35 (14400)    0.0  *
11:40 (14700)    0.9  *
11:45 (15000)    3.0  ***
11:50 (15300)   10.0  **********
11:55 (15600)   11.6  ************
12: 0 (15900)    4.2  ****
12: 5 (16200)    5.7  ******
12:10 (16500)    8.0  ********
12:15 (16800)    5.0  *****
12:20 (17100)    7.2  *******
12:25 (17400)    4.7  *****
12:30 (17700)   13.4  **************
12:35 (18000)    8.2  *********
12:40 (18300)    5.4  *****
12:45 (18600)    6.6  *******
12:50 (18900)    5.7  ******
12:55 (19200)   15.8  ****************
13: 0 (19500)    4.6  *****
13: 5 (19800)    6.4  *******
13:10 (20100)   14.0  ***************
13:15 (20400)    8.6  *********
13:20 (20700)    7.8  ********
13:25 (21000)   13.5  **************
13:30 (21300)    5.4  *****
13:35 (21600)    7.2  ********
13:40 (21900)    3.6  ****
13:45 (22200)    5.4  ****
13:50 (22500)    4.3  ****
13:55 (22800)    5.6  ******
14: 0 (23100)    4.6  *****
14: 5 (23400)    8.1  *********
14:10 (23700)    5.1  *****
14:15 (24000)    8.3  *********
14:20 (24300)    5.1  *****
14:25 (24600)   28.2  *****************************
14:30 (24900)    8.8  *********
14:35 (25200)   11.5  ************
14:40 (25500)   12.3  *************
14:45 (25800)    9.0  **********
14:50 (26100)   17.0  *****************
14:55 (26400)    6.8  *******
15: 0 (26700)   10.6  ***********
15: 5 (27000)    7.8  ********
15:10 (27300)   17.1  *****************
15:15 (27600)    9.1  **********
15:20 (27900)   10.3  ************
15:25 (28200)   13.6  **************
15:30 (28500)   17.6  ******************
15:35 (28800)    6.4  *******
15:40 (29100)    4.0  ****
15:45 (29400)   12.1  *************
15:50 (29700)   12.5  *************
15:55 (30000)    7.2  ********
16: 0 (30300)    5.5  ******
16: 5 (30600)    7.9  ********
16:10 (30900)   90.1  *****************************************************************************************
16:15 (31200)    7.2  ********
16:20 (31500)    8.7  *********
16:25 (31800)    4.3  ****
16:30 (32100)   24.8  *************************
16:35 (32400)   13.0  **************
16:40 (32700)    7.7  ********
16:45 (33000)   11.6  ************
16:50 (33300)   11.0  ************
16:55 (33600)    8.0  ********
17: 0 (33900)    6.4  *******
17: 5 (34200)    9.1  **********
17:10 (34500)    9.1  **********
17:15 (34800)    7.6  ********
17:20 (35100)   14.1  ***************
17:25 (35400)    3.5  ***
17:30 (35700)    4.0  ****
17:35 (36000)    6.4  *******
17:40 (36300)    3.9  ****
17:45 (36600)   13.2  **************
17:50 (36900)    6.8  *******
17:55 (37200)    6.0  ******
18: 0 (37500)    0.0  *
18: 5 (37800)    0.0  *
```

Figure IIID-34.   Average system response time.

Figure IIID-35. Average user response time.

Figure IIID-36. Parallel usage map.

REPORT OF POTENTIAL ABNORMALITIES

USERID	CRASH DESC	AT	ATTN RESP TIME AT DURATION		SRT AT DURATION		ABEND RESP TIME AT DURATION		USER THINK TIME AT DURATION	
ANDY****		0.0	10271.1	6143.8	0.0	0.0	0.0	0.0	0.0	0.0
ANDY****		0.0	16575.0	10440.5	0.0	0.0	0.0	0.0	0.0	0.0
APPEL***		0.0	0.0	0.0	0.0	0.0	0.0	0.0	33854.0	722.7
APPEL***		0.0	0.0	0.0	0.0	0.0	0.0	0.0	34084.3	193.9
APPEL***		0.0	0.0	0.0	0.0	0.0	0.0	0.0	34290.2	232.5
APPEL***		0.0	0.0	0.0	0.0	0.0	0.0	0.0	34522.7	180.5
APPEL***		0.0	0.0	0.0	0.0	0.0	0.0	0.0	35142.0	214.8
APPEL***		0.0	0.0	0.0	0.0	0.0	0.0	0.0	35388.4	269.5
APPEL***		0.0	0.0	0.0	0.0	0.0	0.0	0.0	35657.9	987.6
APPEL***		0.0	0.0	0.0	0.0	0.0	0.0	0.0	36674.2	160.2
ASCHE***	CRASH VICTIM	30325.8	0.0	0.0	19747.3	133.6	0.0	0.0	16750.3	198.7
ASCHE***		0.0	0.0	0.0	20498.6	167.7	0.0	0.0	17062.9	121.3
ASCHE***		0.0	0.0	0.0	29621.0	657.7	0.0	0.0	17560.7	239.0
ASCHE***		0.0	0.0	0.0	30379.5	114.3	0.0	0.0	17827.5	427.3
ASCHE***		0.0	0.0	0.0	32728.1	142.9	0.0	0.0	19455.2	128.9
ASCHE***		0.0	0.0	0.0	0.0	0.0	0.0	0.0	18893.9	185.5
BAKIS***		0.0	0.0	0.0	27979.5	105.3	0.0	0.0	27362.8	302.7
BAGLEY**	NO LOGOFF RECORDED	24917.6	0.0	0.0	0.0	0.0	0.0	0.0	23933.9	122.2
BAKIS***	CRASH VICTIM	30044.2	0.0	0.0	0.0	0.0	0.0	0.0	11256.2	237.1
BAKIS***		0.0	0.0	0.0	0.0	0.0	0.0	0.0	15117.1	517.9
BAKIS***		0.0	0.0	0.0	0.0	0.0	0.0	0.0	18434.2	163.2
BAKIS***	NO LOGOFF RECORDED	40503.6	0.0	0.0	37840.7	243.5	0.0	0.0	19639.4	147.0
BAKIS***		0.0	0.0	0.0	0.0	0.0	0.0	0.0	20002.6	781.9
BAKIS***		0.0	0.0	0.0	0.0	0.0	0.0	0.0	28744.3	187.6
BAKIS***		0.0	0.0	0.0	0.0	0.0	0.0	0.0	29000.9	413.7
BAKIS***		0.0	0.0	0.0	0.0	0.0	0.0	0.0	32818.9	345.0
BAKIS***		0.0	0.0	0.0	0.0	0.0	0.0	0.0	33340.3	108.0
BAKIS***		0.0	0.0	0.0	0.0	0.0	0.0	0.0	33820.9	125.9
BAKIS***		0.0	0.0	0.0	0.0	0.0	0.0	0.0	34048.8	573.6
BAKIS***		0.0	0.0	0.0	0.0	0.0	0.0	0.0	37824.9	362.6
BAKIS***		0.0	0.0	0.0	0.0	0.0	0.0	0.0	38823.5	362.3
BOIS***		0.0	0.0	0.0	15497.4	139.9	0.0	0.0	9658.5	434.9
BOIS***		0.0	0.0	0.0	27190.0	112.0	0.0	0.0	13229.4	752.5
BOIS***		0.0	0.0	0.0	0.0	0.0	0.0	0.0	14049.0	136.9
BOIS***		0.0	0.0	0.0	0.0	0.0	0.0	0.0	15331.6	165.8
BOIS***		0.0	0.0	0.0	0.0	0.0	0.0	0.0	15671.7	864.9
BOIS***		0.0	0.0	0.0	0.0	0.0	0.0	0.0	27095.3	212.9
BROFF***	NO LOGOFF RECORDED	40503.1	0.0	0.0	28546.9	356.7	0.0	0.0	13988.9	107.7
BROFF***		0.0	0.0	0.0	0.0	0.0	0.0	0.0	14500.7	352.8
BROFF***		0.0	0.0	0.0	0.0	0.0	0.0	0.0	15087.2	162.9
BROFF***		0.0	0.0	0.0	0.0	0.0	0.0	0.0	18387.4	154.8
BROFF***		0.0	0.0	0.0	0.0	0.0	0.0	0.0	18705.4	111.0
BROFF***		0.0	0.0	0.0	0.0	0.0	0.0	0.0	29030.1	735.3
BROFF***		0.0	0.0	0.0	0.0	0.0	0.0	0.0	34043.5	104.8
BUBLEY**		0.0	0.0	0.0	9277.0	224.1	0.0	0.0	0.0	0.0
CF2****	NO LOGOFF RECORDED	30156.1	24746.9	143.2	0.0	0.0	0.0	0.0	28427.5	259.8
CF2****		0.0	28891.7	1264.4	0.0	0.0	0.0	0.0	0.0	0.0
CONSIO**		0.0	0.0	0.0	37344.3	179.8	0.0	0.0	18800.5	904.5
CONSIO**		0.0	0.0	0.0	37560.5	187.4	0.0	0.0	19740.0	450.0
CONSIO**		0.0	0.0	0.0	0.0	0.0	0.0	0.0	20523.7	245.0
CONSIO**		0.0	0.0	0.0	0.0	0.0	0.0	0.0	36088.5	209.7
CONSIO**		0.0	0.0	0.0	0.0	0.0	0.0	0.0	36301.1	470.4
CONSIO**		0.0	0.0	0.0	0.0	0.0	0.0	0.0	36799.6	240.0
CONSIO**		0.0	0.0	0.0	0.0	0.0	0.0	0.0	37855.4	1803.8
COOLEY**		0.0	0.0	0.0	0.0	0.0	0.0	0.0	27400.7	231.1
COOLEY**		0.0	0.0	0.0	0.0	0.0	0.0	0.0	27645.9	123.0
COOLEY**		0.0	0.0	0.0	0.0	0.0	0.0	0.0	39335.5	291.0
COOLEY**		0.0	0.0	0.0	0.0	0.0	0.0	0.0	39721.0	130.1
COOLEY**		0.0	0.0	0.0	0.0	0.0	0.0	0.0	40056.0	187.3

Figure IIID-37. Potential abnormalities.

Note in Figure IIID-35 how the mean user responses lengthen before the lunch period and before quitting time. An interesting study would be to measure the effect of overtime or other unusual working conditions.

The system response time history is useful in calling attention to periods of system sluggishness. When such periods have been identified, another display, the Parallel Usage Map, is examined in detail.

A section of the Parallel Usage Map is shown in Figure IIID-36. Each column shows the sequence of commands issued by a given user. Each row shows the mix of commands being executed during an interval of time. The illustration shows eight users but in actual use shows up to 48 users. The principal output from this map is a tentative identification of combinations of commands, users or user practices that seem to cause degeneration of system response.

Finally, Figure IIID-37 is a listing of every "unusual" occurrence experienced by each user on a given day. "Unusual" occurrences are those in which either the system or the user exceeds a predetermined limit of normal performance. For example, one column of Figure IIID-37 tells whether a user was a victim of a system crash. Another column lists the time and duration of each system response the user experienced which exceeded a certain threshold.

This form of output is useful for system consultants to identify which problems are occurring and the number of users affected. The output provides data on the quality of service provided the users, and identifies users having persistent problems which may require special tutoring or assistance.

Obviously such usage data is sensitive and personal, so long as the identity of the user is associated with it. Precautions should be enforced to ensure the privacy of the individual user in much the same way that personnel and medical records are guarded. In the environment described above, the following precautions were taken: (1) The user was notified that usage was being measured at each sign on. (2) No one was given access to data with the names associated except the head consultant. After this use, names are removed and the data used only statistically. (3) The head consultant's use of the data is limited to determining if any users show need for special instruction or assistance, and asking such users if they desire such aid (no copies to management).

In summary, a set of simple charts and tables can provide user-system performance data of value to many different people:

- Management personnel can derive estimates of service quality and its degradation under loading.
- Users can compare individual performance and service with the average for the session.
- System programmers can use the results to design better schedulers or to detect bottlenecks in the system.
- Psychologists and operations analysts can obtain insights on problem solving behavior and performance under various conditions of environment and support.
- Consultants can determine users having chronic problems and offer assistance accordingly.

References

1. H. W. Lynch, "Time Sharing Measurements," IBM Research Report RC 3589, October 1971.
2. M. R. Barbacci, "A Tool for TSS/360 Usage Analysis," IBM Research Reports RC 3017, August 1970.
3. W. R. Deniston, "SIPE: A TSS/360 Software Measurement Technique," *Proceedings of the SJCC*, AFIPS Press, Montvale, N.J., 1969.

E. CONTROL

Introduction

In this section we consider various strategies and mechanisms for controlling the distribution, use, and quality of computer-based services within an organization. We examine allocation policies and contractual arrangements from the perspectives of the user and the computing center, and consider the use of pricing policies and scheduling algorithms as management tools for controlling service resources. Throughout this examination we try to perceive the degree to which *time*, rather than *money*, in fact serves in the short term as the basis for the exercise of control, and how our control strategies should accommodate to that reality.

As noted at the beginning of Section III, basic differences between administrative data processing and computing services call for somewhat different management strategies. The effects of these differences seem most evident in the area of control. Control strategies developed for ADP and later applied to computing services, or vice versa, can and do cause problems. In many cases these problems become evident only after a consolidation of computing facilities has been effected. Often, then, management policies that have long sufficed in a particular narrow usage environment are found to be ill-suited to the new customer set.

To set the stage for the following discussions, let us review some of the differences between ADP and computing services, understanding the differences to be general tendencies rather than universal truths.

ADP tends to be preprogrammed, highly disciplined, and relatively static. There is little choice of mode or extent of usage left to the user. As a consequence, the workload tends to be inelastic. The response requirement tends to be deadline, that is, the output is needed by a certain calendar time. Batch processing and preprogrammed inquiry are the dominant modes of usage.

The use of computing services, in contrast, tends to be less predictable and constrained. There is more choice between types of services and modes of usage, to suit the style of the individual. The work-progress of the user is increasingly dependent on the quality of the support services. His response requirements tend to be the sooner the better. When the user of computing services receives better (faster and/or cheaper) services, he usually responds by resubmitting faster, thus enlarging the workload. This positive feedback creates an elastic workload. The loading tends to peak strongly during normal working hours.

An example of the consequences of these differences can be seen in the effects of direct cost-recovery charging methods, as has been pointed out by Nielsen (1):

"An effect of direct costing stems from the fact that the provision of computer services can be characterized in the short run as a high fixed cost, low marginal cost operation. Thus the cost per unit of computing is greatly influenced by the heavy usage of the facility. When demand is heavy, the cost is low, thereby encouraging even further usage and worsening the turnaround situation. When demand is light, the cost is high, discouraging use of an already lightly loaded facility. In situations where users are required to use the cheapest facilities available, work is driven off lightly loaded systems to more heavily loaded ones; just the opposite of what would be desired for the most efficient utilization of the available resources."

This basic instability described by Nielsen has not precluded the satisfactory use of direct costing in many ADP environments. In such places direct costing has worked because the workload is relatively fixed and few options are available to users—in effect there is nothing to control in the short term. However, applying the same direct costing methods to a computing service environment that offers real choices to the users certainly renders the system more difficult to control.

In the following sections we will take the characteristics of computing services as a point of departure, and attempt to develop and rationalize appropriate control strategies.

Is Pricing the Answer*

Computing service is one of today's scarcer resources. Despite the tremendous growth in the number and capabilities of computers during the last 20 years, the demand for computing still exceeds the available capacity.

---

* This section has been excerpted from Norman R. Nielsen (2) with the permission of the author.

The manifestation of this shortage of computing power is undoubtedly quite apparent to the reader. Either he is unable to obtain all of the computer time or computer resources that he might desire, or he is unable to obtain those resources when he would like them. Long turnaround times in a batch processing system are symptomatic of this latter problem. Thus most computer installations are faced with a resource allocation problem. How should the unlimited computing resources available be distributed among the much greater demands of an installation's user community?

Despite the existence of this problem, there has not until recently been much interest in trying to find better ways of allocating computer resources. The existing situation was agreed by all to be undesirable, but the design of single stream processing systems with off-line batching tended to limit the possibilities for improvement. Now, however, the widespread use of third generation systems has provided many installations with an opportunity to make explicit resource allocation decisions. As a result much interest is developing in the question of computer resource allocation, and discussions on the subject are becoming more frequent.

Computer center managers often react to the resource allocation problem as being something outside their area of concern. A typical reaction would be, "This is a computer center with serious work to do; let the economists play their allocation games somewhere else." Other managers are of the opinion that any allocation scheme which might be used would be unfair to some members of the user community and that it would therefore be undesirable to use any allocation mechanism.

However, there is a fallacy in trying to avoid these problems by not having an allocation mechanism for computer resources. If resource allocation is not done explicitly, it will be done implicitly; there is no such thing as "no allocation." Ignoring the problem will not make it go away; one will only choose an allocation mechanism by default. In most cases the default mechanism is a first-come, first-served (FCFS) procedure. This is particularly true in situations where there is "no rationing" of computing, where everyone can submit as many jobs as frequently as he wishes. Of course, delays in turnaround act as an implicit rationing mechanism. As delays become longer and longer, demand gradually becomes choked off. Each user sooner or later arrives at the point where there is nothing further he can do until he receives some of his previous runs back.

An FCFS type of allocation mechanism is not necessarily a bad one. It treats all jobs equally. If in fact all jobs are of equal importance, then FCFS is appropriate (and, conveniently, quite easy to employ with a computer system). However, this happy situation rarely exists in practice, as is demonstrated by the inability of installations to live with a pure FCFS procedure. It becomes necessary to abridge the basic procedure by use of administrative regulations. The following are illustrative:

1. "No jobs longer than 10 minutes during the prime shift because we want to provide good turnaround."
2. "No jobs with a memory requirement of greater than 25K words will be run during the prime shift."
3. "Hold work from Group B for a while after it is submitted, since they have been using too much time lately."
4. "Process Joe's jobs as soon as possible after they are submitted, since he has a crucial project and a tight deadline."

The fact that resort has had to be made to these types of overriding procedures is a clear indication that the FCFS rule is not serving the need adequately. In other words, the default choice of FCFS is being judged as inappropriate by those who tried to avoid making allocation decisions in the first place. The trouble is that the administrative regulations, exemptions, and other steps designed to temper the effects of the FCFS procedure are often made or determined in practice by the individuals least qualified to make those types of decisions.

In some cases a computer operator will make some of these decisions based upon individual friendships or upon compassion for an individual who can tell a convincing story. In other cases these decisions will be made by the computer center manager. However, while he is technically competent in the computer field, he is generally not in a position to judge the importance of Smith's biochemical analysis relative to Jones' file update—that is, to determine which projects should be exempted from size and run-time restrictions. Further, even if he could make these decisions properly, there are many other more important problems for his attention. Clearly, then, a better means of making decisions about computer resource allocation is required.

Before turning to the question of better decision making procedures, it is appropriate first to consider the question of who should make the allocation decisions. Clearly, the individual or group with the most global view of the goals and priorities of the entire organization (i.e., the organization containing the computer center) should take the lead in allocating computer resources. It is this group that has the purview to determine whether project A is more important than project B. On the other hand, this group will have neither the technical background nor the detailed project knowledge necessary to make detailed resource allocation decisions. Further, there is not even sufficient time available for the group to operate at this level, since the number of decisions necessary to schedule resources on this basis is staggering.

Moving to the other end of the scale, one could let the actual users of the computer make these decisions themselves. They have the detailed project knowledge necessary to specify resource requirements. However, this group of individuals has neither the perspective nor the objectivity necessary to resolve conflicting requirements of different projects.

Another alternative lies in the middle ground. Someone like the computer center manager could make the necessary allocation decisions. However, as had been brought out above, this individual has neither the broad perspective of the organization as a whole nor the detailed knowledge of the requirements of the various projects. Thus, in a sense, he is the least qualified individual to make the allocation decisions.

It is possible to capitalize upon the relative advantages offered by these possible decision making groups (while at the same time circumventing their relative disadvantages) through the use of a two-stage procedure. Under such a procedure each level would make those decisions for which it is best qualified. The top-level policy group would make decisions about the general level of resource utilization by the various projects. The users would make the detailed resource decisions. The management of the computer center would concern itself not with allocating resources but with providing as large a quantity as possible of the most appropriate resources.

First, some units of global resource utilization must be established. These units may be dollars, yen, points, hours, or simply computer units (CU's). The exact quantity to be created for a given period is immaterial; it can be chosen so that allocations and prices (see below) result in convenient denominations. Letting x CU's represent the total amount of computing which can be done at the computer center over the next period (e.g. month), the high level policy committee can then allocate CU's to the various projects or user groups in the organization. A user given $1/10$ of x CU's would in some sense be given 10 percent of the computing resources. Thus the policy group is making the general overall allocation decisions, the decisions which it is best equipped to make.

The next step is to translate these general indications into specific allocation decisions without an excessive expenditure of people and/or computer resources. One mechanism uses a set of exchange rates or prices at which the CU's are convertible into specific resources. Then the user can make decisions as required about the mix of computer services to seek. He does this in the light of his own needs, tempered by the policy guideline (budget). Although each user will pursue his own self-interest, his actions will move the center toward providing an appropriate mix of services which will mesh with the overall goals and priorities of the organization. The situation is somewhat akin to Adam Smith's invisible hand of the marketplace. Such a procedure has threefold benefit. First, the most knowledgeable persons are making the detailed resource decisions. Second, there is now an economic motivation to make good decisions. Third, the decisions work for the good of the entire organization.

The computer center can also use the price structure to motivate desirable behavior. Although users do not intentionally degrade the service of others, they are often inconsiderate. Requests for users to submit jobs with a "process now" or a "process tonight" label generally meet with little success. Perhaps the user feels that he just might want to see those results later in the day; perhaps he wants to process the job now so he can be sure that it will be ready for him. In any event, most jobs are submitted for current processing, thereby needlessly degrading turnaround time. However, by setting different CU exchange rates for current as opposed to overnight processing, the user is encouraged to weight the relative value of these services to him at that point in the project's life.

The effectiveness of this approach has been demonstrated at several installations. As a result, the computer center can process first those jobs for which turnaround is important and then the jobs which are less urgent. In this way, turnaround can be reduced for those users waiting for output. Even if the computer were to process the very same jobs over a given period time, the value of the output as perceived by the users would be greater. Thus, without adding additional equipment, the computer center can increase the value of the services it provides.

It must be noted, however, that the foregoing is to some extent dependent upon a scarcity of resources. If the policy committee mistakenly grants a user far more CU's than he requires, he may well behave in an undesirable fashion. In other words, if appropriate budgetary control and review are not exercised by management in the upper stage, improper or undesirable allocations may well be made at the lower stage. This does not, however, indicate that the procedures employed at the second stage are necessarily improper.

The actual mechanics used in implementing the aforementioned type of allocation procedure will vary from case to case. In one situation the computer may be totally funded by the organization at the outset (i.e., as an overhead expense). The computer committee then allocates the entire resource via CU's. In another situation the computer center may charge real dollars rather than CU's for its services, operating as a separate profit center. In the latter case, decisions are made by the policy committee about the value of the computing which particular projects should perform. There is never any explicit consideration as to what fraction of the available resource is being given to any particular project, since the computer center will "earn" sufficient revenue to provide adequate facilities to enable all those wishing to purchase service to do so. This particular approach, however, is predicated upon the existence of some general level of computing activity. If the level of corporate support should fluctuate sharply, the computer center may have difficulty reacting quickly enough to avoid bankruptcy or saturation.

In discussing the second stage of resource allocation it was stated that the individual users would make the detailed resource allocation decisions through their exchange of CU's for the various resources. This leads to the question of how exchange rates or prices should be determined for the various resources. One might foresee a free market with supply and demand determining prices. However, this would more likely result in chaos than efficient resource allocation. First, it would take a degree of effort for the user to bid on each of the resources. Second, the prices of the various resources could fluctuate sharply and rapidly as demand surged and ebbed from moment to moment. A computer user has a fair degree of flexibility in selecting the mix of resources he is to use for a particular problem at the time he formulates the design of the program or over long periods of time as the program is modified. He generally does not, however, have the flexibility to change significantly the mix of resources required from one day to the next.

Accordingly, the base price structure must be relatively fixed, appearing stable over that period of time during which most users can neither effectively nor efficiently adjust their mix of computing resources. In this connection it may be desirable to offer long-term or advance contracts for various resources, so that a user can protect himself from price fluctuations. For example, when a project manager makes a commitment to complete a particular project by a given date within a given budget, he is in a sense making a commitment to obtain certain computing resources for some fixed expenditure. An advance contract would provide a mechanism for the project manager to shift the risk to the computer center, to gain assurance that he will in fact be able to acquire the necessary computing resources within his budget. These contracts might be offered at either a premium or a discount relative to existing rates depending upon the extent of anticipated rate changes, the value of the planning information which such a contract provides the computer center, and the value of the risk reduction provided to the user.

If a computer center is totally funded internally, then the amount of service which can be provided during a period must approximately be valued at the amount of computer units distributed by the policy body. Prices can be set accordingly by the computer center within this framework. In the case of a center which is earning its revenue, the long-run capital and operating costs can provide the framework within which to set prices.

Note the emphasis placed upon long run. If such a center tries to match cost and revenue in the short run, the use of charging may well backfire. When a new system is installed there is generally substantial excess capacity (programs have to be converted, users educated, etc.). To recover costs with low utilization implies uneconomically high charges on average. Thus users will be discouraged rather than encouraged to use the system. The situation is just the reverse in the later part of a system's life. Demand has been built up, so utilization is high. This implies low prices (to avoid a profit). However, the bargain rates attract further demand to the already overloaded system. The use of long-run costs as a basis for setting average rate levels will mitigate this type of problem, although it will increase forecasting and other problems for a computer center's management.

While the preceding provides an indication of what "revenue" should be generated through the overall price structure, it does not say anything about the level of individual prices. These prices may be set to achieve a variety of purposes. As was brought out in the previous section, particular resource prices may be set so as to encourage or discourage particular types of use. However, the decision making (on whether to use a particular service or resource) is decentralized; the computer center's management does not make any decisions relative to individual projects.

Another advantage accruing to those installations currently operating on a costing basis would be the elimination of enforced idle computer time due to an insufficiency of funds on the part of some users. With a pricing system, there can be poorer and poorer levels of service with lower and lower prices attached. At some point the price becomes sufficiently low that someone is able to pay for additional service. Thus the full resources of the computer system can be utilized without suffering the usual problems of system saturation. It should be noted in this connection, though, that pricing is addressing the problem of system utilization; it is not directly addressing the question of capital and operating cost recovery.

Pricing also permits a computer center's management to play a role in maximizing the value of the services which the center is providing to the parent organization. Over a period of time various resources or services will be underutilized, while others will be in great demand. The prices for these services can, within limits, be adjusted downward and upward, respectively, in order to redistribute demand and improve the overall utilization of the computer resource.

However, the great advantage of a price mechanism stems from the comparison of the prices which the user community is willing to pay for various services with the costs (savings) associated with providing additional (reduced) quantities of those services. Such comparisons enable the manager to make meaningful judgments about configuring the system hardware and software so as to adjust the types and quantities of service offered. Thus adjustments can be made to provide more of those services which are of greatest value to the users and less of those which are of least value. The manager is given a clear indication of the preferences of the users; he no longer has to act upon what he thinks they want or the vocal minority say they want. Management is then in a position in which it can work to provide greater computing power or more valuable computing service to the organization without necessarily increasing the expenditures on computing. Of course, when expansion is warranted, the usage data will provide a clear indication of the areas in which expansion would be most valuable to the organization as a while. In the case where actual dollars are used to purchase computer service or where users can acquire additional CU's with funds from other budgets, management will have a very demonstrable indication of demand and hence of expansion requirements.

Scheduling Strategies

In the previous section it was noted that a properly designed pricing system would give the user a means of declaring his particular needs for service and, at the same time, provide a deterrent against exaggerating those needs.

Once the user has expressed his requirements, the computing facility needs a means of responding sensitively to those diverse requirements. This is accomplished by the service scheduling strategy.

The scheduling of a multi-usage computer service system is a complex exercise. This complexity, in part, results from conflicting demands placed on the scheduler. On one hand, the scheduler is expected to balance demands on the various internal resources of the system in order to maximize throughput (5), i.e. "resource-oriented scheduling"; On the other hand the scheduler is expected to provide system response times which meet the expectations of the users (6), i.e., "service-oriented scheduling."

Generally, it has not been feasible to design a scheduler that can resolve these conflicting demands in anything approaching an optimal manner. In the meantime, the scheduling problem has sometimes been tackled by decomposing it into two separate scheduling operations. In some cases the service-oriented scheduling is accomplished manually, by the operator overriding the resource-oriented software scheduler. In other systems, two separate software schedulers are used, the first acting as a service-oriented job scheduler and the second as a resource-oriented sub-job, or task, scheduler. If these schedulers are tuned empirically to meet their respective objectives, the results are sometimes quite respectable.

Our interest in usage issues draws our attention to service-oriented scheduling. We will examine just a few aspects of this topic, referring the reader to References 8–10, for example, for a more extensive treatment.

Some examples of service-oriented scheduling strategies are:

- First-come-first served (FCFS).
- Round robin (at fixed time intervals jobs are interrupted, job from head of queue serviced next) (RR).
- Smallest-job first.

Professor Leonard Kleinrock has shown, in an elegant paper (7), that a number of these strategies are closely related. He shows that scheduling strategies can be characterized by a single parameter β/α provided the job priority is linearly dependent on waiting time and serving time with incremental rates α and β, respectively, as shown in Figure IIIE-1. With rates α and β taking on positive, negative and zero values, the regions occupied by various strategies are indicated in Figure IIIE-2. The region in the first

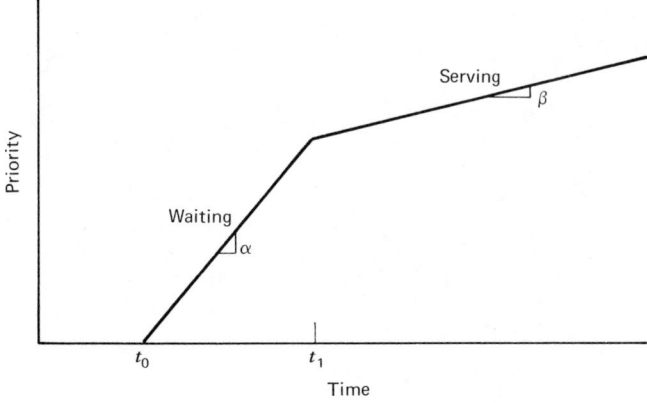

Figure IIIE-1. Behavior of the time-varying priority.

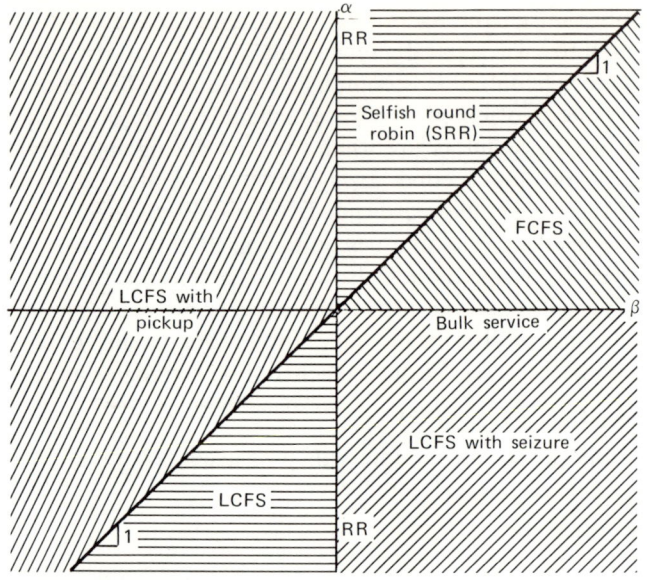

Figure IIIE-2. The structure of the general model.

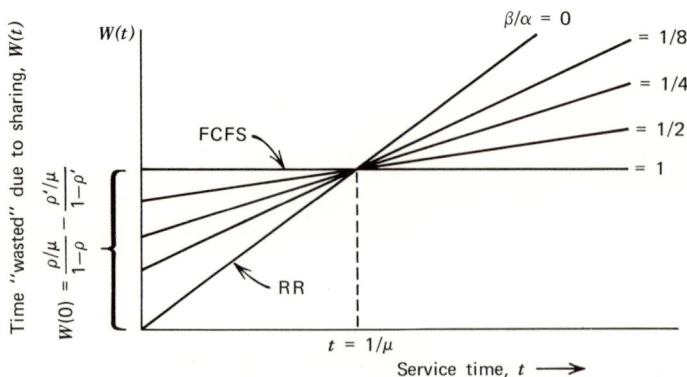

Figure IIIE-3. Performance of the SRR system.

quadrant in which $\alpha > 0$, $\beta \geq 0$ is of particular interest:

- When $0 < \alpha \leq \beta$, the strategy is FCFS.
- When $\beta = 0$, the strategy is RR.
- When $0 < \beta < \alpha$, the strategy is called selfish round robin.*

As shown in Figure IIIE-3, the choice of strategy from this continuum does not affect *mean* waiting time for the entire job stream, but does provide a means of controlling the relative responsiveness to be delivered as a function of job size.

DEADLINE SCHEDULING. We would like now to reiterate an assertion made earlier, in Section IIIB. The assertion was that maximizing the value of services delivered would seem to be a good objective for a computer service system—probably better, for example, than maximizing the utilization of the system.

It was also observed that the value of services delivered could be increased by awarding differential priority to users having greater urgency.

A value-maximizing strategy of this sort could be implemented by a computing installation if sufficient value-time information were provided by the user. Utility functions such as those shown in Figure IIIE-4, along with accurate estimates of service time required, would be sufficient, for example.

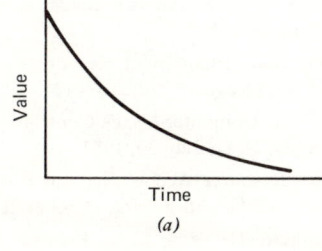

(a)

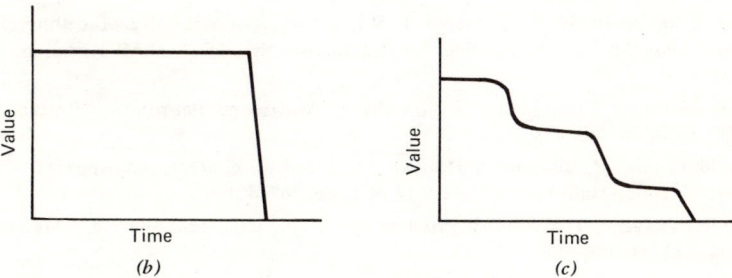

(b) (c)

Figure IIIE-4. User utility functions.

* So called because jobs obtaining service try to maintain the service capacity for themselves.

Given such utility functions, and assuming that service-directed decisions can be considered independently of resource-directed decisions, a reasonable strategy is to select for processing that job whose value will diminish the most during the next time interval.

In fact, utility functions such as those in Figure IIIE-4 are not often available. An approximation to such a value-maximizing strategy is coming into increasing use—referred to as deadline scheduling. The attractiveness of this approximation is based on the fact that most requests for computer service fall naturally into one of two classes:

1. ASAP—The output is needed As-Soon-As-Possible, with a utility function similar to that shown in Figure IIIE-4*a*.
2. DEADLINE—The job completion time is immaterial as long as it meets a specified deadline, with a utility function similar to that shown in Figure IIIE-4*b*.

If, then, users are given the opportunity, and the motivation, to declare for ASAP or deadline service, with the deadline specified—the scheduling strategy can enhance the value of the services delivered any time a deadline job can be deferred in favor of an ASAP job.

References

1. N. R. Nielsen, "Flexible pricing: An Approach to the Allocation of Computer Resources," *FJCC*, 1968, pp. 521–531.
2. N. R. Nielsen, The Allocation of Computer Resources—Is Pricing the Answer?, *Communications of the ACM*, **13**, (August 1970), 467–474.
3. M. M. Lehman, "CASCOM- Computer Usage Control System," IBM Research Report RC 3447, Yorktown Heights, N.Y., July 30, 1971.
4. L. L. Selwyn, "Computer Resource Accounting and Pricing," Proceedings of 2nd Annual SIGCOSIM, (ACM), Gaithersburg, Md., October 26, 1971, pp. 14–24.
5. S. Sherman, Forest Baskett, III, and J. C. Browne, "Trace-Driven Modeling and Analysis of CPU Scheduling in a Multiprogramming System," *Communications of the ACM*, **15**, 12 (December 1972), 1063–1069.
6. D. D. Chamberlin, H. P. Schlaeppi, I. Wladawsky, "Comparative Modelling of Time Slicing and Deadline Scheduling for Interactive Systems," IBM Research Report RC3378.
7. L. A. Kleinrock, "Continuum of time-sharing scheduling algorithms, "Proceedings of SJCC, 1970, pp. 453–458.
8. Harold Lorin, "Parallelism in Hardware and Software: Real and Apparent Concurrency," Prentice-Hall, Englewood Cliffs, N.J., pp. 367–431.
9. M. Greenberger, "The Priority Problem and Computer Time Sharing," Management Science, 12, 11, July 1966, 888–906.
10. J. Blatney, S. R. Clark, T. A. Rourke, "On the Performance of Time-Sharing Systems by Simulation, CACM, 15, 6, June 1972, 411–420.

F. THE QUALITY OF THE MAN-SYSTEM INTERFACE

In this book we have seen many examples of the use of computers in the service of man.

The people who have used the computer in these examples have, for the most part, been scientists or engineers; in a real sense they have pioneered in the use of general computing services.

Clearly, however, the need for these kinds of information services is much broader than that. Businessmen, nonscientific professionals, consumers, service workers, and so on, all have, to some degree, problems of gathering and examining information, deciding on courses of action, reviewing results, and so on. One reason the use of computer services has not spread as rapidly among this wider population is economic—the services simply have cost more than these individuals could justify. As computing costs continue to decrease, this barrier will dissolve—it is only a question of time.

Another barrier exists and will be more difficult to remove: a barrier caused by the strangeness and complexity of the terminals and languages that comprise the interface between man and the information system. Scientists and technologists approached computers with two advantages, as compared to the average person. First, they were used to dealing with abstract concepts and strange notation, so that computer programming did not seem completely crazy. Second, they were accustomed to using complex and expensive devices, of other sorts, in their work. Even with these advantages, scientists have frequently been frustrated in trying to exploit the computer's full benefits, by various flaws in the user–system interface.

Our intent in this section is to call attention to some of these problems, to explore some benefits of computer usage yet untapped, and to describe some exploratory activities which promise to take us in these directions.

Programming Languages for Specialized Application Areas*

Introduction

The purpose of this paper is to provide some of the background and perspective on the existence, classifications, and general characteristics of those languages which are oriented toward a specialized application area.

---

* This section was excerpted from J. E. Sammet, "An Overview of Programming Languages for Specialized Applications Areas," *Proceedings of the SJCC,* AFIPS Press Montvale, N.J., 1972, pp. 299–311. Reprinted with permission of the author.

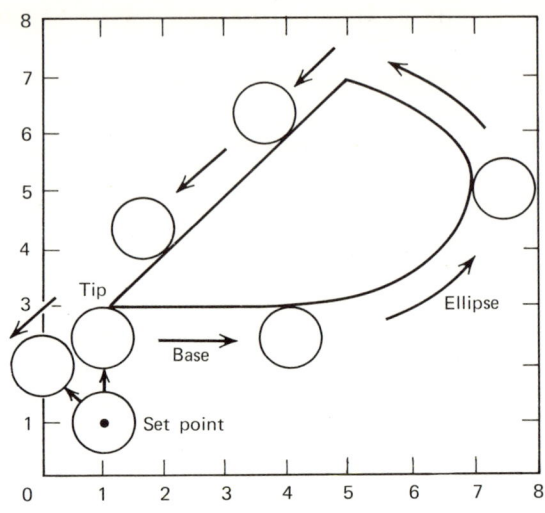

Part Program	Explanation
CUTTER/1	Use a one inch diameter cutter.
TOLER/.005	Tolerance of cut is .005 inch.
FEDRAT/80	Use feedrate of 80 inches per minute.
HEAD/1	Use head number 1.
MODE/1	Operate tool in mode number 1.
SPINDL/2400	Turn on spindle. Set at 2400 rpm.
COOLNT/FLOOD	Turn on coolant. Use flood setting.
PT1 = POINT/4, 5	Define a reference point, PT1, as the point with coordinates (4, 5).
FROM/(SETPT = POINT/1, 1)	Start the tool from the point called SETPT, which is defined as the point with coordinates (1, 1).
INDIRP/(TIP = POINT/1, 3)	Aim the tool in the direction of the point called TIP, which is defined as the point with coordinates (1, 3).
BASE = LINE/TIP, AT ANGL, 0	Defined the line called BASE as the line through the point TIP which makes an angle of 0 degrees with the horizontal.
GOTO/BASE	Go to the line BASE.
TL RGT, GORGT/BASE	With the tool on the right, go right along the line BASE.
GOFWD/(ELLIPS/ CENTER, PT1, 3, 2, 0)	Go forward along the ellipse with center at PT1, semi-major axis = 3, semi-minor axis = 2, and major axis making an angle of 0 degrees with the horizontal.
GOLFT/(LINE/2, 4, 1, 3), PAST, BASE	Go left along the line joining the points (2, 4) and (1, 3) past the line BASE.
GOTO/SETPT	Go to the point SETPT in a straight line.
COOLNT/OFF	Turn off coolant flow.
SPINDL/OFF	Turn off spindle.
END	This is the end of the machine control unit operation.
FINI	and the finish of the part program.

Figure IIIF-1. APT (machine tool control). *Source.* S. Hori, *Automatically Programmed Tools,* Armour Research Foundation of Illinois Institute of Technology, AZ-240, (November 1962).

F. THE QUALITY OF THE MAN-SYSTEM INTERFACE

The earliest of the *major* "specialized languages" seems to be APT, developed at MIT by 1955, for numerical machine tool control. A small program—shown in Figure IIIF-1 illustrates in an intuitive way the type of language with which this paper is concerned. It to perhaps unfortunate—but is certainly quite true—that one of the major reasons for the proliferation of programming languages is that designing and implementing languages are fun, and there is a very large NIH (Not Invented Here) factor that makes even minor deficiencies in an existing language a justifiable cause for the development of a new one. This represents the less productive aspect of the proliferation. However, the important cases (meaning the languages widely used) fulfill a bona fide need for a language that can be used by people who don't really understand programming. The specialized languages help these people work in their own professional jargon. The motivation for the development usually comes when individuals find that for each existing language there are facilities that they want, and which they think the language should legitimately contain, but which are not basically available in the language. It is important to emphasize the "not basically avaiable" aspect, as well as recognizing that there is a value judgment involved on this issue. There are certainly cases where FORTRAN has been used to write payroll programs but it is unlikely that anybody would seriously contend that such usage was appropriate; alternatively, people should not condemn FORTRAN for being ill-suited for writing data processing applications since that was not its intent. Similarly, COBOL has been used to generate differential equation programs, but that is certainly a perversion of its major intent. Thus, in considering whether an existing language should be used for a particular problem, its avowed intent must be kept well in mind. This applies not only to the syntax and semantics of the language itself, but also to the type of the machine or environment for which it was designed. A language suitable for use in a batch system is not necessarily well-suited for use in an interactive mode, even though a compiler or an interpreter for the language can indeed be put into a time sharing system. Similarly, a language which provides very good interactive facilities does not necessarily provide the broad flexibility and control normally found (or needed) in batch programs of great complexity.

In order to more explicitly establish the level of language that is being discussed, the defining characteristics of a higher level language are considered to be the following: (1) machine code knowledge is unnecesary, i.e., the user does not have to know the machine instructions available on any computer; (2) there must be good potential for converting a program written in a higher level language onto another machine; that is equivalent to saying that the language must be basically machine-independent (but since we know that no languages to date are *completely* machine-independent, what is being stipulated is a good potential for conversion to another computer); (3) there must be an instruction explosion, i.e., for most of the statements that the user writes in the higher level language, the computer (through a compilation or interpretive process) should generate many more machine instructions; (4) the notation of the higher level language should be more problem-oriented than that of an assembly language, i.e., it should be more "natural" for the class of problems being solved.

Needs to be Met in Developing the Languages

There are several needs which must be met by a new language or a modification of an existing one. The major needs are functional capability, a style suitable for the application area, and efficiency.

FUNCTIONAL CAPABILITY. The inclusion of specific capability is probably the single most important need to be met by the application-oriented languages. Most of the deficiencies in a particular language actually reflect the omission of functional capabilities which a certain class of users used. For example, the FORTRAN user often wishes to do character manipulation, the COBOL user might wish to do floating point calculations, and the PL/I user might wish to do simulation. In considering functional capability, the three major issues are (a) the specific features which must be included (i.e., commands and data types), (b) the distinction between sub routines and a specific language facility, and (c) the facilities provided by the system. Each of these is now discussed in more detail.

Specific features. The specific features representing the functional capability of *any* language are the operations (i.e., commands) to be performed, and the data types. The kinds of operations to be provided depend completely on the application area, and of course must be consistent with the data types. As a very simple example, the existence of floating point numbers of extremely important in any language to be used for scientific computation, whereas they have little or no importance for business data processing. Therefore, the existence of a floating point or complex number data type is a functional requirement of many scientific problems, and naturally there must be executable statements which can operate on these data types. A less elementary example occurs in the civil engineering field where the ability to calculate the point of intersection of the tangents to two circles may be deemed important enough to incorporate directly into the language. Furthermore, a "point" with coordinates might be defined as a data type with operations provided to calculate areas. In the case of an application involving simulation, some indication of time and time-dependencies in both the data types and commands is absolutely crucial. In the case of a language developed for animated movies, the user must be able to address and manipulate pointers or makers on a screen. In the general area of graphics, a "graphical" data type is normally needed.

Subroutine Versus Language Facility. Since all major languages have a subroutine capability of one kind of another, the question can legitimately be asked as to why the needs cannot simply be met through adding subroutines rather than either developing a new language or adding syntax and semantics to the existing language. It must be emphasized very strongly that there is a fundamental difference between functional capability (which can be represented either directly in the languages *or* via subroutines) and specific language facilities.

The easiest way to show this is by means of an example within the field of mathematics. Suppose a person wished to do MATRIX addition in a language like FORTRAN. One could add a subroutine to perform those calculations and then invoke this facility by writing

$$\text{CALL MATADD (A, B, C)}$$

This is fundamentally different in several ways from writing something of the following kind:

$$\text{DECLARE A, B, C MATRICES}$$
$$C = A + B$$

In the first instance, the user (meaning both the writer and reader of the program) has lost a certain mnemonic advantage and furthermore has the difficulty of remembering the types, sequence, and restrictions on the parameters that he is using. In this particular example, the main difficulty is to remember whether the stated call would provide A as the sum of B and C, or C as the sum of A and B; this is something which must be remembered or looked up in a manual. In the second example, what is happening is far clearer. In addition to the lack of "problem-oriented notation" inherent in using the CALL or equivalent statement, there are implementation difficulties and inefficiencies relative to linkages. In many cases, there is a great deal of extra code generated to invoke a subroutine, although the latter may in fact be quite small and would be more efficient placed in line. Unless the compiler is very sophisticated, it is likely to generate the linkage coding rather than placing the subroutine in line.

While subroutines do serve a very useful purpose in making additional functional capability available to the user, they should not be viewed as substitutes for additions to a language.

System provided facilities. Another aspect of functional capability is the built-in facility of the language and its associated compiler to do things which might need to the programmed in another language. For example, in the languages for computer assisted instruction, it is assumed that they will be used in an interactive mode and hence the language translators automatically provide for input and output from a terminal without the programmer having to specify much (if anything) about input/output. Furthermore, certain types of control flow are assumed by the system and handled automatically. In the case of graphic languages, the language (and its processor) automatically provide the necessary instructions to the graphics equipment.

STYLE SUITABLE FOR APPLICATION AREA. In the development of languages for special application areas, the style plays a major role, primarily because the users are normally not professional programmers. Style in a programming language has many facets, ranging from personal views on the importance (or non-importance) of blanks and punctuation, to the use (or non-use) of a GO TO command, to the selection of a particular word for getting input data (e.g., READ vs. GET). The major identifiable elements of style are vocabulary, personal preferences, and requirements affecting style.

Vocabulary. The second* most important need in a application-oriented language is the vocabulary or professional jargon that is involved. The whole *raison d'etre* of many languages for specialized application areas is to allow the user to write his specialized jargon in a natural manner. Whereas he can certainly develop subroutines to accomplish what he wants, the ability to use his own terminology in a style natural to him is of paramount importance. It is normal that a person outside a particular area will find the nomenclature confusing or not understandable. All figures in this paper reflect this issue, i.e., the programs as written are generally not understandable to any reader outside the specific application area.

Personal Preferences. It is unfortunate—but quite true—that in the development of one of these special-application-languages, the personal preferences of the developer have a significant effect, although they should of course be subordinated to the functional requirements and the vocabulary. For example, people who wish to have short data names and short statements in a language because they like that style may be forced into a different mode because the professional jargon of the field constantly uses long words. (In some systems, e.g., COGO, both short and long forms of

---

* The first is the functional capability.

key words are allowed to provide short cuts for experienced users.) The choice of a fairly rigid format versus a free form, or the selection of specific key words (e.g., READ versus GET) can sometimes make the difference between successful usage of the language versus constant unhappiness by the users. In some instances, people have strong views on punctuation and will change an existing language to eliminate (or include) punctuation in lieu of some other syntactic restriction. (It has been said facetiously that by choosing the correct subset of PL/I one merely has FORTRAN with semicolons.)

Background and past experience with specific equipment often have a strong personal influence. People who have used punched cards extensively tend to favor rigid formats with card columns used as syntactic delimiters. Those who have used on-line terminals generally tend to favor free form. Even in this latter case, there is considerable difference of opinion on the value of limiting each statement to the length of a single line.

The use of very simplistic styles, as illustrated in Figure IIIF-2 primarily consisting of a single key word at the beginning of a line, followed by some parameters, certainly forces one to reconsider the border line between programming languages and powerful macros. Certainly such a style is generally not "problem-oriented" which was described as one of the characteristics of a higher level language. However, such languages (e.g., COGO—see Figure IIIF-2) can be justified as higher level languages because of the distance of these operations from normal machine code. Thus, there is a large amount of information built into the compiler or the interpreter to perform specific functions which are directly related to an application (rather than merely enhancing normal machine code).

It should be emphasized that there is little or not way of determining which of two styles is better; in virtually every case it is a matter of individual taste, preference, previous usage, and jargon common to the application area.

Requirements Affecting Style. It should not be thought that *all* matters of style are arbitrary; some are influenced or forced by specific requirements of equipment—particularly the character set. In other cases, the intended use may affect the style of the language and environment will have a very specific effect. If the language is to be used in an interactive mode, it is pointless to be highly concerned about card columns. On the other hand, if the primary use of the language involves relatively simple statements and a large number of numeric parameters or data, then it may be most effective orient the style of the language toward card columns.

In some instances, the style can be justified on fairly concrete grounds.

438   ISSUES OF MANAGEMENT

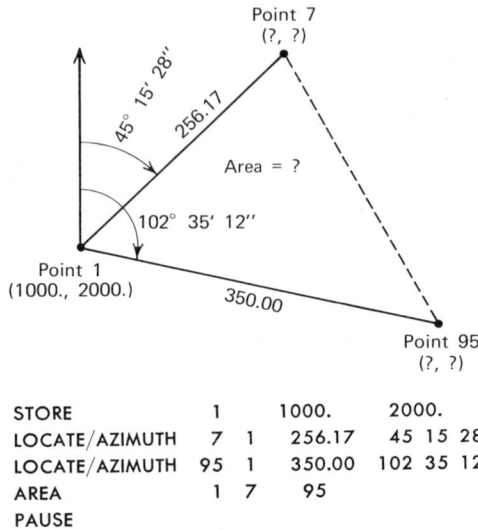

```
STORE           1      1000.   2000.
LOCATE/AZIMUTH  7  1   256.17  45 15 28
LOCATE/AZIMUTH  95 1   350.00  102 35 12
AREA            1  7   95
PAUSE
```

Figure IIIF-2.   COGO (civil engineering). Small COGO program for figure shown. In the figure above, given the coordinates of point 1, the length and azumuth (clockwise angle from north) of lines 1–7 and 1–95, the COGO program shown computes the coordinates of points 7 and 95 and the area of the triangle. In the program, the second line reads: Locate point 7 by going from point 1 a distance of 256.17 at an azimuth of 45 degrees 15 minutes 28 seconds. *Source.* S. J. Fenves, "Problem-Oriented Languages for Man-Machine Communication in Engineering," p. 48. Reprinted by permission from *Proceedings of the IBM Scientific Computing Symposium on Man-Machine Communications*, Data Processing Division, 320-1941, © 1966 by International Business Machines Corporation.

For example, in situations where time is critical (e.g., command and control) there may be much more need for brief fixed formats with little flexibility. In other areas where documentation plays an important role, the desire may be for lengthy free form syntax which clearly conveys the meaning of the program to a large number of person long after the program is written.

EFFICIENCY.   It is obvious that one of the reasons for developing these application-oriented languages is efficiency. This involves the efficiency which comes both from ease of writing the programs and from suitable processors.

One major way in which an attempt is made to increase efficiency is to delete unwanted parts of major language while (perhaps) adding on the functional capability (in the form of new language elements). While the person or group which has a large language available to them is under no obligation to use all of its facilities, it is perfectly clear that they are paying for the implementation of these unwanted features. The common and obvious practical solution to this problem is merely to have a compiler which implements a subset of a language, and this is frequently done. However, to the extent that the individual or group wants to clearly define a certain subset of syntax and semantics and give it a name, he has in effect defined a new language. It is *not* true that all languages can have subsets properly defined, if a program written in the subset is also to run on a compiler for the full language.

The ways in which suitable processors can be obtained are discussed in the next section.

Design Parameters of Special Application Languages

The design parameters of the languages for special application areas essentially reflect the needs which were discussed in the previous section. Thus, the functional capability, a style suitable for the application area, and efficiency are clearly design parameters. However, there are two additional issues which were not discussed in the previous section but which are very significant in the development of these languages, namely the methods actually used to design and implement the languages. It is well-known that those issues are important in the design of any language, but they are perhaps more significant in the languages within the scope of this paper because the intended users are not professional programmers and hence are less likely to be tolerant of unnecessary idiosyncrasies. In more general languages, some of the idiosyncrasies are (unfortunately) forced into existence by the methodology used for language design and/or implementation. Finally, it is possible to summarize the potential language requirements.

METHODS OF DEFINING LANGUAGE. There are three basic methods for defining a language. The first is the most obvious—namely, a straightforward definition. In this instance, the individual or group merely sits down and writes out a definition of the language. Depending upon their sophistication and the complexity of the language, they may use something like Backus Normal Form, or alternatively may simply use ordinary English and examples. A special case of this method involves making specific changes to an existing language, which may involve addition, deletion, changes, or all of these.

The second method of defining a language is through an extensible language system. This is an area which has become increasingly important

Table IIIF-1 Considerations in Language Design

Syntax

1. Form
    Free
    Fixed tabular, as in report writers or decision tables
    Rigid with required parameters, i.e., essentially macrostyle
2. Punctuation
    Critical with many symbols or not very significant
    Blank character is critical delimiter or not significant
    Single or multicharacter
3. Identifiers and Key Words
    Single or few characters vs. lengthy
    Abbreviations optional vs. not allowed
    Specialized vocabulary
4. Full power of a language like PL/I (for systems programming)
5. Declarations—see under Data

Data

1. Types
    Specialized to application, e.g., length
    Many vs. few
    Implicit vs. specifically declared
    Determined by position in statement
2. Declarations
    Grouped by attribute vs. grouped by data item
    Implicit from other syntactic rules
    Default conditions

Semantics

1. Specialized computational routines
2. Non-standard use of common characters (e.g., plus sign)

Program/Control Structure

1. Generally quite simple with no block structure nor compound statements
2. Very powerful (for systems programming)

---

over the past few years, although there is not much evidence of practical systems or significant usage as yet (see Reference 1). In this situation, the developer of the language for a special application area is limited in two ways. First he is limited by the inherent style and capability of the base language, and second, he is constrained by the mechanism given to him to produce the extensions. If the extension facilities do not allow new data types to be added, then he is limited to the syntax and functional operations for new commands. For example, any macro system (e.g., PL/I) tends to allow new commands and/or new syntax to be developed but does not provide for new data types. Alternatively, other extensible systems, e.g., IMP (8) allow for both new commands and new data types, but do not allow for major changes in language style or format.

The third method of defining the language is via some system. In this case, which seems to be the most important and the most promising, the user or application programmer states his wishes to a person who can be defined as a "language designer" who then interacts with a system which produces *relatively easily* a language definition which meets the needs of the original user or programmer. While many people have talked about this for years, relatively little has actually been accomplished—see a later section. In the long run, it is clear to me that we must allow the user ample facilities to easily define and implement his own language subject to whatever constraints and quirks he may have. They key word here is "easily" and that is the major difficulty in achieving the general goal.

METHODS OF IMPLEMENTATION. Just as there are several different ways of defining a language, so there are different broad techniques for implementing them, and to some extent (but not entirely) they match the methods of defining the language. The first and most obvious method of implementation is a specific compiler or interpreter. This would tend to be used most often in a case where a language had been designed from scratch. Second, paralleling exactly the use of the extensible languages is the extensible language compiler or equivalent facility. This method might conceivably be used with a language designed in another way, but it is highly unlikely to be applicable. A third possibility is a very powerful macro assembler which then allows the user quite a bit of flexibility in terms of jargon, lists of parameters, etc., but gives him virtually no flexibility in style and overall format. Finally, roughly corresponding to the user-defined language via a system, is a system which generates a compiler or interpreter. This method of implementation can be used even with the first case where the individual has designed and defined the language from scratch. The compiler generators that have been the vogue for many years come close to satisfying this requirement in theory, although none seem to do it in practice. (See a later section.)

POTENTIAL LANGUAGE REQUIREMENTS. A brief summary of requirements (or considerations) for potential desired language features is shown in Table IIIF-1. Obviously, any one language will only use some of these. However, it is possible to find at least one specialized language which requires or uses each of these approaches or features.

```
QU  WHO DISCOVERED AMERICA?
AA  ERICSON
AB  LEIF ERICSON
TY  YOUR ANSWER WOULD BE ACCEPTED BY SOME.
CA  COLUMBUS
TY  YES
WA  PONCE DE LEON
TY  NO. HE LOOKED FOR THE "FOUNTAIN OF YOUTH." TRY AGAIN.
UN  BL
```

Figure IIIF-3. Coursewriter III (computer-assisted instruction). Example uses the aa and ab operation codes. If the student enters a response of "Ericson," or "Leif Ericson," the message "Your answer would be accepted by some," is typed to the student. After the aa or ab match, the system continues to scan statements until it finds the un statement. It then types the contents of buffer 1. If the student responds with an answer which does not match an aa, ab, ca, or wa statement, only the un argument (the contents of buffer 1) is typed to the student. The contents of buffer 1 might be, "Please try again," Using a buffer in this way saves the author from repeatedly entering the same text for many un statements in the course. *Source.* Reprinted by permission from *Coursewriter I for System/360, Version, 2, Application Description Manual,* Data Processing Division, H20-0587, p. 17. © 1969 by International Business Machines Corporation.

Some Specific Application Areas with Examples

Almost all special application areas tend to look small and homogeneous when viewed from outside, but large and filled with differing problems and issues when viewed by those familiar with the field. A very good illustration of this can be seen merely by glancing at the papers on numerical control programming languages (10). Even though one language—namely APT—predominates, there are still enough technical issues surrounding its utility and implementation to cause the existence of numerous other languages. In particular, 32 others are listed (11).

In the field of computer-assisted instruction, there are over 30* languages utilizing different syntactic and conceptual approaches. Just glancing at Figures IIIF-3 and IIIF-4 for Coursewriter and FOIL, respectively, shows the wide variety of style, ranging from two-letter mnemonics to a PL/I-like language. A comparison of CAI languages can be found in References 23.

The situation in graphics is similar, but with another dimension of concept involved. In the computer-assisted instruction application area it can reasonably be argued that the application is unique and that there is little relevance to existing languages of somewhat wider purpose, e.g.,

* Not all of these are listed in Reference 18.

F. THE QUALITY OF THE MAN-SYSTEM INTERFACE

```
TY WOULD YOU LIKE TO CONTINUE THE EXERCISE?
ACCEPT
    IF 'NO', GO TO FINISH
    IF 'YES, OK'
        NUM = NUM + 1
        GO TO NEXT
    GO BACK PLEASE ANSWER YES OR NO
```

Figure IIIF-4. FOIL (computer assisted instruction). The TY causes the indicated typeout to be made. If the student responds with a NO there is a branch to a statement labeled FINISH. If either YES or OK are typed in the variable NUM has 1 added to it and control is transferred to the statement labeled NEXT. Any answer not including YES, NO, or OK causes the typeout from the system of PLEASE ANSWER YES OR NO and a return of control to the ACCEPT statement. *Source.* J. C. Hesselbart, "FOIL- A File-Oriented Interpretive Language," *Proceedings of the 23rd National Conference of the Association for Computing Machinery,* 1968, p. 94. © 1968 Association for Computing Machinery, Inc. Reprinted by permission.

FORTRAN, COBOL. (However, even in the CAI situation, the case can be made for the desirability of control statement, conditionals, and numeric calculations expressable by formulas as in FORTRAN.) In the field of graphic languages there is certainly a special facility that can be used by many applications (including, for example, computer-assisted instruction). The technical approaches and issues in graphics are as diverse as in other applications. In this case more of an argument can be made for providing the facilities as extensions to existing languages, e.g., GRAF (5), which is an extension of FORTRAN. However, most developers went to the other extreme with entire new languages, for example General Purpose Graphic Language (9). (See Figures IIIF-5 and IIIF-6, respectively.) Some lan-

```
DISPLAY A, B, PDQ, POLE (11), K72A (7, 2, 4)
PDQ = A + POINT (0, XY2) + B
K72A (2, 1; 3) = PLACE (0, 1) + PRINT 13, (YY(I), I = 1, 8) + PLACE (100, 200)
```

Figure IIIF-5. GRAF (addition to FORTRAN to do graphics). The names in the DISPLAY statement are display variables. PDQ is assigned the value which is obtained by first generating the graphic orders of A followed by the orders generated by the built-in function POINT, followed by the orders generated by B. Similarly, the value of K72A(2, 1, 3) is obtained by taking each of the graphic orders indicated in turn. The built-in display function POINT generates orders for plotting the point with indicated coordinates; the built-in function PLACE changes the beam position without plotting, and PRINT plots the indicated string of characters. *Source.* Based on examples in A. Hurwitz and J. P. Citron, "GRAF: Graphic Additions to FORTRAN!" *Proceedings of the Spring Joint Computer Conference,* 1967.

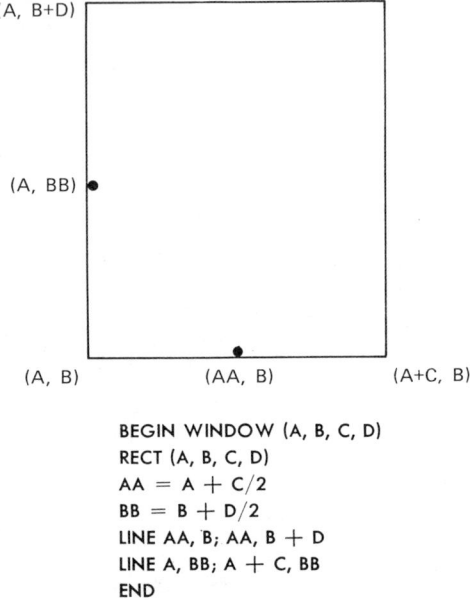

Figure IIIF-6. General purpose graphic language. A subroutine WINDOW is defined where A and B are the coordinates of one corner of a rectangle and C and D represent the horizontal and vertical dimensions. The subroutine to draw a rectangle is called and executed. The drawings of these windows are to have horizontal and vertical lines midway in the window so AA and BB compute the coordinates of the midpoints. The LINE commands cause the "midway" lines to be drawn. *Source.* H. E. Kulsrud, "A General Purpose Graphic Language," *Communications of the ACM,* **11**, 4 (April 1968), p. 253, © 1968 Association for Computing Machinery, Inc. Reprinted by permission.

guages take a middle ground by retaining some of the style of more popular languages, such as ALGOL or FORTRAN, but by no means accept compatibility with them as a constraint. (See for example Euler-G (12).) In each case the developer of the language was reflecting his view of how graphic information should be stored internally, and the most effective way in which it could be displayed and manipulated on a screen. In this application area, the physical environment plays a major role in the development of the language; thus the existence of lightpens, keyboards, push-buttons, etc., must be supported—if they are to be used by the graphic language.

Systems for Developing Languages for Special Application Areas

It is unfortunate, but appears to be a fact, that there are no currently available systems which have actually been used in a practical way for the development of a *significant number* of languages (and their processors) for special application areas. It is not even clear that any of the systems now in prototype stage will ever be satisfactory for that purpose. Virtually all of the systems known to the author have one or more of the following characteristics: (1) they require a compiler expert for their use; (2) they have been used to produce some minor variations on "normal" languages such as FORTRAN, ALGOL, etc.; (3) they are not *really* intended to be used to develop the types of languages discussed in this paper; (4) they give lip service—although little else—to the concept of allowing the average user to be able to define his own language and easily get a processor for it.

In theory, any compiler-compiler, meta-compiler or similarly designated system could be used for this purpose. However, there is different emphasis in most of those developed to date. They have been designed primarily to provide an easy means of implementing known and widely used languages (e.g., FORTRAN, COBOL, ALGOL, PL/I) rather than as a tool for the development of new languages with uncommon requirements, and their processors. Thus the major considerations have pertained to efficiency of the resulting compiler, with an easy way to make minor changes in the syntax. A discussion of the past and potential use of such systems or translator writing systems in general is beyond the scope of this paper. A good survey is given in Reference 3.

Although no systems seem to have been widely, or even significantly, used for developing the types of languages within this paper, several have had limited use and/or have such intent for the future. A brief description of these will now be given.

(a) ICES

The Integrated Civil Engineering System (ICES) provides an overall system within which many language processors suitable for civil engineering can reside and use common facilities (13). There is also the capability of allowing the user to define new languages, or add facilities to one of the existing languages. This is done by means of the Command Definition Language (CDL). Although CDL has not been used very much in practice, at least one language, namely STRUDL (22), was developed using it. (A brief but relatively accessible summary of ICES, including CDL, is in Reference 14.)

(b) REL

The Rapidly Extensible Language (REL) System was (and is) intended for use by researchers in the fields of complex social and environmental process (20). It has a powerful English grammer, thus permitting individuals to communicate with the computer in a fairly "natural" language. In 1970 an experimental system was in operation on the IBM System

360/50 and was used to develop an animated film language and also be some social scientists.

(c) PLAN

The Problem Language ANalyzer (PLAN) has many facets to it, but the only one of interest in this context is its facility to allow the user to define simple new languages in an easy manner (6). A version providing graphics support allows the user to develop his language at an IBM 2250 and also provides him with many built-in graphics facilities (7).

(d) UAL

The User Adaptive Language (UAL) is another attempt to provide a user with the ability to dynamically create and modify a language in an interactive mode (4). This system provides the user with fairly sophisticated programming concepts (e.g., lists), but does not require him to use them.

(e) SDF

The Syntax Definition Facility (SDF) allows the user to define his language by means of illustrative sentences (2). The system indicates whether the input is ambiguous or contradictory to earlier information. By late 1971, it had been used primarily to implement the syntax of fairly standard language subunits, e.g., arithmetic and Boolean expressions.

(f) Extensible Languages

All extensible languages should—in theory—be usable for creating specialized languages. By late 1971, none seem to have been used in this way. See Reference 1.

Brief Comments on the Future

It seems unfortunate but true that the proliferation of higher level languages is likely to continue at about the same rate. The reason for this is that some of the causes and motivations behind the development of these languages rest in quirks of human nature rather than technological progress or lack thereof. Thus, as long as people find it fun to develop languages, as long as they want something which is specifically tailored exactly to their needs, and as long as they are going to find picayune faults with the existing languages, there is very little that technical progress can do to reduce the number of languages. On the other hand, there are some areas in which improved technology will have an enormous effect. For example, the existence of good extensible language systems, or good systems which can easily generate a language and its translator based on appropriate input from a language designer, will have a considerable effect. We might even envision specialized language generators, i.e., a system designed to allow the easy creation and implementation of languages in a single application area, e.g., CAI, graphics. ICES (13) is a simple attempt in this direction for civil engineering.

In the opinion of this author, the ease and efficiency of using a language particularly suited to a specific application area is a desirable result which outweighs the disadvantages of the proliferation. A thorough discussion on the pressures and resources involved in the future development of these specialized languages is given in Reference 20.

Summary

This paper has defined and discussed the class of languages which are designed for use in specialized application areas. These languages include about half of all higher level languages used in the United States at the time of this writing. A discussion of terminology showed why some of the commonly used terms for this class of languages are technically inappropriate.

The major needs to be met in developing these languages were shown to be functional capability, deletion of parts of an existing languages, and a suitable style. Two specific application area, namely CAI and graphics, were used to illustrate the existence of significantly different language styles within the same application area. Although there are a number of systems which purport to allow the user to easily define and implement his own language, and they are mentioned, none have actually been significantly used. A few brief comments on the future indicate that the proliferation serves a useful purpose and will continue.

References

1. "ACM SIGPLAN" Proceedings of ACM SIGPLAN Conference on Extensible Languages, *SIGPLAN Notices,* **6,** 12 (December 1971).
2. R. S. Eanes, "An Interactive Syntax Definition Facility" MIT Electronic Systems Laboratory Report ESL-R-397, September 1969.
3. J. Feldman and D. Gries, "Translator Writing Systems, *Communications of the ACM,* **11,** 2 (February 1968).
4. A. Hormann, A. Leal, and D. Crandell, "User Adaptive Language (UAL): A Step toward Man-Machine, Synergism," System Development Corporation Technical Memorandum, TM 4539, June 1971.
5. A. Hurwitz, J. P. Citron, and J. B. Yeaton, "GRAF– Graphic Additions to FORTRAN," Proceedings of the Fall Joint Computer Conference, Vol. 30, 1967.

6. "Problem Language Analyzer (PLAN) Program Description Manual," IBM Corporation Form GH20-0594.
7. "PLAN Graphics Support for the IBM 2250" (Application Description Manual), IBM Corporation Form H20-0535.
8. E. T. Irons, "Experience with an Extensible Language," *Communications of the ACM,* **13,** 1 (January 1970).
9. H. E. Kulsrud, "A General Purpose Graphic Language," *Communications of the ACM,* **11,** 4 (April 1968).
10. W. H. P. Leslie, Ed. "Numerical Control Programming Languages," North-Holland, Amsterdam, 1970.
11. W. E. Mangold, "Status of NC Language Standardization in I.S.O. (International, Standards Organization)," Numerical Control Programming Languages, W. H. P. Leslie, Ed., North-Holland, Amsterdam, 1970.
12. W. M. Newman, "Display Procedures," *Communications of the ACM,* **14,** 10 (October 1971).
13. D. Roos, Ed. "ICES System: General Description," MIT Dept. of Civil Engineering R67-49, September 1967.
14. J. E. Sammet, *Programming Languages: History and Fundamentals,* Prentice-Hall, Englewood Cliffs, N.J., 1969.
15. J. E. Sammet, "Roster of Programming Languages, 1968." *Computers and Automation,* **17,** 6 (June 1968).
16. J. E. Sammet, "Roster of Programming Languages, 1969," *Computers and Automation,* **18,** 7 (June 1969).
17. J. E. Sammet, "Roster of Programming Languages, 1970," *Computers and Automation,* **19,** 6B (November 1970).
18. J. E. Sammet, "Roster of Programming Languages, 1971," *Computers and Automation,* **20,** 6B (June 1971).
19. J. E. Sammet, "Problems in, and Pragmatic Approach to, Programming Language Measurement," Proceedings of the Fall Joint Computer Conference, Vol. 39, 1971.
20. F. B. Thompson et al., "REL: A Rapidly Extensible Language System," Proceedings of the 24th ACM National Conference, 1969.
21. F. B. Thompson, and B. H. Doster, "The Future of Specialized Languages," Proceedings of the Spring Joint Computer Conference, Vol. 40, 1972.
22. R. A. Walter, "A System for the Generation of Problem-Oriented Languages," Proceedings of 5th National Conference Computer Society of Canada, May–June 1966.
23. K. L. Zinn, "A Comparative Study of Languages for Programming Interactive, Use of Computers in Instruction," University of Michigan Center for Research on Learning and Teaching, February 1969.

Specialized Man-System Interface: A Case Study

The following section illustrates the development of an information system, including language and terminal interface, specifically designed to help solve a technologically caused problem. The problem is the effect of chemicals on humans, and our lack of understanding and control.

Automated Information-Handling in Pharmacology Research*

Pharmacology in its broadest sense involves the multitude of interrelationships between chemical substances and the function of living systems. Since these interrelationships manifest themselves at all levels of physiological organization from the individual enzyme to the intact mammal, research in this area involves concepts and techniques from almost every biomedical discipline. Detailed understanding of the mechanisms of drug action is the best prescription for the discovery of new therapeutic agents and the rational use of old ones.

The breadth and complexity of of the domain of pharmacological inquiry interact to produce a class of information-handling problems as formidable and enticing as any that can be found in the medical area. In recognition of this, the National Institutes of Health (NIH), through its Chemical/Biological Information-Handling (CBIH) Program, is attempting to accelerate the acquisition of new pharmacological knowledge by designing and developing computer-based research tools especially for scientists in this discipline. Working through a tightly interconnected set of contracts with universities and colleges, nonprofit research institutes, profit-making organizations, and government agencies, the CBIH Program seeks to blend the most advanced information science methods into a computer system which can be an almost indispensable logistical and cognitive aid to these investigators. This paper characterizes the current status of these efforts.

The Pharmacological Information-Handling "Problem"

The ultimate goal of pharmacology is a well-validated theory having the following two properties:

1. Given the identify of a chemical substance and the parameters of its administration to a given living organism (e.g., the dose, route, course, etc.), predict the effect, if any, on the behavior of the biological system; and

---

* This section has been excerpted from W. F. Raub, "Automated Information Handling in Pharmacology," *Proceedings of the SJCC*, AFIPS Press, Montvale, N.J., 1972, pp. 1157–1165.

2. Given a desired behavioral end state for a given biological system, predict the specific chemical substance(s) and parameters of administration which can bring about that end state.

Only when such a theory is in hand will it be possible to make an accurate assessment of the therapeutic efficacy of a new substance without extensive testing in animals and human subjects. Only then will one be able to assume withconfidence that a given drug will not have adverse side effects in a particular clinical context.

As is painfully obvious to both pharmacologists and laymen alike, an all-encompassing theory of drug action is nowhere in sight. Present understanding of drug action still is based almost exclusively upon empirical observation. Only a figurative handful of investigators have made extensive attempts to formalize their knowledge through mathematical modelling and the like. Natural language still serves as the predominant medium for the expression and communication of concepts. And textbooks and review articles constitute almost the entire body of organized knowledge.

Nor has information science and technology done much to aid in the development of a broad-based theory of drug action. On the contrary, even the most sophisticated document reference and archival management systems are only marginally useful in helping pharmacologists cope with the plethora of literature which is relevant to their interests. Moreover, outside of a few parochial areas, there are essentially no truly effective data retrieval (as opposed to document retrieval) services. And easy-to-use tools for building, exercising, managing, and communicating models of drug action are much more nearly fantasy than they are routine offerings of the typical general-purpose computer center.

Thus, the pharmacological information-handling "problem" can be stated as a series of interrelated questions:

1. Can one design computer-based information-handling tools which encourage formalistic rather than empirical approaches to the study of molecular structure/biological activity relationships?
2. Can one use these tools to facilitate the interchange of data, procedures, and models among geographically and disciplinary disjoint scientists whose work is relevant to the understanding of drug action?
3. Can one use mathematical models and other formalisms to enhance traditional methods for the storage and retrieval of pharmacological information?

These questions circumscribe the domain of the CBIH Program.

The Prophet System

PROPHET is an experimental information-handling system designed specifically to subserve pharmacology research. It is intended to be a medium through which the latest pharmacologically relevant information-handling methods can be developed, integrated, and made available to practicing scientists throughout the nation. It is viewed as a research tool encouraging more rigorous approaches to the organization and analysis of laboratory and clinical observations as indicated in Figure IIIF-7. Its ultimate goal is to facilitate the acquisition and dissemination of knowledge about mechanisms of drug action across a span of disciplines ranging from molecular biology to human clinical investigation.

The general nature of PROPHET is given in Figure IIIF-8. As shown there, PROPHET is designed to employ a dedicated, medium-sized, time-sharing computer (a Digital Equipment Corporation PDP-10) and to serve a geographically dispersed set of users via remote graphics terminals operating over voice-grade telephone lines. Information-handling procedures and data files reside in the central computer. *Provision is made for eventual interfacing with both utility computers and information services.* A detailed description of the system is given in the document entitled "The PROPHET System: A Final Report of Phase I of the Design Effort for the Chemical/Biological Information-Handling Program."

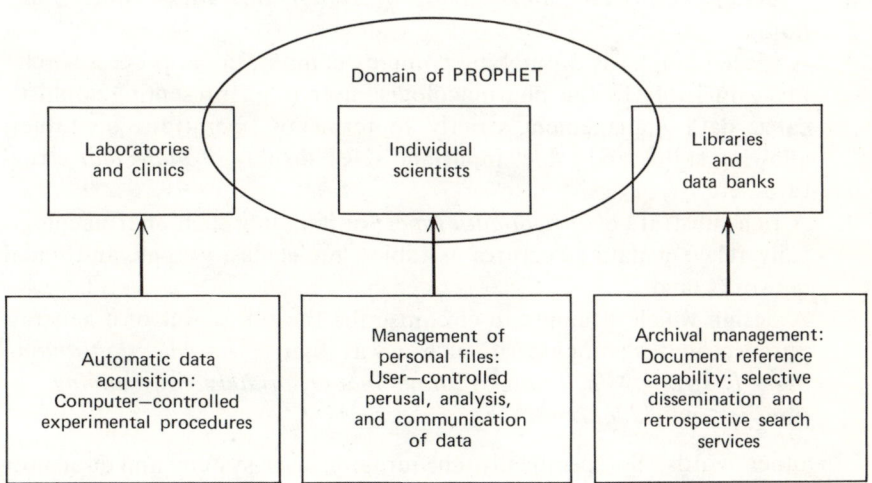

Figure IIIF-7. The PROPHET system in context.

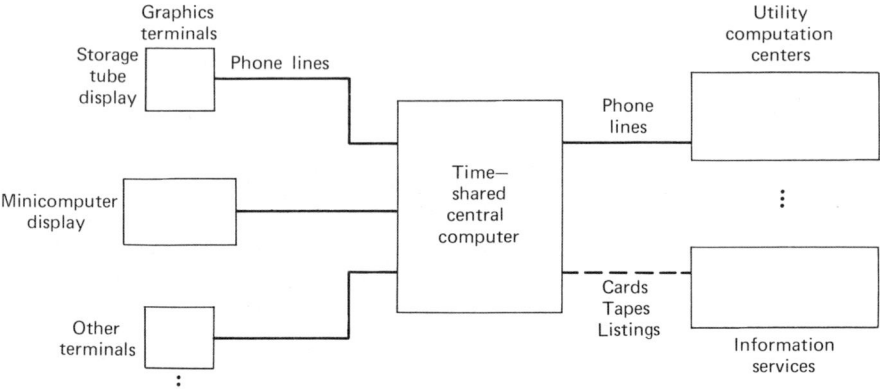

Figure IIIF-8. PROPHET system equipment organization.

The primary features of PROPHET as seen from the perspective of computer technology are five:

1. A powerful interactive command language enabling even a computer novice to effect sophisticated procedures for handling empirical data on chemical substances and their biological consequences;
2. *A simple procedural language* syntactically modelled on PL/1 which is coextensive with the command language and which allows essentially unfettered *interleaving of system and user-defined functions;*
3. A special emphasis on making complex computational processes relatively invisible to the pharmacologist user (e.g., presenting sophisticated data management strictly in terms of operations on tables, allowing stylus and tablet input and CRT display of *molecular* structures, etc.);
4. A rich substrate of *special data types* for handling such pharmacologically relevant data structures as tables, molecules, graphs, and nodal networks; and
5. A design which attempts to circumscribe the full power of a general-purpose digital computer in such a way that *communication among users is strongly facilitated without inappropriately constraining options for individual initiative.*

In other words, by specifically encouraging user-system and user-user interactions within the somewhat rigid context of standard predetermined data types, PROPHET is designed to allow research pharmacologists to handle their personal data files and communicate with their colleagues more effectively than they can any other way.

F. THE QUALITY OF THE MAN-SYSTEM INTERFACE

1. MAKE TABLE unused-name [FROM table-name [FOR relational expression]]

2. ADD $\begin{Bmatrix} \text{COLUMN[S]} \\ \text{ROW[S]} \end{Bmatrix}$ TO table-name [FROM table-name]

3. ENTER $\begin{bmatrix} \text{ROW[S]} \begin{Bmatrix} \text{row-name(s)} \\ \text{row-number(s)} \end{Bmatrix} \\ \text{COLUMN[S]} \begin{Bmatrix} \text{column-name(s)} \\ \text{column-number(s)} \end{Bmatrix} \end{bmatrix}$ OF table-name

4. FILLIN table-name FROM table-name

5. $\begin{Bmatrix} \text{DISPLAY} \\ \text{PRINT} \end{Bmatrix}$ $\begin{bmatrix} [\text{COLUMN[S]}] \begin{Bmatrix} \text{column-name(s)} \\ \text{column-number(s)} \end{Bmatrix} \text{OF]} \\ [\text{ROW[S]}] \begin{Bmatrix} \text{row-name(s)} \\ \text{row-number(s)} \end{Bmatrix} \text{OF]} \quad \text{table-name} \end{bmatrix}$

6. LIST $\begin{Bmatrix} \text{OTHER} \\ \text{log-in identifiicaton} \end{Bmatrix}$ TABLES

7. SORT table-name BY COLUMN[S] $\begin{Bmatrix} \text{column-name(s)} \\ \text{column-number(s)} \end{Bmatrix}$

8. PROTECT table-name

Figure IIIF-9. Summary of table-handling commands.

Although PROPHET, like most complex computer systems, is better demonstrated than described, a few simple illustrations may prove useful. Figures IIIF-9 and IIIF-10 show the system commands for operating on tables and molecules, respectively. Arguments for the commands are given in small letters; square brackets enclose optional portions; braces enclose alternative forms. These two lists are only a fraction of the commands available to the user. Note especially the integration of the various data types—e.g., the data type molecule can be an entry in the cell of a table.

1. MAKE MOLECULE unused-name [FROM display-indication]

2. DISPLAY [CONFORMATION OF] molecule-name [COMPLETE]

3. COMPUTE MODEL OF molecule-name

4. CHEMSET property-name TO value(s) $\begin{Bmatrix} \text{element-indication(s)} \\ \text{number(s)} \end{Bmatrix}$

5. WHAT IS property-name $\begin{Bmatrix} \text{element-indication(s)} \\ \text{number(s)} \end{Bmatrix}$

6. ADD COLUMN[S] TO $\begin{Bmatrix} \text{BONDS} \\ \text{ATOMS} \end{Bmatrix}$ of molecule-name

7. [UN]LABEL property-name of molecule-name

8. ROTATE [DISPLAY] BOND number $\begin{Bmatrix} \text{element-indications} \\ \text{numbers} \end{Bmatrix}$

9. DISPLAY molecule-name WITH molecule-fragment-name

Figure IIIF-10. Summary of molecule-handling commands.

*DISPLAY COLUMNS 1,2,3,19,20 OF MEGAMOUSE$ *

MEGAMOUSE 8R X 20C	1. IMPLANT CELLS	2. DOSAGE (MG/KG)	3. SCHEDULE	19. 11 DAY SURVIVORS /TOTAL	20. MEAN LIFE SPAN
1	1.E7	2.25E2	Q7D,DAYS		
2	1.E7	1.5E2	2,9,16		
3	1.E7	1.E2			
4	1.E7	6.7E1			
5	1.E6	2.25E2	Q7D,DAYS		
6	1.E6	1.5E2	2,9,16		
7	1.E6	1.E2			
8	1.E6	6.7E1			

*DISPLAY COLUMNS 4 14 OF MEGAMOUSE$

MEGAMOUSE 8R X 20C	4. DAY 4	5. DAY 5	6. DAY 6	7. DAY 7	8. DAY 8	9. DAY 9	10. DAY 10	11. DAY 11	12. DAY 12	13. DAY 13	14. DAY 14
1							2		1	1	1
2								1	1		
3						1					1
4				2	3	4					
5	1		1					1	1		
6											
7									1	1	1
8				1	1		3	2		1	2

Figure IIIF-11. Mouse survival time.

The nature of PL/PROPHET, the procedural language, is illustrated in Figures IIIF-11 through IIIF-13 using data drawn from a study of antileukemic drugs being conducted by the Southern Research Institute in Birmingham, Alabama. Figures IIIF-11a and IIIF-11b show selected columns from a user-defined table set up to handle survival time data on mice inoculated with various quantities of L-1210 leukemic cells; the numbers in the cells of Figure IIIF-11b indicate the number of mice which died on that particular day. Note that columns 19 and 20 of the table (Figure IIIF-11a are blank since they are intended to accommodate results derived from earlier columns.

Figure IIIF-12 lists a brief user-defined procedure for calculating the number of 11-day survivors and the mean survival time from the observations recorded in columns 4–14 and storing them in columns 19 and 20. Figure IIIF-13 then gives the result of calling this new function—i.e., an updated version of the table with the derived values in place. Note that the user need take no special action to have his personal PL/PROPHET procedures operate in conjunction with the standard system functions.

```
SURVIVE: PROCEDURE (TABNAM);

DECLARE (I,J,DEATH,SUMDEATH,SURVS) FIXED;
DECLARE TABNAM TABLE;
DECLARE (ENTRYIJ,ENTRY19,NU,TOT) CHARACTER;

NU = ' ';
TOT = '/10';

DO I = 1 TO 8;
   SUMDEATH = 0;
   DEATHDAYS = 0.0;
   DO J = 4 TO 14;
      SET ENTRYIJ TO COLUMN J ROW I OF TABNAM;
      IF ENTRYIJ=NU THEN GO TO ABC;
      DEATH = CINT(ENTRYIJ);
      SUMDEATH = SUMDEATH + DEATH;
      DEATHDAYS = DEATHDAYS + CREAL(DEATH)*CREAL(J);
ABC: END;
   SURVS = 10 - SUMDEATH;
   ENTRY 19 = CSTRING(SURVS).TOT;
   ENTRY20 = DEATHDAYS/CREAL(SUMDEATH);
   SET COLUMN 19 ROW I OF TABNAM TO ENTRY19;
   SET COLUMN 20 ROW I OF TABNAM TO ENTRY20;
END;

RETURN;
END;
```

Figure IIIF-12. Listing of PL/PROPHET procedure.

*CALL SURVIVE (MEGAMOUSE)$ *ERASE ALL$ *DISPLAY
COLUMNS 2,3,19,20 OF MEGAMOUSE$

MEGAMOUSE 8R X 20C	2. DOSAGE (MG/KG)	3. SCHEDULE	19. 110DAY SURVIVORS /TOTAL	20. MEAN LIFE SPAN
1	2.25E2	Q7D,DAYS	3/10	1.3E1
2	1.5E2	2,9,16	5/10	1.46E1
3	1.E2		4/10	1.466666E1
4	6.7E1		0/10	9.1
5	2.25E2	Q7D,DAYS	4/10	1.1E1
6	1.5E2	2,9,16	7/10	1.7E1
7	1.E2		5/10	1.48E1
8	6.7E1		0/10	1.079999E1

Figure IIIF-13. Selected columns of the table "megamouse."

At the present time PROPHET is available on a dedicated PDP-10 computer housed and operated for the CBIH Program by First Data Corporation of Waltham, Massachusetts, and is ready for extensive evaluation by research pharmacologists in the context of their day-to-day activities. It is hoped that the testing period now beginning will help both to refine current concepts and to identify areas for future investigation. It is also hoped that these collaborative projects using PROPHET will result in clear-cut demonstrations of the utility of modern information-handling methods in the search to understand the mechanisms of drug action.

To recapitulate the opening theme, pharmacology offers an enormously rich problem space for those interested in applying computers in the biomedical world. Pharmacology impinges on almost every area of medical science and its progress is heavily dependent on the continuing erosion of disciplinary boundaries. Moreover, its information-handling requirements strain at the frontiers of computer science in almost every direction. And the overwhelmingly important implications for society that accompany even small advances in our understanding of drug action make it urgent that the challenge for further inquiry be accepted.

Expanding the User Community—Interactive TV and Computers

The information handling system just described has laudable goals, as do many other applications previously described. However, if the use of information systems remains limited to an intellectual and economic elite, another social problem is created: a further stratification of society into information "haves" and information "have-nots" (2).

If this problem is to be avoided, a major effort must be made to facilitate the availability and acceptability of computer-based services to a much larger segment of the population. This will require wide-ranging channels of distribution, and system interfaces that are cheap, easy-to-use and non-intimidating to the layman. One of the most attractive ways of approaching this is to use mass-media terminals, already familiar to everyone, and already connected to a widespread distribution network. This approach is being taken by the TICCIT project (6, 7).

Since 1968 MITRE has been actively developing an interactive television system called TICCIT (Time-shared, Interactive, Computer-Controlled Information Television). Through the coupling of commercial television and advanced computer technology, MITRE has attempted to open up new areas for cost-effective computer utilization. Several systems have been developed during the past years, aimed at bringing computer-assisted instruction and other computer services into the classroom and the home.

F. THE QUALITY OF THE MAN-SYSTEM INTERFACE

A significant point in the development of interactive televison was reached in July, 1971, when the country's first truly interactive televison system was demonstrated in Reston, Virginia, by MITRE, as shown in Figure IIIF-14. This system connects standard television receivers in home, schools, and businesses in Reston to MITRE's computer system, via the Reston cable television system. A block diagram of the demonstration system is given in Figure IIIF-15. A great variety of potential interactive services were demonstrated to two thousand government and industry leaders.

In December of the same year, NSF awarded a grant to MITRE to study the technical and economic considerations attendant on the home delivery of instruction and other socially-related services via interactive cable TV. The emphasis in this study is to uncover and resolve the problems associated with the development of an interactive television system serving several thousand subscribers on a daily basis. This study is the first part of

Figure IIIF-14. Touch tone phone link in use.

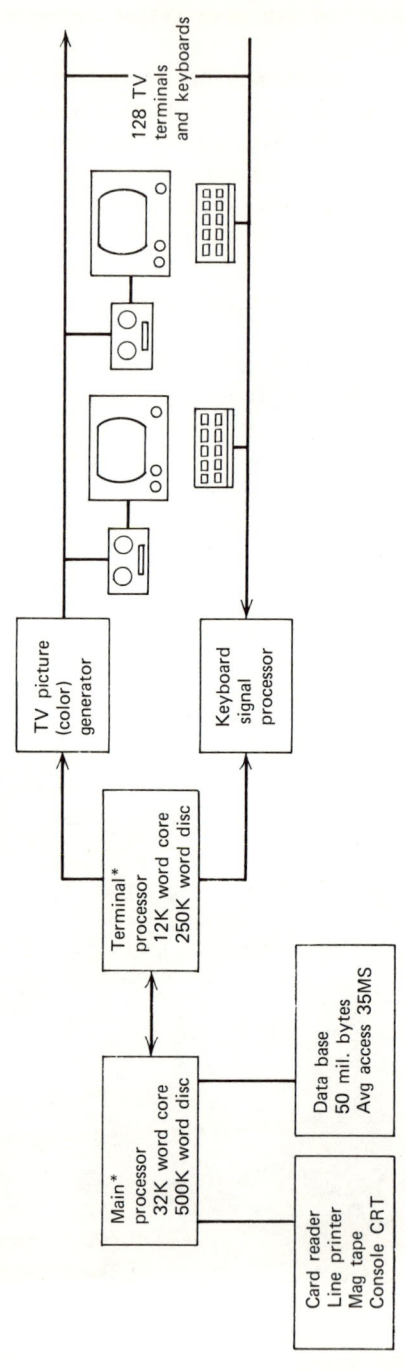

Figure IIIF-15. Demonstration system diagram.

a three-phase program that leads to the installation and evaluation of an interactive television system in a yet to be selected urban community.

The potential uses of such a system, and their importance, stem from certain characteristics:

1. Interactive television is individualized. It responds instantly to the demands of each viewer, permitting him to receive a level of detailed information economically and privately.
2. It is computerized, offering retrieval of information from a tremendous variety of sources, manipulation and computation capabilities and the use of various other computer capabilities that might otherwise be difficult or expensive to obtain in an average home.
3. It provides an unlimited number of entry and delivery points for information transfer (similar to the numbers for telephone and mail) but; in addition, it offers the above mentioned control, storage and access capabilities, plus speed and convenience of retrieval.
4. It is multimedia, providing sight, sound, and personalized computer-service all within one system, giving it the potential of becoming a new kind of common carrier.

Three types of home keyboards will be used in the interactive system: a simple twelve-button keyboard (similar to "Touchtone" pad) will be the standard input device; a full typewriter-like keyboard will also be available to those users who wish to enter textual material or to take a major CAI course. In both cases, a CATV cable will carry the keyboard signal to the computer. A time-slicing digital communications technique will be used to provide each user with the capability of continuously entering data at a rate up to 15 key pushes per second. For the immediate future, however, we recognize that most existing CATV systems do not have two-way capability, and that initially most users will enter the interactive program only infrequently. For this reason, we will provide the interactive capability using existing home Touchtone telephones as entry devices. While there are many reasons why the telephone is far from ideal for the long range, we feel it is a good first step.

References

1. J. McCarthy, "Information," *Scientific American,* September 1966.
2. The Conference Board, Inc., "Information Technology: Some Critical Implications for Decision Makers," Conference Board Report No. 537, 1972.
3. J. M. Shepard, *Automation and Alienation—A Study of Office and Factory Workers,* MIT Press, Cambridge, Mass., 1971.

4. P. Suppes, "The Schools," in *The Computer Impact* I. Taviss, Ed., Prentice-Hall, Englewood Cliffs, N.J., 1970, pp. 203–209.
5. W. F. Raub, "Automated Information Handling in Pharmacology, Research," Proceedings of the SJCC, 1972, pp. 1157–1165.
6. K. J. Stettin, and R. K. Lay, "A Study of the Technical and Economic Considerations Attendant on the Home Delivery of Instruction and Other Socially-Related Services via Interactive Cable TV," Vol. 1, "Introduction and Interim Summary," Mitre Report M72-200, December 1972.
7. W. F. Mason, and R. K. Lay, "The Wired City: Services for Home Delivery via Interactive Cable TV," Proceedings of the ICCC, 1972, pp. 420–424.
8. E. E. David, and R. M. Fano, "Some Thoughts about the Social Implications of Accessible Computing," Proceedings of the FJCC, 1965, pp. 243–247.
9. J. D. Gould, W. J. Doherty, and S. J. Boies, "Bibliography on Behavioral Aspects of On-line Computer Programming," IBM Research Report RC-3513, 1971.

Bibliography

The following periodicals and proceedings are recommended as sources of general information on computer usage and management.

PROCEEDINGS

Proceedings ACM Annual Conference, ACM, 1133 Avenue of the Americas, New York.

Proceedings of the American Society for Information Science, Greenwood Publishing, Westport, Conn.

Proceedings IEEE International Computer Society Conference, IEEE, 345 East 47th Street, New York.

Proceedings IFIP Congress, North Holland Publishing, P. O. Box 3489, Amsterdam, Netherlands.

Proceedings International Conference on Computer Communications, ACM, 1133 Avenue of the Americas, New York.

Proceedings of the National Computer Conference (formerly the Spring and Fall Joint . . .), AFIPS Press, 210 Summit Avenue, Montvale, New Jersey.

PERIODICALS

Communications of the ACM, 1133 Avenue of the Americas, New York.

Computer, Magazine of the IEEE Computer Society, 8949 Reseda Boulevard, Suite 202, Northridge, Calif. 91324.

Computer Decisions, Hayden Publishing, 50 Essex Street, Rochelle Park, New Jersey.

Computing Surveys, the survey and tutorial journal of the ACM, 1133 Avenue of the Americas, New York.

Data Management, the official publication of the Data Processing Management Association, 505 Busse Highway, Park Ridge, Ill.

Datamation, 35 Mason Street, Greenwich, Conn.

Data Processing—The International Journal for Computer Management, IPC Business Press Ltd., Oakfield House, Perrymount Road, Haywards Heath, Sussex RH16 3DH.

The Honeywell Computer Journal, P.O. Box 6000, Phoenix, Ariz.

IBM Systems Journal, IBM Corporation, Armonk, New York.

Installation Management Review, ACM Special Interest Group on Computer Systems Installation Management, ACM, 1133 Avenue of the Americas, New York.

The following books are suggested for general information on computer systems, hardware, and software.

Abramson, N. and Kuo, F. K., *Computer-Communication Networks,* Prentice-Hall, Englewood Cliffs, N. J., 1973.

Beizer, B., *The Architecture and Engineering of Digital Computer Complexes,* 2 Vol., Plenum Press, New York and London, 1971.

Bell, C. G. and Newell, A., *Computer Structures: Readings and Examples,* McGraw-Hill, New York, 1971.

Cardenas, A. F., Presser, L., and Marin, M. A., Eds., *Computer Science,* Wiley, New York, 1972.

Lorin, H., *Parallelism in Hardware and Software,* Prentice-Hall, Englewood Cliffs, N.J., 1972.

Martin, J., *Teleprocessing Network Organization,* Prentice-Hall, Englewood Cliffs, N.J., 1970.

Sammet, J. E., *Programming Languages: History and Fundamentals,* Prentice-Hall, Englewood Cliffs, N.J., 1969.

Sharpe, W. F., The Economics of Computers, Columbia U. Press, New York, 1969.

Watson, R. W., *Timesharing System Design Concepts,* McGraw-Hill, New York, 1970.

The following books and periodicals are recommended for additional information on the application of computing services in various fields of science and technology.

BOOKS

Bisco, R. L., *Data Bases, Computers, and the Social Sciences,* Wiley, New York, 1970.

Bowles, E. A., Ed., *Computers in Humanistic Research,* Prentice-Hall, Englewood Cliffs, N. J. 1967.

Cassell, D. A., *Introduction to Computer-Aided Manufacturing in Electronics,* Wiley, New York, 1972.

Fernbach, S. and Taub, A., Eds., *Computers and Their Roles in the Physical Sciences,* Gordon and Breech, New York, 1970.

Harbaugh, J. W., and Merriam, D. F., *Computer Applications in Stratigraphic Analysis,* Wiley, 1968.

Klerer, M. and Reinfelds, J., Eds., *Interactive Systems for Experimental Applied Math,* Academic Press, New York, 1968.

Negroponte, N., *The Architecture Machine,* MIT Press, Cambridge, Mass., 1970.

Pall, G. A., *An Introduction to Scientific Computing,* Meredith, New York, 1971.

Seely, S., Tarnoff, N. H., and Holstein, D., *Digital Computers in Engineering,* Holt, Reinhart and Winston, New York, 1970.

Spindel, P. D., *Computer Applications in Civil Engineering,* Van Nostrand Reinhold, New York, 1971.

Uttal, W. R., *Real-Time Computers: Techniques and Applications in the Psychological Sciences,* Harper and Row, New York, 1967.

Whitby, L. G., and Lutz, W., *Principles and Practices of Medical Computing,* Churchill Livingstone, Edinburgh and London, 1971.

PERIODICALS

ASIS, Journal of the American Society for Information Science, 1140 Connecticut Avenue, N.W., Suite 804, Washington D.C.

Computers in Biology and Medicine, Permagon Press, Maxwell House, Fairview Park, Elmsford, N.Y.

Computers and the Humanities, Queens College Press, Flushing, N.Y.

Government Data Systems, United Business Publications, 750 Third Avenue, New York.

Journal of Chemical Documentation, American Chemical Society, 1155 Sixteenth Street, N. W., Washington D.C.

Law and Computer Technology, 839 17th Street, N.W., Washington D.C.

Automation, Penton Publishing, 1111 Chester Avenue, Cleveland, Ohio.

The following books are recommended for additional information on particular types of computing services.

Harrison, T. J., *Handbook of Industrial Control Computers,* Wiley, New York, 1972.

Houghton, B., Ed., *Computer Based Information Retrieval Systems,* Archon Books, Hamdon, Conn., 1969.

Meadow, C. T., *Man-Machine Communication,* Wiley, New York, 1970.

Newman, W. M., and Sproull, R. F., *Principles of Interactive Computer Graphics,* McGraw-Hill, New York, 1973.

Reitman, J., *Computer Applications,* Wiley, New York, 1971.

Walker, D. E., Ed., *Interactive Bibliographic Search: The User/Computer Interface,* AFIPS Press, Montvale, N.J., 1971.

Weisman, H. M., *Information Systems, Services, and Centers,* Wiley, New York, 1972.

Author Index

Abbott, R. P., 67–77
Ackoff, R. L., 3, 7
Asimow, M., 7

Barbacci, M. R., 409–418
Beaumont, J. O., 67–77
Beilner, H., 386–408
Billingsley, F. C., 44–53
Bradford, R. A., 201–209
Brennan, J., 97–105
Bunge, M., 2, 3, 7

Clementi, E., 242–247
Cooperman, J. A., 378–386
Clarke, D. C., 35–43

David, E. E., 33
DeLeys, N. J., 220–234
Drucker, P., 325

Eames, C. & R., 8, 9, 31
Eicher, J. P., 220–234

Fano, R. M., 366, 373
Fischer, G., 308, 374–377
Frederickson, D., 358–365
Free, V. H., 86–97
Freeman, R. R., 54–58
Freivogel, M. R., 254–277
Freidman, H. P., 105

Gazis, D. C., 195–200
Ghez, R., 118–122
Gold, M. M., 319–321, 326
Goldstine, H. H., 31
Goldwyn, R. M., 105
Grant, P. M., 35–43
Gritter, R. J., 35–43
Grochow, J. M., 306–308

Hachtel, G. D., 184–193
Helbig, R. E., 155–168
Hines, D. L., 59–66

Kleinrock, L. A., 427–429
Knight, K. E., 16, 17, 31

Koenig, S. H., 115, 122
Koford, J., 136–141
Kolsky, H. G., 106–112

Laughlin, J. S., 247–253
Lay, R. K., 456–460
Lee, K., 141–154
Lusebrink, T. R., 35–43
Lynch, H. W., 378–386, 409–418

McCaslin, J., 326–336
McClure, J. Y., 288–302
McCormick, C. W., 169–183
McCormick, E. J., 33
McHenry, R. R., 220–234
Malozemoff, A., 234–247
Mason, W. F., 456–460
Mataker, E. J., Jr., 86
Mays, C. H., 141
Miller, M., 105
Miller, R. E., Jr., 309, 326–336

Neal, R. H., 169–183
Nelson, P. J., 59–66
Neman, T. E., 86–97
Nielsen, N. R., 419–426

Orr, P. K., 155–168
Osborn, J. J., 67–77

Raimondi, D. L., 35–43
Raison, J. C. A., 67–77
Raub, W. F., 448–456
Reich, H. A., 116–118, 122
Roediger, R. R., 155–168
Rohrer, R. A., 184–193

Sackman, H., 325, 336
Sammet, J. E., 431–448, 462
Savit, C., 77, 86
Schneider, W. A., 86
Sharpe, W. F., 311, 326, 340, 462
Siders, R. A., 3, 4, 7
Siegal, J. H., 105
Simon, E. D., 210–219
Sood, G. W., 123–135

Stettin, K. J., 456–460
Stewart, C., 141–154
Stuehler, J. E., 201–209
Swalen, J. D., 35–43

Tetzlaff, W. H., 378–386

Waldbaum, G., 386–408
Walker, R., 141
Woodson, T. T., 7

SUBJECT INDEX

Interactive services, 12, 13, 20–21, 113–122, 141, 142–153, 452, 459, 463

JOSS, 13, 17, 106

Keypunching, 87, 279, 281, 329–331

Laboratory automation, 13, 18–19, 35–43
Law, applications in, 277–287, 463

Manufacturing, applications in, 127, 201–209, 339, 432, 462
Matrix methods of computing, 94, 170–183
Medical applications, 48, 53, 67–77, 97–105, 247–253, 463
Minicomputers, 200, 305, 337, 367
Monitoring, 41, 67–77, 196–200, 288

Networks, 253, 358–366

Objectives of computer use, 38, 54, 58, 67–68, 79–81, 86, 98, 107, 142, 155, 169, 184, 202, 214, 221, 240, 261, 288–289, 451
On-line, 12, 272, 255, 289
Optimization, 155–168, 184–193

Personalized services, 58–65, 369, 447, 459
PL/1, 127, 393–394, 437, 441, 452
Plotters, 84, 118, 140, 173–174
Prediction, 209, 223
Pricing of services, 419–426
Priorities, assignment of, 263, 312–314, 383
Problem formulation, 5, 105–122, 319–321
Problem solving, 20, 299, 302

Problems of using computers, difficulty of learning and use, 272, 286, 417, 450, 456
  excessive computer time, 74, 165, 170, 246
  excessive waiting, 317, 335, 419–420
  errors, 109, 170
  high cost, 32, 50, 217, 221, 250
  lack of standards, 54, 360–365, 450
  privacy, 369
Process control, 11, 195–200, 201–209

Remote job entry, 20, 253, 263, 360–364
Response time, system, 293, 313, 323–324, 367, 376, 409–417
Response time, user, 323–324, 409–417

Satellite computers, 205, 208, 349
Scheduling of workload, 408, 426–430, 312–314
Security, 262, 279, 339
Sensor-based services, 18–19, 35–43, 67–77, 113–118, 201–209, 195–201
Simulation, 6, 16–17, 137, 139, 220–234, 386–408
System back-up, 337, 365, 369

Terminals, 19, 20–21, 100, 250–253, 272, 366
Text processing, 21, 279–287
Testing, computer-aided, 138, 206
Time-sharing versus batch, 122, 124, 141, 208, 319–323, 332–336, 433
Turnaround time, 252, 350, 383–385, 423

Utilization, 313, 339

Validation, 16, 223–226, 406–407